THE DISTRIBUTION OF
NATIONAL INCOME

Other International Economic Association symposia

＊

THE ECONOMICS OF INTERNATIONAL MIGRATION
Edited by Brinley Thomas

THE BUSINESS CYCLE IN THE POST-WAR WORLD
Edited by Erik Lundberg

INFLATION
Edited by D. C. Hague

STABILITY AND PROGRESS IN THE WORLD ECONOMY
Edited by D. C. Hague

THE THEORY OF CAPITAL
Edited by F. A. Lutz and D. C. Hague

THE THEORY OF WAGE DETERMINATION
Edited by J. T. Dunlop

CLASSICS IN THE THEORY OF PUBLIC FINANCE
Edited by R. A. Musgrave and A. T. Peacock

THE ECONOMIC CONSEQUENCES OF THE SIZE OF NATIONS
Edited by E. A. G. Robinson

ECONOMIC DEVELOPMENT FOR LATIN AMERICA
Edited by Howard S. Ellis assisted by Henry C. Wallich

THE ECONOMICS OF TAKE-OFF INTO SUSTAINED GROWTH
Edited by W. W. Rostow

ECONOMIC DEVELOPMENT WITH SPECIAL REFERENCE TO EAST ASIA
Edited by Kenneth Berrill

INTERNATIONAL TRADE THEORY IN A DEVELOPING WORLD
Edited by R. F. Harrod and D. C. Hague

ECONOMIC DEVELOPMENT FOR AFRICA SOUTH OF THE SAHARA
Edited by E. A. G. Robinson

THE THEORY OF INTEREST RATES
Edited by F. H. Hahn and F. P. R. Brechling

THE ECONOMICS OF EDUCATION
Edited by E. A. G. Robinson and J. E.\Vaizey

PROBLEMS IN ECONOMIC DEVELOPMENT
Edited by E. A. G. Robinson

THE DISTRIBUTION OF NATIONAL INCOME

*Proceedings of a Conference
held by the International Economic Association*

EDITED BY

JEAN MARCHAL

AND

BERNARD DUCROS

MACMILLAN

London · Melbourne · Toronto

ST MARTIN'S PRESS

New York

1968

Published by
MACMILLAN & CO LTD
Little Essex Street London W C 2
and also at Bombay Calcutta and Madras
Macmillan South Africa (Publishers) Pty Ltd Johannesburg
The Macmillan Company of Australia Pty Ltd Melbourne
The Macmillan Company of Canada Ltd Toronto
St Martin's Press Inc New York

Library of Congress catalog card no. 67-16867

Printed in Great Britain by
R. & R. CLARK LTD
Edinburgh

CONTENTS

vii

Contents

ACKNOWLEDGEMENTS

THE International Economic Association wishes to express its gratitude to all the organizations and individuals who helped to make this Conference possible. It could not have taken place without the grants of the Ford Foundation and of UNESCO which have supported the work of the Association. In the particular case of this Conference, these grants were reinforced by the generous assistance given by the Bank of Sicily; to the Bank itself, to its Director-General, Dr. Giuseppe La Barbera, and to our President, Dr. Ugo Papi, who brought our needs to their attention, we are particularly grateful. We owe many debts for their friendly help in overcoming the minor problems of working in a strange city and for their intellectual encouragement to Professor Giuseppe Mirabella of the University of Palermo and his assistant Dr. Gaetano Cesario.

The Conference was held in the beautiful setting of the Hotel Igiea on the outskirts of Palermo. We shall remember both the long views from its terrace and the helpfulness of its staff. But a Conference depends for its success on its programme, its papers, and its discussions. The Officers of the Association would wish to express their great gratitude for what was unquestionably a most interesting and stimulating conference to Professor Jean Marchal, who was the architect of the programme and the chief editor of this volume, to all the authors of the papers, to the participants in the vigorous discussions, and not least to Professor Bernard Ducros, who has managed to convey to a reader so much of the substance of all that was said.

LIST OF PARTICIPANTS

Professor Armen A. Alchian, University of California, Los Angeles, U.S.A.

Professor D. A. Allackverdyan, Association of Soviet Economic Scientific Institutions, Moscow, U.S.S.R.

Professor H. Brochier, University of Grenoble, France

Professor M. Bronfenbrenner, Carnegie Institute of Technology, Pittsburg, U.S.A.

Dr. A. Bruzek, Prague, Czechoslovakia.

Professor M. Negreponti Delivanis, University of Salonika, Greece.

Professor D. Delivanis, University of Salonika, Greece.

Professor B. Ducros, Faculté de Droit and de Sciences Économiques, Dijon, France.

Professor M. Falise, Centre de Recherches Économiques et de Gestion, Lille, France.

Professor L. Fauvel, Secretary-General of IEA, Faculté de Droit, University of Paris, France.

Mr. C. H. Feinstein, Department of Applied Economics, Cambridge, U.K.

Professor C. Föhl, Freie Universität, Berlin, Germany.

Professor E. Gannagé, Beirut, Lebanon.

Professor R. Gendarme, Faculté de Droit, University of Nancy, France.

Professor B. Haley, Stanford University, U.S.A.

Professor E. James, Faculté de Droit, University of Paris, France.

Dr. A. Jeck, University of Munich, Germany.

Dr. Karl Jungenfelt, Industrial Institute for Economic and Social Research, Stockholm, Sweden.

Professor W. Krelle, Institut für Gesellschafts- und Wirtschaftswissenschaften der Universität Bonn, Germany.

Professor J. Lecaillon, Faculté de Droit et des Sciences Économiques, University of Lille, France.

Professor E. Lipinski, University of Warsaw, Poland.

Professor André Marchal, Faculté de Droit, University of Paris, France.

Professor Jean Marchal, Faculté de Droit, University of Paris, France.

Professor G. Mirabella, University of Palermo, Sicily.

Professor K. Ohkawa, Hitotsubashi University, Tokyo, Japan.

Dr. P. N. C. Okigbo, Cabinet Office, Lagos, Nigeria.

Professor Ostrovitianob, Association of Soviet Economic Scientific Institutions, Moscow, U.S.S.R.

Professor G. U. Papi, University of Rome, Italy.

Dr. Luigi Pasinetti, King's College, Cambridge, U.K.

Professor D. Patinkin, The Eliezer Kaplan School of Economics and Social Sciences, The Hebrew University, Jerusalem, Israel.

Professor A. I. Petrov, Association of Soviet Economic Scientific Institutions, Moscow.

Professor E. H. Phelps Brown, London School of Economics, U.K.

Professor E. Preiser, University of Munich, Germany.

Professor P. Nørregaard Rasmussen, Institute of Economics, University of Copenhagen, Denmark.

Professor M. W. Reder, Stanford University, California, U.S.A.

Professor E. A. G. Robinson, University of Cambridge, U.K.

Professor E. Schneider, Kiel University, Germany.

Professor R. M. Solow, Massachusetts Institute of Technology, Cambridge, Mass., U.S.A.

Dr. N. V. Sovani, Gokhale Institute of Politics and Economics, Poona, India.

Professor R. C. Tress, University of Bristol, U.K.

Dr. L. Urban, Prague, Czechoslovakia.

Dr. Julia Zala, Hungarian Central Statistical Office, Budapest, Hungary.

INTRODUCTION

BY

JEAN MARCHAL
University of Paris
Chairman of Programme Committee

AND

BERNARD DUCROS
University of Paris
Rapporteur

UNDER the aegis of the International Economic Association some
forty economists met at Palermo in September 1964 to study income
distribution. The debates proved to be stimulating for those who
were privileged to participate. The purposes of such a Conference,
however, are not completely fulfilled until its proceedings have been
made available to all in printed form. We take pleasure, therefore,
in introducing the reader to the twenty-seven papers submitted to
the Conference together with the summary record of the debates.
Discussions were extensive and lively. If our own experience is
to be trusted, those days of working in pleasant surroundings in a
close-knit community were valuable as well as enjoyable.

The Conference began by looking at the factual evidence in
capitalist, socialist, and newly developing countries. Theoretical
models of income distribution were then dissected and, finally,
policies came in for examination. It was clear that there were conflicting ideas on theoretical, methodological, and doctrinal grounds as
soon as the facts were produced for interpretation. Soviet, Polish,
Czech, and Hungarian economists present gave opportunity for an
interesting investigation into the ways in which the social product
was allocated in socialist countries. Russian colleagues put the stress
on the basic differences in the process and results of distribution in
socialist and capitalist economies. Dr. Bruzek, Dr. Urban, and
Dr. Juliet Zala studied income distribution in Czechoslovakia and
Hungary. Frank and highly informative, their papers and remarks
brought out how centrally-planned economies were trying, for the
sake of economic efficiency, to reintroduce market mechanisms in
the allocation and rewarding of the factors of production. Although
the participants were reminded of the fundamental differences,

these papers showed how socialist and capitalist economic systems were tending to converge.

The study of income distribution in developing countries gave the opportunity to compare the established theory of distribution with a theory in the making. Professor Sovani, in discussing Professor Gannagé's paper, emphasized that data on distribution in developing countries were still scarce, unreliable, and difficult to interpret in the usual theoretical terms. Professor Maria Negreponti Delivanis, Professor Gendarme, and Professor André Marchal were all strongly in favour of a revision of established theory to accommodate the special features relating to the social structures and development level in such economies. A number of English-speaking colleagues maintained, on the other hand, that the apparatus of pure theory was comprehensive enough to deal with all situations.

When it came to market economies, the determination of the distributive shares for labour and capital, considered as central to the theory by most American, British and German economists present, gave abundant opportunity for comparing neo-classical and post-Keynesian theory. If one assumes that income distribution is the intermediate stage between production and income generation, on the one hand, and spending or allocating distributed income to consumption and saving, on the other hand, income distribution can be approached either through production or through effective demand. This would seem to be the basic difference between the neo-marginalist, supply-orientated theory and the post-Keynesian, demand-orientated theory of distribution.

The former approach was brilliantly set forth in several papers. In a paper whose original purpose was to meet the objection against marginal productivity analysis in its usual version — the use of a cardinal measure of utility for inter-personal comparisons, by ordinally measuring utility instead — Professor Reder showed with much inventiveness how marginal productivity could explain the differentiation of labour income as a function of personal abilities, of the cost and social utility of training as valued by market mechanisms.

But how total income was distributed between labour and property remained the central theme of the marginal productivity analysts. In presenting a version based on the Cobb–Douglas functions, Professor Bronfenbrenner made it clear that the neo-classical theory explained income distribution by the process of production — the combination of inputs reduced to the two factors, capital and labour — and not in terms of the way in which income was spent and re-formed as an aggregate. Income distribution was macro-economic since its object was to determine relative shares in total income, but the determining of the shares resulted from the combination of factors within the firm by a profit-maximizing entrepreneur and thus the analysis is entirely based on micro-economics.

Production functions were therefore a fundamental consideration : for a given technology, the reward of a factor would depend on the marginal productivity of its inputs and on the extent to which the quantity of this factor employed relative to the other factor varies in accordance with a change in its relative price. In the case of a relative increase in the use of one factor, one can expect this to be accompanied by a relative decrease in its reward per unit and conversely — always assuming the production function to be un-changed — that a relative increase in its reward will mean its use diminishing in proportion. With a given technology, an increase in the wage rate above the marginal productivity of labour would result in a decrease in entrepreneurs' demand for labour, assuming that they could substitute capital for labour in the combinations of factors.

Do they, however, behave in this way and can they substitute one factor for the other, at any rate in the long run ? At this crucial moment of the reasoning the Cobb–Douglas type of production function comes in. In making a drastic simplification and assuming the elasticity of substitution between labour and capital to be unity, Cobb and Douglas have given a new life to the marginal productivity theory which had been held up for so long by conceptual difficulties of how to impute increase in product between several factors. Econometrical verifications have shown the elasticity of substitution to be near unity in the long run. The stability of distributive shares of labour and capital in the data used for these verifications implies that, if the employment of one factor changes proportion-ately to the other, its reward per unit shall change in the reverse proportion relatively to the other, so that its relative share in dis-tribution (the quantity employed multiplied by its relative unit price) shall remain unchanged. For given production functions, capital and labour may be combined in different proportions according to changes in their relative prices ; conversely the ratio of their rewards per unit may change as a result of variations in the amount of accumulated capital in proportion to the labour force but relative shares of labour and capital will not change.

Technology itself is allowed to change. If technical progress remains neutral, say in Hicks' sense — if it results in an increase at the same rate of both capital and labour productivity — the level of product and factors' productivities will rise. Distributive shares will become larger in absolute amounts, but relative shares will remain unchanged. Thus marginal productivity theory far from being a short-run explanation can be considered as explaining the growth of factors of incomes as the outcome of long-run changes in supply and demand of factors and technology.

The theory can make allowance for technological change. It can be dynamic. But does it escape equally from the objection of being generalized micro-economics rather than being macro-economics proper? There has been, over the last twenty years, a great deal of discussion over the conceptual meaning of an aggregative production function and the difficulties of deriving it from the micro-functions for individual firms. Nevertheless the most decisive debate seems to us to be not in aggregating micro-functions, but in the underlying assumption that one can do without a direct determination of the various classes of incomes as aggregates. Let us admit that in a market economy factors' incomes are distributed within the firm as a result of the combination of factors by the entrepreneur. But does it follow that macro-distribution is nothing but the summing-up of intra-firm income distribution? We are not so sure.

A first ground for doubt — on which our English-speaking colleagues at the Conference seemed to agree in principle but were not ready to put much weight — was that the generalization of micro-economic production functions is based on the assumption that the conditions of production for the representative firm in a given branch or sector extend to the whole economy. In reasoning, for instance, on the share of hired labour it is difficult to admit that the conditions of reward in agriculture or in public administration do not fundamentally differ from those in manufacturing.

There are more general grounds for objection. To state that functional income distribution is entirely a matter of production functions — of the profit-maximizing activity of the entrepreneur and the way he adjusts capital intensity according to the market price ratio of capital and labour inputs — is to assume a definite pattern of relationship between causes and effects in economic

Introduction

theory. It is to assume that distribution is the direct outcome of production and also that, the profit share being determined by the entrepreneurs' profit-maximizing, the share of investment in the national product, as well as other aggregates, will be consequently determined.

Here was the main bone of contention between the neo-classicists and the post-Keynesians whose views were no less brilliantly set forth at the Conference. For the Kaldorians the causality runs the other way round. They start from effective demand and consider the income generating effect of investment expenditure and the part played by investment in promoting growth through increased capacity of production. The post-Keynesian authors do not consider profit as the entrepreneur's maximized individual income, but as the aggregate outcome of investment activity. Therefore, in order to explain distributive shares, instead of looking at the relationship between inputs of capital and labour in the firm's outlays, they rather turn to the overall capital-product relationship.

Investment thus jointly explains growth and distribution. For a given capital-product ratio, a constant ratio of the increase in production capacity (measured as a rate of investment in the product) to the rate of increase of the product, the rate of investment which will allow for balanced growth with permanent full employment of available factors — the Harrodian 'natural' growth — cannot be determined without bringing into the reasoning the investment-saving relationship. Clearly one needs to know what current savings will be at different alternative levels of investment. One is thus led to consider propensity to save, or rather the propensities to save of two different groups, since in our capitalist system capital accumulation by entrepreneurs (and the income inequality which goes with it) implies a systematic differentiation between capitalists and workers. Because of this process of income differentiation — which is related to the way effective demand is generated and not to the distinction between two sorts of inputs in production — the conditions of stability in the process of growth remain a problem which cannot be solved until one has determined how aggregate income, created by the multiplier effect of spending for increasing production capacity, has been distributed between the two groups. As Dr. Pasinetti pointed out, a theory of balanced growth needs the profit and the wage shares as weights of the propensities to save of the capitalists and the workers. Otherwise the overall propensity to save would remain indeterminate.

The Distribution of National Income

If the propensities to save are assumed to be stable and the capital-output ratio constant, according to the Kaldorian model the profit share must vary in the same way as the share of investment in the national product. 'Bowley's law' stating the constancy of the relative shares is turned into a long-run condition of equilibrium for balanced growth since the constancy of the profit share is implied in the constancy of the investment rate. The implications of Bowley's law are not the same as in the Cobb-Douglas version of the neo-classical theory. The constancy of the distributive shares is a condition of stable growth and, for given propensities to save, the same state of equilibrium will persist as long as the capital-output ratio keeps constant, whereas, for given production functions, the neo-classical theory would make this state of equilibrium depend on the flexibility of the relationship between capital and labour — that is, on a high elasticity of substitution between factors.

Which of the two competing theories, neo-marginalist or post-Keynesian, is to be preferred? It seems to us that our debates have thrown much light on this issue, firstly by demonstrating how necessary it was to combine both theories and secondly by showing that they nevertheless remain contradictory.

Attempts at reconciling them were made at the Conference. At the beginning of Professor Solow's paper the reader will find an interesting comparison of the two models, the one characterized as an analysis of the distribution of an homogeneous product between two factors, the other as an analysis of distribution in a two-sector economy where factors remain undifferentiated. The outcome of the comparison is that a satisfactory model ought to be both a two-factor and a two-sector model. The two-sector analysis, however, is brought into the neo-classical, two-factor model only as a step towards a generalized equilibrium 'à la Walras' where the fixing of the rewards for a number n of factors calls for the simultaneous determination of the prices for n goods.

In the special case of two factors, capital and labour, being combined to produce, in two sectors, consumer's goods and capital goods, it ought to be possible to determine simultaneously, in a non-contradictory way, the conditions of the capitalists' and the workers' rewards, approaching the problem both from the side of demand and relative prices of the two-factor inputs, and also from that of demand and relative prices of the two products. For instance, in factor proportions one could use more capital; in sector proportions one could produce more capital goods. But does not the one imply the other? Conversely, an improved remuneration for capital relative to labour could come from capital as a factor being relatively more demanded. But this would mean as well an increased demand for capital goods, resulting in an increase in their relative price. There is surely a pattern of interdependence between the factoral and the sectoral sides and each of the two models remains incomplete in neglecting this sort of interdependence.

If, however, the model proposed by Professor Solow could be called a generalized model in the sense of retaining both the factoral and the sectoral sides in the relationship of interdependence, this had been made possible only by extending the scope of the micro-economic approach. The two-sector analysis had been devised in the same micro-economic terms as the two-factor analysis, and Professor Solow, in the discussion of his paper, was led to state that the limit case of his model was the two-factor *cum* one-product situation — and not one-factor *cum* two-product — a situation where marginal productivity was the only relevant analysis. Thus his model was a generalization of the micro-economic approach, not a reconciliation of the two approaches.

In the course of the debates Professor Reder significantly raised the question of what would come from extending the reasoning to a third factor and a third product. The third distributive share would be univocally determined only in so far as income recipients could be univocally broken up into three homogeneous groups. The breaking up might, however, lead to different conflicting results depending on whether one classified groups according to factor specificity or homogeneity of sectoral products and propensities to buy products. Professor Reder raised this objection on logical and mathematical grounds. We would like to explore its implications *in concreto*. Assuming, plausibly enough, the third factor to be land, the third sector would be agriculture. The distributive share of the third group, farmers, would depend on whether land was more or less intensely used relative to the two other factors and also on what the demand for farm products was relative to the two other sectors' products.

Under these assumptions it is most likely that the third distributive share would be equivocally determined. As a factor's reward it would be the landowners' share in income, land rents. From the sectoral point of view it would be the reward of farmers *lato sensu*, i.e. people engaged in producing farm products. Even in functional distribution these are two different classes of income. Assuming for simplicity's sake that there is no self-employment in agriculture so that people are rewarded either as landowners, or farm labourers, or farmers *stricto sensu*, i.e. entrepreneurs combining rented land and hired labour with their own capital for profit, there is still a major theoretical difficulty.

Having retained three factors and correspondingly three classes of income recipients : workers, capitalists, and landowners, for determining income distribution between the three groups according to the sector from which their income is generated, we have to consider three specific propensities to spend : a propensity to buy consumer's goods produced by the corresponding industrial sector ; a propensity to save or to buy investment goods produced by the other sector of manufacturing activities (since for an equilibrium value of the distributive shares savings are equal to the amount of investment made by capitalists) ; finally, a propensity to buy (or, rather, to consume) products from the third sector, farm products. It might happen that workers, capitalists, and landowners have different propensities to buy manufactured consumer's goods and different propensities to save (and therefore, residually different propensities to buy food products) so that a three-group model is neither under- nor over-determined. The three-group model, how-ever, is most likely to be over-determined, short of assuming personal distribution to be just the same as functional distribution. For instance, wage-earners in the agricultural sector might have a higher propensity to save than wage-earners in manufacturing industries, but one that was very near to that of farmers ; conversely, land-owners might have roughly the same propensity to consume farm products as farmers and other capitalists, whereas wage-earners might have roughly the same, irrespective of whether they are employed in manufacturing or farming activities.

In passing thus to principles of income differentiation — one relating to factors on the supply side and one relating to products on the demand side — homogeneous classes of incomes would tend to be defined in two contradictory ways in a three-group analysis.

One obvious way to escape the contradiction between the two approaches is to give up one of them. If one's interest lies in studying functional distribution of primary income ; if one sees no objection to breaking up all observed personal incomes before redistribution to factor incomes by imputing either a labour or a capital income to self-employed and small entrepreneurs ; if one is convinced that the laws of distribution are nothing but another way of stating the laws of production, i.e. allocating highly substitutable factor resources between alternative aims ; if changes in the structure of the labour force such as an increasing number of wage-earners relative to self-employed and small entrepreneurs really do nothing but conceal the basic fact that the ratio of the real wage rate to the product per head changes as does marginal productivity of labour as a consequence of technological progress, so that once the bias due to structural changes on the observed distributive share of hired labour has been removed the wage-earners' share is proved to be determined by technological factors alone ; if this, and only this, is the purpose of the theory of distribution then the way out of the contradiction must be by giving up sectoral analysis.

For the purely factoral approach there would then be only gains and no losses in retaining its original bi-partite analysis : on one side labour incomes grouped around the big, hard core of industrial wages ; on the other, all non-labour incomes, no matter whether they can be called profit or not, since they have the common character of deriving from the ownership of material means of production. There are many grounds for objecting to income imputation as was pointed out by the senior author of this introduction in the debates, but its logic could not be questioned within the limits of a purely factoral analysis. Very often imputing an income alternately to labour and to capital will lead to conflicting results because in activities where self-employment is found labour and capital are combined in such a way as to make their joint productivity abnormally low ; but in such cases, if income imputation is considered valid, our opinion is that an income at market rate should be imputed to labour, leaving the reward of capital as the abnormally low residual income rather than the reverse. We would agree with Professor Tress's comment that, from a social point of view, in the case of self-employed people such as shopkeepers and small farmers, the reward of the individual's labour is sacrificed to the aim of maintaining the family's inherited assets. If, however, there is to be income imputation, it is better to impute a market wage rate to labour corresponding to a rate that exists in activities where it can be regarded as determined by marginal productivity ; by showing the return on capital to be not enough for maximizing profit, it is implied that resources are not efficiently allocated in such activities. Self-employed people ought to behave as profit-maximizing entrepreneurs or give up self-employment and become wage-earners, all social implications of this being left aside.

Perhaps we have given an extreme account of our neo-classical colleagues' views. If so, this is implicitly a tribute to the sharpness of their analysis and to the uncompromising sincerity with which they argued in favour of their vision of income distribution. If, however, factoral analysis is contradictory to sectoral analysis, there is good ground for opting for the latter.

The same is true, in a way, of the Kaldorian model of distribution, since the consideration of effective demand and different group propensities to save relate to personal, not functional distribution. Starting from investment as an aggregate, the reasoning on the input side is limited to capital as production capacity and labour as level of employment. By assuming — and not demonstrating, the neo-classicists would object — a long-run full employment, and by assuming a constant capital-output ratio — an assumption which seems to tally with statistical observations — the taking into account of conditions of production is elegantly if drastically simplified. Analysis is centred on the determination of the profit share rather than the wage share ; for given equilibrium rate of investment and capital-output ratio, the latter being the reciprocal of the average rate of capital overall productivity (or, rather, the reciprocal of the average rate of the overall joint productivity of factors related to capital alone) the volume of investment as a share of total output is determined ; the determination of the share of profits in total income follows in its wake, leaving the determination of the wage share as a residual.

A bi-partite, if sectoral, analysis could be sufficient for determining the equilibrium rate of investment with full employment growth, since to know the overall amount of saving induced by alternative distributions of income between labour and capital one needs to know the propensities to save of both the wage-earners and the capitalists. The post-Keynesian school would not reject *a priori* the suggestion that a three-sector analysis would be preferable, but only in so far as saving behaviours are proved to be such as to justify the consideration of three different savings functions. Aggregate investment, however, remains the only factor of causality. The risk of loss of rigour and of clarity incurred in shifting from a two- to a three-sector analysis might well outweigh the advantage of such contingent improvement for the post-Keynesian theory.

The post-Keynesian theory has the great advantage of giving an account of the relationship between growth and income distribution, but in doing so it tends to neglect other implications of personal distribution. Income distribution is included in effective demand analysis on the ground that investment is not only inducing growth of real product through capital accumulation but also aggregate monetary income through a multiplier effect. Nevertheless we wonder whether it is possible to make distribution depend on capital accumulation alone, short of a Marxist interpretation of it — and to make anything depend on exogenous investment contrary to the corresponding Marxist analysis. Surely there were some grounds for the objection made by Kaldor's neo-marginalist colleagues that Kaldor's model dealt with the effects of income distribution rather than its causes. One cannot limit the impact of group behaviours on distribution to the results of alternative choices between consumption and saving. The conditions of equilibrium for distribution are not just a qualification of the saving-investment relationship.

Where are the causes ? The alternative neo-marginalist model gives only a hypothetical account of causes. The explanation which it offers is plausible only in so far as one believes in the validity of applying the generalization of the representative firm analysis to the entire economy. Our opinion is that this process of generalizing is objectionable, not only on empirical grounds but also for its implicit contradictions. One has to assume production by large capitalist corporations, but without this implying that market conditions are not close to perfect competition ; to assume manufacturing as the representative sector but without this resulting in trade-union organization of labour ; to assume no lagging sectors nor any advance of service activities, whereas both phenomena are conducive to either perpetuating old forms or the rise of new forms of self-employment activity ; last but not least, to assume the existence of a social pattern in which the state would have no part to play in redistributing income or in modifying the basic conditions of primary income distribution through its varied policies.

Should then the conclusions after confronting these two great alternative theories of distribution so brilliantly presented at the Conference by our English-speaking colleagues be entirely negative ? They ought to be complementary but they finally prove to be impossible to reconcile. An eclectic approach is still possible, as Professor Krelle's paper showed ; in his income distribution model a highly complex pattern of econometric relationship made it possible to consider coherently capital as both production capacity in the macro-economic fashion and as one of the factors of production in the micro-economic fashion. But no matter how interesting this sort of achievement may be for the future of economic theory, we believe that there is another way of getting out of the dilemma and it is this we would tentatively put forward here.

We are inclined to think that both neo-marginalist and post-Keynesian theory, on account of the way they approach income distribution, are subject to one and the same criticism. Economic activity as a circular process is a sequence of operations to be analysed in three steps : production, then distribution, then spending (by this we mean a logical order, not a time sequence). For the supply orientated neo-classical theory causality runs from production — the acts of combining factor inputs — to the distribution of real output. Conversely the demand orientated post-Keynesian theory makes the reasoning start from aggregate spending and works its way back from effective demand to output and the income creation effects of production through distribution. Both approach distribution as an intermediate step and neither pays much attention to the conditions under which incomes accrue to individuals and groups. If it were proved that the distribution process had no autonomy, no alternative would be left other than the neo-classical or the post-Keynesian and, in truth, it would not matter much which one would be preferred : approaching the process of income distribution from the side of production or from the side of effective demand would be two distinct but complementary approaches.

This not being so seems to indicate some measure of autonomy of group behaviours as income recipients in the causal relationship, in so far as people react as collectively conscious groups to the conditions under which social product is allotted through either primary distribution or redistribution of income. This is the starting point of the sociological — or rather the 'socio-economic' — theory of distribution which the senior author of this introduction put forward. Professor Lecaillon, Professor Brochier, and Professor Gendarme also made their contributions to this theory at the Conference.

May we be permitted at this stage to confess that at the end of the debates our belief in the socio-economic approach was even stronger? On purely theoretical grounds if one chooses to analyse the observed data of personal distribution, relative shares clearly cannot be based on factors, but neither can they be based on sectoral analysis alone or on a combination of both factors and sectors which would lead to contradictory results. The theory of distribution to get out of the deadlock must be based on a positive and detailed analysis of the working population and its evolutive pattern. This

Introduction

means reasoning from socio-occupational categories or *catégories socio-professionnelles*.

It was objected that such an analysis was just a lapse into institutionalism : a sin against the purity of theory. But does not this objection confuse theory with such and such an econometric model ? Our concept of *catégories socio-professionnelles* is obtained by crossing two well-defined criteria : one occupational according to the earning process relating to the household's major source of income ; the other sociological according to income disposal process, the household's spending and saving behaviour. This two-criteria classification of personal incomes is in our opinion a better cross analysis than the factor/sector one.

Socio-occupational categories, far from being institutional notions, are currently used in French social accounting — and no one would deny social accounting to be quantitative analysis. Economists who choose to approach distribution from micro-economic analysis have grounds for objecting to this argument, but we cannot so easily accept methodological objections from post-Keynesian economists to a type of analysis devised so as to bridge the gap between social accounting and theory.

Does a socio-economic analysis give a better account of the long-run trends in observed data than the alternative approaches ? Out of six papers dealing with the factual evidence in capitalist countries the four on the United States, Britain, Germany, and Japan by Professor Haley, Dr. Feinstein, Dr. Jeck, and Professor Ohkawa were based on the usual bi-partite analysis and were implicitly geared to verifying the marginal productivity theory. Bowley's law of long-run constancy of capital's and labour's relative shares loomed large in the background. Their authors are to be congratulated for their care in gathering and analysing the data. It would be most unfair to pretend they have given no convincing explanation of observed changes in the distributive shares when these were rather short-run movements and could be related to cyclical fluctuations or violent monetary disturbances, such as the 1923 inflation in Germany, where there was, for a time, a sharp downturn in the share of property because of the vanishing real value of the returns on money claims. Certain movements of the shares were explained by reference to Kaldor's model. For instance Professor Phelps Brown pointed out that it was a fitting explanation of the increase in the profit share in Germany during the rearmament boom in the pre-war period. Professor Falise, using Kaldor's model to interpret Belgian data in a recent ten-year period, did not find the expected correlation between investment and profit. A deflationary bias of the Belgian economy in comparison with its trading partners could well explain why the observed results departed from Kaldorian assumptions.

A secular trend towards an increasing share of labour, however, was observed by Professor Lecaillon in the French data approached from the socio-economic angle, and also in German data and, although less significantly, in the United States and British data — a fact which, as Professor E. A. G. Robinson pointed out, was not usually regarded as a matter for explanation by distribution models. Neo-classical theory might provide an explanation by invoking a systematic bias in the effect of technological progress on distribution between factors ; a 'neutral' progress is a handy assumption for short-run analysis but it needs to be verified in long-run analysis. On the post-Keynesian side one should consider *inter alia* the effects of a changing proportion of replacement expenditure in gross investment which was studied in Professor Rasmussen's paper. In periods of steady growth with a stepping-up of the net rate of investment the consequently decreasing proportion of replacement in gross capital expenditure would rather tend to an increasing profit share than the reverse. One might still suggest another, more general, post-Keynesian explanation in downward movements of the equilibrium rate of investment in connection with similar movements in the saving functions. Nevertheless observations of a diminishing share of profit, especially in the French data, did not relate to periods of diminishing rates of growth alone.

Even if the penalty is to be branded as institutionalists or, in this case, historicists, the authors would suggest that such a trend cannot be accounted for either by changes in factor productivities or in the rate of capital accumulation but by changes in socio-economic conditions of distribution. These conditions have changed partly as a result of changes in productivity and capital accumulation ; but the picture would be far from complete if structural changes in the work force — in the pattern of socio-occupational categories — were not brought in. These are, first, changes in number and proportions of people in different categories. An investigation should be made into factors explaining group cohesion in the formation and distribution of income, as well as into their organization for advancing claims either through pressure on market conditions or on the policy-makers.

The bi-partite analysis should remain a preliminary step in

approaching the basic issue on distribution in these sectors of the economy where the conditions retained in the highly simplified model of a pure market economy are approximated ; the issue there is mainly one of wage-earners versus capitalist entrepreneurs. But to reduce the whole process of income distribution to one of labour versus non-labour income is an undue generalization of the observed process of division of capitalist firms' receipts between wages and gross profits. In the long-run analysis this reasoning often led our authors to conclude that the labour share *lato sensu*, including an income imputed to self-employed labour, had decreased whereas the share of hired labour — a more homogeneous category — had increased, and the share of salaries — a sub-category of the former, still more significant as being more homogeneous, at any rate if it is defined according to socio-occupational criteria and not institutional or legal criteria as used, for instance, in British data — had increased even more. This seemed to us clearly a case for at least a threefold analysis of income division : wages and salaries of hired labour, entrepreneurial and corporate profits, self-employed or mixed incomes. The objection which was most frequently voiced against a three-fold analysis was that it prevented long-run comparisons of resource allocation between capital and labour on a permanent homogeneous basis. Where there is an unchanged pattern of labour and non-labour homogeneous groups of income recipients, such as wage-earners and capitalist employers, one can opt for the study of functional distribution proper, but even in such a case it seems that the endeavour is justified only in so far as group analysis can back up factor analysis.

The Conference was an occasion for trying out distribution theory on grounds of its logical coherence and its capacity to explain observed facts. It had to be submitted to a final test : confronting it with economic policy. Several papers dealt with policy-making. Professor Papi, the then President of the IEA, submitted a paper on state intervention encompassing both the general impact of public finance on distribution and income redistribution policies with risk hedging as a central theme. Professor Fauvel approached farmers' incomes in relation to price support policies.

As was to be expected, incomes policy was on our schedule. Western countries in the post-war years have experienced a process of steady but unbalanced growth with an inflationary bias. As was pointed out by Professor Phelps Brown, contrary to the experience of pre-war years, one does not observe in a period of boom a downward cyclical movement of the labour share ; it seems that the Kaldorian process of re-equilibrium by means of an increase in the profit share, so as to push the savings ratio up to a high rate of investment, fails to operate. And the relationship between investment, distributive shares, and savings, instead of providing a convincing explanation of the re-equilibrium process, rather explains the reasons for state intervention in order to adjust the shares in such a way as to balance savings and investment at full employment level.

Why has the process of monetary re-equilibrium through changes in distributive shares become inoperative ? For some of us marginal productivity theory supplied the answer. A persistent disequilibrium was a clear sign that market forces tending to equate the wage rate to marginal productivity of labour at full employment level were prevented from operating ; if trade unions' bargaining power allowed for the wage rate to be kept above marginal productivity the penalty to be paid for this in a consistent market economy would have been unemployment, but in our economies the policy of full employment at any cost allowed the money wage rate to stay above its constant price *cum* full employment equilibrium level : if then the penalty is not unemployment it has to be upward instability of the price level.

Thus imbalance ought to be related to two factors in combination : trade union organization to allow labour a measure of monopoly on the labour market and governmental full-employment policy, carried out as an unconditional commitment. A return to 'orthodox' monetary policy was therefore advised : at the cost of a brief spell of unemployment a deflationary policy would restore monetary equilibrium and also by its resulting effect of diminishing the employers' demand for labour it would consequently bring down trade unions' bargaining power to a level consistent with equating the wage rate to marginal productivity.

Do market forces respond so as to limit the scope and duration of the unemployment effect ? Will it not be necessary to repeat the deflationary process at intervals with such frequency that it may tend over time to increase uncertainty of expectations of growth ? The price to be paid for securing stability through monetary policy alone may be too high and a majority of the participants at any rate seemed in doubt about this.

The disagreement on prognosis stemmed from a disagreement on the diagnosis of disequilibrium. No matter what one's feelings are about the socio-economic theory of distribution, would not the diagnosis imply some measure of socio-economic analysis ? In their papers on incomes policy in Britain and in France both Professor Tress and Professor Brochier emphasized the reasons which made incomes policy a necessity under changing conditions of the distribution process. It seemed agreed that from a monetary point of view disequilibrium was related to the appearance of a new form of inflation : cost inflation as distinct from demand inflation. Cost inflation, however, is not *per se* a cost-push effect of wage claims. They do not seem to be usually the initial cause of inflation as would clearly be the case if wage rate increased over marginal productivity, all other conditions of equilibrium standing. This proviso does not apply to actual cases ; rather is cost inflation a factor of propagation of inflationary pressures initiated by excess demand such as a stepping up of investment expenditure. Most often cost inflation will be connected with settlements of wage claims because of a previous increase in the cost of living. It should be interpreted as the corporate reaction of people who, rightly or wrongly, believe themselves the losers in the changing conditions of distribution of real income.

If such a phenomenon as bargaining power and therefore group behaviour is relevant to disequilibrium analysis, one ought not to relate it *a priori* to labour unions or to one group alone but consider all income recipient groups in so far as their combined claims might be in excess of social product at the current price level. If one supports a distribution policy, there is thus no alternative to marginal productivity theory but a socio-economic analysis of some sort.

Of course labour enjoys a certain degree of monopoly, but trade unionism is only one of the varied forms of organized group pressure to be considered. The degree of monopoly theory can be reckoned as being an alternative theory to marginal productivity. Professor Preiser's authoritative opinion emphasized significantly enough that, whereas primary income distribution could be approached as a result of production, yet, in his own words, production ought to be envisaged as a struggle between groups, not only for money wages on the labour market but also for price determination by entrepreneurs. Following this line of thought, Professor Preiser said, was recognizing that distribution was not simply the effect, or, so to speak, the by-product, of the whole process of producing, consuming, and investing because a certain distribution was planned by the actors.

From this to a socio-economic theory there is but a single step.

It being agreed that the conditions under which social product is divided between labour and capital are affected by the degree of monopoly of which both categories somehow can avail themselves, the next step might possibly be a more detailed analysis of the actors as socio-occupational classes and of the impact of their specific behaviour on distribution. Distribution as an observed result of the equilibrium process might not tally with distribution planned by the actors ; groups will react if their expectations fail to materialize. If their reactions lead to inflation this is a sure sign that monetary equilibrium and social equilibrium — in Professor Lecaillon's terms — do not coincide. An incomes policy has to be thought of as an attempt at making the two equilibria mutually consistent by new ways of settling conflicting claims on the expected real increment in the social product under the state's sponsorship. One has to reconcile conditions for monetary and for social equilibrium. To deny the autonomy of the latter and analyse group behaviour as if it were nothing but an obstacle to an altogether perfectly determined process of equilibrium might not be the most suitable way of approaching policy issues.

Even in the last session on economic policy conflicting ideas thus emerged. No one would yield on the essentials. Ideas are not to be swapped like stamps or old jokes. What was shared by all of us was what was undivided : a feeling of brotherhood born of a common quest. Though many of the enjoyable memories of Palermo are condemned to remain off the record, we nevertheless hope that the readers of the papers and proceedings will have some stimulation of their interest.

PART I

RECENT TRENDS IN INCOME DISTRIBUTION IN MORE ADVANCED CAPITALIST ECONOMIES

Chapter 1

CHANGES IN THE DISTRIBUTION OF INCOME IN THE UNITED STATES

BY

BERNARD F. HALEY
Stanford University

INTRODUCTORY

THE purpose of the present paper is to present a selection from the wealth of data bearing on changes in the distribution of income in the United States, and to indicate some of the more important structural changes in the U.S. economy that have had an impact on the distribution.[1] Although data available would permit a consideration of income distribution by occupation, by race, by age-groups, by regions, by education, and other variables, attention will be mainly focused on : (1) the changes in the size distribution of income for the United States as a whole since 1929, and (2) changes in the distribution between property and labour in the United States since 1850.

I. THE SIZE DISTRIBUTION OF INCOME

Estimates of the size distribution of personal incomes of families and unattached individuals in the United States are given, in 1963 dollars, in Table 1.[2] The pattern of the distribution is the typical

---

[1] The author is heavily indebted to M. W. Reder for helpful comments on an earlier draft.

[2] Estimates of the whole distribution are not available for years previous to 1929 ; and the reliability of the 1929 and 1941 sets of figures is probably considerably less than that of those for 1944 and subsequent years.

In addition to the estimates made by the Department of Commerce, which are available for most years since 1944, there are also annual estimates by the U.S. Bureau of the Census for the income distribution of both families and persons 14 years of age and over, available for years since 1944, and annual estimates by the University of Michigan Survey Research Center for the income distribution of 'spending units', available for years since 1946. There have also been a number of surveys of family income by the U.S. Bureau of Labor Statistics for individual years, the most recent of which, for 1950, is reviewed by Kravis [13]. The relations between these various sets of data are reviewed by Goldsmith [6]. (For references to the sources and literature see pp. 28–29 below.)

one : strongly skewed, a modal income well below the mean income per family, and a long tail stretching over the upper-income range. Since 1929 the whole distribution has moved upward in real terms, although it was lower than in 1929 during a substantial part of the 1930's. For the entire period 1929–63 the average rate of growth in the mean income (in 1963 prices) was 1·6 per cent.

TABLE 1

SIZE DISTRIBUTION
OF PERSONAL INCOMES OF CONSUMER UNITS 1929, 1941, 1947, 1963

(Dollars of 1963)

Income	Per cent Distribution			
	1929	1941	1947	1963
Under $2,000	30	27	16	11
$2,000–$3,999	38	28	28	18
$4,000–$5,999	16	22	26	20
$6,000–$7,999	7	12	14	18
$8,000–$9,999	3	5	7	12
$10,000–$14,999	6	6	6	13
$15,000 and over			3	8
Average (mean) income per consumer unit	$4,300	$4,599*	$5,520	$7,510

* 1962 dollars.

Sources : U.S. Department of Commerce [3] [4].

Note.—Consumer units consist of families and unattached individuals. Families are units of two or more persons related by blood, marriage, or adoption and residing together. Unattached individuals are persons not living with relatives. Family personal income included wage and salary receipts, other labour income, proprietors' and rental income, dividends, personal interest income, and transfer payments. Certain imputed items are included, such as non-monetary wages, net value of food and fuel consumed by farm-operator families, net rental value of owner-occupied homes, and imputed interest.

As the income distribution has moved upwards, it has also flattened somewhat, the percentage of consumer units in the lower-income classes decreasing, that in the upper-income classes increasing, and the percentage in the modal class decreasing. This tendency for the distribution to flatten is not necessarily accompanied by a reduction in the degree of inequality of the distribution [3, p. 18]. The latter is more clearly revealed in Table 2, which shows the distribution among quintiles and the top 5 per cent of consumer units for selected years.

TABLE 2

DISTRIBUTION OF FAMILY PERSONAL INCOME AMONG QUINTILES
AND TOP 5 PER CENT OF CONSUMER UNITS IN VARIOUS YEARS

Quintiles	Per cent Distribution					
	1929	1935–36	1941	1947	1955	1962
Lowest	13	4	4	5	5	5
Second		9	10	11	11	11
Third	14	14	15	16	16	16
Fourth	19	21	22	22	22	23
Highest	54	52	49	46	45	45
Top 5 per cent	30·0	26·5	24·0	20·9	20·3	19·6

Sources : For the 1929 figures [*31*] ; 1935–36 and 1941 [*8*] ; 1947, 1955, and 1962 [*7*] [*4*].

It is clear that in the period 1929–47 a significant reduction in the inequality of the distribution occurred.[1] This is shown by both an increase in the share of the lowest two quintiles and a decrease in the share of the highest quintile and, even more, in the share of the top 5 per cent of consumer units. The Gini concentration ratio decreased from ·47 for the income of consumer units in 1935–36 to ·41 in 1946 [*13*, p. 204].[2]

Since 1947 the inequality of the distribution has not changed significantly. This is brought out more clearly in Table 3 in which changes in the respective shares of the top and lowest income groups, as estimated by three different agencies, can be compared. The Commerce figures, carried to one decimal place, appear to show a slight decrease in the relative share of both the lowest quintile and the top 5 per cent of consumer units. But the Census and the

[1] Simon Kuznets [*14*, pp. 585, 635] has provided estimates of the share of the top 5 per cent of income recipients, on a *per capita* basis, for the period 1917–48. The tendency revealed by his figures for 1929–48 corresponds with that shown by Table 2. In the period 1917–28, on the other hand, the inequality of the distribution appears on the whole to have increased moderately. Kuznets's 'basic' variant income share (employee compensation, entrepreneurial income, rent, interest, and dividends) for the top 5 per cent increased from 24·6 to 26·78 per cent. The subsequent decline brought the figure down to 17·41 per cent in 1947. The share for the top 5 per cent for his 'economic income' variant (the basic variant corrected for non-reporting of state and local government salaries before 1938, omission of imputed rent, and use of an inappropriate income base in classifying tax data) increased from 26·1 per cent in 1919 to 32·06 per cent in 1928 and 32·12 per cent in 1932. It decreased to a low point of 18·68 per cent in 1944.
[2] The Gini concentration ratio is the ratio of the area between the diagonal line of complete equality and the Lorenz curve of income distribution to the entire triangular area under the diagonal.

5

The Distribution of National Income

Survey Research Center series, available only as rounded off, show no such tendencies. The concentration ratio [*13*, p. 204], which was ·41 for 1944, 1946, and 1950, was ·39 for 1952, ·4 for 1956, and ·4 for 1958, the last year for which it was computed.[1]

Various hypotheses have been advanced to explain the reduction in inequality in the period 1929–47 and the absence of any significant change in inequality in the period since 1947.

TABLE 3

THE SHARE OF THE TOP AND THE LOWEST INCOME GROUP
AS ESTIMATED BY THE DEPARTMENT OF COMMERCE,
THE BUREAU OF THE CENSUS, AND THE SURVEY RESEARCH CENTER

	Family Personal Income (Commerce)		Family Income (Census)		Income of Spending Units (Survey Research Center)	
	Lowest Quintile	Top 5 Per cent	Lowest Quintile	Top 5 Per cent	Lowest Quintile	Top 5 Per cent
1947	5·0	20·9	5	18	4	33
1948	n.a.	n.a.	5	17	4	31
1949	n.a.	n.a.	5	17	4	30
1950	4·8	20·4	4	17	4	29
1951	5·0	21·0	5	17	4	31
1952	4·9	21·0	5	18	4	30
1953	4·9	20·0	5	16	4	31
1954	4·8	20·0	4	16	4	29
1955	4·8	20·3	5	17	4	30
1956	4·8	20·2	5	16	4	31
1957	4·7	20·2	5	16	4	29
1958	4·7	20·0	5	16	4	27
1959	4·6	20·0	5	16	4	29
1960	4·6	19·6	5	17	4	28
1961	4·6	19·6	5	18	4	30
1962	4·6	19·6	5	16	n.a.	n.a.

Sources: Department of Commerce [*7*] [*4*]; Census [*30*]; Survey Research Center [*29*] [*12*, p. 12].

Note.—The Department of Commerce figures are for consumer units (families and unattached individuals). The Census figures are for families only. The Survey Research Center figures are for spending units (a spending unit consists of persons living in the same dwelling and belonging to the same family who pool their incomes to meet major expenses).

[1] However, as Pechman [*22*] has pointed out, the stability shown by the figures may be illusory. It is likely that changes in the tax laws and in tax practices have considerably altered the content of family personal income. Methods of compensating employees designed to avoid high tax rates, use of the preferential capital gains rates, the practice of splitting incomes among family members are illustrations.

(1) Changes in the Relative Importance of the Various Types of Income

As Table 4 shows, the percentage share of wages and salaries increased sharply between 1929 and 1939. It increased again between 1950 and 1953, but has been relatively stable since 1953. Transfer payments also increased during the 1930's and again in the period since 1953.

Self-employment income, which increased in relative importance during the war, has shown a declining percentage share since 1947. Both the increase during the war and the decline since the war are due in considerable part to underlying changes in the relative importance of farm-operator income. In 1947, the mean income of farm-operator families was nearly four times as high as it was in 1936, while the mean income of non-farm families was only a little more than twice as high [*18*, p. 123]. On the other hand, since 1947 the mean income of farm-operator families has risen only 40 per cent, while the mean income of all consumer units has risen about 70 per cent [*3*, p. 16]; and the number of farm-operator families has declined while the total of consumer units has been increasing. At the same time there has occurred a slight decrease in the percentage share of business and professional income in the aggregate of personal income for non-farm families, while the share of wages and salaries in this aggregate has moderately increased [*26*, p. 397]. These latter two changes no doubt have reflected a shift from self-employment to employee status in the non-farm sector.

TABLE 4

PER CENT DISTRIBUTION OF FAMILY PERSONAL INCOME
BY MAJOR TYPES OF INCOME, IN VARIOUS YEARS

(Billion dollars)

Type of Income	1929	1939	1947	Average 1950–55	Average 1956–62	1962
Wages and salaries	59·6	63·3	63·5	66·6	67·1	66·8
Transfer payments	1·7	4·0	6·3	5·7	7·4	8·1
	61·3	67·3	69·8	72·3	74·5	74·9
Self-employment income	17·6	16·3	19·1	15·6	12·5	11·6
Property income	21·1	16·4	11·1	12·1	12·9	13·5

Sources : 1929 and 1939 [*5*]; other years [*3*].

7

Property income (interest, rent, dividends) as a percentage of family personal income declined sharply between 1929 and 1947, and has increased slightly since the latter year. Also, both interest and dividends, but particularly the latter, have been included in the incomes of an increasing proportion of consumer units during the past decade [*17*, pp. 13–14]. Among the circumstances responsible for the decline in the relative share of property income in 1929–47 were : the decline in interest rates, low corporate profits during the 'thirties, and the high corporate income taxes imposed during the war and after.

An increase in the share of wages and salaries, such as occurred particularly in the period 1929–39 and since 1953, would tend to reduce the share of the upper-income groups even if the increase were distributed proportionately to all of the recipients of this type of income ; for wages and salaries constitute a much smaller share of the incomes of those in upper-income groups than of those in lower-income groups. Also, the concentration ratio for wages and salaries is typically lower than for self-employment income or for property income.[1] Since transfer payments go mainly to lower-income groups, the increase in this type of payment has also tended to reduce the inequality of the distribution, although its impact has been relatively small.[2]

The decline in the relative importance of property income between 1929 and 1947 tended also to reduce the inequality of the distribution. There is some basis for believing that this tendency was supplemented by a tendency for property income to become somewhat less concentrated [*13*, p. 224].

The lack of significant change in the inequality of the income distribution since 1947, in contrast to the period 1929–47, is in part related to the mixed impact of changes in the relative importance of different income types.[3] On the one hand the decline in the relative

[1] For the present it is assumed that the concentration ratios for these different types of income were unchanged during the period under consideration. In 1950 the concentration ratio for wages and salaries was between ·31 and ·35 for urban consumer units as compared with ·62 to ·68 for self-employment income, and ·50 to ·60 for property income [*13*, p. 193]. These coefficients were derived from the BLS survey of 1950 income ; and they refer to the inequality of distribution of *after-tax* income of each type.

[2] The Survey Research Center study of 1961 income shows that the lowest quintile of spending units received 29 per cent of aggregate transfer income, the next higher quintile 35 per cent [*12*, p. 23].

[3] Lee Soltow [*26*] shows, for the personal income distribution of non-farm multi-person families, that the decline in inequality between 1929 and 1947 was related significantly to the increase in the percentage shares of wages and salaries and of transfer payments, and the decrease in the relative importance of dividends

importance of property income ended about 1947, and thereafter the share of property income tended upward. Furthermore, in spite of the tendency toward a diffusion of stock ownership mentioned earlier, there appears to have been no significant change in the concentration of net worth of spending units in the period since 1947.[1]

On the other hand the decline in the relative share of self-employment income since 1947 has tended, along with the increase in the share of wages and salaries (particularly in 1950–53) and the increase in transfer payments, to favour a continuation in the tendency toward reduced inequality. There has at the same time been some reduction in the concentration ratios for two of the important components of self-employment income, families headed by 'managers, officials, and proprietors, excluding farm — self-employed', for whom the concentration ratio in 1948 was ·444 and in 1960 was ·399; and families headed by 'farmers and farm managers', for whom the concentration ratio decreased from ·550 in 1948 to ·461 in 1960 [*20*, pp. 152–160].

Changes have also occurred in the concentration ratios for wages and salaries income, and the impact of these changes is considered in the immediately following subsection.

TABLE 5

PER CENT OF AGGREGATE WAGE OR SALARY
INCOME RECEIVED BY EACH FIFTH OF WAGE
OR SALARY RECIPIENTS RANKED BY INCOME
IN VARIOUS YEARS

Quintiles	Per cent of Wage or Salary Income Received		
	1939	1949	1951
Lowest	3·4	2·6	3·0
Second	8·4	10·1	10·6
Third	15·0	18·7	18·9
Fourth	23·9	26·2	25·9
Highest	49·3	42·4	41·6

Source : [*18*, p. 104].

and interest. The lack of significant change in inequality since 1947 he attributes to the relative stability of the percentage shares of the different types of income, except for a moderate increase in the share of wages and salaries at the expense of the share of business and professional income.

[1] Net worth of spending units, the Survey Research Center finds, is much more unequally distributed than is income. No large shift occurred in the concentration from 1953 to 1962 [*12*, pp. 118–121].

9

(2) *Changes in Income Differentials within the Wages and Salaries Sector*

Particularly between 1939 and 1949 important changes occurred in income differentials within the wages and salaries sector. The net effect in that period was to reduce the inequality of distribution of wages and salaries. Table 5 shows the outcome in terms of the quintiles of wage or salary recipients. Since 1949, however, it is doubtful whether any reduction in inequality of distribution of wages and salaries has occurred ; and in fact the circumstances tending to increase inequality appear to have been strong.

The underlying changes are examined at four levels : (a) changes in the relative importance of different industries ; (b) changes within individual industries ; (c) changes in the relative importance of major occupation groups ; and (d) changes in skill differentials and in sex ratios within individual occupations.

(a) The major changes that have occurred in the relative importance of different industries since 1939 have been the relative decline of employment in agriculture and the relative increase of employment in manufacturing ; construction ; retail trade ; finance, insurance, and real estate ; business and repair services ; personal services ; professional services ; and public administration. The proportion of persons employed in agriculture dropped from 19 per cent of the total employed in 1940 to 6 per cent in 1963.[1] Since the coefficient of concentration has been higher for wage and salary recipients in agriculture than in other industries [2] and since the median income of the former group has been persistently much lower than that of wage and salary recipients in other industries, the shift of labour out of agriculture has contributed to the reduction in the inequality of distribution of wages and salaries that occurred between 1939 and 1949 ; and it has tended to offset the counter-effect of an increase in the concentration ratios for wages and salaries in industries generally that has occurred since 1949 [*20*, Table 17, pp. 326, 336].

Second only in importance to the reduced percentage of agri-

[1] Actually the decline in the proportion of persons engaged in agriculture began much earlier — from more than half the work force in 1870 to less than 40 per cent in 1900 [*13*, p. 125].

[2] In 1960 the concentration ratio for wage and salary income of males in agriculture, forestry, and fisheries was ·474 compared with ·355 for professional services ; ·368 for finance, insurance, and real estate ; ·357 for business and repair services ; ·451 for personal services ; ·296 for manufacturing ; ·331 for construction ; and ·244 for public administration — the industries which expanded most between 1949 and 1960 [*20*, Table 17, p. 326].

cultural employment has been the increased importance of employment in government [16, p. 521] [13, p. 218]. The dispersion of wage and salary income is less in government than in other sectors, and earnings per employee are very close to the national average. The share of government employment has increased from about 9 per cent of total employment in 1929 to about 15 per cent in 1950 and has continued at about the latter percentage.

(b) Although the changes in the industrial distribution of the labour force contributed to the reduction in inequality of the distribution of wages and salaries between 1939 and 1949, more important, according to Miller [19, pp. 358–359] were the changes in the dispersion of wage income within individual industries. He found that there was a narrowing of wage differentials for men in all but 5 of 117 industries examined. And Kravis has discerned 'a tendency for earnings in particular industries to "regress" toward the mean for all industries' [13, p. 217] : for example, the finance, insurance, and real estate sector had annual earnings per employee 47 per cent above the national average in 1929, but only 8 per cent above in 1950.

Between 1949 and 1960, however, as has already been noted, concentration ratios for wages and salaries income in each of the census industrial categories increased respectively for male and female workers. At the same time the proportion of female workers increased, particularly in retail trade ; finance, insurance, and real estate ; services ; and public administration ; but in only the first two of these categories was the concentration ratio for women workers lower than for men in 1960 [20, Table 17, pp. 326, 336].

(c) With regard to the distributional impact of changes in occupational structure, it has been estimated that [16, p. 521] :

> Between 1910 and 1955 the percentage of workers in unskilled employment was cut in half, the percentage in semi-skilled work rose by 50 per cent, the percentage in white-collar work doubled, as did the percentage in the 'professional, technical and kindred workers' classification. This change is clearly such as to encourage a narrowing of income inequality.

The change in occupational structure was in the direction of an increase in the proportion of workers in occupations having higher incomes and/or less unequal distributions of income [18, ch. 8, 9] [27, pp. 452–453]. The proportion of service workers and labourers, occupations characterized by relatively high income dispersion and median earnings well below the average, decreased, while the proportion of craftsmen, for whom the income dispersion was somewhat less and median earnings near the average, increased by about one-third between 1940 and 1952. There also occurred a decrease in the income differential between high-paid and low-paid occupations.

Between 1952 and 1960, however, the number of craftsmen, operatives and labourers decreased, while salaried professional workers and salaried managers (other than farm) increased about one-half, household workers about one-third, clerical workers and sales workers about one-quarter, and service workers about one-fifth [*20*, Table 14, pp. 276, 284]. Although the median income of salaried professional workers is relatively high, their concentration ratio is relatively low, and the sex ratio did not change significantly in the period 1952–60. On the other hand, the concentration ratio and median income are both high for salaried managers. In the case of clerical workers, nearly all of the increase was in female workers for whom the concentration ratio is low and the median income higher than for female workers in general. Practically all of the increase in household workers was in female workers also, but in this case the concentration ratio is high and median income low. For sales workers the sex ratio did not change significantly; median income for men is relatively high, for women about average; concentration ratios are high. In the case of service workers nearly all of the increase was in female workers for whom median income is low and concentration ratio is a little higher than average.

Of those occupational categories that decreased in relative importance after 1952, concentration ratios are relatively low for craftsmen, operatives, and labourers other than farm labourers; relatively high for farm labourers. On the whole, the decrease in these categories probably tended to be accompanied by an increase in the inequality of distribution of wages and salaries. The same tendency was probably strengthened by the increase in relative importance of salaried managers, household, service, and sales workers. On the other hand, the increase in the proportion of salaried professional workers and clerical workers may have worked the other way. The net effect of these changes upon the distribution of wages and salaries is uncertain; but it is clear that in the period since 1952, in contrast to 1939–51, no strong tendency towards a decline in inequality accompanied the shifts in occupational structure that occurred.

(d) Within occupations, there occurred a narrowing of inequality of the wage and salary income distribution during and after the war. An important reason for this was the reduction in unemployment that occurred during that period [*18*, p. 116]. There has also been a significant reduction in skill differentials within occupations, possibly due to the broadening of education, the reduction in the proportion of foreign-born in the labour force, the imposition and raising of a minimum wage (or a rise in the 'social minimum'), trade-union pressure as well as reduced unemployment [*24*, pp. 833–845]. However, there is evidence [*30*, No. 33, January 15, p. 6] that the narrowing of differentials among major occupations may have halted, and that it may even have been reversed.

That such a reversal may have occurred is borne out by changes in occupational concentration ratios between 1952 and 1960 [*20*, Table 14, pp. 276, 284]. In the case of the following occupational categories, all of which increased in relative importance during the period, concentration ratios increased : professional (male), clerical (female), sales (male and female), household (female), services (male and female). Concentration ratios also increased for the following occupational categories whose relative importance decreased during the period : craftsmen (male), operatives (male), and labourers (male). Of the remaining occupational categories, the concentration ratio decreased only for professional workers (female), a category whose relative importance increased ; and the concentration ratio remained about the same for salaried managers (male) and operatives (female), the former increasing and the latter decreasing in relative importance.

This rather strong tendency for concentration ratios to increase rather than decrease for different occupational categories since 1952 matched the increase in concentration ratios for wages and salaries that occurred in the different industry categories during the same period. Furthermore, as was pointed out in connection with changes in occupational structure during this period, the increase in the female–male sex ratio, while tending to reduce inequality in the case of clerical workers, worked the other way in the cases of household, sales, and service workers.

Altogether the strong circumstances tending to reduce inequality of the wage and salary distribution for individuals in the period 1939 to about 1950 have been weakened or reversed in the period since 1950.

(3) *Movement of Population from Rural to Metropolitan Areas*

The shift of families and employed labour out of agriculture has of course been accompanied by an increase in the proportion of

The Distribution of National Income

families living in urban areas and a decrease in the proportion living in rural farm areas. But as Table 6 shows, there also has occurred an increase in the proportion of families living in rural non-farm (e.g. suburban) areas. The concentration ratio for all families and that for unrelated individuals both declined between 1947 and 1959 — the former moderately and the latter considerably. Underlying the moderate decline in the concentration ratio for families is the considerable decline in the ratio for rural farm family incomes and the

TABLE 6

NUMBER OF FAMILIES AND UNRELATED INDIVIDUALS, MEDIAN INCOMES, CONCENTRATION RATIOS, AND SHARES OF TOP 5 PER CENT, CLASSIFIED BY URBAN, RURAL NON-FARM, AND RURAL FARM, 1947 AND 1959

	Total (Millions)		Median Income (1959 Dollars)		Concentration Ratio		Share Top 5 per cent	
	1947	1959	1947	1959	1947	1959	1947	1959
All Families	*37·3*	*45·1*	*3,957*	*5,417*	*·378*	*·366*	*17·5*	*16·3*
Urban	22·5	27·6	4,383	5,754	·344	·344	16·4	16·1
Rural Non-farm	8·3	13·6	3,688	5,360	·348	·356	16·2	15·8
Rural Farm	6·5	3·8	2,585	2,801	·493	·456	24·8	20·5
Unrelated Individuals	*8·1*	*10·7*	*1,325*	*1,557*	*·568*	*·512*	*33·3*	*23·2*
Urban	5·8	8·2	1,568	1,801	·548	·495	31·6	22·9
Rural Non-farm	1·3	2·0	927	1,126	·531	·518	25·7	22·3
Rural Farm	·9	·5	877	625	·560	·609	32·7	36·1

Source : [20, Table 1, pp. 36–45].

Note.—These are Census figures ; incomes do not include income in kind or imputed income items. Unrelated individuals are persons (other than inmates of institutions) not living with any relatives.

decline in the relative importance of this sector which has the highest concentration ratio of the three. But the decline in inequality for all families would have been greater during this period if it had not been for the increase in relative importance of the rural non-farm sector of family incomes coupled with the increase in the concentration ratio for this sector. The very fact that the decline in inequality of family incomes in the aggregate since 1947 was so moderate is no doubt related to this circumstance.

The more considerable decline in the concentration ratio in the case of unrelated individuals than in the case of families is the out-

14

come of a decline in the ratio for both urban and rural non-farm individuals, and it occurs in spite of an increase in the ratio for rural farm individuals. Note that these ratios behaved quite differently for unrelated individuals than for families; but the outcome, a decline in the concentration ratios for both families and unrelated individuals, is the same.[1]

We need to explore the possibility that the changes in concentration ratios between 1947 and 1959 shown in Table 6 for different groups of families might have been related to changes during the same period in the average age of the family head or in the number of earners per family. Similarly there is the possibility that changes in concentration ratios in this period for the different groups of unrelated individuals might have been related to changes in average age or in the percentage of non-earners. These possibilities will be considered in succeeding sections.

(4) *Age*

Since 1947 both the percentage of families having heads aged 65 or over and the corresponding percentage for unrelated individuals have increased. However, in both cases the increase has been particularly marked in the lower-income brackets, under $5,000 in the case of family heads and under $3,000 in the case of unrelated individuals (see Table 7). The concentration ratio for this age-group is higher than for any other [*21*, p. 273], in part because of the prevalence of part-time employment or no employment at all for heads of families and individuals 65 years of age or more. Hence this change in the age pattern of the population since 1947 might have been expected to be accompanied by an increase of the inequality of the income distribution for all families and unrelated individuals.[2]

The tendency towards an increase in the age of family heads was particularly marked, between 1947 and 1959, in the case of the rural farm group. For these families, the percentage of family heads

[1] The behaviour of the concentration ratios for unrelated individuals does not correspond with that for *all* individuals above the age of 14 and having money incomes. The concentration ratios were higher in 1959 than in 1947 for all individuals in the urban and rural non-farm groups, and for rural farm females; but slightly lower for rural farm males [*20*, Table 12, pp. 212–251].

An interesting model illustrating the complicated way in which the shift from agricultural to non-agricultural sectors may affect the income distribution is developed by Kuznets [*15*, pp. 12–18].

[2] Soltow [*27*, p. 452] demonstrates statistically that this has been the tendency, but that the effect on the income distribution has been quite small. Cf. Morgan [*21*, pp. 273–274].

aged 55 and over increased from 32 to 36 per cent. The corresponding percentage for heads of urban families increased only from 29 to 30; and that for heads of rural non-farm families remained unchanged at 25 [*20*, Table 3, pp. 76, 98]. Yet in spite of the high concentration ratio consistently found for age-groups 55 and above, the concentration ratio for the rural farm group decreased during the period, and that for urban families remained unchanged. Although the concentration ratio for rural non-farm families increased, this increase was not related to a corresponding change in the average age of the family head.

TABLE 7

PERCENTAGE OF HEADS OF FAMILIES AND UNRELATED INDIVIDUALS
AGED 65 OR OVER, BY INCOME GROUPS,
1947 AND 1960

	Heads of Families (per cent)			Unrelated Individuals (per cent)	
Family Income	1947	1960	Income	1947	1960
Under $3,000	20	31	Under $1,000	43	48
$3,000 to $4,999	6	13	$1,000 to $2,999	26	41
$5,000 to $9,999	7	6	$3,000 to $4,999	10	12
$10,000 and over	11	7	$5,000 and over	19	10
All Families	*11*	*13*	*All Individuals*	*30*	*34*

Source : [*20*, Tables A and B, pp. 6–13].

The fact that concentration ratios for all families and for unrelated individuals decreased in spite of the increase in the percentage of family heads and unrelated individuals in the older age-group may be related to the increase that occurred in the percentage of individuals over 65 receiving social security and other transfer payments during the period. Thus the concentration ratios both for families whose heads were aged 65 or over and for unrelated individuals in the same age-group decreased between 1947 and 1959 relatively more than the average for other age-groups [20, Table 3, pp. 76, 98].

(5) *Increase in Number of Earners per Family*

An increase in the number of earners per family would have no effect upon the inequality of the income distribution if the increases in earnings were to be distributed among the families in proportion to previous income levels. However, as Table 8 shows, the proportion of families with two or more earners has increased relatively more in the lower-income groups (below $5,000) than in the middle- and upper-income groups in the period 1947 to 1960. This does not prove that the increase in the number of earners per family has tended to reduce the inequality of the distribution ; but it does suggest that this tendency may well have been operative.

TABLE 8

PERCENTAGE OF FAMILIES WITH TWO EARNERS
OR MORE, CLASSIFIED BY FAMILY
INCOME GROUPS, 1947 AND 1960

Family Income	1947	1960	Per cent Increase in Proportion
Under $3,000	20	27	42
$3,000 to $4,999	29	39	34
$5,000 to $9,999	56	54	— *
$10,000 and over	54	67	24
All Families	*35*	*46*	*31*

* Decrease.

Source : [*20*, Table A, pp. 6–10].

The increase in the number of families with two or more earners was greatest in the rural farm group, next greatest in the rural non-farm, and least in the urban [20, Table 6, pp. 130, 150]. The decrease in the concentration ratio for rural farm families (Table 6) as compared with the other two groups may be partly attributable to the fact that the proportion of families with two or more earners increased from 27 to 46 per cent between 1947 and 1959. The corresponding percentages for rural non-farm families were 31 and 43 ; for urban families, 39 and 46. The slightly lower percentage in the case of rural non-farm families in 1959 may be attributable to a somewhat lower average age of head than in the case of the other two groups, which likely meant more younger children whose age made it less easy for the wife to work. In 1959, 51 per cent of heads of families in the rural non-farm group were in the 25 to 44 age bracket ; the corresponding percentages for urban and rural farm family heads were respectively 43 and 35 [*20*, Table 3, pp. 76, 98].

In the case of unrelated individuals, the urban group is by far the most important (Table 6). The concentration ratio for non-earners is typically higher than for earners [20, Table 6, pp. 132, 150]. Between 1947 and 1959 the percentage of non-earners increased from 31 to 38, and a particularly marked decline occurred in their concentration ratio. It is possible therefore that the decline in the concentration ratio for urban unrelated individuals was connected with the increase in the number of retired persons (in turn related to the ageing of the population) and to the decline in inequality of income distribution among them.

The rural non-farm group of unrelated individuals is numerically much less important than the urban, but is growing as rapidly. Between 1947 and 1959 the percentage of non-earners remained about the same (about 45 per cent), but the concentration ratio for non-earners declined much more than in the case of earners. Again, the increase in the number of retired persons seems to have been accompanied by a decline in the inequality of income distribution among them.

The rural farm group of unrelated individuals is unimportant in size and is declining. The concentration ratio is much higher for earners than for non-earners, but the increase in the concentration ratio between 1947 and 1959 was particularly marked for non-earners who remained, however, about the same proportion of the group (about 34 per cent).

(6) *Education*

Those family heads with relatively less education are particularly vulnerable to unemployment [21, p. 277]. Furthermore, lack of education constitutes a barrier to income increases for family heads ; while those heads with more education receive more income increases than decreases over time [21, p. 277]. The dispersion of secondary and advanced education among the population, such as has been occurring in the United States, should be accompanied by a reduction in income inequality. It has been shown that this has indeed been the tendency [27, pp. 450–452], but that the effect of the dispersion of education has been quite small as compared, for example, with the effect of the shifts that have occurred in occupations. As Morgan points out [21, p. 279] :

It seems clear that more jobs for women, less unemployment for men, and fewer farmers have had more effect on income inequality than changing age or educational distribution of the population, or even the income tax.

(7) *Regional Shifts: Racial Differences*

Between 1929 and 1946 there occurred a significant narrowing in the relative difference in average-income levels among states and regions in the United States. The coefficient of variation declined from 32 in 1929 to 18 in 1946 [*9*, p. 30]. A slight further narrowing has recently occurred, bringing the coefficient of variation to 16 for 1963.

During the Second World War, when most of the reduction occurred, there was a sharp increase in industrialization and improved utilization of existing labour resources in the South-east and South-west. At the same time, because of high prices and full utilization of resources, income from agriculture was at a high level in the Rocky Mountain and Plains regions as well as in the South. These changes in the efficiency of resource utilization occurred without corresponding shifts in population. Consequently, *per capita* personal income fell, relative to the national average, in the Mid-east, Far West, New England, and Great Lakes states, and rose in the regions previously mentioned.

Since the war, while these same tendencies towards increased efficiency in resource utilization have been operative, there also has occurred a differential population growth by regions to match the increases in state and regional incomes. White population has shifted from the North-east and Central Plains to the South-west and West. There has been a substantial out-migration of Negroes from the South to the North and West. But since growth in personal income by regions has about matched growth of population by regions, *per capita* incomes by regions have changed little, relative to the national average, since 1948.

The migration of Negroes must have tended to reduce inequality of income distribution nationally, since in general the movement carried with it an increase in incomes for the migrants to a level closer to the median. The median income of non-white families in the South in 1960 was $2,735 as compared with the national median for non-white families of $3,190 [*20*, Table 9, p. 168].

The migration of white population from the North-east and North Central regions to the South-west and West no doubt tended also to affect the national income distribution for families, but the direction of the effect cannot be determined. Median income for families was higher than the national median in the case of the two regions from which the out-migration mainly came; it was lower than the national median in the South-west and higher than the national median (and higher than in the North-east and North Central regions) in the West [*20*, Table 9, p. 168].

At the national level, the concentration ratio for the income distribution of non-white families decreased insignificantly from ·363 to ·357 between 1947 and 1960, while that for Negroes increased insignificantly from ·406 to ·414 [*20*, Table 9, pp. 168, 188].

(8) *Conclusions*

Needless to say, the various hypotheses that have been reviewed overlap one another. For example, regional changes, the relative decline of employment in agriculture, and the shift of population from rural to urban areas are all related to the relative decline of agriculture as an industry. The influence of diffusion of education is no doubt related to the reduction in unemployment. However, without regard to implicit duplication of this sort, the preceding analysis can now be summarized.

The decline in the inequality of the income distribution that occurred between 1929 and 1947 appears to have been due mainly to : (1) the increase in the percentage share of wages and salaries in family personal income ; (2) the decrease in the percentage share of property income ; (3) the relative decline of employment in agriculture ; (4) the relative increase of employment in government ; (5) a shift in the occupational structure resulting in a higher proportion of workers in occupations having higher incomes and/or less unequal distributions of income ; (6) a reduction of income and wage-rate differentials within occupations ; and (7) the narrowing in the relative differences in average-income levels among states and regions. A minor role has been played by increased dispersion of education. The change in the age pattern of the population has also played a minor part, but in the direction of increasing inequality.[1]

Of these circumstances, the first, the fourth, the fifth, and the seventh have exerted little influence in reducing inequality in the period since 1947. The second has clearly operated in the opposite

[1] Since the analysis has been limited to the distribution of family income before taxes, the effect of the highly progressive federal income tax has not directly been involved. Indirectly, no doubt, the tax has had some impact on property income through its effect on the distribution of property.

way, and probably also the sixth. In addition the increase in the proportion of families in rural non-farm areas has also tended to increase the concentration ratio of the income distribution — although this tendency was not necessarily additive with the tendency for the relative share of property income to increase. In general the relative stability of the income distribution since 1947 has been due to an approximate balance in the relative strength of these various tendencies — with a slight downward drift, perhaps, to be explained by the continuing movement out of agriculture.

II. THE FUNCTIONAL DISTRIBUTION OF INCOME

The national accounting data that come nearest to showing income 'earned' by the factors of production are those for the allocation of national income. However, the breakdown of the accounting data into wages, interest, rent, and profit does not provide counterpart data to the economic theorist's concepts that go by those names. To give only one example, national-accounting rent is limited to 'rental income of persons' and has little relation to the economist's notion of rent as a return to those resources the supply of which is unresponsive to variations in the returns to them.[1]

Some of these difficulties are alleviated if the accounting figures for interest, profits, and rent are aggregated and treated as a 'property' share to be considered over against a labour share. However, there still remains the essentially insoluble problem that accounting data for the return to unincorporated business enterprise (hereafter called entrepreneurial income) is a joint return to the entrepreneur's capital invested and to his labour expended in the enterprise. Although numerous and ingenious bases for separating the two elements have been suggested, all such devices must necessarily be in some degree arbitrary. But unless one of these devices is adopted, the accounting data leave us with three 'shares' — wages, entrepreneurial income, and property income from incorporated business — that have no counterpart in the theoretical analysis of factor distribution. Since a decline in the proportion of the gainfully employed who are individual proprietors has been fairly steady since at least the middle of the nineteenth century the accompanying upward trend in wages is difficult to interpret. Whether it represents an increase in the share

[1] This and other differences have been frequently pointed out; for example [*10*, pp. 273–275].

of labour as a factor and a decrease in that of property as the other factor cannot be determined because of the impossibility of separating out the wages and property-income constituents of the declining joint income of individual proprietors.

There have been a few pioneer attempts to discover what happened to the relative shares of labour and property in the latter half of the nineteenth century in the United States. A recent study which has revised and combined some of these early results [1] provides us with estimates of the labour and property shares by census years from 1849–50 to 1909–10. This study attempted to separate out an imputed return to labour from entrepreneurial income by assuming that individual proprietors earned for their labour the equivalent of the average annual earnings of hired labour. The residual was attributed to the proprietors' invested capital. (This method of imputation will hereafter be referred to as the labour basis, in contrast to the asset basis which attributes to the proprietors' invested capital the rate of return earned by other property in the form of interest, rent, and corporate profits.[1] Use of the asset basis makes the return to entrepreneurial labour a residual.)

According to Budd's estimates, the share of employed plus self-employed labour decreased from 68·3 per cent of total private income in 1849–50 to 62·4 per cent in 1909–10.[2] In contrast, the share of wages of employed labour alone showed an upward trend (from 41·4 per cent of total private income in 1849–50 to 46·0 per cent in 1909–10) in spite of a steady decline in the wages share in the agricultural sector [1, p. 373]. Between 1850 and 1910 the importance of the agricultural sector, whether measured by income or employment, was reduced about one-half, and mainly because of this reduction the proportion of hired labour to the total gainfully employed in the private sector steadily increased. It was principally the relative decline of agriculture (in which the share of wages was low and declining) and the relative advance of industry (in which the share of wages was high) that resulted in a net increase in the wages share during the period.

The downward trend in the share of employed plus self-employed labour, in spite of the upward trend in the wages share alone, was

---

[1] Following Kravis [13, p. 129]. The author is heavily indebted to Kravis for the presentation of this section.

[2] Budd's results, based on W. I. King's figures, are supported by other estimates of labour's share which Budd derived from Kuznets's figures. These showed a decline in the share of employed plus self-employed labour from 73·4 per cent of net private product in 1869–78 to 62·9 per cent in 1904–13 [1, pp. 385–387].

also due to the relative decline of agriculture. In the case of the share of employed plus self-employed labour, the weight of this share in agriculture was relatively high (though declining) for the period as a whole, as compared with its weight in industry; consequently the strong downward trend of this share in agriculture more than offset the effect of a moderate upward trend of the share in industry. On the other hand, in the case of the wages share alone, the weight of this share in agriculture was relatively low as compared with its weight in industry and consequently the upward trend in industry overbalanced the downward trend in agriculture.

For the period since 1900 the data are both more adequate and more reliable. Table 9, in the first three columns, provides the basic data by decade-average percentages.[1] The advance in the wages share (as a proportion of private income) that Budd found in the period 1850–1910 has a counterpart in the steady increase in the share of employee compensation (as a proportion of national income) in the period since 1900 (see column 1). In our earlier discussion of the size-distribution of family income a similar upward trend in the percentage share of wages and salaries in family income was found for the period 1929–53. As in the earlier period, the upward trend in the wages share of national income since 1900 reflects, at least in substantial degree, the relative decline of agriculture and the shift out of self-employment into wage and salary employment. Both of the latter two changes are also reflected in column 2 of Table 9, showing the decline in the share of entrepreneurial income since 1900 — a downward trend which was also characteristic of the period 1850–1910 for entrepreneurial income as a percentage of private income, and characteristic of the period since 1929 for self-employment income as a percentage of family personal income (Table 4).

Another reason that has been suggested to explain, in part, the rise in the share of employee compensation is the increase in the importance of the government sector. Since our national accounting procedures do not attribute any return to capital employed in government, the expansion of the government sector automatically carries with it a corresponding expansion in the proportion of wages to national income. The importance of this circumstance can,

---

[1] Note that these figures are not comparable with Budd's figures for the earlier period. The latter are based on 'total private income' (which excludes income received from government employment), and are adjusted to the labour basis — the basis which is also employed in column 5 of Table 9. But Table 9 throughout is based on national income, not private income.

The Distribution of National Income

TABLE 9

FUNCTIONAL SHARES IN NATIONAL INCOME,
AVERAGES OF PERCENTAGE SHARES BY DECADES,
1900–1963

	Distributive Shares			Property Share, Various Concepts			
Period	Employee Compensation (1)	Entrepreneurial Income (2)	Interest, Rent, and Corporate Profit (3)	Asset Basis (4)	Labour Basis (5)	Proportional Basis (6)	Economywide Basis (7)
1900–09	55·0	23·6	21·4	36·8	23·0	30·6	28·0
1905–14	55·2	22·9	21·8	38·0	24·4	30·7	28·3
1910–19	53·2	24·2	22·6	38·0	30·6	31·9	29·8
1915–24	57·2	21·0	21·8	34·6	23·9	29·8	27·6
1920–29	60·5	17·6	22·0	32·3	21·9	28·4	28·6
1925–34	63·0	15·8	21·1	27·9	17·2	26·8	25·1
1930–39	66·8	15·0	18·1	23·9	12·7	23·4	21·3
1929–38	66·6	15·5	17·8	23·5	11·2	23·2	21·1
1934–43	65·1	16·5	18·4	24·3	17·0	24·2	22·0
1939–48	64·6	17·2	18·3	25·8	21·5	24·3	22·1
1944–53	65·6	16·4	18·1	24·7	21·5	23·8	21·6
1949–58	67·4	13·6	19·0	26·0*	21·9	23·8	22·0
1954–63	69·9	11·8	18·3	—†	19·9‡	22·4	20·7

* 1949–57. † Not available. ‡ 1954–63.

Source : [13, p. 124]. Column 6 (up to 1930–39) from [11, p. 178]. Figures for 1949–58 and 1954–63 computed by author.

however, easily be exaggerated. Between 1929 and 1963 compensation of employees of government (including military personnel) as a percentage of national income increased from 5·6 to 12·4 per cent.

Three recent studies have examined the behaviour of employee compensation as a proportion of *private* national income or product. One of these [10], for the period 1899 to 1929, shows that compensation of employees as a percentage of the business sector's gross product had no trend, upward or downward, in contrast to the upward trend of employee compensation as a percentage of national income (see column 1 of Table 9). Two studies of the period since 1929 [28, p. 14] [25, p. 620] show respectively (1) that employed labour's share of business gross product rose from 46·2 per cent in 1929 to 53·6 per cent in 1957, and (2) that employed labour's share of privately produced income rose from 55·6 per cent in 1929 to 64·7

24

per cent in 1955. A comparison of these two sets of results with those for employee compensation as a percentage of national income (Table 9, column 1) suggests that the growth of the government sector has not been a major factor affecting the accounting estimates for the shares of labour and property since 1929.

When, however, national-income-originating sectors are more narrowly defined, employee compensation becomes a much more stable percentage. Thus Denison has shown that, for 1929–52, employee compensation originating in each of three sectors — non-farm corporations, non-farm proprietors and partnerships, and farms — as a percentage of income originating in the respective sectors showed no significant trend [2, pp. 256–257]. A more recent study by Phillips [23] uses the device of expressing the share of employee compensation as a percentage of the proportion of employees in the labour force as a means of allowing for structural changes in the economy bearing upon labour's share. These 'wage-parity ratios' showed the same upward trend for employee compensation as a whole as was exhibited in Table 9, column 1. However, when the computation was made for the private sector and for the private non-agricultural sector, in both cases the wage-parity ratio, after increasing during the great depression, showed no significant trend thereafter [23, pp. 171–172]. Hence it can be argued that, when the sector is defined so as to make it reasonably homogeneous, there has been a tendency towards stability of labour's share.

The share of interest, rent, and corporate profit — column 3 of Table 9 — in national income has been more nearly stable than the other two shares as presented in that Table, although it has shown a moderate decline in the period 1930 to the present taken as a whole. A comparable decline in the case of the corresponding share of interest, rent, and dividends in family personal income (Table 4) for the period 1929–47 was attributed to the decline in interest rates, low corporate profits during the 1930's, and the high corporate income taxes imposed during the war and after. The same reasons no doubt contribute to the explanation of the lower level of interest, rent, and corporate profits as a share in national income for the period since 1929. But in the latter case, no return to a somewhat higher level after 1947 (such as we found in the case of this share of family income) has appeared. A possible reason for this difference may be that accelerated depreciation allowances (particularly since 1954) have affected total corporate profits more than dividends. Indeed, total corporate profits in 1963 were 67 per cent above the

1948 level, while dividends as a constituent of personal income were 147 per cent above the 1948 level.

Table 9 also shows, in columns 4 to 7, for four different ways of separating out an imputed property share from entrepreneurial income, four corresponding estimates of the total property share for the period 1900–9 to 1954–63. The asset basis (column 4) yields a higher property share than the labour basis (column 5), since in the former case the return to entrepreneurial labour, while in the latter case the return to entrepreneurial investment, is treated as the residual. (Entrepreneurial income does not run at a high enough level to provide *both* a return to entrepreneurial labour equal to employed labour's average compensation and a return to entrepreneurial investment equal to the rate of return on other property.) Neither of these bases for separating out an imputed property share from entrepreneurial income carries much conviction.

Column 6 (the proportional basis) shows estimates for the property share when the return imputed to entrepreneurial property is determined by the application of a constant percentage division. The particular percentage employed here was 35 per cent.[1] The outcome is a percentage share for property which lies between those derived respectively on the asset and the labour bases. But as Kravis points out [*13*, p. 130], the application of such a constant division not only is arbitrary but also impairs the usefulness of the results for a study of whether relative shares have in fact varied, and if so in what way.

Finally, in column 7 the proportion of entrepreneurial income included in the property share is determined by the current relationship, for each year, between labour and property income in the rest of the economy excluding the entrepreneurial sector. This appears to be as reasonable a basis as any.

The interesting fact, however, is that, for all our ways of computing the property share so as to include an imputed return to entrepreneurs' investment, the share shows a downward trend (and the share of labour shows an upward trend) for the period since 1900–9. The downward trend in the property share is steepest when the asset basis is used, and is least steep when the labour basis is

[1] Kravis [*13*, pp. 129–130]. Actually, for the period 1900–9 to 1930–39, the percentage employed was not constant but varied somewhat from 35. The figures in column 6 for this period are Johnson's [*11*, pp. 176–177]. He estimated that the share of farm operators' income attributable to property varied from about 43 per cent in 1900–14 to about 36 per cent in the 1940's, while the share of non-farm entrepreneurial income attributable to property was about 35 per cent throughout the period.

used. If, in fact, the whole of entrepreneurial income were to be attributed to entrepreneurial labour, labour's share in national income would have even then shown a moderate increase during the period since 1900–9.

Conclusions

National accounting data do not provide figures that can be used satisfactorily to throw light on the applicability of theories of functional distribution. However, on any basis on which entrepreneurial income may be split between labour and property shares, the share of national income attributable to labour has increased during the period since 1900. This outcome is in contrast to the declining relative share of labour (when entrepreneurial income is divided on the labour basis) that was found for the period 1849–50 to 1909–10.

These two opposed tendencies respectively evident in the earlier and the later period of economic development of the U.S. economy are both in considerable part traceable to the same underlying causes — the relative decline of agriculture and the shift out of self-employment into wage and salary employment. But in the earlier period, since for the period as a whole the average share of employed and self-employed labour in agriculture had a relatively heavy weight, the net effect was a decline in the share of employed and self-employed labour. On the other hand, in the period since 1900, agriculture was no longer as important a sector relative to industry, the share of employed and self-employed labour in industry was higher than in agriculture (on the labour basis at least) and rising, and the outcome for the total share was a rising rather than a falling trend.

Another structural change which may have played some part during the later period has been the increasing importance of the government sector for which accounting procedures allow a disproportionate share to employed labour.

The decline in the share of interest, rent, and corporate profits has been moderate. It has continued from 1929 to the present, in contrast to the behaviour of interest, rent, and dividends as a share in family personal income, which has increased moderately since 1947.

When labour's share of national income originates in a sector so defined as to be homogeneous, such as private non-farm business for example, something approximating stability of the share has been characteristic of the last twenty years. But there is still room for considerable scepticism as to how persistent or how general any such tendency may be (cf. [25]).

REFERENCES

[1] E. C. Budd, 'Factor Shares, 1850–1910', *Trends in the American Economy in the Nineteenth Century*, Studies in Income and Wealth, vol. 24, pp. 365–398, Princeton, 1960.

[2] E. F. Denison, 'Income Types and the Size Distribution', *Am. Econ. Rev.*, Proc., May 1954, **44**, 254–269.

[3] Jeanette M. Fitzwilliams, 'Size Distribution of Income in 1962', *Surv. Curr. Bus.*, April 1963, pp. 14–20.

[4] Jeanette M. Fitzwilliams, 'Size Distribution of Income in 1963', *Surv. Curr. Bus.*, April 1964, pp. 3–11.

[5] Selma F. Goldsmith, 'Changes in the Size Distribution of Income', *Am. Econ. Rev.*, Proc., May 1957, **47**, 504–518.

[6] Selma F. Goldsmith, 'The Relation of Census Income Distribution Statistics to Other Income Data', *An Appraisal of the 1950 Census Income Data*, Studies in Income and Wealth, vol. 23, pp. 65–107, Princeton, 1958.

[7] Selma F. Goldsmith, 'Size Distribution of Personal Income', *Surv. Curr. Bus.*, April 1958, pp. 10–19.

[8] Selma F. Goldsmith, George Jaszi, Hyman Kaitz, and Maurice Liebenberg, 'Size Distribution of Income Since the Mid-thirties', *Rev. Econ. Stat.*, February 1954, **36**, 1–32.

[9] R. E. Graham, Jr., 'Factors Underlying Changes in the Geographical Distribution of Income', *Surv. Curr. Bus.*, April 1964, pp. 15–32.

[10] Arthur Grant, 'Issues in Distribution Theory: The Measurement o Labour's Relative Share, 1899–1929', *Rev. Econ. Stat.*, August 1963, **45**, 273–279.

[11] D. G. Johnson, 'The Functional Distribution of Income in the United States, 1850–1952', *Rev. Econ. Stat.*, May 1954, **36**, 175–182.

[12] George Katona, C. A. Lininger, and R. F. Kosobud, *1962 Survey of Consumer Finances*, Survey Research Center, Michigan University, Ann Arbor, 1963.

[13] I. B. Kravis, *The Structure of Income*, Philadelphia, 1962.

[14] Simon Kuznets, *Shares of the Upper Income Groups in Income and Savings*, New York, 1953.

[15] Simon Kuznets, 'Economic Growth and Income Inequality', *Am. Econ. Rev.*, March 1955, **45**, 1–28.

[16] R. J. Lampman, 'The Effectiveness of Some Institutions in changing the Distribution of Income', *Am. Econ. Rev.*, Proc., May 1957, **47**, 519–528.

[17] Maurice Liebenberg and Jeanette M. Fitzwilliams, 'Size Distribution of Income in 1961', *Surv. Curr. Bus.*, April 1962, pp. 9–16.

[18] H. P. Miller, *Income of the American People*, New York, 1955.

Haley — Income Distribution in the United States

[19] H. P. Miller, 'Changes in the Industrial Distribution of Wages in the United States, 1939–1949', *An Appraisal of the 1950 Census Income Data*, Studies in Income and Wealth, vol. 23, pp. 355–420, Princeton, 1958.

[20] H. P. Miller, *Trends in the Income of Families and Persons in the United States: 1947 to 1960*, U.S. Bureau of the Census, Technical Paper No. 8, Washington, 1963.

[21] James Morgan, 'The Anatomy of Income Distribution', *Rev. Econ. Stat.*, August 1962, **44**, 270–283.

[22] J. A. Pechman, 'Comment' (on 'The Relation of Census Income Distribution Statistics to Other Income Data'), *An Appraisal of the 1950 Census Income Data*, Studies in Income and Wealth, vol. 23, pp. 107–115, Princeton, 1958.

[23] J. D. Phillips, 'Labor's Share and "Wage Parity"', *Rev. Econ. Stat.*, May 1960, **42**, 164–174.

[24] M. W. Reder, 'The Theory of Occupational Wage Differentials', *Am. Econ. Rev.*, December 1955, **45**, 833–852.

[25] R. M. Solow, 'The Constancy of Relative Shares', *Am. Econ. Rev.*, September 1958, **48**, 618–631.

[26] Lee Soltow, 'Shifts in Factor Payments and Income Distribution', *Am. Econ. Rev.*, June 1959, **49**, 395–398.

[27] Lee Soltow, 'The Distribution of Income Related to Changes in the Distribution of Education, Age and Occupations', *Rev. Econ. Stat.*, November 1960, **42**, 450–453.

[28] Sidney Weintraub, *Forecasting the Price Level, Income Distribution, and Economic Growth*, Philadelphia, 1959.

[29] *Federal Reserve Bulletin*, July 1954, August 1957, July 1959.

[30] U.S. Bureau of the Census, *Current Population Reports*, Series P-60, No. 33, January 15, 1960 ; No. 41, 21 October 1963.

[31] U.S. Bureau of the Census, *Historical Statistics of the United States, Colonial Times to 1957*, Washington, 1960.

DISCUSSION OF PROFESSOR HALEY'S PAPER

Professor Mirabella thanked the meeting for the honour it had conferred on Palermo. On behalf of the University of Palermo, he welcomed the debate on income distribution. The subject was of particular interest to Mediterranean-type economies. In regions where an attempt was being made to create suitable conditions for 'take-off' or for accelerating the process of autonomous growth, there was conflict between the two principal aims of development policy. It was difficult to achieve overall economic growth and an improvement in income distribution defined as a reduction of the dissymmetry of the distribution curve at one and the same time. This dissymmetry was due, in developing countries, more to

29

the size of the poverty area than to the gap between top and bottom classes in income strata. Inasmuch as the aim was to eradicate poverty the problem of interpreting income differences could not be discussed in the same terms as in the United States. Professor Haley's valuable contribution, which Professor Mirabella had the honour to introduce, was confined to a case study of the richest and most industrialized country in the world, but, even so, it was of great value to those, like himself, more interested in the removal of poverty in developing regions than in the problems of differences of distribution between the extreme classes in rich countries. Professor Mirabella would limit his comments to the first part of the paper in which Professor Haley had made a division into two periods — 1929–47 and 1947–62 — concluding that, in the first period, evolution followed what was generally considered the right path in showing a significant reduction in the number of units in the lowest income bracket, although he drew attention to the shift to the right of the distribution curve and a flattening of the central section of the curve. As Professor Haley had pointed out, this flattening out of the bell-shaped curve did not necessarily mean a lesser degree of income inequality. Nevertheless, assuming that there had been a tendency towards more equality during the first period and more particularly up till 1935, this evolution was scarcely noticeable over the second period between 1947 and 1962. Professor Haley had inferred that the size distribution of income tended to become stable.

The same conclusions were reached in a study recently carried out in Italy and seemed to confirm the tendency towards a crystallization of the income differentials between different groups in market economies today. If one could be sure of that trend, Professor Mirabella would willingly draw the conclusion that it was advisable to concentrate all efforts on accelerated growth, as Galbraith and others had recently suggested, thus enabling an overall rise in the standard of living and capacity to save of *all* classes of society, while, on the other hand, accepting to limit the improvement in income distribution to eradicating the worst inequalities and to raising incomes below a decent minimum.

Professor Haley had analysed seven factors which could have contributed to the evolution of the distribution up to 1947 and its stabilization since then. Among these factors, Professor Mirabella said he would distinguish between the systematic factors, which were always present and which explained similar phenomena in other countries, and factors arising from economic fluctuations or a specific policy whose explanatory value was limited to the period and national economy under survey.

With regard to this second type of factor, specific rather than systematic, it was not surprising to see, in Table 4 of the paper, that the percentage of personal income distributed in the form of wages and transfers rose up to 1947 and then remained at about its usual two-thirds level, while the percentage of property incomes in personal distribution had considerably declined up to 1947, when they gradually began to rise.

The trend towards a declining percentage of incomes accruing to self-employed did, of course, contribute in a large measure to the stabilization of the percentage of wages and transfers during the second period, but Professor Mirabella preferred to class this phenomenon in the category of systematic factors. Excluding this, the evolution observed by Professor Haley confirmed the remarkable influence which fluctuations in economic activity and economic policy, both interacting, could have on income stratification and its modifications. Professor Haley had underlined the importance of modifications in the share of personal income between workers and capital owners between 1929 and 1947 although his conclusions were attenuated by the results in the second part of his paper, based on data of functional distribution. It was of interest to compare these notifications with fluctuations in economic activity in the same period and with the New Deal policy in so far as it was connected with the slump of 1929. Every important slowing down of economic activity brought with it measures of redistribution aimed at starting up effective demand, even if this entailed disequilibrium and inflationary trends later.

In the first factors indicated by Professor Haley — the changes in the relative importance of different types of income — Professor Mirabella perceived the reflection of fluctuations in economic activity and redistribution policies. He thought, however, that economists, more preoccupied with phenomena of a systematic nature, would be even more interested in the results of Professor Haley's analyses which threw light on the role played by factors of this type, whether as a positive influence in the evolution observed during the first period or as a brake to the tendency towards concentration of incomes since the Second World War. Professor Mirabella considered all the factors analysed by Professor Haley as systematic except the first, if one added to this the decline in the relative importance of self-employed. Like Professor Haley, he admitted that the six factors studied by him were too interdependent for it to be possible to isolate their respective influences. However, it did seem possible to find a common origin, if one stressed one of these factors, namely, progress and the spread of education.

On this point he did not agree with Professor Haley who accepted Professor Morgan's theory that education had only played a minor role in diminishing the concentration of incomes or in opposing concentration when the preceding trend was reversed. He wanted to point out that all the factors quoted by Professor Morgan had, essentially, their origins in the spread and specialization of education. Progress in education encouraged women to seek work outside the home. It offered men the possibility of avoiding unemployment and using their capacities to the full. Even more, it encouraged a shift of labour from the land and allowed the public sector to widen the scope of its influence.

Professor Mirabella concluded by returning to his first point. All the factors studied by Professor Haley in the case of the United States were, or soon would be, present in developing countries or regions. This gave rise to hope that sooner or later it would be possible to reconcile the objective of a steady overall growth with curbing the trend towards greater inequality or towards maintaining the social stratification, a trend which had, since Pareto, so often preoccupied economists.

Professor Jean Marchal had noticed that Professor Haley stressed a difficulty encountered by several of the authors who had submitted papers to the present Conference on the evolution of income distribution in different countries as case studies : national accounts did not provide data for breaking up national income into salaries and wages, interest, rents, and profits, which were the income categories retained by the neo-classical theory. Most of the authors had regrouped interest, rent, and profit in a wider concept of profit or property income, as opposed to labour income.

Professor Haley had pointed out that this two-category division removed the difficulty in using national income data. Professor Marchal would agree, with a proviso that this was theoretically justifiable only if one were ready to work on a totally different set of theoretical hypotheses from the neo-classicists. Their approach was micro-economic and placed the entrepreneur at the focal point of their analysis. In hiring the labour force on the labour market, borrowing capital on the capital market and hiring the services of natural factors in scarce supply, the entrepreneur's activity originated wages, interests, and rents, the difference between sales price and production cost generating the profit as his own remuneration.

Economists today, at least implicitly, reasoned within the macro-economic framework of the national economy as such and they were prepared to admit a relationship between *all* employers as controlling the means of production and *all* wage-earners as supplying labour. Out of the bargain between these two major groups of economic agents' profits, in the wider sense of the concept, and wages were determined. Then and only then entrepreneurs who did not actually own the entire supply of other production factors paid back such part of their profits as interest and rent to those who had supplied borrowed capital and rent-producing goods, and what finally remained in the hands of entrepreneurs was their profit in the narrower sense. This second bargain between entrepreneurs and owners of production factors other than labour was a minor one, although the bargaining power of the entrepreneurs in their dealings with the wage-earner group was influenced by their expectations about the outcome of the second bargain. Providing the theoretical consequences of such a departure from the neo-classical approach were made explicit, Professor Jean Marchal preferred this new approach as being more realistic in taking due account of contemporary conditions in a world where group pressures were strongly felt, where trade unions were powerful and where competition was often impeded.

Economists today, then, took up all the national income data to put them in one or the other category of wages and profits *lato sensu*. At this stage Professor Marchal could no longer follow them because of their treatment of income out of self-employment or individual small farmers' and entrepreneurs' incomes. This implied that this type of income could be broken up between labour and capital income, whereas in national income data it appeared neither as a wage nor a profit.

Although admitting that any method of income imputation was arbitrary, Professor Haley had not been able to go without as he had rejected the idea of a threefold income analysis. Professor Marchal would disagree. He believed that a threefold division of income between wages, corporate profits, and income of self-employed and small entrepreneurs was justified for theoretical and practical reasons.

All methods of imputation being arbitrary, they led to conclusions which were not only contradictory but also paradoxical in certain cases. Professor Marchal observed that when working on French eighteenth-century data the imputation of a wage at current market rate for hired labour to the farmers and family labour implied a negative rate of return on their capital as a residual.

Professor Marchal thought that if each author was entitled to use the income categories he had defined according to the purpose of his theoretical analysis, in defining them he had, however, to abide by certain rules, the most important one being that the income categories had to be *homogeneous* with respect to the group behaviours retained in devising the model. In post-Keynesian models, where the identity of *I* and *S* was always a condition of equilibrium, the level and shape of the consumption function was a significant criterion for defining groups. Everyone agreed so far on the propensity to consume out of profits being much less than the wage-earners' and everyone would distinguish between the two types of income on that account. Now, Professor Marchal thought that the propensity to consume of the self-employed and the small entrepreneurs was not so high as the propensity to consume of the profit-earners nor so low as that of the wage-earners. The consumption function of this group was different from either. Therefore this type of income should be distinguished from the two others.

Another criterion was also used for categorizing incomes in models, namely the way the income accrued to its recipient. This depended on the part the income-earner played in production, which in turn determined what were the means at his disposal for acting on the rate of his income. From this point of view Professor Marchal would say that there were three major ways to obtain an income in present conditions : to offer one's labour on the labour market ; to start a corporate business ; to combine one's labour with a small amount of capital. These three possibilities could not be reduced to a simpler alternative and the corresponding rates of reward would vary distinctly. When he had been a member of the French Conseil économique et social, he had noticed that in any debate on national income distribution the group divisions according to conflicting vested interests almost always conformed to this pattern.

Finally Professor Marchal remarked that Professor Haley had constantly brought out this third type of income to qualify his findings. For instance, Professor Haley, having noted that during the period 1840–50 to 1909–10 the income share of both hired and self-employed labour had gone down from 68 per cent to 62 per cent, took care to redress this by saying that the share of hired labour alone had risen from 41 to 46 per cent. He was, of course, right to point out that the gain in the wage-earners' share had been obtained at the expense of the share of self-employed labour. But this confirmed Professor Marchal in thinking that it would be better to distinguish between the two shares once and for all, and to base the theory of distribution on a tripartite analysis.

Although agreeing with Professor Marchal that any method of income imputation was arbitrary, *Professor Solow* wished to comment on what Professor Marchal had said about the paradoxical outcome of imputing a current market wage to farmers' labour. Professor Marchal had said this led to showing up a negative return on their capital. Professor Solow remarked that the reverse procedure, imputing a market rate of return on their capital, would also lead to an abnormally low or negative rate of reward of the farmers' and their families' labour as a residual. The only conclusion should be that returns to both labour and capital were abnormally low in agriculture.

Professor Solow said he could not settle easily for a three-category analysis because, for instance, the incorporation of a family business for tax reasons would mean a change in income distribution although such change had not strictly speaking occurred.

Income distribution theory had really two objectives : one was a study of evolution of distinct social groups, the other being a study of factor prices as well as commodity prices. Admitting that it might be desirable to use the three-part division for the first, the latter, whose objective was more purely economic, implied, however, that one retained the two-part division of income.

Dr. Feinstein pointed out to Professor Solow that if one chose to impute an income to labour the arbitrariness could be diminished and the result made more realistic by imputing to the self-employed a wage at the rate prevailing in their own sector rather than a wage at the average rate over the whole economy.

Professor Solow maintained that one might still obtain an anomalous result in some industries.

Professor Reder observed that such calculations did not take into account certain types of earnings such as windfall gains due to the rise in price of land which did not appear in income statistics. Farming was a form of

34

Haley — Income Distribution in the United States

activity which tended to be run at a current loss but subsidized by capital gains on a longer run. The omission of windfall earnings might help to explain why the imputation methods conceded anomalous results.

Professor Falise agreed with Professor Solow that the need to link the empirical analysis to the theory of factor returns was an essential reason for retaining the two-category division of income. Professor Solow had, however, admitted that the breaking up of mixed incomes between labour and capital was arbitrary. If this was so, could the reason for this not be that entrepreneurial ability as a specific factor had been ignored in setting up a bipartite analysis? Thus any proper reward for the efficiency of the entrepreneur was passed over, although his part could not be reduced to the supply of either labour or capital only.

In bigger corporations managerial efficiency was reflected in the high salaries of executives and in the returns on capital. But it was much more difficult to divide the incomes of smaller entrepreneurs between the rewards of labour, capital, and the ability of the entrepreneur. In small businesses the latter played a particularly important part, as was revealed by the magnitude of the dispersion of returns in firms employing equivalent quantities of labour and capital. Instead of attempting an impossible breakdown of this type of income, Professor Falise said he thought it more opportune to analyse the efficiency of labour, capital, and entrepreneurial ability as a phenomenon of joint productivity. The study of mixed incomes should be conducted in terms of financial returns to the production unit rather than in terms of imputed returns to different factors.

Professor Jean Marchal shared Professor Falise's views. In a rejoinder to Professor Solow's comments on what he had previously said, he stated that he thought the three-category division of income to be relevant not only for studying the evolution of income distribution but also for equilibrium analysis. The three groups were constantly comparing their respective shares in national income — for instance, farmers with respect to industrial wages. If one group thought that its position had deteriorated not only would it exert pressure on the scale of relative rates of reward, but it would do so using different means of action from the other groups. Apart from systematic differences in behavioural functions such as propensity to save which he had already pointed out, the specific differences in the instruments of bargaining power available to each group were one further reason for retaining the three-category analysis.

Professor Solow said he agreed with Professor Jean Marchal about the need for analysing the corporate behaviour of at least three different groups, although he could not see any convincing reason for not pushing further the breaking down of the agreggates into more than three income groups. The distinction between labour and capital, however, remained the significant one for studying the well-defined problem of the allocation of resources.

C   35

The Distribution of National Income

Professor Alchian asked Professor Haley whether, as certain well-known principles suggested that lifetime earnings distribution would be different, that was to say more equal than the distribution of momentary or annual earnings, had Professor Haley, in preparing his paper, found any data on lifetime earnings of specific individuals ?

Having in mind Professor Mirabella's comments on Professor Haley's paper and assuming that women in the labour market were an increasing proportion of the market labour force, Professor Alchian would surmise that economic theory contained some implications about the effect of that change in sex ratio of the labour market force on (*a*) the share of national income allocated to wages as payment for current personal services, and on (*b*) the distribution of income by individuals or family. Had Professor Haley found anything that would support his conjecture ?

To Professor Alchian's first question, *Professor Haley* answered that a few studies of lifetime earnings had been made in conjunction with a recurrent interest in the relation of educational investment to future earnings of individuals. Professor Haley suggested that Professor Reder, whose paper, to be discussed in a later session, had bearings on the matter, might comment on this.

On the second point Professor Haley thought that the increasing proportion of women in the labour force should have varying effects on income distribution by size. In some cases women had entered employment in activities where the coefficient of income concentration was high ; in other cases it had been the reverse and it was difficult to ascertain this mixed impact on size distribution. Besides, the increase in the female sex ratio in the labour force had gone hand in hand with the increase in the number of families with more than one income-earner.

Professor Reder said he was glad to comment on Professor Alchian's first question as he thought it important to distinguish between annual and lifetime incomes in using income statistics to indicate social inequality. Annual incomes almost certainly showed a greater dispersion than life-time incomes because they included the effects of temporary disturbances to normal returns to factor inputs such as illness, unemployment, crop failures, etc. Conversely, windfall gains, unusual amounts of overtime, etc., had the effect of thrusting some people above their normal income station. Unfortunately there were few, if any, studies of incomes for specific persons covering periods of longer than one year. Because of this unfilled need, studies of investment in human capital had been compelled to resort to makeshifts such as treating the average income of persons in a specific age-group in successive censuses as though it were the time path of the income of a typical member of that group.

Professor Reder also wished to comment on Professor Alchian's second question as he thought the difference between annual and lifetime incomes to be especially pertinent to the relationship between the percentages of married women to enter the labour force and the husband's

36

income. In any given year, the higher the husband's income, *ceteris paribus*, the lower the percentage of wives who would enter the labour force. But the percentage of wives who worked increased with the education of their husbands and it was well known that income and education were strongly and *positively* correlated. This paradox had been noted and investigated by Professor J. Mincer. It could, however, be dispelled in the following manner : whereas the relationship between the percentage of working wives and husband's current income reflected a short-run reaction to temporary adversity (the wife's tending to go to work to minimize the dissaving in consequence of the husband's illness or unemployment), the positive correlation between the wives' propensity to work and their husband's educational level reflected the long-run tendency of men to marry women of similar education combined with a known tendency for the percentage of women in the labour force to increase with their level of education.

Professor Delivanis said he had been under the impression that income inequalities tended to diminish in periods of prosperity. Therefore he would appreciate it if Professor Haley could expand on his conclusion to the contrary at the end of the first part of his paper, namely that the intensity of the factors acting in favour of more equality in the distribution of national income had weakened in the United States since 1947.

Professor Haley explained to Professor Delivanis that his conclusion was the summing up of the action of contradictory factors. Among circumstances unfavourable to income equalization he would quote the slowing down in the increase in the real share of wages, the probable termination of the war-time and immediate post-war tendency for wage differentials to narrow, the ageing of the population and the increase in the number of families whose heads were over 65. On the other hand, there had been a slight reduction in income differentials among the states. All things considered, he would, however, maintain that the tendency towards less inequality had not continued except to a very minor degree, if at all.

Referring to figures in Table 9 of the paper, *Dr. Feinstein* observed that the long-run upwards tendency in the wage share had not been a regular trend ; most of the increase took place in the shape of two short jumps after both the First and Second World Wars, as a comparison of the periods 1920–29 and 1949–58 with respectively the periods 1910–19 and 1939–48 would reveal. Had there been any discontinuity in the data to explain this ?

Professor Haley stated that Table 9 was based on a variety of data which he had to piece together, especially for the early years when data were not considered as reliable as they had been since 1929. He had relied especially on the data since 1929 because Denison's and Phillips's studies started from that date and no comparable data were available for earlier years.

The Distribution of National Income

Professor Krelle remarked that in the calculations by Denison and by Phillips, which had been brought into the debate, the labour share remained stable only if one took the labour share in the private sector. This was in accordance with the Marxist concept of the labour share, however, without the corresponding recalculation of the national product data in the calculation. Had this been done, the outcome might have been different. In that case would not the calculation demonstrate a trend in the labour share ?

Short of evaluations with a wider scope than the one which had already been mentioned, *Professor Haley* did not want to pronounce on this. Only these limited studies on the private sector defined as such had been available to him. As his other figures in Table 9, taken from a study by Kravis with the exception of a few computations he had done himself to bring them up to date, contradicted the hypothesis of the stability of the labour share contained in the former, he had thought it advisable to reproduce them as evidence on a controversial question.

Professor Petrov said he had a query bearing on the concept of national income used in several papers. This was very different from the Marxist concept. Marxist analysis distinguished between incomes originating in material production and incomes from non-productive work. It also distinguished between incomes from production and incomes originating from the unproductive state expenditure, taking into account income redistribution by means of prices and by means of taxation. On the other hand, income distribution analysis in capitalist countries was based on a distinction between three social groups : the wage- and salary-earners, the self-employed and individual entrepreneurs, the capitalists.

Professor Petrov criticized these categories as not reflecting the real group divisions. The wage- and salary-earners were not a homogeneous group because they included civil servants, the armed forces, etc., as well. Therefore an increase in, for example, the number of people in the Forces would appear as an increase in the labour share, whereas correctly this should be analysed as a redistribution of primary income by means of taxation.

Professor Petrov wished to stress the distinction between income originating in productive work and income created by primary income redistribution. The incomes accruing to social groups could only be correctly determined at the final stage after redistribution, public expenditure, and taxation had been duly taken into account, and not as primary distribution.

One should consider the effects of indirect taxes and the burden per head of population. Professor Petrov thought that the main proportion fell on people in lower- and medium-income brackets in capitalist countries. According to sources available to Professor Petrov, indirect taxes had increased by 51 per cent in the United States during the period 1954–61, as against an increase of only 13 per cent in national income during the same period. Therefore he thought that the real wage share had fallen meanwhile. If one took into account known data on defence expenditure, price rises, etc., he thought this would demonstrate that the labour share could not have increased or even remained stable during this period.

Professor Brochier had doubts on the significance of the statistics on which one could appreciate equality or inequality of incomes, as far at least as his own experience with French data went. No matter how much more reliable the American data were, he wondered whether they could reflect all the factors making for income dispersion in the final distribution. Professor Haley had made it clear that his figures included incomes received in kind. But did they include such benefits as expense accounts, distribution of bonus shares to executives, and the like ?

If these were not taken into account, a conclusion that income inequality had been reduced was questionable. The trend towards less income inequality had been a very mild one, especially for the period 1929–62 as figures in Table 2 demonstrated. The lowest fifth had not significantly increased its share in national income ; the only major change had been that affecting the share of the upper fifth. As incomes placed in the upper fifth quintile were those more likely to benefit from expense account sheets, bonus shares, etc., Professor Brochier thought that any statement about reduction in income inequality should be interpreted with great care.

Commenting on Professor Brochier's remarks, *Professor Reder* observed that Professor Haley's data did not include the equity of individuals or family in undistributed profits in corporations. This led to understating the degree of inequality in distribution of personal income at any one time since these equities were distributed more unequally than current incomes of any sort. This omission was necessitated by lack of information. He, however, felt uncertain as to the manner in which it affected the trend in inequality.

Before concluding the discussion, *Professor Haley* thanked Professor Mirabella for introducing his paper. As to Professor Mirabella's comment on the bearing of education on income distribution, his own conclusion that education played a minor role in itself referred only to the period 1947–62. Over a period as short as that it was not surprising that changes in the dispersion of educational levels within the population had not played a major part. But Professor Haley was very conscious that in the United States lack of education was associated with a substantial part of unemployment and variations in the level of unemployment affected income distribution. Besides, in the long run, adaptation of education to technology was an important problem.

Concerning Professor Brochier's remark on the meaning of the statistical data, Professor Haley admitted that the reduction in income inequality over the period 1929–47 could be attributable to the way statistics were put together. He thought, however, that a change which appeared to be rather systematic would not just reflect errors in the figures although

The Distribution of National Income

one should recognize that the 1929–41 series were not as accurate as the series since 1947. He would not want to exaggerate the reliability of the data but the change in the top 5 per cent figures in Table 2 had been quite marked.

Professor Haley presumed that some of the points raised by Professor Petrov would come up in discussion in the next session of the Conference at which Professor Petrov's paper was to be discussed. Meanwhile he agreed with him in regretting that adequate data on changes in size distribution of disposable income in the United States were not available. The present data were on family incomes before tax. The effects of indirect taxes on distribution were worth investigating. But increase in indirect and direct taxes needed to be taken into account together in appraising the effect of taxation on distribution. Both in the U.S.S.R. and in the U.S.A. the burden of armament expenditure was very heavy, and therefore real consumable income lower than it would otherwise have been. This had a bearing on disposable income distribution, but our knowledge of tax incidence was not sufficient to appreciate it with precision.

The debate raised by Professor Marchal's statements had brought out all the points at stake. Professor Haley agreed that the existing data did not meet the requirements for analysing income distribution between a wage share and a property share and he would admit that there was a measure of arbitrariness in all the methods of imputation. He did not, however, think it possible to do without one. Professor Marchal's alternative solution implied that one should adapt income concepts and categories to available data. In so far as one was interested in studying saving propensities, Professor Marchal's proposal for breaking down income was relevant. But Professor Haley did not think it relevant to the study of income distribution as such. No matter how difficult it was to provide data in pure homogeneous form for studying functional distribution, Professor Haley would dissociate himself from a theory which altered the distributional concepts on which the theory of the pricing of production factors was based for the sake of meeting the existing statistical data.

40

Chapter 2

CHANGES IN THE DISTRIBUTION OF INCOME IN THE FRENCH ECONOMY

BY

JACQUES LECAILLON

Faculté de Droit et des Sciences Économiques, University of Lille

INTRODUCTORY

A STUDY of the trend of income distribution calls for an approach determined by two considerations :

(a) In view of the historical nature of this trend, no attempt can be made to explain it without also accounting for the expansion and the fluctuations with which it is accompanied.

The mode and structure of the distribution depend to a very great extent on the pattern of production ; but at the same time they govern the volume of savings and the trend of consumption which in turn determine production ; they should therefore make it possible to ascertain whether the sharing of the increased production among the beneficiaries justifies the continuation of expansion or whether on the contrary it jeopardizes its harmonious progression.

Furthermore, the combined analysis of the growth and of the distribution of the national product will serve to highlight their degree of compatibility or their inconsistencies and the ensuing lack of balance.

(b) This first methodological option entails a second one : since distribution constitutes the necessary link between production and the utilization of the national product it cannot be analysed along purely functional lines. It will not suffice to explain the factor costs of production and it will be necessary to ascertain how income derived from diverse sources and remunerating different functions is received and utilized by groups of people following a uniform pattern of behaviour. This I may describe as the sociological approach.

I shall endeavour to apply these principles to the examination of the problem in France, by a brief survey under two heads : [1]

---

[1] Cf. Jacques Lecaillon, *Croissance, répartition et politique des revenus*, Paris, Éditions Cujas, 1964.

41

The Distribution of National Income

I. The relationship between growth and distribution in the French economy.

II. The main features of distribution in present-day France.

I. THE RELATIONSHIP BETWEEN GROWTH AND DISTRIBUTION IN THE FRENCH ECONOMY

Although the documentation available is not always very adequate, I shall try in this first part to present a conspectus of growth and of the trend of distribution so as to identify the links that exist between the two processes of increasing and sharing out the aggregate product.

(i) *General Survey of Growth*

Viewed from its simplest aspect, economic growth may be defined as an increase in the *per capita* product. This increase is accompanied by major changes of a structural nature which are reflected in the changes in the structure of the active population.

(1) *Increase in the* Per Capita *Product*

Several stages are discernible in the trends of production, of population, and finally of the *per capita* product which follows as the result.

(A) *The growth of the product or of the total income* has not been a steady progression. According to the calculations published by the *Institut de Science Economique Appliqué,*[1] the national income at factor cost (in millions of current francs) would appear to have risen from 5,890 million in 1788 to 9,250 in 1845 and 24,100 in 1890, which represents a yearly growth rate of 0·8 per cent between 1788 and 1845 and of 2·1 per cent between 1845 and 1890 ; in view of the relative stability of the currency, these rates calculated in money value appear to represent a real growth. After a period of slow increase over the first half of the nineteenth century, during which the process of industrialization set in, the growth became more pronounced during the second half of the century.

From the end of the nineteenth century onwards we have the calculations of the volume of final production published by the National Institute of Statistics.[2] It emerges from Table 1 that

[1] *La Croissance de revenu national français depuis 1780,* Cahiers, Série D, n⁰ 7, 1952, p. 102.

[2] *Annuaire statistique, Rétrospectif,* 1961, p. 363.

the period of pronounced growth which began in the last century continued up to World War I ; after that, apart from cyclical fluctuations, the indices remain practically stable between the two wars, and in particular between 1924 and 1938 ; and lastly there is the present period, marked by very swift expansion.

TABLE 1

GROSS FINAL PRODUCTION
1896–1959 *

Years	Indices (in Volume) †	Mean Variation per Year as %
1896	100	+2%
1913	140	
1919	(113)	+0·7
1924	151	+3·5
1929	180	
1935	149	−3·1
1938	155	+1·3
1945	(85)	+0·7
1949	167	+1·6
1959	264	
1896–1959		+1·6

* Gross final production, inclusive of imports, covers orders from governmental bodies and also the agriculturists' consumption of their own products and the services procured by housing.
† Chain indices, basis 1896 = 100. Successive calculations 1913, 1929, 1938, 1956.

(B) *The growth in population* [1] has likewise been marked by fluctuations. From the end of the eighteenth century up to 1846, the growth was considerable except for an interval at the time of the Empire (1801–16) ; it is estimated that the total population rose from 25·6 million in 1776 to 35·4 million in 1846, i.e. an increase of some 38 per cent in 70 years.

After 1846 there is a very definite slowing down, with a total population of 39·7 million in 1913, which represents an increase of only 12 per cent over a period of 67 years.

From 1913 (87 *départements*) to 1946 (90 *départements*) there is practically no change over the period as a whole ; the 1946 census shows 39·8 million inhabitants (as opposed to 39·7 in 1913) though

[1] Cf. J. C. Toutain, *La Population de la France de 1700 à 1959*, Cahiers de l'ISEA, Série AF, nº 3, p. 26 *et seq.*

43

The Distribution of National Income

there is a peak of 41·2 million in 1931, followed by a regression. For the active population there is a slight drop : 20·5 million in 1946 compared with 21·1 in 1921.

Since 1946, on the other hand, there has been a steep rise in the total population : estimated at 46·5 million in the census of 7 March 1962 and at 47·6 on 1 January 1963, it was showing by the latter date nearly 7·5 million more than the figure reached on 1 January 1946, i.e. an increase of nearly 17 per cent in 17 years.[1] It should, however, be noted that during this latter phase the active population remained relatively stable, the larger young generation only reaching working age at the end of 1963.

It should also be noted that since the beginning of the twentieth century there is a definite correlation between the population trend and that of production. The increase in the total population, even when not accompanied by a parallel increase in the active population, appears to have provided momentum in the periods of increase of the aggregate production whereas the lack of growth in population seems to have contributed to the halt in economic growth between the two wars.

(C) *The changes of* per capita *output* fall into the same stages. Although caution must be shown in interpreting the figures that are available, it may be recalled that the total population increased by some 38 per cent between 1776 and 1846, whilst the national income at factor cost showed a rise of 57 per cent between 1789 and 1845, which represents a very slight improvement in personal income.

Between 1845 and 1890 on the other hand, the national income at factor cost increased by 16 per cent whilst the population rose by only 9 per cent ; the improvement in *per capita* income thus appears to have been a substantial one, once the difficulties of the 'take-off' period had been overcome.

For the twentieth century we can consult the calculations made by A. Sauvy,[2] according to which the national *per capita* income (in 1938 francs) rose from 5,800 to 7,800 between 1901 and 1913, i.e. an increase of 34 per cent in 12 years.

After a drop caused by the war, the 1913 level was regained in 1922. But the increase then recorded up to 1929 (10,900 francs) was cancelled out by the slump, with the result that the figure obtained for the year 1936 (8,800) was practically the same as that for 1923 (8,200). After World War II, it was not till 1948 that the

[1] M. Croze, 'Chronique de démographie', *Journal de la Société de Statistique de Paris*, October–December 1962, p. 281 *et seq.*
[2] *Annuaire statistique, Rétrospectif*, 1961, p. 360.

44

1936 level was regained. Taken as a whole, this period is thus one of stagnation in the standard of living. The increase achieved from 1948 (8,800 francs) to 1960 (14,900) is on the contrary a very considerable one : nearly 70 per cent in 12 years.

It would thus appear that the growth of population, with the impetus it gives to production, is generally accompanied, in a fully developed country, by a more than proportional increase in the standard of living.

(2) *Changes in the Occupational Structure*

Economic growth is accompanied by changes of a structural nature due to the unequal rate of development in the different branches and sectors of production, which in turn affects the size of the production units, the occupational pattern and the social structure. A simple indication of these changes can be found in the trend of the structure of the active population.

(A) *Over the long period of 1866–1954* this trend was as follows (Table 2) :

TABLE 2

STRUCTURE OF THE ACTIVE POPULATION
(1866–1954) *

Socio-occupational Categories	Numbers		% of Total	
	1866	1954	1866	1954
Farmers	5,404,888	3,978,920	32·1	20·6
Agricultural wage-earners	3,922,407	1,156,400	23·3	6·0
Employers in industry, trade, and liberal professions	2,328,253	2,418,600	13·8	12·5
Wage-earners in industry, trade, and liberal professions	3,654,943	7,952,640	21·7	41·1
Domestic staff	900,964	1,003,980	5·4	5·2
Civil and other public servants	616,435	2,832,960	3·7	14·6
Total active population	16,827,890	19,343,560	100·0	100·0

* According to N. Delefortrie and J. Morice, *Les Revenus départementaux en 1866 et en 1954*, Paris, A. Colin, p. 1.

The main features of this change are well known [1] :

(a) a decline of the active agricultural population both absolutely and relatively, which reflects the process of industrialization and urbanization ;

[1] Cf. Jean Marchal and Jacques Lecaillon, *La Répartition du revenu national*, Paris, ed. Génin, vols. i and ii.

45

The Distribution of National Income

(b) a rise in the number of wage-earners and a relative reduction in the number of individual entrepreneurs, which reflects a process of concentration in industry and trade ;

(c) an absolute and relative growth in the numbers employed in public services, which reflects the increasing intervention of the State in economic life.

(B) *The same features are found to be present and even accentuated in the present-day period* (Table 3). The proportion of people earning their livelihood from the land, whether as farmers or as agricultural wage-earners, which had dropped from 55 to 27 per cent of the active population in 90 years (1866–1954), fell to 20 per cent in a mere eight years (1954–62).

The proportion of wage-earning classes, which rose from 54 to 65 per cent between 1866 and 1954, had reached 71 per cent by 1962. This increase relates more to senior and junior managerial staff and employees than to work-people, in practice. It thus signifies a greater diversification in the wage-earning group and it is no longer possible to speak of a process of proletarianization in the strict sense of the term.

TABLE 3

STRUCTURE OF THE ACTIVE POPULATION
(1954 AND 1962) *

Socio-occupational Categories	Numbers in Thousands		Average % of Total		Variation as %
	1954	1962	1954	1962	1954–62
Farmers †	3,983·9	3,011·6	21·1	15·9	− 22
Agricultural wage-earners	1,136·8	820·7	6·0	4·3	− 28
Employers in industry and trade †	2,418·7	2,124·0	12·9	11·2	− 12
Senior managerial staff	427·5	629·4	2·3	3·3	+ 47
Junior managerial staff	1,124·0	1,478·1	6·0	7·8	+ 32
Employees	2,020·8	2,372·8	10·7	12·5	+ 17
Work-people and foremen	6,266·2	6,914·1	33·3	36·5	+ 10
Personnel in public services	951·3	1,016·0	5·1	5·4	+ 7
Other categories	494·9	589·7	2·6	3·1	+ 19
Active population in employment	18,824·1	18,956·4	100·0	100·0	+ 0·7%

* According to the census figures.
† Including members of the family working on the land.

Finally, the number of wage-earners in the civil and other public services rose by 11 per cent between 1954 and 1962, increasing from 15·2 to 16·7 per cent of the active population in employment.

With the increasing rate of growth in recent years, there has thus been a speeding up of the changes in the socio-occupational structure. These changes have not been without effect on the relative positions of those participating in the distribution of the national income and on their relative shares in it.

(ii) *The Trend of Distribution*

A study of the trend of distribution over a long period encounters two series of difficulties. The first is of a statistical nature : the further one delves into the past, the fewer and the less reliable are the data available. The second difficulty is of a methodological nature, for the very notion of income to be shared out can vary according to the source from which the income is derived. I shall therefore confine my investigation to the general pattern of the changes.

(1) *The Trend of Distribution in the Nineteenth Century*

As already mentioned, the *Institut de Science Economique Appliqué* has estimated the national income at factor cost for the years 1788, 1845, and 1890 [1] by producing a synthesis of the data available at these different times. This income has been obtained by adding to the income distributed to individual citizens and to foreign countries by the various sectors of production the savings which had been set aside by the different undertakings (Table 4).

The familiar trend towards a reduction in the relative share of those drawing their income from agriculture (farmers, agricultural wage-earners, and landowners) will be noted. We also find, at any rate from 1845 onwards, the increase in the share of the wage-earning classes in industry, commerce, and the public services.

As for the share of entrepreneurs in industry, commerce, and the liberal professions, its trend has not always followed the same course: during the first half of the nineteenth century, corresponding to the beginning of industrialization, their share increased, in line, moreover, with an increase in the share of the income derived from stocks and shares (interest and dividends) and a certain stability on the part of wages in industry and commerce ; during the second half of the century, on the other hand, the share of entrepreneurs in

---

[1] *La Croissance du revenu national français, op. cit.*, pp. 102 *et seq.*

47

The Distribution of National Income

the secondary and tertiary sectors and that of interest and dividends showed a decrease whilst there was a sharp rise in the share of non-agricultural wage-earners.

In so far as any conclusions can be drawn from these estimates, it would seem that the pattern of growth had changed from one period

TABLE 4

DISTRIBUTION OF THE NATIONAL INCOME
AT FACTOR COST IN THE NINETEENTH CENTURY

Categories	Income (Millions of Current Francs)			Distribution Percentages		
	1788	1845	1890	1788	1845	1890
Farmers	2,400	2,000	3,700	40·7	21·6	15·3
Entrepreneurs in industry and commerce	630	1,400	2,650	10·7	15·1	11·0
Liberal professions	100	350	500	1·7	3·8	2·1
Partially earned incomes	...	...	...	53·1	40·5	28·4
Ground rents	1,100	1,100	2,400	18·7	11·9	10·0
Interest and dividends	710	1,400	2,000	12·1	15·1	8·3
Business savings	...	...	200	...	...	0·8
Foreign countries	...	...	100	...	...	0·4
Unearned incomes	...	...	...	30·8	27·0	19·5
Agricultural wage-earners	...	1,200	2,300	...	13·0	9·5
Wage-earners in industry and commerce	700	1,100	7,800	11·9	11·9	32·4
Wage-earners in services	...	...	1,150	...	...	4·8
Civil servants	250	700	1,300	4·2	7·6	5·4
Earned incomes	...	...	...	16·1	32·5	52·1
NATIONAL INCOME at factor cost	5,890	9,250	24,100	100·0	100·0	100·0

to the other. Since the annual rate of growth was much higher in the second half of the nineteenth century than in the first, it may perhaps be inferred that the speeding up of growth in the second half of the century was accompanied by a process of concentration which reduced the share of the individual entrepreneurs and made for an improvement in the lot of the wage-earning classes.

48

(2) *The Trend of Distribution from 1913 to 1938*

Private Income. Table 5 is based on the estimates of private income drawn up by Duge de Bernonville and Rivet.[1]

In spite of the reservations which have to be made on account of the incompleteness of these estimates, two conclusions may be drawn from them :

(A) Firstly, the share accruing to the entrepreneurs in industry and commerce and the liberal professions shows a remarkable stability, as does the share of unearned income and more particularly that of stocks and shares. On the other hand, the earlier features of the trend continue as before : increase in the share of wage-earners and decrease in that of farmers, at any rate if the 1913–38 period is considered as a whole.

(B) Secondly, if one confines attention to years between the two wars (1921–38), it will be seen that except for brief periods of fluctuation, the distribution is remarkably stable : a very definite constancy in the relative shares appears to be the essential feature of this phase of our economic history. It had previously been noted that this period had witnessed a complete stoppage of growth and we thus find economic stagnation accompanied by stability in the relative shares of the distribution.

TABLE 5

DISTRIBUTION OF PERSONAL INCOME
FROM 1913 TO 1938
(As % of the total income)

Categories	1913	1921	1929	1935	1938
Wages and salaries	43·2	51·0	47·1	49·8	49·9
Pensions	1·4	2·8	4·6	7·6	5·6
Earned income	44·6	53·8	51·7	57·4	55·5
Stocks and shares	12·4	12·8	11·5	12·3	11·3
Property	7·2	3·7	4·9	7·1	5·3
Unearned income	19·6	16·5	16·4	19·4	16·6
Farmers	23·1	16·2	18·3	10·5	15·8
Industry and commerce	11·0	11·8	11·8	10·5	10·2
Liberal professions	1·7	1·7	1·8	2·2	1·9
Partially earned income	35·8	29·7	31·9	23·2	27·9
Grand Total	100·0	100·0	100·0	100·0	100·0

[1] *Annuaire statistique, Rétrospectif*, 1961, p. 300.

The Distribution of National Income

TABLE 6

DISTRIBUTION OF NATIONAL INCOME
1938–62
(Percentages)

	1938	1949	1950	1951	1952	1953	1954
Remuneration of wage-earners	51·4	53·5	52·1	55·2	56·7	56·5	57·5
Net income from property and enterprise received by families	47·7	41·0	42·6	40·4	38·9	37·5	37·6
Family income	99·1	94·5	94·7	95·6	95·6	94·0	95·1
Net income from property and enterprise received by :							
companies		5·3	6·4	6·3	5·1	5·4	6·6	5·8
administrations		−4·4	−0·9	−1·0	−0·7	−1·0	−0·6	−0·9
NATIONAL INCOME	100·0	100·0	100·0	100·0	100·0	100·0	100·0

	1955	1956	1957	1958	1959	1960	1961	1962
Remuneration of wage-earners	57·5	57·9	58·6	58·3	59·5	58·3	60·2	60·6
Net income from property and enterprise received by families	37·0	36·6	35·9	36·0	34·7	35·3	33·7	33·7
Family income	94·5	94·5	94·5	94·3	94·2	93·6	93·9	94·3
Net income from property and enterprise received by :								
companies	6·3	6·4	6·4	6·7	6·8	7·5	6·9	6·4
administrations	−0·8	−0·9	−0·9	−1·0	−1·0	−1·1	−0·8	−0·7
NATIONAL INCOME	100·0	100·0	100·0	100·0	100·0	100·0	100·0	100·0

(3) *The Trend of Distribution from 1938 to 1962*

For the current period, we have much more reliable estimates of the net national product at factor cost or of national income. The latest accounting statistics provide a breakdown of this income into four categories of remuneration: remuneration of wage-earners, and the net earnings from property and enterprise received by families, by companies, and by administrations (Table 6).[1] This distribution is of a functional nature, but it suggests two comments of some interest.

(A) Firstly, it is seen that families were receiving, either as wages or as earnings from property and enterprise, approximately 94 per cent of the national income throughout the 1949–62 period.

This proportion is remarkably stable: it reaches a maximum of 95·6 per cent in 1951–52 and a minimum of 93·6 per cent in 1960. This stability of the distribution of the national income between families and institutions appears to be confined to periods of average length, over which one can assume the structure of society and the patterns of behaviour to remain fairly stable. Looking at the figures for 1938, it is seen that the share of the institutions (companies and administrations) was much smaller than it is today, the net income of administrations being markedly negative at that time.

(B) Secondly, within the family income, there is seen to be a very pronounced contrast between the remuneration of wage-earners and the net income from property and enterprise. From 1950 onwards, the relative share of earned income shows an almost constant growth at the expense of the net income from property and enterprise received by families; between 1950 and 1962 the share of wage-earners rises from 52·1 to 60·6 per cent whilst the share of property and enterprise drops from 42·6 to 33·7 per cent. This goes to confirm the trends noted over the last century.

There is a contrast, on the other hand, when we look at the immediate past, i.e. the war years and reconstruction period. In comparing the years 1938 and 1950 it is seen that the share of wage-earners showed only a very slight increase: 52·1 per cent in 1950 as compared with 51·4 per cent in 1938. Moreover, other sources [2] show this share to have been 50 per cent in 1938, 43 per cent in 1946, 50 per cent in 1947, and 51 per cent in 1948, 1949, and 1950; it

[1] *Rapport sur les comptes de la nation de l'année 1962*, Paris, 1963, pp. 280–281. For the year 1938, cf. *Annuaire statistique de la France, Rétrospectif*, 1961, p. 356.
[2] P. Bauchet, 'Évolution des salaires et structure économique', *Revue économique*, May 1952, p. 313.

would thus appear to have remained stable over the greater part of the 1938–50 period and even shown a definite drop towards the end of the war when inflation was most severe.

It may thus be concluded that the years 1950 to 1962 represent a comparatively homogeneous period marked by new features which differentiate it from the preceding period and show that a different type of trend brought with it a different pattern of distribution.

(iii) *Forms of Growth and Pattern of Distribution*

If we examine the various conclusions drawn from the statistics available, we are able to distinguish several periods which will throw some light on the nature of the links that exist between growth and distribution.

(1) *The Stages of the Trend*

Four main phases appear to emerge as the historical framework of the problem :

(A) The first period corresponds to the end of the eighteenth century and the first decades of the nineteenth century. It is characterized by the beginning of industrialization and is marked by a relative fall in the incomes drawn from the agricultural sector (income of farmers, agricultural wage-earners, and ground landlords) and by a corresponding increase in the profits and income derived from capital invested in industry and commerce (interest and dividends), whilst the share of non-agricultural wage-earners remains relatively stable.

It may be suggested to begin with that this type of distribution was the only one compatible with a policy of growth. In an economy of this kind, presumably with a very low standard of living for the wage-earners at the outset, any increase in wages at the cost of profits would immediately be followed by an increased demand for staple commodities, i.e. primarily for agricultural products ; in other words, a general increase in wages was liable to produce a fall in the profits of capitalist undertakings and a rise in agricultural income, and consequently to retard the process of development by reducing the financing capacity of the industrial sector.

(B) The second period covers the second half of the nineteenth century and extends up to World War I. The rate of growth gathers speed and the share of agricultural income continues to fall. But a new factor now intervenes : the share of the entrepreneurs in industry, commerce, and the liberal professions, together with that of interest and dividends, which appears to be linked to it, is also seen to fall. The share of non-agricultural wage-earners, on the other hand, shows a significant increase.

The increase in the productivity of labour due to technical progress and to the concentration of undertakings, and the development of trade unionism accompanying this concentration, enabled wage-earners to partake of the fruits of expansion, and to share with the capitalist-entrepreneurs the advantages which the industrial sector was now drawing from the relative decline in agricultural income — a decline which was itself reinforced up to 1892 by the policy of free trade : between 1850 and 1911 the stability of the general price level was accompanied by a doubling of the straight-time wage rate.[1]

The problem of financing the necessary investment may, however, arise when wages increase too rapidly and bring about a fall in profits and in the earnings of capital and a decline in the inclination to save. The situation may become so serious as to interrupt the process of growth for a time. To seek protection against contingencies of this kind, the various groups will endeavour to organize themselves more closely, thus modifying the structure of the economy and setting up obstacles to impede the continuation of development.

(C) The third period corresponds to the years between the two wars and continues till practically the end of World War II. Under the combined effect of the halting of growth in population, of the Malthusian attitude of the groups concerned and of the various forms of protectionism which follow in its wake, there is a slowing down of expansion which finally gives way to near-stagnation, with the result that the pattern of distribution appears to become stabilized. In a stationary economy, the forces of the contractual groups confronting each other do indeed attain a certain equilibrium and there is little prospect of any change in the situation except through the intervention of an outside cause. It is this period that seems to have given rise to the subsequently accepted idea of the stability of the relative shares in distribution over a period of several years.

It may be added here that this phase of stagnation was followed during World War II and the years of reconstruction by a phase of scarcity and inflation which appears to have engendered a kind of 'regressive trend' exemplified by an increase in the share of farmers and the owners of commercial concerns at the expense of that of wage-earners ; the index of the straight-time wage rate in the Paris

[1] *Annuaire statistique, Rétrospectif*, 1961, pp. 217 and 252.

The Distribution of National Income

area, adjusted with the help of the cost of living index, fell from 133 in 1938 to 95 in 1946 (1930 = 100).

(D) Finally, the fourth period brings us to the contemporary scene characterized, since the end of the great post-war inflation, by a rate of growth never previously attained. This is producing a trend that is comparable, in relative terms, to that of the second half of the nineteenth century, with a reduction in the share of the income derived from agriculture and in that of earnings from property and enterprise in industry, trade, and the liberal professions, and an appreciable increase in the share of wage-earners. But the pattern of growth is no longer the same ; for though the rate of growth of the national product has varied from year to year, and though some years have witnessed a slowing down of expansion (1952–53 and 1958–59), there has been no major depression to record. There has thus been almost unbroken full employment and the growth has been accompanied by an upward pressure on prices : from 1949 to 1962 the gross national product increased by 305 per cent in value and by 85 per cent in volume.[1] The upward trend in the general price level thus appears to be playing an increasingly important part in the pattern of distribution and is taking the place of the cyclical rhythm in an economy no longer held back by monetary impediments.

(2) The Links between Growth and Distribution

Two conclusions emerge from this examination of the problem :

(A) In studying the pattern of France's economic growth we can discern a number of basic distribution problems which still remain at the present day :

(a) The first concerns the relationship between agriculture and the rest of the economy in a country where the agricultural sector is not fully industrialized and still employs a large fraction of the active population. This problem is known today as the 'problem of the parity of agricultural income'.

(b) A second problem concerns the sharing of the product of the non-agricultural sectors between those who draw their main source of income from property and enterprise (entrepreneurs in industry, commerce, and the liberal professions) and those whose main source of income is the remuneration for their labour in its widest sense (wages and social benefits).

[1] Rapport sur les comptes de la nation de l'année 1962, Paris, 1963, pp. 278/279.

54

However, the conditions in which the determination of the shares is effected are variable ; when the rate of growth is only slight, it appears to be met by a straightforward shift of the active agricultural population to industry and services and by a kind of substitution of industrial and commercial profits for agricultural revenue, with only a very small increase in the share of wage-earners. A swift rate of growth, on the contrary, implying a high level of employment, is apparently advantageous for wage-earners at the expense of entrepreneurs, farmers, and those drawing unearned income. Lastly, a phase of comparative rigidity of supply and open inflation seems likely to give rise to a contrary process.

(B) On these premises, it may be suggested that the links that exist between economic growth and the pattern of distribution take the form of thresholds :

A trend favourable to the increase of the share allotted to labour appears to presuppose the achievement of a certain rate of growth, the substitution of 'intensive growth' for an 'extensive growth' merely by transferring the factors of production from one sector to the other ; in other words, a reduction in the share of entrepreneurs in industry and commerce (and the corresponding increase in the share of the wage-earners) would seem to depend on the intervention of a concentration mechanism which comes into play only when a certain rate of development is attained. But if this growth is accompanied by serious disequilibrium — if for example it sets in motion an inflationary trend — it is possible that from a different threshold it may prejudice wage-earners and improve the relative position of the other groups.

In order to develop these ideas in greater detail I shall now confine myself to the present period in which the inflationary rise of prices appears in fact to play a steadying role.

II. THE MAIN FEATURES OF DISTRIBUTION IN CONTEMPORARY FRANCE

In attempting to study the pattern of distribution in relation to growth, the analysis can no longer proceed along functional lines but has to become sociological in its approach to the problem. It no longer suffices to explain the make-up of such and such a type of remuneration or of this or the other factor cost. What is now called for is an enquiry as to how income which may be derived from various sources is acquired by the groups of economic units and assigned by them to consumption or to savings.

This change from the customary approach involves taking account not only of the results provided by the market (primary distribution) but also of those of the redistribution effected through the medium of official bodies ; it also calls for a determination of the categories following a uniform pattern of behaviour as regards both the receipt and the employment of income. The latest figures taken from France's National Accounts provide the necessary data for this approach and will enable us to examine successively the categories of participants in the distribution, the evolution of their relative shares, and the subsequent problem of achieving economic balance.

(i) *The Categories of Participants in the Distribution*

In France the National Accounts are based primarily on the concept of the gross domestic product. This is a relatively narrow concept for, contrary to Anglo-Saxon practice, it excludes the services rendered by domestics to families, the services rendered by civil servants and other public officials to the administrations, and the insurance services rendered to families and business concerns.[1] The remuneration of these services, considered to be non-productive, is effected through redistribution operations, that is to say, by transfers which can be taken into account in drawing up the table of final distribution. At the final stage, the value of the gross domestic product is equal to the sum of the incomes available to the various recipients. In 1956, a year for which an exhaustive survey was made,[2] the gross domestic product was shared out as shown in the Table 7.

It will be seen from this Table 7 that families received only 83 per cent of the total income, the remainder going to the various 'institutions' or bodies, or representing the small balance left over from operations of distribution to other countries. We shall therefore now proceed to undertake a brief analysis of the 'families' and of the 'institutions' groups.

(1) *Analysis of the Families Group*

In the French National Accounts system, families are classified by socio-occupational categories according to the occupation of the

[1] Jean Marchal, *Nouveaux Éléments de comptabilité nationale française*, Paris, Éd. Cujas, 1962, pp. 36–37.
[2] 'Étude sur les revenus de 1956', *Études et conjoncture*, June 1963.

head of family, with the result that each category of families may be drawing income derived from different sources (Table 8).

In these circumstances, the categories selected do not all seem to be capable of exerting a significant pressure on the pattern of distribution.

(A) Some of them occupy too small a place and carry too little 'relative weight' to play any decisive role. This is the case of the agricultural wage-earners (1·8 per cent of the total income), services personnel (1·3 per cent), 'other categories' (1·8 per cent), and non-residents (1·5 per cent), all of whom constitute 'satellite' groups, as it were.

(B) Other categories, of greater importance in view of the weight they represent, do not dispose of sufficiently homogeneous sources of income to enable them to show any real uniformity of behaviour in influencing distribution. This is the case of senior management

TABLE 7

DISTRIBUTION OF THE GROSS DOMESTIC PRODUCT
IN 1956

Categories	Available Income Millions of N.F.	% of Total
Farmers	17,230	10·3
Agricultural wage-earners	3,030	1·8
Employers in industry and commerce	26,130	15·7
Senior management and liberal professions	11,690	7·0
Junior management	9,740	5·9
Salaried workers	9,190	5·5
Industrial workers	34,550	20·8
Domestic service	2,160	1·3
Other categories (wage-earners)	2,980	1·8
Non-active	17,660	10·6
Others	1,020	0·6
Non-resident	2,490	1·5
Total of Family Incomes	137,870	82·8
Administrations	7,900	4·8
Companies	15,690	9·4
Financial institutions	1,910	1·1
Balance of distribution operations abroad	3,110	1·9
Total of Incomes (Gross domestic product)	166,480	100·0

staff and the liberal professions (7 per cent of the total income) whose available income comprises 66 per cent as wages and 25 per cent as earnings from liberal activities ; it is also the case of the non-active (10 per cent of the total income) whose resources are composed of net transfers to the extent of 47 per cent, net wages 23 per cent, and gross operating revenue (rents) 12 per cent (Table 8).

(C) On the other hand, the remaining categories are characterized by their considerable relative importance and a certain homogeneity in their sources of income. These are :

(a) Farmers, who receive 10 per cent of the total income and whose resources are constituted, for as much as 83 per cent, by the gross income from their operating earnings.

(b) Employers in industry and commerce who receive 15 per cent of the total income and whose incomes represent 92 per cent of gross business earnings.

(c) Wage-earners : 21 per cent of the total ; incomes received as wages (70 per cent) and social transfers (23 per cent).

(d) Junior management : 6 per cent of the total ; incomes received as wages (80 per cent) and social transfers (11 per cent).

(e) Employees : 5·5 per cent of the total ; incomes received as wages (72 per cent) and transfers (20 per cent).

Experience shows, moreover, that these various categories, and more particularly the first three, play an important part in respect of distribution, in present-day France. Together they received 58 per cent of the total income in 1956.

(2) *Analysis of the Institutions Group*

The participation of units other than families in the distribution of the product in terms of value deprives the concept of *per capita* income of part of its significance, since all or part of the increase of the aggregate income may be absorbed by the institutions. The question then arises as to how these institutions can fit into the theory of distribution ; or in other words how to provide an exact definition of institutional income.

The available income of companies (private companies and public undertakings) raises no particular difficulty in this respect, since it corresponds to their gross non-distributed earnings or gross savings, normally assigned to amortization and to self-financed investment.

The available income of administrations (government, local authorities, social security agencies, etc.) and of financial institutions

TABLE 8

STRUCTURE OF AVAILABLE INCOME OF FAMILIES
IN 1956

(Millions of N.F.)

Socio-occupational Categories	Net Wages	Net Interest and Dividends	Gross Operating Earnings of Families	Gross Income of Individual Entre- preneurs	Net Foreign Receipts	Social Benefits and Net Tax Transfers	Total
Farmers	1,210	350	420	14,400	– 20	870	17,230
Agricultural wage-earners	1,710	—	250	60	—	1,010	3,030
Employers in commerce and industry	400	1,200	1,250	24,800	– 290	–1,230	26,130
Senior management and liberal professions	7,810	1,100	600	3,110	–410	– 520	11,690
Junior management	7,840	290	340	470	– 260	1,060	9,740
Salaried workers	6,660	230	100	500	– 130	1,830	9,190
Industrial workers	24,390	270	340	1,440	10	8,100	34,550
Domestic service	1,490	30	70	40	– 40	570	2,160
Other categories	2,130	30	50	230	– 70	610	2,980
Non-active	4,160	1,640	2,180	1,580	– 200	8,300	17,660
Others	490	—	—	—	—	530	1,020
Non-residents	640	—	—	—	1,770	80	2,490
Total	58,930	5,140	5,600	46,630	360	22,210	137,870

59

(banks and insurance) is on the other hand of an original nature. As such bodies are not considered to be productive, their available income is equivalent to the sum of their savings (which may moreover be negative) and of their consumption, that is to say, of their purchases of equipment and services used to provide other services for the families (roads, information services, military equipment, etc.).

This leads to a twofold conclusion :

(A) In so far as institutional income represents consumption it really amounts to the provision of free services to the families although it is not possible to identify the precise beneficiaries of these services. This redistributive aspect of the action of the institutions, and in particular of the administrations, which leads to the development of collective equipment, probably has a levelling effect on the standards of living. If it were to assume very significant proportions it would obviously have a considerable effect on the problem of distribution ; but this would presuppose a fundamental transformation of the regime by the multiplication of free benefits.

(B) In so far as institutional income represents gross savings, it may be wondered whether the savings do not confer a residual character on it. Unlike the income of families, the income of institutions is not a vital one, at any rate over a short period ; it is thus found that the savings of administrations and companies can become negative, in the event of a major depression, for instance. This sensitivity of savings plays the role of a 'conjunctural shock-absorber' and appears to be conducive to the achievement of economic equilibrium.

In order to probe further into this problem we must now examine the trends of the relative shares of the various categories of participants in the distribution.

(ii) *Changes in the Relative Shares*

Unfortunately, for no period of several years are there any estimates similar to those made for the year 1956 ; use will therefore be made of the figures provided by the National Accounts for the trends of functional remunerations.[1] These figures give a fairly good idea of the movements of the incomes of the main socio-occupational categories and are shown in Table 9 and translated into percentages in Table 10.

[1] Cf. *Les Rapports sur les comptes de la nation*, Paris, Imprimerie Nationale.

TABLE 9

DISTRIBUTION OF DISPOSABLE INCOME
1938–62

(Millions of current N.F.)

Incomes	1938	1949	1951	1952	1953	1954	1955
Net wages	1,570	25,820	35,970	42,760	44,200	48,140	52,890
Net interest and dividends	390	2,190	3,300	3,960	4,100	4,480	4,650
Rent accruing to households (including some imputed income)	240	2,780	3,560	4,080	4,330	5,040	5,320
Gross income from self-employment	1,260	25,320	34,270	38,010	37,950	39,990	42,900
Net external receipts	40	820	930	840	650	810	660
Social benefits, insurance, and tax-free transfers	160	8,120	12,240	14,630	15,460	17,220	19,550
Total disposable income of households	3,660	65,050	90,270	104,280	106,690	115,680	125,970
Consumption of administrations and financial institutions	250	3,330	5,370	8,520	9,520	8,620	8,430
Gross savings of companies and financial institutions	410	9,650	11,410	13,770	15,340	14,890	15,830
Gross savings of administrations	-270	1,520	1,670	-590	-260	1,110	320
Balance of transactions with the rest of the world	-90	-2,080	810	2,310	2,160	860	830
GROSS DOMESTIC PRODUCT	3,960	77,470	109,530	128,290	133,450	141,160	151,380

TABLE 9 (*continued*)

Incomes	1956	1957	1958	1959	1960	1961	1962
Net wages	58,930	66,300	76,030	82,620	90,860	99,870	111,090
Net interest and dividends	5,140	5,610	5,900	6,200	6,520	6,820	7,130
Rent accruing to households (including some imputed income)	5,600	5,940	6,530	7,070	8,110	8,940	10,250
Gross income from self-employment	46,630	51,320	57,880	59,700	66,040	68,280	73,640
Net external receipts	360	560	640	1,370	1,410	1,240	1,630
Social benefits, insurance, and tax-free transfers	21,210	23,430	24,350	26,370	29,720	33,770	41,260
Total disposable income of households	137,870	153,160	171,330	183,330	202,660	218,920	245,000
Consumption of administrations and financial institutions	10,140	11,150	11,320	13,080	13,430	14,360	15,350
Gross savings of companies and financial institutions	16,990	18,620	19,140	20,760	23,690	24,510 }	31,750
Gross savings of administrations	−1,630	−530	4,730	6,370	7,160	7,880 }	
Balance of transactions with the rest of the world	3,110	3,990	4,900	5,180	5,190	6,130	5,630
GROSS DOMESTIC PRODUCT	166,480	186,390	211,420	288,720	252,130	271,800	297,730

TABLE 10

DISTRIBUTION OF DISPOSABLE INCOME

1938–62

(Percentages)

Incomes	1938	1949	1951	1952	1953	1954	1955
Net wages	39·6	33·3	32·8	33·3	33·1	34·1	34·9
Net interest and dividends	9·9	2·8	3·0	3·1	3·1	3·2	3·1
Rent accruing to households (including some imputed income)	6·1	3·6	3·3	3·2	3·3	3·6	3·5
Gross income from self-employment	31·8	32·7	31·3	29·7	23·4	28·3	28·3
Net external receipts	1·0	1·1	0·9	0·7	0·5	0·6	0·4
Social benefits, insurance, and tax-free transfers	4·0	10·5	11·2	11·4	11·6	12·2	12·9
Total disposable income of households	92·4	84·0	82·5	81·4	80·0	82·0	83·1
Consumption of administrations and financial institutions	6·3	4·3	4·9	6·6	7·1	6·1	5·6
Gross savings of companies and financial institutions	10·4	12·4	10·4	10·7	11·5	10·5	10·5
Gross savings of administrations	−6·8	2·0	1·5	−0·5	−0·2	0·8	0·2
Balance of transactions with the rest of the world	−2·3	−2·7	0·7	1·8	1·6	0·6	0·6
GROSS DOMESTIC PRODUCT	100·0	100·0	100·0	100·0	100·0	100·0	100·0

TABLE 10 (*continued*)

Incomes	1956	1957	1958	1959	1960	1961	1962
Net wages	35·4	35·6	35·9	36·1	36·0	36·7	37·6
Net interest and dividends	3·1	3·0	2·8	2·7	2·6	2·5	2·4
Rent accruing to households (including some imputed income)	3·4	3·2	3·1	3·1	3·2	3·3	3·4
Gross income from self-employment	28·0	27·5	27·4	26·1	26·2	25·1	24·7
Net external receipts	0·2	0·3	0·3	0·6	0·6	0·5	0·5
Social benefits, insurance, and tax-free transfers	12·7	12·6	11·5	11·5	11·8	12·4	13·8
Total disposable income of households	82·8	82·2	81·0	80·1	80·4	80·5	82·4
Consumption of administrations and financial institutions	6·1	6·0	5·4	5·7	5·3	5·3	5·1
Gross savings of companies and financial institutions	10·2	10·0	9·1	9·1	9·4	9·0}	10·6
Gross savings of administrations	−1·0	−0·3	2·2	2·8	2·9	2·9}	
Balance of transactions with the rest of the world	1·9	2·1	2·3	2·3	2·0	2·3	1·9
GROSS DOMESTIC PRODUCT	100·0	100·0	100·0	100·0	100·0	100·0	100·0

64

If we confine ourselves to basic trends, there are two problems to be considered ; one concerns the sharing of the aggregate income between families and institutions, the other the sharing between the earnings of labour and those of capital and enterprise.

(1) *The Division of the Aggregate Income between Families and Institutions*

As already mentioned, the fact that in a modern economy not all of the aggregate income is received by families raises the problem of how to integrate the institutions into the theory of distribution. On the basis of experience in France, it would appear that such integration depends on the length of the period chosen for examination.

(A) If a long period is selected for analysis and if account is consequently taken of changes in the structure, it is clear that the role of institutions increases : the development of self-financing policies, the intervention of the state, the creation of social security agencies, are all stepping-stones along the road to 'socialization' in enlightened capitalist countries. It is thus that, in comparison with the pre-war period, the share of institutions has shown a sharp rise, implying a corresponding fall in the share of families from 92 per cent in 1938 to 84 per cent in 1949. This increase is mainly explained by the disappearance of the deficit of administrations and its replacement by positive savings ; it is linked to the introduction of the social security scheme which has given the administrations stricter control over the flow of income by compelling a portion of wage earnings to pass through their books.

(B) Over a medium period of a few years, on the other hand, featuring some measure of stability in structure and behaviour, the sharing of the aggregate income between families and institutions appears to remain comparatively stable : from 1951 to 1962 the families received a steady 80 to 83 per cent of the aggregate income. It would seem in fact that, in the light of established practice, the share of institutions could not go beyond a certain level without causing a reaction on the part of families anxious to protect their real incomes or to ensure their steady increase. It is to this extent that the income of institutions may be considered to present a residual character.

(C) Lastly, over a short period — that is to say from one year to the next — the relative share, not only of each category of institution but also of operations with other countries, is found to be extremely

The Distribution of National Income

variable and to entail contrary variations in the share of families. As already suggested, it plays the role of a conjunctural shock-absorber; a typical example of this is the sensitivity of the gross savings of administrations. This is the reason why, in an economy in which institutions occupy a sufficiently important place to exercise effective control over the flow of income, the problem of general economic equilibrium is more easily solved than in a purely individualistic society. The only question which can arise in an economy of this kind is that of the determination of the level of prices and of activity at which equilibrium will be achieved.

(2) *The Division between Earnings of Labour and those of Capital and Enterprise*

The current period shows, in France, a clean break with the war and pre-war years characterized by stability in the division between the earnings of labour and those of enterprise; in 1951 the share of net wages and social benefits and transfers amounted to 44 per cent of the aggregate income compared with 43·6 per cent in 1938; that of the gross income of individual entrepreneurs 31·3 compared with 31·8 per cent in 1938; that of companies 10·4 per cent as in 1938.

Since 1951, on the other hand, the upward trend in the share of labour in the aggregate income, which is found to accompany the increase in the number of wage-earners over a long period, has again been making itself felt at the expense of the share going to individual entrepreneurs, capitalists, and capitalist companies. Between 1951 and 1962, the share of net wages rose from 32·8 to 37·6 per cent and that of social benefits and transfers from 11·2 to 13·8 per cent; inversely, the share of individual entrepreneurs fell from 31·3 to 24·7 per cent and that of companies from 10·4 to 9 per cent. Within the income of families one may note, in particular, a steady and progressive redistribution in favour of the wage-earners and beneficiaries of transfers and at the expense of farmers, employers in industry and commerce, and members of the liberal professions.

This trend, which runs counter to the established concept regarding the stability of the share of labour in the national income,[1] would appear to be linked to the simultaneous action, in the French economy of today, of three characteristic processes of growth : the process of industrialization and urbanization, the process of concentration and the process of state intervention.

[1] Cf. W. Krelle, 'Un Modèle expliquant la stabilité de la répartition du revenu national, *Revue économiqué*, July 1963.

66

(A) The process of industrialization and urbanization explains the fall in the relative share of farmers in the aggregate income. The income of agriculturists is to a very large extent an operating income produced by the difference between the sales of agricultural products and the costs borne by the producer. These costs consist mainly in purchases of the industrial commodities required for agriculture. In a given state of technique, the operating income therefore depends on the difference between agricultural prices and industrial prices with the result that a poor harvest may finally prove more profitable than a good one, for the inelasticity of the demand for food products has the effect of reducing the monopoly power of the agricultural sector in a period of abundant supply. It may thus happen that the relative share of agriculturists, and consequently their relative personal income, may become smaller.

A further feature of the present situation in France is the fact that as soon as a certain threshold of awareness is reached — and it is a point brought continually nearer with the advance of information media — any fall in the relative standard of living of agriculturists sets off a reaction on the part of the latter who at once bring pressure to bear on the authorities and clamour for subsidies, social benefits, tax-relief, the raising of agricultural prices, and so forth. In other words, the relative share of agriculturists cannot fall below a certain level without jeopardizing political and social order.

Over a longer period technical progress also comes into play and has the effect of reducing the monopoly power of the agriculturists ; the relative income of the farmers can then no longer be maintained except at the cost of an emigration of rural workers to other sectors of the economy. In the last ten years, the active agricultural population has diminished at the rate of 160,000 persons a year ; and as most of the migrants have become wage-earners in other sectors, it may be deduced that a diminution of the share of the agriculturists in the aggregate income has helped to increase the relative share of wage-earners.

(B) The process of concentration affects mainly the non-agricultural sectors and more particularly industry. In these sectors, the individual entrepreneurs, as owners of their undertakings, bear costs which consist primarily of wages, whereas their receipts come from the sale of their production at market prices ; wages and prices are thus the determining factors in their income. These wages and prices frequently depend, however, on the policy of the big firms organized as companies. This being so, if there is competition

The Distribution of National Income

between these big firms — as is the case in an expanding economy open to foreign trade — and if their productivity rises faster than that of the small individual concerns, the gross income of the small entrepreneurs ultimately begins to fall, at least in relative value, thus leading in the long run, at the cost of certain social difficulties, to the disappearance or absorption of the small undertakings.

It is found, however, that this process of concentration is not accompanied by any increase in the share of companies or in that of capital earnings (interest and dividends) in the aggregate income ; in recent years this share has even tended to diminish. This may perhaps be explained by the fact that within the big companies in the forefront of progress, capital does not have the same relation to labour as in the old-fashioned type of enterprise — in other words that progress economizes capital instead of being 'labour-saving'.[1] The adoption of more advanced machinery, which costs more but also works faster and is more productive, means that less of it is needed and capital can be economized. At the same time, the use of this advanced equipment involves the employment of greater numbers of well-paid research workers, engineers, and technicians who more or less offset the reduction in direct and cheaper labour. A more highly concentrated economy also requires increasingly large management and administrative staffs, supervisors, publicity agents, and salesmen. This up-grading of the labour needed for production is effected through the medium of large companies, the development of which, to the detriment of small undertakings and family concerns, appears to be the basis of the mechanism leading to a redistribution of the national income in favour of wage-earners in modern economies.

(C) The process of state intervention is related to that of concentration, for a more highly concentrated economy demands and permits a strengthening of government control. With the transformation of small entrepreneurs and redundant farmers into wage-earners, the state and the social welfare agencies are in a much better position to keep track of the flow of income : wages hold fewer secrets for the tax authorities than do the incomes of private enterprise, and increasing numbers of citizens are being brought into the social security scheme. The substitution of company undertakings for individual undertakings would appear to have the same effect : it becomes easier for the administration to calculate profits and it can if necessary collect a larger share of the earnings of business and

[1] Cf. D. J. Robertson, *The Economics of Wages and the Distribution of Income*, London, Macmillan, 1961, pp. 180 *et seq.*

68

proceed to a more effective redistribution of the aggregate income. At the same time, this extension of the scope of the government entails the creation of new jobs which reinforce the upward trend in the share of the wage-earning classes in the national income.

It may then be wondered how far this bears out the theory that the share of wages is stable over a long period. In the light of what has been said, it would appear that this theory holds good in two sets of conditions :

(a) on the one hand, when the rate of growth is sufficiently low to cause no change in the economic, occupational, and social structure ;

(b) on the other hand, when the economy has reached such a high level of development and maturity that the proportion of wage-earners can hardly increase further, as would appear to be the case in the Anglo-Saxon countries.

As these conditions do not apply in the present French economy, we must try to see what is the effect of changes in the pattern of distribution on the attainment of overall equilibrium.

(iii) *Effect of the Pattern of Distribution on the Achievement of Economic and Social Equilibrium*

The growth of the French economy has proceeded since the war in a climate of near-permanent inflation ; the general index of wholesale prices doubled between 1949 and 1962, in spite of the increasingly strong pressure of foreign competition. In other words, equilibrium could only be attained from year to year at the price of steady depreciation in the value of the currency.

The causes of this phenomenon are complex. We shall here merely examine the extent to which the pattern of distribution shares some of the responsibility either in the origin or in the amplification of the price spiral.

(1) *Pattern of Distribution and Origination of Inflation*

According to Keynesian theory, overall economic equilibrium is achieved when there is equality of savings and investment ($S=I$) and this at all levels of employment. However, since the Great Depression, the public authorities have developed more and more efficient mechanisms of control and intervention ; the existence of a large nationalized sector and the participation of the state in investment policies within the framework of modernization and equipment schemes, are contributing in France to the maintenance of full employment and the continuation of economic growth.

Two comments may now be made in this context :

(A) In an expanding economy which is assumedly functioning at a full-employment level, the achievement of equilibrium, in the Keynesian meaning of the term, presupposes a flow of savings sufficient to finance the necessary investment. However, the change in the relative shares of distribution, to the advantage of wage-earners and to the detriment of capitalist entrepreneurs, may cause a decline in the community's aggregate propensity to save, since the propensity to save of the former is definitely lower than that of the latter, as is shown in Table 11.

This fall in the average propensity to save, due to a phenomenon of distribution, ought to cause, all other things being equal of course, a fall in the rate of investment to allow economic equilibrium to be maintained ; in other words, to bring about a slowing down of the

TABLE 11

AVERAGE PROPENSITY TO SAVE
IN THE VARIOUS CATEGORIES OF FAMILIES
1956 *

Categories	Available Income (in Millions of N.F.)	Gross Savings	% of Savings in Relation to Income
Farmers	17,230	2,910	16·8
Agricultural wage-earners	3,030	180	5·9
Employers in industry and commerce	26,130	9,560	36·5
Senior management and liberal professions	11,690	2,850	24·3
Junior management	9,740	550	5·6
Salaried workers	9,190	110	1·2
Industrial workers	34,550	840	2·4
Domestic service	2,160	90	4·1
Other categories	2,980	190	6·3
Non-active	17,660	200	1·1
Others	1,020	—	—
Non-residents	2,490	—	—
Total	137,870	17,480	12·7

* *Études et conjoncture*, June 1963.

economic growth. In these conditions, expansion can only be pursued at the same pace at the cost of some measure of inflation ; the latter acts as a regulating factor which sets a limit to the rise in the incomes of the groups in which consumption is highest (wage-earners, non-active).[1]

(B) This does not mean that the changes in the pattern of distribution are the only causes of French inflation. These changes merely combine in reinforcing the action of the factors which in recent years have almost continuously encouraged the too rapid development of private and public consumption: aid to under-developed countries, high military expenditure, rapid increase in state benefits for a stable active population, pressure of advertisement and so forth. On the other hand, the phenomena of distribution play a decisive role in amplifying the rise in prices.

(2) *The Pattern of Distribution and Spread of Inflation*

The present-day economy is a group economy. In France the largest socio-occupational categories (work-people and employees, entrepreneurs, farmers) are well organized and exercise fairly effective means of pressure. These various groups see to it, not only that their standard of living is not reduced in terms of absolute value but also that it suffers no reduction in relative value ; and as they each constitute an autonomous decision-making body, a level of stable equilibrium can only be attained if they are all simultaneously satisfied with the share they are obtaining in the national income.

Consequently, the role of the public authorities today consists in ensuring both economic equilibrium in the Keynesian sense and social equilibrium between the groups, the two types of equilibrium not necessarily being compatible. Once full employment is assured the continuation of growth causes an upward pressure on prices ; the adjustments required in the social context will likewise follow an upward trend and will amplify the initial inflation. These amplifying mechanisms are particularly conspicuous in France for reasons of a structural nature, namely :

(A) *The coexistence of a number of large groups*, some of which are expanding (wage-earners) whilst others are contracting (farmers and individual entrepreneurs), but all of which carry economic and political influence. In countries where there is a high proportion of wage-earners inflation by costs is essentially a wages inflation ; the wage race leads to a uniform increase in the rate of remuneration in

[1] Cf. Nicolaï, ' L'Inflation comme régulation ', *Revue économique*, July 1962, p. 546.

all branches, the least productive branches generally falling into line with the pilot industries, with the result that the average rise in wages tends to out-pace the increase in productivity.[1]

In the French economy, a race between wages and profits, between the earnings of industry and commerce and those of agriculture, brings reinforcement to the mechanism of salary comparison.[2] Indeed, the greater the number of organized groups, the greater the risks of outbidding and the wider the spread of inflation.

(B) *The fact that each of the main categories commands a different strategic variable* (wages, agricultural prices, retail price of industrial products, and price of services) and that these variables are directly and mechanically inter-related. Any rise in wages means not only an improvement in the living standard of wage-earners but also an immediate increase in the costs borne by small entrepreneurs ; any increase in agricultural income, and therefore in agricultural prices, means a rise in the cost of living and a fall in real wages. The competition between the groups thus rests on an objective and even quantifiable basis, which further strengthens its automaticity.

(C) *The fact that the groups are groups of families* and not of institutions, i.e. they are groups of consumers. Unlike the income of institutions the income of families is scarcely compressible, since it is a vital and human income ; moreover, families are responsive to the 'effect of imitation' and are protecting a relative standard of living, with the result that a subjective and psycho-sociological factor is added to the mechanical factors previously mentioned.

Thus it is that in the sectors where concentration is not very pronounced, where external competition plays little part and where small family undertakings are numerous (home industries, trade services), a rise in wages tends to produce a proportionate rise in prices, even though wages only constitute one cost factor, since the entrepreneurs seek to maintain their own standard of living in relation to that of the wage-earners.

The position is the same in the agricultural sector ; in recent years, the agriculturists' claim for a reduction of the inequality of earnings has had the effect of stabilizing or raising agricultural prices, even when there has been surplus production,[3] which has

[1] Cf. *The Problem of Price Increase*, OEEC, 1961, pp. 54 *et seq.*
[2] Cf. Jean Marchal, *Cours d'économie politique*, Paris, Éd. Cujas, 1962–63, pp. 363 *et seq.*
[3] *Rapport sur les comptes de la nation de l'année 1962*, Paris, 1963, p. 18. In 1962, the rise in production prices attained 5·2 per cent for transport and services and 4·4 per cent for agricultural and food products, as opposed to only 1·7 per cent for industrial products.

caused a further rise in the cost of living and started a fresh series of wage claims.

The final conclusion thus seems to be that inflation plays a two-fold regulating role, by ensuring the equalization of savings and investment at full-employment level (economic equilibrium), and by adjusting the claims of the various groups confronting each other (social equilibrium). It is somewhat paradoxical that the greater effectiveness of government intervention in respect of full employment has served to some extent to complicate the solution of our social problems. It is to resolve these problems and slow down the rate of price rise that a national income policy is now being advocated.[1]

DISCUSSION OF PROFESSOR LECAILLON'S PAPER

Professor Krelle introduced Professor Lecaillon's paper. He began by commenting on the methodology used and saw in Professor Lecaillon's paper a plea for a sociological approach to the theory of distribution as opposed to the functional approach. Professor Krelle agreed with the author if he meant that the distribution theory should as its ultimate aim consider real sociological groups with similar economic and sociological behaviour instead of the two categories capital and labour. If Professor Lecaillon was thus pleading for a multi-sectoral analysis he could not but agree with him. The theory had to develop in this direction but this would be very difficult owing to the number of groups to be taken into consideration. Professor Krelle drew a parallel with astronomy, reminding his audience how much more complicated three bodies' problems were in comparison with two bodies' problems.

He would, however, disagree with Professor Lecaillon if he meant a substitution of sociological considerations for economic theory. There were enough journalists and politicians already. Nothing could be gained from general sociological remarks without specifying how the social forces produced economic effects and measuring these by means of econometry. What exactly did Professor Lecaillon mean by a sociological approach ?

Proceeding to analyse Professor Lecaillon's findings on French income distribution, Professor Krelle observed that Professor Lecaillon's conclusions were that labour had improved its share in total income. It was interesting to note that Dr. Jeck for Germany, Dr. Feinstein for the

[1] Cf. Jacques Lecaillon, *Croissance, répartition et politique des revenus*, Paris, Éditions Cujas, 1964.

73

United Kingdom, and Professor Falise for Belgium had come to the same conclusions. Professor Haley's conclusions for the United States were also somewhat similar, at least for the period up to the post-war years. In the case of France, Professor Lecaillon's data revealed that this development had continued up till now, excluding the inter-war period when the distributive shares remained stable. Moreover a comparison between Tables 9 and 10 and Table 6 in the paper proved that a study in terms of disposable incomes since 1938 would lead to the same conclusions.

Such findings were what one would expect. On the other hand Professor Krelle had been surprised that Professor Lecaillon's data did not reveal any influence of the business cycle on income distribution. How was it that the changes in distributive shares were so near a trend although 1952/53 and 1958/59 had been periods of depression in France? These findings challenged the theorists. One would have expected the share of labour to go up in a depression and to go down in a boom even admitting that figures had to be rather accurate to prove the influence of the cyclical movement.

Professor Krelle observed that, in order to interpret his findings, Professor Lecaillon had divided the long-run historical evolution of distribution in France into four periods. In the first period the beginnings of industrialization implied that if the share of industrial wage-earners in national income rose this had to be at the expense of the share of farmers and agricultural wage-earners and thus the overall share of labour remained stable. In the second period, when the process of growth and industrialization gathered momentum, and in the fourth after 1948, when growth started again after its interruption during the inter-war period, the share of labour increased both times whereas in the third period between the World Wars economic stagnation had prevented it from rising.

Professor Lecaillon had given two conditions for distributive shares remaining stable ; that the rate of growth should be low enough to allow for no structural changes and that the economy should have reached a high level of maturity so that the proportion of wage-earners could not increase further. Short of a dynamic theory of distribution, and this Professor Lecaillon had not attempted as he was dealing only with facts, Professor Krelle could not see how these two factors and no other could make for stability.

Professor Krelle wished to comment on the reasons Professor Lecaillon had given for the increase of the wage share in the last period. Concerning the effect of a rising price level he would agree with Professor Lecaillon in saying that this *could* bring forth an increase in wage-earners' share but only supposing the rise in the price level had been the result of active wage claims and provided that the rise in prices lagged behind the rise in money wages. The rise in prices could run parallel with the rise of wages ; the former need not be the cause of the latter. Besides,

Professor Krelle was not prepared to accept the idea that the higher the share of wages the higher the rate of growth with full employment.

Concerning the effects of an increasing concentration of production, Professor Krelle would agree with Professor Lecaillon only if he meant by this the elimination of the less efficient firms. He would not agree if concentration meant an increasing degree of monopoly ; the opposite would then be true as anti-trust laws operated to the advantage of labour. Professor Krelle thus thought one should define an optimum degree of monopoly with respect to the level of the labour share.

Professor Krelle had noticed that Professor Lecaillon's data showed an improvement of the labour share even taking into account the structural changes in the working population and the shift from self-employment and farming towards wage-earning jobs in industry. This improvement could not be explained by the structural changes only, in the way Professor Haley had been able to do in his paper on distribution in the United States for the period since the end of the last century. In the case of France the increase in the labour share had not been a purely statistical phenomenon. Professor Krelle suggested the best explanation in this case might be a declining degree of monopoly bringing the situation nearer to an optimum of concentration. What would then be the effects of an increasing concentration of production in Professor Lecaillon's terminology would be smaller differences between average costs of most and least efficient firms. In this should be found the circumstances favourable to an increase in the wage share rather than in an overall increase in productivity which had no effect *per se* on income distribution.

Concerning the relation between income distribution and inflation in a period of full employment with a high rate of growth, Professor Krelle thought that a rising share of labour must lead to inflation because of the wage-earners' high propensity to consume. Figures in Table 11 measuring the workers' average propensity to save seemed to him very low even in comparison with such data in, say, Germany.

Professor Krelle agreed with Professor Lecaillon on the impact of pressure groups on distribution. Social equilibrium could be reached at a point different from the point of economic equilibrium at which prices remained stable. This led Professor Lecaillon to conclude with a plea for an incomes policy. Would Professor Lecaillon say more about what he really meant by an incomes policy ?

Dr. Pasinetti wished to comment on data in Table 11 relating to propensity to save by various social groups. From these data striking differences emerged between proportions of income saved, by farm and non-farm workers, wage-earners and profit-earners, employers and employees. Dr. Pasinetti said that these were important findings, which confirmed the preoccupations of those post-Keynesian economists who had always thought that these differences played a quite important part in determining income distribution and also the distribution of wealth.

These differences in propensities to save were in fact so great that perhaps economists ought to give the matter more attention than they usually did.

Professor Delivanis asked Professor Lecaillon whether the diminution in the share of profits in the French national income could not be explained by two circumstances : first, the nationalization of private industries carried out in France in a period of severe inflation with payment of inadequate indemnities the purchasing power of which had been reduced still further by inflation ; second, fiscal evasion by craftsmen, tradesmen, and professional people.

Professor Delivanis wished to make a general comment on the fact that if an increase in well-being in a developed country with increasing population presupposed excess production capacity or an increase in imports until the new investments yielded an output, the same would apply to a developing country. If these requirements were fulfilled the same developments might be expected in a developing country.

Professor Delivanis pointed out that inflation made investment and saving equal at the full employment level and adjusted the claims of the various groups, but only provided no bottlenecks appeared, e.g., transport or balance of payments. Moreover he emphasized that this so-called social equilibrium reached through inflation was not usually the best.

Professor Lecaillon thanked Professor Krelle for his detailed introduction, remarking that on the question of methodology Professor Krelle had left him little choice : he had to accept the first of the two alternative interpretations of the sociological approach proposed by Professor Krelle or abandon economics for sociology or political science. All the same, his approach to distribution departed from neo-classical theory as a functional, micro-economic analysis. The neo-classical theory was an application of the general theory of prices and its scope was to study returns to production factors in a competitive economy, demand being given. His own approach was macro-economic with a Keynesian stress on effective demand. He did not consider demand as a datum. Analysis of distribution could no longer be functional as demand related to personal incomes after redistribution ; the analysis had to be carried out in terms of propensities and the behaviour of social groups had to be taken into account. This was what he meant by a sociological approach : this was still economic theory.

Professor Krelle had asked about the impact of the business cycle on income distribution. Professor Lecaillon had omitted this subject from his paper as in the recent period the traditional cyclical behaviour had not been apparent in the French economy. There had been phases of recession in the sense of a slowing down of expansion ; yet expansion continued. The trend toward an increasing share of wages had been most pronounced in periods of expansion with stable prices whereas both in periods of recession and of inflation the share of wages failed to increase.

Professor Lecaillon did not think that his point of view was as different from Professor Krelle's as the latter made out. Professor Lecaillon had never written that the higher the share of wages in national income the higher the rate of growth of the economy. He did not think that an increase in the wage share could, as such, be the cause of an increase in the economic rate of growth : on the contrary, an increase in the share of wages was conditioned by a high enough rate of growth. If the share of wages increased too much this would start inflation and inflation was always detrimental to the wage-earners. He agreed with Professor Krelle when he said that an increase in wages was not a source of growth because it led to greater consumption.

Professor Lecaillon wished to indicate to Dr. Pasinetti that his calculations of propensities to save of various groups were in gross terms. Had they been calculated in net terms the discrepancies of the figures would have been narrower.

Professor Lecaillon pointed out to Professor Delivanis that if nationalization of industries had played a part in reducing the share of profits this circumstance could have been operative in the decrease only during the period immediately after the war when nationalization was enforced whereas the downwards trend in profit share has continued since then. Professor Lecaillon agreed that tax evasion tended to lead to underestimation of the share of profits, but social accounting made allowance for this by means of a corrective factor. He agreed with Professor Delivanis that the saving-investment equilibrium and the social equilibrium were not one and the same ; if social equilibrium was attained through inflation this would not be the best way to reach it as inflation had proved to be to the detriment of the weaker social groups.

Chapter 3

THE TRENDS OF INCOME
DISTRIBUTION IN WEST GERMANY

BY

ALBERT JECK
University of Munich

I. INTRODUCTION

EMPIRICAL investigation into the growth and distribution of national income in the long term runs into greater difficulties in Germany than elsewhere. The particularism of individual Federal States with their different tax systems, the two World Wars, the subsequent extremes of inflation and repeated territorial changes, combined with long-lasting scepticism on the part of theorists and official statisticians with regard to such enquiries have left us today with at the best fragments of a reliable picture of national income accounts.[1] The Statistisches Reichsamt (Reich Statistical Office) calculated the national income of the German Reich for the first time in 1925, and thereafter continuously until 1940. The method used was based in the main on income distributed, which means that detailed information on income distribution is given. The Statistisches Bundesamts (Federal Statistical Office), however, has based its national income calculations since 1950 mainly on the net output method.[2] Distribution aspects play a secondary role and the information given is less detailed than in the pre-war period — much to the annoyance of distribution theorists. The following is an attempt in the face of these difficulties to make a reasonably accurate reconstruction of the trends of 'functional' income distribution in Germany since about 1875.

It is often assumed that the German economy, like others, has experienced over the long term rapid growth and a relatively constant income distribution. But if the period after 1950 is ignored, the first half of this century shows almost exactly the reverse picture.

[1] Cf. P. Studenski, *The Income of Nations*, New York, 1958, p. 134, and W. G. Hoffman and J. H. Müller, *Das deutsche Volkseinkommen 1851–1957*, Tübingen, 1959. [2] *Wirtschaft und Statistik, 1954*, p. 63.

78

National income *per capita* in money terms grew considerably, but real *per capita* income shows a negligible increase.[1] In 1913 it was 16·8 per cent greater than in 1893, but also 11·4 per cent greater than in 1925. In 1932 it reached its lowest level (Table 1). Federal statistics show, moreover, that the figures for 1925 and 1949 are very nearly identical — the 1949 figure is 3·4 per cent higher. All in all this means that on balance living standards in Germany hardly changed at all between 1893 and 1949, if real income *per capita* is taken as a measure. This contrasts with an increase of a full 100 per cent (at 1954 prices) in West Germany since 1950, although the tempo has slackened considerably recently.

As for the distribution of income this was characterized up to 1913 by the constantly increasing share going to wages. This trend continued — at a faster rate — through the war and inflation years up to 1931. The trend then turned downwards — under the influence of economic policy, especially under the National Socialists — and finally changed again to an upward trend in the post-war years. Whereas real *per capita* national income in 1950 was not very different from that of 1893, the share going to wages was now just under 60 per cent compared with barely 40 per cent in 1893. It would be premature, however, to conclude from this that the position of wage and salary earners had improved.

Summary. The growth and distribution of national income have been subjected to very strong pressures of a predominantly exogenous character. The two World Wars, and two disastrous inflations which governments had to answer for, combined with the world economic depression to wipe out time after time gains through growth in the German economy. If the West German population are better off today than their grandparents at the end of the nineteenth century, it is thanks entirely to the extraordinary expansion since 1950. The same set of factors has, on the other hand, produced a continuing upward trend in the share of wages and salaries in national income.

II. THE TREND OF INCOME DISTRIBUTION BEFORE 1913

Since there are no figures for the Reich territory, we have to make do with the statistics of the individual Federal provinces

[1] This is a question of broad trends only. Objections on statistical grounds to the method of calculation, especially the matching up of the various parts of the table, are of secondary importance.

TABLE 1
GROWTH AND DISTRIBUTION OF NATIONAL INCOME FROM 1893 TO 1950

	German Reich *				Federal Republic of Germany †								
	1913 Frontiers		1925 Frontiers										
	1893	1913	1913	1925	1925	1928	1931	1932	1933	1936	1939	1949	1950
Nominal *per capita* national income	Marks or Reichsmarks				Reichsmarks or Deutschmarks								
	493	748	766	961	953	1,179	861	680	698	987	1,314	1,349	1,505
	1913=100				1936=100								
	66	100	100	125	97	119	87	69	71	100	133	137	152
Real *per capita* national income ‡	1913 Prices		1928 Prices		1936 Prices								
	Marks or Reichsmarks				Reichsmarks or Deutschmarks								
	640	748	1,162	1,043	808	943	797	708	751	987	1,288	836	939
	1913=100				1936=100								
	85·5	100	100	89·7	82	96	81	72	76	100	130	85	95
Aggregate of wages and salaries as a percentage of national income	39·1§	46·5	61·0	59·9	60·3	64·6	61·8	59·8	55·6	54·0	…		58·6

* Source: *Das deutsche Volkseinkommen vor und nach dem Kriege; Einzelschrift zur Statistik des Deutschen Reichs* No. 24 (1932), pp. 64–71 (quoted subsequently as *Einzelschrift* No. 24).
† Source: *Wirtschaft und Statistik*, 1954, pp. 64–65.
‡ For the comparison between 1893 and 1913 the wholesale price index was used, for all other comparisons the official cost of living index.
§ This figure is for Saxony only (cf. Table 2), but can be taken as reasonably representative for the whole German Reich.

(Bundesländer). For Saxony they go back as far as 1874 (Table 2), for Württemberg and Baden to 1900 (Table 3).

The figures for Saxony cover three complete trade cycles during which the national income increased by just under 300 per cent. The increase for the Reich territory for this period was only 225 per cent, Saxony's share in the Reich national income rising from 7 to 9 per cent (Prussia : *circa* 60 per cent). During this period the population of Saxony increased by 77 per cent ; prices sank on average by about 20 per cent up to 1895, and then rose again by between 25 and 30 per cent [1] up to 1913, which indicates an appreciable growth in real *per capita* national income.

The most remarkable thing, however, is the change in income distribution which went with it. Contrary to the view generally held, this followed a clear trend : the rate of growth of wages and salaries (II) was always higher than the growth rate of the national income (I) and much above that of income from property and entrepreneurship (III). Wage and salary incomes increased by 563 per cent between 1876 and 1913, whilst incomes from property and entrepreneurship only rose by 153 per cent. For almost four decades without interruption the share of wage and salary incomes increased from 28·0 per cent to 47·3 per cent, while the share of property and entrepreneurship incomes fell just as steadily from 52·8 to 34·1 per cent.

This trend is equally valid for periods of recession (1875–79, 1891–94, 1900–04) and for periods of rapid expansion (1880–90, 1895–99, 1905–13), for the years when prices were falling (1876–95) and for the years when prices were rising (1896–1900, 1904–7, 1910–1913),[2] so the concepts of traditional distribution theory are not much help in explaining it. The influence of short-term or cyclical factors is only of secondary importance. They caused only slight deviations from the trend, which reveals no lasting correlations — for example between the growth rate of national income and the increase in the share of wage and salary incomes. It is true that the share of wages and salaries increased faster up to 1895 with falling prices than in the subsequent period with rising prices.

Basically, this trend is not so much a question of a change in income distribution as of a shift in the distribution of income receivers (for which no reliable data can be given, unfortunately) as

---

[1] Estimated from information in *Einzelschrift* No. 24, pp. 64–68, and in Hoffman and Müller, *op. cit.*, p. 14.
[2] *Einzelschrift* No. 24, p. 65, and Hoffman and Müller, *op. cit.*, p. 14.

TABLE 2
NATIONAL INCOME AND ITS DISTRIBUTION IN SAXONY 1874–1913 *

Year	National Income I — Millions	I — Percentage Increase	I — 1876=100	Wages and Salaries II — Millions	II — Percentage Increase	II — 1876=100	Property and Entrepreneurship III — Millions	III — Percentage Increase	III — 1876=100	Undistributed Corporate Profits IV — Millions	Income from Public Property and Enterprises † V — Millions	Shares ‡ of II and III in National Income (II)	(III)
1874	1,216			317§			655			13·0	36	26·1	53·9
1876	1,134	− 6·3‖	100	317	—‖	100	598	− 8·7‖	100	7·8	27	28·0	52·8
1877	1,099	− 3·1	97	334	5·2		562	− 6·1	94	6·9	17	30·3	51·1
1878	1,145	4·2	101	365	9·2		564	0·0	94	7·2	24	31·9	49·2
1879	1,171	3·1		380	4·2		571	1·3	95	6·7	23	32·4	48·8
1880	1,222	4·4	108	403	6·1	127	586	2·6	98	7·0	28	33·0	48·0
1881	1,267	3·7		422	4·8		602	2·7	101	7·3	31	33·3	47·5
1882	1,320	4·2		450	6·6		615	2·2		8·0	34	34·1	46·6
1883	1,365	3·4		465	3·2		637	3·6		8·6	34	34·0	46·7
1884	1,421	4·1		492	5·8		657	3·1		8·8	33	34·6	46·2
1885	1,480	4·2		523	6·2		673	2·4		9·1	36	35·3	45·5
1886	1,533	3·6		554	6·1		687	2·3		9·3	33	36·2	43·6
1887	1,604	5·0		586	5·7		710	3·1		9·5	39	36·5	44·3
1888	1,687	5·2		621	6·0		743	4·7		10·4	41	36·8	44·2
1889	1,795	6·4		668	7·6		780	4·9		11·3	47	37·2	43·3
1890	1,876	4·5	165	704	5·4	222	812	4·1	136	12·5	45	37·5	43·3
1891	1,895	1·0		721	2·3		812	0·0		13·7	44	38·0	42·8

Year													
1893	4·5	778		3·0	1,992		1·6	837		13·1	41	39·1	42·0
1894	3·7	807	237	2·9	2,049		1·9	854		13·6	43	39·4	41·7
1895	6·2	857		4·6	2,143		3·0	879		14·2	46	40·0	41·0
1896	7·3	920		6·4	2,281		5·2	925		14·7	53	40·3	40·5
1897	6·4	979		4·7	2,388		3·1	954		18·3	53	41·0	39·9
1898	7·1	1,049		5·0	2,507		3·2	984		20·5	48	41·8	39·3
1899	6·0	1,111		4·7	2,624		3·5	1,019		22·7	47	42·3	38·8
1900	3·4	1,149		2·2	2,683	362	1·2	1,031	172	22·4	46	42·8	38·4
1901	2·9	1,182		1·6	2,725		1·5	1,047		22·1	33	43·4	38·4
1902	2·1	1,207		1·9	2,778		1·5	1,063		21·4	39	43·4	38·2
1903	4·4	1,260		2·2	2,839		−1·1	1,050		20·8	51	44·4	37·0
1904	4·2	1,312		3·3	2,932		1·8	1,070		20·3	59	44·8	36·5
1905	4·3	1,369		3·7	3,041	564	2·9	1,101		20·0	63	45·0	36·2
1906	5·9	1,449		5·0	3,193		3·9	1,143		22·2	67	45·4	35·8
1907	7·0	1,551		5·6	3,373		4·1	1,191		23·7	67	46·0	35·3
1908	4·1	1,614	337	3·7	3,499		3·5	1,233		26·7	63	46·1	35·2
1909	4·3	1,683		3·6	3,626		2·7	1,266	222	29·7	65	46·4	35·2
1910	5·4	1,775		5·4	3,822		4·9	1,328		30·9	77	46·4	34·7
1911	6·3	1,887		5·7	4,040		4·1	1,383		32·0	93	46·7	34·2
1912	7·2	2,024		5·3	4,255		3·8	1,435		34·9	82	47·6	33·7
1913	4·0	2,104	393	4·7	4,453	663	5·7	1,517	253	37·7	84	47·3	34·1

‡ Undistributed profits of corporations, and public property, and enterprise, as a percentage of national income:

	1876	1880	1885	1890	1895	1900	1905	1910	1913
IV	0·7	0·6	0·6	0·7	0·7	0·8	0·7	0·8	0·8
V	2·3	2·3	2·4	2·4	2·1	1·7	2·1	2·0	1·9

* Combined and calculated from figures by W. G. Hoffmann and J. H. Müller (*Das Deutsche Volkseinkommen 1851–1957*, pp. 87–99).
† Reduced by the interest from public debt.
§ Estimated; this is why 1876 is used as the base year for comparison.

In addition, to compensate for the undervaluation of II and III in the taxation statistics used as source, an additional 16 per cent was added to the national income in each case, which appears in Table 2 as the difference between column I and the sum of columns II to V; the figures in column IV already allow for such an increase.
|| Applies to both years.

83

between the two broad categories of wage- and salary-earners and receivers of income from property and entrepreneurship — something which the process of industrialization always brings with it. Table 3 provides some indications of such structural changes.[1]

The share of wages and salaries clearly increased in Saxony, Württemberg, and Baden from 1900 to 1913. The share of income from capital assets remained constant (Saxony), or increased too. The shares of income from real estate and from trade and industry (here Baden was for a time an exception) declined.

For real estate this can be explained by the inevitable shrinkage which agriculture normally undergoes in a period of industrialization. The figures in Table 3 do not show this very clearly, since during this period the house rent element in income from real estate rose considerably.

The decrease in the share of income from trade and industry was most likely due in the main to two factors of a structural nature.[2] On the one hand the process of industrial concentration meant the squeezing out of small businesses, whose owners then — like almost all newcomers to the labour force — became wage- or salary-earners. Both processes tended to increase the share of earned incomes. On the other hand large businesses chose more and more the form of joint-stock company, so that the former individual entrepreneur became a member of the board, director, or manager, whose income was now classed under wages and salaries. But the profits of undertakings — in the form of dividends, say — were classed as income from capital. The rise of the joint-stock company therefore led to a reduction in aggregate income from small industry and commerce in favour of aggregate wages and income from capital. Since it was the high incomes and the large profits which were involved in this process, the consequences must have been perceptible from both sides.

Economic development between 1875 and 1913 was fairly smooth. It seems permissible therefore to take the internal distribution charges within income from property and entrepreneurship enterprise shown in Table 3 between 1900 and 1913 and the assumptions based on them, and extend them back to the period from 1875. Moreover developments in the German Federal States were so similar that the movements demonstrated for Saxony, Württemberg,

---

[1] Shown in column I. They show also the differing structures in the various Federa provinces, although part of the differences is due to statistical factors.
[2] Cf. *Einzelschrift* No. 24, p. 86.

TABLE 3

INCOME DISTRIBUTION IN INDIVIDUAL GERMAN LÄNDER

1900–28 *

(Percentage shares)

Source of Income	SAXONY I 1899	SAXONY I 1907	SAXONY I 1913	SAXONY II 1913	SAXONY II 1926	SAXONY II 1928	WÜRTTEMBERG I 1913	WÜRTTEMBERG I 1928	WÜRTTEMBERG II 1913	WÜRTTEMBERG II 1928	BADEN I 1900	BADEN I 1907	BADEN I 1913	BADEN II 1913	BADEN II 1926	BADEN II 1928	BAVARIA II 1911	BAVARIA II 1926	BAVARIA II 1928
Labour	45·9	49·4	50·6	49·0	65·6	64·8	47·2	47·1	60·6	62·9	38·0	38·7	41·7	41·2	64·1	64·5	46·2	59·9	61·7
Trade and Industry	28·4	26·5	25·9	27·1	24·1	25·2	18·4	18·4	17·3	16·3	24·5	26·4	24·9	25·7	24·4	22·4	22·0	19·8	18·2
Capital Assets	12·0	11·4	11·8	12·7	6·0	4·9	13·2	14·3	5·4	7·2	10·5	11·5	11·7	13·6	3·7	5·1	9·9	2·2	3·3
Real Estate	13·7	12·7	11·7	11·2	4·3	5·1	21·2	20·2	16·7	13·6	27·0	23·4	21·7	19·5	7·8	8·0	21·9	18·1	16·8

* Source: *Einzelheft* No. 24, pp. 95–97 and 175. Column I refers to the income subject to tax without allowing for tax undervaluation. Column II refers to comparable incomes including additions to compensate for undervaluation. In both cases the sum of incomes is less than the relevant national income, but the distribution structure is not significantly affected. In view of this rearrangement of the material undertaken by the Statistisches Reichsamt the revised figures are suitable for comparisons over time, but less suitable for regional comparisons.

The Distribution of National Income

and Baden can be taken as symptomatic for the German Reich as a whole.

On this hypothesis the following conclusion can be reached. The most notable feature of income distribution in Germany between 1875 and 1913 was the steady increase in the share of wages and salary incomes from barely 30 per cent to barely 50 per cent. The share of property and entrepreneurship incomes in the aggregate decreased markedly. The same is certainly true of incomes from small industry and commerce and from property. In contrast the share of incomes from capital probably stayed constant or even increased. The share of public property and enterprise income fluctuated narrowly around 2 per cent throughout the period. The share of undistributed profits of corporations was less than 1 per cent. In the case of limited companies undistributed profits form about a third of their total income, the outside limits being 25 and 40 per cent.[1]

Structural changes, such as the contraction of agriculture, the increase in the proportion of wage- and salary-earners in the gainfully employed and the rise of the joint-stock companies, must have played an important part in bringing about these readjustments in income distribution. These assumptions cannot be proved in detail, since information as to the statistical evolution of the various categories of income receivers does not exist. For the same reason it is impossible to say whether this extraordinary shift in income shares was associated with a shift in the relative position in distribution of individual types of income receivers ; whether, for example, incomes of workers and employees increased faster on average than incomes of the self-employed in trade and industry, or farmers and owners of capital assets.

III. INCOME DISTRIBUTION BETWEEN 1913 AND 1925

For the war and inflation years no statistical material exists. The only clues are revenue accounts for the provinces of Saxony, Württemberg, Baden, and Bavaria for the years 1913, 1926, and 1928. Nevertheless, an unambiguous picture emerges. The figures in Table 3[2] show that the trends observed earlier continued — with one exception — throughout this period.

[1] Hoffman and Müller, *op. cit.*, p. 29.   [2] Shown in column II.

86

The expansion of the share of wages underwent a remarkable acceleration. The 1913 figure for Saxony was 4·7 per cent higher, for Baden 3·7 per cent higher than for 1899 or 1900 respectively, whereas the increases between 1913 and 1926 were 15·8 and 22·9 per cent respectively. In Württemberg the share of wages was higher by 13·5 per cent, in Bavaria 13·7 per cent higher. On the other hand income from trade and industry, and above all income from property, lost further ground. Contrary to the original trend, the same now applied to income from capital, which the post-war inflation and the devaluation of 1923 reduced to a fraction of its former figure. It never went back again to its 'normal' level.

On the basis of the comparatively uniform developments just described in these Federal provinces the Statistisches Reichsamt estimated in retrospect the national income and its components for the Reich territory in 1913, and compared them with the figures published from 1925 onwards for the German Reich.[1] In what follows we shall use these figures.[2]

National income in money terms (I) in 1925 was, according to these calculations, about 30 per cent greater than in 1913. In real terms (1928 prices), as a result of the 40 per cent increase in prices, it was 6 per cent less than in 1913.[3] Real income *per capita* had gone down by 10 per cent, which means that average living standards had been severely reduced.

The share of wages and salaries (II) in national income (I) increased between 1913 and 1925 from 46·5 to 61·0 per cent. Aggregate wages and salaries in 1925 had risen by 65 per cent in money terms, 17 per cent in real terms over the 1913 total. But if allowance is made for the increase in non-self-employed workers, the result is the same figure for real earned income per worker in 1913 and 1925. Their standard of living had not changed.[4]

However, aggregate income from entrepreneurship and property (III) was down by 9 per cent in money terms, and a much greater percentage in real terms, below the pre-war level, so that its share in national income declined from 53·5 to 39·0 per cent. There were marked differences in the behaviour of individual components, which meant a shift in distribution within income from entrepreneurship and property (Table 5).

Income from agriculture and forestry (IV) in money terms hardly

[1] *Einzelschrift* No. 24, pp. 79–102.
[2] In each case the first rows in Tables 4 and 5.
[3] *Einzelschrift* No. 24, p. 69.　　　　[4] *Einzelschrift* No. 24, pp. 87–89.

TABLE 4

GROWTH AND DISTRIBUTION OF NATIONAL INCOME IN THE GERMAN REICH
1913 AND 1925–40 *

Years	Income from			Percentage Change				1925 = 100			Share of National Income as Percentage			Shares of Wages for the Territory of the Federal German Republic ‡
	National Income I	Wages and Salaries II	Entrepreneurship and Property III	Nominal I	Real † I	Nominal II	Nominal III	I	II	III	I	II	III	
1913	45,600	21,200	24,400	—	—	—	—	79	61	109		46·5	53·5	—
1925	57,397	35,003	22,394	—	—	—	—	100	100	100		61·0	39·0	59·9
1926	60,050	36,465	23,585	4·6	3·1	4·2	5·3	105	104	105		60·7	39·3	59·9
1927	67,285	40,830	26,455	12·0	10·2	12·0	12·2	117	117	118		60·7	39·3	59·8
1928	72,395	44,871	27,524	7·6	4·9	9·9	4·0	126	128	123		62·0	38·0	60·3
1929	72,297	45,436	26,861	0	-0·9	1·3	-2·4	126	130	120		62·8	37·2	61·9
1930	66,199	42,216	23,983	-8·4	-3·1	-7·1	-10·7	115	121	107		63·8	36·2	63·3
1931	53,794	35,576	18,218	-18·7	-10·5	-15·7	-24·0	94	103	81		66·1	33·9	64·6
1932	42,597	27,427	15,170	-20·8	-10·8	-22·9	±16·7	74	78	68		64·4	35·6	61·8
1933	44,049	27,654	16,395	3·4	6·8	0·8	8·1	77	79	73		62·8	37·2	59·8
1934	50,443	31,167	19,276	14·5	11·0	12·7	17·6	88	89	86		61·8	38·2	58·7
1935	56,849	34,441	22,408	12·7	10·5	10·5	16·2	99	98	100		60·6	39·4	56·9
1936	63,599	37,649	25,950	11·9	9·5	9·3	15·4	111	108	116		59·2	40·8	55·6
1937	71,477	41,531	29,946	12·4	11·3	10·3	15·4	125	119	134		58·1	41·9	55·2
1938	79,798	45,673	34,125	11·6	11·6	10·0	14·0	139	130	152		57·2	42·8	54·9
1939	87,187	49,085	38,102	9·3	8·2	7·5	11·7	152	140	170		56·3	43·7	54·0 §
1940	89,782	49,800	39,982	3·0	—	1·5	4·9	156	142	179		55·5	44·5	53·2 §

* Source: collated and calculated from data in the *Statistical Yearbook for the German Reich, 1932* (p. 526); *1939/42* (p. 579); *1941/42* (p. 605) and in *Wirtschaft und Statistik, 1954* (p. 64). The material was regrouped as far as possible according to definitions in current use today and applies to the Reich territory *after* the First World War; up to 1934 without the Saar.
† 1936 prices.
‡ Source: *Statistical Yearbook for the German Federal Republic, 1963*, p. 538. In view of the different economic and social structure of the Federal Republic the share of wages and salaries is always below the figures for the Reich territory; the average income from wage and salaried work is on the other hand always above the figures for the Reich territory (cf. *Wirtschaft und Statistik, 1954*, p. 515).
§ Estimated.

changed, and thus temporarily increased somewhat its share of income from business and property. Calculated at constant prices, however, it was in 1925 about 40 per cent below its 1913 level. Since the number of farmers working on their own account had hardly changed at all, average real incomes, and with them farmers' living standards, suffered the same order of decline.

The share of incomes from trade and industry (v) in national income also declined, but its share in property and entrepreneurship income increased from 37·7 to 48·7 per cent. Aggregate income in money terms was about 20 per cent higher, but in real terms about 15 per cent lower than the 1913 figure. The Statistiches Reichsamt calculated moreover that the numbers of self-employed in trade and industry and the liberal professions had increased, which would imply a fall of between 20–25 per cent in real *per capita* incomes.

Unlike IV and V, incomes from letting and leasing (VII) and undistributed profits of joint-stock companies (VIII) were far below pre-war figures even in money terms. The decreases were 40 and 23 per cent respectively, or 55 and 44 per cent at constant prices. Real incomes of house-owners must have been halved on average. This was due in particular to the introduction of the rationing of accommodation, and rent controls.

Nevertheless the shifts in distribution between the various components of income from property and entrepreneurship were made mainly at the expense of owners of capital assets. This was the result of the inflation and the 1923 devaluation, which destroyed a large part of liquid assets. Income from capital assets (VI) in 1925 was therefore 79 per cent (in money terms) or 85 per cent (real terms) below the 1913 figures. Its share in national income shrank from 12·5 to 2·1 per cent, and as a proportion of income from property and entrepreneurship it fell from 23·4 to 5·3 per cent. Here too individual categories of assets were affected in quite different ways, so that a completely different distribution resulted.[1]

Whereas income from shares in limited companies actually increased in money terms and moved roughly parallel with income from trade and industry, income from dividends fell steeply. The various categories of interest — apart from the relatively unimportant interest on domestic deposits — were almost completely wiped out, as was income on German foreign investment. Of course, owners of such funds probably had other sources of income.

Summary. After 1913 the trend of events was distorted, which

[1] Table 6 on p. 95.

meant a severe set-back for the German economy as a whole, but hurt the wage- and salary-earners least of all. In income distribution between the various categories of income-receiver the pre-war trends already noted were carried further. The share of wages greatly increased, the share of income from trade and industry and real estate fell steeply. The share of income from capital was depressed by exogenous factors to a minimum level.

In contrast to the earlier period, something can be said about the position of the various socio-economic groups. Real average *per capita* income was in 1925 about 10 per cent below that of 1913. Whereas the incomes of owners of monetary assets almost ceased to exist, the average real incomes of shareholders declined by about 80 per cent, that of house-owners by at least 50 per cent, farmers by about 40 per cent, the self-employed in trade and industry and the liberal professions by 20 to 25 per cent. The average real income of employed wage- and salary-earners remained constant in spite of their considerable increase in numbers. To the extent revealed by these figures — they are, of course, only broad estimates — the relative positions of the individual groups shifted, at least temporarily, between 1913 and 1925. This change in income distribution — in every respect a significant one — to the benefit of the wage- and salary-earner and at the expense of all other groups was, however, accompanied by a standstill or reduction in levels of income.

IV. THE DISTRIBUTION OF NATIONAL INCOME FROM 1925 TO 1940

Up to 1930 the evolution followed a normal path, and the trends already noted continued. Then, under the influence of the world depression and changed economic policies, there comes an abrupt change (Table 4). The share of incomes from employment (II) in national income (I) climbed — apart from a short interruption (1926–27) — to a peak of 66·1 per cent in 1931, but from then on (before the trough of the depression was reached, therefore) it fell steadily to 55·5 per cent. Income from entrepreneurship and property in 1940 was, in money terms, 79 per cent higher than in 1925, that of income from employment only 42 per cent higher. Since the numbers of self-employed in trade, industry, and agriculture had remained roughly constant, while the numbers of employed wage- and salary-earners increased by about 3 million (Table 8), these figures do not reveal the full extent of the deterioration in income distribution for employed workers. There were noteworthy shifts in individual positions between 1925 and 1940.

As a causal factor for aggregate wages and salaries the extent of unemployment became very important.[1] Steeply falling employment levels and gradually falling average wage levels caused aggregate earnings from employment to decline from 1930 onwards. Its share in national income increased, however, in 1931, because other incomes declined even faster. This process was halted when the Brüning government, as part of its deflationary anti-crisis policies, began in 1931 to intervene strongly in wage matters, and passed legislation to force through several steep reductions in wages and salaries. The share of income from employment shrank significantly — probably for the first time since 1875. The same thing happened in subsequent years. Succeeding governments, especially the National Socialists, replaced the orthodox deflationary policies with expansionary short-term policies, but held wages generally at the extremely low levels of 1932. Incomes of civil servants remained constant in the following period, while wages and salaries rose very little, so that the growth of aggregate income from employment after 1932 was the result of the rapid fall in unemployment.[2] The share of income from employment went steadily down, since the growth rates of income from property and entrepreneurship were always higher.

The world depression and economic policies from 1931 onwards changed the trends not only in the evolution of wages and salaries, but also of the various components of property and entrepreneurial income (Table 5).

This is most obvious for income from trade and industry (v). As

[1] Percentage change from the previous year :

	Income from Wages and Salaries					
	Aggre-gate	Per Employed Worker	Aggre-gate	Per Employed Worker	Labour Force	
	Current Prices		1928 Prices		Employed	Unemployed
1926	3·2	7·5	2·1	6·4	−4·0	197
1927	11·7	5·6	6·8	1·0	5·8	−35
1928	9·6	8·2	6·7	5·3	1·3	6
1929	1·0	2·5	−0·4	1·1	−1·5	38
1930	−8·0	−2·6	−3·9	1·7	−5·5	64
1931	−16·5	−9·7	−9·5	−2·1	−7·6	46

[2] Cf. J. H. Müller, *Nivellierung und Differenzierung der Arbeitseinkommen in Deutschland seit 1925*, Berlin, 1954, pp. 107 and 139–143.

TABLE 5

INCOME FROM ENTREPRENEURSHIP AND PROPERTY AND ITS DISTRIBUTION IN THE GERMAN REICH 1913 AND 1925-40 *

	Agriculture and Forestry IV		Trade and Industry V		Capital Assets VI		Rents and Leases VII		Undistributed Corporate Profits VIII		Incomes of Public Enterprises IX		Remainder † X	
	Millions	1925=100	Millions	1925=100	Millions	1925=100	Millions	1925=100	Millions	1925=100	Millions	1925=100	Millions	1925=100
1913	5,700	100	9,200	84	5,700	478	900	165	1,200	129	1,100	75	600	35
1925	5,677	100	10,899	100	1,191	100	546	100	928	100	1,450	100	1,703	
1926	5,829	103	10,813	99	1,563	131	637	117	904	97	2,058	142	1,781	
1927	5,939	105	12,022	110	2,107	177	759	139	1,316	142	2,408	161	1,904	
1928	5,816	102	12,187	112	2,784	234	836	153	1,308	141	2,483	171	2,110	
1929	5,754	101	11,768	108	3,181	267	871	160	882	95	2,457	168	2,132	
1930	4,950	87	9,950	91	3,341	281	900	165	400	43	2,318	160	2,124	
1931	4,375	77	7,500	69	3,195	268	900	165	−1,000	...	1,218	80	2,030	
1932	3,695	65	6,000	55	2,298	193	760	139	−450	...	1,008	70	1,859	109
1933	3,865	68	6,420	59	2,403	202	720	132	175	19	913	63	1,899	
1934	4,975	88	7,243	66	2,569	216	775	140	735	79	976	67	1,993	
1935	5,750	101	8,500	78	2,644	222	840	154	1,365	147	1,131	78	2,178	
1936	5,840	103	10,640	98	2,724	229	980	179	2,330	251	1,316	91	2,120	
1937	6,110	108	13,260	122	2,780	233	1,100	220	3,000	323	1,520	105	2,176	
1938	6,400	113	15,910	146	2,980	250	1,200	238	3,900	420	1,500	103	2,235	
1939	6,900	122	17,940	165	3,045	256	1,335	243	4,750	512	1,750	1,202	2,382	
1940	6,900	122	18,500	170	3,200	269	1,400	256	5,600	603	1,945	133	2,437	143

TABLE 5

Percentage Shares in National Income (I) and in Aggregate Income from Entrepreneurship and Property (III)

	Agriculture and Forestry		Trade and Industry		Capital Assets		Rents and Leases		Undistributed Corporate Profits		Incomes of Public Enterprises		Remainder†	
	I	III	I	III	I	III	I	III	I	III	I	III	I	III
1913	12·5	23·4	20·2	37·7	12·5	23·4	2·0	3·7	2·6	4·9	2·4	4·5	1·3	2·5
1925	19·9	25·4	18·9	48·7	2·1	5·3	1·0	2·3	1·6	4·1	2·5	6·5	3·0	7·6
1926	9·7	24·7	18·1	45·8	2·6	6·6	1·1	2·7	1·5	3·8	3·4	8·7	3·0	8·0
1927	8·8	22·4	17·9	45·4	3·1	8·0	1·1	2·9	2·1	5·0	3·6	9·1	2·8	7·2
1928	8·0	21·1	16·8	44·3	3·9	10·1	1·2	3·0	1·8	4·8	3·4	9·0	2·9	7·7
1929	8·0	21·4	16·3	43·8	4·4	11·8	1·1	3·2	1·2	3·3	3·3	9·1	2·9	7·9
1930	7·5	20·6	15·0	41·5	5·0	13·9	1·5	3·8	0·6	1·7	3·5	9·7	3·2	9·8
1931	8·1	24·0	13·9	41·2	5·9	17·5	1·7	4·9	−1·9	−5·5	2·3	6·7	3·8	11·2
1932	8·7	24·4	14·1	39·5	5·4	15·3	1·8	5·9	−1·1	−3·0	2·4	6·6	4·4	12·3
1933	8·8	23·6	14·6	39·2	5·5	14·7	1·7	4·4	0·4	1·1	2·6	5·6	4·3	11·5
1934	9·7	25·8	14·4	37·6	5·1	13·3	1·5	4·0	1·5	3·8	1·9	5·0	4·0	10·3
1935	10·1	25·7	15·0	38·0	4·7	11·8	1·5	3·7	2·4	6·1	2·0	5·5	3·8	9·7
1936	9·2	22·5	16·7	41·0	4·3	10·5	1·5	3·8	3·7	9·0	2·1	5·1	3·3	8·2
1937	8·5	20·4	18·6	44·3	3·9	9·3	1·5	3·8	4·2	10·0	2·1	5·1	3·0	7·3
1938	8·0	18·8	19·9	46·6	3·7	8·7	1·5	3·5	4·9	11·4	1·9	4·4	2·8	6·5
1939	7·9	18·1	20·6	47·1	3·5	8·0	1·5	3·5	5·2	12·5	2·0	4·6	2·7	6·2
1940	7·7	17·3	20·6	46·3	3·6	8·0	1·6	3·5	6·2	14·0	2·1	4·9	2·7	6·1

* Breakdown of column III, Table 4.
† Mainly civil service pensions, which should really be shown elsewhere. In terms of present income distribution concepts the values for columns I and III in Table 4 are in each case too high by these amounts.

for many years past, its share continued to decline from 1925 to 1931. From then on, however, it recovered steadily, and in 1939 was back at the 1913 level. Since the numbers of professional and self-employed in trade and industry declined if anything in this period, there can be no doubt that income distribution in the National Socialist period changed drastically in favour of this group. By contrast, the share of income from agriculture and forestry (IV) increased temporarily between 1931 and 1935, only to resume its downward trend thereafter — in spite of the self-sufficiency (Autarkie) drive and domestic farming policy (Reichsnährstand).

Surprisingly enough the share of income from public enterprises between 1926 and 1930 was larger than in the period of the dirigiste policies after 1933. The opposite is true of the undistributed income of corporations. This was the category of income most subject to fluctuation. From 1936 onwards it expanded at first, with the result that its share in national income became much greater than that of income from capital assets. Underlying this was a fundamental change in dividend distribution policy. In the period before 1933 corporations had always distributed 65 to 75 per cent of their profits to shareholders, partners, etc., but the proportion distributed in 1937 is estimated at only 25 to 30 per cent.[1] The cause of this reversal of traditional proportions lay in a series of economic policy measures taken by the National Socialist Government.

Income from capital assets, drastically reduced and changed in composition by the 1923 devaluation, recorded up to 1931 the highest growth rates, but after that year its growth rates were very small. In money terms it reached its peak in 1930. Its real value (in 1928 prices) increased again in 1931 by 1 per cent, so the setback did not come until 1932 and in comparison with other incomes was not so noticeable. In this period too the various types of income from capital developed very unevenly, and an approach to something like the pre-war structure emerges. This can be followed in detail up to 1931 (Table 6).

Whereas in 1925 income from dividends and holdings in private limited companies formed 37·8 and 28·6 per cent respectively of aggregate income from capital, their shares had shrunk again to 22·1 and 5·8 per cent by 1931. Since, as already indicated, profit distribution habits changed radically from 1934 onwards under the pressure of economic policy, this shrinkage probably continued right up to the new economic regime introduced in 1948. The opposite

[1] Hoffman and Müller, *op. cit.*, p. 48.

94

TABLE 6

THE COMPOSITION OF INCOME FROM CAPITAL ASSETS

Income from	1913	1925	1930	1931	1913–25 Change	1913	1925	1930	1931
	Millions					Percentage of IV			
Holdings in private limited companies	300	341	350	175	+14%	4·9	28·6	10·8	5·8
Dividends from German corporations	1,220	450	920	670	−63%	19·8	37·8	28·3	22·1
Interest on :									
Domestic loans	1,800	100	1,100	1,215	−94%	29·2	8·4	33·9	40·1
Private mortgages and loans	1,200	120	450	455	−90%	19·4	10·1	13·8	15·0
Savings banks deposits	720	120	770	815	−83%	11·7	10·1	23·7	26·9
Domestic bank deposits	150	120	190	245	−20%	2·4	10·1	5·8	8·1
Foreign investments	1,450	105	80	75	−93%	23·5	8·8	2·5	2·5
Of which securities in foreign ownership and portfolios	670	165	610	620	−75%	10·9	13·9	18·8	20·5

Source : *Einzelschrift* No. 24, p. 89.

is true of interest income. Its share in income from capital expanded rapidly from 1925 to 1931 — interest rates were rising. The share of income from fixed-interest securities and savings deposits was higher than ever before. This rising trend must have continued, in spite of falling interest rates, into the later period, since the inflationary increase in money supply from 1936 to 1948 had gone for the most part, as a result of price controls, rationing, etc. into savings accounts or bonds. These assets and the income from them were then largely wiped out by the currency reform of 1948.

Summary. Up to 1931 the evolution of income distribution proceeded on the lines noted for the previous period, and then changed abruptly and decisively. The share of income going to wages and salaries stopped expanding and began to contract, falling from 66·1 per cent of national income in 1931 to 55·5 per cent in 1940, although the number of wage- and salary-earners was still rising fast, as in earlier periods. The share of income from capital assets also declined from 1931 onwards, after having increased from 2·1 to 5·9 per cent. By contrast, the share of income from trade and industry, which

95

had declined steadily up to 1931, now began to recover strongly. Further, from 1935 onwards the retained profits of corporations were tripled. These drastic changes in long-term trends were the result of massive intervention by official economic policy-makers.

V. INCOME DISTRIBUTION 1940–50 AND 1950–53

One difficulty in comparing 1940 and 1950 is the 'Remaining Items' (x) in Table 5. If they are ignored, wages and salaries make up 57 per cent of national income for the Reich area in 1940, with income from property and entrepreneurship taking 43 per cent. The corresponding figures for the territory of the present Federal Republic would have been about 54·7 and 45·3 per cent in 1940. In 1950 the share of wages and salaries was 58·6 per cent (Table 7), that is to say, roughly 4 per cent higher than in 1940.

One-half of this rise was the result of a decrease (about 2 per cent) of income going to public enterprises and retained corporate earnings. The larger private and public undertakings were worse hit by the consequences of the war (war damage, dismantling) than the smaller ones. The other half is explained by the decline in the share of income from property and entrepreneurship paid to households (IV), which, unlike the pre-war period, is no longer shown as a separate item in post-1950 statistics.[1] This decline must have affected income from capital assets in the main, since income from interest was almost wiped out by the 1948 currency reform, and the quota of distributed corporate earnings in 1950 amounted to a bare 7 per cent.[2] The share of income going to independent traders, etc., in farming, trade, and industry and the professions in 1950 must have been about the same as in 1940. The same can be said — in spite of the increased share of wages and salaries — for the relationship between average income of the independently employed and that of employees (Table 8, Row XII), since the former decreased in number up to 1950, while the latter increased. So that although this relationship, and therefore the relative income distribution position of employees, deteriorated from 1931 to 1940, it remained constant on balance between 1940 and 1950.

The first point that emerges from the figures for post-1950 in Table 7 is that the share of income from public enterprise (VI) is smaller than for the period 1925 to 1940. The share of undistributed

---

[1] Column IV of Table 7 is the sum of columns IV to VII of Table 5.
[2] *Statistisches Jahrbuch für die Bundesrepublik Deutschland, 1960*, p. 257.

income of private corporations (v) is, however, somewhat higher than for the years 1937 to 1940. In spite of very different yearly growth rates the two ratios show little change.

In contrast, the ratio of wages and salaries (II) to national income (I) rises, with minor interruptions in 1952, 1955, and 1959, from 58·6 to 64·8 per cent. The share of income from property and entrepreneurship paid to households (IV) declines — again with minor interruptions in 1951, 1955 and 1959 — from 34·7 to 28·3 per cent. In absolute terms wages and salaries increase by 324 per cent, total profits by 226 per cent, those paid to households by 212 per cent only. Both these trends were already characteristic of the evolution of distribution between 1875 and 1931. Although no official statistics exist for the various kinds of property and entrepreneurship incomes paid to households, tentative estimates of its evolution since 1950 can be made.

The proportion of income from farming has shrunk considerably and will go on shrinking in the future. The Federal Government's agricultural policies (Grüner Plan) have aimed — with only partial success — at increasing the average incomes of independent farmers in line with average incomes in the economy as a whole. This is only possible if at the same time the numbers engaged in farming continue to decrease considerably, so that their aggregate share in national income automatically shrinks. Incomes from rents, on the other hand, are probably subject to the opposite trend. They are never in any case more than 1 to 2 per cent of national income. Their share must have risen somewhat, at least in recent years, as a consequence of the gradual easing and/or abolition of controls.

Lastly, there is no doubt that the proportion of income from capital assets has increased considerably since 1950, just as it did after 1925 (see above). This may be inferred in the first place from the rapid increase in the formation of monetary assets with comparatively high interest rates (income from interest). Then again, income from dividends and holdings in limited liability companies must have expanded far faster than the national income. Whereas the growth in undistributed earnings corresponded on average to that of national income, income in the form of distributed profits from 1950 to 1959 grew almost four times as fast, since the proportion of profits distributed went up from 6·7 to 20·6 per cent.[1] (The pre-1933 figure was about 70 per cent!) This trend must have continued in subsequent years. Bearing in mind what happened in these categories

---

[1] *Statistisches Jahrbuch für die Bundesrepublik Deutschland, 1960*, p. 257.

TABLE 7

GROWTH AND DISTRIBUTION OF NATIONAL INCOME IN THE FEDERAL REPUBLIC SINCE 1950 *

	National Income	Wages and Salaries		Incomes from Entrepreneurship and Property									
				Aggregate		To Households			Undistributed Profits of Enterprises with Legal Personality			Public Enterprise and Property		
	I	II		III		IV			V			VI		
			As Percentage of I		As Percentage of I		As Percentage of			As Percentage of			As percentage of	
Year	Millions	Millions		Millions		Millions	I	III	Millions	I	III	Millions	I	III
1950	75,160	44,070	58·6	31,090	41·4	26,110	34·7	84·0	4,280	5·7	13·8	700	0·9	2·3
1951	91,080	53,430	58·7	37,650	41·3	31,880	35·0	84·7	4,690	5·1	12·5	1,080	1·2	2·9
1952	103,770	59,600	57·4	44,170	42·6	35,820	34·5	81·1	6,730	6·5	15·2	1,620	1·6	3·7
1953	112,130	65,770	58·7	46,360	41·3	37,160	33·1	80·2	7,440	6·6	16·0	1,760	1·6	3·8
1954	121,080	71,870	59·4	49,210	40·6	39,700	32·8	80·7	7,440	6·3	15·5	1,870	1·5	3·8
1955	139,460	81,950	58·8	57,510	41·2	45,890	32·9	79·8	9,100	6·5	15·8	2,520	1·8	4·4
1956	154,370	91,820	59·5	62,550	40·5	50,080	32·4	80·1	9,820	6·4	15·7	2,650	1·7	4·2
1957	168,290	100,520	59·7	67,770	40·3	53,660	31·9	79·2	10,980	6·5	16·1	3,130	1·9	4·6
1958	180,140	108,990	60·5	71,150	39·5	56,610	31·4	79·6	11,350	6·3	15·9	3,190	1·8	4·5
1959	193,970	116,830	60·2	77,140	39·8	61,380	31·6	79·6	12,800	6·6	16·6	2,960	1·5	3·8
1960	216,920	131,400	60·6	85,520	39·4	67,490	31·1	78·9	14,560	6·7	17·0	3,470	1·6	4·1
1960†	229,800	139,770	60·8	90,030	39·2	70,910	30·9	78·8	15,480	6·7	17·2	3,640	1·6	4·0
1961	251,600	157,180	62·5	94,420	37·5	74,680	29·7	79·1	15,430	6·1	16·3	4,310	1·7	4·6
1962	272,140	173,870	63·9	98,270	36·1	78,500	28·8	79·9	15,090	5·5	15·3	4,680	1·7	4·8
1963	288,000	186,700	64·8	101,300	35·2	81,400	28·3	80·4	..	..	..	..	..	..

Year	1950 =100	age Increase	1950 =100	age Increase	1950 =100	age Increase	1950 =100	age Increase	1950 =100	age Increase	1950 =100	age Increase
1950	100		100		100		100		100		100	
1951	121	21·2	121	21·2	121	21·1	122	22·1	110	9·6	154	54·3
1952	138	13·9	135	11·5	142	17·3	133	12·4	157	43·5	231	50·0
1953	149	8·1	149	10·4	149	5·0	142	3·7	174	10·5	251	8·6
1954	161	8·0	163	9·3	158	6·1	152	6·8	178	2·7	267	6·3
1955	186	15·2	186	14·0	185	16·9	176	15·6	213	19·1	360	34·8
1956	205	10·7	208	12·0	201	8·8	191	9·1	229	7·9	379	5·2
1957	224	9·0	228	9·5	215	8·3	206	7·1	256	11·8	449	18·1
1958	240	7·0	247	8·4	229	5·0	217	5·5	265	3·4	454	1·9
1959	258	7·7	265	7·2	248	8·4	235	8·4	299	12·8	423	-7·2
1960	289	11·8	298	12·5	275	10·9	258	10·0	340	13·8	496	17·2
1960	(306)	—	(317)	—	(290)	—	(272)	—	(362)	—	(520)	—
1961	335	9·5	357	12·5	304	4·9	286	5·3	361	-0·3	616	18·4
1962	362	8·2	395	10·6	316	4·1	307	5·1	353	-2·2	669	8·6
1963	383	5·8	424	7·4	326	3·1	312	3·7	··	··	··	··

* Source : *Wirtschaft und Statistik, 1963* (p. 582) and *1964* (pp. 9 and 64).
† Up to the first row for 1960 the Bund territory without the Saar and West Berlin. From the second row for 1960 onwards, including the Saar and West Berlin. The effect of this territorial enlargement on distribution is insignificant.

E

of income, it is clear that income from trade and industry must have declined relatively since 1950, since the proportion of total incomes of households from entrepreneurship and property was 6·4 per cent smaller in 1963 than in 1950.

Putting these factors together, a somewhat surprising result emerges. The evolution of income distribution since 1950 has in all probability been a resumption of the long-term trend. It has taken up again where it broke off in 1931 — mainly as a consequence of exogenous factors. Wages and salaries, and income from capital expanded more rapidly, income from farming, and trade and industry more slowly, than national income. The relative size of undistributed corporate earnings is today markedly greater, since the proportion of earnings distributed has not returned to pre-1931 levels, but corresponds more with levels for the years 1933 to 1940.

VI. CHANGES IN AVERAGE INCOMES 1925–63

We have repeatedly emphasized that changes in relative shares of income categories tell us nothing of the position of persons belonging to the various social and economic groups. We have to know at least the relevant average income levels (*per capita* incomes) to be able to say anything about the relative positions of workers, farmers, property owners, etc., in the distribution of income. Although the requisite statistical information was not available, we attempted a few estimates for the period from 1913 to 1925 (p. 90), which showed an improvement in the relative position of wage- and salary-earners, since the real incomes of all other groups had declined absolutely compared with before the war.

From the numbers of self-employed and employees, it is possible to calculate average incomes at least for these two broad categories for the period 1925 to 1963 (Table 8).[1] Comparing figures for 1933 with those for 1925, it is apparent that the relative position of employees (*in* employment) continued to improve. About 6 million unemployed tell the other side of the story, but the fact is that the average income of wage- and salary-earners in 1933 was higher than the average income of those working on their own

[1] Aggregate income from entrepreneurship and property was shown under self-employed, which raises a number of objections, *inter alia*, that self-employed and property owners do not coincide. The resulting average income for self-employed would appear therefore to be too high. Nevertheless row IV should give a fairly true picture of the long-term trend.

account. If we look at the inter-war period as a whole (1925 to 1939) the opposite is the case. Although the ratio (t) of wage- and salary-earners to all gainfully employed rose from 66·6 to 69·5 per cent, aggregate wages and salaries sank from 61 to 56·3 per cent. The growth in average income of employees remained well below the growth in average income of all gainfully employed, so their relative relationship (r) fell from 91·5 to 81 per cent. By contrast the ratio (s) between the average income of self-employed persons and that of employees rose from 125 to 177 per cent.[1] The gap in the relative distribution position of these two groups had therefore increased greatly to the detriment of wage- and salary-earners.

A comparison of the relevant figures for 1938 and 1950 for the territory of the Federal Republic shows an almost identical increase in average incomes for the two groups ; 'r' and 's' are almost unchanged. Since 't' rose from 65·3 to 68·4 in this period, this can be taken as a kind of indicator that the observed increase in the relative share of aggregate wages and salaries is only a reflection of the increase in numbers of wage- and salary-earners.

The trend since 1950 is first and foremost characterized by the increase in the relative share of wage- and salary-earners and the gainfully employed as a whole ; 't' rises from 68·4 to 79·2 per cent. If the average income of wage- and salary-earners between 1950 and 1963 rose as fast as that of all gainfully employed (assumption A), the ratio of wages and salaries to national income in 1963 should have been 67·9 per cent. If it kept pace with the average income of the self-employed (assumption B), this would give a ratio of 71·4 per cent. The actual figure is, however, 64·8 per cent.

Whereas the income of employees increased in absolute terms by 324 per cent, income from property and entrepreneurship rose by 226 per cent compared with 1950. The relationship is reversed if the numbers of income receivers is taken into account. The relative position of the wage- and salary-earners underwent a marked deterioration. The rise in average incomes for employees was 172 per cent, but for self-employed it was 269 per cent. The ratio 's' went up from 153 to 216 per cent, the ratio 'r' declined up to 1960 from 85·7 to 78·8 per cent, although since 1960 the trend is slightly upwards again. Average income of employees is rising somewhat more than proportionally, so that the gap described above is not getting any bigger, at least for the time being.

[1] Cf. E. H. Phelps Brown and P. E. Hart, 'The Share of Wages in National Income', *Economic Journal*, 1952, vol. lxii.

TABLE 8

TRENDS OF GAINFULLY EMPLOYED AND AVERAGE INCOMES (GROSS) 1925–63 *

		German Reich 1934 Frontiers				German Federal Republic									
		1925	1933	1939	1948	1950	1951	1952	1954	1955	1958	1960	1961 †	1962 †	1963 †
I National income	Milliards	57·4	44·05	87·2	47·3	75·2	91·1	103·8	121·1	139·5	180·1	216·9	251·6	272·1	288·0
	1925 and 1950=100	100	77	152	63	100	121	138	161	186	240	289	335	362	383
II Wages and salaries	Milliards	35·0	27·7	49·1	26·0	44·1	53·4	59·6	71·9	82·0	109·0	131·4	157·2	173·9	186·7
	1925 and 1950=100	100	79	140	59	100	121	135	163	186	247	298	357	395	424
III Incomes from entrepreneurship and property	Milliards	22·4	16·4	38·1	21·3	31·1	37·7	44·2	49·2	57·5	71·2	85·5	94·4	98·3	101·3
	1925 and 1950=100	100	73	170	69	100	121	142	158	185	229	275	304	316	326
IV Gainfully employed	Milliards	31·33	27·39	34·15	19·23	20·0	20·52	20·91	21·0	22·83	24·12	24·81	26·59	26·78	26·88
	1925 and 1950=100	100	87	109	96	100	103	105	110	114	121	124	133	134	134
V Employees	Milliards	20·88	16·87	23·74	12·56	13·67	14·29	14·75	15·97	16·84	18·19	19·07	20·73	21·05	21·30
	1925 and 1950=100	100	81	114	92	100	104	108	117	123	133	139	152	154	156
VI Self-employed	Milliards	10·45	10·53	10·41	6·67	6·32	6·23	6·16	6·03	5·99	5·94	5·74	5·86	5·73	5·59
	1925 and 1950=100	100	101	100	105	100	99	97	95	95	94	91	93	91	88
VII Average income of gainfully employed ‡	RM and DM	1,832	1,608	2,553	2,460	3,759	4,439	4,963	5,505	6,109	7,467	8,744	9,462	10,161	10,714
	1925 and 1950=100	100	88	139	65	100	118	132	146	163	199	233	252	270	285

102

VIII Average income of employees§ — RM and DM	1,677	1,640	2,068	2,070	3,223	3,740	4,040	4,501	4,866	5,992	6,891	7,582	8,259	8,767
1925 and 1950=100	100	98	123	64	100	116	125	140	151	186	214	235	256	272
IX Average income of self-employed‖ — RM and DM	2,143	1,558	3,660	3,195	4,917	6,040	7,175	8,165	9,600	11,986	14,896	16,110	17,150	18,138
1925 and 1950=100	100	73	171	65	100	123	146	166	195	244	303	328	349	369
X t=share of V in IV in per cent	66·6	61·6	69·5	65·3	68·4	69·6	70·6	72·1	73·6	75·4	76·9	78·0	78·6	79·2
XI r=ratio of VIII to VII in per cent	91·5	102·0	81·0	84·2	85·7	84·5	81·4	81·8	79·7	80·2	78·8	80·1	81·3	81·8
XII s=ratio of IX to VIII in per cent	125	95	177	154	153	162	178	181	197	200	216	212	208	207
XIII Hypothetical¶ share of wages and salaries in national income — A					58·6	59·6	60·5	61·8	63·1	64·6	66·0	66·8	67·4	67·9
B					58·6	60·0	61·1	62·9	64·6	66·7	68·6	69·9	70·6	71·4

* Sources : Collated and calculated from data in *Einzelschrift* No. 24 (p. 87), in the *Statistical Yearbooks 1939/40* (p. 389), *1941/42* (p. 33) and in *Wirtschaft und Statistik, 1954* (p. 516), *1963* (pp. 582–583) and *1964* (pp. 9 and 64–66).
† Including the Saar and West Berlin.
‡ I divided by IV.
§ II divided by V.
‖ III divided by VI.
¶ Hypothesis (A) : r=constant=1950 ; Hypothesis (B) : s=constant=1950.

Table 9 gives a picture of the proportions of employees' incomes as between wages and salaries. The relative share of salaries in total wages and salaries paid by industry rose from 22·2 to 29·1 per cent between 1950 and 1963. At the same time the number of white-collar workers rose, in accordance with the usual trend, from 14·8 to 20·6 per cent of all employees.[1] Average salaries were throughout very much higher than average wages, but their rates of growth were practically the same. The tendency for the increased relative share going to salaries is accounted for solely by the structural change in the composition of employment. To this extent, then, the distribution of employee incomes as between salaried employees and workers showed no significant change.

VII. CONCLUSION

The evolution of income distribution in Germany can be traced — although only fragmentarily — from 1875 onwards. It is often so strongly influenced by exogenous factors that any general theoretical explanation seems impossible.

However the available statistical picture shows that the generally held thesis of the relative constancy of shares, that is to say the absence of any clear trend towards change over the long term, does not apply to Germany.

The relative share of income from entrepreneurship and property in national income shows a downward trend (1875–1931, 1950–63). Only for the years 1932 to 1940 — as a direct consequence of economic policy — is the contrary true.

The relative shares of income from agriculture and forestry and from trade and industry have shrunk; the share of income from capital assets has either remained constant (up to 1913) or increased (1925–32 and since 1950), after being drastically reduced by the devaluations of 1923 and 1948 respectively. For all three income categories these trends — like that for aggregate income from entrepreneurship and property — underwent between 1932 and 1940 a temporary interruption due to exogenous factors.

Lastly, the relative shares of rents, the undistributed profits of corporations, and income from public enterprises remained more or less constant. Any significant changes here can be attributed wholly to economic policy.

[1] Phelps Brown and Hart, *op. cit.*

TABLE 9

WAGES AND SALARIES: WAGE-EARNERS AND SALARIED EMPLOYEES IN INDUSTRY 1950, 1954–63 *

	1950	1954	1955	1956	1957	1958	1959	1960	1961	1962	1963
Wages and salaries † (millions of DM)	15,170	25,519	29,484	33,808	36,430	38,977	41,254	48,615	57,831	60,642	64,257
Of which:											
Wages	11,809	19,487	22,494	25,641	27,404	28,960	30,303	35,648	39,804	43,559	45,537
Share (%)	77·8	76·4	76·3	75·8	75·2	74·3	73·5	73·3	72·6	71·8	70·9
Salaries	3,361	6,032	6,990	8,167	9,026	10,017	10,951	12,967	15,027	17,083	18,720
Share (%)	22·2	23·6	23·7	24·2	24·8	25·7	26·5	26·7	27·4	28·2	29·1
Wage-earners (thousands)	4,055	5,070	5,498	5,820	5,984	5,979	5,949	6,311	6,435	6,395	6,281
Share (%) ‡	85·2	84·3	84·2	83·9	83·5	82·8	82·1	81·7	81·0	80·2	79·4
Salary-earners (thousands)	706	947	1,029	1,119	1,183	1,240	1,298	1,410	1,511	1,583	1,630
Share (%) ‡	14·8	15·7	15·8	16·1	6·5	17·2	17·9	18·3	19·0	19·8	20·6
Average wage (DM per year)	2,912	3,844	4,091	4,406	4,580	4,844	5,094	5,649	6,185	6,811	7,250
Increase in %		32·0 §	6·4	7·7	3·9	5·8	5·2	9·8	9·5	10·1	6·4
Average salary (DM per year)	4,760	6,373	6,793	7,298	7,630	8,078	8,437	9,196	9,945	10,792	11,485
Increase in %		33·9 §	6·6	7·3	4·5	5·9	4·4	7·8	8·1	8·5	6·4
Ratio of average salary to average wage as a percentage	163·5	165·8	166·0	165·6	166·6	166·8	165·6	162·7	160·8	158·8	158·4

* Sources: *Statistical Yearbook, 1936*, p. 221 and *Wirtschaft und Statistik, 1964*, p. 102–103. For the years 1950 to 1957 clerical staff and self-employed in industry are shown combined. The share of the latter in the total of employed is, however, very small, being always between 0·7 and 0·8 per cent for the years 1958 to 1963. The number of salaried workers (Angestellte) in earlier years was estimated by subtracting wage-earners from the total of gainfully employed, and then subtracting another 0·75 per cent from the remainder to account for the self-employed. This should not lead to significant errors.
The data relates to the Federal territory without Berlin, includes the Saar since 1960, and covers establishments with 10 or more employees.
† Gross wage and salary payments, i.e. without employers' contributions to social insurance.
‡ In the total wage- or salary-earners.
§ Relates to 4 years.

105

The relative share of employees income in national income rose steadily from less than 30 per cent in 1875 to 66·1 per cent in 1931. From then to 1940 its share was pushed back by National Socialist economic policies to 55·5 per cent, and today it has advanced again to 64·8 per cent.

There can be no question of any improvement in income distribution however. There was just as continuous a change in the grouping of income receivers, and the ratio of wage- and salary-earners to all income receivers, i.e. gainfully employed has increased steeply.

Although nothing precise can be said about average incomes for the various groups for the period before 1913, it can be said that between 1913 and 1925 wages and salaries experienced more than proportional increases compared with all other income categories. This trend was not, however, continued. On the contrary, since 1925 the growth in average wage and salary levels remains distinctly below the growth in average incomes of all gainfully employed persons, so that trends in the distribution of incomes up to the present time — in spite of the increasing relative share of aggregate wages and salaries — have definitely been to the detriment of wage- and salary-earners.

DISCUSSION OF DR. JECK'S PAPER

Dr. Jungenfelt, introducing Dr. Jeck's paper, emphasized the great number of empirical and statistical investigations made by Dr. Jeck on detailed data extending over a period going back as far as 1875. He proceeded to sum up what seemed to him to be the main results of Dr. Jeck's study of the changes in income distribution in Germany, first observing that if the shares in national income were divided up into two broad categories, wages and salaries on the one hand and the rest of income on the other, it appeared that the share of the former had been increasing over all the period with the exception of a minor setback in the thirties. Starting from a proportion of about 40 per cent at the beginning, and an even lower one in 1875, the share of wages and salaries reached a figure well above 60 per cent in the sixties, a substantial part of the increase having taken place during the First World War and the years of inflation immediately after.

He also noted that among the different items composing the shrinking residual category the share of what might have been called income or unincorporated business continuously decreased during the period under review with again the exception of the thirties. The share of the income from capital, meaning dividends paid on stocks and shares and interest paid on bonds and bank deposits, had behaved rather peculiarly up to 1913. As a share of total income it was almost constant but during the war and inflation years it was cut back from 12·5 per cent to 2 per cent! It increased again until 1931, but during the thirties there had been a slight tendency for it to fall as a percentage of total income, while in the fifties it had tended to rise again.

Dr. Jungenfelt thought that development in Germany revealed much the same tendency as had already been pointed out for other countries, i.e. an increasing share of wages and salaries, and that this was to some extent due, as in other cases, to the declining importance of non-incorporated businesses; therefore it was not obvious whether the changes had meant any redistribution between capital and labour in the functional sense. But he did not want to intervene in the discussion on how the factor shares should be correctly calculated and would limit himself to commenting on the figures.

He observed that although Dr. Jeck presented no figures for factor shares, he gave estimates of the ratio of the average wage to the average income of all gainfully employed. Dr. Jungenfelt thought that this ratio might be as good an approximation for the labour share in the functional sense as any more sophisticated calculation. As it turned out, this ratio had been decreasing from 1925 while there had been an upward tendency for the share of wages and salaries. This, apparently, had been a period where the increasing share of wages and salaries did not mean any redistribution of income from capital to labour. Indeed Dr. Jungenfelt wondered whether the redistribution had not gone the other way round. This led him to ask Dr. Jeck whether calculations were not possible owing to the lack of available data as he could not make a guess as to what had happened in this respect for the earlier period under investigation.

On figures, Dr. Jungenfelt wanted to make another comment concerning the sharp rise in the wages and salaries share between 1913 and 1925. He observed that the whole period was one of rising prices, and even of especially severe inflation in the latter part. Now he had always believed that this inflation was to a great extent a demand inflation. He was therefore surprised to observe that the wage share had increased. He would have thought that the effect of demand inflation would have been to lower that share. Dr. Jeck had taken care to point to the effect of devaluation and of certain structural factors which could have played a decisive part in this increase. Dr. Jungenfelt wondered, however, whether there had not, also, been a possibility that the large amount of unemployment had been concentrated in the more capital intensive industries. He wanted to ask Dr. Jeck whether this was not the reason for the high level of the wage share in 1925 as compared with the pre-war period.

The Distribution of National Income

Dr. Jungenfelt wanted to make a third comment relating to the business cycle behaviour of the relative shares in Germany. They seemed to be affected by the cyclical movement to only a limited extent as Dr. Jeck mentioned an amplitude of only two percentage points. It seemed to Dr. Jungenfelt a very small figure in comparison with the experience of his own country. In Sweden peaks and troughs in labour share had diverged to the extent of 5 to 7 percentage points from the average on complete cycles : a 10 per cent decrease in labour share such as Dr. Jeck had recorded from 1931 to 1939 would, in Sweden, be explained to a large extent by the 'normal' effect of the business cycle.

Finally, and not without some hesitation, Dr. Jungenfelt added a last comment remarking that development in Germany tended to encourage theoretical analysis. He reminded the participants that Dr. Jeck had divided German development into three different phases. Now he had noticed that each of these phases started at approximately the same income *per capita* level. Keeping this in view, he wondered whether one could not do something like a controlled experiment on German development by selecting a year within each of these three periods when the average amount of capital per employee had been the same and then comparing the income distribution within these years. If this were possible one would have a unique opportunity of analysing the effects of technological change along the lines of the neo-classical theory as the effects arising from capital accumulation would be neutralized by holding capital constant ; technology being left as the sole factor which would change, any changes in income distribution would be related to it.

Professor Falise said that his attention had been drawn to the reversal of the trend in the labour share from 1931 onwards. Would Dr. Jeck say more about the German government policy and the sharp changes in income distribution in Germany in that period ? How had it been possible to keep wages at the abnormally low level where depression had placed them once full employment prevailed again ? How was it that trade profits had been allowed to increase significantly while, in accordance with a policy of repressed inflation, there had been a strict control of prices parallel to the freezing of wages ? Finally, as corporations' undistributed profits had become important, trebling in volume according to Dr. Jeck, to what use had they been put : had they been used for financing private investments, or rather for financing the increase in public works ?

Dr. Jeck said he would prefer to answer Dr. Jungenfelt's questions at the end of the debate, but would reply to Professor Falise's queries now. Concerning the first question, Dr. Jeck stated the purpose of the government's policy had been to keep the wages frozen all the time at the low level reached during the crisis and noted that the salaries of government employees had actually been kept unchanged from 1931 to 1948.

On the second question, concerning trade profits, Dr. Jeck pointed out that there was also a policy of price stabilization and, after 1936, a price stop. But the combination of wage stop, price stop, armament boom and rising productivity had necessarily led to an increase in the level and the share of trade profits, and also to a situation where full employment was reached.

Finally, Dr. Jeck said that the distribution of dividends had been limited by law to a maximum rate of 5 or 6 per cent of capital. This was the reason why for the first time German data revealed a significant increase in the share of undistributed profits. While it had been between 1 and 2 per cent in the nineteenth century, it increased sharply after 1933 and by 1936 it was 6 per cent. Moreover, in connection with dividend limitation new legislation was enacted on incorporated businesses strengthening the powers of managers and correlatively weakening the shareholders' position.

Dr. Jeck would say that over the whole of this period the lowering of the wage share in the national income resulted from two factors : first, a cyclical factor : the share of wages went down in time of steady growth and up in time of depression. Second, changes in the economic system, such as the transformation of a market economy into a planned economy with a high measure of state intervention. These two factors combined together in such a way as to make it impossible to appreciate them separately.

Dr. Jeck answered Professor Falise's query as to whether the figures showing the extent of the decrease in the share of wages were made public, saying that they had been published until 1940 only. In the last two years of that period the publications of the Statistical Office were classified as confidential. As to the period between 1940 and 1950, no figures were available.

Professor Fauvel declared that he, too, had been surprised to find that wages had remained at a low level even after conditions of full employment had prevailed again and wondered what had been the conditions which had allowed for a steady expansion without rising wage rates. This led him to think that it would be of some interest to compare the thirties with the 'German miracle' period from 1951 to 1960. Although he admitted that there was no income policy in the thirties, such a concept being then unknown, he thought that in the fifties there must have been a link between expansion and income policy.

Dr. Jeck answered, pointing out that Germany had almost always been a peculiar case. The 'German miracle' began with the continuous influx of refugees. Because of unemployment trade unions were in a weak position until 1955/56. Economic growth proceeded at a steady pace until full employment was attained, which resulted in a slowing down of growth from an 8 per cent rate to a rate of 5 to 6 per cent. Trade unions' bargaining power was thereby enhanced to such an extent that the unions were able to claim a 10 per cent rise each year after 1956, and figures showed in fact a greater rate of increase in wages after 1959/60.

Dr. Jeck suggested that perhaps a balance of power had now been achieved between trade unions and employers in Germany. The position appeared today more similar to the usual set up in the United Kingdom or the United States than it had ever been before. In any case he was not prepared, however, to use the figures he had found for Germany to build up a general theory because such abnormal factors as wars, devaluation, changes in the economic system had had in that country a much greater impact on the economy than elsewhere. For instance, the 1923 inflation and the resulting depreciation of the Mark by a billion times had led at one stage to an almost complete disappearance of monetary capital. The share of income from capital thus fell from 12 to 2 per cent ; the share of labour increased, but this was partly a matter of calculation because national income as a whole was cut down by the 10 per cent which represented the fall of income from capital. One could thus point out many abnormalities which strongly biased the interpretation of figures. He would advise against taking the developments in Germany as the basis for an income distribution theory as there had been too many disturbing events which could not be brought into a theory, neo-classical or otherwise.

Professor Phelps Brown reminded the participants that Dr. Jungenfelt had already pointed out the exceptional opportunity which the German data offered for testing the neo-classical theory. Professor Phelps Brown suggested that economic conditions in Germany in the thirties had been closely similar to the basic hypothesis in Kaldor's model. Given an exogenous increase in investment, expansion would be financed through a shift in income distribution in favour of the share of profits to the detriment of labour. Before the war rearmament had provided for that exogenous factor and the condition of the Kaldorian process, i.e. that when profits rose wages would not rise equally, had been fulfilled in Germany in 1933/39 as there were no independent trade unions.

Professor James declared that he could not agree that one should not try to build a theory on a case as exceptional as the German one. He thought that the distinction between normal and abnormal in economics was too arbitrary to be retained. Leaving aside anything relating to cyclical movements in the labour share, one should still study the problem of the effects of inflation and deflation on income distribution to try to integrate the German developments into a general theory.

In a situation of latent inflation, in which both the prices for factors of production and consumer goods were controlled, both controls might not be equally effective ; considering both movements as trends, the increase in wages might lag behind the increase in prices and real wages would tend to decrease ; he thought that there was just such a tendency during the post-war inflationary process in Germany.

Dr. Jeck, although admitting that wages lagged behind consumer's prices in time of inflation, was not prepared to give a definite answer in

this particular case : not only had wages been frozen but from 1936 onwards prices were controlled and finally rationing was enforced during
the war ; rationing made it impossible to transform monetary income
into real income and no alternative was left but to save (and after the war,
in 1948, these savings were cut down by the effect of the monetary
reform). Prices for consumers' goods ceased to be reliable as indices of
scarcity. As well as money wages, prices were subject to state intervention to an extent which deprived them of their significance for measuring real earnings. Dr. Jeck did not therefore think it possible to decide
whether wages had actually lagged behind prices.

Professor James replied by pointing out that at the end of the war there
had been a black market on which current prices greatly differed from
ration prices. *Dr. Jeck* admitted this, whereupon *Professor James* went
on to say that, under these conditions, one could suppose that free market
prices had increased enough for wages to lag behind.

Dr. Jeck suggested that one could not judge what the situation would
have been in the absence of control of both wages and prices : wages
would have been higher but prices might have been too.

Professor Alchian observed that one could not conclude that real wage
rates had fallen simply by asserting on one hand that price controls on
consumers' goods were evaded in black markets and on the other hand
that wage controls existed ; the latter were not necessarily effective.
There were many means of thwarting wage controls. In the absence of
specific empirical data nothing could be said beyond Dr. Jeck's penetrating
observations.

Dr. Jeck pointed out that the black market in manpower had remained
very limited while there were three or four millions unemployed on the
labour market. What forbade his giving any definite conclusion were
the disturbances brought about by non-economic factors and the total
disorganization of the social structures after the war.

Referring to Professor James's remarks about applying economic
theory to the situation in Germany just after the war, *Professor Krelle*
thought that this was not feasible. The German economy in that period
was neither a planned economy nor a market economy : it was a totally
disrupted economy and theory cannot apply to chaos.

On the contrary, the 'German miracle' was easy to explain on neo-
classical lines : given the availability of the production functions, of plenty
of manpower including skilled labour, of the basic investments such as
roads and railways which survived the war, all that was needed was to
replace the destroyed or dismantled machinery. Once this had been done,
a comparatively small amount of investment was needed. The process
started at a very low level, thence a very high rate of growth until
1955–56 when growth settled down to a more usual rate, though it was
still a little higher than in other countries. In this context the comparatively low share of labour income and the high level of investment

were significant facts. The post-war growth of the German economy was no miracle, only a probing application of the neo-classical theory of production.

Professor Bronfenbrenner did not think that a theory of distribution need be applicable to every economy. Ideally it should be, but this was a counsel of perfection, not a precept for action. A distribution theory devised for a market economy should not be criticized on the ground of limitations encountered in applying it to totalitarian or collectivist economies. Although it might be of interest to study exceptional cases, one should always ask oneself whether whatever made them exceptional were really unique circumstances or circumstances likely to recur in the future.

Professor Krelle, associating himself with Dr. Jungenfelt on the scope and quality of Dr. Jeck's paper, emphasized that Dr. Jeck had given figures for the period before 1914 which had never been produced before. These showed a substantial increase in the labour share of income. For later periods when figures were more reliable he would say from his own experience of the same computations that figures for the inter-war period depended on which concept of national income was adopted for recalculating the original data to get them in line with new definitions in social accountancy. One got different absolute amounts for income shares according to the way this was done, but in any case the changes in the distributive shares were very similar, the labour share rising in a slump and declining in a boom.

Something similar happened for figures after the war. The German Central Statistical Office had recently produced revised calculations for the period since 1950 : they showed a slight trend for the labour share to go up, while there was no apparent trend in the original figures ; but the labour share remained fairly stable until 1960 and it was worth noting that the significant increase happened during the period 1961–63, in a period when the growth rate went down by half, from a 12 per cent level in 1960 to 5·8 per cent in 1963. Professor Krelle thus thought that the labour share had again moved according to its usual cyclical pattern.

Professor Krelle observed that the labour share in Germany went up substantially in the periods before the two world wars, this being related to a decline in the importance of agriculture and crafts in the national product and the rise of manufacturing industries. There was, however, no definitely orientated change in the inter-war period and, since the Second World War, there had been no decisive sign that the labour share was rising. There might be a tendency, but it would only be clear if the labour share did not decline with the next cyclical increase in the rate of growth.

Dr. Jeck fully agreed with Professor Krelle in thinking that Germany was now at the critical point. Between 1950 and 1963 there were three years with a falling and 10 years with a rising labour share ; in 1950 that share had been 58·6 per cent, in 1963 it arrived at 64·8 per cent. In spite of this one should be cautious in interpreting the phenomena.

Up till now one could not be sure whether the German economy had taken up its former trend or if the evolution apparent after 1950 was only the well-known cyclical movement. He thought some years would have to elapse before we could see if the labour share would remain stable at its present percentage of income. He anticipated, however, that it would move upwards as he could not personally see any fundamental change between this and the former period : the structural shift in manpower observed before 1914 was a process which had not spent itself : Germany still had too many self-employed and too many small businessmen, although their number was decreasing. In the period 1875–1913 there had, of course, been small movements along cycles but their amplitude had not been such as to prevent the labour share from rising in any single year : although its rate of increase fluctuated according to the cycle, the upward trend always remained apparent. This had been the long-run tendency in normal times. This trend was likely to prevail again in our time.

Dr. Feinstein said that he, too, was reluctant to explain the increase in the labour share since 1961 by the cyclical movement as he had remarked that there had been in the past similar slowings down in the rate of growth in Germany without parallel increase in the share of wages. He wondered whether the present development was related to a purely cyclical slowing down of economic activity or rather to the structural change from an abnormally high to a lower and more permanent rate of growth.

The share of labour in Germany had remained until now at a lower level than in the United Kingdom and the share of investment had been higher in the former country. Dr. Feinstein thought that a structural change was now under way tending to bring the German position nearer to that of Britain and the United States through an increase in the share of labour which should lead to a further increase in the share of consumption.

Dr. Jeck pointed out that the increase in the labour share in 1952, 1955, and 1959 had been a cyclical phenomenon. He admitted, however, that there was a structural factor of change tending to increase the proportion of employees in manpower, but he thought that sooner or later this movement would encounter an upper limit. His opinion was that there was a connection between the development of the labour share and the degree of maturity of an economy and it might be that this upper limit had already been reached in the United Kingdom and the United States. Nevertheless German evolution was not so advanced and the share of labour had not reached its ceiling there.

Yet Dr. Jeck wished to make it clear that he did not think it right to say that income distribution in Germany improved in favour of labour *because* the number of employees was growing while the number of self-employed was diminishing : the increase in the share of labour in the national income was not strong enough to make it possible for the average income of employees to grow as rapidly as the overall average income. In Germany the increase in the labour share was matched by an evolution in personal income distribution not to the advantage but to the detriment of employees. One should not judge income distribution only from what functional shares were ; a statistical determination of personal income distribution in homogeneous groups was also needed and Dr. Jeck felt that there should be a better connection in our theory between functional and personal distribution of income.

Dr. Jeck wished to thank Dr. Jungenfelt for his introduction and to answer the questions raised by him.

On the first question of how average income of the different groups could have developed over the earlier period he could not give a definite answer as no figures were available, but as a guess he would say that the average income of wage-earners had been higher and its growth quicker than the average income of farmers. But until 1875 figures were issued for separate *Länder* and there were no nation-wide data : there was a continuous series from 1925 to 1940, then no further figures were available until 1950. Dr. Jeck had thus been forced to assemble material from different sources and he could not get figures for income participants.

In reply to Dr. Jungenfelt's second question as to whether the 1923 inflation was a demand inflation of the sort which could not lead to an increase in the share of wages in national income, Dr. Jeck would answer that this had definitely been a demand inflation with a single source, the government's payments for war damages ; the excess of demand came from no other source. The sharp changes in monetary values made it impossible to calculate the changes in national income during this period and the observed increase in the labour share only reflected the disappearance of part of the national income as a consequence of monetary depreciation.

Dr. Jungenfelt had asked whether the industries with the highest rate of unemployment were not the most capital-using industries. Dr. Jeck thought that it had generally been so but he could not produce precise figures to prove it.

Chapter 4

CHANGES IN THE DISTRIBUTION OF THE NATIONAL INCOME IN THE UNITED KINGDOM SINCE 1860[1]

BY

C. H. FEINSTEIN
University of Cambridge

I. INTRODUCTION

THE 'distribution of the national income' is a phrase which can be interpreted in various ways, depending on the definition of income and on the distributive classification. For the present paper the basic concept adopted is the national income at factor cost, measured before current transfers (whether of dividends and interest paid by companies and public authorities or of grants to persons from public authorities) and before payment of taxes on income. It thus relates to income as it is initially generated in the economic process of production. The main emphasis is on the gross national product but estimates of net national and net domestic product are also considered.

Two types of distributive share are examined. In the first instance the classification effectively follows the basis on which the estimates are compiled, and so relates to various types of income distinguished primarily by their institutional source. As is commonly the case, these categories do not correspond at all closely with the theoretical concept of the distribution of income among the factors of production. In the second stage an attempt is made to estimate, in very broad terms, the changes over time in the overall distribution of the national income between labour and property. These changes are then related to certain macro-economic variables which may help to explain the observed trends.

Finally, since it is important that users of a 'fact paper' designed to provide certain data for analysis and international comparison should be clear about the nature and quality of the data, a brief

[1] I am greatly indebted to W. B. Reddaway and R. C. O. Matthews for their comments and suggestions on a first draft of this paper.

115

TABLE 1
NATIONAL INCOME OF UNITED KINGDOM * AT FACTOR COST
1860–1963
(Averages of 4-, 5-, or 10-year periods)

£ million at Current Prices

Years	(1) Income from Employment	(2) Income from Self-employment Farmers	(3) Income from Self-employment Others	(4) Corporate Trading Profits	(5) Rent	(6) Gross Domestic Product	(7) Net Property Income from Abroad	(8) Gross National Product	(9) Capital Consumption	(10) Net National Product
1860–69	381	54		258	125	818	25	843	50	793
1870–79	512	51		364	156	1,083	51	1,134	65	1,069
1880–89	570	34		387	172	1,163	71	1,234	66	1,168
1890–99	738	37		474	192	1,441	96	1,537	73	1,464
1900–09	908	44		596	230	1,778	125	1,903	99	1,804
1910–14	1,071	56	311	387	250	2,075	189	2,264	119	2,145
1921–24 *	2,514	91	647	560	290	4,102	194	4,296	314	3,982
1925–29	2,490	56	635	535	323	4,039	250	4,289	288	4,001
1930–34	2,453	65	555	516	374	3,963	174	4,137	291	3,846
1935–38	2,834	78	556	724	426	4,618	199	4,817	341	4,476
1946–49	6,493	284	935	1,668	395	9,775	172	9,947	874	9,073
1950–54	9,015	392	1,077	2,484	539	13,507	296	13,803	1,224	12,579
1955–59	12,770	440	1,321	3,439	862	18,832	242	19,074	1,717	17,357
1960–63	16,626	523	1,565	4,406	1,259	24,379	289	24,668	2,198	22,470

* Southern Ireland is excluded from 1921

Per cent of Gross National Product

Years	(1)	(2)	(3)	(4)	(5)	(6)	(7)	(8)	(9)	(10)
1860–69	45·2	6·4	30·6	⎫	14·8	97·0	3·0	100·0	5·9	94·1
1870–79	45·2	4·5	32·1	⎪	13·7	95·5	4·5	100·0	5·7	94·3
1880–89	46·2	2·7	31·4	⎬	13·9	94·2	5·8	100·0	5·3	94·7
1890–99	48·0	2·4	30·8	⎪	12·5	93·8	6·2	100·0	4·7	95·3
1900–09	47·7	2·3	31·3	⎭	12·1	93·4	6·6	100·0	5·2	94·8
1910–14	47·3	2·5	13·7	17·1	11·0	91·6	8·4	100·0	5·3	94·7
1921–24 *	58·5	2·1	15·1	13·0	6·8	95·5	4·5	100·0	7·3	92·7
1925–29	58·1	1·3	14·8	12·5	7·5	94·2	5·8	100·0	6·7	93·3
1930–34	59·3	1·6	13·4	12·5	9·0	95·8	4·2	100·0	7·0	93·0
1935–38	58·9	1·6	11·6	15·0	8·8	95·9	4·1	100·0	7·1	92·9
1946–49	65·3	2·9	9·4	16·8	4·0	98·3	1·7	100·0	8·8	91·2
1950–54	65·3	2·8	7·8	18·0	3·9	97·9	2·1	100·0	8·9	91·1
1955–59	67·0	2·3	6·9	18·0	4·5	98·7	1·3	100·0	9·0	91·0
1960–63	67·4	2·1	6·3	17·9	5·1	98·8	1·2	100·0	8·9	91·1

* Southern Ireland is excluded from 1921.
Source : See Appendix, pp. 137–139.

117

appendix takes up certain familiar problems of national income accounting and indicates the particular treatment adopted in the United Kingdom estimates. It also contains an assessment of the reliability of the estimates and a note on the main sources used.

II. INCOME ANALYSED BY SOURCE

Broadly reliable and consistent estimates of the national income of the United Kingdom are available for all peace-time years from 1860. The main components are set out in Table 1 both in absolute terms and as a percentage of the gross national income. Here and elsewhere in the paper the estimates are summarized in the form of decade averages for the fifty years 1860–1909 and of averages of four- or five-year periods for the forty-one years covered between 1910 and 1963.

Income from Employment

It is sometimes suggested that income from employment is a stable proportion of the national income. Table 1 shows decisively that for the United Kingdom this view is quite incorrect if it is not further qualified : the share of the gross national income received by employees has in fact increased by 50 per cent over the period covered by the estimates : from 45 per cent in 1860–69 to 67 per cent in 1960–63. This very substantial rise has been achieved almost entirely in two abrupt shifts, occurring during or immediately after each of the world wars. During the three peace-time periods the pattern is generally one of stability, although there has been a slow upward drift in the years since 1946.

The distribution of aggregate income from employment between wages, salaries, pay in cash and kind of the Armed Forces and employers' contributions to national insurance funds, pensions, etc. is shown in Table 2. Administrative, technical, and clerical employees are classified as salary-earners ; operatives, together with shop assistants and policemen as wage-earners. This does not correspond *precisely* with certain other social or economic distinctions commonly made,[1] but does represent a meaningful division between two broad groups of workers.

[1] For example, between fixed and variable labour costs, or manual and non-manual workers, or union and non-union labour; or according to degree of training or skill, level of average income or periodicity of payment.

It is an interesting feature of Table 2 that the increased share of the GNP received by employees has gone almost exclusively to salary-earners. Their share of the national income has expanded persistently, from 6·5 per cent in 1860–69 to 16 per cent in 1921–24 and 23 per cent in 1960–63. By contrast, the long-run share of

TABLE 2

THE COMPOSITION OF INCOME FROM EMPLOYMENT
(Per cent of Gross National Product)

| | | | | Employers' | Included in Wages | |
| | | | Forces' | Contribu- | Shop | Farm |
	Wages *	Salaries	Pay *	tions	Assistants	Workers
Years	(1)	(2)	(3)	(4)	(5)	(6)
1860–69	38·7	6·5	..	—	2·8	8·3
1870–79	38·9	6·3	..	—	2·5	6·5
1880–89	38·6	7·6	..	—	2·8	5·2
1890–99	39·5	8·5	..	—	2·9	3·8
1900–09	38·0	9·7	..	—	2·7	3·2
1910–14	34·5	10·8	2·0	—	2·6	2·8
1921–24	38·6	16·2	1·9	1·8	1·8	1·8
1925–29	37·4	17·0	1·5	2·2	2·0	1·6
1930–34	37·1	18·2	1·5	2·5	2·4	1·5
1935–38	37·0	17·9	1·5	2·5	2·3	1·3
1946–49	39·3	19·1	3·6	3·3	..	2·1
1950–54	39·2	19·9	2·3	3·9	..	1·8
1955–59	39·3	21·3	2·0	4·4	..	1·4
1960–63	37·8	23·1	1·6	4·9	..	1·2

* Forces' pay is included in wages before 1910.
.. Not available.
Source : See Appendix, pp. 137–139.

wage-earners has been remarkably constant, remaining within 1½ percentage points of 38 per cent of GNP in all of the sub-periods shown in Table 2 except 1910–14.

It is this overall stability in the share of wages before 1938 which originally attracted the attention of Keynes [16] and Kalecki [15] and was subsequently investigated by Phelps Brown and Hart [20] ; but it is evident from the above data that the seemingly miraculous 'stability of the proportion of the national dividend accruing to labour' [16, pp. 48–49] depends completely on the exclusion from

The Distribution of National Income

the definition of labour of both the large category of administrative, technical and clerical workers and the self-employed.

In Table 3 the aggregate wage and salary bill for selected years is decomposed into two elements : the numbers employed in each category and the average annual earnings per worker.[1] This demonstrates that the fall in the ratio of wages to salaries from 3·2 in

TABLE 3

WAGE- AND SALARY-EARNERS

NUMBERS EMPLOYED AND AVERAGE EARNINGS
IN SELECTED YEARS

	Numbers Employed		Average Annual Earnings		Ratios	
	Wage-earners *	Salary-earners	Wage-earners	Salary-earners	(1) : (2)	(3) : (4)
	(Millions)		(£s)			
Years	(1)	(2)	(3)	(4)	(5)	(6)
1911*	15·18	1·67	50	140	9·1	·36
1924	13·01	2·85	125	245	4·6	·51
1931	12·93	3·17	120	240	4·1	·50
1938	15·04	3·84	130	240	3·9	·54
1951	16·17	5·69	335	450	2·8	·74
1961	16·27	6·93	590	800	2·3	·74

* Including armed forces.
† Including S. Ireland. The total number employed excluding S. Ireland was about 15·95 m.

Source : See Appendix, pp. 137–139.

1910–14 to 2·1 in 1935–38 and 1·6 in 1960–63 is entirely the consequence of a fall in the ratio of wage-earners to total employees. Whereas in 1911 there were over nine wage-earners for every salary-earner, there were only four times as many in 1938 and 2·3 times as many in 1961.[2] Almost 90 per cent of the increase in the labour force in the last fifty years has thus gone into salaried occupations. The effect of this on the distribution of income has been partially

[1] A third element would be the effects of shifts within or between industries from lower- to higher-grade occupations.
[2] Part of this may be due to changes over time in the classification of certain occupations ; and with the pre-1914 statistics it is also difficult to distinguish accurately between salary-earners and small employers or workers on own account. These problems of classification are probably responsible for a considerable part of the estimated increase in the number of salary-earners between 1911 and 1924 [3, p. 45].

counteracted by the fact that the average wage has risen from about one-third of the average salary in 1911 to a little over half in 1938 and to about three-quarters in 1951 and 1961. It looks, therefore, as though since 1938 the additional salary-earners have gone largely into the lowest-paid occupations (such as clerical work and typing) and so pulled down the average salary.

Income from Self-employment

This category covers the income of farmers, indepedent professional persons and other sole traders or partnerships. This third, and largest, segment is itself very varied in composition, ranging from the small tradersman working without assistance to the owners of a large but unincorporated business employing many workers.

The income of the self-employed (employers and workers on own account) combines both the remuneration for their labour and the return on capital invested, and changes in the relative size of such mixed incomes affect the comparison of the distribution of income between labour and property over time or between countries. An attempt is, therefore, made below (p. 124) to apportion the income from self-employment between labour and property, although any such division is inherently arbitrary.

Farmers' incomes (after deduction of actual or imputed rent) (col. (2) of Table 1) were about 6·5 per cent of GNP in 1860–69, but by the 1880's the great contraction of arable farming which began in the late 'seventies had reduced the proportion to just over 2·5 per cent, at which level it was broadly stable until 1910–14. The inter-war years saw a renewed deterioration in the relative position of farming and their share declined to 1·5 per cent. Following the war-time expansion of agriculture there was an improvement to almost 3 per cent of GNP in 1946–49 when the policy of farm subsidies was particularly generous ; but since then there has been a further fall, to just over 2 per cent in 1960–63. Column (6) of Table 2 traces a similar path in the relative fortunes of farm workers and the two combined represent the major components of the diminishing contribution of farming to the gross domestic product, the main omission being the rent of farm land and buildings.

The share of the non-farm self-employed in the national income (col. (3) of Table 1) was 13·7 per cent in 1910–14, the first period in which it can be distinguished — though only very approximately — from corporate profits. The combined share of non-farm self-employment income and gross trading profits was fairly stable before

1910–14, and as incomes from self-employment would almost certainly have been higher relative to corporate income the further back we go,[1] the share of GNP probably had a diminishing trend from 1860–69 to 1910–14. There was a small (and statistically uncertain) increase after the 1914–18 war but since then the share has declined steadily until in 1960–63 it was no more than 6·3 per cent.

The total number of self-employed persons, including farmers, was about 2·8 m. in 1911 (perhaps 2·4 m. excluding Southern Ireland), was fairly steady at around 2·1 m. in the inter-war years, and has been about 1·7 m. in the post-war years. This represents a fall relative to the number of employees from 17 per cent in 1911 to 7 per cent in 1961. The estimated number of farmers in Great Britain and Northern Ireland has shown little change over the fifty years 1911–61[2] and the absolute reduction has been in the other categories of the self-employed, reflecting the conversion of firms to private or public companies and the movement of independent workers into salaried or wage-earning occupations. The effect of this process in swelling income from employment and corporate trading profits at the expense of income from self-employment is considered below.

The average earnings of all self-employed persons were a little over double those of employees in 1910–14, in the inter-war period, and again in 1946–54. In the latest period there has, however, been a decline in their relative income per head to about 1·75 times that of all employees. For farmers alone, average incomes were a little over twice those of employees in 1960–63 ; a higher ratio than in 1910–14 or in the inter-war years (when it was between 1·0 and 1·5) but lower than in the early years after World War II, when their relative incomes were about three times greater than those of employees.

Gross Trading Profits

Gross trading profits (after provision for stock appreciation) of companies, public corporations, and other public enterprises are shown together in column (4) of Table 1. The proportion of GNP accruing to trading profits was 17 per cent in 1910–14 and has been stable at about 18 per cent since 1946. It cannot be estimated separ-

[1] Company formation in Britain did not begin, in most sectors of the economy, until 1856, and did not become widespread until the closing decades of the century.

[2] The figure was 356,000 in 1961 and about 350,000 in 1911 [*1*, p. 3].

ately before 1910–14 but, as suggested above, it is likely that the proportion was below 17 per cent in earlier years and moved upwards as the trend towards incorporation gathered pace.   In the inter-war years there was more deviation from the long-run share of 16–18 per cent with a fall to a trough of 12·5 per cent in 1925–34 and a recovery to 15 per cent in 1935–38.   It is clear, however, that the gain in the share of income from employment over the last hundred years has not been at the expense of corporate profits.

Companies account for the greater part of gross trading profits, but public corporations have grown in importance, increasing their share of GNP from less than 1 per cent in 1921-24 to just over 3 per cent in 1960–63.

Rent of Land and Buildings [1]

The share of the national income received by (or imputed to) the owners of land and buildings (col. (5) of Table 1) has contracted from about 15 per cent in 1860–69 to 5 per cent in 1960–63.   The contraction begins with a steady decline before 1914 when the rent of agricultural land in England and Wales is estimated to have fallen from a peak of about 29 shillings per acre in 1875–79 to 23 shillings a decade later and a low point of 20 shillings in 1900-4 [*22*, p. 41]. In this period landlords bore a considerable part of the burden imposed on agriculture by falling prices, and as agricultural rent fell in absolute terms it naturally represented a much smaller proportion of the national income.

From 1914 the pattern for the share of total rent is one of an abrupt fall after both of the world wars, followed by a recovery which is insufficient to make good the ground lost in the immediate post-war years.[2]   The fall from 11 per cent in 1910–14 to 7 per cent in 1921–24 is largely the result of the imposition of restrictions on the rents of dwellings, the main component of the total.[3]   In 1946–49

---

[1] The definitions of rent are outlined on p. 135.

[2] From 1921 the estimate of rent excludes imputed income from owner-occupied trading property.   In accordance with the current practice of the Central Statistical Office this item is included in trading profits and income from self-employment. The effect of this change in definition is to reduce the share of rent in the 1920's by roughly one percentage point.

[3] Controls were first imposed in 1915, extended in scope in 1919 and 1920, and relaxed a little in 1923 and more widely but still not completely in 1933.   70 per cent of all houses in Great Britain were subject to control in 1931 and in 1937 the proportion was still as high as 44 per cent [*24*, p. 202].   The recoverable rents of these houses were usually from 20 to 30 per cent below the uncontrolled rents of similar houses.

the share of rent was again drastically reduced, to 4 per cent, as the extension of rent control in September 1939 once again prevented house rents from rising as rapidly as other prices. From 1957 rents have been progressively decontrolled and the share of GNP has climbed slowly upwards again, reaching 5 per cent in 1960–63.

Net Property Income from Abroad

The last component of gross national income is the receipts by United Kingdom residents of rent, interest, profits and dividends from overseas, net of property income paid abroad (col. (7) of Table 1). The extensive export of capital undertaken by Britain before 1914 raised the contribution of this item from 3 per cent in the 1860's to 8·5 per cent in 1910–14, when accumulated overseas investments were at a record level of some £4,000 m.

The realizations of dollar securities during the years 1915–20, the loss of securities in enemy countries and in Russia, and some repayment of earlier loans, partly offset by war-time overseas lending, reduced the total of overseas investments by rather more than 15 per cent [*19*, pp. 317–31]. It is this which was mainly responsible for the failure of net property income to rise after the war and for the fall in its contribution to 4·5 per cent in 1921–24. Renewed overseas lending in the 1920's raised the proportion to almost 6 per cent in 1925–29, but in the 1930's defaults, dividend cuts, and official curbs on new overseas lending reduced it to 4 per cent.

In the post-war years it has fallen still further, to little more than 1 per cent in 1960–63. This is due partly to the realization of over £1,000 m. of securities during 1939–45 [*23*, p. 503], partly to the relatively low level of overseas lending since the war, and partly to the growing importance of investment by foreigners in the United Kingdom. In 1960–63 property income paid abroad was equal to half of property income received from abroad, whereas in 1938 the proportion was about 15 per cent and before 1914 it was negligible.

III. DISTRIBUTION BETWEEN LABOUR AND PROPERTY

The Labour Component of Income from Self-employment

Up to this stage we have considered the distribution of the gross national income between categories of a rather mixed character, determined principally by the form in which the estimates are derived. We now turn to an examination of the evolution of what can broadly be described as the distribution between income from labour and income from property. For this purpose income from employment is treated as return to labour; gross trading profits, rent, and net property income from abroad as return to property. Income from self-employment must be divided between the two categories.

There is no direct way in which the labour and property components of the income of the self-employed can be measured, but there are a number of more or less arbitrary ways in which some sort

TABLE 4

ALLOCATION OF INCOME FROM SELF-EMPLOYMENT

(Per cent of total income from self-employment)

	'Labour'	'Property'
	(1)	(2)
1910–14	49·3	50·7
1921–24	51·9	48·1
1925–29	52·0	48·0
1930–34	58·7	41·3
1935–38	63·1	36·9
1946–49	62·8	37·2
1950–54	63·8	36·2
1955–59	70·0	30·0
1960–63	73·5	26·5

Source : See text.

of allocation can be made. The most satisfactory of these would seem to be to estimate the income which a self-employed person would have received as a paid employee in the same sector of the economy ; and then to regard any residual as the return on capital employed. The results of a calculation made on this basis are shown in Table 4. Except for professional persons, all independent employers and workers on own account, including farmers, have been paid a 'wage', generally equal to that of an adult operative in the same industry. In the case of professional persons, however, who effectively employ no physical capital, the whole of their income has been allocated to labour. The estimated breakdown for 1910–14 is particularly uncertain and no reliable estimate on this basis can be made for earlier years.

Assessed in this way the 'labour component' of income from self-employment has risen from 50 per cent in 1910–14 to about 74 per

The Distribution of National Income

cent in 1960–63. The proportions are thus not very different from those of the share of employment income in the national product excluding income from self-employment: 56 per cent in 1910–14 and 74 per cent in 1960–63.[1] The rising share of the labour component is consistent with the final stages of the trend towards incorporation removing the larger profit-earning employers and leaving an increasing proportion of small traders with incomes very little larger than those of the average employee.

The Distribution of Income between Labour and Property

If we now allocate income from self-employment in the proportions shown in Table 4 we obtain the overall distribution of income

TABLE 5

THE DISTRIBUTION OF INCOME BETWEEN LABOUR AND PROPERTY

	Gross National Product		Gross Domestic Product		Net Domestic Product	
	Labour	Property	Labour	Property	Labour	Property
	(1)	(2)	(3)	(4)	(5)	(6)
Years	Per cent of GNP		Per cent of GDP		Per cent of NDP	
1910–14	55·3	44·7	60·2	39·8	64·0	36·0
1921–24	67·4	32·6	70·6	29·4	76·5	23·5
1925–29	66·4	33·6	70·5	29·5	76·0	24·0
1930–34	68·1	31·9	71·1	28·9	76·7	23·3
1935–38	67·1	32·9	70·0	30·0	75·6	24·4
1946–49	73·0	27·0	74·3	25·7	81·5	18·5
1950–54	72·1	27·9	73·7	26·3	81·0	19·0
1955–59	73·4	26·6	74·4	25·6	81·8	18·2
1960–63	73·6	26·4	74·5	25·5	81·9	18·1

between labour and property. Three variants of this are given in Table 5. The first follows directly from the previous estimates and shows the distribution of the gross national product. The second relates to the gross domestic product, excluding net property income from abroad. The final variant is perhaps the most appropriate, in

---

[1] A third method of allocation would be to assume that the return on capital (fixed assets and dwellings) was the same for unincorporated businesses as for the corporate sector, thus leaving the labour component as the residual. A rough estimate on this basis for 1960–63 gives property a 22 per cent share of the income of the self-employed, which is again not very different from the 26 per cent share estimated on the method used in Table 4.

that it takes account of the need to make provision for capital consumption, showing the distribution of the net domestic product between labour and home-produced property income net of depreciation at replacement cost.[1] Whatever variant is considered there is an unmistakable upward trend in labour's share, but one which is almost entirely the result of the shifts which occur during or immediately after both the world wars. In the inter-war years and again in the period from 1946 the distribution between labour and property is remarkably constant. The coincidence of these 'faults' in the level of the distributive shares with the two major breaks in the sources and methods of estimation (see pp. 136–138 below) might justifiably lead the reader to suspect that it is errors of estimation which account for much of the observed discontinuities. It would seem, however, that this is not the case.[2]

When gross national product is taken as the measure of national income labour's distributive share grows by 18 percentage points or roughly one-third between 1910–14 and 1960–63. In the second variant the exclusion of the relatively diminishing contribution of property income from abroad cuts down the overall improvement in labour's share to 14 percentage points. Finally, when provision for capital consumption is deducted from property income the improvement in labour's relative position over the last half-century is restored to 18 percentage points, since capital consumption has increased as a proportion of the national income (see col. (9) of Table 1) and thus of home-produced property income.

A fourth variant, excluding the actual and imputed rental income of dwellings (net of depreciation) from net home property income and from the total, is shown in Table 6. The effect of this is both to depress the increment in the share received by labour to 15 percentage points and to alter the pattern of change over the period. The trans-war discontinuities are reduced, particularly from 1935–

[1] Consideration of net income was not possible in the previous part of the paper because of the absence of separate data on capital consumption for the different categories of property income.
[2] The effect of the probable errors can be seen if we take an extreme case. As is explained in the appendix the main components are subject to a probable margin of error of up to ±10 per cent (or ±5 per cent for some components from 1921 onwards); and the possibility that the aggregate GNP may be too *low* by up to 5 per cent in 1910–14 and 1921–24 is suggested by the comparison with the largely independent estimates made from expenditure data. If, as is probably *not* the case (see p. 136), the whole of the understatements in GNP is in income from labour in the first period (equivalent to an error of 9 per cent) and in income from property in the latter period (equivalent to an error of 15 per cent) there would still be an increase of 7 percentage points in labour's share of GNP or GDP between the two periods.

The Distribution of National Income

1938 to 1946–49, when the increase in labour's share is only 2 percentage points, compared with 6 in column (5) of Table 5 ; but there
is now some sign of a swing to labour in the post-war years. In
view of the extent to which the level of house rents has been influenced by government controls, it is probably this last variant
which best represents the long-run macro-economic distribution

TABLE 6

THE DISTRIBUTION OF NET DOMESTIC INCOME
EXCLUDING RENT ON DWELLINGS
BETWEEN LABOUR AND PROPERTY

	Labour	Property
Years	(1)	(2)
1910–14	68·8	31·2
1921–24	79·8	20·2
1925–29	79·9	20·1
1930–34	81·7	18·3
1935–38	80·3	19·7
1946–49	82·4	17·6
1950–54	82·0	18·0
1955–59	83·5	16·5
1960–63	84·0	16·0

Source : As for Tables 1 and 4.

between labour and property of income directly generated in the
domestic economy.

Even with some allowance for the probable margin of error in
the estimates the evidence for a rising share for labour over the
period 1910–14 to 1960–63 would thus appear to be firmly established. Other variants which might be calculated (for example, by
excluding income from agriculture or from government employment
and property) would alter the details but would not disturb the basic
trends.

It is not possible to bring forward comparable evidence for the
half-century before 1910–14 but it is possible to make a shot at
forming an impression of what happened. The procedure is too
involved and uncertain to warrant detailed description here,[1] but

[1] We know from the data in Table 1 that the share of income from employment
in the domestic product (either gross or net) rose by 5 percentage points between
1860–69 and 1910–14. The problem is then to make a 'best guess' of the extent
of two countervailing trends : the probable fall in non-farm income from self-
employment relative to corporate profits, and the probable rise in the labour
component relative to total income from self-employment.

leads to a view that any change there may have been over these fifty years was inconsiderable. The outside limits would appear to be a fall of one percentage point in labour's share of the domestic product or a rise of 4 percentage points.

Conclusion

If we now take the estimates in Table 6 as our 'reference series' we are in a position to pronounce our final verdict. Once provision is made for capital consumption, and if net property income from overseas and rents of dwellings are excluded, the evidence suggests clearly that from immediately before World War I to the present time there has been a secular upward trend in labour's share. It increased very markedly between 1910–14 and 1921–24; was steady between the wars; rose again, though only very weakly, during or immediately after World War II; and has continued to creep upwards in the post-war period.

Those willing to accept evidence of very much lower credibility might add that there is no warrant for thinking that any significant change occurred between 1860–69 and 1910–14.

IV. SOME MACRO-ECONOMIC IMPLICATIONS

Any attempt at explanation of the observed trends would be beyond the limited scope of this paper. However, since the data presented have been confined entirely to national aggregates it may be helpful, as a final factual contribution, to set out the corresponding data for certain ratios commonly invoked in macro-economic theories explaining the changes (or the stability) in distributive shares.[1]

There are two basic identities underlying this type of approach. The first is:

$$\frac{P}{Y} = \frac{P}{K} \cdot \frac{K}{Y} \qquad (1)$$

where P = Property income

Y = Total income or output

and K = Capital stock

P/Y and P/K are appropriately measured at current prices but K/Y,

[1] Cf. [*17*] and [*21*].

the capital-output ratio, should logically be at constant prices, so that the identity ought to be :

$$\frac{P}{Y} = \frac{P}{K} \cdot \frac{Q_K}{Y'} \cdot \frac{p_K}{p_K} \tag{2}$$

where Q_K, the quantity of capital, is obtained by deflating K by p_K, an index of capital goods prices ; and Y' is real output, equal to Y deflated by p_Y, an index of national output prices.

The second identity is :

$$\frac{P}{L} = \frac{Q_K}{Q_L} \cdot \frac{R'_K}{R'_L} \tag{3}$$

where the additional variables are :

L = Labour income = $Y - P$

Q_L = Quantity of labour

R'_K = Real return per unit of capital = $\dfrac{P}{Q_K} \div p_Y$

R'_L = Real return per unit of labour = $\dfrac{L}{Q_L} \div p_Y$.

In order to represent the concepts in identities (2) and (3) by actual series it is necessary to define the basic terms more precisely, and we take :

Y' = Gross domestic product at 1958 prices.

P and L = Property and labour components of GDP as in Table 5 cols. (3) and (4).

Q_K = Gross stock of reproducible fixed assets at 1958 prices.[1]

[1] For fixed assets a case could be made for using the net rather than the gross stock and our choice was dictated largely by the very much better data available for the latter. Rough estimates of the net stock at 1958 prices suggests that it varied as follows as a ratio of the gross stock :

1910–14	·70	1930–34	·60	1950–54	·56
1921–24	·61	1935–38	·60	1955–59	·58
1925–29	·61	1946–49	·55	1960–63	·60

If the net stock had been used in place of the gross stock the ratio of the 1960–63 value to the 1910–14 value of the variables involved would have been as follows :

	Net Stock	Gross Stock
P/K	·59	·51
$Q_{K/Y}$	·90	1·04
R'_K	·71	·62
Q_K/Q_L	1·44	1·67
R'_K/R'_L	·36	·31

These values can be substituted in the last row of the two summary tables on p. 131 representing the 'actual' behaviour of identities (2) and (3).

There is no data on the degree of utilization of fixed assets or on changes in hours worked by capital.

Q_L = Employed labour force.[1]

Estimates of these five series and of the two price indices p_K and p_Y are given in Table 7, and the ratios derived from them are set out in Tables 8 and 9.

The ratios in Table 8 correspond to identity (2) above. The proportionate changes over the period 1910–14 to 1960–63 can be summarized as follows :

	$\dfrac{P}{Y}$	$\dfrac{P}{K}$	$\dfrac{Q_K}{Y^i}$	$\dfrac{p_K}{p_Y}$
1910–14 to 1935–38	·75	·72	1·13	·93
1935–38 to 1960–63	·85	·71	·92	1·32
1910–14 to 1960–63	·64	·51	1·04	1·22

Note: The above figures measure the ratios at the second date as a proportion of their value at the first date.

The fall of 14 percentage points (or 36 per cent of the original ratio), in the share of property income in GDP (i.e. from almost 40 per cent in 1910–14 to 25·5 per cent in 1960–63) can thus be expressed as the outcome of a fall of about 50 per cent in the average rate of return on capital (new and old taken together), partly offset by the rise of 22 per cent in the price of capital goods relative to the general price index. As Table 8 shows this rise comes almost entirely between 1935–38 and 1946–49 and it should be said that the data on changes in capital goods prices over the war years are extremely uncertain. The average capital-output ratio displays its accustomed stability over the long-run but is at a higher level in the inter-war years when there is presumably an unusually low degree of utilization.

Identity (3) is represented in Table 9 and the overall changes are summarized below :

	$\dfrac{P}{L}$	$\dfrac{Q_K}{Q_L}$	$\dfrac{R^i_K}{R^i_L}$
1910–14 to 1935–38	·65	1·28	·51
1935–38 to 1960–63	·80	1·31	·61
1910–14 to 1960–63	·52	1·67	·31

The data on inventories is very uncertain and for this reason they are omitted. For what it is worth the estimates show approximately the same rate of growth between 1910–14 and 1960–63 as the gross stock of fixed assets given in Table 7. There is also no estimate of the value of the stock of land in use.

[1] Adequate data on hours worked are not available, but it should be borne in mind that between 1910–14 and 1921–24 there was a reduction of some 10 per cent in hours worked by manual labour. Subsequent changes in hours worked were very much smaller.

TABLE 7

INPUTS OF LABOUR AND CAPITAL, INCOME AND PRICES

Years	P Gross Domestic Property Income	L Labour Income	Y^1 GDP at 1958 Prices	Q_K Gross Fixed Assets (excl. Land) at 1958 Prices	Q_L Employed Labour Force	p_Y GDP Price Index	p Capital Goods Price Index
	£ million			£'000 million	million	1958 = 100	
	(1)	(2)	(3)	(4)	(5)	(6)	(7)
1910–14*	790	1,196	10,450	41·4	18·59	19	15
1921–24	1,205	2,897	9,580	45·9	17·53	43	32
1925–29	1,190	2,849	10,680	49·4	18·44	38	27
1930–34	1,146	2,817	11,040	53·7	18·65	36	25
1935–38	1,384	3,234	12,970	58·3	20·51	36	26
1946–49	2,516	7,259	15,665	63·3	23·11	62	64
1950–54	3,555	9,952	17,495	70·0	23·60	77	81
1955–59	4,829	14,003	19,780	80·2	24·35	95	96
1960–63	6,218	18,161	22,530	92·6	24·95	108	104

* Excluding Southern Ireland.

Source: (1) Col. (4) of Table 5 × col. (6) of Table 1.
(2) Col. (3) of Table 5 × col. (5) of Table 1.
(3) (1) + (2) ÷ (6).
(4) For 1946–63 based on estimates by G. A. Dean [9]; earlier years from [12] adjusted to the level given by Dean for 1938.
(5) See Appendix, p. 137.
(6) Derived from estimates of GDP (from expenditure data) at current and at 1958 prices. See [11] and [18], Table C.
(7) From [18], Table F.

Over the 50-year period a fall of almost 70 per cent in the 'price' of capital relative to the 'price' of labour has been associated with a rise of only 67 per cent in the quantity of capital per worker, with the result that the ratio of property income to labour income has fallen to 52 per cent of its original level, i.e. from ·66 to ·34. The gross stock of fixed assets has more than doubled over the period while the numbers at work have gone up by only a third. The

TABLE 8

RATIOS 'EXPLAINING' THE SHARE
OF PROPERTY INCOME IN GDP

	$\dfrac{P}{Y}$	$\dfrac{P}{K}$	$\dfrac{Q_K}{Y^1}$	$\dfrac{p_K}{p_Y}$
	Ratio of Property Income to GDP	Average Rate of Return on Capital %	Average Capital-output Ratio	Ratio of Price Indices
	(a)	(b)	(c)	(d)
1910–14	·398	12·7	4·0	·79
1921–24	·294	8·2	4·8	·75
1925–29	·295	8·9	4·6	·71
1930–34	·289	8·5	4·9	·70
1935–38	·300	9·1	4·5	·73
1946–49	·257	6·2	4·0	1·03
1950–54	·263	6·3	4·0	1·05
1955–59	·256	6·3	4·0	1·01
1960–63	·255	6·5	4·1	·96

Source: Numbers in brackets refer to columns of Table 7. (a) = (1) ÷ [(1) + (2)]. (b) = (1) ÷ [(4) × (7)]. (c) = (4) ÷ (3). (d) = (7) ÷ (6).

resulting increase in capital per worker (as shown in Table 9) was most rapid from 1946–49 to 1960–63, but the ratio in the inter-war years is distorted because only the labour series is adjusted for unemployment. If allowance is made for this the rise in Q_K/Q_L would presumably have proceeded at a more steady pace throughout the period.

Column (a) of Table 9 shows that apart from a sharp fall between 1910–14 and 1921–24, the average rate of return on all capital has, in real terms, been fairly stable, though there is some suggestion that the rate has been slipping downwards since 1950–54. However, the rate in the inter-war years was presumably depressed by the relatively high level of unused capacity, and if adjustment could be made for this the real average rate of return on capital might show a more steady long-run downward trend with perhaps a cyclical recovery in the late 'thirties. In sharp contrast to this, the real 'wage' of labour (col. (b) of Table 9) has almost exactly doubled over the period, rising by over 30 per cent between 1910–14 and 1935–38 and by a further 50 per cent by 1960–63. The result of these two divergent trends is that the relative 'price' of labour has risen more than threefold over the last fifty years.

TABLE 9

RATIOS 'EXPLAINING' THE RATIO
OF PROPERTY TO LABOUR INCOME

	$R^l{}_K$	$R^l{}_L$	$\dfrac{P}{L}$	$\dfrac{Q_K}{Q_L}$	$\dfrac{R^l{}_K}{R^l{}_L}$
	Real Rate of Return per Unit :			Ratios of	
	of Capital %	of Labour (£s per Worker)	Property to Labour Income	Quantities of Capital and Labour (£s per Worker)	Return per Unit of Capital and Labour
	(a)	(b)	(c)	(d)	(e)
1910–14	10·0	338	·660	2,227	2·97
1921–24	6·1	386	·416	2,618	1·59
1925–29	6·4	409	·418	2,679	1·56
1930–34	5·9	421	·407	2,879	1·41
1935–38	6·7	443	·428	2,842	1·51
1946–49	6·4	503	·347	2,739	1·27
1950–54	6·6	546	·357	2,966	1·21
1955–59	6·3	604	·345	3,294	1·05
1960–63	6·2	673	·342	3,711	0·92

Source : Numbers in brackets refer to colums of Table 7. (a) = (1) ÷ [(4) × (6)]. (b) = (2) ÷ [(5) × (6)]. (c) = (1) ÷ (2). (d) = (4) ÷ (5). (e) = [(a) ÷ (b)] × 100.

APPENDIX

1. *Concepts and Definitions*

The concepts of national income used in this paper represent the basic social accounting aggregates and their estimation raises a number of familiar issues. In general the estimates are intended to be consistent in all significant respects with the official estimates currently prepared by the Central Statistical Office. These are described fully in *Sources and*

Methods [5] and in *National Income and Expenditure, 1963* [6], and the reader is referred to these publications for further details. The following paragraphs do not attempt to discuss these issues but merely to indicate the particular convention adopted on matters which would affect the present estimates of income shares.

(i) *Imputation.* To a very large extent the economic activities brought within the scope of the estimates are those in which goods or services are actually traded for money. The major exceptions to this are the inclusion in wages and salaries of certain payments in kind ; in farmers' incomes of the value at farm prices of farm produce consumed by the farmer's household ; and in the treatment of rental income (see paragraph (ii) below). No income is imputed to housewives for their unpaid chores ; or to owners of consumers' durables (other than houses) for the services rendered by such assets.

(ii) *Rent of land and buildings.* For 1921–63 the estimates of rent represent the income derived from the ownership of land and buildings after deduction of actual expenditure by the owners on current repairs, maintenance and insurance. Where the property is owner-occupied an imputed rent is, with one exception, included in rental income ; this applies to private dwellings occupied by their owners, to buildings owned and used by public authorities, and to owner-occupiers of farm land and buildings. The one exception is that the income imputed to owner-occupiers of trading property is included in trading profits (of either corporate or unincorporated bodies) and not in rental income. The rental income imputed to the owners is that, in principle, which represents the amount which would be received if the property were let unfurnished, with the tenant responsible for rates, repairs, and insurance. Where rents paid by tenants of houses are subsidized by public authorities the rental income is calculated as the full economic rent, i.e. the subsidy is regarded as contributing to the rental income.

For 1860–1914 the estimates are partially derived from a different source but the definition is the same except that for this period income imputed to owner-occupiers of trading property is included in rent, and the deduction for repairs, etc., is based on a statutory allowance, not on the actual expenditure.

(iii) *Capital gains and losses.* The estimates take no account of capital gains or losses arising from the sale of real or financial assets.

(iv) *Interest and dividends.* All interest and dividend payments (including national debt interest) are regarded as transfer payments not as factor incomes, and profits are measured before such payments (or receipts). One consequence of this definition is that financial concerns make a 'loss' in the national accounts equal to the excess of management expenses over bank charges, commissions, etc., charged for specific services. Since other trading profits are measured before payment of bank interest and other interest payments this would have no effect on aggregate profits if all financial services were rendered to trading bodies. However, some financial services are rendered to persons (e.g. as customers of banks) and if that part of the 'loss' were imputed to persons as a form of consumers' expenditure then total expenditure, profits, and total income would be higher than on the present basis.

(v) *Public authority trading income.* Three classes of trading surpluses (or deficits) are distinguished in the accounts. Only the trading incomes of those bodies which aim, broadly, to cover their costs over a period are included in trading profits. The trading deficits of public bodies which are deliberately run at a loss are treated as subsidies, not as trading losses ; and the trading profits (after provision for depreciation and interest) of the Post Office are treated as a tax on expenditure (because of its position as a state monopoly).

(vi) *Capital consumption.* The estimates of capital consumption are designed to allow for capital resources used up in current production as a result of wear and tear, obsolescence and accidental damage. They do not include repairs nor do they provide for depletion of mineral assets. They represent an estimate of the cost of replacing capital consumed by identical assets purchased at current prices (not at the original cost of the assets) but do not allow for technological progress.

There is an important asymmetry in the estimates which should be noted. From 1921 onwards the income estimates are derived before provision for depreciation and it is estimates of capital consumption of the above type which are deducted to obtain net income series. For 1860–1913 the estimates are derived on a net basis and the amount allowed for depreciation for tax purposes (at original cost) is unknown and so cannot be added back. To obtain gross incomes our estimates of capital consumption are added back but these are not necessarily equal to the initial deduction.

(vii) *Stock appreciation.* From 1921 onwards stock appreciation (whether positive or negative) is excluded from the estimates. For earlier years no estimates of this item are available.

2. Reliability of the Data

An assessment of the reliability of the basic estimates can be made in two ways. At the level of aggregate income a comparison can be made with a largely independent estimate based on expenditure data, available from 1870 [*11*]. Averaged over periods of five or ten years the expenditure estimate is always higher than the income estimate, the discrepancy varying between 6 and 7 per cent of the expenditure estimate until 1909, dropping to 5·5 per cent in 1910–14, 4·6 per cent in the 1920's, and 2·4 per cent in the 1930's. From 1948 it is negligible, e.g. it is 0·7 per cent in 1960–63. There are a number of factors, affecting both sides, which might account for the persistence of a significant discrepancy before the

1930's, but my impression is that, in general, it is due more to under-estimation of incomes than to over-estimation of expenditure. Possible causes of the former include inadequate allowance for evasion of tax on incomes from self-employment and trading profits, for non-wage incomes below the tax exemption limit and for the addition to wages and salaries from supplementary earnings. The first two of these are more likely sources of under-estimation than the third.

A second indication of the reliability of the component series can be obtained from subjective judgements of the 'range of reasonable doubt' attaching to the estimates. Such judgements have generally been made by those responsible for compiling the series underlying the estimates in Table 1 ; [1] they suggest that for the main components the probable margin of error is up to ±10 per cent before 1914 ; up to ±5 per cent for wages and salaries and ±5 to 10 per cent for other items in the inter-war years ; and up to ±3 per cent for wages, salaries, and trading profits from 1948 to 1963, but ±3 to 10 per cent for income from self-employment and rent.

3. *Sources Used*

(i) *Income estimates.* From 1946 all the basic series are official estimates (for 1946–59 from [6] and 1960–63 from [7]) except that the 'residual error' between the expenditure and income estimates of the gross domestic product has not been treated as a component of income.

For 1860–1938 the estimates are taken from or based on the following sources : [2]

Income from employment : 1870–1913 : Bowley [2] and Feinstein [10] ; [3] 1920–38 : Chapman [8].
Income from self-employment, profits, and rent : 1870–1913 : Feinstein [10] ; [3] 1920–38 : unpublished estimates by P. E. Hart [13] and by Feinstein.
Stock appreciation : 1870–1913 : no provision made ; 1921–38 : Feinstein [12].
Net property income from abroad : 1870–1913 : Imlah [14] ; 1920–1938 : Board of Trade.
Capital consumption : 1870–1913 : unpublished estimates by Feinstein ; 1920–38 : Feinstein [12].

(ii) *Employment estimates.* For 1946–63 estimates of the employed population are given in [4], together with estimates of the number of

[1] See for example [2], p. 74, [8], p. 234, and [5], pp. 36, 92, and 166–67.
[2] The estimates for 1870–1962 are (with a few very minor modifications) the same as those given on an annual basis in [11].
[3] It should be noted that the estimate of net national income in [10] is un-changed, but the classification of salaries, income from self-employment and trading profits has been appreciably revised.

The Distribution of National Income

employees. Estimates of the number of self-employed were derived
from these series and from the 1951 Census of Population. The numbers
of salary- and wage-earners underlying the national income estimates
of salaries and wages are not published, but an estimate of the breakdown
of the total number of employees was made for 1951 from the Census
and for 1961 from the *Ministry of Labour Gazette*, July 1962, p. 264.

For 1920–38 Chapman [*8*] gives separate estimates of the number of
wage- and salary-earning employees at work each year. Estimates of the
number of self-employed workers were derived from the 1921 and 1931
Census of Population.

Estimates for 1910–14 were based on Bowley's figures for 1901 and 1911
[*2*, p. 91] and [*3*, p. 7].

REFERENCES

[*1*] J. R. Bellerby, 'The Distribution of Manpower in Agriculture and
Industry, 1851–1951', *The Farm Economist*, ix, 1958.

[*2*] A. L. Bowley, *Wages and Income in the United Kingdom since 1860*
(1937).

[*3*] A. L. Bowley and J. Stamp, *Three Studies on the National Income*
(1938).

[*4*] Central Statistical Office, *Annual Abstract of Statistics* (1963).

[*5*] Central Statistical Office, *National Income Statistics, Sources and
Methods* (1956).

[*6*] Central Statistical Office, *National Income and Expenditure, 1963*
(1963).

[*7*] Central Statistical Office, *Preliminary Estimates of National Income
and Balance of Payments, 1963* (Cmnd. 2328, 1964).

[*8*] A. L. Chapman, *Wages and Salaries in the United Kingdom, 1920–1938*
(1953).

[*9*] G. A. Dean, 'The Stock of Fixed Capital in the United Kingdom in
1961', *Journal of the Royal Statistical Society*, 127 (Series A), 1964

[*10*] C. H. Feinstein, 'Income and Investment in the United Kingdom,
1856–1914', *Economic Journal*, lxxxi, 1961.

[*11*] C. H. Feinstein, 'National Income and Expenditure of the United
Kingdom, 1870–1962', *London and Cambridge Economic Bulletin*,
June 1964.

[*12*] C. H. Feinstein, *Domestic Capital Formation in the United Kingdom,
1920–1938* (1965).

[*13*] P. E. Hart, *Studies in Profits, Savings and Investment*, vol. i (1965).

[*14*] A. H. Imlah, *Economic Elements in the Pax Britannica* (1958).

[*15*] M. Kalecki, 'The Determinants of Distribution of the National
Income', *Econometrica*, 6, 1938.

[*16*] J. M. Keynes, 'Relative Movement of Real Wages and Output',
Economic Journal, xlix, 1939.

Feinstein — Income Distribution in the United Kingdom

[17] I. B. Kravis, 'Relative Income Shares in Fact and Theory, *American Economic Review*', xlix, 1959.

[18] London and Cambridge Economic Service, *Key Statistics of the British Economy, 1900–1962* (1963).

[19] E. V. Morgan, *Studies in British Financial Policy, 1914–1920* (1952).

[20] E. H. Phelps Brown and P. E. Hart, 'The Share of Wages in National Income', *Economic Journal*, lxii, 1952.

[21] E. H. Phelps Brown and B. Weber, 'Accumulation, Productivity and Distribution in the British Economy, 1870–1938', *Economic Journal*, lxiii, 1953.

[22] H. A. Rhee, *Rent of Agricultural Land in England and Wales, 1870–1946*, Central Landowners Association (1949).

[23] R. S. Sayers, *Financial Policy, 1939–45* (1956).

[24] R. Stone, *The Measurement of Consumers' Expenditure and Behaviour in the United Kingdom, 1920–38*, vol. i (1953).

DISCUSSION OF DR. FEINSTEIN'S PAPER

Professor Tress, introducing Dr. Feinstein's paper, said that he had noticed in the present Conference some pretty definite, competing theories : the disposition of the contributors on the facts of the mature, Western-type economies was to select for presentation those facts which were available in relation to these theories. Throughout his paper, Dr. Feinstein had thus concentrated his attention on those data which had bearing on the national income as initially generated in the productive process and its distribution between factor shares.

Professor Tress regretted that the single-mindedness of Dr. Feinstein's purpose had led him to omit from his study of income distribution in Britain all references to the size distribution of personal incomes, contrary to Professor Haley in his paper for the United States. Though Professor Tress knew that data on the distribution of family incomes by income brackets were sparse in the United Kingdom in comparison with the United States, he reminded his listeners that some official data based on raw figures relating to tax returns had been published for the periods before and since the Second World War : Dr. W. B. Reddaway had used these to essay estimates in the distribution of real income. Professor Tress admitted, however, that, as had been pointed out by Professor R. M. Titmus, tax avoidance made these data unreliable.

Regarding the data offered by Dr. Feinstein, Professor Tress wished to associate himself with Dr. Feinstein's own cautionary observations (p. 137 of the paper) on the tendency for the United Kingdom national income to be under-estimated before 1948. He had, however, a more critical comment to make regarding the presentation of data in averages for periods, generally of ten years before 1910 and of five years since, wars intervening. For three different reasons he would have liked to see the annual data brought into the study.

Firstly, as Dr. Feinstein drew attention at one stage in his paper (p. 127) to the 'faults' in the level of distributive shares occurring during and after each of the two world wars, he would have thought that one needed the annual data to identify these 'faults' as occurring at these specific dates. Secondly, Professor Tress would have thought them also necessary in so far as it might have been of interest to study the movements of relative incomes during the trade cycle, as an average figure over a whole period might conceal a downward and an upward movement of an income share alternating between the beginning and the end of the period.

Finally, Professor Tress had noticed that the figures in Tables 1 and 2 in the paper showed that gross trading profits as a proportion of the gross national product had fluctuated quite appreciably, even when expressed in quinquennial averages. As over the period 1946–63 the four five-years' average figures varied from 16·8 to 18 per cent, he thought that Dr. Feinstein's conclusion that the proportion had been stable about 18 per cent since 1946 and was 17 per cent in 1910–14 did not take sufficient account of the variability of the quinquennial data and perhaps of a still greater variability of the annual data from which they had been calculated. Professor Tress also wanted to underline the still greater dispersion of the quinquennial averages during the interwar period, when they ranged from 12·5 to 15 per cent and he did not think that the author had done full justice to these fluctuations of the share of profits in contenting himself with the statement that 'in the interwar years there was more deviation from the long-run share of 16–18 per cent' (p. 123 of the paper).

Professor Tress had noted that in Part III of his study Dr. Feinstein had attempted to derive an exhaustive pair of series for labour income and property income, although he had observed that the British data on the distribution of factor incomes actually related to institutional categories, i.e. wages and salaries from employment, income from self-employment profits and rents. Dr. Feinstein did this claiming that a two-fold division of incomes between a labour share and a property share would correspond more closely with the theoretical concept of the distribution of income among the factors of production. In this matter of a functional versus an institutional classification Professor Tress felt that he would rather fall in line with Professor J. Marchal's comments earlier that day. Professor Tress suspected that the familiar division of income into labour income and income from property was less a functional distinction between two types of factor income, from the services of labour and capital respectively, than it was a sociological distinction between 'workers' and 'owners'.

Supposing the distinction to be a functional one, Professor Tress suggested that one ought at least formally to recognize the need to extract the capital element in wages and salaries where an investment in education and training was involved; and to extract the labour element in profits where these accrue to an owner-entrepreneur as distinct from a sleeping shareholder. By the same token it was not satisfactory to classify all the income of professional persons within the self-employed class as being labour income, as did Dr. Feinstein on the score that they 'effectively employ no physical capital' (p. 125 of the paper).

In attempting to distribute the mixed income of self-employed between its labour and property components, Dr. Feinstein attributed to the labour component the income which a self-employed person would have received as a paid employee in the same sector of the economy, with the residual as the return to capital employed. While taking for granted that any procedure of this sort was arbitrary and admitted to be so, Professor Tress wondered whether it might not have been more realistic to apply a market rate of return to capital employed and to treat the residual as labour income. He would have preferred the alternative procedure. Not only had he noticed that Dr. Feinstein did this in the case of professional incomes where capital was assumed to be zero, but Professor Tress pointed out that in the case of small farmers and small shopkeepers it was often the family labour which was exploited for the sake of the parental capital.

Moreover, Professor Tress was puzzled by the results of Dr. Feinstein's method. As observed by Dr. Feinstein, the trend towards incorporation had been very pronounced; this should tend to leave the self-employed sector, other than the professions, increasingly to the small traders, 'with incomes very little larger than those of the average employee' in Dr. Feinstein's own words (p. 126). Professor Tress was thus somewhat puzzled to observe (p. 126 again) that Dr. Feinstein's rough estimates for 1960–63 produced a result in which the calculation on the basis of a capital return, the residual share being that of labour, was more favourable to labour than the calculation on the basis of an imputed wage which only gave to labour 74 per cent of self-employed income, comparing with 78 per cent with the former method.

Proceeding to Part IV of the paper, Professor Tress would restrict his comment in order not to trespass on the coming discussions of the theoretical papers with which this part of Dr. Feinstein's paper was closely related. He would comment on two points.

The first was a point of methodology. Dr. Feinstein had said that the decrease in the share of property income between 1910–14 and 1960–63 could be expressed as the outcome of two phenomena: a fall of about 50 per cent in the average rate of return on capital and a rise of 22 per cent in the relative price of capital goods, the second partly offsetting the effect of the first. Professor Tress only saw in this statement a problematical way of defining the variation of the share P/Y by means of formulating a simple identity of the form: $P/Y \equiv P/X \, . \, X/Y$ where X was not necessarily the capital (K) but any unknown that it had been chosen to introduce. Dr. Feinstein's statement might provide us with an hypothesis as to why that fall had happened, but it was not an explanation in itself.

If one thought that the quantity of capital affected the share of property income, Professor Tress suggested that the right procedure would be to formulate a regression equation with P/Y as the dependent variable and K as a determining variable (P. E. Hart had analysed the U.K. data for 1870–1960 in this way). Then one remained free to recognize that K was not the only significant variable.

Professor Tress believed that one could introduce other variables, including in particular institutional forces where these can be quantitatively represented. He cited especially the role of trade unions pressure which Kalecki brought into his later work and which Professor Phelps Brown and P. E. Hart also featured in their joint study. He pointed out that this had been lately analysed by A. G. Hines by relating trade union strength and the change in money wages. Trade unions pressure not only was measurable, but its expression should not be limited to a trend variable and one should try to take its fluctuations into account.

Professor Tress wanted to make a second main point : what could the British experience, as represented by Dr. Feinstein's data, tell us about what had been, in another paper to be discussed in a later session, described as 'magic constants' or 'stylized facts' of macro-economic distribution theory ? Personally he noted five features. First, within the last half-century the quantity of real capital had doubled while the working population had increased by only one-third. Second, allowing for the under-use of capital between the wars, the capital-output ratio had maintained its proverbial constancy at a ratio of about 4. Third, consistent with the relative move of 5 : 3 in the additions to capital and to labour, the real wage of labour had almost exactly doubled. Fourth, in contrast, the real rate of return on capital had fallen, with the result that the price of labour, relative to the price of capital, had risen more than threefold. Last, 'Bowley's law' of constant long-run relative shares of the national product going to labour and property did not hold : Dr. Feinstein had admitted that there was 'an unmistakable upward trend in labour's share' although he had considered it as almost entirely the result of the shifts or 'faults' which occurred during or immediately after the two world wars. Professor Tress thought that these were the facts as far as the British economy was concerned which any macro-economic theory of distribution had to accommodate.

Dr. Feinstein said he wished to make it clear that, having been asked to prepare a paper on facts, he had interpreted his commission as referring to functional and institutional distribution and not to size distribution. He also understood from the title of the paper he was asked to present that the phrase 'the evolution of the distribution of national income' referred to a long-run study, leaving aside annual data and thus, as he thought that cyclical fluctuations were outside his brief, he did not want to go into a discussion of this subject. About the breaks or 'faults' in the evolution, Professor Tress might well have been right in suggesting one needed them to explain these peculiarities ; unfortunately figures did not exist on a comparable basis for the two periods when the breaks occurred, that is when one would have liked to have been able to compare what had happened year by year.

Concerning the division of self-employed people's incomes between labour and capital Dr. Feinstein was not sure that it was fruitful to discuss various methods knowing they were all arbitrary. None of them was satisfactory, yet he thought that if one limited the scope of the study to industries where self-employment was not important, as was the case in manufacturing, this arbitrariness tended to be less significant.

Dr. Feinstein was in agreement with Professor Tress when he stated that identities were not explanations. It was true that he used the word 'explanation' in Table 18, but he purposely put it in inverted commas, not suggesting that he was providing an explanation when he just meant to indicate a direction for further research towards an explanation of the observed changes. He had indeed no satisfactory explanation to offer about the sudden upwards shifts in the labour share during the war periods. Disagreeing with Professor Tress, he did not think, however, that a severe fall of real returns on capital provided the explanation which was sought, even assuming that the amplitude of the change would have been sufficient.

Professor Robinson returned to one of Professor Tress's criticisms of Dr. Feinstein. Professor Tress had challenged Dr. Feinstein's use of averages of five- and ten-year periods : was that general criticism, or had Professor Tress grounds for thinking that there had actually been significant year-by-year variations ?

Professor Tress answered that his comment was meant to be interrogative. He did not know whether there had been such variations and it was the use of averages itself which provoked him into putting the question as he had noticed that the data related to a limited number of years for the pre-war period in comparison with the later period : he wondered whether averaging over a number of years would have been significant in such a case.

While admitting that the interpretation of the data was made more difficult by the occurrence of the cyclical movements, *Dr. Feinstein* reminded him that the purpose of his study had been to give an account of what had happened to the wages and profits shares over the whole period of the last fifty years.

Professor Patinkin declared himself in agreement with Dr. Feinstein's statement that a year-by-year study was not significant when what was intended was to ascertain a trend over the long period.

It still seemed to *Professor Tress* that there was a difference, when referring to a constant, according to which sort one meant : whether a constant which fluctuated year by year or a constant which was not affected by cyclical variations. Both sorts were actually to be found in the macro-economic theory of distribution and it seemed to him that there was some point in making it clear whether one meant the first sort relating to data which were not apparently constant but could be considered as such provided a correction factor was applied.

Dr. Feinstein said that he had thought of constants in terms of long-run trends, around which there would be year-to-year fluctuations.

This debate on how to interpret constancies led *Professor Patinkin* to put a question referring to Table 2 in the paper : in it the proportion of wages was a constant and the whole increase in the labour share appeared to be due to rising salaries. Considering the different ways the two components of the labour share had behaved it seemed to him of importance to make clear on which ground the distinction between the two kinds of labour income had been based : was it simply on the difference between payments by the hour and payments by the week ; or was it on a classification by occupational categories ? If the distinction was according to the second criterion it seemed to imply that the investment of capital into human beings had been going on in a steady way while the remuneration of unskilled work had remained constant.

Dr. Feinstein answered that the distinction was based solely on occupational categories but he did not think this was the explanation for the difference in relative shares because the wage-earners' category was not limited to unskilled workers. Indeed some wage-earners were more highly skilled than many salary-earners.

Professor Patinkin replied, pointing out that to him the question was more complex : was a miner, for instance, today using the same skill as formerly, or had he acquired new skill ? This was really the issue and he wondered whether there was not a real difference in investment in human capital between wage-earners and salary-earners on that account.

To this comment *Dr. Feinstein* answered that so far as he knew there was no evidence to establish the answer to this question.

Professor Solow asked whether a salaried worker was defined by reference to an occupational class, irrespective of the way the worker was paid. *Dr. Feinstein* answered that it was so. The division between salaries and wages did not line up with any other distinction.

Professor Robinson pointed out that the importance of design staffs was increasing in modern industries to such a point that there might perhaps soon be the same problems of redundancy with them as with operational workers. As design staff were included in salary-earners this was one of the reasons why there was an increasing proportion of salaried workers in the working force.

Professor Solow added that in the last hundred years when the salary share in the gross national product had been multiplied by four, the number of salary-earners had also been multiplied by four while the number of wage-earners had remained constant.

Professor Gannagé, who was in favour of a threefold classification of income on account of the arbitrariness of the methods used to allocate mixed incomes between a labour share and a property share, had noticed that in order to do this Dr. Feinstein had defined property income in a different way from Professor Ohkawa in the next paper to be discussed. A methodological problem was involved : how should the income to be imputed to capital of the self-employed people be determined ?

Dr. Feinstein replied that no matter how imperfect were the methods of allocation, the division between labour and property shares seemed to him to be necessary in any case as a threefold distinction made it impossible to determine what was the comparative evolution of incomes out of labour and incomes out of capital.

Concerning the problem of the share of capital in the incomes of one of the groups of self-employed, the farmers, *Professor Robinson* had noticed that the data provided by Dr. Feinstein were in gross terms. This meant that part of the income was then in the form of depreciation allowances for wear and tear of machinery, and the more so when machinery was short-lived, as was the case with agricultural implements. He had been much interested by the data which Professor Lecaillon made available in one of the papers previously discussed, which were also data in gross terms ; they showed the high level of French farmers' savings in proportion to their incomes and yet as Professor Lecaillon had been led to point out during the discussion of his paper, this surprisingly high level of French farmers' propensity to save was in part certainly the result of the calculation having been done in gross terms. In the British instance, also, one could suppose that the gross incomes of farmers included a substantial proportion of allowances for capital depreciation and their comparison with incomes of other groups might have led to different conclusions if it had applied to data in net terms. He thought that in any case reasoning on gross data brought in one more difficulty in interpreting the results.

Professor Krelle would have liked to see how the figures Dr. Feinstein gave on p. 116 and p. 117 in his paper compared with figures produced by Professor Phelps Brown in his 1952 study on distribution. In the latter the proportion of wage-earners' incomes was found to be fairly stable. Professor Krelle wanted to know to what extent the two sets of data led to similar conclusions. Did Dr. Feinstein ascribe the increasing share of labour to the rising number of employees in industry ? And was the share of workers, in the restricted sense of being the share of wage-earners, stable ?

Dr. Feinstein stated that the figures in Table 2 of his paper corresponded to Professor Phelps Brown's. He had divided labour income between wages and salaries and the share of wages did seem stable ; yet the distinction between the two categories did not correspond closely with any other economic or social distinction, and he did not feel that the occupational classification was sufficient justification for hypotheses which depended on the stability of the share of wages and ignored the increasing share of salaries.

The question put by Professor Krelle led *Professor Bronfenbrenner* to wonder whether the Marxian theory remained as it was originally, classifying salaries as part of the surplus value, only the wages of manual workers being classed as labour income. He wondered what would have been the outcome of a calculation of labour income on the British data according to this principle. He pointed out that the Labour Research Association in the United States was engaged in a recalculation of American data on the 'Marxian' basis.

Dr. Bruzek pointed out that in Marxian analysis the distinction to which Professor Bronfenbrenner had referred could not be reduced to a clear-cut distinction between salaries and wages. The former were as a matter of principle paid out of surplus value but there were exceptions to the rule. If a technician was working in a factory in such a way that what he did had repercussions on the material product, his work was a productive one and consequently his salary was of the same kind as the remuneration of a wage-earner. On the other hand if the same technician had a job which meant that he did not contribute to the formation of the material product, then the rule would apply : what he earned was truly a salary and what he produced was not even value. It was thus the contribution to material production which ruled the division between productive and non-productive work, but this was a very difficult distinction in practice.

Mrs. Zala observed that, although the share of self-employment was nowadays negligible in the Hungarian economy, a few years ago economists in her country had still been concerned with making a distinction between labour and property incomes in the self-employment sector, and this for two reasons.

First, farmers' incomes fluctuated to a remarkable degree from one year to the next as did the crops. However, farmers' expenditure on consumption remained fairly stable. So the Hungarian economists deemed it right to assume that the consumption expenditure of farmers tended to correspond to their labour earnings while the fluctuating part of their income was treated as the return on property.

Second, in order to make long-run comparisons as to the respective evolutions of labour and property incomes it was necessary to remove the effects of structural changes in the social system on the shares of labour and property. This was done through the same method as the one used by Dr. Feinstein in his paper. Only in such a way did it become possible to make long-run comparisons in a country like Hungary where agriculture had gone rapidly through rather momentous structural changes in the recent past.

Professor Solow wanted to make further comments on the breaks occurring in the series, though they had already been mentioned in the discussion, as he thought it interesting to try and find some explanation.

He first intended to comment on the change in the rate of return on capital : what were the reasons for such a sudden drop as the one mentioned in Tables 8 and 9? Although his knowledge of the economic history of Britain was limited, he thought it correct to say that the whole decade of the twenties had been a period of depression in the United Kingdom and it was well known that the rate of profit on capital was sensitive to the rate of its utilization : had that decade been less depressed the trend would have been smoother.

Second, he wondered whether U.K. social accounting procedures were as quaint as those of the United States where the output of government operations was measured solely by the input of labour employed in this sector. If it was so in Britain, a sharp increase in government product happening during each of the two war periods might have explained the drops in the share of capital occurring in the same periods.

Dr. Feinstein answered that in the United Kingdom a large part of government operations was also measured in terms of labour input. He did not think, however, that this had been determinant and that excluding government activities would be enough to eliminate the observed increase in employees' share.

On the first point raised by Professor Solow, *Professor Robinson* admitted that, obviously, the twenties were a period of depression in, for instance, cotton, steel, and coal, as compared with 1913. This, however, was not the point really in question. The real problem was : why was it that when conditions much similar to those in the 1910–14 period had prevailed again in recent years, the return on capital had not yet come back to the 10 per cent rate which prevailed in that period ?

Professor Patinkin asked Dr. Feinstein the reasons that had led him (p. 129 of his paper) to take out incomes transferred from overseas, and also rents. Had these items been put into the evaluation the secular trend in the labour share would have continued to prevail. So he would have preferred to see them included, especially in the case of a country like Britain where foreign investments were a characteristic feature.

Though reminding Professor Patinkin that he had kept overseas incomes in the figures of Table 5, *Dr. Feinstein* said he had preferred to leave them out in order to restrict himself to the study of domestic income and the domestic stock of capital relating to it. He had meant to study not the national income, but the income distribution within the country. Concerning rents, he pointed out that his reason for excluding them was that these were the sort of income which had been most interfered with by the government since the First World War.

Professor Patinkin wondered whether these measures of control had been really effective as the practice of 'key money' tended to prove the contrary. If the effect of these measures had been to fix rents at a level lower than market price would it not have been better to apply a correction factor rather than to exclude the whole of rents from the evaluation ?

147

The Distribution of National Income

Dr. Feinstein observed in reply that this was inconsistent with the usual procedures of social accounting and that one simply did not know what would have been the position in the absence of rent control. The alternative was either to study the evolution of income excluding rents or to study it including the rents at their official rate.

Professor Rasmussen pointed out that this problem was rather similar to, for instance, the one connected with the treatment of monopoly profits in the national accounts when from certain points of view it was thought advisable to exclude the monopoly element in them. It might have been difficult to estimate hypothetically what the total of rents would have been without control, but he thought that even a rough estimate might have been preferable to excluding the item altogether.

Dr. Feinstein summed up his position by stating that although he might concede that for certain reasons one might have preferred leaving the rents in, he still thought that, in that case, they ought to be at their official rates, without any correction.

Chapter 5

THE DISTRIBUTION OF NATIONAL INCOME IN BELGIUM, 1953-62[1]

BY

M. FALISE

Centre de Recherches Économiques et de Gestion, Lille

I. INTRODUCTORY

RESEARCH on the distribution of income is of fairly recent origin in Belgium. The problem did come up more than once in connection with other work,[2] but nobody investigated the facts systematically until the Department of Applied Economics in the University of Brussels began to do so.[3] Its work became both a stimulus and a help in drawing up official national accounts ; the results were published in 1963 and cover the period 1953-62.

Given the fragmentary nature of earlier information, the paper which follows concentrates on the same period ; an attempt will be made to present and interpret the principal features of the structure of income and its changes.

A brief outline in Section II of the characteristics of the Belgian economy and of its course during the ten years under consideration will be followed by a presentation of the essential facts emerging from the national accounts (Section III : The Facts).

These overall results will then be interpreted in terms of current theory ; this will show up the difficulties of adapting the neo-Keynesian theory of income distribution to the Belgian economy and, more generally, to the economy of any country heavily dependent upon foreign trade (Section IV : Tentative Interpretation).

Finally, partial analysis more in line with neo-classical theory will deal with differential movements of profits, wages, and productivity

---

[1] Translation from the French by Elizabeth Henderson.
[2] See, in particular, D. Crespi, *Les Salaires belges*, Colin, Paris, 1960; M. Frank, *Analyse macro-économique de la fiscalité belge*, Brussels, 1960; L. Dupriez, *Monetary Reconstruction in Belgium*, New York, 1947, and the annual estimates of national income and its components in *Bulletin de l'Institut de Recherches Économiques et Sociales de l'Université de Louvain*.
[3] *Cahiers économiques de Bruxelles*, especially Nos. 2, 16, 17.

149

in a number of separate sectors (Section V: Partial Analysis). This paper, therefore, is not concerned with the mere presentation of facts, but will try to apply some modern distribution theories to a specific situation.

II. RECENT TRENDS OF THE BELGIAN ECONOMY

The economy of Belgium displays all the structural characteristics of a mature industrial country. Industrial activities as a whole — including mining and quarrying, manufacturing industry, electricity, gas and water, building, transport and communications — accounted for half the national product in 1962; agriculture contributed no more than 6·6 per cent, and services are highly developed. The changes since 1953 were those one would expect in a highly industrialized country: relative contraction of the primary sector (mining and quarrying, agriculture, forestry, and fisheries accounted for 12·9 per cent of the national product in 1953 and for 9 per cent in 1962); stability of the share of manufacturing industry (31 and 31·1 per cent, respectively), of the combined share of electricity, gas, and water (2·1 per cent) and of transport and communications (7·9 and 8·3 per cent respectively); development of the tertiary sector (38·8 and 41·5 per cent respectively).[1]

As has been shown, among others, by A. Lamfalussy,[2] the traditional sectors play an important part in industrial activity. In 1956, mining and quarrying, the textile, and the base metal industries together provided 44 per cent of industrial output, as against 20·1 per cent in the United Kingdom and 23·1 per cent in the OECD countries as a whole. The proportion is somewhat less nowadays, as a result of the sharp relative decline of mining and quarrying and the less pronounced one of the textile industry; but it is still higher than the average of European countries. In 1962 the first-named group of industries still contributed about one-third of the value added by all extractive and manufacturing industry.

As regards the use of domestic resources, the share of private consumption fell slightly from 71·4 per cent in 1953 to 68·8 per cent in 1962; gross domestic capital formation, though subject to considerable cyclical fluctuations, increased its share of the total

---

[1] *Bulletin de l'Institut National de Statistique*, June 1963, p. 1205.
[2] A. Lamfalussy, *Investment and Growth in Mature Economies*, Macmillan, London, 1961.

from 15·9 to 19·3 per cent, while the proportion of public consumption expenditure remained more or less stable (between 10 and 12 per cent). Over the period under consideration, the Belgian economy has also become more and more open : in 1953 the country exported 29·4 per cent of its national product, in 1962 36·3 per cent, and the corresponding import figures show a similar increase from 29·1 to 36 per cent of GNP.[1]

Belgium is traditionally a free trade country, with low tariffs and few as well as lenient quantitative import restrictions. With the advent of the Common Market, the country opened up even more to foreign trade, especially with its fellow members of the EEC. The structure of Belgium's exports is fashioned by its industry ; they consist largely of marginal supplies of semi-finished and standardized goods with a high price elasticity, and export demand is supported in large part by the importing countries' inability to produce enough to meet a rapid expansion of domestic demand.[2]

From 1953 until 1960 the dominant trend was one of relative deflation, but lately it flattened out somewhat. In 1959 the index of gross national product in 1953 francs was 116·2 (1953=100), which implies the rather slow growth rate of 2·6 per cent ; in 1962, the index was 131·4, as a result of more rapid expansion.

At the same time, prices rose less than anywhere else among the OECD countries (with reference to the base year 1953, the retail price index was 112·6 in 1962 in Belgium, 144·7 in France, 130·7 in the United Kingdom, 118·3 in Germany and 113·4 in the United States).[3]

Balance-of-payments surpluses raised official reserves from 859 million dollars at the end of 1953 to £1,622 million at the end of 1962 — an increase far in excess of the increase in the stock of money and quasi-money or in capital inflow. The situation of relative deflation was reflected also in fairly high unemployment, which was to all intents and purposes mopped up during boom periods (1957 and 1962), but was as high as 5 to 6 per cent of the labour force during the years of recession.

A last important point to note is the high sensitivity of the Belgian economy to cyclical fluctuations. The index of industrial production dropped from 124 to 116 in Belgium between 1957 and 1958, whereas

[1] *Bulletin de l'Institut National de Statistique*, June 1963, pp. 1241–1242.
[2] A. Lamfalussy, 'Essai sur la croissance économique et la balance des paiements de la Belgique', *Bulletin de l'Institut de Recherches Économiques et Sociales de l'Université de Louvain*, March 1959.
[3] OECD General Statistics, September 1953.

it remained stationary in the Netherlands and continued to climb, though more slowly than before, in France, Germany, and Italy. A similar situation had developed in 1952–53. This high sensitivity is explained by the weak expansion of domestic demand and the strong dependence of exports upon a sustained rate of growth in the principal buyer countries.

The development of industrial production and GNP (in 1953 francs) during the period under consideration is shown in Table 1.

TABLE 1

INDICES OF INDUSTRIAL PRODUCTION AND GNP
IN BELGIUM, 1953–62

	1953	1954	1955	1956	1957	1958	1959	1960	1961	1962
Industrial Production	100	106	116	123	124	116	122	129	135	143
Gross National Product	100	103·8	105·6	112·3	115·4	114·2	116·2	122·5	126·5	131·4

These, then, are the principal features of the Belgian economy relevant for an explanation of the process of distribution of income : industrialization is advanced but the structure of industry is old ; relative deflation is evident in a low growth rate and high unemployment ; the economy is highly sensitive to cyclical fluctuations and to all intents and purposes enjoys price stability, while foreign reserves are getting more and more plentiful. When we speak of relative deflation, this applies to the average of the ten years under consideration ; obviously, the statement is less true of the boom years and especially today, in the general situation of overall employment throughout Europe. Lastly, the economy of Belgium is greatly — and increasingly — dependent upon foreign trade, and the high price elasticity of Belgian exports is an important aspect to be taken into account in discussing global adaptation processes in income distribution.

III. TOTAL ANALYSIS, PART I: THE FACTS

The relative incomes shares accruing to the different factors of production during the period 1953–62 are shown in Table 2.[1]

[1] *Bulletin de l'Institut National de Statistique*, June 1963, p. 1227.

The figures reveal a number of major tendencies.

(1) The wages share has grown considerably, from 53·8 to 58·6 per cent. The increase has taken place largely at the expense of the incomes of individual entrepreneurs and companies (other than joint stock companies), that is, in practice, farmers, traders and independent artisans ; their combined income share dropped from 29·4 to 25·1 per cent.

These figures are a reflection mainly of a structural change in the labour force. Official Belgian statistics provide no annual estimates of the labour force, but according to a recent study by the Ministry of Employment and Labour [1] the index of the number of wage-earners rose from 101·84 in 1953 (1948 = 100) to 108·97 in 1960, while the index of the labour force dropped from 103·29 to 103·11. Between 1953 and 1960, therefore, the proportion of wage-earners in the labour force rose from 66·9 to 71·7 per cent.

The increase in the wages share therefore corresponds more or less to the increase in the proportion of wage-earners in the labour force. We shall discuss later what implications this has for the theoretical interpretation of income distribution in terms of the shares of labour incomes and capital incomes respectively. But it is immediately obvious that in the light of this structural change these shares were in fact more constant than the figures of Table 2 suggest. Here, then, is a first fact to underline. The share of mixed capital-and-labour incomes (farmers, traders, artisans, and companies other than joint stock companies) contracted to the benefit of the wages share, largely as a result of population transfers or changes in juridical status.

Looking more closely to see what sectors are responsible for this transformation, we note the dominant part played by the outflow of manpower from agriculture. Between 1953 and 1960 the number of independent workers and employers diminished by 70,000 ; [2] of these 68,000 came from agriculture, forestry and fisheries, and 18,000 from trade, banking, and insurance, while their number increased by 17,000 in services and contracted slightly in manufacturing industry. What happened was clearly that manpower diminished and productivity per head increased in agriculture and trade.

(2) Within the wage bill itself, the most significant fact is the growing proportion of indirect wages : employers' social insurance

---

[1] *Aperçu de l'évolution de la population active belge pour la période 1948–1960*, pp. 80–81 and 134–135.
[2] Ministry of Employment and Labour, *op. cit.* (footnote 1), pp. 58–95.

TABLE 2

DISTRIBUTION OF NATIONAL INCOME AMONG FACTORS OF PRODUCTION

(Per cent)

	1953	1954	1955	1956	1957	1958	1959	1960	1961	1962
1. LABOUR INCOMES										
(a) Wages and salaries of workers subject to social insurance	30·7	30·2	30·2	30·7	31·6	31·9	31·5	31·2	31·3	32·5
(b) Incomes of workers subject to certain special social insurance provisions	2·3	2·3	2·3	2·4	2·4	2·5	2·4	2·5	2·6	2·6
(c) Employers' contributions to social insurance	4·8	4·7	4·9	5·0	5·5	5·6	5·4	5·6	6·0	6·2
(d) Incomes of workers not subject to social insurance	12·5	12·4	12·6	12·3	12·3	13·4	13·6	13·5	13·3	13·6
(e) Adjustments, errors, and omissions	3·5	3·3	3·1	3·4	4·0	3·9	3·8	4·3	3·7	3·7
Total of Labour Income	53·8	52·9	53·1	53·8	55·8	57·3	56·7	57·1	56·9	58·6
2. MIXED LABOUR-AND-CAPITAL INCOMES										
(a) Farming, gardening, and forestry	5·8	5·4	5·3	4·8	5·3	4·9	5·1	4·9	5·5	4·6
(b) Liberal professions	2·5	2·6	2·5	2·5	2·4	2·6	2·7	2·7	2·7	2·7
(c) Traders, independent artisans, and companies *	20·5	20·7	20·4	19·9	18·4	18·1	18·4	17·9	17·8	17·6
(d) Adjustments	0·6	0·5	0·3	0·4	0·7	0·7	0·5	0·7	0·5	0·2
Total : Mixed Incomes	29·4	29·2	28·5	27·6	26·8	26·3	26·7	26·2	26·5	25·1
3. WHOLLY CAPITAL INCOMES										
(a) Interests	3·0	3·2	3·3	3·4	3·4	3·7	3·9	4·1	4·3	4·5
(b) Rent	8·5	9·1	8·8	8·4	8·0	8·0	7·9	7·3	7·1	6·6
(c) Dividends, profit shares, gifts	2·7	2·6	2·8	3·1	3·1	2·9	2·6	2·8	3·0	3·0
Total : Capital Incomes	14·2	14·9	14·9	14·9	14·5	14·6	14·4	14·2	14·4	14·1
4. UNDISTRIBUTED COMPANY PROFITS	2·0	2·6	3·3	3·3	2·4	1·7	2·4	2·5	2·9	2·7
5. DIRECT COMPANY TAXATION	2·1	1·9	1·8	2·1	2·0	1·8	1·7	2·0	1·8	1·8
6. PUBLIC CAPITAL INCOMES AND PROFITS FROM PUBLIC ENTERPRISE	1·0	1·1	1·1	1·0	1·2	1·0	1·0	1·1	1·0	1·0
7. INTEREST ON THE PUBLIC DEBT	− 2·5	− 2·6	− 2·7	− 2·7	− 2·7	− 2·7	− 2·9	− 3·1	− 3·5	− 3·3
Net National Income at factor cost	100·0	100·0	100·0	100·0	100·0	100·0	100·0	100·0	100·0	100·0

* Other than joint stock companies.

154

contributions accounted for 4·8 per cent of national income in 1953 and for 6·2 per cent in 1962. Even then, these figures represent only employers' payments with respect to their own workers, and exclude all transfer payments, social security or otherwise, which accrue to wage-earners through the redistributive mechanism of public finance. But these, too, have grown rapidly, as shown in Table 3.[1]

TABLE 3

CURRENT INCOMES OF INDIVIDUALS

	Receipts per cent of Total									
	1953	1954	1955	1956	1957	1958	1959	1960	1961	1962
Wage-earnings	49·2	48·7	49·1	50	51·8	51·7	50·7	51·4	51	52·5
Earnings of individual entrepreneurs and companies (other than joint stock)	27	27	26·6	26·5	25	23·6	24	23·6	23·6	22·4
Capital incomes accruing to individuals	13	13·7	13·9	13·8	13·4	13·4	12·9	12·8	12·8	12·6
Social security transfers to wage earners and independent workers	7·4	7·6	7·3	7·4	7·6	8·7	9·7	9·3	9·6	9·6
Other net current transfers from the state	3·2	2·8	2·9	2·2	2·1	2·3	2·2	2·4	2·4	2·3
Current transfers from the rest of the world	0·2	0·2	0·2	0·1	0·1	0·3	0·5	0·5	0·6	0·7
Total	100	100	100	100	100	100	100	100	100	100

Social security transfers have risen from 7·4 to 9·6 per cent of individual incomes, the increase being only partly offset by a relative decline of other current transfers from the state. Table 3, incidentally, confirms the conclusions drawn from Table 2 : the wages share has increased, the share of mixed incomes has declined, and the proportion of capital incomes has remained constant.

(3) Capital incomes accruing to individuals, generally speaking, acount for a remarkably stable share of national income. However, there were certain divergent developments within this composite item. The proportion of interests has risen in connection with the higher propensity to save at rising standards of living (private consumption expenditure absorbed 79 per cent of current expenditure by individuals in 1953, and the figure then dropped steadily to 75·5 per cent in 1962), and in connection also with a relative shift of savings to time deposits, special deposits, and savings deposits, away

[1] *Bulletin de l'Institut National de Statistique, op. cit.* p. 1258.

from less remunerative current accounts. The proportion of dividends, profit shares, and gifts was subject to slight cyclical fluctuations, while that of rent has had a falling tendency, especially since 1959. This latter appears attributable mainly to the market situation, in so far as a growing supply of housing enabled demand to be met without upward pressure on rents.

(4) The share of undistributed company profits fluctuated sharply, with a drop from 3·3 per cent in 1956 to 1·7 per cent in 1958. Like dividends and profit shares, this item is governed mainly by general business conditions, but undistributed profits fluctuate more than distributed ones, because companies tend to keep their dividend distributions as stable as possible.

(5) The share of direct company taxation follows business conditions with a time lag, which is easily explained by the delays of tax collection. Generally speaking, the share is very stable, as is also the share of public capital incomes and profits from public enterprise. Interest on the public debt has been accounting for a slightly rising proportion, especially during the last three years; this implies that the public debt rose faster than national income.

Public expenditure in Belgium accounts for a mounting portion of total expenditure and hence plays an important part in sustaining economic activity. Between 1953 and 1962, government expenditure at current prices increased by 80 per cent, whereas the corresponding figure for private expenditure is 52·3 per cent.

(6) These last figures underline the redistributive functions of public finance, which have become more and more important over the course of the ten years under consideration. Table 4 shows the composition of current government revenue and expenditure.[1]

As was noted before, the share of social security charges in total current revenue has risen, and so has the share of social security transfers in total current expenditure. The proportion of revenue from direct taxation contracted even more in the case of companies than of individuals, in spite of progressive income taxes on a growing national income. Part of the explanation is, no doubt, widespread tax evasion; but it is also true that in times of reasonable social stability the public authorities have no particular reason for raising the rates of direct taxes and find it easier to increase the proceeds of indirect taxation, which in any event grow spontaneously thanks to the rapid expansion of the consumption of certain heavily taxed goods, such as luxury goods, alcohol, petrol, and others.

[1] *Bulletin de l'Institut National de Statistique, op. cit.* p. 1257.

TABLE 4

A. PERCENTAGE COMPOSITION OF CURRENT EXPENDITURE

	1953	1954	1955	1956	1957	1958	1959	1960	1961	1962
Public consumption	57	57	52	50	47·10	52·46	51·25	51·70	48·60	49·10
Subsidies	3·78	5·50	4·16	6·01	5·48	5·81	5·10	4·82	4·55	4·82
Social security transfers to wage-earners and independent workers	31	32·70	29·65	30·10	29·56	34·70	37·21	35·80	35·20	34·64
Other net current transfers to individuals, including non-profit making private institutions	13·32	11·40	11·67	9·14	8·26	8·85	8·36	9·15	8·85	8·10
Current transfers to the rest of the world	0·12	0·40	0·37	0·28	0·25	0·24	0·14	0·24	0·06	
Public saving	− 5·22	− 7	+2·16	4·47	9·35	− 2·27	− 2·16	− 1·61	+2·56	+3·28
Total	100	100	100	100	100	100	100	100	100	100

B. PERCENTAGE COMPOSITION OF CURRENT REVENUE

	1953	1954	1955	1956	1957	1958	1959	1960	1961	1962
Capital income and profits from public enterprise	3·8	4·4	4	3·8	4·3	3·5	3·5	3·9	3·4	3·1
Less : interest on the public debt	− 9·6	− 10·1	− 10·3	− 10·2	− 9·8	− 9·8	− 9·9	− 10·6	− 11·4	− 10·4
Indirect taxes	45·1	46	47	47·5	45·7	46·6	48	48·5	50	49·2
Direct taxes on individuals (including non-profit-making private institutions)	28·8	26·6	26·7	25·5	26·3	25·4	26·4	24·6	25·4	26·4
Social security charges with respect to wage-earners (workers' and employers' contributions) and independent workers	23·3	24·6	25	25	25·7	27·6	25·9	26·7	26·6	26
Direct taxes on all companies regardless of juridical status	8·1	7·6	6·8	7·7	7·3	6·5	6	6·8	6	5·5
Current transfers from the rest of the world	0·5	0·9	0·8	0·7	0·5	0·2	0·1	0·1	0	0
Total	100	100	100	100	100	100	100	100	100	100

157

IV. TOTAL ANALYSIS, PART II: TENTATIVE INTERPRETATION

The mere presentation of the major facts concerning the Belgian economy has already, in most cases, brought to mind a plausible explanation. But we should like to go beyond these isolated interpretations and attempt a coherent analysis of the behaviour of the principal variables, that is, profits, wages, the profit and wages share in national income, productivity, employment, prices, and foreign trade. We shall proceed along two lines: first, we shall examine how far the observed facts fit into a neo-Keynesian model of income distribution, and then we shall suggest another type of analysis which seems to us more suitable for the Belgian economy.

A. *A Neo-Keynesian Model — Statistical and Logical Difficulties*

The theory to which we refer more particularly here is that put forward by Nicholas Kaldor on more than one occasion,[1] and developed further by Luigi Pasinetti.[2] However, Pasinetti's refinements make the theory even more difficult to apply to empirical data, and in any event, our conclusions apply equally to the Kaldor and Pasinetti versions.

Let us briefly recall the main features of Kaldor's model. The data are:

Y national income

W wages

P profits

β wage-earners' marginal propensity to save

α profit-earners' marginal propensity to save

$S_W = W$ wage-earners' saving

$S_p = P$ profit-earners' saving

---

[1] See especially 'Alternative Theories of Distribution', *Review of Economic Studies*, vol. xxiii, no. 2, March 1956, pp. 94–100; 'A Model of Economic Growth', *Economic Journal*, vol. lxvii, no. 268, December 1957, pp. 591–624; 'Economic Growth and the Problem of Inflation', *Economica*, August 1959. Compare also J. Marchal's report to the Congress of French language Economists, *Revue d'Économie Politique*, 1960.

[2] L. Pasinetti, 'Rate of Profit and Income Distribution in Relation to the Rate of Economic Growth', *Review of Economic Studies*, October 1962, pp. 267–280.

The basic equation is

$$I - S = S_W + S_P = \alpha P + \beta(Y - P) \tag{1}$$

$$= (\alpha - \beta)P + \beta Y$$

hence

$$\frac{I}{Y} = (\alpha - \beta)\frac{P}{Y} + \beta \tag{2}$$

and

$$\frac{P}{Y} = \frac{I}{Y} \cdot \frac{1}{\alpha - \beta} - \frac{\beta}{\alpha - \beta}.$$

This means that the share of profits (and, consequently, of wages) in national income depends upon the marginal propensity to save both of wage-earners and profit-earners, as well as upon the ratio of investment to income. Assuming the coefficients α and β to be constant, P/Y is all the higher the higher is I/Y. In Kaldor's analysis, I/Y is the independent variable, and if we assume that in a growing economy this variable I/Y remains constant beyond a certain level of development, the respective income shares of wages and profits do not change either.

Adaptation comes about through the mechanism of demand variations in relation to supply assumed to be inelastic in the presence of full employment of the factors of production, the demand variations themselves being attributable to investment variations. If investment, and with it demand, increases, prices rise in relation to costs, and so do profits and the income share of profits. Since profit-earners have a higher propensity to save than wage-earners, saving increases and so adapts itself to investment.

Thus we have two independent relations, the significance of which we shall test with reference to the Belgian economy :

(1) Demand variations attributable to investment variations ;
(2) Demand variations leading to corresponding price and profit variations.

Two main facts have to be checked against empirical results.

(1) Do I/Y and P/Y vary in the same direction ?
(2) Are the income shares of profits and wages constant ?

We have no statistical data in Belgium which would allow us to estimate the coefficients α and β. But if we assume with Kaldor that they are constant, I/Y and P/Y must move in the same direction, and this is a matter which we can verify statistically. We have figures for gross domestic capital formation during the period 1953–62, and so it was possible to calculate the ratio I/Y. To estimate the ratio P/Y, we used two different series :

(a) capital incomes only (private capital), incomes and undistributed company profits — items 3 and 4 in Table 2 ;

(b) incomes under (a) plus mixed incomes (item 2 in Table 2), after correcting the latter for the structural changes in the labour force mentioned earlier.[1]

In both cases we found near-zero correlation, the changes in P/Y and I/Y having been in the same direction for five of the years considered and in opposite directions for four years ; nor did we get any better results with lagged correlation. Aggregate statistics relating to the Belgian economy do not confirm a correlation between P/Y and I/Y.

There is nothing to suggest that a more refined analysis would reveal the facts to fit Kaldor's analysis any better. The Belgian economy has certain characteristics which make it unamenable to neo-Keynesian distribution theories. First of all, the existence of margins of underemployment during large parts of the period caused the increase in demand to be translated into an increase in production and employment rather than into price rises. But even during the full-employment years 1956 and 1957 we found no parallelism between P/Y and I/Y. The explanation lies in the very open nature of the Belgian economy.

Exports absorb nearly twice as much of national product than does gross capital formation, and they are also the motive element in the economy and the first to feel the impact of cyclical fluctuations. In other words, the influence of investment on demand is weak.

Furthermore, the high price elasticity of exports, low import tariffs, and the traditional nature of a considerable part of economic activities combine to keep the Belgian economy permanently in a state of international competition in sectors where price changes very quickly lead to opposite demand changes. The Belgian economy enjoys little protection, either institutional or natural, and as a result prices are very stable.

It has been seen that the period 1953–62 was one of relative deflation for the Belgian economy. Since absolute price rises in Belgium were less than in the principal competing countries, no

---

[1] We divided successive indices of the real wage bill by the corresponding indices of the ratio of wage-earners to a practically constant labour force. In this way we recalculated W/Y and P/Y without the influence of the structural change in the labour force.

Kaldor-type relation — which implies that demand increases raise prices and, hence, profits — can have been at work, even at times of full employment.

On the contrary, when unemployment had practically disappeared in 1957 and 1962, full employment led to a rise of wage costs in excess of productivity, and since, for the reasons mentioned, prices could not go up in corresponding measure, the share of profits in the national income declined. The two fundamental relations of Keynesian distribution theory, that is, investment-demand and demand-prices-profits, are not, therefore, applicable to an open economy.

This was, of course, only to be expected, since Kaldor's model is built on the assumption of a closed economy. Yet this exercise in shadow-boxing was perhaps not useless, in so far as it showed the model to be inapplicable in a concrete situation. The important point is that the assumption of a closed economy is not introduced just to simplify the exposition, but is a necessary condition of the functioning of the model.

In other words, it seems impossible to adapt the theory so as to make room for the complications deriving from foreign trade. Because exports in practice depend neither on the consumption function nor on the savings function, the model is invalidated as soon as exports play a major part in the economy. If we add a high price elasticity of both imports and exports, such as exists in the Belgian economy, the relation demand-prices-profits also falls, and therefore the theory cannot be made more valid by assimilating exports to investment. In an open economy the analysis of income distribution along neo-Keynesian lines definitely seems to lead nowhere.

B. *An Alternative Explanation*

One of Kaldor's fundamental assumptions is borne out fairly well by the Belgian figures, and that is the relative constancy of the ratio of profits and wages to national income. Once we eliminate the influence of structural changes in the labour force from the income share of wages and mixed incomes, we indeed find a very marked stability on the average over the period under consideration. The increase in the wages share (Table 2 : from 53·8 per cent in 1953 to 58·6 per cent in 1962) corresponds approximately to the increase in the proportion of wage-earners in the total labour force (from 66·9 per cent in 1953 to 71·7 per cent in 1960).

Around this long-term stable trend we find considerable cyclical fluctuations; the wages share diminished in 1954–55, remained stationary in 1956, rose in 1957–58, dropped again in 1959, 1960, and 1961 [1] and climbed in 1962. It follows that the share of profits rose during most of the upswing, and fell at the height of the boom (1957 and 1962) as well as during the recession — which, incidentally, was very short (1958).

These developments cannot be explained by a Kaldor-type analysis in an open economy characterized by high price elasticity. We must, on the contrary, assume that prices remain practically stable, and this implies that profit variations are attributable not to price variations at constant costs, as in Kaldor's model, but to cost variations at constant prices — or, in other words, to variations in the productivity of the factors of production.

To test this assumption, we calculated annual indices of average productivity and average real wages in manufacturing and extractive industries; profit indices are not available at this level of analysis.

Straight lines fitted to the two series have a practically identical slope. If we denote by y an annual time span, by x' the index of real wages in manufacturing and extractive industries, and by x'' productivity in these same industries, the equations of the fitted straight lines are

$$x' = 3·9836\,y + 98·88$$
$$x'' = 3·629\,y + 101·19$$

This result confirms the stability of income shares. On the assumption of constant prices, the fact that real wages and productivity rise in the long run at the same rate implies constancy of the income shares of profits and wages.

This similarity of movements over a ten-year period is not, however, reflected in the annual, let alone the quarterly, figures. On quarterly changes in real wages and productivity we found an insignificant correlation of 0·03, and even on annual changes the correlation was only 0·45. The much more satisfactory coefficient of 0·8682 was obtained for a lag correlation, allowing two years between the rise in average productivity and the rise in average real wages. We conclude that in the industries concerned real wages adjust to productivity within two years on the average.

[1] In spite of a very slight rise in 1960 with respect to 1959, the year quite clearly fits into the downward movement 1959–61.

How are we to explain this fact and how can we reconcile it logically with the observed cyclical fluctuations in the income shares of profits and wages ?

We must, at this stage, introduce two other variables which are important in the Belgian economy, namely, underemployment and the part played by exports. In the light of the respective annual series, we can put forward the following interpretation.

At the beginning of an upswing (1953–55 and 1959–61), productivity increases are translated into profit increases ; absolute price levels can remain stable and this means an improvement of relative prices in relation to foreign competition, Belgium being in a permanent state of relative deflation. As a result, exports are stimulated and, in fact, expand during the early upswing faster than at any other time.[1] Underemployment is absorbed, but not completely, and for this reason wage claims are less forceful and real wages cannot follow the productivity rise at once. At this stage, therefore, the share of profits rises at the expense of the wages share.

Thanks largely to export expansion, the economy then gradually reaches full employment (1956–57 and 1962–63). Wage claims, strengthened by full employment and stimulated by knowledge of prior profit increases, succeed in raising real wages quite substantially — witness the much more rapid increase in real wages in 1956–57 and 1962–63 in comparison with earlier years.

But full employment slows down or indeed arrests the growth of productivity (an increase of 2·8 per cent in 1956 and practically none in 1957 compares with rises of 6·8 and 5·1 per cent, respectively, in 1954 and 1955 ; similarly, we find a rise of 2·7 per cent in 1962 and 1·5 per cent in 1961, compared with 4·3 and 7·6 per cent, respectively, in 1959 and 1960).

Prices can now rise more easily than before, but international competition imposes severe limits, so that higher prices cannot compensate a wage rise much in excess of productivity increases. At this moment, the income share of profits declines to the benefit of the wages share, and the index of real wages climbs up fast enough to make good its earlier lag and catches up with the productivity index.

[1] Export expansion owes something also to a quantitative factor, namely, that in the countries which import most Belgian goods domestic supply falls behind domestic demand. But Belgian exports rise most rapidly not at the moment of greatest strain in the principal importing countries, but a little earlier. On the other hand, the high price elasticity of Belgian exports certainly implies that a relative price advantage stimulates exports considerably. Finally, we find the rather satisfactory correlation coefficient of 0·75 between annual export increments at constant prices and annual productivity rises.

This situation continues during the recession (1958), with diminishing divergences; wages still rise, industry makes price sacrifices in order to keep its markets and, since productivity begins only slowly to improve again, the wages share keeps growing and the profits share shrinking, both movements gradually losing impetus. When recovery sets in, the whole process starts all over again and the income shares move in the opposite direction.

These are the outlines of our interpretation, which allows for the main features of the Belgian economy, namely, relative deflation, high price elasticity and trade dependence, growing importance of exports as the mainstay of economic activity, unemployment and an accentuation of wage claims at times of full employment. All in all, the facts and calculations do not seem to invalidate the argument that in the long run the income shares of profits and wages are constant, which implies a mechanism of cyclical adaptation: the share of profits rises during recovery and most of the upswing, and declines when full employment is reached and later, in the recession. Furthermore, we find: a significant lag correlation between real wages and productivity; deceleration of the export expansion in the full-employment situation and recession and acceleration during the upswing; a satisfactory correlation between annual productivity increases and simultaneous annual export increments at constant prices.

V. PARTIAL ANALYSIS

Beyond total analysis lies the wide open field of partial analysis, by which we can throw more light on the structure of income distribution. We have tried to compare developments in a number of different sectors with the help of annual indices of average physical productivity, nominal and real wages, production, employment, and nominal and real distributed profits.

But at this stage of the analysis we encounter many crippling statistical deficiencies, even for the period 1953–62 under review. For this reason only those conclusions will be presented here which appear sufficiently well founded. The logic of our argument is of classical origin: comparative analysis of different labour markets in terms of labour supply and demand, demand for labour being derived from the marginal productivity in value terms.

To estimate the latter, the only series we could use were those of average physical productivity, there being no price indices to deflate output in different sectors. However, we were able to make some cross-checks against price developments, and it is in this light that we shall interpret the facts. Such sectoral profit figures as we have refer only to distributed profits, and that unfortunately deprives the series of much of its interest and relegates it to second place in the analysis. The sectors for which we possess all the information we needed are coal mining, other mining and quarrying, the iron and steel industry, metal manufactures, textiles, tobacco, food, beverages, leather and hides, chemicals, paper and board, and non-metallic minerals.

The first fact which catches the eye is that there is much less dispersion of wage changes than of productivity and profit changes. We have calculated for the various sectors a dispersion index showing the scatter of real wages, real distributed profits and productivity around their respective average, in terms of annual increases and the total increase over the period considered. The results are shown in Table 5.

TABLE 5

ANNUAL AND TEN-YEAR CHANGES

PERCENTAGE DISPERSION OF SECTORAL INCREASES

AROUND THE SIMPLE ARITHMETIC MEAN $(\sigma/\bar{x})$

	1954	1955	1956	1957	1958	1959	1960	1961	1962	1962/3
Increase in :										
Real wages	196	71·6	57	54	581·6	187·6	74	48	67·8	18·14
Productivity	122·4	92·3	97·8	149·6	950	118·4	113·8	247	107·45	61·87
Real profits	688·5	181	76·3	132·8	211·3	814·5	130·3	110·6	417·4	143·52

It will be seen that dispersion is much more pronounced in the case of productivity and profits than in wages. If we replace physical productivity by productivity in value terms, allowing for price changes, the order of dispersion remains the same. We conclude, and this is important, that the demand for labour, which depends upon productivity in value terms, is not a determining factor for changes in the average wage level. In spite of differential productivity changes, the separate sectors display much the same processes of wage increase.

This confirms the results of other studies to the effect that the inter-sectoral fan of wages has hardly changed in Europe during the last ten years.[1] Inter-sectoral productivity variations can, therefore,

[1] OECD, *The Problem of Rising Prices* (by W. Fellner, Milton Gilbert . . .), May 1961.

give us an explanation of employment or profit variations rather than of wage variations.[1] In terms of wage increases, inter-sectoral differences are small and the absolute movements of wages are more closely connected with supply than with demand.

In an economy like that of Belgium, where trade unions are powerful and widespread, the cross-elasticities of labour supply are strong and employers must follow the general movement if they want to keep their personnel.

If labour supply is considered as an exogenous variable determining the absolute rise of wages, the differential development of demand for labour shows its effects mainly in a differential development of the employment indices. From this point of view we can classify the different sectors as in Table 6.

TABLE 6

COMPARATIVE MOVEMENTS OF EMPLOYMENT, 1953–62

Group I Sectors with Growing Employment	Group II Sectors with Stable Employment	Group III Sectors with Declining Employment
Chemicals	Food	Textiles
Paper and board	Beverages	Leather
Non-metallic minerals	Iron and steel	Tobacco
	Metal manufactures	Coal
		Other mining and quarrying

If we introduce into this tabulation certain indications drawn from an examination of productivity, output, and wages, we can expand the classification as in Table 7.

Such a classification corresponds to the whole set of information we were able to collect. From the theoretical point of view, the behaviour of the various items can be classified according to the logical scheme outlined above.

(1) In Group I, demand for labour and productivity in value terms increases faster than labour supply (represented by the average rise in wages); wages can rise a little more than average and employment can grow.

[1] This observation applies to movements more than to absolute levels. To the extent, for example, that relative wage levels corresponded in 1953 to relative productivity levels, it is at least likely that they still do so. The correspondence has diminished to the extent that relative variations in productivities and wages diverged.

166

TABLE 7

CLASSIFICATION OF SECTORS BY CHANGES IN WAGES
PRODUCTIVITY IN VALUE TERMS, AND EMPLOYMENT

Sectors	Analytical Definitions	Economic Effects
GROUP I Chemicals Paper and board Non-metallic minerals	Marginal (value) productivity rises faster than wages Output grows faster than average physical productivity	Rapid growth of : —wages —employment —output and productivity
GROUP II Iron and steel Metal manufac. Food Beverages	Marginal (value) productivity and wages rise at similar rates Output and average physical productivity grow at similar rates	Wages rise at the average intersectoral rate Employment is stable Output and productivity grow fast (steel, metal manuf.) or moderately (food, beverages)
GROUP IIIA Coal Tobacco	Marginal (value) productivity rises less fast than wages Output grows less fast than average physical productivity (tobacco) or declines while physical productivity rises (coal)	Wages rise less fast than the intersectoral average Employment declines Output rises slightly or declines Productivity rises at less than average rates
GROUP IIIB Textiles Other mining and quarrying	Marginal (value) productivity rises as fast or faster than wages Output grows markedly less fast than average physical productivity	Average rise of wages Decline of employment Growth of output, but much stronger rise in productivity

167

(2) In Group II, movements of the demand for labour and of labour supply are of the same amplitude ; wages rise at the average intersectoral rate and employment remains stable.

(3) In Group IIIA, productivity in value terms rises less than labour supply ; employment declines and wages rise at less than the average rate.

(4) Group IIIB is somewhat more difficult to analyse. Productivity in value terms (demand for labour) increases as much as labour supply, which should mean stable employment. But employment declines, because physical productivity grows faster than output. This apparent contradiction is explained by the fact that the demand curve for labour changes its shape in rising and becomes much more inelastic. This is how we can register at one and the same time a decline in employment and an increase in marginal (value) productivity in excess of the wage rise.

This transformation of the labour demand curve in the direction of much less elasticity reflects an economic characteristic typical of sectors with a low capital-output ratio and a slow expansion of demand for the sector's products.

What happens is that the slow expansion of demand sets limits to the possible expansion of output. Labour is attracted to other sectors where wages are higher, and the resulting manpower shortage is an incentive to mechanization ; productivity grows and, indeed, sometimes quite considerably so over the course of a few years. In these conditions, the quantitative demand for labour contracts strongly and the labour demand curve, while rising thanks to higher productivity in value terms, turns toward the left — which means that it becomes much more inelastic — and becomes vertical at much lower levels of employment than before. (The marginal product of additional workers beyond this point would be worth nothing because their products could not be sold.) The apparent paradox of the curve for IIIB can be explained both in graphical and in economic terms.

A graphical illustration of the four types of development is given in the chart opposite.

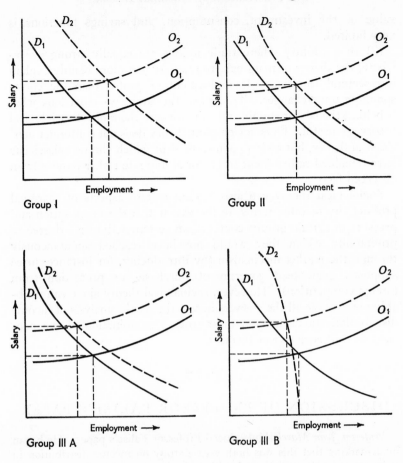

VI. CONCLUSION

In the course of our study, we have used analytical tools belonging to different theories : a neo-Keynesian model, the theory of marginal productivity, explanations of labour supply movements in terms of trade-union behaviour (sociological theory).

It may be worth recalling two conclusions regarding the analytical significance of these different approaches.

(1) A neo-Keynesian type of analysis of income distribution is all the less applicable to any given economy the more open it is to international trade. Total analysis is not excluded, but the explanatory

value of the investment, consumption, and savings functions is very limited.

(2) In a country where trade unions are equally strong everywhere, the theory of marginal productivity can more readily explain intersectoral variations of employment or profits than the corresponding wage changes. To explain the latter, we must look what is behind the labour supply and this is where the tools of sociological theory are useful. Thus sociological theory does not contradict neo-classical theory, but adds to it in a field in which the neo-classicists have remained rather silent so far, or at any rate rather remote from observed facts.

Sociological theory can also explain certain aspects of marginal productivity in value terms, to the extent that the organisation and pressure of certain groups confer upon certain activities a degree of profitability which they would not have reached spontaneously through the market mechanism (by introducing, for instance, price supports, guaranteed government purchases or protection from foreign competition). However, sociological theory alone can probably not provide all the answers here ; the partial analysis of income distribution stands to gain most from a combination of the neo-classical and sociological theories.

DISCUSSION OF PROFESSOR FALISE'S PAPER

Professor Jean Marchal introduced Professor Falise's paper. He began by remarking that this was both a case study on income distribution in Belgium and a theoretical work with wider bearing. The first part of the paper dealt with primary distribution. Professor Falise's findings indicated that during the period under study, 1953/1962, the share of labour had increased substantially and the share of distributed property incomes had remained stable whereas the share of non-distributed corporate profits had fluctuated strongly. At the same time public expenditure had played an increasing part in modifying primary distribution by redistribution of income.

Professor Falise had tried to present a theoretical interpretation of his findings according to the usual two-fold classification of incomes into labour and property incomes. Professor Marchal objected to this method for several reasons. It implied breaking up the incomes of self-employed and the profits of non-corporate businesses into imputed labour and capital incomes. Everyone agreed that any method of imputation was highly arbitrary but nobody seemed prepared to draw what Professor Marchal thought to be the necessary conclusion : that this type of incomes was a category entirely distinct from both profits and wages. There was all the more reason for so doing in this case as these incomes had amounted to from 25 to 29 per cent of Belgian national product.

As a second objection Professor Marchal remarked that the twofold analysis tended to confuse the distribution of disposable incomes after redistribution with the primary distribution. Wages and profits were first defined as returns to labour and to other production factors respectively. Then one went on applying to these factor returns propensities to consume and to save which should correctly have been related to the incomes received by workers and non-workers, redistribution being taken into account.

Professor Falise had tried to interpret his findings in the light of Kaldor's model in which P/Y, the share of profits in national income, depended on I/Y, the share of investment, assuming propensities to save out of profits and out of wages to be constant. Now Professor Falise had not found any correlation, simultaneous or lagged, between the two ratios, even when he added mixed incomes to profits in the calculation of P/Y. Professor Falise had thought that the conditions of unemployment prevailing during part of the period he studied might have explained why his findings deviated from the model but the two ratios did not fluctuate in the same way even in periods of full employment.

Professor Falise had therefore looked for another explanation of the lack of parallelism in the changes. This he found in the openness of the Belgian economy. The Kaldorian model applied to a closed economy. Thus conditions in the Belgian case allowed for a high measure of price stability contrary to Kaldor's assumption which led to the conclusion that any increase in effective demand brought about by the increase of I/Y would induce a rise in prices relative to costs and therefore a proportionate increase in profits. Professor Marchal wished to emphasize that not only was this a fundamental difference in Kaldor's and Falise's assumptions, but that Professor Falise had shown that it was not feasible to bring in international trade as an afterthought because this altered the basic assumptions in the model.

Professor Falise was thus led to propose an alternative hypothesis. Whereas in Kaldor's model profits varied according to the variations of prices, costs being assumed to be constant, in Belgium their variations were to be explained by the variations of costs in relation to constant prices, in other words by variations in factor productivity. According to Professor Falise's calculations of correlation changes in wages tended to conform to changes in productivity with an average two-year lag. A high volume of exports and underemployment were two important characteristics of the present Belgian economy. In periods of expansion Belgian prices would remain fairly stable whereas they rose abroad ; Belgian exports increased and productivity went up ; so long as unemployment pressed on the level of wages the profit share would increase. Real wages would tend to increase with full employment and this at a time when the rate of growth would tend to decrease ; as competition on foreign markets prevented prices from rising, the profit share would decrease and the wage share increase. In the following period of recession, owing to the lag in the adjustment of wages to productivity, the wage rise would continue for some time whereas exporters would cut their prices in order to remain competitive on foreign markets and profits would go down until conditions allowing them to rise again prevailed in the next upward turn of the business cycle.

Professor Marchal said he had three remarks to make concerning Professor Falise's theoretical developments. He first emphasized that this was a purely cyclical analysis on a ten-year period, leaving aside all long term movements in income distribution. He also wished to stress that Professor Falise's analysis applied under rather unusual conditions. It did not apply to economies less dependent on exports and in which full employment was a more or less constant feature. Moreover, he was not even sure that it would hold in the Belgian case in the near future as member countries of EEC were pledged to co-ordinate their business cycle policies. This seemed to Professor Marchal to imply that Belgium should take steps to remove the bias towards deflation which had been a characteristic feature of its economy in relation to other EEC countries. Professor Marchal also wished to remind his audience that Professor Falise's theory as well as the Kaldorian model were based on the twofold division of incomes which he had already objected to and which shed no light on redistribution and its effects.

In the second part of his paper Professor Falise had studied the sectoral changes in wages rates. He found that the dispersion of the sectoral variations were much less in terms of real wages than in terms of productivity. From this he had concluded that those changes in demand for labour which were related to variations in productivity in each industry did not play an important part in differentiating the level of wages and their sectoral changes. Thus the theory of marginal productivity in an economy with strong trade unions did not throw light on relative variations in wages. In each industry employers were compelled to conform to the general trend in wages in order to keep their labour force. This left the supply of labour as the determinant factor in the wage differentials and the changes of relative wage rates. The sectoral changes in demand for labour only played a part in the differentiation of sectoral levels of employment.

In Professor Falise's model the supply of labour was an exogenous variable but he was anxious to find out what was behind the variations in the labour supply. Professor Falise felt the need for a sociological approach as the neo-classical theory said very little about the factors which determined the labour supply. Professor Marchal fully agreed. A theory of wage differentials could not consider the pattern of the various groups' behaviours as an exogenous datum but would have to integrate their interrelationship. One should take into account not only trade unions' attitudes towards employers and towards each other, but also the behaviour of employers and farmers as well-organized pressure groups.

As Professor Falise himself had noticed, the latter could exert pressures tending to make sectoral monetary returns rise above their market level and this tended to increase the marginal productivity of labour in the same sectors. Professor Marchal thought that one should also consider the pressures exerted by either workers, employers, or farmers to improve their share in disposable income through redistribution of primary income. Professor Marchal agreed that the sociological theory did not contradict the neo-classical theory but enlarged the scope of distribution theory in throwing light on facts which the neo-classical theory passed over or interpreted in a far from realistic manner.

Dr. Pasinetti gave credit to Professor Falise for having taken his readers where angels might have feared to tread, namely in an attempt to verify how observed data could fit in a theoretical model of income distribution. Dr. Pasinetti said, however, that he would be much more cautious than Professor Falise in drawing the conclusion that Kaldor's model was not applicable. Professor Jean Marchal had already pointed out limitations in Professor Falise's analysis of the Belgian case in the sense that Professor Falise considered a short period whereas Kaldor's analysis referred to the long run ; besides, the Belgian economy was very open to foreign trade and, during the period considered, had been subject to deflationary pressures. It was agreed that prices had not been very flexible in Belgium during the period under review but Dr. Pasinetti did not think that this would be a criterion on which Professor Kaldor would himself rely for testing his model. Surely, Professor Kaldor would not assume prices to respond immediately to short-run and temporary changes in effective demand. He would pay much more attention to the long run.

Dr. Pasinetti did not think that any explanation in terms of structural changes would conflict with Kaldor's model. In fact, he found it easier to interpret Professor Falise's structural analysis in terms of the Kaldorian model than in terms of marginal theory. The main difference, he thought, in trying to put one against the other was whether one assumed that investments (or effective demand in general) determined profits or whether one assumed the relationship to be the other way round. If, as he thought, one chose to make the first assumption, not only investment but also foreign trade would have to be taken into account. Therefore Dr. Pasinetti thought that Professor Falise's findings were not incompatible with Kaldor's theory.

Professor Lecaillon had noticed that Professor Falise in testing the applicability of Kaldor's model to the Belgian case had not taken into account the trend phenomenon of a shift of the labour force from self-employment and farming towards wage-earning jobs in the industrial sector, in order to appreciate whether there had been a parallelism of evolution of the profits share and the investment share in the national product. This omission was implied by reasoning entirely in terms of the primary, functional distribution.

It seemed to Professor Lecaillon that this way of reasoning entailed a certain lack of realism as Kaldor's model was concerned with growth as well as distribution of income. This implied that the shift towards wage-earning jobs could not be considered as an exogenous phenomenon. Besides there was a certain lack of consistency in ignoring that structural changes of this sort led to changes in the distribution of personal disposable incomes as well as to changes in factors incomes. Now, propensities to consume and to save were related to disposable incomes. If for example small farmers became industrial wage-earners their propensity to save would decline. How could this sort of change be reconciled with the assumption of constant propensities on which Kaldor's model, if not Falise's, was based?

Professor Negreponti-Delivanis, referring to Professor Falise's reasons for the non-applicability of Kaldor's model to the Belgian economy, thought that its deflationary bent was more relevant than its openness. More than the fact that exports were higher than investment in proportion of national product, permanent conditions of deflation hindered the Kaldorian process as an increase in I/Y should lead to an increase in P/Y only in so far as prices would rise while wages were lagging behind.

A state of deflation would on the contrary mean that prices remained stable. Then any increase in investment would tend to provoke an increase in the wage share, especially in periods of full employment as 1956–57 and 1961–62 in Belgium. Professor Negreponti-Delivanis remarked that, according to Professor Falise's figures, the share of wages had risen from 53·8 per cent in 1953 to 58·6 per cent in 1962 whereas the share of profits had gone down from 29·4 to 25·1 per cent during the same period.

She thought that such a deviation from the implications of the Kaldorian model was related to the deflationary bent in the Belgian economy whereas it might apply to an economy as open as the Belgian one providing that it was not deflationary. Therefore she suggested that Professor Falise's conclusions should be modified in consequence.

Professor Krelle was surprised that Professor Falise had not found any correlation between profits and investment. The studies of investment functions in various countries had always shown a good correlation between both. He suggested that as much of Belgium's investment goods were imported the study of correlation should be extended to the corresponding part of imports. Had Professor Falise done so he might perhaps have found a good correlation.

Falise — Income Distribution in Belgium

Professor Falise thanked Professor Jean Marchal for his introduction. He agreed with Dr. Pasinetti about the limitations of his analysis. As had been remarked by Professor Marchal and Professor Lecaillon his study spanned only a short period of time ; this was due to the lack of available data before that. He agreed with Professor Marchal that the basic conditions with which he had dealt might not prevail in the future ; the change might already be under way. Figures for 1963 would have proved it if he had been able to include them in his study.

Concerning the drawbacks inherent in the usual division of incomes shares between wages and profits, Professor Falise observed that he had selected as samples for his study industries such as mining and manufacturing in which self-employment was small in proportion to the labour force. In his calculations he had taken into account the sectoral shifts in the working population. Professor Lecaillon had questioned the stability of propensities to consume : Professor Falise wished to make it clear that he had not had to use evaluations of propensities for his calculations. Therefore this methodological criticism could not be directed at him.

Answering Dr. Pasinetti's comments on the applicability of Kaldor's model to the Belgian economy, Professor Falise thought that international trade tended to make prices less flexible. He thought it relevant to emphasize the comparatively high degree of price rigidity in the Belgian case. Besides, if Professor Falise was prepared to take into account the high share of exports in effective demand, he would maintain that it was impossible in an open economy to identify exports with investment and imports with savings because variables which applied to exports and imports were different from those which determined investment and saving.

Bearing in mind Dr. Negreponti-Delivanis's comments, he thought that he had already sufficiently underlined the impact of deflation on the Belgian economy. Deflation was not an absolute ; however the Belgian economy had been in a state of deflation throughout the period which he had studied.

He agreed with Professor Krelle's remark that imports of investment goods should be taken into account. He would have liked to include them in his calculations, just as he wished he could have excluded the effects of public investment and of changes in inventories. But one had to take into account that there had been during the period under review a fairly big increase in other forms of the capital-widening, as opposed to the capital-deepening type of investment. This had meant extending the use of capital in a way which had not resulted in any appreciable increase in productivity. Finally Professor Falise wished to underline that an important feature of the Belgian economy was the abnormally high proportion of personal savings in the total of savings. Therefore self-financing was proportionately less important than in other countries and the level of the propensity to save out of personal incomes might help to explain the lack of correlation between profits and investment.

The Distribution of National Income

Professor Reder wished to know how it was that the events of 1960 in the Congo had not had any more apparent impact on Belgian national income and its distribution.

Professor Falise agreed that the independence of the Congo had actually had little influence on the Belgian economy in comparison with its psychological and political repercussions. To explain how little the distribution of income in Belgium had been affected one should remember that the major corporations established in the Congo did not employ many Belgian wage-earners on the spot. Besides, even before the period of independence, these corporations enjoyed the status, not of domestic, but of foreign concerns in the Congo. The loss of assets resulting from the political situation there had also been mitigated by the distribution of substantial dividends to Belgian shareholders.

Dr. Bruzek was concerned about the phenomena of tax incidence as a cause of deviation of the share of wage-earners in disposable incomes from their share in the distribution before taxation. To what extent did Professor Falise's evaluations of the wage-earners' share take taxation into account?

Professor Falise answered that he had used the data of national income at factor cost, therefore excluding indirect taxes and including direct taxation. He admitted that the final distribution of disposable income after tax might thus be modified. He thought however that the redistribution effect of progressive taxation tended to be cancelled out by the effects of tax evasion.

Chapter 6

CHANGES IN NATIONAL INCOME DISTRIBUTION BY FACTOR SHARE IN JAPAN [1]

KAZUSHI OHKAWA
Hitotsubashi University

I. INTRODUCTORY

SINCE around 1920,[2] striking changes have occurred in the Japanese economy. The past four decades have witnessed the drastic post-war adjustment following excessive expansion during World War I ; the shock of the Great Depression ; the mobilization in preparation for military and imperialistic expansion ; the great impact of World War II and the unprecedented spurt which immediately followed the end of the rehabilitation period. There were, moreover, the radical institutional reforms implemented in the occupation period. The question of the effects of all of these events on the distribution of national income is an important one which deserves attention.

On the other hand, there is the question of whether there is any long-term pattern of change underlying the effects of the exogenous factors we have mentioned, and the extent to which such a pattern of change in the distribution of income can be systematically analysed and interpreted by our conventional concepts and methods. The aim of this paper is to give a preliminary answer to this question. Its emphasis, consequently, will be mainly on the identification of the effects of underlying economic forces rather than on the impact of specific historical events.

The following discussion will be concentrated on the distribution of income by factor shares, leaving the problem of size distribution entirely untouched. The scope will be confined to the private

[1] I am greatly indebted to Professor Alan H. Gleason of International Christian University for helpful suggestions in the preparation of this paper.
[2] For the purpose of this paper a long-term series of national income distribution is desirable. Unfortunately continuous data are available only after 1919.

177

domestic economy excluding the government sector and the relationship with the 'rest of the world'. Using conventional concepts of national income accounts, three broad components — compensation of employees (W_1), income from assets (A_1), and income of unincorporated enterprises (Y_2) will be considered and a major attempt will be made to analyse the behaviour of aggregate factor shares in the non-agricultural sector. The main results of our analysis will be summarized in the concluding remarks. Statistical sources and procedures will be briefly stated in the Appendix.

II. STRUCTURAL CHANGES AND SECTORAL SHARES

The aggregate factor shares can be conveniently regarded as consisting of two kinds of shares — structural shares and sectoral factor shares. Given two sectors, corporate and unincorporated, the structural shares are defined as Y_1/Y and Y_2/Y, where $Y_1 = A_1 + W_1$ and $Y = Y_1 + Y_2$. During economic growth, the share of output produced by corporate enterprises tends to increase (that of unincorporated enterprises tends to decrease), representing broadly the rate of modernization of the economy. Sectoral breakdowns by income produced, however, can only be approximated here. So far as the shares of distributed income reflect these, they can be used as 'structural shares'. The labour share (assets share) can be defined as $W_1/Y_1 (A_1/Y_1)$ with respect to Y_1 and is measured directly. With respect to Y_2, $W_2/Y_2 (A_2/Y_2)$ can only be measured by some kind of artificial imputation. Nevertheless, an attempt is made to do this and to obtain an estimate of the aggregate factor shares. The aggregate labour share may be defined as follows, as a combination of the structural shares and sectoral factor shares, in which the structural shares, in effect, serve as 'weights' for the sectoral factor shares, although they have an independent significance of their own.

$$\frac{W}{Y} = \frac{W_1}{Y_1} \cdot \frac{Y_1}{Y} + \frac{W_2}{Y_2} \cdot \frac{Y_2}{Y}.$$

In the case of a mature economy Y_2/Y may be insignificant, but in Japan's case, where the traditional sector is still important, the behaviour of the structural share requires attention. If agriculture is included, Japan reached the point of equal shares of Y_1/Y and Y_2/Y around 1920. (A ratio of 40 : 60 is witnessed if rent is included in Y_2 instead of Y_1.) After 1920, Y_1/Y increased (Y_2/Y

decreased) gradually toward a ratio of 63 per cent (37 per cent) in 1938 and reached 72 per cent (28 per cent) in 1944 due to rapid structural changes during the war. Because of the disastrous impact of World War II, the structural shares in 1949 went back where they were in 1920. Since then, however, the share of the corporate sector has increased very rapidly in response to the post-war recovery and, by 1962, had almost reached the level attained in 1944. Such structural shifts are a good indicator of the striking changes that have occurred in the Japanese economy during the past forty years.

We turn our attention next to the movement of the sectoral factor shares especially in relation to the behaviour of the structural shares. To begin with the modern sector, the long-term behaviour of the labour share (W_1/Y_1) is shown in Fig. 1. W_1/Y_1 decreased roughly from 70 per cent to 56 per cent during the pre-war period. Starting with an abnormal high level (over 90 per cent) in the years immediately after World War II, the post-war trend of its decrease is distinctly steeper. The level of about 70 per cent in 1962 is close to the share realized in 1921–23. Two things may be especially noted. First, the changes in pattern can best be understood by dividing the whole period under consideration into four phases: I (1919–30), II (1931–38), III (1939–52) and IV (1953–62). A broad picture of the share behaviour during these phases is as follows: constant (I), decrease (II), abnormal variation (III), and decrease (IV). It is interesting to see that apart from short-term business fluctuations, the labour share movement shows an association with long-swings in terms of the growth rate of aggregate output [1]: a constant trend during phase I associated with the downward phase of the growth rate, and the trends of decrease in phases II and IV are associated with the periods of upswings or spurts of output growth. Secondly, there is a noticeable rise in the general level between the pre-war and post-war periods which occurred during phase III.

A negative association of the labour share with swings in output growth suggests the following mechanism: during an upward phase, an accelerated increase of productivity due to an increased domestic fixed investment and technological progress takes place, accompanied by a certain lag of wage increase, while during a

[1] See K. Ohkawa and H. Rosovsky, 'Economic Fluctuations in Pre-war Japan: A Preliminary Analysis of Cycles and Long Swings', *Hitotsubashi Journal of Economics*, October 1962. The long swings in terms of the growth rate of real GDP are identified as follows: 1905 (trough), 1919 (peak), 1931 (trough), 1938 (peak), 1953 (starting point of the post-war upswing after the end of the rehabilitation period).

The Distribution of National Income

downward phase, a parallel process between wage and productivity increase tends to occur. These relationships will be analysed in detail later. The change in level of the labour share which took place during phase III, however, requires special explanation. This was caused partly by post-war abnormalities and partly by the institutional changes mentioned previously which were introduced into Japanese society immediately after the war. The effects of the former probably had ended by around 1953. In the case of the institutional changes, the dissolution of the Zaibatsu, which liquidated monopoly elements, may have had a downward effect on the share of income from assets and the nation-wide development of trade unions may have affected labour's relative share through the strengthening of labour's bargaining power. In comparing the pre-war and post-war spurt periods, the average level of the labour share rose from 64 per cent to 74 per cent. This is due mostly (if not entirely) to the effects of the institutional changes.[1] Thus the net result of both these types of changes as a whole through the entire period under consideration is that the most recent labour share turns out to be approximately equal to the highest pre-war level, which stood at around 70 per cent in early years of the twenties.

Next, in treating the income of unincorporated enterprises, W_2/Y_2 is obtained by the following method of imputation. Disregarding the unpaid family workers' contribution, this 'mixed' income is assumed to be the compensation of the heads of the unincorporated enterprises, and the value of their labour per person is regarded as equal to the average compensation of employees in the corresponding sectors. The agricultural and non-agricultural sectors require separate treatment.

The labour share for non-agricultural unincorporated enterprises as shown in Fig. 1 (by notation W_2/Y_2), shows movements similar to those of W_1/Y_1, though with wider fluctuations, and also similar to the swings in GDP, except during the abnormal phase III. This suggests that aggregation of this sector and the corporate sector is plausible.

The behaviour of the labour share for agricultural unincorporated enterprises does not seem to be closely associated with W_2/Y_2. Its level, moreover, is much lower throughout almost the entire period under consideration. In most years of the twenties and thirties, the

[1] The behaviour of labour's relative share in factory manufacturing presented by Umemura shows a movement similar to the behaviour described above. See M. Umemura, *Chingin, Koyō, Nōgyō*, Tokyo, 1961, chap. 4.

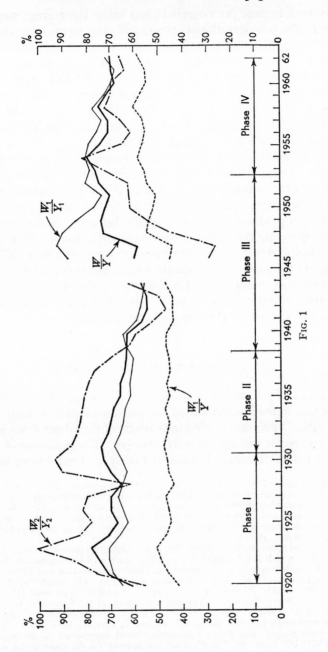

Fig. 1

agricultural income per household was below the average wage income in the non-agricultural sector, and even went down close to 50 per cent of the average wage income in the years of the Great Depression. This of course does not represent exactly the gap of real income between farmers and wage-earners. But still it reflects the severely depressed situation of farmers at that time. The post-war rise in its level, however, is remarkable. This is the combined result of the Land Reform, which abolished traditional landlordism through elimination of absentee ownership of land, and of terms of trade which became favourable to agriculture through various government policies. Despite these factors, its share tended again to decline relative to the average wage income in the non-agricultural sector during the recent spurt due mostly to the lag in the increase in agricultural productivity. Such peculiar behaviour makes us reluctant to aggregate this sector with the corporate sector. The use of the agricultural wage rate would create another operational difficulty, though in principle this would be a more reasonable approach for the purpose of imputation. The aggregation, therefore, will include only the non-agricultural sector.[1] (Hereafter the notations in (1) above will be used for the non-agricultural sector.)

III. AGGREGATE FACTOR SHARE

In Fig. 1, W_1/Y, and W/Y are shown. W_1/Y appears to be almost unchanged in the pre-war period and increased rapidly in early post-war years. This reflects combined effects of the labour share in the corporate sector and the structural changes. The behaviour of W/Y is to be noted. In phase I, it shows a fairly level trend from around

[1] Examination of W_2/Y_2 for eleven sectors of the economy using each sectoral W_2 shows that its performance over time is similar in all sectors except agriculture despite considerable differences in magnitude. In agriculture, hired labour is not widely used and the wage rate is of a highly seasonal nature. Our method of imputation therefore tends to be much less meaningful. These are further reasons for excluding agriculture.

A device to avoid such an imputation is to adopt the concept of 'participation income' (P), which is the sum of W_1 and W_2. As is well known, Simon Kuznets analysed a wide range of international data, both cross-section and historical, in applying a dichotomy of P versus A in aggregate terms. His broad finding is that A (and accordingly P) tends to be constant or slightly decreasing (P slightly increasing). See S. Kuznets, 'Quantitative Aspects of the Economic Growth of Nations, IV: Distribution of National Income by Factor Shares', *Economic Development and Cultural Change*, vol. vii, no. 3, Part II, April 1959. Japan's case reveals roughly that P has a decreasing trend interrupted by the impact of World War II. However, I don't think this approach is the most useful one for our purpose.

1921, though the annual fluctuations are relatively large, remaining at an average level of about 70 per cent. In phase II, it shows a declining trend. During phase III, it dropped sharply and recovered to a level over 70 per cent. Through phase IV, apart from fluctuations associated with the business cycle, it shows a trend declining toward 70 per cent — the pre-war level of the twenties. If the movements during phase III are excluded as being abnormal because of the war, we can say that the aggregate relative labour share tends to be constant in the long-run, with variations from phase to phase associated with fluctuations in output growth.

The phase-to-phase fluctuations of W_1/Y_1 and W/Y are more or less similar. A big difference between them is that the post-war average level of W/Y remains almost equal to the pre-war average level, while the post-war level of W_1/Y_1 shows a distinct rise as was previously noted. In Table 1, the relationships and changes in averages of our major ratios are shown according to phases, excluding the abnormal war period.

TABLE 1

MAJOR SHARES BY PHASE AVERAGES
(%)

	1920–30	1931–38	1953–62
W/Y	70·1	68·2	72·3
W_1/Y_1	66·2	63·5	74·2
W_2/Y_2	80·4	80·5	68·5
Y_1/Y	70·1	73·3	76·9
(W_1/Y)	46·4	46·5	57·1
Y_2/Y	29·5	26·3	22·0

A relative constancy of average W/Y throughout the three phases results from the counter-balancing movements of W_1/Y_1 and W_2/Y_2. The post-war increase of W_1/Y_1 is, to a large degree, offset by a sharp drop in post-war W_2/Y_2.[1] The average structural shares $(Y_1/Y, Y_2/Y)$ change rather moderately from phase to phase, but

[1] In reality, some part of employees' compensation recorded in the national income accounts is paid by the unincorporated sector. To that extent, W_1/Y_1 is overestimated and W_2/Y_2 underestimated. This is the reason why the figure for W_2/Y_2 is illogically smaller than the figure for W_1/Y_1 in 1953–62. According to the survey of the National Tax Bureau, the average percentage of wages paid by unincorporated enterprises was 3·9 per cent of the total compensation of employees during 1953–62. W_1/Y_1 becomes 71·0 per cent and W_2/Y_2 79·6 per cent for 1953–62, if this percentage is assumed. This may not be far from reality. Such data are not available for pre-war years, but I think the percentage required for adjustment may be smaller than the post-war one.

The Distribution of National Income

the average conceals a very rapid change within the post-war phase. Thus their effects on W/Y are, on the average, not great. Why did the level of W_2/Y_2 decrease so markedly in the post-war period? The income per unincorporated enterprises increased relative to the average wage level probably due to an increase in its relative productivity, accompanying a decrease of underemployment in this sector as compared to the pre-war situation. In fact, the number of unincorporated enterprises in the non-agricultural sector began to decrease from 1954 after showing a long-sustained increasing trend, except during the abnormal war and early post-war periods. This may reflect the wearing out of less efficient or profitable firms, hastened by growing job opportunities in the corporate sector during the post-war spurt.

IV. CHANGES IN FACTOR PRICES AND FACTOR QUANTITIES

The factors responsible for the changes in the income share are wage rates (w), labour employment (L), rate of return to capital (r), and capital stock (K). The annual rates of increase in these components in terms of 5-year moving averages are given in Table 2.

TABLE 2

RATES OF COMPOUND ANNUAL CHANGES
IN FACTOR PRICES AND FACTOR QUANTITIES
(%)

Phases	w	L	$w+L$	r	K	$r+K$
I (1922–31)	2·70	1·31	4·01	0·72	3·28	4·00
II (1931–37)	2·00	2·97	4·84	2·15	4·84	6·99
III (1951–54)	5·71	4·36	10·07	1·98	4·54	6·52
IV (1954–58)	3·46	4·78	8·24	3·19	10·15	13·34

From these figures we may further derive the following relationships:

Phases	$(w+L)-(r+K)$	$K-L$	$w-r$
I	+0·01	1·97	1·98
II	2·15	1·87	0·28
III	+3·55	0·18	3·73
IV	5·10	5·37	2·70

Remarks : Because of the use of 5-year moving averages and the lack of capital stock data for some years, each phase is represented by a smaller number of years than is actually covered by the phase. This technical disadvantage, however, does not, I believe, much affect our interpretation.

The difference between $(w+L)$ and $(r+K)$ can be used as an approximation of the difference between the rate of change in Lw and the rate of change in Kr. It may be seen that in phase I the difference is nearly zero, in phases II and IV it is a large negative figure and in phase III it is a large positive figure. These differences are consistent with the behaviour of W/Y revealed previously. These different movements may be explained as follows. In the twenties, though with some fluctuations, the labour share maintained a fairly constant level because the greater rate of increase of capital stock relative to labour employment $(K-L)$ was largely offset by the greater rate of increase of wages relative to the rate of return to capital $(w-r)$. In the thirties, the capital intensity increased almost at the same pace as in the twenties, though the rate of increase in both labour and capital was accelerated. But wages increased much less than the rate of return to capital. This was due to the abnormal expansion toward the war mobilization. In the post-war period of rehabilitation, the capital intensity remained almost unchanged through a process of capital widening along with an accelerated rate of increase in labour employment, and the wage rate increased substantially (a recovery process) with an increase of the rate of return to capital. Lastly, in the phase of recent rapid growth, we can see an unprecedented high rate of increase of capital with an increasing trend in the rate of return to capital. The rates of increase in both wages and labour employment were not small, but $w-r$ dropped far below $K-L$.

Concerning the changes in rates occurring throughout the whole period, certain general observations may be made. First, with the exception only of the thirties, the wage rate increased much faster than the rate of return to capital. Second, the capital intensity increased continuously, except during the rehabilitation period, implying that a greater rate of increase of capital stock was realized despite a relatively high rate of continuous increase in labour employment. Third, the variations from phase to phase in the shares of income are mostly influenced by the two counter-balancing movements of factor prices and factor quantities and consequently on distinct long-term trend is seen throughout the entire period under consideration.

V. CONCLUDING REMARKS

(1) Our analysis of the distribution of national income by factor shares reveals striking changes during the past eventful forty years in Japan. Exogenous and institutional factors are found to be specifically responsible for some of these changes. In particular, it is noted that the average level of the labour share in the corporate sector reveals a sharp rise from the pre-war to the post-war period and that this can be attributed to the post-war institutional reforms. Throughout these changes in the corporate sector, however, the factor shares tend to reveal a systematic behaviour closely associated with long-term upward and downward movements in the growth rate of output. Imputed factor shares of unincorporated enterprises behave in similar fashion in the non-agricultural sector. The degree of underemployment, however, seems to be a key factor in determining the average level of these shares. With respect to agricultural income, the post-war improvement due to institutional reforms is noted.

(2) The aggregate labour share obtained by imputing average wage income to the labour of unincorporated enterprises (agriculture excluded) appears to be quite stable in its level, with long-term fluctuations similar to those of the corporate sector. The variation in average aggregate factor shares from phase to phase is explained by the relationship between the rates of change in factor returns and the rates of changes in factor quantities. A fact to note is that during spurts in the past, a strong force pushing down labour's relative share has been evident. The incentive for investment is shown by a larger marginal rate of return to capital than its average one. This suggests the mechanism of the high rates of capital accumulation, which operated in the growing process of the Japanese economy. From a long-term point of view, however, no definite trend of decrease in the aggregate labour share is witnessed. This seems to be primarily the result of the offsetting impact of the post-war institutional reforms which favoured its levelling-up.

(3) Lastly, a few words on a long-term trend for the future. The distribution pattern of national income revealed above was, I believe, heavily characterized by a sustained existence of flexible supplies of labour. The Japanese economy, however, now stands at the threshold of the new phase of semi-limited supplies of labour. The rate of increase in the labour supply is expected to decline sharply in the

near future for demographic reasons. This will have an important impact on the future pattern of national income distribution. Less flexible labour supplies will tend to be the basic force which resists the factors which would tend to decrease labour's relative share in the phase of accelerating the rate of growth.

STATISTICAL APPENDIX

(1) W_1 excludes compensation of government employees. A_1 is the sum of corporate income (corporate savings, direct taxes on corporations) and income from personal assets (dividends, rent, and interest, excluding government payments of interest). The income of the corporate sector is $Y_1 = W_1 + A_1$. Y_2 is the sum of the incomes of unincorporated enterprises in agriculture and non-agriculture. Thus defined, the sum of Y_1 and Y_2 is the allocated income of the private domestic economy (Y). In dealing with the aggregate income share of the non-agricultural sector, the rent income paid to the owners of agricultural land is excluded from A_1.

(2) The data for national income distributed are composed from three sources: Yudo Yamada's revision of S. Hijikata's estimates for 1919–29, the unofficial estimate of the Economic Planning Agency for 1930–44, and the official EPA estimates for 1946–62. As for the pre-war series, there remains some inconsistency between these series of total income distributed and our series of total income produced estimated in K. Ohkawa and others, *The Growth Rate of the Japanese Economy since 1878*, Tokyo, 1957. (In calculating the rate of changes in real wage and capital return for the period 1931–1937, the rate of increase in the income produced in the non-agricultural sector, presented in this volume, was used to adjust the EPA series of income distributed.) As for the post-war series, the work of revision is now going on at the EPA. Therefore, these data cannot be regarded as final, and their reliability is limited. However, I believe that they can be used for our present purpose of analysing broad changes disregarding short-term fluctuations. The first series is taken from Y. Yamada, *Nippon Kokumin Shotoku Shiryo*, revised edition, Tokyo, 1962. With respect to some small items such as compensation of government employees, rent income of owners of agricultural land, etc., the unpublished data of the EPA were kindly made available.

(3) The number of employees and unincorporated enterprises are taken from the two sources mentioned above. Where data were not published, however (for example, the number of farm households), the EPA's worksheets were made available. The number of unincorporated enterprises of the non-agricultural sector for the years 1919–29 is the writer's own tentative estimate. It is obtained by linking the data for the censuses in 1920 and 1930 broken down into ten sectors.

(4) With respect to factor prices, the wage rate is tentatively calculated by dividing the total compensation of employees by the number of employees and deflated by a general deflator, and the rate of return to capital is calculated by dividing the similarly deflated income from assets for the non-agricultural sector by the series of capital stock estimated in net real terms. The pre-war capital stock series was made available by S. Ishiwata's unpublished work and the post-war series was derived from the EPA's series estimated by Akabane (*Shihon Suttokku to Keizai Seicho*, Tokyo, 1962). The two series are not strictly comparable in terms of their levels because of some differences in scope and methods of estimation. However, the figure for capital stock is adjusted as far as possible to correspond approximately to the non-agricultural sector of the private domestic economy. Weighted series are not available for both the wage rate and the rate of capital return. The pre-war general deflator is an unpublished series tentatively compiled by the writer. The post-war one is the EPA's published series, and no satisfactory link between the two is, as yet, available. Therefore, in this study, no long-term link was attempted between pre- and post-war years.

DISCUSSION OF PROFESSOR OHKAWA'S PAPER

Professor Brochier wished to underline the special interest of a study of income distribution in Japan owing to the exceptional position of the Japanese economy. Until a very recent period labour had been freely available. The institutional peculiarities of the Japanese labour market with its system of permanent employment reduced the mobility of the labour supply. The economic structure was a 'dual' one with a relationship between a traditional and a modern sector in which the former was under the dependence of the latter rather than competing with it on equal terms. Finally the very steady process of economic growth had been carried through pronounced fluctuations which might reveal a connection between changes in income distribution and variations in the pace of growth.

These features came out clearly in Professor Ohkawa's paper. In accordance with the requirements of a study dealing with a dual or two-sector economy Professor Ohkawa had distinguished between, in his own terminology, sectoral shares and structural shares, the sectoral shares being the ratio of income originating in either the corporate sector or the traditional sector to total income and the structural shares being defined as the respective shares of labour and property within each sector. This meant that the overall share of labour in the usual sense was indirectly determined by adding the labour shares in the corporate and traditional sectors weighted by the respective weight of the two sectors in total income, the same applying for the overall share of property.

Professor Brochier summarized Professor Ohkawa's findings. The share of labour employed in the corporate sector and in the non-agricultural firms within the traditional sector displayed the well-known tendency to decrease in periods of boom and to increase in periods of slower growth. In the long run, however, the overall share of labour had kept fairly constant. Professor Brochier wished to emphasize that, as had been observed by Professor Ohkawa, it had tended to remain constant only as a result of compensatory movements in the two structural shares : after the war the sharp decrease in the share of labour employed in the traditional sector had been offset by the increase in the corporate labour share, the two movements in opposite direction being probably related from 1954 onwards with the reversal of the trend towards an increasing number of non-agricultural small businesses and with the widening of job opportunities offered by corporate businesses in the post-war boom years.

The stability of the overall factor shares was also the result of compensatory movements in Professor Ohkawa's analysis, in the sense that relative variations in factor quantities had tended to be offset by relative variations in the opposite direction in the rates of earning on labour and on capital. In these findings Professor Brochier saw a conclusion which agreed with the neo-classical theory and he would think them very similar to those obtained by Kuznets. He would, however, like to add that if the share of labour had not shown its tendency to decrease, this was to a large extent due to the post-war institutional reforms. For the coming period, as the free availability of manpower which had had such bearing on the process of income distribution studied by Professor Ohkawa was no longer a dominant feature of the Japanese economy, Professor Brochier would think that this recent development should tend to curb any trend towards a decreasing share of labour in national income.

He had noticed that Professor Ohkawa had calculated the income of the self-employed by imputing to them an income for their labour according to the average of wages in the two sectors together ; knowing how rich the statistical data on wages in Japan were, he wondered whether it would not have been better to use the average rate of wages within the same sector rather than an overall average.

Keeping in view the well-known fact that many of the small firms in the traditional sector were badly equipped and inclined to substitute free family labour for capital Professor Brochier would have thought that Professor Ohkawa's structural share of labour should have been bigger in the traditional sector than in the corporate sector where the production units were mostly of the capital-using type. He had therefore been much surprised to note that Professor Ohkawa's evaluations revealed only a small discrepancy in percentage between both the shares even after allowing for correction made to Table I data (note (4), p. 188) taking into account the relative overvaluation of the corporate labour share due to national accounting procedure. This correction did not substantially alter the outcome of the comparison and Professor Brochier hoped that Professor Ohkawa would say more about the reasons for this apparently anomalous result.

Professor Brochier also wondered what bearing the peculiar Japanese institution of permanent employment had had on income distribution. He would suggest that the phenomenon of compensatory movements in the two sectoral labour shares already mentioned had been a wider one than supposed in Professor Ohkawa's paper. Professor Brochier thought that at the same time the Japanese labour market was characterized by a great immobility of manpower employed in the modern sector (due to the permanent employment system) and by an easy transmission of cyclical movements from the modern to the traditional sector, agriculture included to the extent that the small family businesses tended to hire the excess of agricultural manpower in peak periods. It helped to understand the reasons for the constancy of the overall labour share in the national income : only the recurrent excess of agricultural manpower had allowed for the adjustment of supply to demand of labour in the rest of the economy and especially in the corporate, modern sector. Moreover, Professor Brochier thought that Professor Ohkawa's study, being in terms of factor quantities and prices, had both the advantages and limitations of a market analysis and his opinion was that it should have been extended to take into account the institutional background.

Professor J. Marchal wished to comment on the way Professor Ohkawa divided income participants into groups as he thought Professor Ohkawa did not take sufficient account of the institutional or sociological background of the distribution. The total income in the corporate sector was easily broken down into labour and property incomes. In dividing up the income in the traditional sector Professor Ohkawa had assumed, at least implicitly, that the small entrepreneurs and self-employed people in the traditional sector paid no wages to hired labour and that (exception taken of what was said in note (4), p. 188) all wages were supposed to be paid by incorporated businesses. Professor Marchal suspected that this assumption led to an overestimation of the share of labour in the corporate sector relatively to the traditional one : Professor Ohkawa estimated wages paid by small entrepreneurs to be 3·9 per cent of the total and this figure was surprisingly low in comparison with other countries.

Professor Ohkawa took no account of the labour supplied by unpaid family manpower in his evaluation of the labour share. Even if one admitted that hired labour was of no real importance in the traditional sector, surely unpaid family labour had a great part in it. Again, he thought it necessary to impute an income to them ; in not doing so Professor Ohkawa overvalued the shares of other groups in income distribution.

Professor Ohkawa imputed to small entrepreneurs and self-employed the same wage as the average wages earned by wage-earners employed by corporate businesses, their property income being calculated as a residual. Professor Marchal objected to this procedure. Although allowing for the labour input of the small businessman or the self-employed, this wrongly neglected the work of family helps : had an income been imputed to it in the same way, the total imputed labour income could well have appeared higher than the total income actually originating in this sector leaving a negative amount for the residual property income — a very paradoxical outcome.

Professor Marchal therefore wondered whether this procedure of income imputation to labour was correct. When Professor Ohkawa observed that the labour share in the traditional sector calculated in this way behaved, at least when agriculture was excluded, in the same way as the labour share in the corporate sector, Professor Marchal wondered whether this was not partly due to the method used for calculating the former. Farming excluded, was there anything in this conclusion beyond stating that industrial production in the traditional sector moved in the same way as production in the corporate sector ?

Professor Marchal thought that in any country where a substantial proportion of the national product originated in non-corporate businesses one should break up the income between three sectors: the corporate sector, the sector of small firms engaged in manufacture and trade, and the sector of farming. Whereas in the corporate sector the division between wages and profits was the obvious procedure, in the two other sectors one should not try to divide incomes in this way as the income originating there could not be reduced to wages and profits ; small entrepreneurs' incomes and farmers' incomes should be considered as such within a theory of distributive shares between social categories.

Professor Bronfenbrenner would have preferred the data to be presented in a different way, more along macro-economic lines, by aggregating the data on the overall share of labour and the data on farmers' incomes. For convenience sake this could be called 'proletarian' income. One would then be led to the conclusion that, although the share of industrial wages and salaries rose steadily, proletarian income had been falling since 1955, this being due primarily to the shift of manpower from farming to industry.

Kuznets' conjecture about the behaviour of the labour share in a developing economy had been already evoked : in early stages, capital being rare and labour freely available, the share of labour decreased, while in the later stages it rose as skilled labour became scarce. Professor Bronfenbrenner would suggest that Japan was now at the turning point in this development. His own interpretation of Kuznets' conjecture was that the decisive factor in it was not modernization of the economy as such, but the labour market changing from one on which there was an unlimited supply of labour at the subsistence level to one on which labour had become scarcer.

Professor Bronfenbrenner wished to comment on the so-called system of guaranteed lifetime employment. This covers only the larger firms ; even there it did not apply to their entire labour force as a large part of it was classified as 'temporary' or employed by sub-contracting firms. The proportion of permanent employees was in fact not much greater than in the U.K. or the U.S.A. Contrary to what had been often stated by non-Japanese economists one should not relate the system's origin to the feudal background of the Japanese society: it developed at about the time of the First World War, as an attempt by Japanese employers to retain the skilled workers who were becoming rarer on the labour market.

Professor Patinkin thought that Professor Bronfenbrenner's last statement seemed to imply that by promising permanent employment to their labour force employers attempted to hold skilled labour. But he could not see how this could induce labour to remain where it was employed if other employers simultaneously offered it the same advantage.

Professor Bronfenbrenner answered, pointing out that firms trained their skilled workers along highly 'firm-specific' lines, and that each company offered permanence to its own trainees. In this way each firm protected itself against its labour force being snatched by outside firms, and the system made for less and not more mobility of labour between firms.

Professor Brochier pointed out that the system tended to perpetuate itself. As few workers were willing to leave their employers one presumed that those who had done so had in fact been sacked, hence the reluctance they met from prospective employers. The man who left a guaranteed lifetime employment of his own accord would more or less become a social outcast.

Professor Krelle did not see how the cyclical movements in the two sectoral labour shares could be reconciled with what Professor Ohkawa and Professor Brochier had said about the respective behaviour of firms in the traditional and in the modern sectors of the economy. Since employers in the traditional sector freely hired and fired their labour force and it could find employment in the other sector the share of labour should be more stable than if they retained their labour force permanently. Now he had observed from data in Table I almost the reverse : the traditional sector seemed to retain its manpower and behaved just as it would in European countries where craftsmen and farmers (with the exception of capitalist farming) kept their labour force, whereas employment in corporate businesses fluctuated according to cyclical movements. Either the employers did not behave as had been said or the explanation had to be revised.

Professor Ohkawa said he would like to answer the questions which had been put to him before the discussion proceeded further as they were in several instances linked.

After thanking Professor Brochier for his introduction he answered his three questions. Concerning the division of 'mixed' income, although any method of imputation was somewhat arbitrary, he thought he had chosen the most adequate method in preferring imputing a wage to labour, leaving a return to capital as residual. His main reason for doing so had been that the amount of capital used by small Japanese entrepreneurs was very small and less competitive with the corporate sector. Kuznets' findings covering a number of countries had shown that whether an income was imputed to labour or to capital the outcome was that the returns on either factor in the small enterprise sector were much less than the current returns in the corporate sector. Thus his own findings for Japan were no exception.

Professor Ohkawa imputed a labour income to the small entrepreneurs under the assumption that the unpaid work of their wives and children had no part in national income. He knew that this was a bold assumption but he did not think it far from the truth. Data in Table I should be understood keeping in mind this assumption. The 3·9 per cent figure (in a footnote to his paper) which provoked both Professor Brochier's and Professor Marchal's doubts as a percentage of wages paid by small entrepreneurs in the total wage-bill was the result of his own calculations for the post-war period as this could not be calculated for the previous period owing to lack of data.

Before answering the third and last question put by Professor Brochier Professor Ohkawa observed that Professor J. Marchal had rejected any method of income imputation as being arbitrary. Professor Ohkawa wished to emphasize that he could not agree with the method of income division which Professor Marchal had proposed as a substitute to imputation. The share of labour, W_1/Y in Professor Ohkawa's own terminology, was made up of two different components : the share of wages in the corporate sector and the structural share of this sector's income in the national income. From Professor Ohkawa's own point of view studying changes in the second component was not the true scope of the theory of income distribution by shares ; these changes were only a reflection of the historical evolution of the economic structure. Therefore he entirely disagreed with a suggestion which assumed that the changes in the second component *were* the changes in the labour share in income distribution.

Professor Brochier's last point was of interest, but Professor Ohkawa thought that foreign students of the Japanese economy tended to overstate the scope of the peculiar institution of guaranteed lifetime employment and its effects on labour mobility. It started when the large firms had felt the need for retaining a skilled labour force the supply of which was becoming scarcer, but there had always been an elastic supply of unskilled labour. Besides, signs of change had appeared recently and, having in mind Professor Patinkin's observation, Professor Ohkawa said that the system now tended to disintegrate under the pressure of new circumstances of labour shortage.

Concerning Professor Krelle's question about the effects of cyclical movements on the labour shares in the two sectors, the shift of labour from the traditional to the modern sector could be explained by means of a theory of 'job opportunities'; the inflow of labour in the modern sector was accelerated in periods of boom when employers' demand for labour increased and decelerated in slack times. Professor Ohkawa thought that this movement was not related in a significant way with changes in income disparities between the two sectors. Professor Ohkawa admitted that it was not easy to see how the mechanism operated regarding the changes in relative labour shares in Table I.

Professor Nørregard Rasmussen asked for an explanation of the extremely high share of the corporate sector in the national income. He assumed that a figure of the order of 75 per cent could not be found in any other country even excluding agriculture and government.

Professor Ohkawa answered this by saying that excluding agriculture had been one of the reasons for this high percentage at least for the pre-war period when farming still had a big share in the national income. Amongst the other reasons he would point to the trend towards incorporation of family businesses, even amongst the smaller ones, for fiscal and other reasons since the war.

Dr. Negreponti-Delivanis wondered whether the free availability of manpower had fostered the growth of the Japanese economy or had hindered it under the weight of the non-working population. She also wanted to ask Professor Ohkawa whether when stating an increase in the labour share in national income this meant an increase per head of worker, as the existence of a substantial amount of unemployment during the period of rapid growth in Japan should have been an obstacle to an increase in real wages per head.

Professor Ohkawa said that the flexible supply of labour had greatly supported the steady growth of the Japanese economy but it could not be thought to have been its positive cause. A rapid progress of technology together with the high rate of investment had been the real factors for growth. On Dr. Negreponti-Delivanis' second point he replied that in his calculations he had taken changes in the number of wage-earners into account.

Dr. Pasinetti asked Professor Ohkawa whether data were available on non-distributed profits to appreciate the part they had played in financing the high rate of investment.

Professor Ohkawa said that data were available, especially for the post-war period, but the ploughing back of profits in his opinion had not been an important factor in rapid capital formation as would have been expected judging from the experience of other countries. In the case of Japan bank credit had played a more important role.

Professor André Marchal wondered whether Professor Ohkawa's evaluations of wages included social benefits. In Japan there were two sorts of employees : those employed by large companies enjoyed substantial social benefits such as housing whereas the workers of smaller firms and sub-contractors did not. Any comparison between the wage shares in the corporate and the traditional sector would be biased if it did not cover social benefits.

Professor Ohkawa observed in reply that the scope of his paper had been a study of the long-term movements of the factors shares. He confined himself to the problem of primary distribution and did not try to analyse problems of income redistribution.

PART II

INCOME DISTRIBUTION
IN SOCIALIST ECONOMIES

Chapter 7

DISTRIBUTION OF THE
NATIONAL INCOME IN THE U.S.S.R.

BY

A. I. PETROV

Association of Soviet Economic Scientific Institutions, Moscow

I. INTRODUCTION

A PLANNED socialist economy is characterized by its own principles of distribution. These principles are radically different from
the principles of distribution under capitalism, with its uncontrolled
economic development, continuous aggravation of class inequality
and antagonistic contradictions which organically restrict the
potentialities of the capitalist economic system for expansion. The
Soviet economy is based on public ownership of the means and
instruments of production and the national income is the collective
property of the workers to be used for the progress of society as a
whole. The purpose of planning the production and distribution of
the national income is to speed up economic development and to
secure the uninterrupted improvement of the material and cultural
welfare of the nation.

The principles and methods of the distribution of the national income in the U.S.S.R. are consistent with the socialist system of social
organization. The socialist system has done away with all kinds of
profits derived from exploitation and an end has been put to capitalist
property, exploitation of man by man and expropriation by a
minority of the products created by the work of the majority. 'He
who does not work, neither shall he eat' is the fundamental law of
socialist society. An able-bodied member of a socialist society can
provide for himself and his family in no other way than by personally contributing to some kind of socially useful activity, which
may be manual or mental labour in the field of material production,
culture, science and technology, or services. At the same time,
under the U.S.S.R. Constitution, the Soviet people enjoy a guaranteed right to work and therefore there is no unemployment in the

199

country, nor can there be any. Members of a socialist society who have become old or ill have the right to old-age or disability pensions. The social funds set aside from the national income are making an increasing contribution towards meeting the requirements of the workers and will expand and grow in importance along with the general progress of society. The nation uses these funds for financing all kinds of social services, free education, free medical assistance and for other benefits and grants made available to the workers.

The problems raised by the national income, its growth, distribution and utilization are of vital importance to the workers of all countries and have always been a subject of great interest for economists. The first attempts to analyse the nature of incomes and to evolve techniques for their evaluation date back to the period before the advent of capitalism. These early economic works were entirely empirical and lacked a scientific approach to the nature of incomes and their sources. The classification of incomes of different social groups was arbitrary and untenable.

For example, we can mention the table of incomes in England in the late seventeenth century compiled by Gregory King. This table included lords, barons, knights, squires, gentry, crown and other officials, lawyers, the clergy, commissioned officers and so on in the 'productive' class, while farm labourers, industrial workers, and peasants were classified as a non-productive class which also comprised paupers, beggars, soldiers in the ranks, and the like.

Bourgeois political economy of the early capitalist period and particularly such outstanding economists as Adam Smith and David Ricardo, later followed by Say, Rodbertus, Sismondi, and others, also dealt with these problems, but failed to provide a correct solution. Karl Marx was the first to give a scientifically substantiated interpretation of the nature of incomes, their origin and distribution under capitalism and, in general outline, under socialism.

Adam Smith and David Ricardo came quite close to a correct scientific understanding of the nature of the social income, although they did not distinguish it from the social product. They had a correct understanding of the various categories of incomes in a capitalist society, and specifically the incomes of the bourgeoisie and landlords which are in effect profits derived from labour that was not recompensed. Unlike these great thinkers, popular political economy of the period that followed discarded a scientific approach to the problem of income formation and distribution and achieved a complete confusion of the whole issue. Lenin pointed this out in his work *The Development of Capitalism in Russia,* in which he attacked the futility of an empirical approach to the concept of the national income and its distribution in isolation from its inherent background of the reproduction process as a whole and divorced from social and class relations.

Modern bourgeois political economy is characterized by an empirical approach to the nature of various categories of incomes (wages and salaries, profits, and so on). Incomes are treated as a sum of money received by a person or a group of persons in exchange for goods or services rendered. (In some cases, an income is received not in cash, but in kind, as is the case with the issue of food and clothing to servicemen, meals provided for farm hands by employers, and the like.) As regards the income of a country as a whole — its national income — it is treated simply as a sum of the different incomes. Under this concept, all incomes are regarded as completely independent and derived from separate sources, such as compensation for services rendered through provision of labour, capital or management. This concept is based on the following fundamental principles : (a) denial of the class nature of income distribution under capitalism and, consequently, denial of the existence of exploitation and incomes derived therefrom ; (b) treatment of material production and so-called services (culture, science, government, defence) as one category ; (c) absence of the category of social income as a specific part of the entire social product considered in relation to the conditions of its reproduction, which, in the final analysis, is the source of all incomes and not their sum. As a result of this interpretation of the concept of the national income, its actual amount is grossly overrated, as incomes received by individuals or companies engaged in services are added to the overall figure.

There are a number of other incorrect procedures in calculating the national income which are also responsible for the overestimation of its actual amount. Contradictions inherent in this conception of income are evidence of the fact that it conflicts with the economic processes observed in actual practice. The treatment of all categories of incomes as completely independent of one another not only ignores exploitation, but also denies redistribution of incomes in any form or shape, for example, through direct or indirect taxation. However, in a modern capitalist state, the burden of taxation is too heavy to be ignored as an economic factor and an instrument for redistribution of income, all the more so as taxation hits the working masses hardest. In practice, professional economists cannot but admit that the funds obtained from taxation are spent precisely for financing government, defence and, partly, some social services (education and so on). Out of these funds the state also pays civil servants, servicemen, and others. However, if we are to accept the concept of the separate source of all such incomes, civil servants and similar categories of salaried personnel are themselves producing the equivalent of their incomes and, therefore, no national taxation is required to meet the expenses the state incurs to pay them. This situation brings out in bold relief the glaring contradiction between economic practice in actual reality, on the one hand, and the artificially constructed and erroneous concept of the independent origin of all categories of incomes, on the other. The untenability of this concept is further emphasized by the exceptions its authors are compelled to make as regards interest on war debts and pensions paid to veterans and retired servicemen, since such incomes can in no way be regarded as compensation for services rendered. However, it stands to reason that many other categories of incomes, such as incomes of servicemen, are basically of the same nature.

A number of economists argue that the income distribution may be practically — or completely — independent of the system of ownership prevalent in a society or in a country. Modern bourgeois economists go as far as to allege that not only is just and fair distribution of incomes under capitalism possible, but that there is a process of levelling off of incomes going on in various social groups of capitalist society. However, these allegations are disproved by well-known facts. All categories of capitalist incomes (profits, rent, interest) grow at a faster rate than the growth rate of wages of industrial workers or incomes of small farmers.

The economic theory of Marxism–Leninism postulates that the categories of incomes and their distribution are intrinsically connected with, and dependent on, the relations of production and forms of ownership. In a society characterized by the domination by the private capitalist system of ownership, categories of incomes and their evolution are determined by the economic laws of capitalism. The capitalist system is based on an unequal distribution of material wealth and has as its inherent features class antagonism and exploitation of workers. There can, therefore, be no equalization of incomes under capitalism and no justice in the way they are distributed. The select few of capitalist society appropriate for themselves the lion's share of the entire social income, and this situation will prevail as long as capitalism exists.

Marxism–Leninism regards the national income as an objective economic category and as a specific part of the gross social product created in the field of material production. The public product includes all material values created or provided in the course of production in a given year. It comprises, among other categories of commodities and services, the means of production designed to meet the requirements of uninterrupted reproduction and, therefore, excluded from the commodities and products that make up an income. On the other hand, the national income is composed of the commodities and products (in kind or in terms of their value) which are produced by the total of labour in a given year and which can, therefore, be treated as income and used for consumption or accumulation. The national income is a basis for the existence and development of any society. Various categories of incomes draw on the overall national income of the country and, therefore, it is not individual income categories that make up the national income, but, on the contrary, all these categories originate from one common source and their relative shares in the overall national income depend on the system of distribution predominant in the society in question.

It follows, therefore, that the relationship between incomes is that between parts of the overall product of labour created in a given year. At the same time, it would be erroneous to treat the national income as a mechanical sum of incomes, because, apart from incomes created in the field of material production, there are several categories of derivative incomes, i.e. incomes received by people engaged in services, government, defence, and so on. Derivative incomes come from already distributed incomes created in the sphere of material production. They are built up either from the money paid by people engaged in material production in compensation for the services that they receive, or through the redistribution of incomes, or by the deduction of a certain share of incomes through direct and indirect taxation and earmarking of the funds thus obtained for various national and local needs, including payment of salaries to civil servants, servicemen and so on. In view of the above, the quantitative growth of the total of incomes as such cannot be regarded as indicative of the growth of the social income in terms of its real value. The sum of all individual incomes may go up on account of the growth of the number of civil servants, the strength of the army and so on, while the real value of the social income will remain unchanged or even go down.

The modern categories of labour and human activity outside the sphere of material production proper (such as science, teaching, health services and the like), important and useful as they and their progress are for human society, cannot be a source of income or of any social product. These useful activities and services outside the domain of material production, and the people engaged in them, operate and exist at the expense of the social income derived from material production. However, while emphasizing the predominant role of material production in social development, we do not intend to underrate the tremendous importance of many activities designed to meet the spiritual needs of people. At the same time, it is to be reiterated that these activities owe their existence and development to the material resources of society and basically depend on the manner in which these are distributed.

II. CALCULATION OF THE NATIONAL INCOME

When planning and calculating the actual volume of the national income, Soviet planners proceed from the estimation of the currently produced national income. The currently produced national income is part of the gross social product created through the application of labour in the sphere of material production. The sectors of material production responsible for the creation of the social product and formation of the national income include both those which involve production or processing of goods and those which do not affect the use value of commodities, but have as their functions the transportation and distribution of goods.

The sectors of production which result in new material values include industry, both mining and manufacturing, agriculture and construction : other sectors of material production are transport (of commodities), communication (other than that required to meet the needs of individuals), wholesale and retail trade, the supply of equipment for the means of production, procurement (purchases) of agricultural raw materials, and so on. Transport of goods, trade, and supply are included in the sphere of material production because of the fact that the total value of any specific commodity and the social product, as a whole, is bound to incorporate costs of transportation of goods from the producer to the consumer and costs of commodity distribution. It is acknowledged, therefore, that although no new material values are produced in the process of transportation and distribution of commodities, the value is increased, as added to it are costs incurred to complete the commodity production process and deliver the produced commodities to consumers. However, the aggregate social product is the gross product and, as such, it is a measure of the growth of production of material wealth, part of which has to be reassigned back to production to maintain its uninterrupted flow, just as out of a crop of wheat a certain proportion has to be laid aside to be used as seed for the next year. Out of the total of new material wealth, a certain part goes to replace the means of production, the raw and semi-processed materials and the fuel expended in production and to cover depletion and depreciation costs. The means of production expended in a given year come in part from the output of the preceding years, while part of them is produced in the same year. Only after the expended means of production, raw materials, and the rest have been deducted from the gross social product (or from the gross output of separate industries) can the remaining part of the material wealth (in kind and in terms of its value) be placed at the disposal of society as its income — that is to say, used for consumption or accumulation.

According to the 1959 estimates, material expenditure on production represented 50·8 per cent of the gross social product, and thus 49·2 per cent could be used as the income of society, i.e. available for consumption and accumulation. The balance of gross output over material expenditure on production forms the net output in each sector of material production, while for the national economy as a whole this balance represents the total national income. Already in 1937, 99·1 per cent of the national income of the U.S.S.R. originated in the socialist economy and less than 1 per cent comprised the income created by small-scale private enterprises which did not employ hired labour. At present, the socialist economy accounts for practically 100 per cent of the national income of the U.S.S.R.

The rapid economic expansion in the U.S.S.R. ensures uninterrupted growth of the national income. Thus, in 1962 the national income of the U.S.S.R. was three times that of 1950. The corresponding increase for the United States was 45 per cent; for Great Britain, 28 per cent; for the Federal Republic, 133 per cent; Italy (1961 in comparison with 1950), 86 per cent; for Japan (1961 in comparison with 1950), 171 per cent. The growth of the national income in the U.S.S.R. is based on a continuous increase in productivity which is responsible for a major share of economic expansion. At the same time, the high growth rate of the national income and

accumulation ensures full employment of all the able-bodied population in industry, agriculture, construction, public education, public
health, and other activities.

In 1962, the overall national income in the U.S.S.R. amounted to
over 60 per cent of the U.S. national income, while the income
per capita of the population was more than 50 per cent of the
American figure.

The Soviet national income in 1962 amounted to 198 billion
dollars in absolute value, while the U.S. national income (as estimated in accordance with Soviet evaluation techniques), amounted to
329·4 billion dollars. In the same year, the *per capita* income in
the U.S.S.R. was estimated at 894 dollars, while that in the United
States (as estimated in accordance with Soviet evaluation techniques)
amounted to 1,766 dollars. If estimated in accordance with the
evaluation techniques used in the capitalist countries (i.e. with
incomes generated outside the sphere of material production regarded
as independent incomes and added to the basic figure) the *per capita*
income in the United States amounted in 1962 to 2,431 dollars.
Under the development plan for the Soviet Union's national economy
covering the period until 1980, the national income of the U.S.S.R.
is due to grow almost 2·5 times in the first decade of the plan and
5 times over twenty years.

The national income is a composite economic concept in the sense
that it combines a material and a cost (monetary) content. An important prerequisite for effective utilization of the national income
is a balanced composition of its material elements, part of which is
available for consumption, while the other part is reserved for
accumulation. The part assigned for consumption should comprise
material values of appropriate character, i.e. consumer goods in
quantities sufficient to meet the demands of the population and non-
productive organizations. The share reserved for accumulation is
chiefly made up of means of production (basic capital and operating
funds) required for planned investment and economic expansion.
Under socialism, the commodity-monetary form of reproduction of
the social product and income operates through the incomes of the
population and of enterprises ; these incomes enable labour, consumption, and economic efficiency to be assessed on a cost-to-ouput
comparison basis. One of the major objectives of planning is to
ensure a proper balance between the material elements of the gross
and net product on the one hand, and between the material and
value structure of production on the other.

It follows from what has been said that planning of the distribution and production of the national income should proceed in parallel and be properly co-ordinated. Planning of production and planning of distribution are interrelated, with production taking priority. The objective of planning, therefore, is to provide for the highest possible level of production and of national income, to establish an optimum relationship between consumption and accumulation, and at the same time to ensure the growth of money and real incomes of the workers as a consequence of higher labour productivity.

This purpose is achieved by drawing up an integrated financial plan designed to co-ordinate and balance the incomes and expenditure of the sectors of material production, agencies, and organizations engaged in the non-productive sphere and also the monetary incomes and expenditure of the population. The plan is used as a basis for planning the demand and supply of consumer goods and services.

In practical planning, the features of the national income mentioned above involve evaluation and analysis of the material composition of the national income and of its ultimate use for consumption and accumulation. Plans must also cover the distribution of basic incomes of the population and enterprises and redistribution of the latter in accordance with the ultimate objectives for the use of the national resources.

III. PLANNING OF ULTIMATE UTILIZATION OF THE NATIONAL INCOME IN U.S.S.R.

The distribution of the national income must be consistent with its ultimate utilization, and planning therefore covers, among its principal aspects, the absolute amounts of, and proportions between the funds for consumption and the funds for accumulation.

The share of accumulation (with other expenditures) varies from 26·8 to 28·2 per cent and the share of consumption from 73·2 to 71·8 per cent of the total of the utilized national income.

These proportions have for a long time been typical of the Soviet national economy and are regarded as most conducive to speeding up the country's economic development, and thus to an uninterrupted and rapid growth of the fund of consumption at a rate close to the growth rate of the entire national income.

The Distribution of National Income

TABLE 1
NATIONAL INCOME IN THE U.S.S.R.
1959–62
(Billions of roubles at prices of the current year)

	1959	1960	1961	1962
Total utilized National income	132·9	142·7	151·0	162·9
Of which :				
Consumption	97·3	104·5	108·1	117·0
Accumulation and other expenditures	35·6	38·2	42·9	45·9

(The utilized income is the produced income less losses and undistributed expenditure ; in 1962 the produced income amounted to 165·1 billion roubles.)

The funds for consumption are represented by the total of material wealth available for the personal needs of the population, for the maintenance of social services, for public utilities and other public service enterprises (schools, colleges and universities, amusement and recreational establishments, sanatoria, hospitals, public services, passenger transport, etc.) ; the funds for consumption also include material expenditures on science, research, and government.

TABLE 2
CONSUMPTION IN 1959–62
(Billions of roubles at prices of the given year)

	1959	1960	1961	1962
Total consumption	97·3	104·5	108·1	117·0
Including :				
Personal consumption of the population	88·0	93·9	96·7	104·5
Material expenditure on public services	7·2	8·2	8·7	9·5
Material expenditures of scientific and research establishments and government departments	2·1	2·4	2·7	3·0

When estimating the total of material wealth to be used to meet the requirements of the population in total and in terms of *per capita* consumption, material expenditure on public services has to be added to the volume of personal consumption proper since, in the final analysis, this expenditure must be regarded as a category of personal consumption. On the other hand, expenditure on science and research establishments and on government departments, indispensable though they are if society is to function, cannot be included in personal consumption.

The funds for accumulation can be defined as that part of the national income which is allocated for expansion and development of the socialist economy and for non-productive public investment (such as new housing or construction of cultural and public service establishments) and for maintaining reserves and special funds to meet emergencies.

The funds for accumulation cover additions to basic funds (new industrial and housing construction, other construction projects, equipment and machinery, cattle, and so on), additions to stocks of raw materials, fuel, finished goods, stocks in the wholesale and retail trade, agricultural produce reserves, uncompleted construction, new additions to government material reserves and to the reserves of agricultural products possessed by the population.

TABLE 3

FUNDS FOR ACCUMULATION, 1959–62

(Billions of roubles at prices of the given year)

	1959	1960	1961	1962
Accumulation and other expenditures	35·6	38·2	42·9	45·9
Including :				
Increase of productive funds	13·7	15·7	15·6	20·1
Increase of non-productive funds	9·1	9·6	9·7	9·3
Increase of material reserves and stocks	12·8	12·9	17·6	16·5

The outstanding feature of accumulation in the U.S.S.R. is that a significant share of the total funds available for accumulation is allocated to new non-productive investment: construction of housing, schools, theatres, hospitals, development of city transport facilities and the like. In view of the fact that new non-productive investment is directly available for use by the individual consumer, its share can be added to the share of current consumption in material wealth. These two shares in the national income added together make up the total of the funds used for consumption. In 1962 this total amounted to 123·3 billion roubles, or 76 per cent of the utilized national income.

IV. PRINCIPLES GOVERNING THE DISTRIBUTION OF THE NATIONAL INCOME IN THE U.S.S.R. AND THE DETERMINATION OF INCOMES OF PERSONS ENGAGED IN PRODUCTION

In the U.S.S.R. the national income is distributed in the form of personal incomes and incomes of socialist enterprises. As the product of the collective labour of all members of a socialist society, created with the aid of publicly-owned means of production, the national income is the joint property of all working people of the country. But this is not to say that the total national income is intended for distribution among individuals. The society and the nation require funds for economic expansion and development. A share of the national income must be reserved for building up public consumption funds, for the maintenance of the system of government, and for defence. When discussing the distribution of the aggregate social product under socialism, K. Marx, F. Engels, and V. I. Lenin all pointed out that it is economically necessary to make several deductions from the social product before it is distributed among producers. The deductions are required to cover the means of production used and to meet various needs of society as a whole : socialist accumulation, maintenance of schools and hospitals, and of non-able-bodied persons, and the like. In accordance with this fundamental principle, the national income is divided into two basic parts : the part created by labour required to meet the producer's own needs or necessary labour, and the part created by labour for society or surplus labour. Hence, necessary labour creates the necessary product, while surplus labour is responsible for the surplus product.

The part of the income equivalent to necessary labour is distributed among individual producers engaged in manual and mental activities in material production, the distribution being made in accordance with the quality and quantity of labour contributed by each producer. It is obvious, therefore, that producers do not receive equal shares, as the amount of compensation given to a producer is related to his contribution to social production or other socially useful activity. V. I. Lenin repeatedly emphasized the paramount importance of material incentives for efficient production under socialism and for stepping up labour productivity.

Distribution according to labour is the economic law of socialism. Under socialism, which is the first stage of communism, the productive forces have not yet been sufficiently developed, nor has a sufficient abundance of products been attained, to enable a socialist society to adopt a system of distribution according to people's needs. Psychologically, labour itself has not yet become the most vital necessity for members of society. The socialist principle of payment according to labour takes into account the skill of a mental or manual worker and the complexity of the work done. This principle ensures just distribution, since the criterion followed in socialist distribution is equal pay for equal work regardless of sex, age, race, or nationality.

The primary incomes of workers engaged in material production originate in the initial distribution process of the national income. The fact that there are various forms of recompense for labour in the U.S.S.R. is due to the existence in the country of two forms of socialist property. In state-owned enterprises this recompense is made in the form of wages and salaries paid in cash. Workers employed by state-owned socialist enterprises are mostly paid at piece-rates. The piece-rate system in all its variations (direct piece rates, piece rates with bonuses and so on) stimulates the growth of labour productivity and makes for improved efficiency. In its turn, higher labour productivity makes it possible to raise wages and salaries since, under socialism, the growth of labour productivity and wage and salary increases are directly interrelated. The growth of labour productivity must, however, be faster than that of wages and salaries, since the former leads to more rapid expansion of public funds, including funds allocated for public consumption.

The Soviet economy also employs the time-rate system which has two basic forms : ordinary time rates and time rates with bonuses. This form of payment also takes into account the skill and experience of workers, while time rates with bonuses, employed on a large scale for assessing the work of engineers and managerial personnel, provide a powerful stimulus for the introduction of new technology and fulfilment of production targets. The wage-rate system and norms establish a basis for a proper wage scale, based on the skill of the worker, his efficiency, the quality of the work done, and other criteria.

In the U.S.S.R., a major role in establishing a balanced and stream-lined system of labour organization and of wages and salaries is played by the trade unions. Trade-union sections at the factory level, with the assistance and support of all workers, conclude collective agreements with the management which cover the basic issues relating to the conditions and wages of the employees of the enterprise involved.

The principle of distribution according to labour also extends to collective farms with their co-operative socialist property, i.e. property owned by a restricted group. Income distribution on the collective farms has a number of specific features. The amount of compensation to a collective farmer depends on the output of his collective farm and, consequently, is to a certain extent affected by the weather and climatic conditions of the year. Collective farmers receive a sizeable proportion of their income in kind, i.e. in the form of agricultural produce. The incomes in cash and in kind are distributed among the collective farmers according to the number of work-day units which each farmer has to his credit. The work-day unit is a unit of work and is based on a daily norm for unskilled work. All work done by a collective farmer is evaluated in terms of work-day units, the number of work-day units awarded for each operation being determined according to the complexity of the operation and the amount of labour and skill it requires. Remarkable performance shown by a collective farmer in his work entitles him to extra bonuses in cash and in kind.

In recent years, a number of collective farms have adopted a progressive system of payment in cash. The most advanced collective farms with a high output have introduced fixed guaranteed payments to collective farmers in equal shares throughout the year. These farms have sufficient funds in their accounts to enable them to offset transient effects of output fluctuations in different years on the amount of compensation paid to the collective farmers. The collective farmers make their living mainly from the incomes received by them on the basis of the number of work-day units they have put in in the year for which they draw compensation. In addition, the collective farmers supplement their basic income by income from their individual holdings (vegetable gardens and privately-owned cattle). Under the collective farm regulations, a collective farmer and his family may possess as their personal household a small plot of land (the size of the plot varying in different regions of the country) and a restricted number of livestock and poultry.

V. CALCULATION OF THE INCOMES OF SOCIALIST ENTERPRISES

As has been explained above, the process of the primary distribution of the national income involves, as its major aspect, the estimation of the sum total of the incomes of the producers employed in socialist enterprises. This estimate is based on the necessary product and correlated with it. Also estimated in the same process is the sum total of the incomes of state-owned and co-operative enterprises and collective farms which comes from surplus labour related to the surplus product. This part of the income, which is the material embodiment of labour contributed by producers to meet the needs of society as a whole, may be described as a net income. In practical finance, the net income assumes the form of the incomes of state-owned and co-operative enterprises and collective farms.

The net income of state-owned enterprises includes the net product of the enterprises less the funds reserved for paying the employees. The principal elements of the net income are profits, the so-called turnover tax and some other revenues of lesser importance. The greater part of the incomes of enterprises is transferred to the centralized fund controlled by the state, to be used for financing economic development, i.e. new investments and other appropriations, and also social services, government, and defence. The part of the enterprise's income which it retains for use at its discretion goes to finance improvement and modernization projects. The enterprise also draws on this fund to pay bonuses to employees and finance cultural and social projects at the factory level.

Collective farm finance does not make use of the category of profits calculated in terms of money, but operates with the net income. The net income is the difference between a collective farm's production and the sum total of incomes in cash and in kind (the latter category expressed in appropriate monetary terms) distributed to the collective farmers in accordance with the work-day units that each farmer has to his credit. The net income of a collective farm is used to build up the farm's economic and production potential, to finance social and cultural projects and to make payments to the state.

According to the 1959 statistics, the primary distribution of the national income was shown by the following figures : in the total national income, wages and salaries, collective farmers' incomes received from the collective farm and from their individual households and other emoluments paid to the labour force of the country accounted for 53 per cent, while 47 per cent was taken by all categories of the surplus product : profits, the so-called turnover tax and other sources of revenue.

VI. REDISTRIBUTION OF THE INCOMES OF ENTERPRISES AND POPULATION

An important advantage of the planned socialist economy is centralized control of the major part of the surplus product turned out by socialist enterprises. This enables the state to carry on planned economic development through channelling investments into appropriate sections of the economy. The public consumption fund is also built up under centralized control. Redistribution of the national income is effected by the socialist state, which collects the greater part of the incomes of state-owned enterprises and a limited portion of the incomes of the collective farms and population and concentrates the funds thus received, to be subsequently appropriated under the national budget, the budgets of Union republics and smaller administrative units. Part of the accumulated funds is transferred to the banking system. The redistribution funds incorporate approximately two-thirds of the total profits of state-owned enterprises, all payments of the so-called turnover tax which is in the form of a fixed profit, a sizeable percentage of the payments made by the enterprises to the social security fund, the income tax paid by the collective farms and some other minor payments made by the enterprises into the budget. As regards payments made by the population, the state collects a progressive income tax and thus transfers a certain proportion of personal incomes to the budget.

The income tax and other payments made by the population account for only 7·8 per cent of all budget revenues. In a few years, the income tax now paid by industrial and office workers will be completely abolished. At present, industrial and office workers whose incomes are below the average level, are exempt from the income tax.

Another form of redistribution of incomes within the population is through the payments made for various services, such as transport, entertainment (theatres, cinemas, etc.), personal services and the like.

The next stage in income redistribution is the allocation of funds for financing the national economy, for capital investment, building up operating capital, and similar purposes. Income redistribution is also a source of the incomes received by people employed outside material production (i.e. in social services, government, and defence) as well as a source of funds required to meet the material expenditure incurred by non-producing agencies and organizations. All benefits received by the population through the social security system also come from the same source.

Funds appropriated for social services, including social security, make up the public consumption fund. The public consumption fund is built up primarily from the funds of the state, but contributions to it are also made by co-operatives, collective farms, and trade unions.

The public consumption funds cover expenditure for the following items : free education and medical assistance, sickness benefits, maternity leaves, paid vacations, old-age and disability pensions, allowances for large families and to unmarried mothers, scholarships and stipends, and also other benefits, subsidies, and grants.

In 1963, the total expenditure from the public consumption fund amounted to 35·4 billion roubles, as against 31·9 billion roubles in 1962. In 1963, the salaries of about 4 million doctors and other medical personnel and 6 million people employed in the public education system and cultural institutions were paid out of the fund. The state and the collective farms paid pensions to 26 million people. Over 5 million students received government scholarships. Over 6 million mothers of large families and unmarried mothers received assistance grants at the expense of the state. The public funds paid for over 9 million rest home and sanatorium vouchers issued to working people free or at reduced prices. Kindergartens and crèches maintained mainly at the expense of the state or collective farms took in about 10 million children. In 1963, *per capita* expenditure from the public consumption fund totalled 154 roubles. The importance of this figure becomes particularly apparent if we bear in mind that the total *per capita* consumption in the same year amounted to 517 roubles. When analysing the utilization and distribution of the national income, allowance has to be made, in addition to the public consumption fund, for investments in new housing and the construction of cultural and service establishments and utilities which are an important contribution to the development of the services placed at the disposal of the population. Thus, in 1963 alone, about

2 million new apartments with all modern conveniences were built in cities, towns, and townships. Moreover, the collective farmers and intellectuals residing in the countryside built over 400,000 new homes with the financial assistance of the state. The number of apartments built in towns and townships in the last decade has exceeded 17 million, while about 6 million new homes went up in the countryside.

An appreciable proportion of the surplus product is paid back to the working people through free services, benefits, grants and subsidies, and various kinds of social security, or through the development of community institutions and establishments. Thus, in 1960 the surplus product in terms of money amounted to 67·5 billion roubles (as estimated in the prices of the year and from the ratio between the surplus product and the national income in 1959). Out of this total, 16·3 billion roubles were allocated for building up circulating capital and reserves, 2·8 billion roubles covered material expenditure on scientific and research institutions and government departments with the total spent on the above-mentioned items amounting to 32·6 billion roubles. The rest of the surplus product totalling 34·9 billion roubles was transferred back to the consumption fund either for the needs of current consumption or for the development of non-productive spheres : housing, public health, public education, personal services, etc.

In socialist society, the surplus product is utilized in the interests of the whole of society. This also applies to the part of the surplus product allocated for investment in material production, since economic expansion is a major prerequisite for economic progress and, consequently, for the improvement of the living standards of the working people.

VII. ULTIMATE DISTRIBUTION OF THE NATIONAL INCOME

The processes of distribution and redistribution culminate in the ultimate incomes of the population and of the non-productive establishments on the one hand, and of enterprises and industries for material production on the other hand. The ultimate incomes define the shares of the national income received by the persons and enterprises concerned. These incomes are determined as an algebraic sum of all income and expenditure and, consequently, take into account the balances of all kinds of redistribution. The sum total of all ultimate incomes is equal to the overall national income.

The ultimate incomes of the workers define the amount of the material wealth actually consumed by the population and the growth of the population's property, such as private homes, stocks and reserves for consumption and for households, privately-owned livestock and poultry, etc. The ultimate incomes of the population are estimated according to social groups.

The ultimate incomes of enterprises and industries for material production take the form of additions to equipment, machinery, new industrial construction and so on, and to stocks available for production and sale.

The ultimate incomes of organizations and agencies operating outside the field of material production are achieved through the consumption of resources required to keep them in operation, and through additions to their equipment and so on.

VIII. TRENDS OF REAL PERSONAL INCOME IN THE U.S.S.R.

The real income index for the population is obtained by comparing, for two years or more, the sum total of the population's ultimate incomes measured at comparable prices *per capita* of the population or per actively employed person, and estimated for the whole population or separately for industrial and office workers and for farmers. The real incomes of the population (as well as the ultimate incomes) include :

(a) all kinds of emoluments (wages and salaries, compensation received by the farmers from their collective farms in accordance with the number of work-day units earned, scholarships, subsidies, and other payments from the social security fund, interest paid by the state savings banks on deposits and government bonds, etc.) less taxes, compulsory payments and donations, payment for services (passenger transport, communications, entertainment, etc.) ;

(b) incomes in kind evaluated in terms of money ;

(c) material expenditures in social and personal services.

In 1962, the real incomes of industrial and office workers had increased 2·2 times as compared with the 1940 figure, while the real incomes of peasants had risen 2·6 times in the same period. Despite the fact that in the last few years the share of the national income appropriated for economic development and defence exceeded the original estimates of the 1959–65 seven-year plan, the real income per actively employed person in the five years of the seven-year plan (1959–63) showed a 20 per cent increase. The economic plan for 1964 and 1965 envisages a further 7 per cent increase in the real income of workers. In 1965 the wage and salary fund will exceed the original estimate for the year. The public consumption funds will increase in 1964–65 by over 5 billion roubles and will total 40 billion roubles or about 170 roubles *per capita* of the population annually, as compared with 154 roubles in 1963. The plan for 1964–65 envisages salary adjustments for persons employed in non-productive fields. The minimum monthly wage is to be brought up to 40–45 roubles. These steps are in line with the general policy of wage and salary increases for industrial and office workers in the low income brackets so as to reduce the disparity between the higher and lower wage brackets. The long-term plan for labour envisages wage disparity reduction through upgrading the skills of low-paid workers, replacement of unskilled labour by skilled labour, and economic expansion at a rate that will provide jobs for all able-bodied citizens, including newcomers to industry and workers made redundant on account of technological progress. The 1964–65 plan also envisages pay increases for teachers, medical personnel, and workers in the civil services.

IX. PROSPECTS FOR THE GROWTH OF THE NATIONAL INCOME AND CHANGES IN ITS DISTRIBUTION PATTERN

Under the programme of the economic development of the U.S.S.R., the material and technical basis of communism will have been created by 1980. This programme of gigantic economic expansion which envisages a five-fold increase of the country's national income in the twenty years from 1961 to 1980 provides for continuous growth of the resources allocated for the improvement of the material and cultural well-being of the people. In the U.S.S.R., economic expansion is not regarded as an end in itself, but has as its aim the maximum satisfaction of the constantly growing requirements of all members of our society. 'Everything for the sake of man, for the well-being of man' is the motto of a socialist country.

Along with a tremendous quantitative growth of resources earmarked for consumption, the current twenty-year period will witness important changes in the distribution and utilization of the national income.

The essence of these changes is as follows :

The real incomes of collective farmers in the twenty years will advance at a faster rate than those of industrial and office workers with a view to eliminating the distinctions between living standards in cities and towns on the one hand and the countryside on the other.

The real incomes of persons in the low income groups will grow more rapidly than those of other sections of the labour force.

As labour productivity goes up and more resources become available for consumption, scientifically substantiated and rational standards of nutrition and, more widely, consumption will be adopted.

The proportion of the public consumption funds in the overall amount of real incomes will be greatly increased. By 1980, consumption chargeable to the public consumption funds will account for approximately a half of the real incomes of the population (as compared with a quarter at present). In the twenty years it is planned to increase the annual public consumption funds more than tenfold.

The number and scope of the requirements satisfied out of public funds will progressively grow. Apart from larger appropriations for social security, scholarships, etc., it is planned in the twenty years covered by the plan to effect a gradual transition to free accommodation for patients at sanatoria, free dispensation of medicines, rent-free housing with a modern apartment for each family, free transport facilities and some kinds of personal services, and for free meals (dinners) at enterprises and offices and for collective farmers at work. In the second decade, it is also planned to set up many new crèches and kindergartens with a view to giving each family, if it so desires, the possibility of keeping its children in a crèche or kindergarten free of charge.

In total, in ten years (i.e. by 1970), the *per capita* real income in the U.S.S.R. will double. By the end of the twenty-year period, these incomes will grow over 3·5 times and will exceed the present level of incomes of the workers in the United States by 75 per cent. Larger public consumption funds and free distribution on a wider scale are prerequisites for the transition to a system of distribution in accordance with the principle of communism : 'From each according to his abilities, to each according to his needs'.

The Distribution of National Income

In the coming period of communist construction, payment according to labour will, however, remain the chief source of the incomes of the workers. The U.S.S.R. will also retain money as common tender and as the system of distribution, on the basis of monetary and commodity relations. Under socialism, monetary-commodity relations with their specific features are an indispensable economic form of reproduction.

Such economic concepts as money, incomes, profits, and the like are employed in the U.S.S.R. as effective instruments for planned organization of the economy, for the optimum guidance and control of economic development and as an instrument of just distribution of the products created by the collective labour of the members of socialist society.

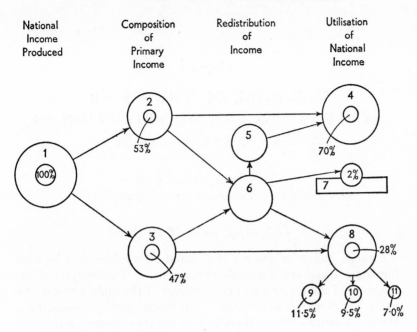

1. National income produced
2. Wages and the other kinds of payments
3. Surplus product
4. Private consumption of persons and material expenditure in the public utilities
5. Derivative and additional income of persons
6. Fund for redistribution of income
7. Material expenditure on science and administration
8. Accumulation and other expenditure
9. Increase of fixed productive funds
10. Increase of fixed non-productive funds
11. Increase of current and reserve funds

Chapter 8

THE ROLE OF THE U.S.S.R. STATE BUDGET IN DISTRIBUTION OF NATIONAL INCOME

BY

D. ALLACKVERDYAN
Association of Soviet Economic Scientific Institutions, Moscow

I. THE ROLE OF THE BUDGET

THE state budget of any country should be considered as its most important social and economic phenomenon. The analysis of the structure of the revenue and expenditures of the budget reveals the nature and functions of the state. The budget vividly demonstrates the dependence of the composition of the state revenue on certain economic principles and shows also the purposes and class distribution of state spending. The predominant form of ownership of the means of production, the type of public production, the corresponding economic relations characteristic of a certain economic formation — all these determine the character, sources, and purposes of the funds accumulated in the state budget.

Thus specific political and economic conditions, and not *a priori* definitions, determine the true role of the state budget in the distribution of the national income.

The state budget is at the same time a very important and effective instrument of economic policy of the state. An increased role of the budget in redistribution of the national income expresses the rising economic role of the state. But if the funds of the budget are spent in unproductive ways, especially for military purposes, this means that the budget is not fulfilling its real objectives.

The budget cannot exert an independent influence on the development of the economy. We should not take seriously any attempts made by some bourgeois economists of the West to present the state budget as some special 'regulating force'.

It is widely known that at present a capitalist state makes use of different regulating measures, one of which is the budget policy.

222

In accordance with Keynes' theory of 'deficit financing', some economists of the West suggest using the budget as a 'regulator of the economy' which should 'balance the economy' and find resources to satisfy the so-called 'collective needs' through 'the control over the distribution of the national income.'[1] That is why some economists regard taxes as an 'instrument of redistribution of income between the rich and the poor'.

In the long run they think the so-called 'national economic budget' is formed along with the state budget and this allows, within the framework of private ownership, planned regulation of personal consumption and investment as a kind of antidote against crises and unemployment and as a way to achieve on this basis 'full employment' and 'a balanced economy'.

It should be noted that these 'theories' contain nothing new or original. Émile de Girardin advocated similar theories in the middle of the nineteenth century. He considered the budget as a means of achieving socialism. The same ideas were proclaimed by Otto Bauer in the twenties of the twentieth century.

Marxist–Leninist economic science rejects the idea that budgetary relations can determine the economic basis of a society and contends that the budgetary relations depend entirely on the basis of the economic structure of society. Thus attempts to reform the budgetary relations are incapable of altering those principles and proportions which are characteristic of the distribution of the national income under the constitutions of domination of private ownership of the means of production. V. I. Lenin pointed out that 'regulation of economic life, if it is to be taken seriously, entails nationalization of banks and syndicates'.[2]

The public socialist form of ownership profoundly changes the social and economic nature of the state budget. With the appearance of the socialist method of production and of the socialist state, the content and purpose of the state budget and its role in the distribution and utilization of the national income are radically changed.

In so far as the main means of production under socialism are concentrated in the hands of the state, the latter becomes an organization which directly carries out functions of control over the economy of the country. The budget of the socialist state becomes accordingly the budget of the whole national economy. Under socialism the budget is one of the important instruments of the complete state

[1] E. James, *History of Economic Thought in the 20th Century*, 1959.
[2] V. I. Lenin, *Works*, t. 25, p. 311 (Russian edition).

control over the national economy. The budget as well as the whole national economy is subject to planning. It is the principal plan — the balance of the Soviet State.

II. THE FUNCTIONS OF THE BUDGET IN A SOCIALIST ECONOMY

If we are to summarize the main characteristic features of the budget of the Soviet State, they may be presented as follows :

(1) the revenues of the budget are principally derived from inter-economic savings ;

(2) the resources controlled through the budget are utilized on a planned national economic basis for productive purposes ;

(3) there is a permanent excess of the revenues of the state budget over its spending and transfers to budgetary reserves ;

(4) the budgetary system is truly democratic ;

(5) the unity of the whole budgetary system is determined by the unified economic basis of the society — by the socialist economic system and by the public ownership of the instruments and means of production.

The national economic purpose of the budget of a socialist state implies a necessity for the creation and utilization of a centralized fund of financial resources, first of all to meet the needs of enlarged reproduction and secondly to provide for rising living standards of the working masses.

The study of the role of the state budget of the U.S.S.R. in the establishment of the whole economy is concerned with two aspects : firstly, the continuously satisfactory commodity-money relations ; and secondly, the production, distribution, and utilization of the national income. In these conditions, the state budgetary resources derived from the national income always have a monetary aspect.

The national income is the source of the financial resources of the Soviet State. In 1963 it reached over 170 billion roubles, having increased 2·5 times against 1952, ensuring steep growth of the revenue of the state budget. From 1952 to 1962 the state budget of the U.S.S.R. increased correspondingly from 49·8 billion roubles to 84·3 billion roubles. In 1963 the incomes were 87·7 billions of roubles and expenditures 86·2 roubles.

Through the state budget, the Soviet State carries out distribution and redistribution of the national income with the aim of providing financial resources for the needs of the national economy and to maintain the institutions and organizations in charge of health, culture, education, administration, and defence. At present about one-half of the national income of the country is distributed through the state budget of the U.S.S.R.

The resources available for distribution through the state budget are limited not only by the volume of the national income and the corresponding total of accumulated and centralized net income but also by the natural-material structure of national production. This means that the sums allocated in the plan for financing gross investment, for maintenance of the non-productive sphere, and similar purposes, must inevitably correspond to a certain volume of the means of production (equipment, raw materials, construction materials, and so on) and consumer goods (commodity funds for retail sale). In practice some deviations are allowed which are chiefly made possible by uneven fulfilment of plans in different branches of the national economy and by offsetting errors in planning.

Such small discrepancies are of a temporary and local character and may be comparatively easily eliminated with the help of direct planned regulation of production and, with the help of the state budget, through utilization of available reserves.

The Soviet State through the budget exerts a carefully planned influence upon the structure of public production, and especially upon the structure of productive accumulation through the distribution and redistribution of the national income. Acting at the intermediate stage of the reproduction cycle — at the distribution and redistribution stage — the budget exercises a decisive influence on the establishment of the proportions of the final distribution and utilization of the national income, and especially on the element of accumulation.

Though the budget cannot create or enlarge the natural-material resources for accumulation, it creates conditions for the most effective utilization of the available financial, material, and manpower resources through the distribution of the accumulation fund among branches of the national economy, among the economic regions and republics of the Soviet Union, and between productive and non-productive sectors.

In recent years in the determination of incomes and expenses of the state budget the following progressive trends have been observed:

(i) the increase of the portion of the centralized fund of financial resources which is concentrated in the budgets of the republics;

(ii) the increase of the share of the budgetary funds which is derived from deductions from profits ;
(iii) the increase of budgetary allocations designed primarily to provide financial resources for development of the most progressive branches of the national economy, and which play a decisive role in the creation of the material-technical basis of communism ;
(iv) the increase of the budgetary resources made available for utilization as a public consumption fund.

The Soviet State through the state budget solves the following concrete problems :

First, it accumulates money resources for the provision of the centralized state fund of monetary resources ;

Second, it spends the accumulated resources for the expansion of production, for financing social-cultural programmes, administration, and defence;

Third, it secures financial control over production, distribution and effective utilization of the national product and national income.

The role of the state budget of the U.S.S.R. in the distribution and utilization of the national income is revealed in concrete terms by an analysis of the structure of its revenue and expenditures. Its significance as an instrument of planned distribution is determined first by the proportion which it covers of the national resources ; second, by the sources of the budget revenues, and, third, by the use of the budgetary resources in the process of their further distribution.

The centralized state net income in the state budget of the U.S.S.R. is secured through distribution and redistribution of the national income in the following ways :

(a) the transfer to the budget of a part of inter-economic savings of socialist enterprises, mainly through two channels — the turnover tax and deductions from profit ;
(b) the transfer to the budget of deductions made under state social, property and life insurance ;
(c) from the taxation and other compulsory and voluntary payments of collective farms and individual persons.

III. THE MAIN SOURCES OF REVENUE

In contrast to the budgets of capitalist countries, where taxes and loans are the main sources of the state funds, the chief place in the revenues of the state budget of the U.S.S.R. belongs to receipts from inter-economic savings and incomes generated in production. This means that the taxes play a minor role in the budgetary revenues of the U.S.S.R. In 1964 receipts from state and co-operative enterprises and organizations will amount to 84·6 billion roubles, or 92·2 per cent of the whole budget, and in 1965 to 93·6 billion roubles, or 92·5 per cent.

The fact that the steady growth of the budgetary revenues is accompanied by changes in the sources of these revenues is natural in the case of the Soviet State budget. In practice it is illustrated by the steady growth of the share of receipts from the socialist economy, and particularly from the state-owned sector, with the simultaneous decline of the absolute size and the share of total resources received from the taxation of individuals. The savings of the socialist economy represent nine-tenths of the state revenue in the U.S.S.R. while the taxes paid by individual persons represent some 7 per cent.

Through the state budget of the U.S.S.R. the main part of the cash saving of the national economy is imposed mainly in the form of turnover tax and deductions from profits of the state enterprises and economic organizations. Since 1930, with the adoption of tax reforms, many different previously existing payments to the state budget (more than 86) have been unified into two kinds of payment — turnover tax and deductions from profit. They form about 70 per cent of all revenues of the state budget of the U.S.S.R. Profits and turnover tax in the U.S.S.R. are of the same economic character. They are concrete forms of the realization of the value of the additional product (net income). As a result of the steady growth of the profitableness of the socialist enterprises of the Soviet Union, considerable changes of the proportions arising from profits and turnover tax respectively are to be found. During the past decade and especially since the reorganization of the management of industry and construction in 1957, the rates of growth of profits have considerably outstripped the rates of growth of turnover tax, though both have been increasing. Thus, profits increased by 80 per cent between 1958 and 1963, while turnover tax increased by less than 11 per cent.

This means that changes in the ratio between profits and turnover tax are in favour of profits. In 1950 the ratio between profits and turnover tax was 1 : 4·5 ; in 1955 it was 1 : 2 ; in 1958 it was 1 : 1·5 ; while in 1963 the total of profits had come to exceed that of the turnover tax. This trend in the ratio between profit and turnover tax will continue into the future. By the end of the seven-year plan in 1965 the ratio between profits and turnover tax will be approximately 1·25 : 1.

In its turn the change in the ratio between profits and turnover tax has exerted an influence leading to change in the structure of the revenues of the state budget of the U.S.S.R. This took the form of considerable changes in the relative contributions of turnover tax and deductions from profits.

Thus while in 1950 the turnover tax formed 55·8 per cent of the whole of the revenues of the budget and deductions from profits contributed only 9·5 per cent, in 1963 they represented 38·6 and 29·8 per cent respectively.

In absolute terms the total deductions from profits in 1963 amounted to 26·1 billion roubles as compared to 4 billion roubles in 1950 — an increase of approximately 6 times ; the yield of the turnover tax during the same years increased from 23·6 billion roubles to 33·8 billion roubles, or by 46·3 per cent. In 1965 the turnover tax is expected to yield 37·6 billion roubles, or 37·2 per cent of all budget revenues and the deductions from profits 29·5 million roubles, or 30·3 per cent of all budget revenues.

IV. THE USE OF THE BUDGETARY RESOURCES

To assure the best use of the national income, the principle of a combination of planning of the centralized and decentralized finances is used. In this connection it is very important to secure a proper balance between the share of the national income used in centralized forms, through the state budget, and the share which remains at the disposal of enterprises, for decentralized use. The division of the net income of the Soviet society between the income of enterprises and centralized net income of the state is planned with consideration of the interaction of the three main factors : the whole volume of that part of the national income which forms the net income of the society ; the requirements of the national economy and of the state for the financial resources to meet the needs of accumulation and public consumption; and the necessity to establish satisfactory conditions for the productive operations of enterprises not financed by the state. But whatever these proportions may be, the leading role is with the centralized finances.

Accumulation of resources from the national income in the state budget is not an end in itself, but a necessary condition for the centralized supply of financial resources to meet the needs of material production and the non-productive sector. Derived from the national income, the centralized state fund of financial resources concentrated in the state budget is divided in accordance with the plans. This redistribution of the budget resources determines the use of that part of the national income which they represent.

In the course of working out the national economic plans and the state budget (they are worked out and approved simultaneously), the structure of available funds in the national economy, the progressive changes within the planned period and the structure of the national income created on this basis, and the necessary natural-material aspects (the relation between means of production and consumer goods) are all taken into consideration. All this predetermines in turn the volumes of socialist accumulation and consumption in the national economy and the division of the resources of the state budget (taking account of inter-economic savings) into the part available for development of material production and the part allocated to the non-productive sector.

Thus the role of the state budget of the U.S.S.R. becomes apparent in two directions: first, on terms of planned distribution of the socialist accumulation, with the purpose of ensuring the optimum branch structure of the national economy and the most rational regional distribution of production; second, in terms of financing those branches of the non-productive sector which furnish services free of payment to the population at the expense of the centralized fund for public consumption.

V. RESOURCES FOR THE NON-PRODUCTIVE SECTOR

The sphere of material production is varied and the purpose is to find the optimum proportions which meet all the financial needs of the different branches of production. The problem is not only to provide financial resources, but also to find the best balance of allocations within the whole sector of material production. The effectiveness of the material and monetary reserves used, and a punctual and adequate 'return' to the national economy also depend to a great extent on this balance. It is no less important to find the proper direction of resource allocation in the non-productive sector. Steady growth of outlays on education, public health service, culture and science with simultaneous reduction of expenditure on general administration and defence is normal for the state budget of the U.S.S.R. Outlays on defence are not inherent to the Soviet State budget but are enforced from without. From the point of view of the utilization of the national income they are considered as losses, productive deductions to the detriment of the development of the national economy and the raising of the welfare of the people. Karl Marx is well known to have said that military expenditures mean nothing more than throwing a part of national wealth into the sea. Thus it is much more rational to use this part of the national income for peaceful purposes instead of piling up ever new mountains of arms and spending a lion's share of the budget on defence. The constructive programme of the Soviet Union for universal and complete disarmament is of vital importance for the peoples of the whole world, if we remember that annual military expenditures amount to 120 billion dollars and one way or another some 100 million people are concerned with military production.

The Soviet Government found it possible to envisage in the budget for 1964 a 600 million roubles cut of expenditures on the armed forces of the U.S.S.R. In consequence in 1964 the outlays on defence will fall to 14·6 per cent of all budget spending (13·3 billion roubles) as compared to 16·1 per cent in 1963. The resources released will be used for peaceful purposes.

In 1964 budget expenditures to finance the national economy will absorb more than 42 per cent of the whole, and expenditures to meet social-cultural needs will take 36 per cent. This means that almost four-fifths of budget spending will be used to finance the national economy and to meet social-cultural needs. Expenditures for financing the national economy are required for the expansion of production and imply the utilization of that part of the national income which forms the accumulation. Expenditures designed to meet social and cultural needs are primarily connected with the maintenance and use of the public consumption fund.

VI. THE POLICIES GOVERNING INVESTMENT

At present the governing principle of distribution of the financial resources to meet the needs of material production can be defined as the achievement, in the interest of society, of the best results at lowest cost. The primary solution of this is achieved through the system of investment, which accounts for the major part of the accumulation fund. The indivisible centralized investment plan, worked out with the help of the balance method, serves these ends.

The balance of investments is of special importance in the national financial balance. It is necessary in order to discover the total volume of fixed asset formation resulting from the volumes of investment and of the bringing into operation of new fixed assets in all the various branches of productive and non-productive activities after taking account of construction already completed at the beginning of the year. With the help of the balance of investments, the absolute volume of the accumulation fund and its share in the national income can be determined as a whole ; the way of using the accumulation fund which will yield the highest national-economic result and achieve optimum national-economic proportions is at the same time discovered.

The building up of the material and technical basis of communism in the U.S.S.R. has in the first stages been associated with a tremendous volume of investment. During the twenty years down to 1980, the total of investment in the Soviet national economy is expected to be approximately 2 trillion roubles. This is six times the total of all investment undertaken during the whole preceding period of Soviet power. In the U.S.S.R., more than one-fifth of the national income is used for investment. That is why the problem of increasing the effectiveness of investment and of shortening the pay-back period is especially acute. In practice it involves the reduction of the amounts of investment per unit of output, that is the creation of larger productive capacities with a given volume of accumulation, leading ultimately to the expansion of the material basis of the growth of the national income.

The concentration in the budget of the greater part of the monetary savings of the national economy permits the Socialist state to organize from the national income the large monetary funds necessary to ensure optimum rates and proportions of enlarged reproduction. In this way high effectiveness of use of the accumulation fund is achieved throughout the national economy, because waste of resources is prevented.

Inter-branch and inter-territorial division of the national resources is determined through the state budget because it is expedient to use a part of the savings made in some branches and administrative regions to meet the needs of other branches and regions of the country. It is not economically expedient to use incomes and savings entirely at the point of their creation. For instance, the need for investment in each individual branch may not directly and immediately depend on the net income generated in it. Apart from the budget, it would not be possible to supply additional resources to those branches which are most progressive and need inter-branch redistribution of the national resources through the state budget of the U.S.S.R. to ensure their development.

In the Soviet Union the task of accelerating the development of the chemical industry has been made an objective. This necessitates a corresponding redistribution of financial resources through the state budget. The general volume of output of the chief chemical products is to increase 3–3·3 times during the seven years 1964–70. The realization of this programme requires over 42 billion roubles, including the expenditures on the development of a chemical base for agriculture which are estimated at approximately 10·5 billion roubles. The economic effect of such a volume of investment in the chemical industry will be shown in the general volume of net income which as a result of chemicalization of industry and agriculture in the period from 1964 to 1970 will amount to 57 billion roubles. Consequently, the gain will amount to 15 billion roubles. Thus within a short period of time not only will the investment financed from the state budget be paid back but also the source of accumulation of resources for the state budget will be further increased.

For the year 1964, an amount of 2,092 million roubles has been assigned to finance investments in the chemical industry, or 44 per cent more than in 1963 ; a further 2,757 million roubles are to be allocated in 1965, or 32 per cent more than in 1964. During the two years, 82 chemical plants and works will be put into service and construction of 37 plants will be started. The realization of these great chemicals programmes will lead to radical qualitative changes in the principal spheres of material production.

VII. THE PUBLIC CONSUMPTION FUND

The necessary allocations are envisaged in the state budget of the U.S.S.R. to ensure the free education and medical services of the population, payments during sickness, paid regular vacations, paid vacations during pregnancy and childbirth, pensions and other allowances. These allocations form the public consumption fund. Expenditures for these needs of the population from the public consumption fund reached 34·5 billion roubles in 1963 compared to 31·9 billion roubles in 1962.

A large part of the expenditures of the state budget of the U.S.S.R. thus represents the allocations to the social-cultural needs, including social insurance. The budget of social insurance in the Soviet Union is one of the methods of financing the public consumption fund from the resources of enterprises, organizations and institutions. The fund of social insurance is calculated as a certain percentage of the wages and salary fund. The size of deductions is differentiated by branches of the economy, depending on the type of production. The largest items of expenditure from the budget of state social insurance are pensions, allowances on temporary disability, on pregnancy and childbirth. They consist of about 95 per cent of the total expenditures of the social insurance budget.

The resources from the state budget are transferred to the population not only directly, through pensions, allowances and the like, but also through the financing of a broad system of social-cultural services, mainly free of charge, as well as through house construction, training facilities, and the like.

VIII. THE RELATION BETWEEN THE STATE AND THE REPUBLICS

In recent years considerable changes have been made in the relations between the state budget and the budgets of the separate republics. Before the reorganization of the management of industry and construction, the distribution of the national income was mainly effected through the state budget. After the reorganization of 1957, the role of the budget of the republics of the Soviet Union was considerably increased.

The handing over of almost all industry to the republics of the

Soviet Union had an inevitable repercussion on the development and structure of the republican budgets. The budgets of the republics of the Soviet Union increased almost threefold from 17·6 billion roubles in 1956 to 47·3 billion roubles in 1963 — and their share in the state budget of the U.S.S.R. during the same years increased from 31·2 to 54·9 per cent. The state budgets of the republics account for approximately one-half of the whole volume of the national income of the country, accumulated and disbursed through the state budget of the U.S.S.R.

The expenditures of the budgets of the republics of the Soviet Union in respect of the national economy increased threefold, from 7·5 billion roubles in 1956 to 22·7 billion roubles in 1963. Sixty per cent of all allocations for development of the national economy were financed in 1963 from the budgets of the republics of the Soviet Union.

The budget resources of the republics are mainly used to finance the national economy and social and cultural arrangements to the extent of more than 95 per cent. Thus in the Soviet Union a strong financial basis for development of all national republics within the brotherly family of the U.S.S.R. is built up.

While considering the role of the state budget in the distribution of the national income we should have in mind the question of those allocations used for providing economic assistance to foreign states in accordance with agreements between governments. Both the agreement signed by the states which are members of the Council of Economic Co-operation on the multilateral payments and the establishment of the International Bank of Economic Development will contribute to the further development of economic relations among socialist states. This is the first international bank in world history which operates on the basis of complete respect for sovereignty and full equality of all member states, irrespective of their share in the capital of the bank. In all this we are concerned with a new type of international relations in the economic and financial field.

DISCUSSION OF PROFESSOR PETROV'S and
PROFESSOR ALLACKVERDYAN'S PAPERS

Professor Haley said he was grateful for this opportunity of confronting his views on income distribution with those of Marxist economists. To the Soviet economists, a preoccupation with the question of factoral distribution or with the allocation of national income between wages and property income must appear to be a problem peculiar to capitalist economies. In a socialist economy there was no allocation of income as a return to the owners of capital since ownership of means of production resided in the state. There was no preoccupation with the inequality of the personal or family distribution since the major source of this inequality — the inequality in the distribution of wealth — in a capitalist economy was reduced to a minor element in the socialist economy. In the latter the major problem of income distribution was that of determining the appropriate allocation of resources to consumption, for the economy as a whole, as against social investment and the maintenance of social services.

Hence Professor Petrov approached the subject of income distribution in the U.S.S.R. from quite a different point of view from that characteristic of the papers on Western economies which had been presented earlier in the Conference. The major part of Professor Petrov's paper was devoted to an explanation of the principles of national income accounting that had been developed in the U.S.S.R. in contrast to those adopted in free enterprise economies.

Professor Haley observed that it suited the purposes of Soviet economies to define national income as the net value of material goods produced in a given time period excluding the value of personal services that did not directly enter into the production of material goods. It followed that national income thus computed fell considerably short of the amount that would have been arrived at if the national income concept used by bourgeois economists had been employed. It did not follow, however, that the wages earned by those who produced personal services were neglected by Soviet economists : they simply regarded these wages as arising from a secondary distribution of the social product which followed upon the primary distribution of national income and as having been made possible by the surplus produced by those engaged in material production.

Professor Haley thought that this different way of treating the national income was derived from the Marxian concepts of production and surplus value. The socialist economists might possibly add that it had the advantage, for economic planning, of stressing the high priority of material production in a relatively underdeveloped economy : only as the productivity of labour in the industrial and agricultural sectors could be increased

I 2   235

was it possible for labour to be diverted from these sectors to the provision of educational, military, medical, and administrative services. Yet surely any such inference could be misleading and would involve the same sort of mistaken concept of the independent origin of different types of incomes that Professor Petrov — wrongly in Professor Haley's opinion — attributed to bourgeois economists.

At any rate the Soviet concept of national income served to emphasize the fact that, as Professor Petrov pointed out, the planning of income distribution and the planning of production were interdependent. Thus the real income of the worker depended heavily on the major planning decision as to the proportion of the national income taking the form of consumer goods as against the proportion taking the form of accumulation and other expenditures. But the real income of the worker also depended heavily on the proportion of this latter category of national income which was devoted to the provision of social services. And of course in the long run the real income of the worker was favourably affected by a high rate of new investment in production.

The distribution of income *among* the workers in the U.S.S.R. however depended first and foremost on the structure of wage rates. Thus Professor Petrov, in addition to providing figures for the major categories of national income for the period 1959–62 and explaining how the aggregate of personal incomes were derived from the production process as distribution and redistribution occurred, indicated the principles underlying the determination of individual wages. Professor Petrov had said that these were related to the worker's 'contribution to social production or other socially useful activity'. Wages were adjusted to differences in skill and the complexity of the work done and so as to ensure 'just' distribution. The wages system was designed to provide strong incentives to efficiency — thence the extensive use of piece-rates, the coupling of time-rates with bonuses, the relating of the farmers' income from the collective farm to the output of the farm. Therefore wage income was necessarily unequal among workers and households. Professor Haley, however, wished that Professor Petrov had gone on to give his readers some idea of how great the resulting inequality of wage incomes in fact was.

He would also have been interested to know what the resulting income distribution by size of household income was. Given the ownership by the state of nearly all capital goods, differences in wealth played a small part in shaping the income distribution. But wage differentials, the private incomes of farmers, bonuses paid to managerial personnel, the favourable income differentials provided for engineers, scientists, and doctors, all of these aspects of the income distribution had a bearing on the resulting household income pattern. What was the outcome ?

Finally Professor Petrov had rightly stressed the importance of the public consumption funds which covered expenditure for free education and medical assistance, sickness benefits, paid vacations, old-age and disability pensions, family allowances, etc. These must have amounted to a value of about 27 billion roubles in 1959, as compared with a total wages bill of 97 billion roubles. In 1963 total expenditure from the public consumption funds amounted to over 35 billion roubles and Professor Petrov had anticipated that by 1980 consumption chargeable to these would account for about one-half of real income as compared with about one-quarter in the present period. Yet Professor Haley hoped that Professor Petrov might throw further light on the degree of income inequality in household income as distinct from public services income.

Professor Ohkawa said that he much appreciated the opportunity he had been given of introducing Professor Allacverdyan's paper. In the first Professor Allackverdyan had explained the role of the state budget in the distribution of national income in the U.S.S.R. distinguishing between two aspects of budgeting : how to raise the revenue to meet the requirement of expenditure ; how to allocate the funds thus obtained between different social needs.

Beginning with the revenue, Professor Ohkawa had been interested to learn that there had been a noticeable shift from turnover tax to the deductions from profits in the state revenue and that it was planned that this evolution should continue into the near future. Why such a change took place and was planned to go further was not explained in Professor Allackverdyan's paper but Professor Ohkawa would guess that this was related to structural changes in the Soviet economy. The turnover tax receipts came, to a great extent, from the sales of farm products whereas the profit deductions were raised on the concerns in the industrial sectors. The progress in industrialization therefore might be the main cause of the shift. Would Professor Allackverdyan tell him whether his conjecture was right ?

On the expenditure side, Professor Ohkawa wished to draw attention to two points. The first was the problem of attaining the optimum proportion between the state (or centralized) budget and the republics' (or decentralized) and individual enterprises' budgets. This problem was closely connected with the 'planned distribution of socialist accumulation' with regard to 'branch structure of the national economy' and territorial or regional distribution. Professor Allackverdyan had said in his paper that, since the reorganization of 1957, the role of the republics' budgets had increased significantly. Why had this reorganization been undertaken and what changes in national income distribution had resulted from it ?

Secondly, how could one ensure optimum rates and/or proportions of 'enlarged reproduction' in Marxian terminology ? In bourgeois terminology this was the familiar problem of attaining an optimum pattern of expenditure on consumption and investment or alternatively an optimum consumption/saving pattern. With regard to investment, Professor Allackverdyan referred to the shift to chemical industries in connection with the so-called 'chemicalization of agriculture'. Professor Ohkawa observed that the investment required by this sort of structural change was truly momentous. What effects on the distribution of national income should one expect from such a change ? Would this simply result in a change in the composition of investment, or would it imply raising the rate of investment in proportion to national income ?

As the optimum rate of enlarged reproduction had to be attained through planning procedure this led Professor Ohkawa to raise a last point. On page 225 of his paper Professor Allackverdyan had written that in practice some deviations from the planned allocations in monetary and real terms for the financing of gross investment, for the maintenance of the non-productive sphere, etc. were allowed in connection with the uneven fulfilment of plans in the different branches of the national economy and with separate errors in planning. Professor Allackverdyan had nevertheless thought that 'such partial disproportions were of temporary and local character' of the sort which could be rather easily eliminated by direct production planning and by allocating reserve funds from the state budget. This Professor Ohkawa viewed as an adjustment process corresponding to the working of the price mechanism in private enterprise economy. What were then in practice the optimum criteria in planning procedure ? Professor Ohkawa would appreciate Professor Allackverdyan's answering this particular question as well as the others he had previously raised.

Professor Reder said he had found Professor Petrov's paper very stimulating. He had, however, been somewhat puzzled by Professor Petrov's statement on p. 201 of his paper that 'modern bourgeois political economy' conspicuously lacks a scientifically substantiated theory of the social income and 'is characterized by an empirical approach to the nature of various categories of incomes (wages and salaries, profits, etc.)'. Contrary to Professor Petrov's view most bourgeois economists would not consider the choice of income categories a matter of scientific accuracy, but one of convenience. What should be done was to study regularities of behaviour as they appeared in alternative systems of accounts and then choose the system in which those relations under investigation appeared most clearly. There was no *a priori* reason why any one set of categories should be superior for all purposes.

Professor Reder observed that Professor Petrov's assertions (p. 202) that under capitalism the inequality of distribution increased according to a secular trend were inconsistent with the facts presented in a number of papers at this Conference, quoting Professor Haley's paper as an instance. Conclusions running contrary to Professor Petrov's assertions might be mistaken. These were, however, the findings of careful study and he would have liked Professor Petrov to refute them specifically.

Professor Reder did not agree with Professor Petrov's statement (p. 202) that 'if we [were] to accept the [capitalist] concept of the separate source origin of all such incomes, civil servants and similar categories of salaried personnel [were] themselves producing the equivalent of their incomes and, therefore, no national taxation [was] required to meet the expenses the state [incurred] to pay them'. He could not accept this deduction. Taxation was necessary to pay civil servants but this did not mean that the output they produced was of no value ; it simply meant that the people were not compelled to buy these services which were distributed free of labour cost so that civil servants' salaries had then to be subsidized.

He wished that Professor Petrov had supported his claim to a higher degree of justice in income distribution having been attained by socialist states with a comparison of statistical evidence in socialist and capitalist countries. A degree of justice in income distribution could not be measured. But a first step was to set forth how incomes were distributed by sizes, by families, by regions, etc. In his paper to the Conference Dr. Bruzek had made a good beginning and it was to be hoped that similar figures would become available for U.S.S.R. In this way one could create a science of comparative economics which would transcend differences in systems and ideologies. One would have to begin by carefully comparing statistical records, and not by ignoring the evidence of statistics collected in countries belonging to another economic system.

Professor Lecaillon said he would first comment on the distinction between productive and non-productive sectors relating to the Marxist definition of national income. As Professor Reder had pointed out this was largely a matter of convenience. On this not only Russian and English-speaking economists' opinions differed. In French social accounts public administration was not regarded as productive whereas in the U.S.A. and in the U.K. public servants' salaries were included in productive services. Now Professor Lecaillon had noticed that Professor Petrov in his paper had introduced wholesale and retail trade in the productive branches of the economy. Was this not departing from the original Marxist conventions ? He did not think that French Marxists would agree with this. They subdivided the non-productive activities into socially useful ones, e.g. doctors', and the parasitic ones including defence and police forces and tradesmen as well. Professor Lecaillon was ready to concede to them that there was at least an argument that went in favour of excluding retail trade ; in a capitalist economy if tradesmen's profit margins were increased because, under monopolistic conditions, retail prices went up what was just an increase in prices would result in an increase in national income. Was the inclusion of retail trade as productive in the U.S.S.R. a recent development and what were the reasons behind it ?

As Professor Petrov had rightly stressed the importance of the final distribution amongst groups, Professor Lecaillon would have liked to be given figures showing the evolution of income shares of different groups such as farmers, industrial workers, and non-productive workers

These shares must have evolved as in any economy. The hypothesis that part of the workers were unproductive and therefore were paid wages out of the surplus value led French Marxists to recognize an objective opposition between those who produced surplus value and those who shared the surplus with the capitalists. Did this lead to the same risk of conflict between the two groups of workers within a socialist economy ?

Professor Lecaillon had a last query concerning the wage policy mentioned by Professor Petrov tending to reduce wage differentials and improve the non-productive workers' wages. What were the criteria for reducing these differences ? Were they economic or political ?

Dr. Negreponti-Delivanis had noticed that Professor Petrov had stated that in capitalist countries rents, interests, and profits increased more rapidly than wages and salaries. She was surprised by this statement as the statistics officially published in the more advanced capitalist countries showed a decline in the share of rents and interests and a slight rise in the share of wages and salaries, the share of profits remaining stable. She would like to hear Professor Petrov's comments on this point.

Professor Petrov had stated that *per capita* income was 1766 dollars in U.S.A. as against 894 dollars in U.S.S.R. It seemed to Dr. Negreponti-Delivanis that one could not draw conclusions about the comparative standards of living from these figures. One needed to know what was the ratio of capital goods to consumer goods in both countries. The higher the proportion of capital goods in the national product in U.S.S.R. in comparison with U.S.A., the lower should be the standard of living in U.S.S.R. in comparison with U.S.A., other things being equal.

Dr. Negreponti-Delivanis would like to know, roughly, what was the kholkoz farmers' share of income out of their private properties in the national income, however small this might be. Professor Petrov had written that the socialist economy covered practically 100 per cent of national income.

Finally she had been surprised to read in Professor Petrov's paper that in 1959 wages and salaries amounted to only 53 per cent of total income in the primary distribution. This seemed a very low percentage in a socialist economy where the great majority of people were wage- or salary-earners. In capitalist countries this percentage was higher. How could this figure be explained ? Was the scope of redistribution so wide that it could compensate for the much greater proportion of wage earners ?

Professor Papi said he was rather surprised that Pareto's law of income distribution had not been mentioned. Did the distribution conform to it in U.S.S.R. ? Could Professor Petrov tell him what was the difference between minimum and maximum income in the various sectors of production ?

Professor Brochier wished to comment on the distribution of consumption expenditure into individual and collective consumption. Not only was this a problem relating to both Professor Petrov's and Professor

Allackverdyan's papers but it was a problem that no society today could escape from. The national product could be distributed either as personal disposable money incomes or under the form of public expenditure as free collective services. What were the criteria of choice in U.S.S.R. and were they purely political ?

Professor Brochier thought that in any society other than a purely liberal one there was a great margin of unsatisfied collective needs so that the share of collective consumption could increase almost indefinitely. This would especially apply to a collectivist economy like U.S.S.R. How then was the share of collective consumption determined ? Was it in preparing the plan or the budget and was there a marked tendency for it to rise in proportion to total consumption ? As it was envisaged in U.S.S.R. to distribute some consumer's goods freely in a more or less distant future Professor Brochier thought there would be some such trend in total consumption. Then the problem would arise of how to preserve the incentive to work in a society where the proportion of free consumption was steadily increasing. Would it not be necessary to increase factors leading towards inequality in distribution, e.g. bonuses to stimulate productivity ? Professor Brochier said he would like to know what were the policy measures used to attain the required distribution of national income. This could be done by measures other than the fixation of the wage scale, e.g. differential tax rates bearing heavily on the non-essential consumption of luxury products. It was a problem relevant to economies which were not entirely planned.

Professor Falise said he thought that both Professor Petrov's and Professor Allackverdyan's papers somewhat over-emphasized the contrasts between socialist and capitalist economies. Professor Petrov had stressed the differences in the concept of national income in the two systems and criticized the bourgeois economists' definition of national income as the sum of separate individual incomes (p. 201 of his paper). Yet he himself concluded (p. 217 in his paper) by stating that in U.S.S.R. the sum of 'ultimate' incomes was equal to national income. Clearly in either system one had to distinguish between incomes originating in productive activities and transfer incomes originating in public expenditure as a redistributive process. Thus the difference in the definition of national income came down to a difference in the definition of what was a productive activity, national income being in any case nothing but the sum of incomes.

From Professor Falise's point of view the problem of the remuneration of the workers was another instance of over-emphasizing the differences. In capitalist countries as well as in U.S.S.R. labour was paid according to both criteria of quantity and quality. The real difference seemed to Professor Falise to lie in the criteria which were chosen for ascertaining both quantity and quality : a market criterion versus a criterion of strict definition by public authority.

Referring to Professor Allackverdyan's paper (p. 227) in which it was

241

stated that in contrast to the budgets of the capitalist countries in which taxes and loans were the main sources of the formation of state funds, in the U.S.S.R. budget the main sources of revenue were receipts from incomes and savings originating in the productive sphere of the economy, Professor Falise doubted whether the difference was as drastic as Professor Allackverdyan made out. In capitalist countries the financing of public expenditure by state borrowing as an alternative to taxation came from domestic savings. On the other hand the Russian type of budget financing implied that sales prices in the productive sphere were fixed higher than the factor costs and this was an alternative to indirext taxation.

Professor Jean Marchal said that he could not agree with Professor Petrov's criticism (p. 201 of his paper) addressed to contemporary bourgeois economists for not distinguishing between 'social income' and 'social product', the latter being the source of all incomes and not their sum total. He thought that the distinction in French social accounting between gross national product and net national product came close to the Russian distinction between social product and social income. There was of course a discrepancy due to the exclusion of services by the Russian, but the discrepancy was made narrower by the exclusion of public administration from the productive activities in French social accounts.

Concerning the Marxist distinction between material products and services, Professor Petrov has recognized 'the tremendous importance of many [non-productive] activities designed to meet the spiritual needs of people' (p. 204 of his paper), but insisted, however, that 'these activities [owed] their existence and development to the material resources of society'. Would it not be permissible to say the existence and the development of the society's material resources aimed at satisfying the many spiritual needs of the population and that the former were dependent on the latter and not the other way round ? Professor Marchal thought that the distinction between productive and non-productive activities was, as such, legitimate but this did not entail the latter being subordinated to the former.

Professor Marchal referred to Professor Petrov's statement (p. 207) about the share of capital accumulation (and expenditure other than consumption) fluctuating around 26·8 per cent/28·0 per cent in the period 1959–62 as being the proportion of national income 'most conducive to speeding up the country's economic development'. Would Professor Petrov comment on this ? How had this proportion been arrived at as being the most favourable for the growth of the economy ? Was it considered as a constant, irrespective of the level of the social product ?

Professor Petrov had written (p. 210) that 'the part of the income equivalent to the necessary labour [was] distributed among individual producers engaged in manual and mental activities in material production [. . .] in accordance with the quality and quantity of labour contributed by each producer'. Professor Marchal would like to know what was the objective criterion devised for measuring the quality of work. How was, for instance, an accountant's and an unskilled worker's work-day compared in value?

As Professor Petrov had said (p. 217) that 'the ultimate incomes of the population [were] estimated according to social groups', Professor Marchal hoped that Professor Petrov would tell the meeting which were the social groups retained in the final distribution and how their income shares had developed.

Professor Marchal confessed some surprise at Professor Allackverdyan's assertion that 'only the public socialist form of ownership radically changed the social and economical nature of the state budget' and at his denial of the budget as an instrument of economic regulation in capitalist countries. Did this really mean that in these countries the state budget could not have any influence on the rate of growth and on income distribution? Professor Marchal would have thought that short of nationalization of private industries and banking there were many effective fiscal means of influencing production and income distribution.

Professor Krelle hoped that Professor Allackverdyan would comment on the third and fourth of the features he had listed on p. 224 of his paper as being characteristic of the Soviet state's budget. By '[a] permanent excess of the revenues of the state budget over its spending and transfers to budgetary reserves' did he mean that the budget was systematically overbalanced? What did Professor Allackverdyan mean by 'the true democratism of the budgetary system'?

Professor Petrov thanked Professor Haley for his profound and coherent exposition of the basic concepts in his paper and also for his comments and critical observations. Professor Petrov was glad that his colleagues had shown such interest in Soviet economics and he would try to answer their questions within the limited amount of time available.

He would first take the principles and practice of distribution of individual incomes in the Soviet Union as based on both quantity and quality of work. Whereas the quantity was estimated according to productivity, quality was a question of qualification of the worker relating to the diversification of operations. In industry there were seven grades of qualification. The system of remuneration of labour according to the worker's qualification gave a material interest to the worker and stimulated the rise in productivity. Distribution according to the principle of labour used in production was just in abiding to the principle of equal pay for equal work and also because there were no incomes other than labour incomes. Collective consumption financed out of social funds covering such essential needs of the population as medical services, education, etc., was about 50 per cent of total consumption. Although social funds were of great importance for the smaller income recipients, direct remuneration of labour was the principal form of income and the differentiation of workers' incomes was based on diversity in qualification.

243

The Distribution of National Income

Professor Petrov said that comparing the productive and non-productive spheres of the economy, the number occupied in non-productive branches such as education, transport, etc., had been 19 per cent of the total in 1963 as against 15·3 per cent in 1953. The incomes of the non-productive workers were 20 per cent of all individual incomes. Professor Petrov wished to make it clear that he did not deny the great importance of science, medical care, education, etc., but he did not think this was an argument for including the workers engaged in these activities in the same category as those producing material value. The general tendency was to enlarge the sphere of cultural and scientific activities and to diminish administrative staff. Trade was inside the productive sphere because its costs were included in the price of the products sold and its exclusion would make it impossible to balance the production/consumption sheet.

Concerning the criticism of what he had written about a decreasing trend in the wages share in the national income of capitalist economies Professor Petrov stated that he had not had in mind any particular economy at any definite period in writing this. He would not deny that in various countries at various moments the share of wages had risen either in primary or final distribution but taking into account rising prices, increasing burden of taxation, etc., he would not think it had been generally so. One had also to be careful not to underestimate the effect of unemployment. The burden of indirect taxes mostly fell on mass consumption goods so that it was not proportional to income : the smaller the income the heavier the burden.

Professor Petrov stated that the consumption of the population had been about 70 per cent of national income in 1959. This figure included only material values and the inclusion of services would enlarge the sum. The high rate of capital accumulation helped to carry out a programme of housing and the building of cultural establishments on a large scale and to raise the general level of consumption (from 1959 to 1963 the real income of workers had risen by 20 per cent). It had been said in the course of the discussion that the comparison of *per capita* average incomes in U.S.S.R. and U.S.A. was biased by the higher rate of capital accumulation in U.S.S.R. This comparison must be made for income and consumption of workers in both countries and this should give a different result because of consumption from non-labour incomes in U.S.A.

Comparing gross national product in capitalist countries' social accounting and social product in the calculations of Soviet economists Professor Petrov thought the difference between the two consisted in the inclusion in social product of all productions even those of intermediate products as they usually appear in input-output tables.

Professor Petrov thought that the discussion had made it clear that Soviet economists were confronted with many unsolved problems. National income and social accounting were still open to research and international co-operation was called for and would certainly prove profitable in this field.

Professor Allackverdyan said he was very grateful to Professor Ohkawa for the introduction to his paper. About his estimation of the part played by the state budget in capitalist countries he would not deny that nowadays this included various regulatory measures but its role was not decisive in regulating the economy. The base of the economy depended entirely on the conditions of material production and this could not be changed by budget control.

Professor Allackverdyan agreed with Professor Ohkawa that the structural change in the budget revenue, i.e. the decrease in the turnover tax in the total state revenue and the increase in the deduction of profits in proportion, was related to the progress of industrialization. The turnover tax had played a momentous role in the past as the instrument for a centralized redistribution of resources between the branches of production. The turnover tax was a tax only in name as it was part of the same profit on state enterprises as that which was ploughed back in investment. The major part of the turnover tax receipts came from industry, not agriculture, as had been suggested by Professor Ohkawa.

The decentralization measures in 1957 had enhanced the role played by the budgets of the Soviet republics in distributing the national income. Whereas about 30 per cent of national income was distributed through the budgets of the republics before the reform now this proportion was about 50 per cent.

Professor Allackverdyan said that an optimum investment/consumption proportion in expenditure implied aiming at the maximum efficiency through the minimum expenditure. Research in the optimizing process was now carried out in U.S.S.R. by means of mathematical methods and computing machines. Professor Allackverdyan thought Professor Reder had been right in stating that the way to ascertain which economic system and set of analytical income categories were the best was through a comparison of their economic performance.

Professor Allackverdyan stated that the annual excess of budget revenue over expenditure was utilized to form a reserve fund of credit resources available to state banks. Of all credit, 50 per cent was from budget resources. By the democratic character of the budget Professor Allackverdyan meant a process of choice ordering the determination and fulfilment of objectives in which due allowance was made for the budget rights of local administrations.

Chapter 9

THE MAIN FACTORS AND METHODS OF THE INCOME DISTRIBUTION IN THE CZECHOSLOVAK SOCIALIST REPUBLIC

BY

ANTONIN BRUZEK

I. THE CRITERIA OF A DISTRIBUTION POLICY

THE problem of the distribution of the national income is very important in all types of economies, in spite of the fact that the forms and aims of distribution are different depending on the type of ownership of the means of production. On the one hand it is necessary to examine the question of how the quantity of products produced is or ought to be distributed ; on the other, the distribution of income has a great influence on production. In other words, this means that the distribution is not only a question of equity in the distribution of income and of rise in the standard of living, but also an incentive for or a brake to economic growth. Therefore I think that it is necessary to examine the distribution of income from these two points of view. From the human and economic point of view it is not right to maintain excessive differences in incomes, but neither is it possible or useful to introduce conditions of absolute equity in the distribution of income.

In socialist countries both inadequate and excessive differences in the income distribution in comparison with the work done by individuals have a negative influence on economic growth. The main reason lies in the fact that a levelling of income does not create sufficient incentive to work because in this case nearly everyone receives the same money income regardless of the amount of work done. Therefore, proceeding from the present economic level it is necessary in the socialist countries to maintain and even increase a certain differentiation of income according to the work done. The higher the contribution to production, the higher the income received, and conversely. If this condition is not fulfilled, economic growth is slowed down and as a consequence incomes cannot rise sufficiently.

Excessive differences in income are to be rejected not only from the human point of view but also because lower or higher incomes in comparison with the corresponding contributions to production do not create incentives to work. If incomes are lower than the relevant contribution to production, people show no interest in their work, cannot renew their capacity to work to a sufficient extent, usually cannot improve their qualifications, etc. These factors act as a brake to production.

If incomes are too high — that is higher than the pertinent contributions to production — this is not only unjust, but in many cases fails to provide an incentive for more and better work, higher qualifications, and so on. It is, of course, very difficult to determine what are the correct incomes for the work done and what is the influence of the distribution on economic growth, but it is useful and necessary to examine this question.

II. DISTRIBUTION POLICIES IN CZECHOSLOVAKIA

Let us now consider how this problem is solved in Czechoslovakia. In the socialist countries a so-called 'net material product' (national income), which is defined as the total value of goods and productive service minus the value of intermediate commodities consumed in the process of production, is created and distributed. Economic activities not contributing directly to material production, such as public administration and defence, passenger transportation, communications not serving material production, educational and scientific services, medical services, financial services, personal, cultural and social services and similar activities, are not included. The national income as computed in Western countries is therefore always higher. In the United States it was higher in the last twelve years by 22 to 30 per cent.

The net material product is created by only a part of the people (productive) but is distributed among all people — productive, non-productive, and non-working. In the first stage of distribution (first distribution), the net material product is divided into two main parts : the first part is the so-called 'product for the producer', which takes the form of wages and salaries, paid in the sphere of material production ; the other part is the so-called 'product for society'.

It is possible to compare the latter only from the quantitative point of view to some extent with the terms used in Western countries — 'income originating in business' (but only in agriculture, mining, construction, manufacturing, wholesale and retail trade, goods transportation), after deduction of all wages, salaries, and supplements to wages and salaries, and after addition of indirect taxes from durable and non-durable goods. This comparison is not perfect, but it serves our purpose. In other words it is possible to say that the 'product for society', which in Western countries is equal to the corporate profits before tax, the income of unincorporated enterprises and the net interest and inventory valuation adjustment in the above-mentioned industries, including indirect taxes in the socialist countries takes the following forms :

(a) net income of state enterprises (profit) ;
(b) centralized net income of the state (turnover tax) ;
(c) social insurance taxes ;
(d) trading surcharge ;
(e) net income of co-operatives.

This first stage of distribution is carried out in the sphere of production.

With this kind of distribution money incomes were received only by workers in the productive sphere and by socialist (state and co-operative) production and trade enterprises. Money incomes were not received by employees in the non-productive sphere and by persons who do not work.

This is achieved in the second stage of distribution (re-distribution) by means firstly, of the state budget, services, and the credit system.

The state, as the owner of the main means of production, has the possibility and is compelled, on the one hand, to accumulate money incomes and, on the other, to distribute them, because it has to ensure the development of the national economy and the non-productive sphere.

This is ensured in the following way : a part of the above-mentioned incomes goes to the state budget. The first part of the 'product for society' (profit) remains at the disposal partly of the enterprises and partly of the state budget. The turnover tax, which represents the difference between the prime cost of production and the wholesale price after the deduction of the trading surcharge, is fully centralized in the state budget. An additional income of the state is the contribution to national insurance, a part of the net income of co-operatives in the form of agricultural tax and also income tax from wages and salaries, various fees, and the like.

The non-productive sphere (services) receives contributions from the state budget (subsidies) and from the population, as well as from the productive sphere for services rendered to them.

The re-distribution of money incomes in the credit system plays a relatively less important role than the state budget and services. Receipts are gained from the productive sphere (interests, etc.) from the population (savings, interests, etc.) and from the state budget.

By means of the distribution and re-distribution of incomes we receive final incomes which can be divided into two main parts : the first part represents the sum total of incomes, which are earmarked for the personal consumption of the population ; the other part is represented by incomes which remain in socialist enterprises and in the hands of the state for accumulation and for government expenditures on goods other than for personal use.

III. THE PRINCIPLES DETERMINING RELATIVE INCOMES

Let us examine now in detail the main principles and methods which are used for the distribution of incomes among individual workers in Czechoslovakia. This distribution takes two basic forms :

(i) people may receive incomes related to their work in the productive or non-productive sphere (wages, salaries, rewards) ;

(ii) people may receive incomes without any relation to the work done in the form of money income or in kind (pensions, scholarships, gifts, medical care, education, social security, cultural services, family allowances, etc.).

The main part of such incomes is based on work and takes the form of wages and salaries. Work is paid for on the basis of quantity, quality, and its usefulness to society. There is equal pay for equal work, but there are no equal incomes. It means that those who contribute most toward economic development will therefore benefit most. In such a way the personal income distribution should promote the most rapid growth. The system of workers' wages ensures a greater interest in higher qualification and consequently in higher earnings for those who do the socially most important work and those who work under the most difficult conditions. A planned economy makes it possible to introduce bonuses for wage- and salary-earners to stimulate the fulfilment and surpassing of planned targets, to effect economies in raw material and to improve the quality of products. Besides this, rewards are paid for exemplary work from the 'enterprise's workers' fund', which is one part of the profit, from special funds of the government, a ministry or the Central Council of Trade Unions.

With the social productivity of labour and the volume of production rising, wages and salaries can be increased. But it is not only a question of nominal wage increases. Their real value rises also. The rise of the real value of wages can be seen from a comparison with 1937, when average wages and salaries amounted to 764 crowns a month. In 1962 the average was 1,391 crowns. Taking 1937 as 100, we find that the index for 1962 was 182·0. During the same period the cost of goods and services rose from 100 to 114·1. The index of real wages rose therefore by 59·5 per cent.

A more detailed indication of the trend of wages and salaries in the past ten years is evident from the following table:

TABLE 1

THE WAGE FUND AND NOMINAL AND REAL WAGES *
IN CZECHOSLOVAKIA, 1953–62

Year	Average Number of Wage and Salary Workers (in thousands)	Wage and Salary Fund (millions of crowns)	Average Monthly Wage (crowns)	Index of Nominal Wages and Salaries	Index of the Cost of Living of Households	Index of Real Wages of Workers and Employees
1953	4,029	52,459	1,085	100·0	100·0	100·0
1954	4,178	58,068	1,158	106·6	96·7	110·3
1955	4,267	60,713	1,186	109·3	94·1	116·2
1956	4,386	64,814	1,232	113·5	91·7	123·8
1957	4,514	68,002	1,255	115·7	89·9	128·7
1958	4,572	70,321	1,282	118·2	89·7	131·7
1959	4,682	73,562	1,309	120·6	87·6	137·7
1960	4,829	78,162	1,349	124·3	85·1	146·1
1961	5,000	82,946	1,382	127·4	84·5	150·8
1962	5,152	85,987	1,391	128·2	85·6	149·8

* The Unified Agricultural Co-operatives and apprentices excluded.

Source : *Statisticka rocenka C.S.S.R. 1963*, str. 115, 41. *Czechoslovak Economic Papers*, **2**, 1962, p. 199, 204.

The above figures show that the growth of real wages was influenced both by an increase in nominal wages and by a reduction in the cost of living. It was made possible by the rapid growth of the national income (net material product), whose level was higher in 1962 in comparison with 1953 by nearly 80 per cent (in comparison with 1948 the index is 272).

The general growth in wages and salaries was not the same in all sectors of the national economy and the level of average wages and salaries also varies somewhat. It corresponds to the theory that the income of individual workers is dependent on the quantity, quality, and the usefulness of their work to society.

TABLE 2

AVERAGE MONTHLY WAGES AND SALARIES
IN DIFFERENT INDUSTRIES

(Crowns)

	1955	1962
National economy, total	1,186	1,391
A. Material production, total	1,206	1,421
1. Industry	1,279	1,482
2. Construction	1,350	1,545
3. Agriculture	898	1,174
4. Forestry	1,064	1,315
5. Transport	1,262	1,544
6. Communications	1,019	1,259
7. Material and technical supply	1,171	1,358
8. Trade	985	1,104
9. State purchase	1,064	1,228
B. Non-material production, total	1,103	1,273
10. Transport	1,259	1,495
11. Communications	1,019	1,259
12. Science and research	1,452	1,590
13. Municipal services	990	1,043
14. Housing	701	806
15. Public health and social security	987	1,146
16. Education, culture, etc.	1,036	1,254
17. Administration and justice	1,193	1,391
18. Banking and insurance	1,180	1,307
19. Social organizations	1,231	1,334

Source : *Statisticka rocenka C.S.S.R., 1963*, p. 116.

The average level of incomes is higher in the sphere of material production than of non-material production (the ratio of non-material production to material production was 89·6 per cent in 1962). The ratio within the material production sphere between the highest income (construction) and the lowest (trade) income is 71·4 per cent, and within non-material production 50·7 per cent (the highest incomes are in science and research and lowest in housing). Differences exist also within individual sectors of the economy. For instance the differentiation in industry (mining and manufacturing) in 1960 was as follows :

TABLE 3

RELATIVE INCOMES IN DIFFERENT INDUSTRIES
IN 1960

Fuel	100·0
Metal mining and metals	82·9
Electric energy	79·4
Heavy machinery	78·5
Chemicals and allied products	71·2
Food industry	63·8
Consumer-goods industry	60·0

IV. THE EXTENT OF INEQUALITY

From the above-mentioned figures it is quite clear that there is inequality in the distribution of incomes, which has its origin in the work done. The reason consists in the fact that the abilities of individual workers are different ; different also is the level of productivity of labour in individual industries ; the reason is also to be found in the division of labour among individual workers (e.g. mental and physical work, etc.) and in the different degrees of usefulness of the individual industries for society. Equity lies in the fact that for the same work everybody must receive the same income.

It has already been said that these differences are absolutely necessary under the present economic conditions of the country, as there is no other way of distributing incomes (an equal share for everyone or a share according to the needs), if we do not want to slow down economic growth. There is no other way of distributing incomes in a society where all the means of production are socialized.

But real equality or inequality in the distribution of incomes is not dependent only on the work done, but also on the size of families and on the number of family members who are employed. With the same income in two families there is a different income *per capita*, if, for example, the number of children varies. This is quite evident from the following table :

TABLE 4

AVERAGE NET YEARLY INCOME
OF PARTICULAR SOCIAL GROUPS OF HOUSEHOLDS
ACCORDING TO THE SIZE OF HOUSEHOLDS IN 1960 *
(Average income *per capita* in crowns)

Social Groups of Households		Households					
	General Average	with 1 Member	with 2 Members	with 3 Members	with 4 Members	with 5 Members	with 6 Members and more
Workers	7,187	12,690	10,013	8,192	6,844	5,964	5,039
Employees	8,375	14,092	11,478	9,284	7,678	6,740	5,587
Members of UAC †	5,748	7,757	6,800	6,459	5,737	5,049	4,321
Private farmers	3,905	5,717	4,652	4,861	4,082	3,553	2,787
Farmers working in industry and running private farms	5,718	11,300	8,670	7,381	6,066	5,386	4,460
Pensioners	5,853	5,598	5,799	6,687	6,207	5,117	4,312
Artisans, etc.	7,292	10,126	6,902	7,668	9,447	6,163	5,192
Others	3,843	3,295	4,175	4,166	4,222	3,927	2,511
Total (1960)	7,040	8,430	8,320	8,066	6,933	5,950	4,872
Total (1958)	6,358	7,536	7,792	7,325	6,437	5,362	4,200
Index (1960/1958)	110·7	111·1	106·8	110·1	107·7	111·0	116· 0

* Based on a sample budget inquiry covering 31,000 households.
† Unified Agricultural Co-operatives.

Source : *Statisticka rocenka C.S.S.R.*, *1962*, p. 375. *Czechoslovak Economic Papers*, **2**, p. 236.

V. WELFARE SERVICES

These different incomes, based on work, are not the only indicators of income. The state offers the working people other material advantages and services, which on the one hand raise their material and cultural level and on the other reduce the differentiation of incomes among individuals in society caused by social factors (number of children, etc.). This is done on the one hand in the form of money incomes (children's allowances, subsidies for workers, lunches in canteens, scholarships for university sudents, subsidies for newly married couples, pensions, social insurance, etc.) and on the other in the form of various amenities and services (free medical care, medicines and spa treatment, cheap housing, free tuition in all schools and universities. In all schools, except universities, pupils and students receive all text-books, copybooks, pencils, and other school aids free of charge. Very cheap meals and cultural facilities are available for children in schools and nursery schools, etc.). This so-called social component of wages in the case of a family of four amounts to something like an additional 40 per cent of gross average wages.

This form of distribution plays a very important role in the whole system of distribution at present and its role will permanently increase in the future in relation to the distribution according to the work done. In this connection it is necessary to examine the correct proportions between these two forms of distribution. Too slow a growth of the latter type of distribution does not eliminate the social differences in the income distribution and slows down production if the means provided for schools, medical care, etc., are insufficient. On the other hand, if this growth is too high (e.g. higher than the growth of production), the influence on production may be negative, as it is not possible to increase wages to a sufficient degree and in such a way as to increase labour incentives.

VI. CONCLUSION

From all that has been said, it is quite evident that the distribution of incomes in socialist countries can, in a high degree, influence the rate of economic growth. If this influence is to be positive, it is necessary to use such forms of distribution that ensure that incentives work better. From this point of view the distribution of the national income must be considered one of the most important factors which influence economic growth and thus create conditions for the faster growth of incomes.

Chapter 10

THE STATE BUDGET AND NATIONAL INCOME DISTRIBUTION

BY

Dr. L. URBAN

I. THE GROWING ROLE OF THE STATE BUDGET

SINCE World War II we are witnesses to the fact that, in almost all countries, the significance of the state budget for national income distribution has been steadily growing. The Federal budget expenditures in the U.S.A. represented only 9·8 per cent of the national income in 1929, and, during the years immediately before World War II, 12·2 per cent, while in Britain they represented about 22 per cent; in the post-war period this figure is substantially higher: in recent years in the U.S.A. it amounts to 18–20 per cent, in Britain it exceeds 20 per cent, in Western Germany it amounts to 16–17 per cent. This means that the redistribution of the national income by means of the state budget (its receipts and expenditure aspect) has become an important instrument of economic policy and planning.

We can follow a similar process in Czechoslovakia. If before the war the state budget redistributed about one-fifth of the national income, then in the post-war period more than one-half of the national income (net material product) is redistributed through the state budget.

To a certain extent we have here to deal with similar processes taking place in countries with different social and economic institutions. It is of course evident that in the socialist countries the redistributional function of the state budget is much more important, as is apparent from the higher share of the state budget in the national income.

A more profound analysis would show that besides particular

255

The Distribution of National Income

quantitative differences, which need not necessarily be substantial, a greater difference lies in the structure of the state budget both on the receipts and expenditures side. In particular, these structural features make the state budget in the Czechoslovak Socialist Republic one of the most important instruments for economic planning which itself presupposes a number of fundamental changes in the distribution of national income. The state budget in Czechoslovakia therefore plays an important role in ensuring a high and steady rate of growth of national income.

II. RECENT TRENDS IN CZECHOSLOVAKIA

We can get some idea of this role if we recall the structure of the state budget in pre-war Czechoslovakia. In 1937 it amounted to 13·9 million koruna ; 30·6 per cent of its expenditures were used for military purposes, internal security, and state administration, 17·4 per cent for cultural and welfare measures (including education and health services), 42·3 per cent for state enterprises (which were partially working with a deficit), and only 7·8 per cent were investment expenditures ; 9·7 per cent of expenditures were used as state debt reimbursement.

In the post-war period the expenditure structure, on the other hand, shows the following features :

TABLE 1

DISTRIBUTION OF STATE EXPENDITURE IN CZECHOSLOVAKIA
1955–63

	Total	The National Economy	Culture and Welfare	Defence and Security	Administration
1955					
in million kčs	86,039	43,865	28,276	10,429	3,469
in per cent	100·0	51·0	32·9	12·1	4·0
1956					
in million kčs	89,887	48,093	28,779	9,606	3,409
in per cent	100·0	53·5	32·0	10·7	3·8
1957					
in million kčs	97,919	53,155	31,932	9,319	3,513
in per cent	100·0	54·3	32·6	9·5	3·6

Urban — The Budget and Distribution in Czechoslovakia

TABLE 1—*contd.*

	Total	The National Economy	Culture and Welfare	Defence and Security	Administration
1958					
in million kčs	94,530	45,317	36,927	8,933	3,353
in per cent	100·0	47·8	39·1	9·4	3·6
1959					
in million kčs	95,913	45,703	38,415	8,789	3,006
in per cent	100·0	47·6	40·1	9·2	3·1
1960					
in million kčs	103,406	51,341	40,286	8,783	2,996
in per cent	100·0	49·6	39·0	8·5	2·9
1961					
in million kčs	111,915	57,222	42,441	9,512	2,740
in per cent	100·0	51·1	37·9	8·5	2·5
1962					
in million kčs	123,201	64,747	44,831	10,854	2,769
in per cent	100·0	52·6	36·4	8·8	2·2
1963					
in million kčs	125,815	65,620	46,117	11,332	2,746
in per cent	100·0	52·2	36·5	9·0	2·2

Source: *Statistical Yearbook of the Czechoslovak Socialist Republic, 1962*, p. 474. *Statistical Yearbook of the Czechoslovak Socialist Republic, 1963*, p. 478.

It is *prima facie* evident that in the post-war period, besides a great increase in the volume of the state budget, approximately one-half of its expenditure is being permanently used for the development of the economy (80 per cent of this sum is used for investment), more than one-third, on average, are expenditures for cultural and welfare measures, and expenditures for the defence of the country and for administration are a relatively small portion of the total (11 to 12 per cent).

This relatively high increase in expenditure must of course be in harmony with the corresponding changes in the state budget receipts. The majority of the receipts in the pre-war budget came from taxing the population. Today taxes, duties, and other payments from individuals represent 10 to 11 per cent of the state budget receipts. The decisive part of budget receipts consists in payments by socialist enterprises. A more detailed picture of this can be seen in the following table:

TABLE 2

STATE BUDGET RECEIPTS IN CZECHOSLOVAKIA
1955–63

	Total	Receipts from the Socialist Sector of the Economy	Taxes, Duties and other Payments by the Population	Other Receipts
1955				
in million kčs	86,209	73,128	10,256	2,825
in per cent	100·0	84·8	11·9	3·3
1956				
in million kčs	90,304	77,244	10,730	2,330
in per cent	100·0	85·5	11·9	2·6
1957				
in million kčs	98,240	85,092	10,683	2,465
in per cent	100·0	86·6	10·9	2·5
1958				
in million kčs	94,725	80,406	11,312	3,007
in per cent	100·0	84·9	11·9	3·2
1959				
in million kčs	96,230	81,771	11,313	3,146
in per cent	100·0	85·0	11·7	3·3
1960				
in million kčs	103,593	89,070	11,268	3,255
in per cent	100·0	86·0	10·9	3·1
1961				
in million kčs	112,534	97,255	11,777	3,502
in per cent	100·0	86·4	10·5	3·1
1962				
in million kčs	123,322	107,066	12,498	3,758
in per cent	100·0	86·8	10·1	3·1
1963				
in million kčs	125,877	108,873	12,767	4,237
in per cent	100·0	86·5	10·1	3·4

Source : *loc. cit.*

The changes described above in the expenditure and receipts structure of the state budget in the Czechoslovak Socialist Republic are connected with the profound social and economic changes which have taken place in this country. They reflect the fact that the means of production have been removed from private ownership and have become socially owned (in state or co-operative form).

These important changes in the manner of distributing national income, which are reflected in the volume and structure of the state budget, make it possible to concentrate considerable economic resources and overcome obstacles, which would probably be impossible to surmount given the existence of private ownership of the means of production. On the other hand, the availability of so large a share of the national income not only makes it possible, but makes it necessary, to produce a long-term economic plan, calculated with regard to the given possibilities and expected trends of development.

In this way, in spite of the general increase in the state budgets of all industrially developed countries, a relatively marked difference remains between the socialist and capitalist countries as far as the receipts and expenditures structure of the state budget is concerned. We have to take this difference into account when evaluating the role of the state budget in economic policy, as well as in long-term planning, both of which influence the development of the national income.

III. THE INFLUENCE OF THE BUDGET ON DEVELOPMENT

In the next part of this paper we shall try to specify what is the economic influence of the expenditure items of the state budget in Czechoslovakia on the long-term development of national income, as well as on its composition.

As has already been stated, more than half of the expenditures of the state budget in the Czechoslovak Socialist Republic are used for the development of the economy. The appropriations of the state budget for the economy have to cover the investment expenditures for new enterprises and their current assets, technical development, price subsidies, coverage for eventual losses of particular enterprises, financial aid to individual agricultural co-operatives, the formation of state material reserves, geological research, and other purposes.

The significance of centralized allocations from the state budget is that they ensure the construction of expensive investment projects of State-wide importance, such as, for example, power-dams, electric power plants, iron and steel mills, etc., and in this way ensure an accelerated rate of growth of production and labour productivity in the key branches. But at the same time it must be clear that there are also many requirements in that part of the economy which it is neither necessary nor useful to finance directly from the state budget. It has proved more useful to use for their financing the decentralized resources of individual enterprises, or credit, or both. This is the method used to finance small investments, the majority of increases in current assets of enterprises, as well as some expenditures for technical development, etc.

Because the state budget concentrates such an important share of the national income (one-half is being used for the development of the national economy in key industries), it is possible to create the conditions where the state budget is an instrument of accelerated growth.

TABLE 3

GROWTH OF THE CZECHOSLOVAK
NATIONAL INCOME AT CONSTANT PRICES

(1948 = 100)

1950	.	. 121	1958	.	. 218
1954	.	. 162	1959	.	. 232
1955	.	. 179	1960	.	. 251
1956	.	. 188	1961	.	. 268
1957	.	. 202	1962	.	. 272

Source: *Statistical Yearbook of the Czechoslovak Socialist
Republic, 1963*, p. 42.

Of no less importance is the fact that the structure of national income formation and distribution is influenced, in decisive manner, by the state budget. First of all there is the relationship between accumulation and consumption, which is in the long run determined by the receipts and expenditures of the state budget. Through the state budget other important relations in distribution are also influenced. The relationship between productive and non-productive activities is influenced in such a way as to be in harmony with economic possibilities and needs. Furthermore, in manufacturing we have to deal with important mutual relationships between the development of mines and metallurgical works, power, engineering, and those branches producing consumer goods; in the non-productive sphere, between defence and state administration, health services, education, etc. The state budget makes possible the regulation and distribution of resources between new investments, refitting of older plants, wages, material costs, etc. And finally the state budget makes it possible to perform a relatively extensive redistribution of the national income inside the country in such a way as to reduce differences in the economic level of individual regions in the country.[1]

The economic policy of the Czechoslovak State, which uses the state budget as one of its most important long-term planning instruments, was therefore able to ensure full employment of the labour force, as well as full use of productive capacities. Unemployment in all its various forms has been done away with. This has also made possible the utilization of available resources for the growth of national income. The mobilization of a large part of all resources in the national economy through the state budget has enabled a substantial growth of the national income compared with the pre-war period, absolutely as well as *per capita*. During the period 1948–1962 our national income grew 2·7 times and on a *per capita* basis 2·5 times.

Relatively high present increases in the national income have created the basis for a regular growth in the nominal as well as the real incomes of the population.

TABLE 4

INDEX OF REAL WAGES
OF WORKERS AND EMPLOYEES
(1953 = 100)

1955	.	. 116·2	1960	.	. 146·1
1957	.	. 128·7	1961	.	. 150·8
1959	.	. 137·7	1962	.	. 149·8

Source : *Statistical Yearbook of the Czechoslovak Socialist Republic, 1963*, p. 41.

IV. THE INFLUENCE OF THE BUDGET ON CONSUMPTION

As far as the volume and structure of consumption are concerned, they are influenced by the state budget in a slightly different way than is the case of proper investment activity. First of all a high

---

[1] In spite of the fact that the redistribution of the national income, as far as the ratios between accumulation and consumption is concerned, is one of the most important economic relationships, which the state budget, through its expenditures part, aims at setting, a number of authors point out the fact that in Czechoslovakia at the moment there is no immediate linking up between the expenditures of the state budget and the final redistribution of the national income.

employment rate is achieved by means of investment activity, financed by the expenditures of the state budget. Also the steady growth of the national product and national income makes it possible to increase the real incomes of various groups of the population.

The state budget also directly influences the volume and structure of the so-called social component part of consumption. This is the part of consumption which is not paid for by the individual (in the majority of cases), but from social funds and is practically distributed according to needs. It is true that the state budget is not the only source for financing social consumption. The expenditures of enterprises and co-operatives for these purposes, various profit-sharing schemes, so-called enterprise funds in industrial enterprises, special social and cultural funds in agricultural co-operatives, as well as the assets of various organizations (above all trade unions), serve the same purpose. In spite of this, however, the centralized expenditures of the state budget for cultural and social measures pay for an overwhelming share of the social consumption of the country.

We can roughly classify the social consumption expenditures covered by the state budget into the following groups :

(a) Transfers which serve for the final consumption of the population and are part of the money incomes flow, but which are not the direct outcome of distribution according to work done. Social security benefits, children's allowances, old-age pensions, etc., belong to this category.

(b) Expenditures which serve for the final consumption of the population but which are not accompanied by a flow of money income to the population and therefore make possible the direct distribution of services and material commodities. This includes free medical care, education, culture, etc. These are services of a non-productive character which, however, significantly influence the living standard of the population.

(c) Expenditures which cover the material consumption (including investments) of those institutions which grant services to the population, such as hospitals, schools, etc.

(d) Expenditures for final consumption of employers in this sphere, which are connected with a money flow of income from the state budget. This includes the salaries of teachers, doctors, medical staff, etc.

A number of circumstances cause the steady growth of expenditures for welfare and cultural purposes. The growth of social consumption can, for example, be caused by an increase in the number of old-age pensioners and in the amount paid out in pensions, because of a longer life span, of increasing average incomes, of the growing number of years spent in jobs, etc. It may also be necessary to increase the salaries of certain professions, for example in the health services and education, so as to maintain a suitable relationship with regard to the growing wages of those employed in manufacturing.

V. WELFARE EXPENDITURES

The complicated task of economic and social development, as well as the growing wants of all people, force the government to use the resources of the state budget earmarked for social consumption with the greatest possible care. It is important in this connection that government expenditures of a cultural and welfare nature should in themselves be an efficient instrument for solving various economic, political, educational, social, and sanitary problems, which are the result of relatively accelerated economic growth. The system of sickness benefits and old-age pensions is, for example, constructed in such a way as to help to decrease economically unfavourable employment mobility on the one hand and at the same time to induce the transfer of workers into key industries or new plants. The construction of nurseries and of other welfare institutions has an important place in the effort to induce married women to accept employment. High expenditures for the development of universities and colleges increase the skill of employees. Accelerated economic growth in connection with fast technical and scientific development and increasing productivity of labour, all become very demanding as far as this field is concerned.

By means of welfare expenditures the structure of consumption of various social strata of the population is influenced in the long run as well as in the short run. Through all this, various social inequalities based on various sizes of families, on the difference between life in the town and in the country, between those who are employed and those who are retired, can be gradually removed (by children's allowances, the distribution of free school books and other means of meeting needs of children in school). The following table gives information on the share of incomes from social consumpton funds in various social groups of households in 1961.

TABLE 5

RELATIVE IMPORTANCE OF SOCIAL CONSUMPTION FUNDS

Households	Shares of Different Forms of Distribution (percentages)		Percentage by which the Social Consumption increases Labour Earnings
	Reward for Labour	Social Consumption	
Workers	75·4	24·6	32·5
Employers	76·0	24·0	31·6
Members of agricultural Co-operatives	80·5	19·5	24·1
Independent farmers	85·7	14·3	16·8
Retired persons	39·5	60·5	153·1

When comparing national income distribution in countries with various social systems and when comparing standards of living we must take into account data about the volume and structure of social consumption. At present the social consumption in Czechoslovakia is already on a relatively high level. Budget expenditure for welfare and culture represented in 1963 approximately 3,500 kčs *per capita* annually, that means as much as 300 kčs a month. At present approximately 72 per cent of the total incomes of individuals is distributed according to labour and 28 per cent is distributed from social consumption funds. Social consumption therefore increases the labour income of the population by 40 per cent.

VI. SOME REMAINING PROBLEMS

This high level of social consumption brings with it a number of complicated problems that still await solution. We shall indicate the most important of them :

(1) Which types of material and non-material consumption should be financed entirely from the funds of the whole Society, which should be paid for partially by the state, and which by the consumer ? This is a problem as far as culture is concerned, as well as some forms of medical care, etc.

(2) Which free services should be offered to all citizens (school education, etc.) and which to particular social and income groups, for example to the employed mothers ?

(3) In what form should social consumption be realized ? in kind (school books, medicine) or as money incomes (children's allowances), preferential rates, etc. ?

(4) Which measures should be financed centrally from the state budget and to what extent and which from decentralized resources of enterprises, co-operatives, and other organizations (for example nurseries for children, cultural, physical cultural, recreational institutions).

As is evident from what has been said above, it is the task of the economic authorities, as well as economic science, to look continually for new paths of development of the system of social consumption, financed by the state budget. It is necessary continually to keep in mind the limited resources available and the aim of harmonious development and efficiency. Our point of departure here must always be that it is impossible to distribute more than has been produced and that thus the amount devoted to social consumption can only be raised by a growth in the available resources, by the growth of the national income.

The national income is distributed in accordance with this principle and this of course is reflected in the structure of the expenditures side of the state budget.

DISCUSSION OF DR. BRUZEK'S AND DR. URBAN'S PAPERS

Dr. Negreponti-Delivanis introduced Dr. Bruzek's papers. It described, she said, the process of income distribution in Czechoslovakia giving a clear idea of distribution in socialist economies. According to Dr. Bruzek, national income should be distributed so as to avoid creating inequalities, but in a way that was conducive to a satisfactory rate of growth. This second objective explained why socialist countries in the present period made allowance for income inequalities, although, as Dr. Bruzek said, these should not be disproportionate : fixing the wages at too low a level would weaken the incentive to work ; on the other hand, fixing the wages at a level higher than the workers' contribution to production would remove incentives to improve work efficiency. The degree of income inequality permissible in a socialist economy was therefore related to the objective of economic growth.

Dr. Negreponti-Delivanis noted that Dr. Bruzek had distinguished between primary and secondary distribution, and also between individual and collective distribution, the basis of the distribution being, in all cases, the net material product defined according to the socialist concept. Primary income was distributed between two categories only : the workers employed in the productive sphere and the enterprises, either state concerns or co-operatives. Dr. Bruzek thought that on a purely quantitative basis the latter income would compare with corporate profits and other income originating in business before tax in a capitalist economy. Workers employed in the non-productive sphere and persons who did not work did not participate in primary distribution.

This made a process of income redistribution necessary. The distinction between incomes distributed to individuals and collective incomes related to the secondary or final distribution. Collective consumption corrected certain income discrepancies, such as those related to the size of the family, family allowances adding for instance 40 per cent to the gross income of the bread-winner in a family of four. Although forecasting that the scope of collective consumption would increase, Dr. Bruzek concluded that a too steady rate of increase would be just as detrimental to economic growth. The relation between individual and collective distribution was thus considered by Dr. Bruzek as an optimum problem.

Dr. Negreponti-Delivanis was not sure she understood how differences in remuneration could be based on differences in productivity in a planned economy. In a socialist economy differences in workers' productivity would mainly depend on the quantity and efficiency of capital used in different sectors. Differences in workers' productivity would therefore relate to the planning process of allocating capital between sectors rather than to differences in workers' efficiency. She had, for instance, noticed in Table 2 in the paper that building was the best-paid activity in the material productions whereas housing was the lowest-paid in the non-productive sector : how could this be explained ? She would suggest that this sort of discrepancy was related to the ordering of priorities in production planning and not to productivity, the level of workers' incomes being fixed in each sector according to the ranking of the sector in the planning of priorities.

Referring to Table 1 in the paper, which showed a drop of 15 per cent in the cost of living index for households between 1953 and 1962, Dr. Negreponti-Delivanis thought this a rather unexpected development in an economy aiming at a high rate of growth. In developing economies a high rate of growth was usually only attained through inflationary pressures. How was it that the growth of the Czechoslovakian economy made an exception to the rule ? Could the reason be that the cost of living index only included foodstuffs and other essential commodities, the prices of which had been fixed at an abnormally low level ?

As Dr. Bruzek had admitted that income inequalities were temporarily required for rapid growth, would he give an opinion of the problem of incentives to growth which would arise once such inequalities had been abolished ?

Dr. Negreponti-Delivanis had noticed that in Table 2 public utilities such as transport were only in part included in non-material productions. Was not the distinction between, say, carrying raw materials to a plant as being productive and carrying the workers to the same factory as being unproductive, arbitrary ?

Dr. Negreponti-Delivanis said in conclusion that she had gained the impression from Dr. Bruzek's paper that differences in the process of income distribution in socialist and capitalist countries were not as great as the prima facie evidence would suggest.

Dr. Bruzek answered Dr. Negreponti-Delivanis' questions. Concerning the sectoral wage differentials he maintained that differences in sectoral rates of growth had to be taken into account : nominal wages increased more rapidly in sectors where the rate of growth was higher. Nominal wages, however, must increase more slowly than average productivity. Dr. Bruzek pointed out that what was under the heading of housing were the wages of workers engaged in housing administration. The wage rates in these jobs were rather low : there was a shortage of labour in this sector.

Dr. Bruzek remarked that the decrease in the cost of living index in Czechoslovakia had no deflationary implications. Whereas in Western countries a rise in real wages was usually attained by nominal wage rates rising faster than prices, the increase in real income in Czechoslovakia was obtained only partly by increasing nominal wages, and partly by lowering prices. The cost of living index in Table 1 related to a complete sample of consumption goods. The average price level had actually been lowered every year with the exception of 1952 and 1953.

Dr. Bruzek was of the opinion that income inequalities would continue for the next twenty years or so. They would progressively be reduced, but incentives for efficiency, acquisition of skill, and so on would have to be retained. Thus wages had been raised very recently in such activities as mining and building to meet a shortage of labour in these sectors.

Dr. Negreponti-Delivanis asked Dr. Bruzek whether in such cases wage increases were not justified by the objectives of economic growth rather than by higher productivity.

Dr. Bruzek said that this was true in so far as labour shortage was the reason for increasing wage rates in these instances. He was aware of the difficulties met in distributing transport activities between productive and non-productive spheres. This was a tricky problem subject to different solutions in different socialist national accounting systems. In Eastern Germany, for instance, all transport activities were included in the material product.

Professor Föhl introduced Dr. Urban's paper on the part played by the state budget in income distribution in Czechoslovakia. Dr. Urban had started out from the observation that the ratio between budget expenditure and the national income had considerably increased during the last thirty years both in Western and in socialist economies. There was, however, a marked difference in so far as in a socialist economy the state budget had to take care of investment in industrial enterprises in addition to all those tasks it performed in Western economies.

Professor Föhl would have liked to know what percentage of national income was represented by the state budget in Czechoslovakia so that a comparison could be made, in terms of national income percentages, of the components of expenditure for culture and welfare, for defence and security and for administration with similar figures for other economies.

The expenditure on development headed 'National Economy' in Table 1 in the paper amounted to somewhat above 50 per cent of the state budget, 80 per cent of this being spent on investment (net investment, Professor Föhl assumed). Professor Föhl regretted that the expenditure on investment had not been broken down so as to distinguish between the capital expenditure on public utilities and infrastructure such as roads, railways, and the like which were included in Western states' budgets, and net investment on production capacity which in Western economies were taken care of by private enterprise. He hoped that Dr. Urban could give him some information on the division between the two sorts of capital expenditure.

Turning to the receipts side of the budget, Professor Föhl was not surprised to find that about 86 per cent of the total amount was received from the socialist sector of the economy — the turnover tax and profits of the state enterprises — that is from what would be called indirect taxation in Western economies. Conversely this meant that direct taxation on paid out incomes of the working population amounted to next to nothing. Labour incomes were net incomes but this did not mean that in a socialist economy public activity rained from heaven and was not paid for by a part of labour product. Instead of paying taxes on their incomes the wage-earners paid for the cost of public activity by being charged higher prices which included indirect taxes and the profits of the state enterprises.

Dr. Urban had written that these peculiarities in a socialist economy made it possible to overcome obstacles which would probably be impossible to surmount under private ownership. Professor Föhl doubted this and asked Dr. Urban to indicate what obstacles exactly he had in mind.

Referring to Dr. Urban's remark that from 1948 to 1962 national income in Czechoslovakia had increased 2·7 times and *per capita* 2·5 times, Professor Föhl thought this to be a very satisfactory result. Still, having calculated the annual growth rates from the figures in Table 3 in Dr. Urban's paper he had found that they were normally between 6 and 8 per cent, which could compare with what had been achieved by a number of Western countries. The outcome of the comparison did not surprise Professor Föhl as he was aware that Czechoslovakia, far from being an underdeveloped country, had been known for the high skill of her labour and had already owned a world famous industry before she became a socialist state.

Professor Föhl was more surprised by the comparison of the index figures for 1961 and 1962 as they implied a growth rate of only 1·5 per cent over the year. He regretted that this was the very last figure in Table 3 and would appreciate if Dr. Urban could give him the figure for 1963.

Professor Föhl observed that this apparent slowing down of growth was to a certain extent confirmed by the figures given in Table 4 for the real wages, the index of which did not rise at all in 1962, indeed it slightly dropped in comparison with the year before. He was rather surprised that such changes in growth rates could occur in a controlled economy.

Dr. Urban had devoted the last part of his paper to the question of social consumption, that was the part of the total consumption which was not paid for by individuals. Professor Föhl observed that all the kinds of social consumption listed by Dr. Urban existed in practically all Western economies as well. Thus the difference could only be a gradual one. As Dr. Urban had written that out of the total of individual incomes 72 per cent were distributed according to labour, leaving 28 per cent for social consumption benefits, Professor Föhl would guess that this difference was small as Western countries were not far from these figures.

Dr. Urban had been right to emphasize that when comparing standards of living in different economies one must keep the amount of social consumption in mind, but this should be qualified. Professor Föhl said that the fact that labour in Western countries paid for social consumption by income taxes out of their gross incomes and by contributions to the social security system, whereas in socialist countries labour paid for it by buying other commodities at higher prices than otherwise, did not make any difference. Thus when comparing standards of living one should either exclude social consumption on both sides and compare socialist incomes with net Western incomes, or compare socialist incomes, including social consumption, with gross Western incomes.

Professor Föhl wholeheartedly agreed with Dr. Urban's concluding statement, i.e. that it was impossible to distribute more than had been produced. This went for all systems and all economists should keep it in mind.

Dr. Urban, before answering Professor Föhl's questions, thought it necessary to underline the fact that the evolution of the Czechoslovakian economy towards socialism had proceeded through several stages as this had a bearing on the study of income distribution there.

As in other socialist countries private property in the means of production had been eliminated and economic development was based on a new pattern of income distribution allowing the state to allocate a very large part of the national income and to concentrate the greater part of the surplus product in government hands.

This meant that a large part of the funds not only could but had to be allocated through planning and therefore ought to be used in the most efficient way. This raised many problems. If one looked at the way the question of allocating funds for optimal growth had been approached, it was useful to distinguish two different stages through which economic policy had passed.

In the first stage in new socialist economies as well as in the U.S.S.R. before the war, the central government not only centralized the funds but also used them in a direct way. In Czechoslovakia this stage went on from 1948 to 1958.

During this period growth was based on a more intensive use of production factors which had been under-utilized before the war, especially in the agricultural sector where there had been some disguised unemployment. If Professor Föhl had been right in stating that Czechoslovakia was an industrialized country even before the war, nevertheless in the pre-war years the rate of growth had been low whereas it had been very high in this period.

But from 1957 onwards this reserve of factor resources tended to run out, this being particularly true for manpower, Czechoslovakia having already reached the highest percentage of women in labour force in any Eastern European country with a 42 per cent figure. Product growth tended to be limited to the increase in population.

A second stage began in 1958–59, characterized by a tendency to decentralize the allocation of funds, part of which were no longer used by government but retained by enterprises. This evolution towards decentralization was also marked by a more extensive use of market mechanisms concurrently with planning. As yet the evolution was not complete and Dr. Urban would say that the economy was now right in the middle of a process of transition.

Turning to Professor Föhl's specific questions, Dr. Urban said that whereas he had written in his paper that one-half of the national income was redistributed by the budget, figures available for 1962–63 now showed the proportion to be even higher.

It was true that the rate of growth had slowed down in the last few years ; available index figures proved that the national income had been roughly at the same level in 1963 as the year before. The reason for this was to be found in the structural changes now in process : new industries had a high rate of growth but to the detriment of other activities, and this tended to push down the growth rate as an average on the whole economy. The need to finance a large amount of investment in new industries in the present stage of transition was the reason why the increase in real wages had come to a halt in 1962, as Professor Föhl had noticed.

Dr. Urban thought that the obstacles which private ownership of the means of production raised against development were a complex issue. Instead of giving a general answer to Professor Föhl's question, Dr. Urban would rather give a specific example of what he had had in mind. Under a capitalist regime the economic development of the Western regions of Czechoslovakia before the war had not led to growth in the eastern part of the country. The socialist regime had succeeded in linking the one to the other and in eliminating the disparity in development. Dr. Urban did not think that private ownership would have done so.

Dr. Urban agreed with Professor Föhl that social consumption shares in national income were comparable in Eastern and Western economies. He nevertheless thought it to be somewhat higher in socialist economies and social consumption in these countries, being financed out of the surplus product, contributed more towards equality than in Western countries.

Professor Alchian wished to raise again the question put by Dr. Negreponti-Delivanis about the principle retained for breaking down transport activities between material product and non-productive activities. He had, besides, noticed that Dr. Bruzek had used in his paper the terms 'contribution to production' and 'social usefulness of work'. Were they the same ? As he thought not, what was the criterion of distinction and who was entitled to decide what was the contribution to production and the social usefulness of work ?

Dr. Bruzek stated that among the transport activities those which were a continuation of the process of production belonged to the sphere of material production. Everyone would agree that transporting crops from the fields to the farm or transferring goods in process from one workshop to the next within a factory were part of production and one did nothing but generalize this observation in extending the same rule to all transport of goods.

Dr. Bruzek thought that the term 'contribution to production' had a wider meaning than 'social usefulness of work' as referring to the quality as well as the quantity of work done. As far as social usefulness of work was concerned all activities were not equally useful to society ; production of equipment goods had the highest social usefulness in that it made possible the very existence of consumption goods industries.

The evaluation of contribution to production was an issue which related to fixing wage rates by the appropriate government authority : most often the Ministry of Production for material production, the Ministry of Finance usually for non-productive activities, or the Ministry of Education, and so on.

Criteria had been devised for ranking people according to their qualifications and skills. They were applied by a special section within each enterprise and once his ranking was determined each worker earned according to his work's return.

Dr. Pasinetti had several questions to ask, the first being addressed to Dr. Urban who at the end of his paper had listed a series of problems connected with social consumption. Dr. Pasinetti pointed out that the issues were quite similar to those which economists engaged in welfare economics had been discussing in the West and he would like to know what sort of solutions were given to them in a socialist economy.

Dr. Bruzek's paper had raised the question of wage differentials. This seemed to Dr. Pasinetti to raise a three-fold problem : there was first the problem of what the structure of wage rates should be at a given point of time, second the problem of how to let wage rates in different industries move through time and how to control their movements, this admittedly being an issue closely connected with those of an income policy to be discussed in a later session of the conference ; finally there was the problem of using wage differentials as incentives. How were these three separate problems solved in a socialist economy ?

Both Dr. Bruzek's and Dr. Urban's papers prompted Dr. Pasinetti to put a final question about relations between money wages and the general level of consumer goods prices. In Western countries allowing money wages to increase at the rate of growth of productivity was an accepted (though not an achieved) policy objective. It implied that one had given up hope in falling prices. If Dr. Pasinetti had understood correctly, in socialist countries the objective was to bring down consumer prices, money wages being kept constant. If it was so, had it been possible in Czechoslovakia to prevent money wages from rising ?

Professor Brochier wished to make some comments at this stage of the discussion as they were closely connected with Dr. Pasinetti's first question. Professor Föhl had already observed that the share of social consumption in socialist economies was not very different from that of capitalist ones. But Professor Brochier thought the fact that, in the latter, goods for social consumption were produced under a market economy by private enterprise made an enormous difference in terms of the effects of social consumption on the distribution of national income. Of course, both in Western countries and in socialist countries, expenditure on social consumption as such tended to reduce income inequalities. The way these goods were produced and marketed tended however to increase inequality in countries like France where, for instance, the production of pharmaceuticals, paid for by social security benefits, permitted the private businesses producing these commodities to make abnormally high profits.

Another significant problem was the determining of an optimum distribution of resources between social and individual consumption expenditure. Professor Brochier was amongst those who thought that the share of social consumption was under optimum in France and he feared that under the pressure of private consumption expenses increasing hap-hazardly, the consumption pattern would tend to drift further away from optimum. The fact that only the production of goods for individual consumption was stimulated by the market mechanisms in a profit economy was a factor of imbalance. As an example, he would quote the way the needs for mass leisure were fulfilled in France. An increasing population, shorter working hours and higher incomes had, in a short time, enlarged the demand for holiday amenities at the sea and in winter sport resorts. These needs were met by private enterprise. There was intense speculation on available sites. Rent incomes went to a few private interest groups who tended to monopolize nature's amenities for their own benefit. Professor Brochier was of the opinion that determining the extent of mass consumption and the way its need should be filled was a political choice which should be subject to planning rather than market mechanism.

Dr. Bruzek said that social consumption in Czechoslovakia mainly benefited the lower income brackets of the population and thus tended to reduce inequality. An optimum division between social and private con-sumption was a difficult issue as the rate of growth of social consumption could be fixed too high and in Czechoslovakia recently it had been found necessary to lower the rate of its increase although in absolute terms social consumption went on rising. Dr. Bruzek thought that the rate of increase should not be higher than the rate of growth of national income as a whole. But there were other means of tending towards reducing social inequalities. Thus, in Czechoslovakia, where housing rent rates had for long been fixed at too low a level, there had recently been an increase in cases where the occupier did not have a large family. This would lead to flat exchanges and favour a more equitable pattern of occupation.

Dr. Bruzek turned to the relation between money wages and consumer prices, stating that the principle in a socialist economy was to combine both increase in wages and decrease in prices. Lowering prices had nevertheless caused difficulties because of the insufficient elasticity of supply of many commodities whose prices were already fixed too low at the start. In these cases to apply the principle without limitation would lead to more shortages. The principle could conflict with the need for a policy of price flexibility in order to remove structural imbalances between supply and demand. The rule of decreasing prices should be enforced only as a long-run tendency. For newly produced goods it could apply only if prices were initially fixed high enough as was done now. Another reason for allowing money wages to rise in relation to productivity increase was the fear that if they were kept constant incentives to increase labour productivity might disappear.

Professor Papi asked Dr. Bruzek whether there were market mechanisms in the Czechoslovakian economy and, if not, which authority was entitled to fix incomes and prices.

Dr. Bruzek said that the recourse to market mechanisms was becoming more and more extensive. Prices were set by commissions sitting within Ministries and, for new products, they fixed prices according to what was charged for similar commodities already marketed. The interplay between supply and demand was taken into account. Prices for new products in high demand were fixed accordingly.

The new trend in policy towards more price flexibility was more or less marked according to the different sorts of products. A threefold distinction had to be made. For food and other essentials such as clothing, any change in price had to be approved by central governmental authorities. Prices for a second group of commodities were set by a lower authority, the Conseil supérieur des entreprises, but only within certain limits. For a third group of products the production units themselves had power to set the prices. As a rough estimate one could say that 70 per cent of the prices were still subject to fixing by central government whereas 20 per cent fell in the second category, leaving 10 per cent for the third.

The determination of incomes entailed distinguishing between the non-productive activities where wages and salaries were related to level of qualification, university degrees and so on, and jobs in the productive industries where the wage bill varied according to the measure of fulfilment of planned targets by the labour force. Overreaching the target by 10 per cent would bring a 2 to 3 per cent increase in the wage bill whereas the workers' pay would go down to less than the planned wage rate if they failed to fulfil it.

Dr. Pasinetti observed that a high rate of increase in productivity in capital producing industries was such as to make the fulfilment of targets in other industries easier. Were there mechanisms of adjustment which could take into account this sort of inter-industry effect?

Dr. Bruzek said that the rate of wage increase must be, in all cases, lower than the rate of productivity increase. Besides, the latter was not fixed once and for all, but changed every year. Actual increases in productivity, however, could be related to distortions such as changes in assortments of produced goods in comparison with what had been specified by planning. The production units' returns were analysed, and if profits were discovered to have been made by dubious means they were cut down for not having conformed to the Plan.

Professor Papi objected that principles of this sort could not apply to the agricultural sector as productivity there was not dependent on human will only. *Dr. Bruzek* said that, of course, crop variations influenced farmers' incomes.

Dr. Negreponti-Delivanis wanted to know how the cost of production was calculated in a Socialist economy. *Dr. Bruzek* said that the price structure was made up of several components. The cost of production was a first component which broke down into two : material cost, and wages and salaries. By adding the margin of profit for enterprises in the productive sphere one got the wholesale price. Besides these two components retail prices for consumers goods included the turnover tax, wages and salaries in the sphere of trade, and profit in the trade activity. Dr. Bruzek observed that in this way prices of means of production were lower than they ought to be.

Dr. *Negreponti-Delivanis* asked whether no interest was charged on capital. Dr. *Bruzek* said that this was deducted from the profit of enterprises and thus was an incentive not to waste loan funds.

Dr. *Negreponti-Delivanis* asked who would benefit from the profits. Dr. *Bruzek* said that the fraction not retained by the enterprise for stock-building was transferred to the state budget for financing investments, in a proportion of 90 per cent and the rest, that was about 10 per cent, was available for increasing the welfare fund of the enterprise.

Dr. *Pasinetti* asked what the reasons were for dividing up the surplus of receipts over costs between profits and turnover tax in a socialist economy.

Centralizing resources was in any case the basic principle, said Dr. *Bruzek*. If part of the surplus, however, was in the form of profit, the reason was that enterprises should be given an interest in the returns of their activity. Still, in theory, there was no difference between turnover tax and profits as both were part of the surplus value.

Dr. *Pasinetti* observed that thus the existence of profit was not related to the need for financing the enterprise's investments. Dr. *Bruzek* replied that the principle of centralizing the greatest part of surplus value made it possible to accumulate capital and redistribute it according to the needs of the different sectors of the economy.

Dr. *Feinstein* presumed that allowances for capital depreciation were included in material costs. He wished to know on which principle and by whom they were calculated. In cases of changing prices were they reckoned at original cost or replacement cost?

Dr. *Bruzek* said that depreciation allowances were fixed by planning authorities. They were valued at constant prices but subject to revision from time to time.

Professor Tress wondered about a possible effect of fixing actual wages according to the achievement of production targets. If the output of a given industry exceeded the target level this implied raising a quantity of material input larger than forecast. If the elasticity of supply of the raw materials was not infinite other industries would run short of supplies of it to the detriment of their own output. How were workers in enterprises doing well to be persuaded that their level of production had to be less in order that others do better?

Dr. *Bruzek* recognized this as being a serious problem. Shortages of material were not unknown. In order to prevent such a situation developing the accumulation funds included buffer reserves. But determining their optimum amount was another problem as overfreezing of resources had to be avoided as well as shortages. In practice this meant that shortages could not always be prevented. When enterprises went on short time for reasons of that sort which were not of their own making they were compensated for the loss of production but their profits decreased all the same.

Professor Tress wondered whether under such circumstances there was not a possibility of too much of certain commodities being produced at the expense of others which were in higher demand.

Professor Föhl, although making allowance for the difference between state ownership and centralized economies and private enterprise and decentralized economies, wished to emphasize how much the basic problems that had to be solved in both economies were similar.

In all cases for given scales of rewards and sets of relative prices people showed definite preferences for certain jobs and certain commodities. In socialist economies trouble started the moment private people were even partially asked to state their preference, freely. It then became necessary to fix wages in such a way as to channel the supply of labour towards the jobs required by planning ; and the same applied for consumer goods, the prices of which had to be fixed so that articles produced would be accepted by the consumers according to their price demand function.

In the U.S.S.R. there had long been discussion on whether it was advisable to bring back the rate of interest as an income category. Professor Föhl confessed that he did not understand why this should have been taboo for so long as, if there was profit, why not interest as another part of capital income?

In his own paper, to be discussed later by the Conference, Professor Föhl had tried to show that one should create a structural profit so that the least successful entrepreneurs must receive a zero profit, this being a condition for maintaining full employment in a competitive market economy. In this sort of economy, with profit equal to zero for the marginal producer in each industry, any increase in money wages must lead to increasing costs and prices. Although having no influence on the national income distribution, any money wage rise under full employment was then a cause of inflation. The only policy which could then succeed in curbing inflation was progressive taxation of net profits as this was the only measure which would have a bearing on income distribution without having any influence on full employment, the marginal producer being left in the same situation as before tax, and gross profits, as opposed to net, being the same as before tax. The problem was then how to convince the taxpayers of the necessity of increasing the tax burden on incomes.

No problem of this sort arose in a socialist economy and would not in any monopolistic economy, no matter whether centralized or decentralized. Investment could be increased without starting inflation as price increase would necessarily bring down consumption.

But in their turn socialist economies had a problem of inflation once they decided to go a step further towards a market economy through letting people spend their wages freely. To prevent inflation it became necessary to act upon private people's behaviour in indirect ways such as by means of incentives just as in Western countries. Professor Föhl wished to stress that in his opinion the problem of curbing inflation was not related to the characteristics of either the capitalist or the socialist system as such but to the fact that an economy was of the competitive pattern as opposed to the monopolistic one.

Dr. Feinstein observed that if the rate of depreciation was calculated so as to include a provision for new investment over what was wear and tear on accumulated capital, was this not bringing the rate of interest in by the back door ?

Dr. Bruzek said that the scope for capital redistribution was not made less through this, as enterprises could receive more or less of the centralized capital funds beyond their own funds for depreciation allowances.

Dr. Urban agreed with Professor Föhl that basic economic problems were the same in socialist and in capitalist economies and he thought that there was no automatic way of solving them in either economic system although he could not quite agree with Professor Föhl's analysis of the two systems as tending to become more alike.

Chapter 11

MAJOR FACTORS DETERMINING THE DISTRIBUTION OF THE NATIONAL INCOME IN A CENTRALLY PLANNED ECONOMY

BY

Dr. JULIA ZALA

Hungarian Central Statistical Office, Budapest

I. THE DIFFERENCES OF CONCEPTS

I WOULD like to begin by summarizing the differences between the present concepts of national income as applied by the socialist and by the Western economies. To define these divergences is necessary if we are to make the problem of planning the distribution of the national income comprehensible.

In the socialist countries the national income encompasses only the sectors of so-called material production, that is it fails to cover the scope of services. Moreover in the socialist countries the national income is calculated at consumer prices, that is including the turnover tax, and not at factor cost.

In the national income, however, logically not only those working in material production and the companies participate but also the whole population and the 'non-productive agencies' as well. Consequently in the socialist countries the distribution of the national income means — as resulting from the concept of the national income — a multiple planning task. The issues are the following :

(1) The national income is primarily divided into two main parts :

  (a) personal income of those working in material production ;
  (b) centralized original incomes (profits of productive companies ; taxes, primarily turnover tax paid by them, bank charges, insurance fees, etc.).

(2) Redistribution of the national income :

    (a) all individual incomes ;

    (b) centralized final (derived) incomes (material outlays of the public sector, investments, amounts spent on building up state reserves).

(3) End use of the national income :

    (a) consumption of the population ;

    (b) public consumption ;

    (c) investments ;

    (d) increasing stocks.

Though closely interconnected the three types of distribution of the national income are not of the same rank from the point of view of planning.

The so-called original distribution — into the personal incomes of those working in the material production and centralized original income — is featured by the magnitude of the following factors or, better to say, by their changes :

(1) within all earners the ratio of those employed in the sectors of material production ;

(2) the average wage and income levels ;

(3) level of the national income.

It is a well-known fact that the number of those employed in the sectors of material production shows a relatively slower increase in every developing economy than that of the aggregated number of the employed (irrespective of whether there is full employment or any unemployment). For increasing productivity involves a relative decline of the labour input of production and the number of workers employed in the servicing, scientific, and administrative sectors is relatively increasing. From all this it follows that in the course of economic progress within all earners the ratio of those employed in material production is falling back.

II. RECENT TRENDS IN HUNGARY

In Hungary the numbers and ratios of all active earners and, within the total, of those employed in the sector of material production have moved as follows in recent years :

TABLE 1

NUMBERS OF WORKERS IN HUNGARY
1958–63

(1000s)

Year	Numbers of all Active Workers (net of Pensioners)	Numbers Employed in Material Production	Ratio
1958	4,671	4,006	85·8
1959	4,754	4,054	85·3
1960	4,827	4,118	85·3
1961	4,776	4,028	84·3
1962	4,765	3,983	83·6
1963	4,805	4,002	83·3

The average level of earnings of those employed in material production and the trends of change do not essentially differ from the earnings of those employed in other sectors of the economy. The average level of wages and incomes is not determined by whether someone is employed in the sector of material production or not, but rather by qualifications, professional experience, and the difficulty of the work performed, and in some fields by the relative shortage of manpower. (E.g. in Hungary the earnings of building workers have been stepped up to a more than average extent, there being a great lack of manpower in this sector.) Thus when it is a question of the primary distribution of the national income as a whole we can generally disregard the relative change of the wages level of those employed in the sectors of material production.

It follows that in planning it is the change of the number of those employed in production and the increase of the average earnings that determine the magnitude of the first element in the original distribution (personal income of those employed in material production).

As has been pointed out, as a result of the steady increase of productivity the number of those engaged in production is scarcely rising, and as a result of increasing mechanization the rise of average incomes is lower than that of productivity. Thus the ratio of the personal incomes of those engaged in material production within the national income shows a relative decline.

In Hungary the figures have shown the following trend in recent years :

TABLE 2

PERSONAL INCOME
OF THOSE ENGAGED IN MATERIAL PRODUCTION
AS PERCENTAGE OF THE NATIONAL INCOME AT CONSTANT PRICES

1960	52·4%
1962	50·7%

It follows from the above that, since the national income is growing faster than the personal income of those employed in the sectors of production, the centralized original income is increasing within the national income. This is what makes up the overwhelming part of the revenue side of the budget and to a smaller extent the funds left at the disposal of the productive companies. The increasing proportion of the centralized original incomes is justified by the general, well-known laws of economic progress and by the special requirements of the advance of the socialist countries alike.

Let us first examine the factors which prevail in any developing country, irrespective of its social system.

(a) The incomes of those employed outside the sectors of material production must be met from the centralized net incomes. And since the ratio of those employed in services, science, culture, health, supply is steadily increasing in the course of the social development a relatively bigger share of the national income has to be secured to meet these incomes. The extent of increase is determined here also by the increase in the numbers so employed.

The average earnings of those employed in this sector increase in general to the same degree as the earnings of those employed in the sectors of production and — at least in the long run — we need not expect any change of the ratio.

(b) In developing countries the proportion of the national income represented by the amounts spent on the development of the infrastructure is, and must be, steadily increasing. The source is in this case also the centralized original income. This is the second general law governing the growth of the ratio of the centralized original incomes.

In addition, in the countries with a socialist social system there exists also a special factor necessitating the increase of the ratio of

281

the centralized original incomes. It follows from the transitional social order of the socialist countries that in the course of development the ratio of gratuitous state grants (and those offered at preferential prices) is increasing faster than the personal incomes actually depending on work performed.

The state covers to an increasing extent the health, cultural, housing, educational, recreational, old-age welfare, etc., requirements of the population from the central revenues free of charge or at rather preferential prices.

In Hungary the amounts paid partly or fully by the state in the form of state grants, as a percentage of all personal incomes, have shown the following trend in recent years :

1960	21·6%
1961	22·3%
1962	23·0%
1963	23·2%

In effect these are the major items whose growth rate should be quicker than the original income of those engaged in material production, and this is why the rate of centralized original incomes must grow within the national income.

There are other essential requirements also which must be met from the centralized original incomes. With these latter, however, there is not — and certainly not permanently — a need that their growth rate should exceed that of the national income. These items are investments expanding production, amounts spent on the increase of stocks and reserves, and military expenditures. In connection with these items it is rather the optimum size (with military expenses : the political aspects ensuing from the international situation) that are relevant. This, however — important as this problem is and much as it is connected with our subject — is not a topic of the present Conference, nor of this paper.

III. THE DIVISION OF THE NATIONAL INCOME

I mentioned at the beginning of my paper that the distribution of the national income has several aspects which, however, from the point of view of planning are not equal in importance. The planning of the primary distribution of the national income as described above is mostly a technical question; in fact it is nothing but the extrapolation of the well-known trends of development.

The important decisions on economic policy arise when the ratios of the end use, mentioned above as the third aspect of the distribution of the national income, have been established.

Since in a centrally planned economy the national income is — in *ultima analysi* — the aggregate of material goods, the planning agencies have to decide what share of the national income the population may consume, how much the consumption of the public sector should be, what should be the share of the productive investment, how much can be earmarked for the development of the infrastructure, and how much should be allocated for the increase of stocks and reserves.

If we disregard the possibility of raising foreign loans, there is no source other than the national income on which to rely for the above purposes. So the decisions concerning distribution are greatly influenced by the magnitude and growth rate of the national income itself.

It is well known that there must be a close connection between the ratio spent on productive investment and on the rate of growth of the national income. Experience has, however, shown that there is no, or at least a very doubtful, direct implication that 'the larger the share of the national income spent on productive investments the greater the rate of economic development, i.e. growth of the national income'.

It is known not so much on the basis of exact economic calculations but rather on that of empirically collected statistical evidence that if this rate is too low (4–5–6 per cent) we can only expect a small-scale economic development. Economic evidence as to what can be regarded as the upper limit — in other words how far it is possible to increase the share of the national income spent on productive investments and at the same time secure that the growth rate of the national income shall also increase — hardly exists. Thus in the centrally planned countries this most important planning decision is still partly based on empirical data.

In Hungary the ratio between the rates of investment and of growth, when compared with that of other countries, has shown a favourable trend, but for the time being we have no scientific proof that it can be at the same time considered the optimum. To solve this problem on a scientific level is a task — and probably a very complex one — still facing economists.

IV. THE PLANNING OF CONSUMPTION

In what follows I wish to discuss the item most important from the point of view of the distribution of the national income : the planning of the population's consumption and income.

Between personal consumption as a proportion of the national income and the aggregate of the individual personal incomes there is a close connection, but the two are not the same. As mentioned earlier, in the socialist countries personal consumption covers only the material consumption of the national income; it does not include the value of services. However, people spend their individual incomes also on services. Thus if we wish to establish the numerical connection — from the aspect of planning or statistics — between consumption and the aggregate of incomes the value of the services of the population also has to be taken into account. We can present the following data for Hungary.

TABLE 3

PERSONAL CONSUMPTION AND INCOMES
IN HUNGARY, 1959–63

(Billion forints)

Year	Value of the Material Consumption of the Population	Value of the Services used	Consumption and Services together	Total Incomes of the Population
1959	92·1	16·3	108·4	
1960	97·4	18·1	115·5	118·1
1961	97·9	18·9	116·8	120·5
1962	101·7	20·2	121·9	126·7
1963	106·9	21·6	128·5	137·1

The value of the material consumption and of the services is almost identical with the total incomes of the population. The insignificant (2–4 per cent) difference comes from the fact that the population do not actually 'consume' their individual incomes in the current year but save, repay earlier loans, and make also some fiscal payments. (E.g. taxes, membership dues, but their extent is not substantial in Hungary.)

When planning the total incomes of the population the primary central decision has to be taken by the planning agencies as to the rate of increase. When the investments are planned, as is well known, one must consider what rate of investment is best for increasing the rate of the national income. When planning the consumption (and accordingly the income of the population) the rate of growth of the national income determines the increase of the consumption.

In the planning of the consumption (and the total income of the population) the following two aspects have to be observed :

(1) it should permanently and steadily increase, i.e. there should be no recessions ;

(2) in general it should not exceed the rate of growth of the national income.

Over and above these considerations the distribution of incomes among the main groups of the population (first of all between the wage-earners and the peasantry) is a most important decision. When taking this decision the following have to be considered :

(1) In the process of the large-scale transformation of agriculture, productivity has increased more in agriculture than in industry which had already been operating on the large scale ; thus there has been a flow of manpower from the peasantry to the wage-earning class. This process is reflected in the restratification of incomes as well.

TABLE 4

RELATIVE INCOMES IN AGRICULTURE
AND OTHER OCCUPATIONS
(Billion forints at constant prices)

Year	Incomes from Wages	Total Incomes from Agriculture	Agricultural Incomes as Percentage of Wages and Salaries
1960	57·7	27·3	47·3
1961	59·1	26·7	45·2
1962	62·0	28·8	46·4
1963	67·6	30·4	45·0

(2) As to the magnitude of incomes per earner there prevails a discrepancy between the two main strata of the population. To some extent the way of living of the peasantry differs from that of the wage-earners living mainly in towns. (The peasants live in their own houses, they need not pay local

fares.) Consequently the incomes for peasant earners can be planned at a lower amount than those for workers and employees even though we should find an identical consumption level desirable — which, by the way, is a target in the centrally planned countries.

However, the incomes of the two strata are different even apart from the mentioned gap. This discrepancy is temporary and steadily decreasing as the cultural and hygienic requirements of the peasantry — which can be covered from their incomes — are increasing.

The incomes per earner have shown the following trend recently in the two major strata of Hungary's population :

TABLE 5

CONSUMPTION OF THE PEASANTRY
AS PERCENTAGE OF THE CONSUMPTION OF WORKERS
AND EMPLOYEES

Year	Total	Food	Clothing	Health and Culture
1962	82·8	99·8	78·5	46·8
1963	84·1	99·0	80·4	47·3

The distribution of income is secured through two principal means : through the distribution of money incomes and through consumers' prices.

The principal forms of distributing money incomes in a centrally planned economy are wages and salaries, other personal grants (family allowances, sick money in case of illness, pensions, etc.), the money incomes of members of producers' co-operatives and procurement of the commodities derived from the household plot.

V. THE PROBLEMS OF DEPENDANTS

The magnitude of money incomes can be planned with an adequate degree of accuracy. The central control of the efflux of money in accordance with the plan is effected in different money incomes. (Wages are controlled through direct wages control, procurement indirectly through procurement prices flexibly changed according to the agricultural crop, family allowances and pensions through central measures determined by the circumstances.) In spite of the different degrees of efficiency the total flow of money incomes is controlled by the state to a reasonably satisfactory degree of accuracy. As a result, and with fixed consumer prices, it has proved possible to eliminate fully any inflationary tendencies.

Much more restricted, however, is the scope of influence of a socialist state on the actual distribution and stratification of total incomes. The state exercises control, it is true, over the incomes of workers, but the earnings of the individual workers are not the same things as the actual average income levels of persons living in one family. As is well known — and this is similar in all social systems — the family incomes are greatly influenced by the ratio between earners and dependants, and sometimes in a greater degree than the income of the individual earners.

In a centrally planned economy this problem arises in a special form. The variance of the individual average incomes around the mean is much smaller than in the market economies. Here we have no groups which are not gainfully occupied, we have no individual incomes which are 20 to 30 times higher than the average. However, it also follows that a worker whose work is valued by the state through the wage accorded to him at 3 times the average will be living on the same income level as the worker whose income is about the average, only because there are relatively more dependants in his family.

Such cases are not exceptional and in this way incomes (and through them living conditions) can be actually restratified in a manner which does not correspond to the central concept inherent in the wages policy.

The problem is mitigated by family allowances, by subsidies affecting the prices of articles consumed by children, by the general pension and health insurance system, but, notwithstanding, the problem is not entirely solved by these measures.

VI. CONCLUSION

The above aspects of the distribution of the national income and of the few problems arising in the Hungarian planning practice do not, of course, cover the full scope of the problems. And it was not the purpose of this paper either. Yet I hope to have succeeded in giving a picture of some particular features of the distribution of the national income in the planning system.

———

DISCUSSION OF DR. ZALA'S PAPER

Dr. Feinstein introduced Dr. Zala's paper. One of its two main themes was the distribution of national income between wages and surplus in Hungary as a case study of a centrally planned economy. As Dr. Zala had mentioned that the trend in the wage share was a declining one, average wages not rising as rapidly as output per head, Dr. Feinstein would have liked to find figures about how much of the national income, defined according to the socialist concept as output of material goods at market prices, was paid in wages and how much was retained either by productive enterprises or by the Hungarian state budget.

On page 280 in her paper Dr. Zala had written that 'as a result of increasing mechanization the rise of average incomes [was] lower than that of productivity'. Dr. Feinstein did not think that increasing mechanization required of itself a lag in the rise of wages. Dr. Zala gave, however, three reasons for the declining share of wages in national income, the first being the increasing proportion of the labour force employed outside the sectors of material production in services, administration, and so on, which had to be paid out of surplus value, as a consequence of increasing productivity. Furthermore an increasing proportion of national income had to be devoted to infrastructure. Dr. Zala described these two reasons as 'laws of economic progress'. Although this seemed to Dr. Feinstein too strong a term for assessing these phenomena, he agreed that these trends were independent of the particular social system. But Dr. Zala added a third factor which was specific to a socialist economy or rather to a system in transition to Communism : an ideological preference which required an increasing proportion of income to be available in the form of free goods or of subsidized goods. This was to provide the basis for a transition at some stage from distribution according to ability to distribution according to need.

A second theme in Dr. Zala's paper, closely related to the first, was distribution of national income between investment and consumption. The decision as to what proportion of national income was to be devoted to investment was clearly of crucial importance for the planners. Once the investment ratio had been determined on what appeared to be the empirical basis of trial and error, the growth of national income was determined and as a result of this the growth of wages was given. Personal saving being negligible, personal consumption tended to amount to the same as personal income if services and also grants of various kinds were included on both sides.

Dr. Feinstein was interested to learn more about the way prices were determined and what was the bearing of the turnover tax on them. He would like to know what was the division of the national income between personal and centralized income and how the distribution of the latter between enterprises and the state operated. How was it decided what should be retained in the enterprise ?

Dr. Zala had said on page 283 of her paper that, contrary to what was expected, experience had shown no close and evident relationship between investment ratio and rate of growth of national income. Dr. Feinstein would interpret this as meaning that not only the amount of investment but also the form it took were relevant to the rate of growth of national income. Then how was a choice made between the different types of investment ?

The final point which Dr. Zala considered was distribution between different social groups, distribution between peasants and wage-earners, distribution between households as opposed to individual wage-earners, this latter raising the problem of dependents. Dr. Feinstein wished to know more about the way the different social groups within the sphere of material production fared in income distribution. As Dr. Zala had written on page 287 that the variance of individual incomes around the mean was smaller than in market economies, he would appreciate it if she could produce the actual data for Hungary.

Dr. Zala said she was grateful to Dr. Feinstein for his introduction of her paper as she had feared that the problems of a socialist economy would not be fully understood.

As Dr. Feinstein had pointed out, the principle of developing infrastructure faster than national income was not properly a law ; what she had meant was that in practice it appeared to be a necessity, and one which was experienced by all developing countries.

Dr. Zala said that the present price-determining policies needed complete revision. A distinction had to be made between what they were and what economists would like them to be. The turnover taxes fell upon consumer goods simply because in the early stages of socialism it was thought that investment goods prices should be below cost, the surplus being levied upon consumer goods. In this way the proceeds of the heavy 60 per cent turnover tax on clothing were largely used for subsidizing investment in agriculture, this being necessary as food was marketed at relatively low prices. Thus it was supposed that the sacrifice on clothing expenditure by the consumers would be to the benefit of agriculture. But in fact the low prices charged on food resulted in slower growth for agriculture, and at the same time clothing expenditure was restricted.

Dr. Zala was of the opinion that consumer prices should be readjusted to reflect marginal factor costs although whether it was possible to measure it and if so how was another question. She thought that as a first step it would be enough to charge prices which would cover the full costs and would at the same time allow for equilibrium between supply and demand. At the present moment, however, production capacity was not adequate to meet all demands at such prices.

For the moment investment was not decided on scientific criteria. Planning in Hungary of course conformed to the principle of balancing saving and investment. This was a means of answering an overall problem but of course it did not answer the question which investment and which sector should have priority. Improving the working of the price system would help in solving this sort of problem but then foreign trade might interfere.

Dr. Zala said that most of the centralized income was transferred to the budget as investment was centrally decided. But some income was retained by the enterprises and this was the main source for a small amount of investment expenditure for lowering the enterprises' own costs of production. Besides this, according to a system which was peculiar to Hungary, the workers got a share of the enterprise's net income (amounting to, say, two weeks' earnings) and if there was still some surplus left over it was available for staff welfare.

Professor Brochier had noticed that whereas Dr. Zala had written in her paper that the level of incomes of workers employed in material production and of workers employed in other activities were rather similar, a comparison of the figures in the tables on page 280 and page 281 of the paper led to quite another conclusion, namely that in 1962 workers employed in material production were 83·6 per cent of all wage-earners and received only 50·7 per cent of the national income. How could these figures be reconciled with the written statement ?

Dr. Negreponti-Delivanis observed that Dr. Zala had written on page 280 of her paper that in some sectors such as building the determination of the wage rates was influenced by the relative shortage of manpower available in the sector. Did this mean that supply and demand on labour as such determined the wage rate or did it rather mean, as she would think, that planning priorities were the main factor in determining what the wage rates should be ?

Dr. Negreponti-Delivanis had been surprised to read on page 285 of the paper that farmers' incomes still amounted to 45 per cent of the total wages and salaries. This seemed a high figure for a socialist country in the process of rapid industrialization. As farmers' incomes were usually not so high as industrial workers' wages, she would presume that the percentage of the farming population in the total employed population was still higher than 45 per cent and she would like to know what was the actual figure in Hungary.

Professor Lipinski thought it was as much a problem for capitalist as for socialist economies to achieve optimum efficiency. In order to improve efficiency in the working of the socialist economic system, he told the Conference, in Poland a new occupation, that of economist to the enterprise, had been created. Economists, attached to the executive staff, were there to find out new methods of optimizing resource allocation.

He also wished to underline how increasing the wages' share in national

income in the form of social consumption could favour economic development. Social consumption turned out to be human investment by
improving the health of the population, raising the level of technical
knowledge, etc. At the start investment had to be heavily concentrated
on building infrastructures and heavy industries with little rise in consumption as an immediate result, but the time had come to increase
investment in light industries. Raising standards of housing, health,
education of the population were ways of increasing productive forces.

Professor Bronfenbrenner, referring to Professor Lipinski's remark that
capitalist economies were no more able to solve the problem of optimiza-
tion than socialist economies, thought that there was still an advantage
in a market economy as providing an insurance against wrong or arbitrary
decisions by governmental authorities. Professor Bronfenbrenner was
grateful to Dr. Zala for having left out ideological infrastructure and he
was sorry to introduce ideological considerations himself but he would
suggest that market mechanisms operated positively against extremely bad
state interventions and especially against the inflationary bias they so
often had.

Professor Solow thought that the main difference in income distribution between a socialist and a market economy was that in the latter distribution was tied up with the price system (although subject to modifications by taxes and subsidies). In a market economy allocation of resources
came through people responding to prices and some of the prices to which
economic decisions responded were, directly, incomes, such as wages, or
indirectly, determined incomes. If the pattern of income distribution
thus emerging from the price system was deemed inappropriate, there
remained the possibility of redistribution as a correcting factor. On the
other hand although a socialist economy could substitute some degree of
decentralization, e.g. in awarding higher wages to workers in the building
industry on account of labour shortage in this activity, incomes were
mainly determined by arbitrary decisions.

From the figures in the table on page 284 of Dr. Zala's paper Professor
Solow had calculated, by comparing total consumption and total incomes
of the population, that there had been a steady increase in the rate of
personal savings from 2·4 per cent in 1960 to almost 6·0 per cent in 1963.
Would Dr. Zala comment on this as he was interested to know what the
reasons were for the increasing trend in personal savings ?

Professor Robinson wondered whether Professor Solow had not given
an idealized picture of a market economy. Socialist economies had no
monopoly of arbitrariness. There were many instances of arbitrary
decisions in Western Europe in fixing taxes on fuel, on coffee, and so on.

Professor Rasmussen wanted to mention that a working group established
by the Economic Commission for Europe had attempted on the one hand
to adjust the national accounts of one or two Eastern European countries
to the Standard National Accounts (SNA) of Western Europe and at the

same time had tried to adjust the accounts of Western European countries to the definitions of Eastern Europe. Had anything of that kind been done in Hungary ? Previous work done in the ECE (Professor Rasmussen referred to an article on this problem by Jackson, published some years ago by the International Association for Research in Income and Wealth) pointed to a difference in the national income on the two definitions of up to 20 per cent. Professor Rasmussen asked whether Dr. Zala would be able to give a rough estimate for Hungary.

Professor James thought there would be differences in income distribution patterns in Eastern European countries according to their level of development and the wage share would be bigger in an already highly developed country like Czechoslovakia in comparison with Hungary. As Professor Lipinski had said before, in a country like Poland the infrastructure of the economy had to be built first ; once this had been done it became possible to enlarge the share of wages and consumption in the national income. Thus Professor James thought that the same principle of income distribution could not apply to all the People's Democracies irrespective of their degree of economic development.

Professor James was interested to see how Marxist economists were anxious to bring some measure of market economy into the socialist system. Would not a reforming of the price policy on the lines Dr. Zala advised have the effect of bringing socialist economies closer to the Western ones? He would like to know Dr. Zala's opinion on this.

Dr. Zala said that she had wanted to avoid ideological discussion but some of the speakers in the debate had provoked her to a brief answer on ideological grounds. Far from being a dogma divorced from facts Marxism, as any scientific approach to facts, was an exercise in criticism. It was based on experience and one must not think of planned economies as controlled by more or less arbitrary decisions taken by a few powerful men in the way Professor Bronfenbrenner had suggested. Decisions were based on the work of many individuals in planning commissions, in enterprises' staffs, etc., and there was wide scope for discussion before arriving at a decision. In this way planning had been a way of solving problems in the short run : it was now starting to give answers to longer run problems.

Dr. Zala would give specific answers to some of the questions which had been raised in the course of the debate. She maintained that the figures which Professor Brochier had compared, in order to indicate a distortion in income distribution to the detriment of the workers in the material production activities, were not comparable : whereas the figures in the table on page 280 related to the ratio of workers employed in material production to the total number of employees, the figures in the table on page 281 related to the percentage of the personal incomes received by these workers in the whole national income, profits being included. As the share of profits was large this lowered the second proportion considerably.

Concerning Professor Solow's question about the rising proportion of savings in individual incomes, it was a matter of discussion in Hungary as to whether this trend was a good thing or not. Dr. Zala personally did not see any reason for favouring a rise in savings out of private incomes, at least in the present period when savings were formed by the state out of centralized income. As for the explanation of why the ratio was increasing, one had to remember that it was an extremely small proportion of private incomes at the beginning. A quick increase in committed savings could provide an explanation : as income level rose and more durable consumer goods were available, people started saving in order to buy them.

On a further question by *Professor Solow* suggesting that people might save for retirement purposes, *Dr. Zala* said that, old-age pensions not being very high, this might be so.

Dr. Zala observed that at the moment the rate of interest on personal savings was 5 per cent in Hungary and this was under discussion as being too high.

Dr. Zala was in a position to answer Professor Rasmussen's query as she had been engaged in the study to which he referred. According to this method of reciprocal valuation national income in Hungary, recalculated according to Britain's system of social accounting, would be 7 per cent higher than in the original calculations.

Dr. Zala said that she could not answer Dr. Feinstein's question about income concentration in statistical terms as she had not the necessary data available. But taking as an instance a relatively high family income with husband and wife both having relatively highly qualified jobs, say 12,000 forints per month, this would amount to four times the average household earnings.

Dr. Zala agreed with Professor James when he said that income distribution patterns in socialist countries had to be adapted to the level of economic development in each country. But as her paper had been on income distribution in Hungary alone she had not envisaged that aspect of the problem.

PART III

INCOME DISTRIBUTION
IN UNDERDEVELOPED COUNTRIES

Chapter 12

THE DISTRIBUTION OF NATIONAL INCOME IN UNDERDEVELOPED COUNTRIES[1]

BY

MARIA NEGREPONTI-DELIVANIS
University of Thessaloníki

INTRODUCTORY

ONE of the first things that becomes clear when one starts to think about the problems of income distribution in the less developed countries is that the analytical tools we are accustomed to use for economically advanced countries won't do. We need something different. Modern models of income distribution may, like Kaldor's,[2] assume full employment of the factors of production in a highly capitalistic economy; or they may, like Boulding's,[3] rest on the assumptions of underemployment of factors and perfectly elastic supply; but our analysis will have to work with underemployment and inelastic supply for as long as underemployment lasts.

Nor can we apply to the case of underdeveloped countries such older distribution models as the Keynesian,[4] even though they do deal with underemployment. Keynesian underemployment has its setting in an advanced capitalistic — and hence, industrialized — economy with excess capacity; excess capacity is due to deficient demand, and demand is deficient, first, because the marginal propensity to consume diminishes once primary needs are satisfied, and secondly, because the propensity to invest diminishes as a result of decreasing marginal efficiency of capital.

Underemployment in the less developed countries is also due to

[1] Translation by Elizabeth Henderson.
[2] N. Kaldor, 'Economic Growth and the Problem of Inflation', *Economica*, August 1959, pp. 212–227, and November 1959, pp. 287–299.
[3] K. E. Boulding, *A Reconstruction of Economics*, New York, John Wiley (London, Chapman and Hall), 1950; 'The Fruits of Progress and the Dynamics of Distribution', *American Economic Review*, May 1953.
[4] J. M. Keynes, *The General Theory of Employment, Interest and Money*, London, Macmillan, 1936.

deficient demand, but there are important differences which have an essential bearing on income distribution.

First of all, underemployment in an underdeveloped economy is certainly not due to too low a propensity to consume. On the contrary, it is common knowledge that the governments of these countries often have to turn to the Central Bank to finance consumption, which, incidentally, explains the inflationary pressures endemic in underdeveloped economies. In these conditions the marginal propensity to consume in the economy as a whole must surely be unity or more, which implies either absence of net investment or even disinvestment.

Secondly, the propensity to invest is indeed too low in underdeveloped countries, but not because of any diminution of the marginal efficiency of capital when all the more profitable investments have already been made. Theoretically, at least, the marginal efficiency of capital should be especially high in an underdeveloped economy ; if the propensity to invest is nevertheless insufficient, the reasons are, first, that risks are very great, secondly, that there are no external economies such as are indispensable for the normal functioning of the investment mechanism, and thirdly, and most important, that the market for industrial products is small. We shall have occasion to return to this last point later, in connection with the very considerable extent of self-consumption of agricultural produce in the less developed countries.

It follows that underemployment in the less developed countries has practically nothing to do with excess industrial capacity in the accepted meaning of the term. The problem is certainly not that more has been invested than should have been ; the problem is that not enough has been invested. Even in an underdeveloped economy there may, to be sure, occasionally be some excess industrial capacity in places ; but its causes are altogether different from those one would expect in an economically advanced country, and in any event its effects would be negligible in an economy where agriculture predominates and industry contributes only very little to the national product. If there is excess industrial capacity in an underdeveloped country, the reason may be either that an over-hasty investment is later abandoned, or that deliberate excess capacity is associated with the degree of monopoly ; the latter case most often occurs when the presence of foreign companies creates a dual economy. In any event, such excess capacity as may be found in an underdeveloped economy never implies over-investment in the Keynesian sense.

In these circumstances, our analysis must start out from the assumption of structural underemployment due to an insufficient propensity to invest. If industrial profits are comparatively high, we have to assume that entrepreneurs do not invest their profits, but prefer either to hoard them or to transfer them, if possible, abroad. Underemployment in an underdeveloped economy refers only to the factor labour and to a lesser extent, to the factor land, in the sense that land might be cultivated more intensively.

In the first part of this report we shall briefly examine existing models of income distribution and explain why none of them is applicable to the less developed countries. In the second part, we shall put forward a tentative model of income distribution in an underdeveloped economy.

I. INCOME DISTRIBUTION IN UNDERDEVELOPED COUNTRIES AND EXISTING DISTRIBUTION MODELS

The first difficulty is that none of the existing models is suitable for considering the categories of income in underdeveloped countries. This is true of the models of the classics and neo-classics, Marx, Keynes, and the neo-Keynesians alike.

The classical and neo-classical division of incomes into three categories is very general and would at first sight appear to be applicable to any economy, regardless of its stage of development. Yet the classical model of distribution neglects four important circumstances :

(1) It neglects subsistence-consumption which is very large and accounts not only for the main income of the bulk of the population, but for more than half the total national product.

(2) It neglects the incomes of middlemen in the trade in agricultural products ; these are conspicuously high in underdeveloped countries, owing mainly to the inadequacies of transport between rural and urban areas and to the absence of proper marketing and any kind of farmers' organization, which in turn is due to the dispersion of farms and the low educational level of farmers.

(3) It neglects the possibility of structural underemployment existing precisely because a country is underdeveloped.

(4) It neglects, finally, the role of money, that is to say, the effects of inflation and deflation on the manner of income distribution.

Marx, on the other hand, considers only two groups of income recipients, the workers or proletariat, and the capitalist or bourgeois class. He does, it is true, recognize the existence of other groups, such as farmers, artisans, government officials, etc., but these are anomalies destined to disappear. It is precisely this element of evolution, which dominates the whole of Marx's work, which makes it so difficult to apply his theory to underdeveloped countries. These countries will indeed evolve until, some day, they become developed countries, but what is of interest at the moment is to find out how national income is distributed in these countries now. It is most regrettable that Marx's categories do not fit the underdeveloped countries, because of all the existing models his is the one which otherwise gives the best account of the peculiarities of income distribution in these countries. There are, however, a number of things which the Marxian model, too, neglects.

Firstly, it neglects the fact that in underdeveloped countries the industrial sector is of scarce importance in the economy as a whole, and that the struggle between industrial entrepreneurs and workers concerns only a small part of the total active population in countries where 80 or 90 per cent of it may be engaged in agriculture. But the problems of income distribution among the agricultural population differ radically from those of the industrial sector. In underdeveloped countries agricultural incomes more or less coincide with subsistence-consumption for two reasons : first, the standard of living of the farmers is so low that they can consume only a negligible amount of industrial products ; and secondly, by the same token, farmers use practically the whole of the income they get from the sale of their products to buy other agricultural products, which they need equally badly but do not produce themselves.[1]

Secondly, it neglects the fact that the large extent of self-consumption makes it impossible to classify agricultural incomes under the heading either of wages or of profits.

Finally, the Marxian system is set in the very long period, since it envisages changes in techniques. But a distribution model for an underdeveloped country should abstract from changes in existing techniques. It might indeed be said that the very term underdevelopment implies a given state of techniques, in so far as the application of more advanced techniques means the end of the stage

[1] Apart from direct subsistence-consumption, we shall in this report take into account also indirect subsistence-consumption, that is, the income farmers get from selling their produce to other social groups but use to buy additional agricultural products from each other.

of underdevelopment and the beginning of the take-off. Consequently, a model of income distribution in an underdeveloped economy must be a short-period model describing a stationary situation.

Nor is the Keynesian model of distribution applicable to underdeveloped economies, because the situation of underemployment with which it is concerned differs very much from the kind of underemployment which is characteristic of these economies, as we noted before. There are also other reasons why the Keynesian model is inapplicable.

(1) The Keynesian model assumes that a shift in income distribution to the benefit of groups with a high propensity to consume can, via the multiplier, intensify the country's economic activity. But nothing is less certain in an underdeveloped country, where the supply especially of the industrial sector is inelastic for the following reasons. First, the propensity to consume in underdeveloped countries is insufficient not as concerns agricultural products, but as concerns industrial ones, precisely because the standard of life is so low. Any increase in the purchasing power of the poor classes will cause the latter to buy more agricultural products; they will buy very few industrial products before their vital needs are satisfied, and these are unlikely to be satisfied so long as the country remains underdeveloped. If, on the other hand, the incomes at least of farmers are not raised, any increase in the effective demand of other poor classes can have only a very small influence on the economy as a whole, just because so high a percentage of the total active population is engaged in agriculture. Even supposing that a redistribution of incomes to the benefit of the poor classes does increase the propensity to consume sufficiently to induce entrepreneurs to undertake new investment, there will soon be bottlenecks in capital, means of transport, foreign exchange, and skilled labour. The first need of underdeveloped economies is for structural changes to eliminate the factors which impede all progress and prevent the multiplier from coming into play; a change in income distribution takes second place.

(2) The Keynesian model fails to make one distinction which, in our view, is essential for any distribution model applicable to underdeveloped economies, the distinction, that is, between the propensity to consume industrial products and the propensity to consume agricultural products.

(3) Lastly, like the other models we have discussed, the Keynesian

model uses income categories which do not fit the conditions of underdeveloped countries.

Before trying to construct a model applicable to underdeveloped economies, we still have to take a look at the so-called sociological theories of income distribution, the principal proponent of which is Professor Jean Marchal. We shall refer to several of his articles published since 1950 [1] and to the three published volumes of the work he wrote jointly with Professor J. Lecaillon.[2] A new model of income distribution is to appear in the fourth volume now in preparation.

The great interest of the sociological theories of income distribution resides in their treatment of structural evolution and in their explanation of the manner of distribution in terms of the struggle among the different social classes sharing in the distribution of income. These categories of social classes will be the subject of the fourth volume of the work mentioned above.

Nevertheless, even the sociological theories of distribution do not seem to be of very much help in the case of underdeveloped countries, for the following reasons.

(1) The main criticism levelled by sociological theorists at other distribution models is that the latter take no account of structural change. But structural change is irrelevant for an explanation of income distribution in underdeveloped economies, in so far as under-development implies absence of structural change. What we need to do, instead, is to examine what bearing existing structures have at any given moment on income distribution in underdeveloped countries.

(2) The trade-union movement, for example, which plays so important a part in Marchal's theory, counts for little or nothing in an underdeveloped country where industrialization has hardly begun, the number of industrial workers is negligible in relation to total active population, the standard of living of the working classes is extremely low and permanent unemployment widespread. Even if there were trade unions, they would, in these circumstances, have no chance of doing anything to influence the distribution of national income.

---

[1] Jean Marchal, 'Les facteurs qui déterminent le taux d'intérêt dans le monde moderne', *Revue Économique*, July 1950 ; 'The Construction of a New Theory of Profit', *American Economic Review*, September 1951 ; 'Approches et catégories à utiliser pour une théorie réaliste de répartition', *Revue Économique*, March 1952 ; 'Esquisse d'une théorie moderne des salaires et d'une théorie générale de la répartition', *Revue Économique*, July 1955 ; 'Wage Theory and Social Groups' in *The Theory of Wage Determination*, ed. John T. Dunlop, Macmillan 1957.

[2] Jean Marchal and J. Lecaillon, *La Répartition du revenu national*, vol. i, ii, and iii, Paris, 1959, 1960, 1961.

(3) It is true that in many underdeveloped countries there is a foreign sector with a much higher degree of monopoly than is the rule elsewhere in the economy; but apart from this foreign sector and from all those who are directly or indirectly connected with it, the market of underdeveloped countries appears to be much less monopolistic, and therefore more competitive, than the market of developed countries. One of the reasons is that industry, which more than other sectors creates inequalities among competitiors, is of scarce importance in underdeveloped countries; additional reasons are that subsistence-consumption on the part of the bulk of the population limits the size of the market, and that the number of skilled and semi-skilled workers is very small.[1]

(4) While in developed countries government influences income distribution by means of differential taxation, practically nothing of the kind happens in underdeveloped countries. Statistics show big differences of income distribution in developed countries before and after taxation, distribution being much more even after taxation than before. In underdeveloped countries, distribution is much the same before and after taxation.[2]

Sociological factors, therefore, seem not to count in underdeveloped countries, and the struggle between the different social classes seems to be of no help in explaining the distribution of income.

We are led to the conclusion that what we need to do is to construct a new model for application to underdeveloped economies. This is a difficult task and one which demands years of work. The tentative construction we shall now put forward in this paper may be called a model only by convention. We shall try to stress certain factors which, while of essential importance in an underdeveloped economy, are nevertheless most often neglected. Yet without them no explanation of income distribution in underdeveloped countries seems at all possible.

II. A MODEL OF INCOME DISTRIBUTION IN UNDERDEVELOPED COUNTRIES

In building a model, the first thing to do is to define its structural setting, and then the *sine qua non* conditions of its internal logic.

[1] For more detail, see M. Negreponti-Delivanis, *Influence du développement économique sur la répartition du revenu national*, Paris, SEDES, 1960, pp. 92–99.

[2] United Nations, *Preliminary Report of the World Social Situation*, New York, 1952, p. 133.

The Distribution of National Income

(i) *The Structural Situation*

Any model which is to explain the distribution of national income in an underdeveloped economy must take account of such structural factors as have a direct or indirect bearing on income distribution. The main factors to be so considered are the following :

(1) More than 70 per cent of the total active population are engaged in agriculture. This means that there are far more recipients of incomes other than wages than in developed countries. But is it right, as most existing models do, to classify agricultural incomes as profits ? Surely not, and less than ever in an underdeveloped economy. In economics, the income category 'profit' is associated with entrepreneurs, whose principal function, apart from producing, is to invest. They can do so only if they earn enough not only to cover their consumption expenses, which is a matter of no interest in the context of income distribution, but also to have something over for investment. But the standard of living of farmers is extremely low in underdeveloped countries, and for this reason we only create difficulties for ourselves if we insist on describing agricultural incomes as profits.

(2) In an underdeveloped country, there are no big changes in the economic magnitudes from one year to another. We are, therefore, probably not far wrong in assuming a stationary economy. Apart from the other difficulties mentioned, it is, in these circumstances, neither necessary nor indeed particularly useful to try to construct a dynamic model of distribution. Once the time factor becomes important, the underdeveloped economy is, in fact, on the eve of its take-off. It follows that our model should also assume constant techniques.

(3) An underdeveloped economy typically suffers from permanent unemployment, which begins to be absorbed in a continuous fashion only when the economy enters the take-off stage. For the reasons indicated in the introduction, unemployment concerns only unskilled labour.

(4) Sociological factors are of little import in an underdeveloped country, in the sense that they can contribute nothing to a redistribution of income.

(5) Finally, underdeveloped countries are always subject to inflationary pressures, most often due to the government's inability to cover its consumption expenditure by taxation. Inflation leads to a rise in the nominal salaries of public officials ; entrepreneurs, on

the other hand, do not use their rising profits for new productive investment, but prefer to hoard or at least to increase the liquidity of their business by refusing to extend more credits.

(ii) *The* sine qua non *Conditions of the Model*

(1) The relative importance of the propensity to consume agricultural products and of the propensity to consume industrial products is not the same in underdeveloped and in developed countries. In developed countries, an increase in the purchasing power of wage-earners benefits mostly the demand for industrial products and to a much lesser extent the demand for agricultural products. This is not so in an underdeveloped country, for the following reasons :

(a) The standard of living of industrial wage-earners and public officials is extremely low ; consequently, both will first of all increase their consumption of agricultural products, and industrial products come second at some distance.

(b) If 70 per cent of the active population belong, by assumption, to the primary sector, the number of industrial wage-earners and public officials accounts, in any event, for only a small proportion of the population. The next question, therefore, is whether farmers are consumers of industrial products. It would seem that in an underdeveloped economy farmers are, on the whole, so poor that they consume only a negligible amount of industrial products. In these circumstances practically the whole of the demand for industrial products comes from industrial workers, public officials, and from a third category of income recipients to be discussed presently, namely, traders in agricultural products.[1]

This being so, we feel justified in assuming right away that in an underdeveloped economy the propensity to consume agricultural products is far greater than the propensity to consume industrial products. The matter is somewhat complicated by the fact that the propensity to consume industrial products reacts differently to inflation in the three cases of industrial wage-earners, public officials, and agricultural traders. The behaviour of one group may offset the behaviour of the others. Supposing, for example, that the

---

[1] Industrial entrepreneurs also consume industrial products, but we assume that their consumption expenditure does not reflect changes in their profits, and that profit changes influence only investment.

government has recourse to the Central Bank in order to raise the nominal salaries of government employees. This generates inflationary pressures which, owing to the time lag of wages behind prices and profits, diminish the real wages of industrial workers. These latter are forced to restrict their consumption of industrial products and, in the perspective of the economy as a whole, their behaviour almost offsets the rise in the consumption of industrial products on the part of public officials. A distinction has to be made, therefore, between the behaviour of that share of national income which accrues to industrial wage-earners, and the behaviour of the share accruing to public officials.

(2) The share of profits in national income depends upon the share of investment in national income, while the share of wages depends upon the share of consumption in national income — it being understood that we mean profits and wages in industry. We assume, in common with most modern models of income distribution, that only entrepreneurs are in a position to save part of their income, whereas workers consume all of theirs.[1] This assumption is obviously much more realistic in an underdeveloped than in a developed economy. Furthermore, the entrepreneurs' propensity to invest is a function of the economy's greater or lesser propensity to consume industrial products. As has been stated under (a) above, this propensity seems to be weak in underdeveloped countries and inflationary pressures do not seem to help matters. But, if the propensity to invest is small in an underdeveloped economy, it does not follow at all that the share of profits in national income is also small. It must not be forgotten that stock increases raise the share of investment in national income and that, therefore, other things being equal, the share of profits in national income can also rise.

(3) Our third assumption is that the agricultural population consumes only agricultural products. This is not an unrealistic assumption in an underdeveloped economy where agriculture is not yet mechanized and where the standard of living of the farmers is so low that they cannot even provide for their subsistence needs. This is why we can also assume that even if farmers manage to sell some of their produce to the towns, they will use the proceeds to buy other farm products which they urgently need but do not themselves produce. This is also a form of subsistence-consumption.

Our assumptions so far about the relations between the industrial and the agricultural sector may be summarized as follows :

[1] N. Kaldor and K. E. Boulding, *op. cit.*

(a) In an underdeveloped economy the propensity to consume agricultural products is made up of the propensities of farmers, industrial workers, public officials, and agricultural traders ;
(b) by contrast, demand for industrial products is exercised only by industrial workers, public officials, and agricultural traders, but not by the farmers who account for more than 70 per cent of total active population.

In these circumstances, we have to look for an answer to two extremely important questions. First, why is it that the standard of living of farmers is so low in underdeveloped economies, where the propensity to consume agricultural products is very high ? Secondly, why is it that farmers sell, through the intermediary of agricultural traders, a certain amount of agricultural produce to the towns without demanding, in return, any of the products of the secondary sector ? Other things being equal, this implies that the behaviour of the farming community as a whole has a deflationary effect on the system, and also that the farmers must have certain resources which they hoard. But we cannot make such an assumption for an underdeveloped economy.

We thus need two additional assumptions, which, incidentally, fully correspond to actual conditions in underdeveloped countries. These additional assumptions are :

(1) That the standard of living of the farmers is so low because, while they provide the means of existence not only for themselves but also for the people in the towns, allowance has to be made for the incomes of middlemen in agricultural trade and also of taxes which the farmers pay to the government. Both diminish agricultural incomes and prevent them from rising above the subsistence level.

(2) Apart from the frequent recourse of government to the Central Bank, the bulk of public expenditure is covered by taxation of farmers. Other groups of income-earners no doubt also pay taxes, but first of all well over half the total active population is in agriculture, and secondly governments in underdeveloped countries do not place a heavy tax burden on industrial entrepreneurs, in the hope of inducing them to invest more.

We may take it, therefore, that farmers meet practically the whole of the tax bill and in this way exercise an indirect demand for industrial products via the public officials. This is why the system is not deflationary in spite of subsistence-consumption on the part of the farming community.

Our model of income distribution will have five income categories, namely, the profits of industrial entrepreneurs, the wages of industrial workers, agricultural incomes, the incomes of agricultural traders, and the incomes of public officials. Our model is stationary and set in the short period. We shall use it for macro-economic and sociological analysis, in the sense that we shall examine the incomes of different social classes, but without reference to any struggle among them which might call forth a redistribution of income. The model is in equilibrium when $I=S$. Since we assume continuing inflationary pressures without their having any, or more than a very small, influence on investment and the level of employment, we shall have to explain how the system regains equilibrium.

We assume an inflationary system. A rise in the general price level, though affecting agricultural and industrial products in unequal measure, will raise investment (stocks) as against saving (hoarding) for three reasons :

(1) the share of wages in national income falls, because the level of employment remains stationary while the purchasing power of industrial workers decreases ;

(2) entrepreneurs begin to increase their stocks, in view of an elasticity of demand which equals or even exceeds unity — which signifies $I\ S$;

(3) when entrepreneurs begin to sell their stocks, they earn large profits, and since, by hypothesis, they do not feel induced to invest, they increase their hoarding.

In this way we come to a new equilibrium point $I=S$ with neither national income nor income per head of the population any higher than before.[1]

It is now time to describe in detail the model we have outlined above. We shall use the following notation :

Y National income
W Wages of industrial workers
C Consumption by industrial workers
P Profits of industrial entrepreneurs
C_2 Consumption by industrial entrepreneurs
A Incomes of farmers
C_a Subsistence-consumption by farmers
P_c Profits of agricultural traders

---

[1] Both national and *per caput* income obviously increase in monetary terms, but not in real terms.

C_1 Consumption by agricultural traders
W' Salaries of public officials
C' Consumption by public officials

$\dfrac{n_1}{AP}$ Number of industrial workers in total active population

$\dfrac{n_2}{AP}$ Number of industrial entrepreneurs in total active population

$\dfrac{n_3}{AP}$ Number of farmers in total active population

$\dfrac{n_4}{AP}$ Number of public officials in total active population

$\dfrac{n_5}{AP}$ Number of agricultural traders in total active population

T Taxes paid to government by the farmers (including expansion of the monetary circulation)
S Saving on the part of industrial entrepreneurs (in the form of hoarding)
I Investment (in the form of stocks)
a_1 Propensity to consume industrial products
a_2 Propensity to consume agricultural products.

The identities of our model are as follows :

(1) $\quad Y = W + P + A + W' + P_c$
(2) $\quad Y = C + (I + C_2) + C_a + C' + C_1$
(3) $\quad I = S.$

The variables in these identities may be written in the form of the following functions :

(1) $\qquad C = F_c\left(\dfrac{W}{Y}\right)$

(2) $\qquad I = F_I\left(\dfrac{P}{Y}\right)$

$\qquad C_2 = F_2\left(\dfrac{P}{Y}\right)$

(3) $\qquad C_a = F_a\left(\dfrac{A}{Y}\right)$

(4) $\qquad C' = F'\left(\dfrac{W'}{Y}\right)$

(5) $\qquad C_1 = F_1\left(\dfrac{P_c}{Y}\right)$

We now need to determine all the terms in brackets, that is, $\frac{W}{Y}$, $\frac{P}{Y}$, $\frac{A}{Y}$, $\frac{W'}{Y}$, and $\frac{P_c}{Y}$ according to the conditions of our model.

(1)
$$\frac{W}{Y} = \frac{C}{Y} = f_1 \left(a_1,\, a_2,\, T,\, S, \frac{n_1}{AP} \right)^{\text{I}}$$

or $\quad \dfrac{\partial W/Y}{\partial a_1} > 0, \quad \dfrac{\partial W/Y}{\partial a_2} < 0, \quad \dfrac{\partial W/Y}{\partial T} < 0, \quad \dfrac{\partial W/Y}{\partial S} > 0, \quad \dfrac{\partial W/Y}{\partial n_1/AP} > 0.$

The share of industrial wages in national income is obviously the same as the share of C, since we assume that only entrepreneurs are in a position to save, or rather to hoard, part of their income. The share of C in national income is the larger, the higher is the workers', officials' and agricultural traders' marginal propensity to consume industrial products in relation to the total active population's propensity to consume agricultural products. We thus introduce into our model the influence of a non-proportional price rise on the share of wages in national income. Industrial workers, whose income is low, are interested first and foremost in agricultural products. Consequently, it is to their advantage, in the case of a general price rise, to have agricultural prices go up less fast than the prices of industrial products. This development is a function of the relative values of the propensities to consume agricultural and industrial products.

The share of wages in national income rises when hoarding by industrial entrepreneurs increases, because this means that investment diminishes, and vice versa. Finally, T represents the taxes which farmers pay to the government, and which the government uses chiefly to pay the salaries of its employees. Any increase in T therefore aggravates inflationary pressure in underdeveloped countries and consequently diminishes the share of industrial wages in national income and raises the shares of industrial profits and of the incomes of public officials.

(2)
$$\frac{P}{Y} = \frac{(I + C_2)}{Y} = f_2 \left(a_1,\, a_2,\, T,\, S, \frac{n_2}{AP} \right)$$

or $\quad \dfrac{\partial P/Y}{\partial a_1} > 0, \quad \dfrac{\partial P/Y}{\partial a_2} < 0, \quad \dfrac{\partial P/Y}{\partial T} > 0, \quad \dfrac{\partial P/Y}{\partial S} < 0, \quad \dfrac{\partial P/Y}{\partial n_2/AP} > 0.$

The share of profits in national income depends upon the share of investment. According to the conditions of our model, the share of

---

[1] The propensities to consume a_1 and a_2 are here considered as independent variables because they are greatly influenced by price variations in the course of inflation.

investment is the larger, the higher is the workers', officials', and agricultural traders' propensity to consume industrial products.[1] Since real national income is assumed to be more or less constant during the whole period of underdevelopment,[2] these three groups' propensity to consume industrial products depends

(1) upon the size of the incomes of these three groups, which are the only ones that can consume industrial products. Once they have reached a certain standard of living, these groups will indeed begin to spend more on the consumption of industrial products, but they can do so only at the expense of a diminution of agricultural incomes and subsistence-consumption ;

(2) upon a rise in the numbers of industrial wage-earners, public officials, and agricultural traders in the total active population; other things being equal, this implies a reduction in the number of farmers in the total active population.

On the other hand, the share of profits in national income rises when T increases because

(1) the public officials' propensity to consume industrial products rises, either through an increase in their *per caput* income at unchanged numbers, or through an increase in their numbers at unchanged *per caput* income ;

(2) in our model, an increase in T intensifies the inflationary pressures which are endemic in underdeveloped economies, and thereby raises the share of profits in national income ;

(3) an increase in T also diminishes the propensity to consume agricultural products in the economy as a whole, in so far as it implies a diminution of subsistence-consumption.

Finally, an increase in saving (in the form of hoarding) diminishes the share of profits in national income, since it reduces investment (in the form of stocks).

(3) $$\frac{A}{Y} = \frac{C_a}{Y} = f_3\left(a_1, a_2, P_c, S, T, \frac{n_3}{AP}\right)$$

or

$$\frac{\partial A/Y}{\partial a_1} < 0, \quad \frac{\partial A/Y}{\partial a_2} > 0, \quad \frac{\partial A/Y}{\partial P_c} < 0, \quad \frac{\partial A/Y}{\partial S} > 0, \quad \frac{\partial A/Y}{\partial T} < 0, \quad \frac{\partial A/Y}{\partial n_3/AP} > 0.$$

[1] The share of the entrepreneurs' consumption in national income may be considered as stable in the short period. We have included it in the model only for the sake of completeness.

[2] Barring the case of an increase in population, when we assume instead that incomes per head are constant.

For reasons already explained, the standard of living of farmers in underdeveloped countries depends upon the share of subsistence-consumption in national income. This share is a function of the whole active population's propensity to consume agricultural products. When this propensity is high, farmers have a better chance to exchange part of their produce for other agricultural products which they do not themselves produce.

But total agricultural income is reduced by that amount of agricultural produce which serves to pay agricultural traders as well as the taxes with which the government pays the wages of its employees. Agricultural income therefore diminishes whenever either the number or the incomes of agricultural traders or public officials increases. When, on the other hand, entrepreneurs reduce their stocks and hoard more, the farmers' share in national income should increase, since hoarding raises the income share of industrial workers and these latter expand their demand for agricultural products.

$$(4) \qquad \frac{W'}{Y} = \frac{C'}{Y} = f_4\left(a_1,\ a_2,\ T,\ S,\ \frac{n_4}{AP}\right)$$

or $\quad \dfrac{\partial W/Y}{\partial a_1} > 0,\quad \dfrac{\partial W'/Y}{\partial a_2} < 0,\quad \dfrac{\partial W'/Y}{\partial T} > 0,\quad \dfrac{\partial W'/Y}{\partial S} < 0,\quad \dfrac{\partial W'/Y}{\partial n_4/AP} > 0.$

The share of public officials in national income depends upon the amount of taxes paid by farmers and upon the number of officials in the total active population. According to our assumptions, it would also seem that W'/Y increases during inflation but diminishes when hoarding increases, because, other things being equal, less hoarding implies a weakening of inflationary pressure in the economy as a whole.

$$(5) \qquad \frac{P_c}{Y} = \frac{C_1}{Y} = f_5\left(a_1,\ a_2,\ C_a,\ T,\ S,\ \frac{n_5}{AO}\right)$$

or

$$\frac{\partial P_c/Y}{\partial a_1} < 0,\quad \frac{\partial P_c/Y}{\partial a_2} > 0,\quad \frac{\partial P_c/Y}{\partial Ca} < 0,\quad \frac{\partial P_c/Y}{\partial T} < 0,\quad \frac{\partial P_c/Y}{\partial S} > 0,\quad \frac{\partial P_c/Y}{\partial n_5/AP} > 0.$$

The share of agricultural traders in national income equals the farmers' income less subsistence-consumption and taxes. Whenever, therefore, higher taxation diminishes subsistence-consumption, it diminishes at the same time also the share of agricultural traders in national income.

The traders' share is the higher, the more the rate of increase of the propensity to consume agricultural products exceeds the rate of increase of the propensity to consume industrial products. Since an increase in the entrepreneurs' hoarding has favourable effects on the income share of industrial workers, it must have the same favourable effect also on the share of traders' profits in national income.

$$(6) \qquad T = A - (C_a + P_c)$$

Taxation is now not difficult to determine. According to the assumptions of the model, T equals total agricultural income less subsistence-consumption and the profits of agricultural traders.

The above model of income distribution is, I believe, applicable to underdeveloped countries. The principal conclusions to be drawn from it may be summarized as follows :

(1) Although in underdeveloped countries the whole economy's propensity to consume agricultural products is far higher than its propensity to consume industrial products, the standard of living of farmers is extremely low. One reason for this state of affairs is that, in the absence of transport facilities and of any kind of organization among the dispersed farmers, traders in agricultural products are in an extremely strong position ; another reason is the taxation imposed by government on the farming community.

(2) The share of industrial profits in national income is higher than appears justified in the light of an underdeveloped economy's insufficient propensity to consume. The reason is that inflationary pressures, which must be assumed to be always present in an underdeveloped economy,[1] benefit the profit share in so far as they depress the share of industrial wages. But, for reasons explained above, entrepreneurs prefer hoarding to productive investment. In an underdeveloped country, therefore, an increase in industrial profits does not normally raise the propensity to invest ; the propensity to invest depends upon the whole economy's propensity to consume industrial products, which in turn is insufficient in an underdeveloped country. As a result, the price level keeps rising continually in underdeveloped countries, even though nothing like full employment has been achieved. But the rising tendency of prices influences neither the level of employment nor the volume of productive investment.

(3) Under the influence of the inflationary pressures endemic in underdeveloped countries, the income share of profits, P/Y, and the

[1] D. J. Delivanis, *L'Économie sous-développée*, Paris, 1964, chap. 15.

income share of public officials, W'/Y, both develop in the same upward direction. The profit share and the share of industrial wages, W/Y, on the other hand, move in opposite directions : the first grows and the second falls during inflation. Similarly, the income shares of public officials, W'/Y, and of agricultural traders, Pc/Y, also move in opposite directions, since W'/Y rises during inflation under the impact of an increase in T, while P_c/Y diminishes.

DISCUSSION OF DR. NEGREPONTI-DELIVANIS'S PAPER

Professor André Marchal said that all models implied simplification and could but diverge from the complexities of the real world. Dr. Negreponti-Delivanis had thus taken upon herself a delicate task in constructing a model of income distribution for underdeveloped countries.

He would begin by saying what this model was not. It was not, Professor Marchal would suggest, a classical or a neo-classical model. In contrast with classical or neo-classical models, such features of underdevelopment as the abnormally high incomes out of trade on farm products had been brought in. Nor did it neglect structural underemployment which it related to a specifically low propensity to invest. The impact of monetary factors was also included.

Nor was it a Marxian model. Such a model would seem better adapted to the problems of distribution in underdeveloped countries but in differentiating between only two groups, a capitalist versus workers' type of model would not fit into economies where the industrial sector had not yet developed and where the farming population might amount to 80 per cent of the total labour force. Agricultural incomes were very near subsistence level and they should not be treated as either wages or profits. Furthermore the Marxian model was based on changes in technology related to the very long period whereas Dr. Negreponti-Delivanis's model related to stationary economics and was therefore limited to the short period.

A Keynesian model would also have been insufficient for Dr. Negreponti-Delivanis's purpose as the income multiplier was of very limited application to underdeveloped countries as the elasticity of domestic supply of manufactured products was not high enough and the effective demand for these products was restricted by the abnormally low income level of the farming population in combination with an insufficient proportion of people employed outside the agricultural sector. In comparison with Keynesian models in so far as they had usually considered an overall consumption function, a distinct feature of Dr. Negreponti-Delivanis's model was in differentiating between a high propensity to consume farm products and a specifically low propensity to consume industrial products.

Her model could not be called a sociological model. The dynamics of income distribution through structural changes and tensions between social groups were not relevant to non-evolutive situations : Dr. Negreponti-Delivanis's model related to countries which were not yet industrialized and where workers' unions were not an important factor in shaping income distribution. These economies were operating under competitive rather than monopolistic conditions as the agricultural sector was predominant. A sociological model would stress the impact of income redistribution but this was left out of Dr. Negreponti-Delivanis's model because in these countries public finance did not significantly alter the final distribution.

Professor André Marchal summed up the model's assumptions and then described how it explained the distribution of national income between the five groups retained ; entrepreneurs and wage-earners in the industrial sector, farmers, traders in farms products, and civil servants.

Professor Marchal wished to draw Dr. Negreponti-Delivanis's attention to some points he would think questionable. He wondered to what extent one could in fact explain income distribution in underdeveloped countries by an entirely static model. Fortunately enough all underdeveloped countries could now in some sense be called developing countries. Bearing this in mind Professor Marchal would advocate some loosening of the static limitations of the model although he was aware of the almost unsurmountable difficulties which Dr. Negreponti-Delivanis would have encountered in building a truly dynamic one.

It seemed to Professor Marchal that Dr. Negreponti-Delivanis had not given enough stress to one essential feature of all underdeveloped economies which made a strong impact on income distribution, namely their dual character. These economies broke down into two disjointed parts, a modern industrialized sector being superimposed on a traditional sector with little communication between the two. Thus would not income distribution be ruled by different principles in each ?

Professor Marchal was in entire agreement with the author in not having included farmers' incomes within the category of profits. But he would have gone a step farther towards income differentiation in distinguishing between different kinds of profits according to the sectors in which they were ploughed back. In this connection profits which were transferred abroad should have made up a distinct category.

He would not only distinguish between profits according to their sectoral origins but also according to different groups of profit earners. Foreign capitalists who invested in underdeveloped countries most often formed one financial group or belonged to a pattern of joint interests. Thus criteria for investment decisions did not reflect the interests of the domestic producers in agriculture, trade, and industry as they would if these people had access to a competitive capital market within the country. Investments were decided instead on a criterion of profitability relating to overseas markets and not to the domestic market of the country in which they were made. More often than not this would benefit banking or trading activities and primary producers rather than domestic manufacturing producers.

Did this not imply carrying the analysis of income distribution in underdeveloped countries along the lines of the so-called sociological models? In this connection Professor Marchal would give up models based on capital formation and adjustments of the overall saving and investment ratios and, contrary to Dr. Negreponti-Delivanis, he thought that underdevelopment called for a sociological analysis in terms of 'active' and 'inactive' labour force.

The existence of structural unemployment was one of the model's basic assumptions and this should have led to putting the stress on labour rather than on capital as a productive resource. The reason why the traditional society was not as successful in saving and accumulating productive capital as the advanced societies was that a large part of its population was not employed in productive jobs, productive employment being defined in terms of demand, not of labour productivity.

Doubtless capitalism had changed underdeveloped countries, increasing social product and raising the standard of living. But this had been achieved through a new pattern of relations with the outside world and if these economies had benefited from the multiplier effect of industrial development abroad, this had had counter-effects such as the disappearance of craft industries in countries like India.

Once it had been admitted that underdevelopment was a problem of productive employment of the labour force rather than of capital formation one could no longer put aside its close relationship with institutions. Professor Marchal thought that in this connection any model ought to take into account such data as the occupational structure of the population and such changes as shifts in employment from the agricultural to the industrial sector and their effects on income spending and effective demand. This was what was, in fact, meant by a 'sociological' approach to income distribution.

Professor Papi said that he had been very impressed by the way Dr. Negreponti-Delivanis had used modern analytical methods in her paper. Although he would congratulate her on her attempt to adapt them to underdeveloped economies, he wondered whether such an endeavour as model building was leading in the right direction. He thought that models were used for describing economic conditions which varied according to countries whereas to him science should always be *reductio ad unum*. It should strive for logical categories comprehensive enough to account for all circumstances.

Professor Papi wished to make a specific comment on the way the role of the state had been narrowly restricted in the model. The state's part in taxation and inflation was taken into account, but the state as an active force in promoting development and its relation with the outside world were ignored.

Dr. Negreponti-Delivanis's model also neglected the indispensable share of public investment in improving human resources. This he much regretted as he was of the opinion that investing in men conditioned the productivity of all material investments.

Dr. Zala said that although she was well aware that the making of any model implied some simplifying and abstracting from real facts, she would however have thought it necessary to include in this model an external sector. As those were open economies one could not neglect international trade. The model being based on an investment cum saving relationship, adjusting investment to domestic savings would make for a very low rate of growth, if any at all. One should not neglect foreign capital in order to increase the employment of human resources and raise the standard of living.

Professor Gendarme said that he had no intention of reproving Dr. Negreponti-Delivanis for having yielded to the current fashion in economics of model building as the model which she proposed was original and useful. He wondered however whether there was not an excessive over-simplification of the conditions observed in underdeveloped countries.

He thought that a model of this sort would have to reflect the twofold nature of underdeveloped economies and this not only in explaining sectoral imbalance but also regional imbalance.

Like Professor A. Marchal, he regretted that this was an entirely static model. Economics of development were economics of structural change and one had to take into account the shift of labour from agriculture to the modern sector, at the very least. One could not put aside dynamic considerations and distinguish between a period before take-off and a period of autonomous growth. Facts had shown that during the period of take-off there was a risk of loss of speed contrary to over-optimistic expectations. Thus he would rather have had a long-period model. A much longer span of time in consideration would also have allowed for the inclusion of the demographic element in growth which a model of income distribution for overpopulated countries could not ignore.

To assume that the farmers consumed little more than farm products seemed also somewhat of an over-simplification as it implied the absence of the demonstration effect. Professor Gendarme observed that country people in underdeveloped economies were incited to buy more and more imported manufactured products and that this threatened village crafts and industries with extinction.

To treat underdeveloped countries as if they were closed economies also seemed to Professor Gendarme to be questionable. As a matter of fact most of them were fully open and it was rather arbitrary to choose to ignore such facts as the impact of specializing in primary products, or the dependence of capital formation on foreign investment. Foreign aid as a policy of international redistribution of income in favour of the poorer countries was also an emerging feature which had to be considered in relation with income distribution in underdeveloped countries.

Professor Tress wished to make a comment on the use of models. As Professor Papi, in questioning their usefulness, had addressed the conference in general rather than Dr. Negreponti-Delivanis, Professor Tress would contribute to a reply in citing one instance from his own experience where, called upon to resolve the very practical tension between three underdeveloped countries in common market relationship, the construction of an analytical model had been essential to the arbiters in order to arrive at an understanding of the problem and a fair solution of it.

His object in criticizing Dr. Negreponti-Delivanis's paper therefore was to improve it, not to destroy it. Like Professor Gendarme he too had been surprised by the assumption that demand for industrial products was not exercised by farmers. In very primitive economies it was true that farmers might enter the cash economy only to acquire sufficient cash to pay taxes but, as Professor André Marchal had pointed out, underdeveloped countries were developing countries and the fact that Dr. Negreponti-Delivanis's model included an industrial sector confirmed this feature. Now the experience in developing countries was that, as farmers acquired additional income, they bought tools, then prestige goods, e.g. clothes, shoes, corrugated roofing, bicycles, i.e. they purchased industrial products, either domestic or imported.

Professor Tress could not agree either with the assumption that the bulk of public expenditure was covered by taxes paid by farmers. According to his own experience, in underdeveloped countries as elsewhere it was extremely difficult to extract revenue from farmers. Some revenue might be obtained for local government ; some for central government through marketing boards for export crops ; but the main sources of central government income were to be found in other ways : in taxing incomes of public servants and company employees, for whom tax returns were easily available ; in taxing companies and, last but not least, in levying customs and excise duties on manufactured products, produced locally or imported.

Hence, in so far as farmers contributed to central revenues it had to be through the purchase of industrial products. He would thus detect an internal inconsistency in Dr. Negreponti-Delivanis's paper in assuming on the one hand that farmers paid the bulk of government revenue and on the other hand that they did not buy industrial goods.

Professor Falise observed that Dr. Negreponti-Delivanis's reasoning assumed that the share of wages in national income was a positive function of saving whereas the share of profits behaved in the reverse way.

She supported this by positing that when saving increased investment decreased, hence the decrease in the profit share and, conversely, the increase in the wage share.

But Professor Falise wondered how Dr. Negreponti-Delivanis was able to reconcile this form of reasoning with the customary I and S identity which was retained by her model. He could not see why the profit share should decrease when investment expenditure was cut down. This could be supported only by identifying investment with accumulation of inventories and excluding fixed capital formation.

This implicit way of defining investment seemed to him open to question as excluding investment in production capacity in developing countries. He was not sure either about the definition of saving in the model : was it not identified with undistributed profits and if so did the share of profits in her model still include the whole profits or only non-distributed profits ?

Professor Krelle also thought that the model implicitly excluded any investment in fixed capital. This seemed to him an unduly pessimistic assumption as denying any chance of growth to underdeveloped economies and he thought that the model ought to be revised in this respect.

Like Professor Falise he could not understand what was the I and S relationship in the model ; either I and S were allowed to diverge or they should be identical ; either they were defined in monetary terms or in real terms, but they could not be all this at the same time. If investment and saving were defined in real terms as he thought Dr. Negreponti-Delivanis intended, then he could not understand why a condition of identity of I and S was posited in the model.

No matter how interesting he thought Dr. Negreponti-Delivanis's endeavour, Professor Krelle would point out that her model had not yet been tested and the value of any model could not be ascertained until one had tried to solve its equations for given values of the parameters. Econometrics only could decide whether some internal inconsistencies had not crept into a model. Some indications of how income distribution changed for different values of the parameters should have been given as there was no *a priori* proof of the stability of the results.

This being a Keynesian model, much depended on the propensity to consume. One could not be sure that consumption functions were linear functions and again one could decide this only by attempting to solve the model by giving its parameters values likely to apply to a given economy.

Professor Gannagé observed that if Dr. Negreponti-Delivanis's model took certain implications of the dual structure of underdeveloped countries into account in distinguishing a modern industrialized sector from an agricultural one and in differentiating propensities to consume accordingly, it should also have included an external sector because, in many cases, the modern sector of the economy tended to coincide with foreign capital interests in the country. International oil companies in Middle East countries could be cited as an instance. Leaving out this sort of relationship would tend to limit the scope of the model to entirely stationary economies or subsistence economies. As practically all underdeveloped countries had already gone beyond that stage, it was to be regretted that foreign trade had not been brought within the scope of the model.

Dr. Bruzek said that he had been much interested in Dr. Negreponti-Delivanis's paper and especially by the criticisms which she addressed to the Marxian model of income distribution on account of its lack of applicability to underdeveloped countries. He would agree with her that it did not fit them without restriction. He thought however that some of its features would be of great help in analysing income distribution in relation to underdevelopment.

Dr. Bruzek did not think that Dr. Negreponti-Delivanis correctly interpreted Marx's thought in writing (p. 300 in the paper) that whereas Marx recognized the existence of groups other than the proletariat and the bourgeois, such as farmers, craftsmen, and so on, he saw in these 'anomalies destined to disappear'. Marx had never said so : he said that these people must exist in every society.

Dr. Bruzek observed that the Marxian approach stressed the importance of the large farmers employing much hired labour. It would be useful to know what was these people's share in total agricultural product and in national income in various underdeveloped countries. Dr. Bruzek would think that in many cases, in South America for instance, these proportions would prove to be high. The Marxian model had much significance in explaining income distribution in developing countries as the process of development must favour the larger production units not only in industry but also in farming. The small farmers could remain preponderant only in a subsistence economy.

He thought that the Marxian model would also apply to the relations between developed and underdeveloped countries in explaining why the underdeveloped countries' terms of trade deteriorated. The opposite trends towards decreasing raw material prices and increasing manufacturing prices meant that an increasing part of the value in primary producing countries' exports was taken away by industrial countries and the changes in international distribution of incomes as a result could not be ignored.

Professor Fauvel compared econometric models to *modèles de haute couture*; they were glamorous but very uncomfortable to wear. Dr. Negreponti-Delivanis's model was a very sophisticated way of approaching income distribution in underdeveloped countries. But its relevance to observed facts seemed to him to be limited by unduly restrictive assumptions.

It had already been pointed out how difficult it was to reconcile the assumption that farmers did not buy industrial goods with the evidence of cash crops. Professor Fauvel thought that another assumption in the model equally open to criticism was that underdeveloped economies were under constant pressure of inflation. He would think that during the whole colonial period the reverse had been the case, as was indicated by the almost constant surpluses in the balance of payments of these countries. In the present period, supposing that the high rate of increase in public expenditure in newly independent states and a higher rate of capital formation would lead to inflation, this would call for constructing a model of growth without inflation whereas a static model like Dr. Negreponti-Delivanis's was devised in a way which prevented its use in policy making.

Professor Ohkawa wished to congratulate Dr. Negreponti-Delivanis for her contribution to an issue which until now had been approached from the point of view of classical theory. In other models the stress had always been on the supply and production side of the analysis of under-development rather than on the expenditure and demand side. Their starting point had been the assumption of permanent underemployment or of a flexible supply of labour at subsistence level. Since the subsistence level was treated as either historic data or as determined by an insufficient productivity of farmers, these models could not give any comprehensive explanation of the mechanism of national income distribution. Dr. Negreponti-Delivanis's unconventional endeavour in starting from the demand side of the problem of underdevelopment was to be commended.

Real conditions in the so-called underdeveloped economies varied too much from one country to another to make it worth while trying to increase the complexity of a single model. Professor Ohkawa, however, thought the model was not to be criticized for being oversimplified. The first require-ment of a model was simplicity. On the expenditure side, therefore, he would suggest a further generalization.

Thus Dr. Ohkawa was not sure whether Dr. Negreponti-Delivanis had been right in assuming a higher propensity to consume with regard to farm products than to industrial products. Was such a very peculiar assumption really indispensable for the sake of the model ? He would have thought that it should have been possible to construct as good a model without such an assumption and it might have turned out to be a better one in being of more general application.

Professor Nørregard Rasmussen questioned the determinacy of the model. He would have liked Dr. Negreponti-Delivanis to state more explicitly what she assumed to be exogenous. He further would have wished for a more detailed explanation of the reasonings behind the behavioural equations.

Professor Patinkin said that he could not agree with Dr. Negreponti-Delivanis's point of departure that the theory of distribution in an under-developed economy must be fundamentally different from that of a developed country. Although the debates until now had made him aware just how widely this opinion was held amongst his French-speaking fellow economists, he could see no obvious reason for this. He would think that in these countries individual behaviour could be analysed by means of indifference curves in the same way as in other economies and if it were so the analytical framework of marginal productivity theory must provide as good a starting point as in the general case.

Nor, if a Keynesian model was preferred to marginal theory on general grounds, could Professor Patinkin see why it should be deemed necessary to alter it in order to make it adequate to underdeveloped countries. The only reason given had been that one ought in this case to differentiate the propensity to consume according to income groups. But this was relevant to developed countries as well. Models had already been made by Klein for instance, differentiating consumption functions between groups. Although this might be more of a semantic than methodological point, he would maintain that Dr. Negreponti-Delivanis's model remained fundamentally a Keynesian model.

Professor James regretted that Dr. Negreponti-Delivanis, in constructing her model, had left a gap. Was there no room for the category incomes out of speculation on land and especially building sites which played an important part in developing countries even before take-off ?

Professor Jean Marchal was pleased to see that Dr. Negreponti-Delivanis based her model on a differentiation of groups according to the social pattern prevailing in underdeveloped countries. He thought, however, that the criteria which she had retained for differentiating groups were insufficient. Relating them to propensity to invest and propensity to consume farm and industrial products seemed to him one step in the right direction but to this he would add another consideration, i.e. group behaviour as characterized by the way each group strived to maintain within certain limits its relative income share under the pressure of competing groups in income distribution.

This seemed necessary to Professor Jean Marchal in order to give a full account of the inflation process built into the model. Dr. Negreponti-Delivanis posited a differentiated increase in prices with respect to the agricultural and industrial sectors and she explained shifts in the point of monetary equilibrium but the reasons for the inflationary process were not explained in her model.

Doubtless Dr. Negreponti-Delivanis assumed that the government increased the quantity of money in circulation in order to pay for a rise in public servants' salaries, but why had the government to pay higher salaries to the civil servants ? Obviously this was under the assumption of the civil servants claiming a rise on account of an increasing lag in their incomes in comparison with the income in other social categories. Inflation should therefore be related to income distribution and a more comprehensive theory of income distribution than the one on which the model was based would have to be devised.

Dr. Negreponti-Delivanis thanked Professor André Marchal for introducing her paper. Her model had been criticized as static but she had thought it necessary to distinguish between underdevelopment as a stationary state and a take-off-phase, the study of which obviously belonged to dynamics. Income distribution being very different at these two stages one and the same model could not apply to both and thus she had been induced to limit the scope of her study. Her model was not however entirely static as inflation was a built-in feature and it tried to explain how inflation had a bearing on income distribution.

She was ready to admit that she had neglected the twofold nature of underdeveloped economies as she thought that before a certain level of development had been reached there was an almost complete absence of sectoral integration between the modern and the traditional economies : the modern sector could not influence income distribution in the traditional sector in any significant way.

Professor Marchal had been right in suggesting that she should have distinguished between different categories of profits. She had been aware of the advantage in doing so but this would have made her model more cumbersome.

To Professor Papi's general remark about models Professor Tress had already furnished an answer and Dr. Negreponti-Delivanis would just add that devising a model was nothing more than setting a theory in a coherent framework.

Professor Papi had criticized her for neglecting the part of the state. Dr. Negreponti-Delivanis wished to point out that she had brought into her model the Government operations which had a bearing on income distribution, such as taxation, and public expenditure on civil servants' salaries, and their inflationary financing through Central Bank loans to the state. In underdeveloped countries state intervention operated to the detriment of the poorer classes and its consequences on income distribution were very different from what they were elsewhere.

As Dr. Zala had observed her model would have been more complete if she had included foreign trade and foreign investments, but she would think that foreign trade became important only after a certain level of development had been achieved.

Professor Gendarme, in referring to the demonstration effect, had objected with some reason to her assumption that farmers did not spend their incomes on industrial products in any significant measure. But it was not so much a matter of whether farmers wanted these goods as whether they could afford to buy them. This would also answer a similar observation by Professor Fauvel. She intended to improve her model and Professor Tress's remarks would help her.

To Professor Falise's query about how equilibrium would be reached under her model's assumptions, Dr. Negreponti-Delivanis answered that in her model investment was in the form of inventories and saving in the form of holding idle cash balances. Under inflationary conditions wages would lag behind prices and profits and as the wages share decreased there would be increasing accumulations of inventories by the entrepreneurs. As long as entrepreneurs anticipated prices continuing to rise, I would tend to be bigger than S. When they started selling out their inventories, profits would be high and as she assumed them to invest in inventories only their cash holding would then increase and thus the I and S condition of identity would be satisfied.

Dr. Negreponti-Delivanis was not at all surprised by Professor Krelle's remark that her model excluded the possibility of economic growth, as she had reduced investment to inventories and saving to cash holding because she had wanted to emphasize the vicious circle in development. In answer to Professor Krelle's second observation she would say that her identities were in real terms but that the I and S equilibrium was achieved in monetary terms through price fluctuations.

Whereas she agreed with Professor Gannagé's observation that her model applied only to subsistence economies and not to semi-developed economies, she could not agree with his criticism of her not having included an external sector in her model because foreign trade and investment had only a significant impact on semi-developed economies. Opening the model as Professor Gendarme and several other speakers including Professor Gannagé had suggested would have made the model more cumbersome and this had been another reason why she had restricted her model to a closed economy.

Dr. Negreponti-Delivanis pointed out to Dr. Bruzek that if in her paper she had started by criticizing all the available models including the Marxian one, this had been with the proviso that out of them all the Marxian model seemed to her the closest to the facts. She thought, however, that its emphasis on the industrial sector was a major obstacle to applying it to countries not yet industrialized. She regretted being unable to answer Dr. Bruzek's question about the part played by big landowners in underdeveloped countries as she had no available data. She would think this varied widely according to the structure of the different countries.

Professor Ohkawa had been right in stressing that all the underdeveloped countries had not the same characteristics, but she would think that there were some common significant features : specifically distinct propensities to consume agricultural and industrial products was one of them.

Dr. Negreponti-Delivanis wished to make it clear to Professor Patinkin that she did not claim originality for differentiating between consumption functions in constructing her model. Contrary to Professor Patinkin she thought that basic differences in economic structures made for fundamentally different forms of income distribution in underdeveloped countries as opposed to developed ones.

Although Professor James had been right in regretting that her model had not included incomes out of land speculation, she could not yet see how she would bring them in.

Negreponti-Delivanis — Distribution in Underdeveloped Countries

Dr. Negreponti-Delivanis thanked Professor Jean Marchal for his observations, especially about the connections between inflation and income distribution theory. His suggestions would help her to improve her model as, contrary to Professor Fauvel, she believed inflation to be a characteristic of underdeveloped economies. Not only was this a basic assumption in her model but she had tried to explain inflation as an endogenous phenomenon.

Chapter 13

THE DISTRIBUTION OF INCOME IN UNDERDEVELOPED COUNTRIES

BY

ELIAS GANNAGÉ

University of Beirut

INTRODUCTORY

THE study of the phenomena of income distribution in under-developed countries encounters difficulties of a conceptual and statistical order to which attention must be drawn at the outset. The concept of income, already diversely construed in the developed countries, gives rise to a still greater variety of interpretations in regard to more backward countries. There is not one standard notion of income but several varieties. The results will be different, according to whether the individual or the family is taken as the unit of production and consumption and whether or not account is taken of non-monetary incomes (i.e. in kind), the proportion of which is far from negligible in a subsistence economy. Likewise, the geographical partitioning of territory in the underdeveloped areas adds still further hazards to any attempt to ascertain individual incomes, so great is the diversity of mentalities and attitudes even within the rural areas. The tasks performed by women, the size of the family unit, the differences in the monetary remuneration of services are so many factors which often render it useless to try to isolate personal income, for it is found to cover activities and services of a totally different nature.

When it comes to the methods of evaluation, one discovers the dearth and inadequacy of the information available. The countries for which statistical data are obtainable in regard to the distribution of income are not very numerous. The main surveys carried out in the field concern the countries of Asia (India, Philippines, Ceylon, Malaysia)[1] and certain countries in the Middle East (Lebanon),

[1] India : *National Sample Survey*, 4th Round, no. 18, The Cabinet Secretariat, Calcutta, 1958. Philippines : *Family Income and Expenditures*, National Economic Council, 1958. Ceylon : *Survey of Ceylon's Consumer Finances*, Central Bank of Ceylon, Colombo, 1954. Malaysia : *Budget Survey, 1957–58*, Department of Statistics, Kuala Lumpur.

and Central or Latin America (Puerto Rico, Salvador, Mexico, Colombia). These data, although of considerable use to the investigator, seriously curtail the significance of any generalized findings, by reason of the very narrow field of observation they cover. This obstacle might perhaps have been overcome, had it not been further complicated by serious deficiencies in the data that were available. For the underdeveloped countries the information that we find is derived not so much from systematic and co-ordinated surveys as from assessments or opinions formulated by astute investigators with a gift for figures. But however useful these assessments may be, they are contingent on the personal appreciation of the investigator and therefore liable to wide error. The ingenuity of the assessor tends to make up for the deficiency of methodical data.

The purpose of these reservations is to emphasize the inevitably restricted scope of the present study. With this preliminary word of warning, and within the limitations of the conceptual and statistical difficulties referred to, we shall examine the distribution of income first by categories and then by sectors. In conclusion we shall endeavour to assess the significance of these findings, in the light of a comparison of the phenomena of distribution in underdeveloped countries with those in countries that are fully developed.

I. DISTRIBUTION BY CATEGORIES OF INCOME

The data available in respect of the phenomena of income distribution in underdeveloped countries enable a variety of results to be obtained, according to whether the data relate to individuals or families, whether they are confined to a short period or concern cumulative income over a long period, whether they concern primary distribution or take into account the mechanisms of redistribution.

But before embarking on a detailed analysis, attention must be drawn to the relativity of the statistical methods used to measure the degree of inequality of incomes. The conventional method still is to take the difference found between the highest and the lowest percentages in the whole group of categories of income. But this is not the only system. Recourse may be had to coefficients of concentration, to coefficients of variation or to the standard deviations of the logarithms of income which are synthetical indices designed to measure, by means of a single figure, the inequality of distribution.[1] The choice between these different methods is a difficult one, for they are all imperfect ones, placing the emphasis on different aspects of the distribution of income. Thus, though the indices of concentration (Lorenz curves) remain the best assessment,[2] they are nevertheless still too much affected by the size of the slices pertaining to the recipients of high incomes while disregarding the impact of the relative differences between categories of incomes. And inversely, the use of coefficients of variation or of the standard deviation of the income logarithms attaches too much importance to the relative differences of income, by using the dimension of the mean as a strategic factor in the calculation of these indices. The fact remains, however, that the combined utilization of these three indices may give a fair approximation of the degree of inequality of income distribution in an underdeveloped country. It remains to be seen, however, whether the statistics available are sufficient for these different indices to be obtained simultaneously.

With these methodological considerations in mind, it will be easier to group the implications of the comments we now propose to make :

(1) *Distribution by Individual Beneficiaries or by Family Slices*

A question to be settled at the outset is whether distribution by individual beneficiaries or by families is best suited for an assessment of the phenomena of distribution in underdeveloped countries. It is true that, as a rule, the distribution by individuals is the one that best reflects the disparities that proceed from the pattern of production. This, however, encounters almost insuperable difficulties in the young countries. How is it possible to determine the share of income that reverts to each member of a family in property that is indivisible, handed down from generation to generation and that constitutes the main assets in a subsistence economy ? How is it possible, too, to assess those who participate in the family production process for their share of work in kind ? The reservations made regarding the utilization of distribution by individuals cannot be disregarded in countries where the family averages four or five persons and where, therefore, the younger members of the population, generally under 15 years of age, represent a preponderant weight in the traditional productive system. If one were merely to

[1] See H. T. Oshima, 'Comparisons of Size Distribution of Family Incomes with Special Reference to Asia', *Review of Economics and Statistics*, 1962, pp. 439–445.
[2] See J. Morgan, 'Anatomy of Income Distribution', *Review of Economics and Statistics*, 1962, p. 270.

utilize the individual as the basic unit of distribution, one would be overlooking a large portion of the total personal income owing to the impossibility of isolating that share and then calculating its value in figures.

There has therefore been a recent trend, in the young countries as in the more advanced ones, to adopt the distribution of income by categories. By enabling the difficulties just mentioned to be overcome, this type of distribution covers the whole of the personal income of the population, for there is no attempt to identify the earnings accruing separately to each member of the family. It has above all the advantage of throwing more light on the 'welfare' status of a country, by reflecting the needs of the population. The idea of distribution among families according to the sum total of their income signifies distribution among consumer units, in which the productive capability of the individual is replaced by the capacity to spend or to utilize the income.[1]

It is of course necessary for the size of the family to remain constant, to allow of comparisons between one period and another and to facilitate comparisons between countries. This is not always the case, however, and adjustments may have to be made.

Finally, both distributions — among individuals and among families — are useful, for they correspond to two different viewpoints, that of production and that of employment. Their combined utilization depends on the availability of statistics ; but in fact most of the data concern distribution by family categories.

Information relating to the distribution of income among individual beneficiaries is scarce ; it is provided by the study made by UNO, in 1952, on a comparatively restricted number of underdeveloped countries. Thus, the wealthiest tenth of the population receives 39, 44 and 41 per cent respectively in Ceylon for the year 1950 and in Salvador and Puerto Rico for 1947. Inversely, in the same countries, one half of the individuals registered in the census receive between 16 and 27 per cent of the total or personal income.[2] The latest statistics available are those of Ceylon for 1952/53 ; the

---

[1] Kuznets describes this very well when he writes 'Distributions among individual recipients are highly valuable as constitute components, but they cannot substitute for distributions among consuming units, i.e. units which are affected by changing in the production system that constitute economic growth.'—S. Kuznets, *Quantitative Aspects of the Economic Growth of Nations*, 'VIII, Distributions of Income by Size', *Economic Development and Cultural Change*, vol. xi, no. 2, Part 2, 1963, p. 7.

[2] See T. Morgan, 'Income Distribution in Developed and Underdeveloped Countries', *Economic Journal*, 1956, pp. 160–164.

wealthiest 5 per cent of the population receives 32·4 per cent of the income.[1]

Furthermore, if reference is made to the rate of concentration as a measurement of inequality, this rate amounts to 50 per cent for Ceylon, 59 for Salvador, and 46 for Barbados.

However, these data are too limited to allow of any generalized assumption. We must therefore turn to the distribution of personal income among categories of families, for which the statistical data cover a larger number of countries. In this connection, for Table 1, we have taken three Asiatic countries (India, Ceylon, Lebanon), six Latin American countries (Mexico, Colombia, Salvador, Guatemala, Barbados, Puerto Rico) and one European country (Italy), where the regional development is unequal. For most of these countries, the ordinal distribution of family income per quintile has been obtained from direct sources, without having to resort to any interpolation.

TABLE 1

DISTRIBUTION BY FAMILIES
OF PERSONAL INCOME BEFORE TAX

	1st Quin-tile	2nd Quin-tile	3rd Quin-tile	4th Quin-tile	5th Quin-tile	5% at the top	0–60%	2nd, 3rd, 4th Quin-tile
India (1950)	7·8	9·2	11·4	16·0	55·6	33·4	28·5	36·6
India (1955–56)	—	—	14·8	19·7	46·8	23·6	33·5	—
Ceylon (1952–53)	5·1	9·3	13·3	18·4	53·9	31·0	27·7	41·0
Lebanon (1960)	—	—	—	—	60·0	31·5	25·0	—
Mexico (1957)	4·4	6·9	9·9	17·4	61·4	37·0	21·2	34·2
Colombia (1953)	—	—	—	12·2	56·4	41·6	31·4	—
Salvador (1946)	—	—	—	15·7	52·1	35·5	32·2	—
Guatemala (1947–48)	—	—	—	15·8	55·4	34·5	28·8	—
Barbados (1951–52)	3·6	9·3	14·2	21·3	51·6	22·3	27·1	44·8
Puerto Rico (1953)	5·6	9·8	14·9	19·9	49·8	23·4	30·3	44·6
Italy (1948)	6·1	10·5	14·6	20·4	48·4	24·1	31·2	45·5
Brazil (1957)	—	—	—	—	63·0	—	—	—

Sources: Utilization of the data published by Kuznets, *Quantitative Aspects of the Economic Growth of Nations*, viii, 'Distribution of Income by Size', *op. cit.*, Table 3, pp. 13–14. For the Lebanon, see R. Delprat, 'Première ébauche d'un modèle de croissance globale pour le Liban', *Travaux de Séminaire d'Études Économiques et Financières*, n⁰ 3, Beirut, p. 102.

A close study of these figures appears to call for the following comments.

[1] *Survey of Ceylon's Consumer Finances, op. cit.*, Table 1.

For the low-income groups — such as those corresponding to the three first quintiles or 60th of the poorest families, the proportion of personal income devolving to them represents at the most a third of the total income. What is very striking is the only slight divergency in the results, ranging from 27 to 33 per cent with the exception of Mexico. This means that in the underdeveloped countries as a whole, the low-income family groups are all practically at the same level of poverty in respect of income distribution. It may be taken that two-thirds of the families belonging to the poorest categories receive barely a third of the total available income.

The picture is different when we come to the categories of families belonging to the higher slices. The 20th of the wealthiest families receives between 50 and 60 per cent of the total income. At a still further stage of analysis — underlining even more emphatically the extreme inequality in the distribution of income — the 5 per cent of the wealthiest families take between 22 and 40 per cent of the total income. It will be noted in this context that, contrary to the position in respect of the shares received by the lower groups, there is greater disparity in the shares of income from one country to another, according to the pattern of the economic and social structures.

Lastly, it emerges from the two foregoing comments that an important qualification must be added. The countries in process of development are characterized, not so much by the poverty of the lower categories or the wealth of the higher ones, as by the smallness of the intermediary groups between the wealthiest and the poorest. If we leave out the first and fifth quintiles we find that the shares accruing to the other groups amount to less than half the total income ; they vary between 36 and 45 per cent. An even more significant feature is the very marked drop from the top quintile to the fourth quintile. For the countries taken as a whole, there is a fall from the level of 50 to 60 per cent to that of 16 to 20 per cent. Thus, the transition from the top category to those immediately below it is not a gradual movement but a violent drop. This break in the income scale is a feature of the interim phases through which the countries pass in the first stages of their development.

From these three series of comments on income distribution by family categories, the conclusion is that there is deep-seated inequality of distribution of the available incomes, marked by the absence or only small proportion of intermediary groups. This is further confirmed by the concentration index, the average rate of which, for a group of underdeveloped countries, apparently works out at 0·47.[1]

Furthermore, to the extent that these statistical indications allow of any generalization, the distribution of income by individuals reveals greater inequality than by family categories, since the splitting-up of the members of the family into individual units seems to bring down the average income of the weakest groups.

These findings are not confirmed in the case of totally under-developed countries where a subsistence economy still prevails. This is true of Malaysia and of several rural areas in Asia, Africa, and America. Here with the national product reduced to the covering of subsistence costs, we find a state of diminished inequality or of equality in poverty.[2] This is no longer the position, however, in most of the uncommitted countries, which, owing to the introduction of methods of commercialization, the spread of industrialization and the effects of town development, are going through a period of development clearly marked by a wider dispersion of income, indicative of the state of inequality already mentioned. Thus, with the exception of primitive economies, the assumptions we have put forward are valid for all the countries undergoing development and characterized by an underlying *territorial* or *functional* duality. The inadequacy of the statistical data, their scant significance owing to the omission of a great deal of information, are defects which necessitate a cautious approach to the problem but they nevertheless confirm the inequality and the discontinuity in the distribution of income in the underdeveloped countries.

(2) *Distribution over a Short or a Long Period*

We have so far been examining the distribution of annual income. The question now arises as to how far the conclusions we have drawn are modified when the income over a longer period is considered. The answer has to remain an arbitrary one so long as we are unable to draw on statistics recording the evolution of the family income. Without a series of figures showing the evolution of the yearly

[1] According to the work by Kuznets, *Quantitative Aspects of the Economic Growth of Nations*, viii, 'Distribution of Income by Size', *op. cit.*, p. 17. These countries are India, Mexico, Ceylon, Barbados, and Puerto Rico.

[2] This is a theory supported mainly by H. T. Oshima, first in the *Economic Journal* of March 1956 — 'A note on Income Distribution in Developed and Underdeveloped Countries' — and later, on a more discriminating note, in the *Review of Economics and Statistics*, November 1962, 'The International Comparison of Size-Distributions of Family Incomes with Special Reference to Asia'.

receipts of the households no conclusion can be formulated as to the effect of the accumulation of incomes on the degree of inequality in income distribution. From this point of view it is premature to hope for data covering a long period for the countries in the process of developing, where statistical information is only just beginning to be collected.

In this long-period context we come to the problem of the mobility of income : *absolute mobility* to the extent that the individual or family units move up from a low-income category to a higher one ; *relative mobility* when some units are climbing up the income ladder and at the same time others are moving downwards.

The determinants of mobility depend on the accidental or temporary elements included in the make-up of personal income. In underdeveloped countries, where the export sector is predominant, technological changes in the utilization of the natural resources or a perceptible change in the price of raw materials will certainly cause a more pronounced mobility of income, to the benefit of some units and to the detriment of others. However, any policy tending to elude or to control perturbations of an internal nature and above all those of an international nature, weakens the rate of internal mobility of income. But what is valid for a short period does not hold equally good for a study of income levels over a long period. This is not to say that a sustained and regular growth does not cause significant mobility, through the influx of capital into the subsistence areas and through the transformation of the production system. In backward countries, bent on accelerated development, absolute mobility is certainly closely linked to the take-off phases. But once these first stages of development are over it gives place to relative mobility, with a different pattern of income for the specific structures of each phase of development. The significance of this internal mobility cannot be expressed in figures nor studied in detail ; it remains a matter for conjecture as far as the underdeveloped countries are concerned. But once the traditional societies begin to experience periods of rapid development, prior to the stage of complete industrialization, they are liable also to move from absence of mobility to extreme mobility of income. From one generation to the next, we no longer find the same rich nor the same poor ; class or social group consciousness fades out. This, of course, is an extreme hypothesis, rarely borne out in fact. However intensive the internal mobility, it remains circumscribed within certain limits. A situation of poverty or wealth is handed down from a given unit to its descendants, with relative changes occurring within the categories of poverty or wealth but nevertheless leaving the stable groups of the population with some significance.

To sum up, though in studying the phenomena of income distribution the degree of income mobility must be taken into consideration, the effect of the rate of mobility remains slight for a traditional society, attains its full significance for the semi-developed countries and sometimes fades away for certain countries, where the internal mobility changes the structure of the social groups beyond all recognition, as the result of highly accelerated development.

(3) *Functional or Secondary Distribution*

In opposition to functional distribution which reflects the earnings of the factors of production (remuneration of employees, incomes of entrepreneurs, income from property), we have secondary or oriented distribution. The mechanisms of this redistribution operate through the medium of taxation and the volume of public expenditure on social welfare, leaving aside all elements of public investment since it would be difficult to apportion them between the various categories of income.

Disregarding this last difficulty, we find that the transition from the initial distribution to oriented distribution is effected successively by deduction of the taxes affecting each category of income and by adding to this the sum of social expenditure. Social expenditure comprises on the one hand transfer expenditure taking the form of cash benefits and on the other hand benefits in kind. Two categories appear within the transfer expenditure : subsidies which represent an indirect transfer of purchasing power, and the various forms of monetary benefits (different forms of assistance, social security, grants, etc.) which constitute direct transfers proper. As for the benefits in kind they cover all the social services provided free of cost by the state : education, health, housing, etc.

We must now see to what extent the combined effect of the mechanisms of taxation and social expenditure produces a significant transformation in the initial distribution by categories of income. Statistical data are scarce and confined to a few countries, which restricts the scope of our conclusions. According to the studies made by Kuznets [1] these effects appear to be minor ones. The

[1] See Table 7 in *Quantitative Aspects of the Economic Growth of Nations*, 'VIII, Distribution of Income by Size', *op. cit.*

resulting adjustments to the initial distribution of income in Guatemala and Salvador are very slight. In Guatemala, for 1946 the poorest 60th of the population passes from 32·2 to 32·8 per cent and the wealthiest 5 per cent from 35·5 to 35 per cent, after deduction of taxes and addition of social expenditure. The same occurs in Salvador, where for 1947–48, the poorest 60th varies from 28·8 to 30·1 per cent and the wealthiest 5 per cent from 34·5 to 33·2 per cent. These are minor adjustments, representing barely 1 to 4 per cent of the original income.

The validity of the earlier conclusions would appear to call for some reservations when one takes into account the attenuation of the degressive character of the fiscal system and the increase in social expenditure in recent years. In most of the underdeveloped countries there has been a recent trend towards a system of progressive taxation, either by generalization and stiffening of the income tax or by the introduction of indirect taxation, the rates of which are seen to vary according to whether the commodities are necessities or luxuries. The reforms now in progress in Latin American and Middle East countries seem to point to the introduction of more effective mechanisms although it is still too early to give any statistical data confirming this new trend.

TABLE 2

PERCENTAGE OF SOCIAL EXPENDITURE
IN RELATION TO PUBLIC EXPENDITURE IN THE MIDDLE EAST

	1958	1959	1963	1964
Egypt	15·7	15·4		
Syria	16·4	18·6		
Iraq	7·6	7·6		
Lebanon	14·2	16·5	17·3	18·4
Jordan	8·3	10·6		
Israel	19·3	19·8		

Sources : Budgets of the respective countries.

As regards the social expenditure, this has certainly increased. Since World War II, the health and education drive has been considerable, whereas welfare and social security benefits do not show as rapid a progression. But in spite of this effort, the percentage of social expenditure remains low, not exceeding some 20 per cent of the total public expenditure. This is confirmed by the statistics for the Near East countries, which we may take as an example. With the exception of Israel, the social expenditure of these countries is devoted almost exclusively to health and education, with little or no direct transfer expenditures for social security. Here again, sweeping statements must be avoided, for the coming years will witness the adoption, in these countries, of social security legislation which will undoubtedly have repercussions on the relative volume of social expenditure.

Are we to conclude, on the strength of these new trends appearing both in the Middle East and in Latin America, that there is an appreciable change in the initial distribution of income ? It is difficult to give a positive reply, for though it is possible to proceed from a horizontal redistribution to a vertical one, it still has to be decided what are the proportions of the transfer from the higher income groups to the lower ones. In fact, where public expenditure represents only a small percentage of the national income, state intervention will inevitably be restricted in any attempt at a positive redistribution of income. In the Latin American countries, public expenditure represents a low percentage of the national income, varying between 10 and 15 per cent. This emerges from the figures shown in Table 3.

TABLE 3

PERCENTAGE OF PUBLIC EXPENDITURE BY THE STATE
IN RELATION TO THE GROSS NATIONAL INCOME
IN LATIN AMERICA

	1945–47	1955–57
Argentine	18·2	18·7
Brazil	11·8	14·2
Chile	13·1	15·9
Colombia	12·0	17·4
Cuba	12·9	21·8
Mexico	10·5	8·1
Venezuela	15·8	20·5

Sources : J. Ahumada, 'Economic Development and Problems of Social Change in Latin America', in *Social Aspects of Economic Development in Latin America*, Table 8, p. 133, vol. i, UNESCO, 1963, Statistics of the Economic Commission for Latin America.

In the Middle East the picture does not appear to be the same. Except in the case of the Lebanon, the relative size of public expenditure is greater ; it varies between 25 and 30 per cent of the national income, as shown in Table 4. The budget ceases to be a mere accounting document ; it becomes an instrument of economic policy and also a means, if not of achieving redistribution of income, at least of improving the conditions of the poorest categories of the population.

TABLE 4

PERCENTAGE OF PUBLIC EXPENDITURE
BY THE STATE IN RELATION TO NATIONAL INCOME
IN THE MIDDLE EAST

	1953	1954	1956	1957	1959	1960	1961	1963
Egypt		22·7	30				24·8	
Iraq	19·7		29					
Israel		24·2		27·3				
Jordan					32·1	30·0		
Lebanon	8·2	8·8		12·7			15·7	19·2
Syria		12·2		10·6		23·2		

Sources : Ahmad Adjari : *Statistiques économiques et sociales, Asie du Sud-Ouest*, SEDES, Paris, 1961. Lebanon : *Dossier de base pour l'avant-projet du Plan Quinquennal 1964–1968*, Ministère du Plan, Mission IRFED-LIBAN. Egypt : *10 ans de révolution* (Atlas Statistique), Département de la Statistique, Cairo. Jordan : *The National Income for Jordan*, Department of Statistics, Jordan. Syria : 'Le revenu national en Syrie en 1961', in *L'Économie et les finances de la Syrie et des pays arabes*, January 1962. Iraq : N. Haddad, 'Le revenu national iraquien', in *L'Économie et les finances de la Syrie et des pays arabes*, January 1962.

It thus emerges that, however strong the determination of the state to effect a positive redistribution by technical means combined with taxation and social benefits, there can be no hope of changes in the spontaneous distribution of income, so long as the level of *per capita* income remains low. In this connection it may be queried whether changes in the sector distribution of income are really an effective instrument of redistribution.

II. DISTRIBUTION AND ECONOMIC DEVELOPMENT

The conclusions reached in the first section of this study concern the spontaneous distribution of income. We must now, against the background of economic development, see how this initial distribution is modified. The factors we shall take into account for this analysis are the transformations occurring in the importance of the various sectors of the economy, the degree of inequality of income

337

distribution within the respective sectors and lastly the changes in the 'functional distribution' or sharing by type of income.

(1) *Inter-sector Distribution of Income*

The close relationship between the stage of development and the distribution of income is an established phenomenon. In pre-capitalist economies where a subsistence economy still prevails and where agriculture therefore constitutes the main activity, there can be no question of considering the possible effect which differentiation of incomes between sectors may have on the degree of inequality in the distribution of the various categories of incomes. Some inequality of course exists, confined to the agricultural sector. This, however, is more a question of reduced dispersion, or rather of equality in comparative penury.[1]

The inter-sector modification of income occurs when in the succeeding stage of development a modern and industrial sector comes into being alongside the agricultural subsistence sector. With the transition of the labour force from the primary to the industrial sector, significant differences begin to appear between the sectors. With a low level of productivity and a high percentage of labour in the agricultural sector, the income of the modern sector can only be regarded as a higher multiple of that of the agricultural sector. Thus, if we consider the product per inhabitant occupied in the agricultural and non-agricultural sectors respectively, it is found that for Latin America as a whole, for example, the non-agricultural product for the period from 1945–47 to 1955–57 remains 3·4 times higher than the agricultural product.[2] So strongly marked a differentiation between the sectors enhances the inequality of income distribution. This is confirmed by numerous examples from other countries, such as India. Kuznets's survey of 41 countries clearly shows the correlation that exists between the proportion of the labour force in the agricultural sector and the rate of concentration of income. When the countries in question are more developed ones, in which the percentage of agricultural labour varies between 10 and 25 per cent, the index of concentration is about 10 per cent. On the other hand, for the more backward countries, where agricultural labour repre-

---

[1] This is the theory of H. T. Oshima in 'A Note on Income Distribution in Developed and Undeveloped Countries', *Economic Journal*, March 1956.
[2] J. Ahumada, in *Social Aspects of Economic Development in Latin America*, p. 140.

sents between 60 and 70 per cent of the total labour force, the rate of concentration attains 35 per cent.[1]

This inter-sector differentiation of the *per capita* income is not without importance for countries that are in the process of industrialization. Inequality of income distribution often has a catalytic effect on economic development, in so far as it serves to attract technicians, engineers, and skilled labour to the modern sector. Any attempt to achieve complete equality between the sectors or as little inequality as possible would interfere with the normal functioning of the economy and particularly that of the modern sector, eager to attract entrepreneurs, capital, and skilled manpower. The main determinants of these inter-sector disparities, during the stage of semi-development, are town development and industrialization. With the commercialization of production, the advent of urban occupations, the expansion of construction, transport, and public services, there is an inevitable increase in the income of the modern sector. During this phase, the agricultural units remain at the pre-capitalism stage, are self-sufficing and their trade is confined to the village circle. Hence the accentuated inter-sector inequality which is typical of any country just starting to develop. At this point, one must try to ascertain to what extent the *intra-sector distribution* of income reinforces or neutralizes the *inter-sector differences* in respect of *per capita* income.

(2) *Intra-sector Distribution of Income*

The effect of the intra-sector distribution of income is a point of some importance. We shall have to determine the amplitude of the differenitation of income within the agricultural sector and the urban sector in turn. We have comparatively few statistical data to draw upon for this purpose. With the help of what information is available, concerning a small number of underdeveloped countries, we shall try to formulate a few observations, applicable to the uncommitted world as a whole.

In the first place, the distribution of income within the agricultural sector shows a lesser degree of inequality than that within the non-agricultural or urban sector.

In the cases of India, Ceylon, or Puerto Rico, the rates of concentration are respectively 40, 45 and 32 per cent for the agricultural

[1] S. Kuznets, *Quantitative Aspects of the Economic Growth of Nations*, 'VIII, Distribution of Income by Size', *op. cit.*, Table 5, B, p. 20.

TABLE 5

DISTRIBUTION BY CATEGORIES OF INCOME FOR THE AGRICULTURAL AND NON-AGRICULTURAL SECTORS

	% of Total Number	Relative per capita Income	Categories							Rate of Concentration
			0–20% or 1st Quintile	21–40% or 2nd Quintile	41–60% or 3rd Quintile	61–80% or 4th Quintile	81–90%	91–95%	Top 5%	
India—Families (1950)										
1—Rural	84	—	8·8	10·3	12·5	17·1	12·8	9·6	28·9	0·40
2—Urban	16	—	3·6	4·4	5·8	9·2	8·2	7·3	61·5	0·69
Ceylon, individual beneficiaries (1952–53)										
1—Agriculture, forestry, fishing	52	100	5·5	9·8	13·5	18·4	13·5	9·4	29·9	0·45
2—Others	48	158	3·4	7·7	12·1	19·0	14·6	10·4	32·8	0·52
Puerto Rico—Families (1953)										
1—Agriculture, forestry, fishing	31	100	8·0	12·3	16·4	22·4	12·8	9·5	18·6	0·32
2—Others	69	163	4·8	10·0	14·3	21·6	16·0	10·0	23·3	0·43

Sources : Kuznets, *Quantitative Aspects of the Economic Growth of Nations*, 'VIII, Distribution of Income by Size', *op. cit.*, Table 4, p. 50.

or rural sector, whereas they attain 69, 52, and 43 per cent for the urban or non-agricultural sector. True, the greater diversity of occupations and industries may partly explain a wider dispersion in the pattern of non-agricultural income. But the chief cause must be sought in the migration of the population from the rural area towards the modern sectors. Those who were without employment or whose earnings did not exceed the marginal productivity of their work were quite willing to accept a place at the bottom of the income scale in the industrial sector. This naturally had the effect of increasing the degree of inequality between the low-income categories and the economic or financial élite belonging to the higher categories.

Secondly, in so far as the agricultural sector continues to carry most weight, in terms of the large size of its labour force, the relative inequality within the main sectors of production will have but little impact on the distribution of the aggregate income by categories. It will not tend to reinforce to any great extent the effects of the differentiations between the sectors. Agriculture remains the predominant sector where the traditions and long-established practices maintain the populations in a state of inequality marked by a relatively narrow and stable measure of dispersion. However, with economic development, featuring the phenomena of industrialization and town development, the importance of the agricultural sector, in terms of the population it represents, diminishes to the benefit of the modern sector. The intra-sector distribution of the non-agricultural sector, with its greater weight, will very appreciably augment the overall inequality of income distribution. This is yet further proof that the inequality of distribution is a phenomenon inherent to the process of economic growth, in countries which go over to a system of decentralized economy.

In the third place, it is not going too far to say that the intra-sector distributions, though they may reinforce or diminish the effects of inter-sector inequalities, are incapable of neutralizing them completely. However great the diminution in the dispersion of income within the non-agricultural sector, it does not suffice to overcome the high degree of inequality between the sectors, which characterizes countries in the process of development. It may be wondered whether, in countries with a socialist regime, a systematic policy of public services at the local level (water, electricity, education, etc.) can succeed in overcoming the inter-sector disparity of income. There are no statistics to throw light on this question.

In this connection, it is by no means unlikely that economic development may create forces that reduce the inequality of income distribution. Social security benefits, in that they cover a large proportion of the wage-earning population and produce a vertical redistribution of income by means of a progressive fiscal system can do much to reduce the disparity of income. The provision of free education for the poorest strata of the population is noteworthy as a factor neutralizing or attenuating the inter-sector inequalities. Caution is nevertheless called for in proceeding with this equalization of income, so as not to compromise development by encouraging consumer expenditure. In this context we shall now examine the effect of development on the functional distribution of income.

(3) Structural Distribution of Income

Economic development has an even more far-reaching effect on the functional distribution of national income or its apportionment by type of income. Three categories of payment may be distinguished in this respect : the wages or salaries of employees or officials, the earnings of non-corporate undertakings and lastly the earnings of property which include the dividends of companies, interest, rent effectively paid or counted in the case of owner-occupied residences. In the underdeveloped countries marked by their essentially dualistic structure, the earnings of property predominate.

Persons living on a fixed income constitute the privileged social class, whether their income is derived from ground rent or from the income produced by the fixed wage-rate in a regime of strong competition between native workers.

The phase of semi-development is seen to produce, as a result of the contacts and exchanges between the subsistence sector and the modern sector, deep-seated changes in the functional distribution of income. The income from property continues, indeed, to have a decisive weight even though its composition is totally different. It is no longer ground rent but the profits of companies, in the form of dividends, which are the major component of income from property. The spread of limited liability companies, with their implications of *distribution of dividends* and of *corporate savings*, is a powerful factor in favour of a greater inequality of income distribution. We must not, however, exaggerate the importance of the earnings of property (dividends +corporate savings) in developing countries. The volume of capital per head is too small to encourage any great concentration of property earnings (mainly dividends) in the hands of a few property owners. Furthermore, in most cases the entrepreneurs represent a not insignificant portion of the labour force ; their income comes under the category of individual undertakings and is therefore not counted as the earnings of property.[1] These are all factors powerful enough to attenuate the inequality of distribution, which may be caused by the effect of income from property. The concentration of wealth, in the form of shares and of dividends, is not sufficiently pronounced in the backward countries to become a determining factor in the unequal distribution of income.

In any event, the growing size of the share of wages and salaries [2] will be conducive to a greater equality of income, assuming that it will be slowed down or halted by the effects of the earnings from property. But there is no reason for not assuming, with Kuznets, that the lack of social mobility between the various income groups and the absence of any progressive taxation system will intensify the concentration of property earnings in the hands of the high-income classes [3] and foster greater inequality in the distribution of income. This means that, without taking into consideration the political and social background of a country, it is difficult to judge the effect of economic growth on the functional distribution of income.

We have attempted to show to what extent the spontaneous distribution of income is modified by the effect which development may have on the inter-sector and intra-sector distribution and likewise on functional distribution. The conclusions we have been able to reach, as the combined result of statistical analysis and simplifying assumptions, take on a different significance when they are viewed in the light of a comparison of the phenomena of distribution at international level.

III. INTERNATIONAL COMPARISONS OF DISTRIBUTION

The phenomena of distribution have a limited significance until they are placed in an international context. The effect of time on the

[1] In this context, for an over-detailed interpretation, see H. T. Oshima, 'A note on Income Distribution in Developed and Under-developed Countries', *Economic Journal*, March 1956, pp. 156–160.

[2] As an example, for Puerto Rico, the remuneration of the wage-earning classes increased as a percentage of the net national income, from 56 to 67 per cent between 1940 and 1958. During the same period, the profits of undertakings fell from 35 to 31 per cent and ground rents from 9 to 5 per cent. See W. Baer, 'Porto Rico : An Evaluation of a successful Program', *Quarterly Journal of Economcis*, 1959, Table VI, p. 654.

[3] S. Kuznets, *Quantitative Aspects of the Economic Growth of Nations*, 'VIII, Distribution of Income by Size', *op. cit.*, pp. 47–48.

distribution of the categories of income in a given country is certainly worth studying attentively, but the conclusions drawn must be revised when they are examined in terms of space. Comparisons between periods and comparisons between countries are complementary to one another and combine to produce a relatively accurate picture of the phenomena of distribution in the underdeveloped countries.

In this connection we must begin by mentioning the difficulties attending any international comparison of distribution phenomena. We shall then attempt to discern the international factors affecting income distribution, and lastly we shall try to formulate the main distribution differences which distinguish underdeveloped countries from the more advanced ones.

(1) *Difficulties of International Comparison*

At international level, the phenomena of income distribution are difficult to compare in that they encounter factors which produce divergencies and in that they call for adequate statistical methods.

Among the factors necessitating adjustments in order to render valid or less erroneous any comparison between countries, special mention must be made of the personal income in the underdeveloped countries. Resulting from the predominance of a subsistence economy, such income is not counted in the backward rural areas, whereas it is of course included in the monetary and homogeneous economy of developed countries. This means that the income of backward countries is underestimated and the necessary adjustment involves calculations which can only be very approximate.

The treatment of taxes and transfer expenditures must also be taken into consideration. In so far as the shares of income are conceived as corresponding to the process of production, we have to exclude income tax and add all the benefits in kind provided by the state. This reduces the degree of inequality between advanced and underdeveloped countries. Inversely, where, by the application of a policy of redistribution, the direct or indirect taxes are subtracted from the flow of personal income and the benefits of all categories added, the differences in the inequalities of income distribution are accentuated between the two categories of countries. This is particularly true when account is taken of the transfer expenditures effected by the state in favour of the poorest classes. As instances of this, we may mention old-age pensions and social security benefits.

It is not possible to ignore the importance of tax evasion, in any

344

attempt to compare distribution phenomena at international level. In the underdeveloped countries, where the high-income categories practise tax evasion on a large scale, the distribution of income will inevitably appear to be less unequal than it is in reality. Thus in any comparison with the advanced countries, where tax evasion is comparatively less rife, there will be a tendency to underestimate the degree of inequality of income distribution in the young countries in relation to the industrialized nations.

These considerations by no means exhaust the whole range of adjustments needed to diminish the errors stemming from a different concept of the phenomena of distribution in the various countries. They are merely an indication of the prolonged effort that will have to be made to achieve some degree of uniformity in this field.

When we turn to the statistical methods designed to determine the inequality of distribution for the purposes of international comparison, none of the evaluations are found to be entirely satisfactory. Among the various methods which can be used — comparison of the highest and lowest quintiles, use of the coefficients of variation or the standard deviations of the income logarithms, utilization of the concentration indices — the choice will depend on the aim in view and on the aspect of income distribution on which light is to be thrown. However, this is ultimately conditioned by the data available. It is for this reason that Kuznets, without systematically eliminating the synthetic indices [1] gives his preference to the measurement of inequality, depicting at least the structure of distribution by categories, showing up the information resulting from the small number of sources available for the underdeveloped countries.[2] For the remainder of this study we shall therefore use the international comparisons effected by both Kuznets and Kravis in an attempt to formulate the chief characteristics and differences of income distribution between developed and backward countries.

(2) *International Differences in the Distribution of Income*

To bring out the chief characteristics of the two categories of countries, we may modify Table 1 and establish a comparison of the wealthiest and poorest categories of families in turn.

---

[1] See the interesting attempt by Oshima to utilize a synthetic index by resorting to the standard deviation in relation to a perfect distribution by quintiles, *Review of Economics and Statistics, op. cit.*

[2] Kuznets, *Quantitative Aspects of the Economic Growth of Nations*, 'VIII, Distribution of Income by Size', *op. cit.*, p. 11.

The Distribution of National Income

TABLE 6

PERCENTAGE OF INCOME RECEIVED
BY THE WEALTHIEST 10 PER CENT AND 5 PER CENT OF FAMILIES

Underdeveloped Countries	10% at the Top	5% at the Top	Developed Countries	10% at the Top	5% at the Top
India (1950)	43·0	33·4	United States (1950)	30·3	20·4
Ceylon (1952–53)	40·6	31·0	Great Britain (1951–	30·2	20·9
Lebanon (1960)	—	31·5	1952)		
Mexico (1957)	46·7	37·0	West Germany (1950)	34·0	23·6
Colombia (1946)	48·4	41·6	Denmark (1957)	30·7	20·1
Salvador (1946	43·6	35·5	Netherlands (1950)	35·0	24·6
Puerto Rico (1953)	32·9	23·4			

Sources: Kuznets, modified Table 3, *Quantitative Aspects of the Economic Growth of Nations*, 'VIII, Distribution of Income by Size', *op. cit.*

A comparison of the high-income groups, as shown in Table 6, first brings to light the fact that the percentage of income received by the wealthiest families is much higher in the underdeveloped countries than in the developed ones. In the former, the 5 per cent of the families at the top of the scale receive an average 30 to 35 per cent of the total income, whereas the corresponding shares vary between 20 and 25 per cent in the developed countries. Similarly, for the 10 per cent of the wealthiest families it is seen that the percentages attain 40 per cent and more of the total income in the case of the young countries, while they are no higher than 30 to 35 per cent in the older ones.

TABLE 7

PERCENTAGE OF THE
FAMILY INCOME RECEIVED BY THE 60TH REPRESENTING
THE POOREST FAMILIES

Underdeveloped Countries		Developed Countries	
India (1950)	28·5	United States (1950)	32·0
Ceylon (1952–53)	27·7	Great Britain (1951–52)	33·3
Lebanon (1960)	25·0	West Germany (1950)	29·0
Mexico (1957)	21·2	Denmark (1952)	29·5
Colombia (1953)	31·4	Netherlands (1950)	29·5
Salvador (1946)	32·2		
Puerto Rico (1954)	30·3		

Sources: Kuznets, modified Table 3 in *Quantitative Aspects of the Economic Growth of Nations*, 'VIII, Distribution of Income by Size', *op. cit.*

346

On the other hand, when we look at the low-income slices, the differences are found to be slighter, as shown in Table 7.

The poor are of course poorer in the underdeveloped countries than in the industrialized ones, but they are confined to a much narrower segment. The 60th representing the poorest families accounts for an average 25 to 30 per cent of the total income for countries in their infancy, whereas the percentages range between 29 and 33 per cent for the developed countries. Thus, in poverty, the shares received are seen to converge and their difference is of little significance.

It will be seen from these comments that the pattern of income distribution is different in developed and underdeveloped countries. The latter are characterized not only by the greater wealth of the categories at the top of the income scale but above all by the narrow segment representing the intermediate groups. Table 8 shows the intermediate groups to represent about 35 per cent of the total income in the underdeveloped countries whereas they attain over 55 per cent in the developed countries. Still more significantly, there is a more accentuated drop from the top 20th to the fourth 20th in the underdeveloped countries than in the industrialized ones. This is the sign of a profound inequality of incomes in the backward countries, typified particularly in the smallness of the moderate income categories, though these show relative equality among themselves.

This international comparison cannot be concluded without mentioning the differences in regard to the structural distribution of income. There is doubtless an upward trend in the share of the wage-earners in the developing countries, which brings their income structure closer to that of the developed countries.[1] But the main difference still exists in the form taken by the income from property. In the underdeveloped countries, property earnings begin by taking the form of ground rent and later, in the semi-development phase, are mainly seen as dividends, with the introduction and establishment of joint stock companies. In the developed countries, the profits of companies, instead of being distributed as dividends, are absorbed by income tax or reinvested as non-distributed profits. Needless to say, this difference increases the inequality of income for

---

[1] For greater detail, see I. B. Kravis, *Structure of Income*, University of Pennsylvania, 1962, pp. 263–265. The share of wages and salaries rises from 46·6 per cent in 1938 to 48·9 per cent of the total income during the post-war period, for a set of underdeveloped countries. The idea of this evolution, mentioned by Kravis, originates from the work of Kuznets.

TABLE 8
DISTRIBUTION OF FAMILY UNITS ACCORDING TO INCOME
(Percentages)

	Underdeveloped Countries						Developed Countries				
	India (1950)	Ceylon (1952–53)	Mexico (1957)	Colombia (1953)	Salvador (1946)	Puerto Rico (1953)	United States (1950)	Great Britain (1951–52)	West Germany (1950)	Denmark (1952)	Netherlands (1950)
Top 20th	55·4	54·2	61·4	56·4	53·1	49·8	45·7	44·5	48·0	47·0	49·0
Fourth 20th	16·0	18·4	17·4	12·2	15·7	19·9	22·3	22·2	23·0	23·5	21·5
Third 20th	11·4	13·3	9·9	—	—	14·9	16·2	16·6	16·5	15·8	15·7
Second 20th	9·2	9·3	6·9	—	—	9·8	11·0	11·3	8·5	10·3	9·6
Bottom 20th	7·8	5·1	4·4	—	—	5·6	4·8	5·4	4·0	3·4	4·2

Sources: Table 3 of Kuznets's modified *Quantitative Aspects of the Economic Growth of Nations*, 'VIII, Distribution of Income by Size', *op. cit.*

Gannagé — Distribution in Underdeveloped Countries

the underdeveloped countries and reduces it for the developed ones. As an illustration, in the United States, for the 1949–51 period, half of the company profits were absorbed by taxation.[1]

Synthetic methods also provide confirmation of these international differences in income distribution. According to the findings of Kravis, taking an index of concentration rate equal to 100 for the United States in 1950, the indices for Puerto Rico, Ceylon, and Salvador respectively work out at 120, 115, and 136.[2]

This shows these three countries to have a higher degree of inequality than the United States. But these aggregate figures can obviously not show the structure of income distribution or reveal the features peculiar to the underdeveloped countries. They are significant only to the extent that they are the result of a profuse crop of statistical data.

The combined use of synthetic and conventional methods of assessment having thus enabled us to work out the international differences between the family income categories, we must now look briefly into the causes of these variations between the different countries.

(3) Determination of Differences in Inequality of Income Distribution

The causes of difference are numerous and vary from one country to another. We do not propose to give an exhaustive list of them. Our aim will rather be to formulate explanatory hypotheses of general scope, by resorting to the method of structural analysis.[3] It must here be noted that it is in the 'dualist' or 'pluralist' character of the underdeveloped economies that we must seek the explanation of the differing degrees of inequality in income distribution. We must first consider dualism from the territorial aspect. An underdeveloped economy is made up of highly dissimilar areas. Here one finds modern zones of development, featuring all the mechanisms of the modern market ; there one finds rural zones, practising an economy of exchange to a limited degree, largely cut off from the rest of the country. The inadequacy of communications, the fidelity to ancestral traditions are barriers which restrict or render illusory the

[1] I. B. Kravis, 'Relative Income Shares in Fact and Theory', *American Economic Review*, December 1959, pp. 931–932.
[2] I. B. Kravis, 'International Differences in the Distribution of Income', *Review of Economics and Statistics*, 1960, p. 409.
[3] See E. Gannagé, *Économie du développement*, Presses Universitaires de France, Paris, 1962, Part I, chap. iii.

contact between the rural and the urban areas. It is therefore not surprising to find deep-seated inequality in income distribution in such countries, where the agricultural labourer still suffers from the evils of a powerful feudalism, whilst the workers in the modern sector are beginning to experience the benefits of the monetary wage-scale whereby they are rewarded according to their ability. These barriers are further strengthened to the extent that the agricultural areas, still at the stage of a subsistence economy, reveal a paternalistic structure of property, characterized by the existence of a small number of large landowners as opposed to a great number of workers living under their dependence. Even high taxation of land or agrarian reform modifying the distribution of property will not lead to integration of the country's different regions unless frequent and regular contacts are established between the centres of development and the areas still living under a domanial economy.

In addition to this territorial dualism there is also *dualism in the social structures* which further enhances the inequality of income distribution. First, there are all the differentiations, due to racial discrimination, all too familiar in countries such as those of Black Africa, Latin America, or even South-East Asia. As an example, we have only to think of the difference of income seen in the case of the Ceylonese Tamils whose income is double that of the Indians.[1] Race, as an expression of dualism, is destined to disappear. At the present time, education, in so far as it is confined to certain social categories and denied to the lower groups (peasant masses), constitutes the chief source of discrimination and heterogeneity between the various strata of the population. Equality of opportunity for all classes of society is the ultimate condition of all attempts to do away with social barriers and hence achieve greater equality of income. Mobility from one category to the other throughout the whole scale of incomes, that is the touchstone of the disappearance of all social barriers.

Nevertheless, whatever the nature of these disparities — regional, social, or other — they correspond to a particular phase in economic development of which dualism is the underlying feature. Viewed in terms of time, the phase of dualism is situated between a homogeneous and barely mechanized subsistence-economy and an economy of growing industrialization. That the pre-industrial phase shows a small degree of inequality in income distribution, is today confirmed by the actual experience of the underdeveloped and of the

[1] Central Bank of Ceylon, *Survey of Ceylon's Consumer Finances*, Table 15.

advanced countries during their first phase of industrialization. But does this warrant an equally firm assertion that the temporary phases of dualism or of semi-development imply an aggravation of the inequality of income distribution ? At this stage now reached by a fair number of underdeveloped countries, it would seem quite likely [1] on the strength of the statistics already quoted and in comparison with the income distribution seen in the more advanced countries. However there are no grounds for affirming that this aggravation of the degree of inequality is an inherent feature of the transitory phase and that there might not be other forms of distribution that would be compatible with periods of accelerated growth. As for the periods succeeding the phases of semi-development, any generalization on the subject would be rash. It would be hazardous to affirm a reduction in income inequality as some people seem inclined to deduce from the experience of the fully developed countries. Numerous factors will intervene, tending either to increase or to reduce the degree of inequality. Future prospects are difficult to determine ; they are the result of the economic policy, of the pace of industrialization, of the regional localization of investments, in a word, of staking on or expressing a preference for structures expressed as long-term objectives.

IV. CONCLUSION

By way of conclusion, let us try to formulate the lessons emerging from this study. From the point of view of distribution by categories of income we find great inequality in the underdeveloped countries, both for individual and for family units, and this is enhanced by the absence of intermediate groups. The mobility factor, in both absolute and relative terms, is conducive to less inequality over a long period, when the country embarks on the initial stage of development. The same trend is encouraged by the combined effects of taxation and social expenditure, though only to a limited degree so long as the level of *per capita* income remains low.

The inter-sector modifications due to changes in the industrial structures entail more marked differences in the distribution of income in countries undergoing development. In the same context, the intra-sector distribution of income, though capable of increasing

---

[1] S. Kuznets, 'Economic Growth and Income Inequality', *American Review*, March 1955, pp. 1–28.

or diminishing the inter-sector inequalities, is nevertheless not able to neutralize them to the extent of imposing a different pattern on income distribution. As for structural distribution, it shows the growth of the share going to wages and salaries at the expense of ground rent or profits properly so called.

The international comparison of distribution phenomena throws further light on these considerations. It is seen that the wealthiest social categories represent a higher percentage in the underdeveloped countries than in the more advanced ones. Looking at it from the sector angle, though it is true that differences in distribution within the agricultural sector are not very marked, it must however be noted that in the non-agricultural (or industrial) sector, the inequality of distribution is slighter for the advanced countries than for the young ones. A further point worth recalling is the different incidence of the earnings of property (dividends and collective saving) which may serve to reinforce the international differences of income.

Finally, it may be queried whether income inequality is a phenomenon inherent to the growth of countries. There is no outright proof of this. The answer depends on the structures and system of each country. A certain degree of inequality of distribution is broadly compatible with economic development if those receiving the largest shares devote their surplus income to the investments desired by the public authorities, corresponding to a certain consensus of society, expressed in the perspective of indicative planning. Otherwise it is preferable to adopt a policy of income equalization, if it is found that the income in the hands of the wealthiest categories is used to reinforce monopolistic practices, to produce goods of little use to society as a whole or to obtain luxuries. At this point the choice ceases to be an economic one and becomes a social and *a fortiori* a political option.

BIBLIOGRAPHY

W. Baer, 'Puerto-Rico: An Evaluation of a Successful Development Program', *Quarterly Journal of Economics*, November 1959, pp. 645–671.

E. Gannagé, *Économie du développement*, PUF, Paris, 1952, pp. 167–188.

I. B. Kravis, 'Relative Incomes Shares in Fact and Theory', *American Economic Review*, December 1959, pp. 917–950.

I. B. Kravis, 'International Differences in the Distribution of Income', *Review of Economics and Statistics*, November 1960, pp. 408–416.

I. B. Kravis, *The Structure of Income*, University of Pennsylvania, 1962.

S. Kuznets, 'Economic Growth and Income Inequality', *American Economic Review*, March 1955, pp. 1–28.

S. Kuznets, *Quantitative Aspects of the Economic Growth of Nations*. 'IV. Distribution of National Income by Factor Shares'. 'VIII. Distribution of National Income by Size' in *Economic Development and Cultural Change*, April 1959 and January 1963.

R. J. Lampman, 'The Effectiveness of Some Institutions in Changing the Distribution of Income', *American Economic Review*, May 1959, pp. 519–528.

S. Lergott, 'The Shape of the Income Distribution', *American Economic Review*, June 1959, pp. 328–348.

T. B. Lim, 'Redistribution of Income in Under-Developed Territories' in *Income Redistribution and Social Policy*, ed. by A. T. Peacock, J. Cape, London, 1954.

J. N. Morgan, 'The Anatomy of Income Distribution', *Review of Economics and Statistics*, August 1962, pp. 270–273.

T. Morgan, 'Distribution of Income in Ceylon, Puerto-Rico, The United Kingdom', *Economic Journal*, December 1953, pp. 821–834.

T. Morgan, 'Income Distribution in Developed and Undeveloped Countries — A rejoinder', *Economic Journal*, March 1956, pp. 161–164.

G. Myrdal, *Une Économie internationale*, PUF, Paris, 1958, pp. 186–188, pp. 253–255.

United Nations, 'The National Income and its distribution in Underdeveloped countries', *Statistical Studies*, Series B, no. 3, New York, 1951.

M. Negreponti-Delivanis, 'Le développement économique et la répartition du revenu national', *Tiers-Monde*, October–December 1962, pp. 565–598.

M. Negreponti-Delivanis, 'Influence du développement économique sur la répartition du revenu national', SEDES, Paris, 1960.

H. T. Oshima, 'A Note on Income Distribution on Developed and Undeveloped Countries', *Economic Journal*, March 1956, pp. 156–160.

H. T. Oshima, 'The International Comparison of Size Distribution of Income with Special Reference to Asia', *Review of Economics and Statistics*, November 1962, pp. 439–445.

M. G. Reid, 'Survey of Ceylon's Consumer Finances', *American Economic Review*, December 1956, pp. 956–964.

G. Rottier, 'La redistribution des revenus en 1949', *Économie Appliquée*, 1953, pp. 479–510.

C. S. Shoup, *A Report on the Fiscal System of Venezuela*, 1959.

Ceylon—Central Bank of Ceylon, *Survey of Ceylon's Consumer Finances*, Colombo, 1954.

India—The Cabinet Secretariat, *National Sample Survey*, April–September 1952, Calcutta, 1959.

Malaya—Department of Statistics, *Budget Survey*, 1957–58.

Philippines—National Economic Council, *Family Income and Expenditures 1957–58*, Series No. 4.

The Distribution of National Income

DISCUSSION OF PROFESSOR GANNAGÉ'S PAPER

Professor Sovani said he was glad to have been asked to introduce Professor Gannagé's paper. This was an excellent study of a problem made difficult by the insufficiency of available data. Not only were data on income distribution in underdeveloped countries rare, as Professor Gannagé had pointed out, but Professor Sovani would like to add that even in cases where the available data have been collected systematically they were of limited use because they classified incomes according to categories which often did not reflect the actual pattern of occupational earnings in underdeveloped countries. For example, the occupational structure in countries like India and other South Asian countries was extremely undifferentiated and a functional distribution of income in their case might not signify much. In India a peasant proprietor was not only a small entrepreneur but also a wage-earner and the wage work he undertook might not necessarily be in agriculture. In village industries and handicrafts also the workers might be partly working in agriculture. Under such conditions the separation of incomes as profits, wages, and salaries, etc., was extremely difficult and, what was more, was artificial so far as the functioning of the economy was concerned.

Professor Sovani would also like to draw attention in this connection to the deficiency of the data used in Professor Gannagé's paper in respect of India. For instance, the data for 1955–56 income distribution were those calculated by Lydall with the aid of income tax data and data on consumer expenditure collected by the National Sample Survey in its 10th round. In dovetailing these two Lydall had made two bold assumptions. He had assumed that Pareto's law of income distribution applied to India as much as to other countries. In order to put the data on income tax on a *per capita* basis he also assumed that the average number of persons covered by each tax assessment was 3 and Mr. Sovani thought that these two assumptions were highly questionable. He had only given this as an example but data on income distribution in underdeveloped countries were not reliable and he would be more cautious than Professor Gannagé before drawing any theoretical conclusions from them.

He agreed with Professor Gannagé in stressing that one of the more noteworthy features of income distribution in underdeveloped countries was the very small importance of middle incomes groups. In these countries the distribution of income from the lowest to the highest brackets did not present a gradient but there was a gap between the lowest and the highest. Turning to the distribution of income over the long term Professor Gannagé had observed that absolute income mobility was slight in traditional societies and in his opinion the full significance of the phenomenon was linked to the so-called 'take off'.

354

Professor Sovani would like to enter here a caveat as he thought that the word 'take off' was being used in a rather loose way in the discussions. He wished to remind the conference that the International Economic Association had published a book on this in which it appeared that the 'take off' was hardly a definite or identifiable or quantitatively valid concept.

But apart from the loose use of this term he would also like to question the hypothesis that mobility of income was linked with what he would simply describe as economic development. Professor Sovani believed income mobility, as well as social mobility, to be a function of occupational mobility. What is more, he knew of cases where it had been argued that the presence of mobility of this kind had prevented rather than helped economic development while its absence had helped it in others. For instance he would refer to Levy's study ('The Contrasting Factors in the Development of Japan and China', in *Economic Growth: India, Brazil, Japan*, ed. by Kuznets *et al.*, Duke University Press); Chinese society in the nineteenth and earlier centuries being a very open one, whenever any merchant made money he aspired to be a landlord, purchased land and abandoned trade and as a result the mechant class, drained of talent, could not become strong and active so as to bring about an economic transformation of the country. In contrast, contemporary Japanese society was closed. As a result of the absence of social mobility the merchant class became powerful enough to transform the economy.

Professor Sovani did not agree with this analysis. His only point in drawing attention to it had been to show that the role this sort of mobility could play in economic development was not fully known. It could be regarded as either a refractory or a catalytic agent.

In the second section of his paper Professor Gannagé envisaged distribution in relation to economic development and observed that, whereas property income was initially preponderant, wages and salaries and corporate incomes became important when a modern sector developed. Did this evolution make for more or less equality in income distribution? It seemed to Professor Sovani that Professor Gannagé's comments were quite ambivalent and he would like him to give a more definite statement on this.

Professor Sovani desired to draw attention to one point made in this connection by Professor Gannagé who thought that the main cause for intrasectoral income differences must be sought in the migration of people from rural areas to cities. As the people, unemployed or underemployed in agriculture, who went to the towns were prepared to take up jobs in the non-agricultural occupations at the lowest rung of the ladder, this made for greater inequality within the non-agricultural sector.

Now there was accumulating evidence to show that the pattern of urbanization in the underdeveloped countries was completely different from that which had been observed in Europe or the U.S.A. For instance

Indian data indicated that it was not always the poorest people in the rural areas who migrated to cities ; that cities often grew more by the natural increase in their population than by immigration from rural areas ; that migrants to the cities often did better than the local urbanites ; that the incidence of unemployment among migrants was less than that among the local people. With these facts in mind one could not but be very sceptical about the hypothesis advanced by Professor Gannagé.

In the last section of his paper in which Professor Gannagé had discussed the comparison of income distribution between developed and underdeveloped countries, Professor Gannagé had observed that, generally speaking, income distribution was more unequal in underdeveloped countries than in the developed ones. He had concluded his study by stating that there was no clear evidence as to whether inequality was a phenomenon inherent in the economic growth of countries. In this connection Professor Sovani felt that it would be useful to investigate further the relationship between inequality of income distribution and savings in an economy as this might perhaps furnish a link between income distribution and economic growth.

Professor Papi asked Professor Gannagé whether he thought that Pareto's law of income distribution would apply over the long period in underdeveloped countries. He was surprised that Professor Gannagé had taken such a partial view of the part played by the state. He had mentioned the role it played in influencing income distribution by means of redistributive policies but Professor Papi thought that in rapidly developing countries one ought also to take into account the increasing amount of state expenditure on public utilities and public works. Only countries which had already long ago solved the problem of building up the infrastructure required for the take-off of the economy into self-sustained growth could afford to ignore their importance. Professor Papi did not think that the figures given by Professor Gannagé about the proportion of public expenditure in national income, such as 19 per cent for Israel, faithfully reflected the part played by the state.

Professor Gendarme thought Professor Gannagé had rightly mentioned the dual economic structure amongst the main causes for income differentiation in underdeveloped countries and wished to add a few comments.

There was generally a contrast between poorer and richer areas within the same country and the resulting inequalities in average incomes per head were severe enough to constitute a risk of dislocation of the state. In many countries this could be described as a conflict between the industrialized North and the poorer agricultural South. Growth of the Northern over Southern areas would benefit the poorer South through a demonstration effect and more directly by absorbing the surplus of labour kept unemployed in the South. The migration of people to the North might however deprive the South of much needed skilled labour and the competition from industries set up in the North might ruin the South. Which effects were likely to prevail was hard to say. The increasing demand in the North might stimulate industries in the South but production in the South might not be able to respond to the stimulus.

The analysis of regional imbalance in income distribution was ambiguous and there was much uncertainty over the policy of regional investment. Investment might be either concentrated or dispersed. If one chose to concentrate investment on the richer areas where it was more profitable, one ran the risk of enlarging the gap in development between the richer and the poorer areas. If on the other hand investments were spread over the whole territory, the rate of growth might be less.

Professor Gendarme, however, thought advisable a certain measure of concentration of investment. Governments were all too tempted to spread money over the whole country in order to gain political support and had less difficulty in implementing small-scale projects than large schemes. This was to be resisted as only bigger projects could have polarization effects.

Professor Patinkin questioned the use of the ratio of public expenditure in national income as an index of the government's influence on the economy as Professor Gannagé had done in pp. 336–337 of his paper. This might be misleading in comparing government interventions in different countries through public expenditure as a whole. One ought to take into account the way it broke down into different components as the proportion of, say, expenditure on defence might vary widely from one country to another.

In order to measure the full effect of public expenditure on income distribution one would need a picture both of distribution of the tax burden and of the benefits of these expenditures.

Professor Papi having questioned whether this sort of ratio showed the full impact of government action on economic life, Professor Patinkin observed that in the case of Israel the figure quoted by Professor Gannagé as being 19·8 per cent reflected only the percentage of current budget expenditure in national income but this was adequate for the purpose of the analysis and Professor Gannagé did not intend the figures he gave to be interpreted as Professor Papi had interpreted them.

Dr. Negreponti-Delivanis wished to make some comments in support of Professor Gannagé's statement that there was more inequality of distribution in the industrial sector than in the agricultural one. This did not mean that there was no income inequality in the latter but two factors tended to limit its extent there. Farm products were sold under fairly competitive conditions whereas the modern industrial sector was functioning under monopolistic conditions as was proved by the existence of excess production capacity. Technical progress, which could be considered as the main factor for increasing income inequalities, had less impact on agriculture than on the industrial sector in the underdeveloped economies.

The Distribution of National Income

Professor Tress was surprised to find no reference in Professor Gannagé's paper to the effects of trade unionism on income distribution in developing countries. In his own experience the appearance of trade unions in the industrial and public sector (including school teachers) of considerable political power, effectively advancing wage claims, was an important feature.

Professor Tress wondered whether there was not a certain element of complacency as well as of truth in Professor Gannagé's statement (p. 339 of the paper) in which he described the increasing gap in average incomes between the traditional and the modern sectors as often having 'a catalytic effect on economic development, in so far as it (served) to attract technicians, engineers and skilled labour to the modern sector'. He thought he detected a disposition in Professor Gannagé's paper to identify economic development with industrial development whereas Professor Tress would have preferred to emphasize the importance of agricultural development.

The evacuation of those with any education from agriculture should hinder agricultural development while the growth of an urban working-class with comparatively high wages for those in employment was accompanied by considerable unemployment and thus, by migrating to cities, many people were just shifting from overemployment in agriculture to unemployment in industry.

Professor Krelle observed that in his conclusion Professor Gannagé had stated that while income distribution was more uneven in underdeveloped countries some measure of inequality was good if the rich people used their incomes in the right way. But obviously, Professor Krelle thought, they did not, otherwise the country would not be underdeveloped.

Professor Gannagé had concluded that to the extent it was so measures should be taken in order to make income distribution less uneven and that then the choice was no longer an economic but a political one. Professor Krelle would appreciate it if Professor Gannagé would comment on this. Did he mean that a free market economy should be abandoned for some sort of planned economy? Or did he simply advocate an income redistribution policy or state interventions such as land reform, incentives to invest, luxury tax, tariff on imports, etc., which could be included in planning but did not alter the economic system as such?

Professor Reder declared that he could not share Professor Gannagé's confidence in using data on size income distribution in underdeveloped countries and comparing them with similar data in developed countries as he had done on page 348 in the paper. If figures were hardly reliable in developed countries, they were still considerably less so in under-developed ones. They were derived from necessarily inadequate surveys. The more variable the incomes were the less accurately they were reported. Furthermore it became more difficult to measure incomes as more were received in kind and this made for a great difference in reliability of data between a market economy and a subsistence economy.

358

Having this in mind Professor Reder would suggest that one should substitute for income per head better indices for measuring economic welfare such as calories consumed per head, square footage of housing, etc. Professor Reder thought that Professor Gannagé should have been less definite in drawing any conclusions with available data.

Professor Jean Marchal thought that Professor Gannagé should have been more affirmative in answering (p. 351 in the paper) the question whether the stage of semi-development should involve increasing inequality of incomes. From past experience Professor Marchal thought this worsening in income distribution necessary in order to increase savings and to provide for incentives to production.

On the other hand he was equally convinced that the following stage should imply a reduction of inequality. While increasing income levels would be accompanied by the spread of education, increasing consumers' needs, greater aspiration to welfare, along with this the increase in other forms of saving, either corporate or public, made income inequality a less necessary requirement for a high level of personal savings. At the same time inequality of remuneration as an incentive to development would be made less urgent.

Professor James, referring to Professor Gannagé's statement (p. 337 in the paper) that in Middle East countries the state budget was becoming an instrument for income redistribution policy, wondered whether this would work out to the benefit of the poorer people. It was usually assumed by authors that redistribution operated towards reducing income inequalities but Professor James was inclined to question this : were not the privileged classes able to guide budget expenditure along lines favourable to themselves ?

Professor Gendarme said that he would support this. His opinion was that undoubtedly redistribution did not operate in favour of the poorer classes.

Professor Gannagé first took up Professor Sovani's remark on the use of the word 'take off'. The word was used in the English translation of his paper but he had purposely refrained from employing it when writing his paper. He referred to an acceleration of growth. Taking for granted that there was such a stage of accelerating growth in the process of development he believed there was some connection between the rapid move from a subsistence to a modern economy and a greater income mobility.

Professor Gannagé had been interested by Professor Sovani's remarks about the way farmers moved to the industrial sector and perhaps his paper gave too pessimistic an account of the consequences of the shift of population from countryside to towns.

Professor Gannagé thought that Professor Tress had been right in referring to the appearance of trade unions in developing countries. This was a new issue and one could not yet assess its full impact on these countries. But whereas trade unionism might have a great impact on African countries Professor Gannagé thought that in many countries unions were founded for defending producers in specific industries rather than for advancing wage claims.

Both Professor Krelle's and Professor Marchal's observations referred to the paper's conclusions and Professor Gannagé would comment on them jointly. He had purposely left the question of policies open as he would rather let readers make their own conclusions. He personally thought that the choice was specific, not general. Each country must find its own solution and he did not think that the choice should be reduced to a clear-cut alternative between Socialism and Capitalism.

Whether development would, in the long run, lead to more or less inequality was a tricky question. Could less-developed countries achieve a large increase in gross national product without passing through a phase of proletarian poverty? Would ways be found of avoiding what the Western countries had experienced in the early stages of their industrial development?

Chapter 14

REFLECTIONS ON THE APPROACHES
TO THE PROBLEMS OF DISTRIBUTION
IN UNDERDEVELOPED COUNTRIES

R. GENDARME
University of Nancy

I. INCREASING CONCERN WITH PROBLEMS
OF DISTRIBUTION

ALTHOUGH the problem of income distribution in economies of
the capitalist type has been studied since the creation of the classical
school — that is since the very beginnings of economic science —
the question of distribution in underdeveloped economies has so far
remained in the shade. In dealing with these economies, authors
have devoted more time to analyzing the forces that limit production
and the means of promoting development. This attitude seems
logical in respect of such types of economies, where the essential
problem is production rather than distribution. There seems little
point in attempting to distribute a national income which is increasing slowly if this would give rise to new problems by further com-
plicating a situation that is tricky enough already.

Since the achievement of independence by these countries, however, the egalitarian ideology prevailing in the industrial nations has
had its effect on public opinion. The attractiveness of the Russian
and Chinese experiments with their egalitarian distribution models
has also left its mark. Among the poverty-stricken masses of the
uncommitted nations (the Third World) the preoccupation with
distribution is now unquestionably more acute than the concern for
production. Independence was expected to bring about a radical
change in the standard of living, but some of the 'brothers' who are
now copying the habits of and granting themselves incomes as high
as the former colonialists can be heard proclaiming that a long time
will have to elapse before the fruits of development can be shared.
In a psychological climate of this type it becomes difficult to insist

on the absolute priority which should be given to production, for the government must attempt to curb the demands of the different social groups. It is possible that the answer to these movements of protest may only be found in very low growth rates or in very high ones.

As a fundamental problem of economics, distribution has been viewed by writers in different fashions. The classical authors examined the number of income categories and their nature, the socialists stressed the conflicts between the rich and the poor, and the econometrists the quantitative distribution of the mass of the national income among individuals. In an approach with highly sociological leanings, J. Marchal puts forward a theory of incomes in which he insists on the particular character and specific behaviour of the social groups who receive them.

It is of interest to re-examine these approaches to the problem in the light of underdeveloped economies rather than of their industrialized counterparts.

II. THE CLASSICAL APPROACH

The classical approach is attractive, since it deals with economies where industrialization has only just started. Do not the European economies of the eighteenth century have some features in common with those of the insufficiently developed economies of today? Since Smith and Ricardo, the traditional income categories are wages, profits, interest, and land rent. What is their importance in an underdeveloped economy? Are there not, alongside the conventional forms of revenue, other categories of remuneration whose parasitic character is prejudicial to development? Without claiming to exhaust the subject, this approach can provide food for thought.

In contrast to industrialized economies, wages form a relatively unimportant income category in the insufficiently developed economies. What it represents depends on the degree to which the economy has developed (20 to 25 per cent of all remuneration in the countries of Central Africa). As in the economies observed by the classical authors, a weakness can be discerned in the level of wages in the underdeveloped countries. This can be accounted for in several ways:

—the non-existence or weakness of trade unions;
—the competition on the labour market due to the expansion of population (a whole army of unemployed in reserve);

362

—the recourse to capital-saving investments to solve the unemployment problem ;
—the competition of manufactured products from the industrialized countries.

If some of the national groups in these countries draw high salaries, this is because they are a privileged minority possessing professional qualifications and profiting from the shortage of qualified manpower. Generally, the high salaries are paid to foreign executives for whom the salary is broken down into :

—a wage equivalent to that earned in their country of origin ;
—an overseas differential ;
—a series of advantages in kind.

It is noteworthy that the wages paid to a country's nationals lose their individual nature and assume a family or tribal character with a large number of more or less remote cousins living at the expense of the person who has found employment. However, there is a concealed ambiguity in the term 'total of wages' since a large proportion of it may be paid to agricultural workers. If sociological studies were undertaken in an underdeveloped country, they would show that all too often the situation of the agricultural wage-earner is close to that of serfdom or slavery. Even when it exists, social legislation is not applied in the countryside, so that the manager or owner of a large agricultural estate is completely free to decide on how much he will pay his employees. Sometimes, payment is made in kind. Furthermore, in some countries, the use of money for purposes of remuneration is insignificant. In Brazil, the rural worker has to buy the goods he needs at the 'big house', the headquarters of the estate, and pay for them with work tickets which are not accepted on any other estate. Generally, this rural wage is not a permanent feature and may vary from one month to the next depending on the kind of agricultural work to be done ; in the off-season it may drop to a ridiculously low figure : the bare minimum sufficient to maintain the future labour force.

As for profits, neither the earlier nor the more modern authors are agreed as to whether they stem, in fact, from remuneration for risks taken, remuneration for the entrepreneur function, remuneration for innovations, or whatever it may be. In view of the uncertainty of the explanations, it is quite understandable that attempts to work these ideas out in detail for underdeveloped countries should be risky. In my view, a distinction should be drawn between profits made by the very large concern or international unit, by the large or medium-sized entrepreneur and by the small entrepreneur.

With large international concerns, high profits seem to be explained by the difficulty of obtaining a foothold in the industry (cf. the case of the petroleum industry, the large plantations, the import-export companies connected to the shipping companies) which, in turn, leads to 'quasi-incomes' for the entrepreneurs. These high profits may provide the underdeveloped economy with substantial resources in the case of successful exploitation of plantations or minerals (e.g. oil royalties), which are sometimes quite out of proportion to the real needs of the country (Kuwait). However, it is wrong to think that the large foreign firms working the rare resources have any kind of influence on employment in underdeveloped countries. These industries use powerful technical equipment and highly qualified personnel; in Venezuela, for instance, the petroleum industry employs only 2 per cent of the active population. Hence a minority wallows in luxury while the greater part of the population stagnates in misery; an even more serious fact is that whereas the oil flows in abundance, agriculture is declining and an agricultural country like Venezuela is no longer capable of feeding its inhabitants. It seems that when resources are rare and working is confined merely to their extraction or the production of vegetable matter, the effect on the volume of employment and on the income of the population is relatively slight. Often, moreover, the profits made do not remain in the country but are repatriated. W. H. Stead gives some very significant figures which show the difference between profit rates in underdeveloped and developed countries.

The companies justify these rates by the magnitude of the risks incurred. Might not this be merely an application of the theory of monopoly profit? The situation also appears to be favoured by the attitudes of these countries' governments which are more anxious to encourage the setting-up of an industry, if necessary by granting it tax privileges and protection, than to promote or limit the competition.

In respect of the large or medium-sized undertaking, the temptation would be to revert to the type of explanation offered by Schumpeter but in a different sense. Profits are no longer the remuneration drawn by innovators, but that drawn by negotiators. In these economies, profits stem from the application of favourable social and fiscal legislation, of the fixing of advantageous exchange rates, of the perseverance exercised in persuading people to invest their capital in the company, etc. The pioneer entrepreneur may have existed at the beginning of capitalism, but he has been replaced by the diplomat entrepreneur in the underdeveloped countries.

TABLE 1

PROFIT RATES IN PUERTO RICO AND IN THE UNITED STATES

Industry	Profit Rate in 1955 in per cent after Tax	
	American Firms in Puerto Rico	All Companies of the same Sector in the U.S.A.
Food	11	9
Textiles	19	5
Clothing	37	6
Chemicals	29	14
Rubber goods	65	13
Leather articles	37	8
Machinery	73	9
Electrical equipment	67	13
All firms	35	12

Source : W. H. Stead, *The Economic Development of Puerto Rico*, National Planning Association, 1958, p. 78.

As regards the small craftsman or trading firm, it is possible to give several types of explanation. Either the profit is the difference between the subsistence minimum at cost price and the price offered by the buyer without reference to the cost price of the article : it is frequently possible to lose on one article and to earn on another. By proposing very high prices at first and then lower ones afterwards, the seller attempts to derive maximum benefit from the buyer's revenue. Or else, and this is valid for the trader in the bush, the profit becomes a remuneration for an income due to the situation : a comfortable margin can be taken on everything, from oil lamps to aspirin tablets.

In an economy suffering from a chronic shortage of capital, it is only to be expected that interest will play a less important part than it does in the capitalist economies. In fact the supply of capital, like the demand for funds to be invested, is very low.

For a considerable time in China during the concessions and in Indonesia, interest played no part in loans. Each loan was accompanied with guarantee conditions laid down by the lender country such that the economic and tax administration virtually fell into the foreigners' hands. For example, one common practice was for lender banks to take mortgages on State taxes or first-category income tax, while the government was forbidden to change anything at all during the duration of the loan. Furthermore, the lenders reserved the right to organize the collection of taxes themselves if necessary. There were also cases where income taxes were specially created with a view to guaranteeing such loans.

In addition underdeveloped economies do not possess institutions that are capable of draining off savings and the financial markets are non-existent. The lack of a market machinery makes it impossible to assess the yield of private capital. Analysis in terms of micro-decisions comparing the yield of capital with its cost seems quite unreal since the chief obstacle encountered in the formation of capital is the structural conversion of the economy. Frequently the banking system is represented by banks of foreign origin which undergo the influence of the leading world-wide economic and financial centres, as a result of which the domestic interest rate lacks independence. In addition, in an underdeveloped economy, various sectors such as building, agriculture, trade, etc., bear different rates of interest. The differences between sectors seem greater than those between short-term and long-term rates. With such diversified markets, it is impossible to speak of an interest rate.

Research on the underdeveloped countries shows a capital deficit which has to be made up by foreign countries or the international organizations. The supply of foreign capital rather than the interest rate thus assumes importance. It is no doubt true that private capital may be attracted by a high interest rate but, in reality, the part played by these movements of capital remains a minor feature. The supply of foreign capital to the underdeveloped economies manifests itself above all through public capital or international public capital. The volume supplied depends no longer on the interest rate but on the national income or the strategic aims of the industrialized nations. The interest rate plays a minor role in the reimbursement of loans abroad or from the international organizations. Nevertheless in this respect the rates applied, which vary between 5 and 6 per cent, seem too high and constitute a threat to the currency. This risk is all the more serious since the governments of underdeveloped countries tend to over-estimate their reimbursement capacity.

From Adam Smith in his chapter 'On income' (Book A of the *Wealth of Nations*) to the analyses of Alfred Marshall (Chapter 6 of the *Book of Principles*) via Stuart Mill (the chapter devoted to 'peasants, landowners, and farmers'), the older economists have insisted on the importance of the land as a factor in production. No such preoccupation is to be found in modern authors, whether they be Keynesian or post-Keynesian; industrialization and its consequences have pushed this problem into the background. In analyzing a primary economy, however, should we not go back and give land rent its full importance ? The laws governing the land are of vital importance in underdeveloped economies where agriculture remains the chief form of activity. By land rent in this case, we mean first the fixed or proportional payment that the landowner demands from his tenant farmers or share-croppers. It can be seen from reports and investigations that the rates applied, which are not necessarily the legal rates, are too high. As a general rule, the reduction or abolition of land rent could help to increase the productive capacity of the land. It is difficult to believe that in countries where landowners take 50 per cent of farmers' output without doing anything for them in return, agricultural output would not rise appreciably if the farmers were relieved of this burden. This first form of land rent is frequently connected with profits from industry or trade ; for the large landowners of Latin America, capital is seldom used primarily for agricultural investment ; it is first invested in industrial or commercial undertakings so that, when the economic situation deteriorates, the agricultural sector is the most hard-hit since all the available capital is required by industry and trade. The high level of rents is not an exclusive feature of the countryside ; in the towns the price of land reaches prohibitive levels and the prospect of a high yield attracts a great deal of capital that would have been more useful in industry. According to some writers, the building industry absorbs half or three-quarters of national savings in certain Latin-American countries. However, land rent can also be understood as differential income, a gift of nature received by the owners of the most fertile or best situated land. Now, in underdeveloped countries the degree to which the land is fertile varies widely, depending on whether irrigation is available or not, and the relative absence of means of communication tends to increase the importance of this second category of rent.

Alongside these sources of revenue, whose essential feature it is that they contribute less to development than they do in the industrialized countries, we find others which are patently parasitic and do not correspond to any increase in the national product. These are gambling, money-lending, speculation, and smuggling.

The chief characteristic of games of chance in underdeveloped countries is that they are organized in such a way as to arouse the interest of the poorest strata of the population. In view of the low wages, the underemployment, and the impossibility of saving anything, the poor see this activity as the only possible means of acquiring the minimum of capital which would enable them to find a more lucrative occupation. Their hope of winning gives rise to a further vicious circle ; they gamble so that they will be less poor but they are poorer because they gamble. Very often the inhabitants of the underdeveloped countries do not even understand the mechanics of gambling. If a man wins once, he thinks that he will win again and his desire to gamble increases.

The existence of games of chance in the underdeveloped countries modifies the framework of income distribution and the structure of consumption. Gambling strengthens the feeling of domination of the richer class over the poorer classes. Usually the people who organize the games at week-ends in the countryside are the landowners or money-lenders and the peasants are thus dispossessed of part of what they earned during the week. This reinforces the concentration of wealth and widens the gap between rich and poor. By gambling every day, the peasants and workers reduce their consumption of essential articles, such as foodstuffs or medicine. In addition, the people who profit from gambling spend the money either on luxury consumer goods or for the purpose of strengthening their political position. If this second alternative is borne in mind gambling would be one of the factors which help to preserve an unequal distribution of income in the underdeveloped countries.

Money-lending in its generalized form is a phenomenon which commonly accompanies low incomes. The inability of primitive populations to appreciate what the future may bring makes the individual improvident. The present is more important. Hence they contract debts with disconcerting ease to tide themselves over a poor harvest, to provide a dowry for a daughter, to buy a taxi, or for funeral ceremonies. The rates granted range from 50 per cent in Madagascar to 100 per cent in the Far East. At the end of a year, since the debtor cannot pay back the loan, he contracts another with the same money-lender and is further bogged down in debt. The business usually ends with the debtor's home being sold; the sale is advertised in such a manner that the mortgaged house is bought at half the price by someone acting on behalf of the money-lender. It is quite understandable that under such conditions there should be little inclination to invest, since capital yields 10 to 12 times more in money-lending transactions.

Speculation occurs when an individual or group buys or arranges for others to buy goods at a time when they have fallen below their normal price with a view to reselling them subsequently, either in the same place or elsewhere.

What is easier than speculation in an underdeveloped economy? Everything is favourable to it: the economic climate, the attitude of entrepreneurs, the way in which agricultural produce is collected, the property and exchange laws. For instance:

—The fluctuations in export prices and the stock-piling possibilities of the large international units; in respect of jute, speculative patterns drove up the rates by 88 per cent in 1960 and then in 1961 they dropped by 36 per cent. The exaggerated propensity for liquidity on the part of entrepreneurs prompts them to maintain a good part of their assets in the shape of stocks.

—Local planters' ignorance of the prices; in Madagascar, for instance, it is not unusual for a middleman to buy vanilla or coffee at 20 to 30 per cent below the current world prices.

—The scarcity of building land; the most common practice is to place a building under an expropriation order with the complicity of the local authorities and then to remove the threat as soon as it has been bought at a low price.

—The pressure exerted by exporters and importers to obtain a rate favourable to their interests in a multiple exchange rate system.

Naturally smuggling exists in our industrialized countries where many individuals go to extremes of ingenuity in order to get the better of the customs officers. This has nothing in common, however, with smuggling in an underdeveloped economy; these countries have frontiers of an extraordinary length patrolled by a handful of customs officers, who are easily bribed. It is not enough to institute regulations, they have to be respected as well. At the present time, however, the governments of underdeveloped countries cannot ensure that certain laws are respected, particularly those regarding the bringing in or taking out of certain sorts of merchandise. For instance the frontier of the Niger Republic with Nigeria is more than 800 kilometres long and a few francs' increase in the price of ground-nuts in Nigeria causes ground-nut exports from Niger to drop by 10 to 20 per cent. The spread of smuggling contributes to the creation of false incomes without a productive counterpart. Does not the magnitude of these false incomes, all other things being equal, depend on the degree of poverty of a country ?

Lastly, it should be noted that the classical authors have omitted to allow for the earnings of nationals residing abroad, part of which is repatriated to their own country. This situation eases the employment market of the underdeveloped economy and in cases where profits are repatriated, may prove a factor favourable to growth. Countries like Algeria and the Lebanon fall into this category. In the Lebanon, remittances from emigrants account for 100 million Lebanese pounds per annum or 7 per cent of the national income.

III. THE MARXIST APPROACH

The Marxist approach to the theory of distribution makes certain premises which may appear questionable. In other ways, however, inasmuch as it attempts to describe certain mechanisms, its explanatory value seems more applicable to underdeveloped economies than to industrialized economies.

Like the division of capitalist society into two classes, the division of underdeveloped society into two classes does not stand up to serious analysis. The proof of this is to be seen in Communist China during the agrarian reform, where these classes had to be created artificially.

According to Mao Tse-tung himself (*Selected Works*, vol. i, p. 162, para. 5), Chinese rural society can be divided into four different classes :

(1) *Landowners* : i.e. those who possess land but who do not work themselves, or only carry out secondary activities. They live by exploiting the peasants. Methods used to exploit them include tenant-farming, money-lending, hiring of employees, etc.

(2) *Rich peasants* usually owning their land. Generally speaking these peasants have the best means of production and a certain amount of operating capital.

(3) *Middle-class peasants* who generally own land but may rent part of it. They own their agricultural implements and they live entirely by their labour. Nevertheless, they are sometimes exploited by landowners and money-lenders.

(4) *Poor peasants and agricultural workers*: the poor peasants possess either their patch of ground and inadequate implements, or simply inadequate implements; they are exploited by means of the tenant system, money-lending, and the sale of labour. The agricultural workers possess neither land nor tools and live chiefly from selling their labour. Roughly speaking, the strategy used in agrarian reform is that of Lenin; reliance on the poor peasants and union with the middle-class peasantry to crush first the landowner class and then the rich peasants. In short, a revolution making use of the middle class.

In addition, in underdeveloped economies, the struggle does not seem to have been between the capitalist and the proletarian classes but between the colonizers and the colonized. Nations have replaced the classes and the clash has been between rich nations and poor nations with the working-classes making no effort to unite beyond their own frontiers. Sometimes the lines along which the split took place were entirely different from those predicted by Marx with foreign high-capitalism sympathizing with the nationalist movements and the revolution directed against the 'poor white', i.e. against the foreigner with the lowest income. It is symptomatic, incidentally, that after the American War of Independence, some of the large companies continued their activities just as before.

Lastly, although the Marxist thesis of increasing pauperization is no longer defended by any serious and non-sectarian economist since the most capitalist country in the world is the United States where the workers' standard of living is highest, it may nevertheless be true that some underdeveloped countries are sliding into a vicious spiral of indebtedness. Some enquiries in Thailand have enabled rural indebtedness to be followed closely. The amount of the average debt per family (allowing for monetary variations) has risen from 163·34 baths at the beginning of the century to 223·82 baths in 1934 and 421 baths in 1953. The problem is never-ending. A growing debt accentuates the need for money and forces the peasant to sell his crop before the harvest at a very low price. Then, in order to tide things over and provide for future sowing, he has to borrow again at higher rates.

This rural indebtedness has two effects :

—It increases the instability of holdings ; quite logically, leases can be cancelled if the rent is not paid. Enquiries made in Burma showed that only a third or a quarter of all farmers had cultivated the same plot of land for more than three years, while the number of those whose tenure did not date back for more than a year varied from one-sixth to half of the total.

—It increases the concentration of land-ownership. The minute size of the rural holding obliges the small owner to borrow. He cannot free himself from the debt because of the size of his land and the money-lending rates. The only course open to him is to sell the holding when the sum of his debt is equivalent to its value. The fact that money-lenders can buy land in this way turns tens of thousands of people each year into landless peasants.

Therefore although we may reject the dogma of the growing pauperization of workers under a capitalist regime, and many authors have done so, it seems much more difficult to contest the increasing pauperization of the peasant in an underdeveloped economy.

IV. THE ECONOMETRIC APPROACH

The approach to distribution advocated by Pareto and the econometrists provides a number of quantitative indications for the underdeveloped countries ; however it soon comes up against insurmountable obstacles of documentation and interpretation.

The process commonly employed to express the inequality of incomes consists of using the Lorenz curves ; the Y axis represents the accrued percentages of the national income, the X axis the accrued percentages of the people drawing this income. If the income were distributed equally, it would follow a diagonal starting from the point of origin of the abscissae and going towards the upper right-hand corner of the square. The greater the convexity of the curve, the greater the inequality of income distribution ; this seems to be one of the characteristics of distribution in the under-developed economies. According to the IRFED experts who have plotted such curves, it can be seen that in the Western countries 35 to 40 per cent of the population draws an income higher than the average, as against 18 per cent in the Lebanon and about 8 per cent in Colombia. It should be noted that the statistics used to plot these graphs were obtained from tax documents.

As far as the underdeveloped countries are concerned, these figures tend to under-estimate the true situation. In fact :

—no allowance is made for false incomes derived from money-lending, gambling, speculation, or smuggling, which are not checked by the tax authorities ;
—the various advantages and benefits received by skilled workers and people employed in industry and trade are not taken into consideration ;
—the poorly paid minor civil servant often has a second job.

The econometrists have also tried to establish a correlation between the concentration of land and the concentration of incomes. In order to do so they have calculated a land-concentration index with the Gini formula. This index varies between 0 and 1. The value 0 corresponds to a uniform distribution of the land between all the owners and the value 1 to a situation where all the land is concentrated in the hands of a single proprietor.

Hector Corréa [1] has obtained the following land-concentration factors :

Bolivia	1950	0·954
Venezuela	1956	0·909
Mexico	1950	0·852
Brazil	1950	0·838
West Germany	1949	0·675
Netherlands	1950	0·550
Belgium	1950	0·474

However, these statistical analyses do not take us very far if we do not compare them with the sociological or legal facts. Hence, in Mexico, where the concentration index is very high, 27 per cent of the land is in the hands of communities and there can be no question of a concentration of private property.

The Gini coefficients have to take as their basis a table of agricultural holdings classified according to their size. Although we can generally find statistics giving the number of holdings with an area between 0 and 1 hectare, 1 and 5 hectares, 5 and 10 hectares, and so on, the number of owners within these limits

[1] *Travaux du Centre Européen de Nancy*, 1964.

is seldom known. Now there is a difference between the distribution of land by owners and its distribution by holdings. On the one hand, a single person may possess several holdings and the concentration of ownership is therefore higher than that of the holdings. On the other hand, one holding may be owned by several people and the concentration of holdings be higher than that of ownership. All these shades of diffe ences are necessary and many quantitative interpretations do not make allowance for them. Lastly, even after his sophisticated calculations the econometrist arrives at the same conclusion as the economists, namely that the distribution of land in the underdeveloped countries is poor and that agrarian reform is the first step towards development.

If we wish to measure the link between political stability and inequality of income distribution, we find another point of view which should stimulate the imagination of the econometrists ; the construction of a political stability index. However, even if they succeeded in eliminating the anomalies due to the differences in the duration of presidential mandates and managed to take constitutional reforms, ministerial changes, etc., into consideration, the results would still be rather disappointing. For instance, by studying the correlation between political stability and land concentration, it would be possible to find either that land concentration leads to the fusion of economic and political power and thus to governmental stability or else that a high concentration of landownership causes social unrest and brings about governmental instability. There is no relationship between the two variables. Nothing can replace knowledge of local history on the subject. All too often econometric analysis has a tendency to establish a relationship between two factors which vary simultaneously but have no established link of causality. This is, in fact, the concealed obstacle often encountered in correlation studies.

V. THE SOCIOLOGICAL APPROACH OF JEAN MARCHAL

Professor Jean Marchal has tried to formulate a new approach to distribution based on a classification of social groups. Jean Marchal proposes that the society analysed be divided into social categories appropriate to its structure ; he then considers distribution as a 'battlefield' for the sharing-out of the national income which prompts him to look for the dominant groups, the main conflicts and the tactics used.

We cannot take over the social categories of Marchal as they stand, since the social structures of developed and underdeveloped countries are quite different. A realistic analysis of distribution in under-developed countries could single out the following categories :

(1) *Servants* : in view of the importance of domestic service in the underdeveloped countries and the natural aptitude of certain tribes or races for this type of work, this activity cannot be disregarded. In Egypt, this social-cum-professional category represents 12 per cent of the total urban population. This does not mean, however, that there is equality within the group. For example, a middle-class Haitian [1] pays his boy 9 dollars a month, plus food and accommodation, while an American pays between 20 and 30 dollars for the same work. When the American experts and their families left Haiti in 1962, 2,500 servants whose luxury-standard wages kept 20,000 to 30,000 people were reduced to unemployment.

(2) *The urban sub-proletariat* : whereas in the industrialized countries manual workers form the majority of the proletariat and are considered as the least favoured social class, this is not so in underdeveloped countries. In many respects, workers in modern industries form a privileged class provided they have a stable occupation. The real outcasts are the sub-proletarians : labourers and occasional day-rate workers, 'deruralized' country-people who have not become urbanized, illicit street vendors and people with minor trades such as bootblacks, pedlars, porters, cycle-rickshaw drivers, and so on.

(3) *The artisans* form a third group, but care should be taken to distinguish between the traditional crafts practised by tailors, jewellery-makers, shoemakers, blacksmiths, basket-weavers, potters, etc., and modern skills exercised such as mechanics, welders, and electricians. Sometimes artisans occupied in traditional craft are menaced by modern techniques and may go to swell the urban sub-proletariat.

(4) *Factory wage-earners* : in the underdeveloped countries, the total of wages earned by this category represents a figure of much less than 30 per cent of the national income, as against some 60 per cent in the industrialized countries. In the former they appear to belong to the middle-class already.

(5) *The rural proletariat* : this is made up of landless peasants

---

[1] *Croissance des jeunes nations*, no. 26 (1963).

(agricultural labourers), smallholders, share-croppers, and tenant farmers.

In Iran out of 2,700,000 families, 60 per cent are landless and 23 per cent possess less than 1 hectare.[1]

In Ecuador the lowest income level corresponds to almost the whole of the rural population.[2]   Out of a population of slightly more than 3 million inhabitants, nearly 500,000 receive no monetary income at all and more than a million are reduced to an income of 30 to 40 dollars per year, which is barely enough to keep them at subsistence level.

(6) *Civil servants* : their aptitude for acquiring wealth and power seems to be creating an embryo class of civil servants in the underdeveloped countries.   Their intellectual training and their knowledge of administrative organization enable them to secure a share of the power and may even lead to important political appointments.   In 1957, 52 per cent of the ministers of all the territories of former French West Africa were civil servants ; the proportion in former French Equatorial Africa — 56 per cent — was even higher.[3] This social group is tending to become self-absorbed and to form a real class.   J. Binet records that the sons of civil servants alone account for 25 per cent of the numbers at the Conakry Lycée.[4]

(7) *The army* : a recent creation in underdeveloped countries, the army does not yet form a closed and traditional caste although its behaviour can have a strong influence on economic and political trends.   In an underdeveloped state, the army is one of the rare dynamic and progressive-looking forces.   Having broken with traditional family beliefs, young officers are responsive to modern ideas, concerned about transforming their country and in revolt against injustice and corruption. The army represents a force which is both social and patriotic. As a social force, it is hypersensitive to the latent discontent of the population ; as a patriotic force, it embodies the unity and the pride of the young state and, by its prestige alone, it is capable of carrying a large part of the population along with it.

[1] 'Progrès agricole et structure traditionnelle en Iran', by A. Wallerstein, *Revue Tiers-Monde*, no. 3, 1960, p. 341.
[2] 'La répartition des richesses et le développement', by Paul Berger, *Croissance des jeunes nations*, no. 20, 1963.
[3] J. Binet, 'Naissance de nouvelles classes sociales', *Revue Action Populaire*, September–October 1961.
[4] J. Binet, *op. cit.*, p. 261.

(8) *The bourgeois and aristocratic classes* : their composition is not very homogeneous. They include :

—The landowners : the more marked the concentration of holdings, the greater the importance assumed by this social group. According to the official statistics, the rural population of Brazil is 39 million inhabitants, representing 54 per cent of the total population. Almost half of all the cultivated area of the country belongs to only 1 per cent of this rural population. This group, which is economically the wealthiest and politically the most influential, can obstruct any attempt to alter the distribution ; according to a study made by the Getulio Vargas foundation, half the electoral college of the state of Minas Gerais in Central South Brazil is controlled by a minority of 12,000 landowners.[1]

—The old aristocracy, regardless of whether it derives from the old feudal structures or descends from a race of conquerors, may maintain both a certain degree of wealth and a measure of power in some countries or areas. In Morocco, the former feudal rulers (caids, pashas, sheikhs) have kept part of the property they accumulated during the French Protectorate. In the North Cameroun, the Peul or Toucouleur conquerors formed the greater part of the ruling classes.

—The liberal professions : doctors, pharmacists, lawyers, and so on form too small a minority to have any influence at all on distribution. Although they were long thought of as the élite and held governmental posts until independence, their role is now on the decline. They can keep the political reins in their hands only as the representatives of other more powerful or more dynamic groups.

—Local traders and entrepreneurs, usually engrossed in their own business and ignorant of the administrative machinery, are generally excluded from political power.

(9) *Foreigners* also form a hybrid social group. Among them, pride of place must go to the representatives of the large international companies whose decisions affect the national income of underdeveloped countries. For example, the yield on the foreign capital invested in the country by the large international firm depends exclusively on the policy of its

[1] Quoted by Guimarès in *Le Monde*, 4 March 1964.

directors ; the effect of domination is felt all the more strongly if the large firm is more closely connected with foreign than with local capitalism.

In addition to the personnel of these large firms, mention should be made, for reference, of the group of foreigners with high living standards such as technicians and teachers. These people have no direct influence on distribution and, since they are paid by the ex-dominating power, their salaries have no repercussion on the state budget. However, as these foreign technicians are very well paid, the governments of underdeveloped countries are obliged to align the wages of local technicians with those of foreign technicians. Surely this shows a new aspect of Duesenberry's demonstration effect ?

Sometimes a foreign group monopolizes certain forms of trading activity. This was the case with the Mozabites in Algeria, the Djerbians in Tunisia, the Syrians and Lebanese in Central Africa and the Chinese in the Far East. In these cases, there is a combination of race and social-cum-professional category.

A more important feature is the presence of foreign experts who, depending on whether they belong to the Eastern or the Western worlds, guide the underdeveloped countries towards a socialist or capitalist distribution pattern.

The model built by Jean Marchal contains only six fundamental social groups : unskilled workers, executives, entrepreneurs, farmers, and money-lenders ; here we have nine, without taking sub-categories into account. If we acknowledge the multiplicity of social groups required in order to analyse the concrete situation in the underdeveloped countries, the situation is liable to be complex in the extreme, since the homogeneous character and strength of these groups will vary according to the different cases. The theory then loses its generalized character and becomes a study of the particular features of each economy. This approach no doubt provides information on the dominant social groups as far as income distribution is concerned. It is easy to list the army, the civil servants, the land-owners and the foreigners under this heading. Collusion between landowners and foreigners and alliance between landowners and the army or other combinations can create certain structures of income distribution and a disinclination for change. But it is difficult to go further than that and to specify the chief conflicts and their nature or to provide an idea of distribution as a function of the stages in economic growth. The approach of Jean Marchal needs to be supplemented on these points.

The very notion of major conflicts occurring over distribution in the underdeveloped countries goes beyond the context of social groups: allowance has to be made for historical, ideological and political factors and it is sometimes difficult to state whether these arise from racial hatred, for instance, or from a determined desire to alter the distribution. It might be of interest to give a table summarizing the main social conflicts over distribution which may flare up in an underdeveloped country (Table 2).

Without wishing to comment at length on this table, it should be pointed out that strikes play no part as a means of pressure on income distribution in underdeveloped countries. Very often their place is taken by the *coup d'état* or the revolution. If accurate statistics were available, it would perhaps be found that the frequency of *coups d'état* is equal to that of our strikes. Just as our strikes have become less violent, so the *coups d'état* tend to become more pacific, as we saw from the example of the telephone consultations between the military leaders of Syria. Generally speaking, the *coup d'état* is inspired by motives connected with distribution. In Brazil, the fall of Goulart was provoked in order to thwart the agrarian reform ; in Zanzibar, the revolution was triggered off by the 80 per cent African majority against the 15 per cent Arab minority which held the land and dominated trade in the staple resource, cloves. Even when a *coup d'état* has been started for purely political ends, it is rare for it not to alter distribution : one of the first acts of General Nguyen Khanh after he took over in South Vietnam was to raise soldiers' pay by 20 per cent, a rate of increase which has seldom been obtained in a capitalist country as a result of a strike.

Trade unions, on which Jean Marchal dwells at some length, do not appear in our table. This should come as no surprise since the situation of trade unions in the industrialized countries is completely different from that in the underdeveloped countries. In an industrialized country, when the trade unions agitate they know that in claiming a greater share of the profits as a return for their work, they are asking for a proportional reduction in the share accruing to the capital invested. In the underdeveloped countries, their scope is very different ; any excessive demand for consumer goods or for articles manufactured in the country or imported from abroad makes prices rise and upsets the financial forecasts on which all long-term plans are based. Restrictions on consumption are absolutely essential

379

The Distribution of National Income

TABLE 2

SOCIAL TENSION OVER DISTRIBUTION
CAPABLE OF OCCURRING IN UNDERDEVELOPED
COUNTRIES

Major Conflicts	Means of Domination used by the Stronger over the Weaker	Means of changing Distribution
Town against country	Increased migration from the country to the urban centres; investment and infrastructure in towns. Urban political movements	Planning by fiscal means
Rich areas against poor areas	Dispersion of credits over entire country so as to maintain the initial advantage of the rich	Grants, large public works schemes or setting-up of industries in poor areas
Landowners against rural proletariat	Property, loans, usury, pressure on political authorities	Agrarian reform
Army + discontented against privileged classes	Material strength. Social and patriotic prestige	Coup d'état
Civil servants against other social groups	Intellectual training, administrative knowledge, exclusion of other groups from political power	Access of other groups to schools and universities; participation of other groups in political assemblies
Foreigners against nationals	Colonial pacts. Large international concerns	Decolonization, nationalization, royalties
Nationals among themselves	Nobility, conqueror or caste prestige, religion	Revolution or facilitation of social advancement

if the planners' objectives are to be upheld and the formation of capital hastened. Counting on consumption in an underdeveloped economy can provoke inflation and multiply the obstacles in the planners' path. The aim of all concerted action on the part of the workers must be to increase output and the national income in order to guarantee economic development. Hence, in contrast to the trade unions of the industrialized countries which stand as the defenders of consumption against production, the trade unions of underdeveloped countries must gamble on maximizing national production at constant prices. This implies that the trade unions will have to give up their function as claimants and will impose on themselves a limitation on wages at all levels and co-operation with the state to avoid social unrest during the period of development.

This attitude is not without its dangers and sometimes the political authorities use trade unions to achieve their own ends. In Argentina, under Peron, the government exercised absolute control over the trade unions and there was virtually a complete identity between political and trade-union action. In such cases trade unionism becomes a political instrument of the authorities and cannot oppose them.

Still referring to our table, we might wonder whether social advancement in the underdeveloped country is possible in two ways :

—firstly by education, with individuals swelling the civil-servant class. In societies that are still primitive economic power offers less attractions than political power ; in point of fact, political power is often conceived as a 'short-cut' which permits the acquisition of wealth without engaging in economic activity. The simple fact that a person can read and write places the subordinate employee above the mass of the illiterate population and gives him a prestige that he can use for his personal ends.

—or secondly, through the army for people not able to obtain sufficient education. Because of its egalitarian recruitment, the army brings together men from the most varied backgrounds and the social hierarchy can be quickly scaled. In addition, even when it is not directly in power, the army forms what is called a 'factor of power'. In Argentina, at the present time, there is a 'gabinete militar' which guides policy and dominates government decisions.

In the light of these comments, we find two different attitudes towards distribution: one advocated by civil servants, tending to increase their salaries and power and to herald a technocratic society, the other defended by the young officers and non-commissioned officers and proposing more radical social reforms. Might not the U.S.S.R. have experienced a phase of technocratic and military direction in the first years of its development ? Would it not have found itself faced with two different routes, had not communism moulded the technocracy and the army into one ?

Professor Marchal's approach gives no guide to the link between distribution and the historical stages of growth. Taking up a simplified pattern after the manner of Rostow, we can distinguish four stages of growth : primitive society, society in the pre-take-off stage, society on take-off and society arriving at maturity.

Three social categories are usually found in primitive societies, namely people of servile condition, free men, and the aristocracy. Distribution is founded on a social or political hierarchy produced by history or by custom. The aristocracy, with which the power of decision rests, is remunerated primarily according to its degree of sovereignty; economic activities come a poor second. The lord in the feudal system and the patriarch in the tribal system ensure a redistribution of the product rather than a distribution. Sometimes, there is a redistribution among the feudal chiefs in order to ensure the political stability of the state. In Saudi Arabia, for instance, each of the 322 royal princes draws an income of 30,000 dollars per annum (15 million old francs). This phase is characterized by an economic stratification and a stratification of access to political power. The uneven spread of income stems from social and political immobility. In this first stage, the system of distribution drawn up by François Quesnay takes on a particular significance, with a single source income, the land, paying for the other activities. Does not this description resemble the situation in some underdeveloped countries where the army, especially when it is popular, and thousands of monks are sustained by the population ?

In society at the pre-take-off stage, there is a multiplicity of social groups belonging to four types of social structure : the old structure (landowners, artisans, tenant-farmers, etc.), the imported structure (foreigners), the disintegrating social structure (urban sub-proletariat) and the new structure (civil servants, the army, the capitalist class in its embryonic state). Distribution depends on the political power of these groups and the balance of forces. This is the period when conflicts begin between social groups inside the underdeveloped country and it is characterized by a wide income scatter. The inequalities of urban incomes, in particular, may be considered as being greater than those of the rural population. The tensions become all the more violent as the groups endeavour to change the distribution pattern without any increase in the mass of the national income.

In the take-off period, the opposition between social groups results in the elimination of some of them (e.g. landowners) and strengthens the feeling of cohesion in the remaining groups. Three groups can take the initiative for development : the technocratic civil servants, the army, or the entrepreneurs. In the underdeveloped country, the first two hypotheses seem more likely because of the weakness of the entrepreneur class. Sometimes this entrepreneur class exists (cf. Latin America), but its influence on development is disconcerting. The excessive store its members set by profit prompts them to discard their valid output for others from which they expect miracles.[1] Hence came the successive waves of enthusiasm for coffee, cotton, or rubber and the eventual collapse and resulting economic disaster. The speculator mentality and the unwillingness to invest so as to be free to profit from exceptional bargains are factors which are harmful to development and explain the scant influence exerted by this class on growth. Take-off will occur, all other things being equal, when a government is capable of confiscating the profits of growth for its own benefit and of judiciously reinvesting them in the economy. Viewed in this light, take-off would be brought about by a new distribution of the national income. The inequality of incomes would be pushed as far as possible since part would be allocated to growth and the privileged groups, while the remainder of the population would be kept at the bare minimum level. In some cases, maximum boosting of the strategic position of the country is undertaken so that substantial foreign aid can be obtained.

In the period of maturity, we can witness a rebirth of the multiplicity of social groups leading to a self-imposed limit on incomes, an increase in the progressiveness of taxation and a resulting tightening-up of the range of incomes. People tend to prefer safety to risks, whence a partial elimination of the remuneration for risk and the introduction of the concept of 'insurance income'. These insurance incomes, which are received by opposing social groups, tend to weaken the antagonism between them. A concerted policy and the implementation of an incomes policy then becomes possible.

[1] Albert O. Hirschman, *The Strategy of Economic Development*. New Haven, Yale University Press, 1958, p. 20.

Fundamentally, the classical authors only considered the major income categories corresponding to the small number of social classes in existence during the take-off period. Jean Marchal has studied distribution at the last stage of growth where the classes lose their homogeneous composition and splinter into a host of social groups, each seeking its own interest.

VI. A POSSIBLE NEW APPROACH

We wish to propose an approach to distribution in the underdeveloped countries based on the characteristic feature of their economies, namely their dualism. This approach could open up new perspectives; it disregards the social and professional categories but, in contrast, it stresses sociological, economic, geographical, and ethnic criteria.

If the sociological criterion is examined, attention is focused on the two types of society existing in an underdeveloped economy : an urban society responsive to progress and innovation, and a rural society bound by tradition, i.e. the town-country axis. Distribution is then considered as a combination of urban and rural incomes. This problem was brought into prominence by Simon Kuznets [1] who found that, first, the average rural income is habitually lower than the urban average; second, the inequality in the percentages within the income distribution in the rural population is less great than in the urban population. These two findings enable a tentative statement to be formulated, namely that the increase in urban population required by the growth in number and size of towns would lead to an increasingly larger percentage of people moving towards the more unequal of the two distributions. This is further strengthened by the fact that *per capita* productivity in urban employment increases more rapidly than in agriculture. When allowance is made for the town-country axis, it appears that the inequality of incomes in an underdeveloped economy will increase throughout the development process.

If the economic dualism is taken into consideration, the particularity of distribution in the underdeveloped countries lies in the existence of two distinct wage levels, one applying to the traditional sector covering the greater part of agriculture, small business and crafts and

[1] 'Economic Growth and Income Inequality', *American Economic Review*, March 1955, p. 1 *et seq.*

the other to the modern sector. The dualism of wages between the two sectors can be explained on the one hand by the imperfect mobility of the workers which reflects the marginal difference in productivity between the two sectors, but also by the fact that legislation on the minimum wage,[1] on health insurance and on family allowances are applied and are in fact applicable only in modern firms; furthermore, the rise in the cost of living in the towns (of rents, in particular) strengthens the tendency for wages in the modern sector to increase.

As regards the price of capital (i.e. interest) the situation is inverted and it seems more costly in the traditional sector than in the modern sector. Several reasons can be proposed : access to the banks is easier in the modern sector, the practice of usury endures in the traditional sector ; it costs less to set up machinery in coastal towns than in the countryside where means of transportation are often completely lacking ; machinery lasts longer in towns than in the country because of better standards of maintenance, etc.

Let us turn now to the profit aspect, where we see a number of sectors of activity such as petrol refining, steel, chemicals, cement, pharmaceutical products, etc., which use technical and financial procedures that are not available to local artisans and small industries. These branches make high monopoly profits. On the other hand, there are a number of activities where modern techniques are faced with stiff competition from small independent producers (e.g. shoes, bricks, clothing, road transport). In this particular instance, there is a self-limitation of profits which comes from competition between sectors and not from competition between a large number of firms of the same size as was the case in Europe in the nineteenth century.

The isolation of the peasants in the traditional sector is responsible for the appearance of a new income category, the middlemen. They correspond to the remuneration given for providing a distribution service. L. W. Shannon has calculated that, in India, 50 per cent of the price paid to peasants is used to pay middlemen.[2]

If the geographical criterion is chosen, our thoughts spring immediately to the very marked disparities existing in developing countries between the different regions. This regional inequality has its influence on distribution. In this respect, Myrdal writes : [3] 'in assessing regional inequality, if we take as simple a yardstick as

---

[1] In almost the whole of the north-east of Brazil, there is virtually no wage for the rural worker ; tenant-farmer legislation is non-existent.

[2] L. W. Shannon, *Under-developed Areas*, Harper, New York, 1957, p. 15.

[3] G. Myrdal, 'Théorie économique et pays sous-développés', *Présence Africaine*, Paris, 1959, p. 46.

the proportion of the country's total population living in regions where the average income is less than two-thirds the national average, we will find that this proportion amounts to a very low percentage in Great Britain and Switzerland, to about 10 per cent in places like Norway and France, and almost 30 per cent in Italy, Turkey, and Spain'. If we apply this criterion to the so-called underdeveloped countries, it can be postulated that the proportion ranges from 50 to 75 per cent. Moreover, whereas these regional gaps are tending to narrow in the developed countries, they are tending to widen in the backward economies in the absence of any intervention from the state. This discovery is significant since it raises the delicate problem of the regional redistribution of the national income.

If the ethnic criterion is adopted, the profound difference in income distribution by race is brought to light. According to M. Capet,[1] in 1951, the white minority in former French West Africa represented 0·3 per cent of the population and possessed 16·4 per cent of the national income, while the Africans accounted for 99·7 per cent of the population and received 73·6 per cent of the national income.

Even after the ending of colonial status, income discrimination on a racial basis still exists, and accession to independence has changed nothing in this respect. Theodore Morgan [2] has attempted to give an idea of the income distribution by race in Ceylon :

TABLE 3

INCOME DISTRIBUTION BY RACE IN CEYLON

Races	% of Families in Sample	Rupees per Month (average income)
Europeans	0·01	...
Other non-defined races	0·2	219
Indian Moors	0·2	215
Eurasians	0·9	207
Malayans	0·4	144
Ceylonese Moors	5·0	117
Ceylonese Tamils	12·0	107
Indian Tamils	10·0	106
Sinhalese	71·0	89

[1] M. Capet, *Traité d'économie tropicale.* Librairie générale de Droit et de Jurisprudence, Paris, 1958, p. 253.
[2] T. Morgan, 'Income Distribution in Developed and Underdeveloped Countries', *Economic Journal*, December 1953, pp. 821 *et seq.*

With less complete statistics, we have recorded the following substantial differences in the average annual *per capita* income for Madagascar :

TABLE 4

INCOME DISTRIBUTION BY RACE IN MADAGASCAR

Races	Average Annual Income (C.F.A. francs)
Indians and Chinese	1,000,000
French	850,000
Réunion Islanders	300,000
Malagasies	22,000

It can be concluded from these statistical analyses that :

—The oldest race, the original inhabitants of the country, is to be found at the bottom of the income scale ;
—The racial differences maintain a psychological climate favourable to income inequality and tending to perpetuate traditional inequalities ;
—The racial differences are no doubt much greater than those found in certain Western countries in respect of partially assimilated peoples (the Negroes in the U.S.A. for example.)

VII. CONCLUSIONS

At the end of this kaleidoscopic review of the problem of income distribution in underdeveloped countries and having examined the problem under all its facets, I feel prompted to make three observations :

(1) There is a marked lack of information on distribution in underdeveloped countries. Little reliable quantitative data exists on distribution of the national income in underdeveloped countries.
(2) The figures obtained from national statistics for this type of study are open to question. The self-consumed fraction of the agricultural product is now estimated at only a sixth in industrialized countries, while in an underdeveloped country it may be more than half. In a developed economy, national statistics attempt to make the aggregate totals homogeneous,

but in a backward economy they should reflect the heterogeneity of the sectors, regions, races, and so on. Transposition of the methods merely gives a false picture of the facts.

(3) It is quite possible that the inequalities of income in underdeveloped countries will persist for the next few decades. This will be due not only to growth requirements but also to the absence of dynamic forces capable of combating the concentration of private fortune effectively. Except in those countries which have gone beyond the take-off stage, there is little chance of seeing an increase in the income of the lower classes.

In fact, as Alfredo Pareto has already stressed : 'income distribution depends on the distribution of the qualities enabling men to grow rich, but also — and perhaps to a greater degree — on the location of the obstacles impeding the use of these faculties'.

DISCUSSION OF PROFESSOR GENDARME'S PAPER

Professor Ducros said that he thought that the timing of Professor Gendarme's paper was particularly apt, following as it did a session in which methodological problems of adapting distribution theories and models to underdeveloped countries had proved to be one of the main points of contention. Some speakers had advocated a drastic revision of the standard analysis of distribution whereas others denied any necessity whatsoever.

In a stimulating, provocative paper, Professor Gendarme criticized the usual analytical methods which he classed under four headings : the classical approach, the Marxist approach, the econometrical approach, and the sociological approach. Professor Ducros was dubious about the use of the English term 'approach' which implied that each of the four 'approaches' was a mutually exclusive way of dealing with the same problem. This was obviously not true. If one could oppose the Marxist and classical approaches, he did not think it possible to make such a simple distinction between the more modern sociological and econometrical 'approaches'. One could, of course, oppose sociological theory and neo-classical theory, but this latter did not figure in Professor Gendarme's paper. From quite another point of view one could oppose an institutional and an econometrical approach. But one should not, he considered, confuse these two types of alternatives in such a way as to

388

conclude that econometrics and sociological analysis were mutually exclusive. This would be regrettable as both types of analysis had their own place and were necessary to a complete study of income distribution.

Professor Ducros thought that Professor Gendarme, in summing up the classical theory in relation to distribution in underdeveloped countries, had weighed quite fairly the pros and cons. He would agree with him that, in focusing their income distribution theory on land ownership and the differential rent, the classics had tried to explain situations which were much akin to those in underdeveloped countries today. Professor Ducros regretted, however, that in his criticism of the classical approach Professor Gendarme had not clearly distinguished between two kinds of objections, i.e. those relating to a purely functional conception of income distribution and those relating to a theory of distribution founded on factor prices only.

Although there was a close connection between both, had Professor Gendarme criticized the factor prices theory of distribution as such this might have led him to give proper recognition to the neo-classical theory when listing the 'approaches'. Professor Ducros had been interested by what Professor Gendarme had written (pp. 368–370) about' parasitic' incomes earned by money-lenders, middlemen, and the like. But why did these kinds of people fare so well in underdeveloped economies? Professor Ducros thought that there would be some close connection between this type of gain and grave imperfections in the functioning of market mechanisms and this, at any rate, the neo-classical theory could take in its stride, explaining its bearing on factor remunerations.

Professor Ducros none the less preferred an income distribution theory based on personal rather than on functional distribution, as did Professor Gendarme. Professor Gendarme's brave endeavour to adapt personal distribution theory to conditions in underdeveloped economies led Professor Ducros to suggest two lines of thought.

Having in mind what Professor Gendarme called either 'parasitic incomes' or 'false incomes' and their importance in final distribution, Professor Ducros thought there was first an urgent need to rethink the distinction between earned income and transfer incomes. In Western societies the distinction between the two was clear-cut : earned incomes were accruing to one simple, well-defined unit of income and expenditure — the household in social accounting terms — and the public sector, as including public finance and the social security system, was alone instrumental in redistributing incomes in accordance with the limited object of correcting some of the social consequences of productivity and price mechanisms.

In being transposed to other human circles the distinction between income earned by productive agents and transfer incomes became blurred : in between there was room for many factors of social solidarity which made for some percolation of primary incomes into wider social groups — no longer was the household the income receiving and consuming unit, but the larger family, the tribal group or political clientele, replaced it. This, as well as other institutional factors mentioned by Professor Gendarme, such as corruption, smuggling, and gambling could be described as factors making for a diffusion of income through larger and more imprecise units than defined by standard national accounting.

Professor Ducros said that he had insisted on this point with a view to giving an answer to a vexed problem. Economists were always impressed by how large income disparities were in underdeveloped countries. Giving their explanations for income inequality was a favourite subject. But Professor Ducros would like to reverse the question : how was it that so many people could get along, however badly, with incomes apparently under subsistence level ? In some cases there was clearly a case for redressing statistical data which were biased so as to underestimate incomes, especially those received in kind, as had been pointed out by Professor Reder in a former session of the Conference. But Professor Ducros would venture to suggest that through the permeability of income, so to speak, hidden redistribution diminished income inequality and enabled the poorest to survive.

In adapting income distribution analysis to underdevelopment a second and more general object should be the way personal incomes were received independently of redistribution. In this connection, as an example of specific conditions in underdeveloped countries, Professor Ducros pointed to the frequent occurrence of the same person having several jobs, each supposed to be full time. It was understood by personal distribution theory that the same household could have several distinct sources of income at the same time, but this was something of a paradox for the theory when the same man could get simultaneously several incomes from one and the same capacity to work. This sort of situation briefly mentioned by Professor Gendarme was again a case of scraping a living. Any observations — and especially those based on tax returns data — which ignored such facts would give an incomplete and biased account of income distribution in underdeveloped countries.

Professor Gendarme's main interest had been to classify income groups as social categories. Professor Ducros thought that the most stimulating developments in his paper were those relating to the society in transition. He had attributed the originality of the societies in the process of transition to the appearance of three new classes : a class of capitalists, still in an embryonic state, of civil servants and of army officers, the last two being the really powerful emerging forces (p. 376 in the paper). As he had written *supra* (p. 381), it might be that social climbing should no longer be related to money-making through capital accumulation but to education giving access to public service and army careers.

No matter how relevant this was to social conditions in transitional societies, Professor Ducros would, however, question the significance of this analysis. To what extent could this really help in determining income distribution ? Army officers, for instance, could form a social group but would this group still stand on its own not as, say, a pressure group but as a social-occupational category in a distribution theory ? Professor Ducros feared that this could lead to confusion between politics and economics and he felt uncomfortably confirmed in his fear when Professor Gendarme (p. 379 in the paper) made a parallel between army *coups d'état* and workers' strikes. He would rather not bridge the gap between an instrument of political power, no matter its economic implications, and a means of advancing money claims, no matter its political implications.

Professor Ducros was aware of the role played by civil servants and the army in these countries but he wondered whether such features, which seemed so important in a society in transition, were not themselves transitory. The present set-up might simply mean that whereas these countries had rapidly succeeded in establishing a numerous, powerful, and well-paid body of civil servants and army officers, they had not yet been able to build up prosperous industries on a nation-wide basis. The rise of a class of entrepreneurs might follow if development was carried through under a fairly liberal regime, or of a class of managers if socialism prevailed, or of a combination of both classes under a mixed regime.

Professor Ducros concluded by saying that although he felt drawn towards the sociological approach to income distribution he would not go as far as defining economic systems on the basis of group behaviour because he thought that the differentiation of groups and the pattern of social tensions was no more than a reflection of the prevailing economic conditions in a given society at a given moment. The economist, unlike the political scientist or the sociologist, should reason on the assumption that social tensions were the expression rather than the cause of economic phenomena.

Professor Bronfenbrenner said that he thought it misleading to base distribution theory on group analysis because any such groupings are often arbitrary. He failed to see why one set of five, ten, or fifteen groups was more relevant than any other.

Nor would he make a clear-cut distinction between developed and underdeveloped countries on this point. Differences in social patterns amongst underdeveloped countries were at least as important as between developed and underdeveloped ones. In some countries, especially in the Far East, classification according to social groups might lead to the following : students ; priests of one or more major religions, these two groups being the most powerful social forces ; then the many indigenous castes, and last and least, such underprivileged foreigners as, for instance, Koreans in Japan or Chinese in Thailand.

Professor Bronfenbrenner detected some one-sidedness in certain illustrations introduced by Professor Gendarme in support of his theses. To the host of facts which he gave in his paper one could add still more :

robbery, for instance, as a form of taxation and therefore of income and wealth redistribution. All these of course were facts, but how representative were they? What did they signify? Would not criminal profits or gambling gains be found outside underdeveloped countries and was not speculation on land and building sites as intense in other countries? It would require only a little blackening of the process of distribution in the U.S.A. to give a picture similar to Professor Gendarme's.

Professor Bronfenbrenner had also detected in the paper some idealization of young army officers wishing to reform society. If he thought there was some value in positing laws of sociological behaviour in economics he would be ready to propose, as Bronfenbrenner's nth Law, that when any group of young army officers seized power to reform society there was a 99 per cent chance they would be corrupted themselves before they got started on the job.

Professor Delivanis thought that Professor Gendarme had been very harsh on speculators (p. 369 in the paper). In less developed countries, political and economic conditions being unstable, a positive return on investment might not last for long. The expectations of gains might be higher than in developed countries but so were the risks of capital losses.

Concerning the data which Professor Gendarme had quoted (p. 386) about income inequalities according to ethnic groups in former French colonies in Western Africa, Professor Delivanis thought that such inequalities were not due to market mechanisms but to repercussions of political conditions in that period. The paying of local civil servants there according to French salary scales was a good illustration of this point.

Professor Gendarme had written that 'in underdeveloped economies the struggle [did] not seem to have been between the capitalist and the proletarian classes but between the colonizers and the colonized' (p. 371). Professor Delivanis would like this statement to be qualified so as to take into account the existence in many countries of a class of poor whites who were amongst the exploited rather than the exploiters.

Professor Solow thought that there was more loss than gain in talking of 'alternative' approaches. The fourfold distinction made by Professor Gendarme in his paper related to different schools of thought which might be trying to answer quite different questions.

Professor Gendarme's paper offered many interesting insights into distribution but nowhere did he try to answer such traditional questions as : how would a gift of capital affect the rate of profit in the receiving country? How would changes in tariffs affect real wages? These were questions which Professor Solow felt a distribution theory should answer.

Professor Solow suspected that what seemed on the surface to be an explicit struggle between social groups might be the reflection and not the cause of economic facts. There had been much talk of the impact of trade unions on income distribution in the previous session of the Conference. Obviously one ought to try to measure the influence of collective bargaining on wage levels. Now this was difficult but all the available evidence pointed towards its having only a small effect. Thus one should be very cautious in assessing the role played by social forces in income distribution.

Professor Patinkin feared that the line of reasoning in Professor Gendarme's paper would make for complete indeterminacy of income distribution. For instance Professor Gendarme had written : 'Even when it exists social legislation is not applied in the countryside, so that the owner or manager of a large agricultural estate is completely free to decide on how much he will pay his employees' (p. 363). Now if it were so, why would he pay them anything ? The wage rate could be zero !

Referring to the Table on page 380 where Professor Gendarme had listed social tensions over distribution in underdeveloped countries he questioned how specific they were with respect both to countries and distribution. Not only were they to be found in other countries but he was not sure that they could occur only over distribution and not on grounds other than economic.

Professor Gendarme said that he was surprised that Professor Ducros and Professor Solow had criticized him for having opposed 'approaches'. Such an opposition was neither in the spirit nor in the letter of his paper : he had just meant to give a list of the various methods through which income distribution could be approached.

Professor Ducros had criticized him for not having mentioned neoclassical theory but Professor Gendarme did not believe it to be applicable to underdeveloped countries.

In respect of national accounting, whereas Professor Ducros had suggested that one should try to revise national income analysis to fit income distribution in underdeveloped countries, Professor Gendarme thought there were too many obstacles in the way of national income evaluation in these countries to make the results sufficiently reliable. It could lead to paradoxical results. For instance, value added in the public sector being reckoned at factor costs meant that an increasing number of public servants, even if they were redundant, would increase national income.

Professor Gendarme agreed with Professor Ducros' remarks on the importance and specific nature of transfer incomes in underdeveloped economies and admitted the implied criticism for his not having tackled them in a more systematic way in his paper. Even though there was no mention of the word in his paper he had, however, recognized the importance of transfer income by stressing that in less-developed countries there were many activities representing distribution without production. Professor Ducros had also pointed to the superposition of incomes ; this clearly existed in certain cases and he agreed with Professor Ducros' analysis.

Professor Ducros had criticized him for confusing economics with

393

politics. Professor Gendarme would answer that it was very hard to draw a line between the two in countries where they were so closely connected. He was not sure that a clear distinction could always be made between them even in developed countries. Could Professor Ducros distinguish in, say, France between a purely economic strike and a political one ?

Professor Delivanis had thought him fierce with speculators but Professor Gendarme's intention had been to stress the fact that the speculator-mentality of entrepreneurs led them to hold outsize cash balances instead of spending on investment and this could hinder economic growth.

Professor Gendarme wished to say before the debate was closed how surprised he had been not to have been asked how the demographic factor related to income distribution and development. This seemed to him a basic issue. Would too much pressure of population on resources prevent development ? Any drastic conclusion would have to be qualified in the light of recent observations. Within certain limits, it seemed that an increasing population could press on resources in a way conducive to development. It was still an open problem and Professor Gendarme regretted that it had not been discussed.

Chapter 15

THE DISTRIBUTION OF NATIONAL
INCOME IN AFRICAN COUNTRIES

BY

PIUS OKIGBO

Embassy of Nigeria, Brussels

I. INTRODUCTORY

OUR problem is to examine the distribution of national income in
African countries. It divides easily into two branches : the distribution of the national income functionally, that is, by factor shares,
and the distribution of personal income by size. Each of these two
branches has its own special interest for developing countries and
particularly for countries that have only recently emerged from
colonial or dependent status. Each of them has also been canvassed
in the literature but the setting has invariably been in the context of
the highly industrialized countries. An analysis of the problem
posed can be undertaken for a single country if the data permit of
an intertemporal comparison or for a group of countries if the data
permit of international comparisons. Neither procedure is easy in
African countries and it will be a partial object of this paper to
indicate the gaps in the data, the approximations possible in the
absence of suitable material and what further work needs to be done
to bridge the gap.

II. FACTOR SHARES

The problem of the functional distribution of the national income
is as old as economics itself. It featured significantly in the works
of Ricardo and Marx. The interest was twofold : how are the
relative shares of labour, capital, and land determined ? Secondly,
is there a pattern in their behaviour over time ? In the Ricardian
scheme, rent was determined on a marginalist principle — by the
difference between the product of labour on 'marginal' land and

the product of labour on good land ; the share of wages and profits, on the other hand, was determined as a residue or a surplus such that an increase in the wages fund necessarily reduces the share of profits. Marx went further than Ricardo and argued that as wages were tied to the subsistence level, a rise in the wage bill necessarily brought capitalist production nearer to its crisis through a reduction in profits. In a capitalistic system, therefore, the share of wages in output must be held down even when output per head was rising. This tendency can only be averted though the organization of the working class which will reduce the degree of exploitation by winning some of the surplus value back to labour. As Kaldor [1] has pointed out, this hypothesis leads, at best, to a constancy in the share of labour.

Herein lies one of the reasons for an interest in the problem of functional distribution in neo-colonial economies. The division of productive factors between labour (contributed mainly by the dependent country) and capital (contributed mainly by the dominant country) is particularly appropriate for the application of the Marxian doctrine of exploitation. It is a doctrine in which the dominant power is bound to be the villain. If the share of wages in the output is falling, it is a sign of the weakness of the working class of the dependent country ; if the share is constant, it is only a sign of the reduction of the degree of exploitation by the colonial power.

In newly independent countries this type of argument can no longer hold the same fascination as it held previously. The nationals of the newly independent countries can no longer throw at the door of the imperialist metropolitan powers the charge of exploitation. Now they have to face the charge — if the Marxian thesis is still fashionable — of exploitation of Africans by Africans themselves and this is bound to evoke stronger social protest than exploitation of Africans by colonial powers.

No doubt there is another source of interest in the problem of income distribution. The study of business cycles has raised the question whether the relative shares tend to be affected differentially in the various phases of the business cycle. There is no conclusive evidence on this although the available data suggest that the relative share of labour has maintained remarkable stability in the short and in the long run in the United States and in Britain.

From this it is easy to move into the issues raised by economic

---

[1] Nicholas Kaldor, 'Alternative Theories of Distribution', reprinted in *Essays on Value and Distribution* (London, Duckworth, 1960), p. 218.

growth. Recent interest in the process of growth has thrown up anew some old questions : will the relative shares of factors show the same stability in the process of growth as has been observed in the United States and in the United Kingdom ? Will the rapid economic growth of newly emerging African countries result in the immiseration of the poor ? Unquestionably, the rapid growth in *per capita* incomes is the most important objective of policy since it is almost always accompanied by an improvement in the incomes of the lowest income groups. However, the distribution of income can become more unequal if the incomes of the lowest groups increase less fast than those of the higher groups. In this situation, there is a relative not absolute immiseration of the poor. These questions are of more than academic interest for they provide some clue to the social and political stability of many an African country.

There is evidently no unanimity about what the data show for the developed countries. Using the United States Department of Commerce data, Denison[1] came to the conclusion that, between 1929 and 1950, the share of employment income in the national output rose secularly, and that the share of labour as a whole (after corrections have been made for the income of self-employed) also rose during the period. For the period 1920–29, Kuznets[2] found little change in the relative share of labour. These data provided the basis for Fellner's judgement that over the long haul of fifty to a hundred years there has been some rise in the relative share of labour in the Western world.[3]

The other set of evidence comes from Kalecki.[4] His analysis of figures for 1881–1924 and 1911–35 for the United Kingdom and for 1919–34 for the United States of America showed remarkable stability in the share of labour. There were, of course, variations in between the terminal dates. However, from Tables 1 and 2 below we see that the share of wages in the home-produced national

[1] E. F. Denison, 'Distribution of National Income : Pattern of Income Shares since 1929', *Survey of Current Business*, June 1952.
[2] Simon Kuznets, 'Economic Growth and Income Inequality', *American Economic Review*, **55**, 1955 ; also 'Long-Term Changes in the National Income of the United States of America Since 1870', *Income and Wealth*, Series II (Bowes and Bowes, 1952).
[3] William Fellner, *Trends and Cycles in Economic Activity* (New York : Holt, 1956), p. 263 ; but see also L. J. Zimmerman, *Economic Growth, Development and Progress* (forthcoming) in which he argues that this is probably not valid for the first phase of development in spite of increases in *per capita* income.
[4] M. Kalecki, 'The Distribution of the National Income', AEA *Readings in the Theory of Income Distribution* (Blackiston, 1949), pp. 199–200 ; see also, *Theory of Economic Dynamics* (London : Allen and Unwin, 1954), pp. 28–41 ; more recent figures are available but we cannot enter into this controversy here.

397

The Distribution of National Income

income of Britain was very much the same in 1924 (40·6 per cent) as in 1881–85 (40·0 per cent) and the share of manual labour in the national income varied only between 40·7 per cent in 1911 and 43·7 per cent (in 1931) in the interval 1911–35. Similarly, Table 3 shows that in the United States the shares of manual labour in the national income varied in the period 1919–34 from 34·9 per cent in 1919 to 39·3 per cent in 1923 but otherwise was relatively stable.

TABLE 1

RELATIVE SHARE OF WAGES
IN THE HOME PRODUCED NATIONAL INCOME
OF GREAT BRITAIN

Year	Per cent
1881–85	40·0
1901–05	39·8
1911–13	37·1
1924	40·6

Source : Kalecki, *Theory of Economic Dynamics*.

TABLE 2

RELATIVE SHARE OF MANUAL LABOUR
IN THE NATIONAL INCOME OF GREAT BRITAIN

Year	Per cent	Year	Per cent
1911	40·7	1929	42·4
1924	43·0	1931	43·7
1925	40·8	1932	43·0
1926	42·0	1934	42·0
1927	43·0	1935	41·8

Source : Kalecki, 'The Distribution of the National Income'.

TABLE 3

RELATIVE SHARE OF MANUAL LABOUR
IN THE NATIONAL INCOME OF THE U.S.A.

Year	Per cent	Year	Per cent
1919	34·9	1926	36·7
1920	37·4	1927	37·0
1921	35·0	1929	36·1
1922	37·0	1930	35·0
1923	39·3	1931	34·9
1924	37·6	1934	35·8

Source : Kalecki, 'The Distribution of the National Income'.

Many explanations have been offered for this observed pheno-menon. On the one hand, the influence of the development of trade unionism in Britain and the United States could have con-tributed to the maintenance of labour's share in the product. But so also has the existence of monopoly tended to increase the share of profits. Similarly, changes in the movement of raw material and other prices relative to wage costs, changes in the composition of output, the changes in the rate of investment as well as in the pro-pensity to consume of the workers relative to the capitalists — each of these as Joan Robinson [1] has reminded us, provides a partial explanation. Most of the attempts to measure the share of labour use the Cobb–Douglas production function ; it is therefore hardly surprising the result should show a relative constancy.

However interesting this line of enquiry may be we cannot pursue it here ; our first task is to establish the facts in respect of the African countries. We run almost immediately into two major obstacles. First, there is no single African country for which a respectable time series exists or whose time series, if it exists, is sufficiently articulated. Second, we can make meaningful international com-parisons only if our data are strictly comparable for several countries. This last problem, however, is less serious since the francophone countries in Africa all have a reasonably uniform system of accounts (unlike the English-speaking group who on the surface follow the UN Standard system but, in practice, have often incomparable data). [2]

For an analysis of factor shares national accounts data are now available for the following countries for the years shown in brackets after them : Nigeria (1950–57), Ghana (1958–60), Kenya (1955–60), Uganda (1955–60), Senegal (1956–59), Ivory Coast (1958–60), Dahomey (1955–59), Sudan (1956–59), Mali (1959), Upper Volta (1956–59), Niger (1956–60), Togo (1956–58), Congo (Brazzaville) (1956–58), Gabon (1956–60), Tchad (1956–58), Cameroun (1951–59).

Now, how far can we go with these accounts in displaying the relative shares of factors in these economies ? We offer two sugges-tions. First, we can attempt to show the share of employment income

---

[1] Joan Robinson, *Collected Economic Papers*, vol. ii (Oxford : Blackwell, 1960), pp. 145–158. Attention may be drawn here to J. T. Dunlop's *Wage Determination under Trade Unions* (New York, 1944), pp. 176 *et seq.* for additional determinants of the share of wages in the national income over the business cycle.

[2] See the admirable attempt by P. Ady and M. Courcier, *Systems of National Accounts in Africa* (OEEC, 1960) to make the two systems directly comparable. Of the English-speaking territories, Nigeria followed the output approach, Ghana the income and expenditure methods.

relative to the national income for the group of African countries for which national accounts data exist. It is not possible, in the present state of statistical knowledge, to probe this in depth for any single country in the same way as Kalecki or Denison have done for the United Kingdom and the United States. In the absence of firm data on the number of self-employed it is not easy to adjust the share of employment income to reflect the share of labour as a whole. The process of change from a predominantly traditional economy to an exchange economy will generate a movement from self-employment in agriculture to wage employment in the other sectors.[1] It is difficult to speculate on what the figures for African countries should look like if we were to show the share of labour.

Second, we can attempt to show the relative share of urban to rural income. This division of the national income between the rural and urban sectors is of greater interest in developing than in the developed countries because it reflects the degree of commercialization of activity and the stage of economic progress. An approximation to rural income can be obtained from the income originating in agriculture, while the residue (secondary, tertiary and other) can be classified as urban income. Crops are valued at producer prices and the value added by trade in agriculture is treated as part of urban income.

Table 4 below shows the share of employment income in the national output of several African countries. Several qualifications must be made to any interpretation we attach to these figures. First, employment income covers wages and salaries in establishments employing ten or more persons. Since wage-earning employment in agriculture (outside of the plantations) and in retail trade are invariably in establishments employing less than ten persons, the coverage of the figures excludes the two most important activities. In some countries (e.g. Ghana) some adjustment has been made (no details are available) to allow for smaller establishments; in others (e.g. Nigeria) no such adjustments have been made. The second is that wage income figures exclude payments in kind and other hidden emoluments. In the higher reaches of the civil service this can represent a substantial sum. Third, the sources of the data are not uniform — some come from direct employment and earnings surveys; some, as in the Congo (Leo.), represent an extrapolation (to 1958) of the only extant survey (1950); some, as in the Rhodesias,

[1] See L. J. Zimmerman, *Economic Growth, Development and Progress* (forthcoming), pp. 120–122.

Okigbo — Distribution in African Countries

represent an amalgamation of several sources : surveys of employment and earnings, censuses of agriculture and production, censuses of population. Finally, the whole basis of the enquiries is made all the weaker by the lack (total in some countries) of suitable demographic data.

TABLE 4

SHARE OF WAGES IN THE NATIONAL INCOME
OF SELECTED AFRICAN COUNTRIES (1958)

Country		Income from Employment	GDP at Market Prices	Employment Income % GDP
Congo (Brazz.)	(mill. CFA)	(1958) 11·1	18·4	60·3
Rhodesia and Nyasaland	(mill. £)	(1958) 220·6	471·8	46·8
Congo (Leo.)	(mill. BF)	(1958) 27·5	63·5	43·3
Kenya	(mill. £)	(1958) 85·5	208·0	41·4
Madagascar	(mill. CFA)	(1956) 30·9	89·5	34·5
Senegal	(mill. CFA)	(1959) 41·6	120·8	34·4
Gabon	(mill. CFA)	(1956) 4·3	13·5	31·9
Cameroun	(mill. CFA)	(1959) 26·3	89·0	29·8
Uganda	(mill. £)	(1958) 32·5	119·9	27·1
Ghana	(mill. £)	(1958) 92·0	341·4	26·9
Dahomey	(mill. CFA)	(1959) 7·0	29·8	23·5
Mali	(mill. CFA)	(1959) 11·6	60·1	19·3
Ivory Coast	(mill. CFA)	(1960) 22·9	131·0	17·5
Tchad	(mill. CFA)	(1958) 5·2	35·9	14·5
Niger	(mill. CFA)	(1960) 5·7	43·6	13·1
Togo	(mill. CFA)	(1958) 3·0	23·6	12·7

Source : P. Ady and M. Courcier, *System of National Accounts in Africa*, 1960. M. Courcier and G. Hegarat, *Planification en Afrique*, vol. 3.

We now draw attention to the low proportions for Tchad, Togo, Niger, Mali, Ivory Coast on the one hand and for Gabon, Congo (Brazzaville), Rhodesia, Kenya, and Congo (Leo.) on the other. The wide variation cannot be accounted for by statistical differences alone. Again in Table 5 showing the share of rural income in the gross domestic product of selected African countries, we draw attention to the relatively high figures for Niger, Tchad, Mali, Togo, and Dahomey. Since the two sets of figures in Tables 4 and 5 reflect the degree of commercialization of activity, it is not surprising that the same countries should show up on the same side of the line in each case. However, we must restrain ourselves from jumping to

strong conclusions : the figures do not tell us more than they purport
to tell, namely, that at any given point of time there is a wide variation in the economic structure and in the degree of urbanization in
African economies. To read more than this into the figures would
be to make unwarranted inferences.

TABLE 5

DISTRIBUTION OF NATIONAL INCOME
BETWEEN RURAL AND URBAN SECTORS
IN SELECTED AFRICAN COUNTRIES

Country	Year	GDP at Factor Cost mill. units (1)	Rural Income mill. units (2)	Col. (2) as % of Col. (1) per cent (3)
Niger	(1959)	42·7	36·9	86·4
Tchad	(1958)	34·7	25·4	73·2
Upper Volta	(1959)	37·5	26·0	69·0
Dahomey	(1959)	26·5	17·9	67·5
Mali	(1959)	55·0	35·7	64·9
Togo	(1958)	21·7	14·1	64·9
Ivory Coast	(1960)	115·3	71·2	61·8
Nigeria	(1957)	910·0	555·7	61·6
Cameroun	(1959)	82·4	49·8	60·4
Madagascar	(1956)	76·1	41·6	54·7
Congo (Brazz.)	(1957)	16·0	6·9	43·1
Senegal	(1959)	91·6	37·4	40·8
Gabon	(1960)	24·7	7·6	30·7

Source : H. Leroux and Jean Pierre Allier, *Planification en Afrique*, vol. 4.

III. PERSONAL INCOME DISTRIBUTION

We now turn to the distribution of personal income by size. The
mathematics of personal income distribution is fully developed in
the literature and has been applied to the data of developed countries.
In most cases, the comparison between countries and periods has
been undertaken with the aid of Pareto's law (other measures of
inequality or concentration, for example the Gibrat measure, have
also been developed). These measures have helped to refine the
statistics of distribution and to bring out the pattern observed in the
more advanced countries.

Available evidence also suggests that Pareto's constant α for incomes before taxes has risen in most advanced countries during the last forty years.[1] An agrarian community tends to have a greater degree of homogeneity and therefore more equal income distribution (this may be disputed by the evidence in the Middle East). Greater urbanization and industrialization will generate job differentiation and encourage income inequalities with increasing *per capita* incomes. This tendency will continue for a while until countervailing forces are set in motion which tend to reduce the inequalities. These forces consist of social welfare schemes, widening opportunities for education, greater occupational mobility, and development of tax systems.

In the Western world while there has been a shift towards a more equal distribution of personal income, at the same time there has been no significant change in the relative share of labour in the national output. For this disparity Fellner offered three reasons.[2] First, corporate income taxes are not deducted from the total income in relation to which the share of labour is determined. But personal incomes do not include corporate income taxes which appear to have risen relatively to national income. Second, the same observation holds true of undistributed profits. Consequently, the share of the top income classes in a personal income distribution does not reflect in full the significance of what is allotted to them in the statistics of functional distribution. The third reason is that in the aggregate of wage incomes there has been a shift towards smaller income differentials which do not show up in the pattern of functional distribution.

In the face of statistical difficulties in African countries, we have attempted two types of analysis which under-score the problems involved. First, we have set out the pattern of income distribution available from tax data in Nigeria. Table 6 shows the distribution of personal income before taxes. We are restricted by the data to a definition of income derived from the requirements of fiscal authorities. In Nigeria, the definition of income for tax purposes covers wages and salaries and income receipts from property but excludes gifts and allowances. This last source could be quite substantial for the upper bracket. Consequently, an analysis of incomes based on tax data is bound to understate the incomes in the higher income

[1] See for example, H. F. Lydall and J. B. Lansing, 'Distribution of Personal Income and Wealth in the United States and Great Britain', *American Economic Review*, 49, March 1959, pp. 43–66 ; Jan Tinbergen, *Selected Papers* (Amsterdam : North Holland Publishing Co., 1959), pp. 222–262.

[2] William Fellner, *op. cit.*, pp. 267–270.

brackets and thereby distort the picture of the degree of inequality between high and low incomes. The most glaring weakness of the data is clearly the fact that the lowest income range relates to incomes under £500 per annum. In a country where *per capita* incomes are less than £35 per annum, it is obviously absurd to demarcate the lowest income group at £0–£500 per annum. Without doubt, the distribution at the tail end is likely to be relatively even ; but we are interested in the tail because it is where the bulk of the population is to be found.

A further qualification is that the data are taken from tax returns in Lagos Federal territory and refer only to the inhabitants of Lagos in 1959 or to those outside Lagos who fall within the income tax net (elsewhere, most Nigerians pay direct or poll tax). As there is bound to be a high concentration of civil servants and expatriate income earners, the district covered by the figures cannot be considered fully representative of the country.

Additional complications are introduced by systematic errors in the response to tax enquiries. In Nigeria, in the absence of adequate demographic data, it is difficult to estimate the extent of tax evasion or avoidance. The system of assessment of non-wage incomes is very arbitrary and rough. As a result, only wage incomes are fairly adequately covered and there is bound, therefore, to be a bias in the records.

From Table 6 we see that 90 per cent of income units (the definition is taken from tax sources) earn approximately 44 per cent of the aggregate income. At the top of the scale, 2 per cent of the income units earn approximately 22 per cent of the total income or over £2,000 per annum per tax unit.

It would indeed be helpful for further work in this field to have similar data for other countries and to have a fuller breakdown of the £0–£500 income class in Nigeria. Only by this means will it be possible to draw any inferences about the spread of inequality from country to country or of the extent of inequality in a single country.

The reasons for inequality of incomes (and of earnings) have been investigated by economists. It would be otiose for us to indulge here in that discussion. However, we can use the spread of differential reward for skills as a basis for comparing the inequality in income distribution in different countries. For example, in Tables 7 and 8 we have set out in absolute and in proportionate terms the earnings in different occupations in different countries in Africa. We have taken the earnings of general manual labour as a bench

TABLE 5

DISTRIBUTION OF PERSONAL INCOME BEFORE TAXES IN NIGERIA (1959)

Income Class £	Number of Income Units	Percentage of Income Units	Cumulative (from low Income upwards) Income Units	Percentage of Cumulative (upwards) Income Units	Cumulative (downwards) Income Units	Percentage of Cumulative (downwards) Income Units	Aggregate Income £000	Percentage of Aggregate Income £000	Cumulative (upwards) Aggregate Income	Percentage of Cumulative (upwards) Aggregate Income	Cumulative (downwards) Aggregate Income £000	Percentage of Cumulative (downwards) Aggregate Income
	1	2	3	4	5	6	7	8	9	10	11	12
Under 500	138,392	90·00	138,392	90·00	153,763	100·00	19,213	43·98	19,213	43·98	43,688	100·00
500–599	681	0·44	139,073	90·44	15,371	10·00	370	0·85	19,583	44·83	24,475	56·02
600–699	774	0·50	139,847	90·95	14,690	9·55	494	1·13	20,077	45·96	24,105	55·17
700–799	620	0·40	140,467	91·35	13,916	9·05	464	1·06	20,541	47·02	23,611	54·04
800–899	907	0·59	141,374	91·94	13,296	8·65	758	1·73	21,299	48·75	23,147	52·98
900–999	764	0·50	142,138	92·44	12,389	8·06	721	1·65	22,020	50·40	22,389	51·25
1000–1099	880	0·57	143,018	93·01	11,625	7·56	950	2·18	22,970	52·58	21,668	49·60
1100–1199	810	0·53	143,828	93·54	10,745	6·99	930	2·12	23,900	54·70	20,718	47·42
1200–1299	1,025	0·67	144,853	94·21	9,935	6·46	1,275	2·92	25,175	57·62	19,788	45·30
1300–1399	954	0·62	145,807	94·83	8,910	5·79	1,283	2·94	26,458	60·55	18,513	42·38
1400–1499	941	0·61	146,748	95·44	7,956	5·17	1,362	3·12	27,820	63·68	17,230	39·44
1500–1599	985	0·64	147,733	96·08	7,015	4·56	1,519	3·48	29,339	67·16	15,868	36·32
1600–1699	869	0·57	148,602	96·64	6,030	3·92	1,430	3·27	30,769	70·43	14,349	32·84
1700–1799	625	0·41	149,227	97·05	5,161	3·36	1,091	2·50	31,860	72·93	12,919	29·57
1800–1899	609	0·40	149,836	97·45	4,536	2·95	1,123	2·57	32,983	75·50	11,828	27·07
1900–1999	531	0·35	150,367	97·80	3,927	2·55	1,033	2·36	34,016	77·86	10,705	24·50
2000–2999	2,543	1·65	152,910	99·45	3,396	2·20	5,979	13·69	39,995	91·55	9,672	22·14
3000–3999	515	0·33	153,425	99·78	853	0·55	1,723	3·94	41,718	95·49	3,693	8·45
4000–4999	166	0·11	153,591	99·89	338	0·22	730	1·67	42,448	97·16	1,970	4·51
5000–9999	151	0·10	153,742	99·99	172	0·11	924	2·12	43,372	99·28	1,240	2·84
10000 and over	21	0·01	153,763	100·00	21	0·01	316	0·72	43,688	100·00	316	0·72
Total	153,763	100·00					43,688	100·00				

TABLE 7

DIFFERENTIAL HOURLY EARNINGS
IN DIFFERENT OCCUPATIONS
1956

Industry	Nigeria (pence)	Northern Rhodesia (pence)	Sierra Leone (pence)	Sudan (piastre)	Union of South Africa (pence)	Congo (Leo.) (B.F.)	Cameroun (C.F.A. Francs)	Senegal (C.F.A. Francs)	Ivory Coast (C.F.A Francs)
Bakery (ovenmen)	—	5·5	—	5·5	45·0	6·60	40·25	68·15	59·40
Textiles									
Labourers	—	5·5	—	—	—	5·25	—	31·00	28·20
Spinners	—	—	—	—	—	6·00	—	43·30	45·70
Weavers	—	—	—	—	—	—	—	68·15	75·45
Printing									
Labourers	9·90	5·5	—	3·5	—	4·50	22·25	31·00	28·20
Hand compositors	20·0	10·5	—	7·0	70·8	22·00	50·0	68·15	75·45
Machine compositors	32·0	10·5	—	7·5	79·1	24·50	47·50	68·15	75·45
Machinery Manufacture									
Labourers	—	—	7·5	3·5	13·4	4·50	—	—	—
Fitters	—	—	18·3	9·5	76·7	10·25	—	—	—
Construction									
Labourers	9·0	5·5	7·5	3·5	23·5	4·50	22·25	31·00	28·20
Painters	10·0	10·5	18·3	6·0	74·5	9·50	38·00	53·80	59·40
Bricklayers	18·0	10·5	—	—	79·5	6·60	38·00	44·30	59·40
Steel erectors	18·0	15·5	18·3	8·5	79·5	9·00	35·00	53·80	59·40

Source : ILO, *African Labour Survey* (Geneva, 1958).

TABLE 8

DIFFERENTIAL EARNINGS IN DIFFERENT OCCUPATIONS

1956

Industry	Nigeria	Northern Rhodesia	Sierra Leone	Sudan	Union of South Africa	Congo (Leo.)	Cameroun	Senegal	Ivory Coast
Bakery (ovenmen)	—	100	—	157	191	147	181	220	211
Textiles									
Labourers	—	100	—	—	—	117	—	100	100
Spinners	—	—	—	—	—	133	—	140	162
Weavers	—	—	—	—	—	—	—	220	277
Printing									
Labourers	100	100	—	100	—	100	100	100	100
Hand compositors	222	191	—	200	301	490	225	220	277
Machine compositors	360	191	—	215	337	545	213	220	277
Machinery Manufacture									
Labourers	—	—	100	100	57	100	—	—	—
Fitters	—	—	244	273	327	228	—	—	—
Construction									
Labourers	100	100	100	100	100	100	100	100	100
Painters	111	191	244	172	317	211	171	174	211
Bricklayers	200	191	—	—	338	147	171	143	211
Steel Erectors	200	282	244	243	338	200	157	174	211

Source : ILO, *African Labour Survey* (Geneva, 1958).

407

mark for reference and compared with them in different African countries the remuneration for different types of skills.

The results shown in Table 8 are certainly interesting. The range in the earnings of construction labour relative to machine compositors is lowest in Rhodesia and highest in Congo (Leo.) and midway between these two extremes is Nigeria. The influence of education, of availability of particular skills, of social policy, are all bound to have important consequences on the range in differential earnings for different occupations.

We now return to the questions with which we opened the discussion of this section. After examining the patterns of personal income distribution in ten countries, three of which (Ceylon, Puerto Rico, and El Salvador) are underdeveloped, Kravis came to the conclusion that there is a greater equality of income in the more advanced countries than in the less advanced countries and that economic development generates 'forces that operate to make the income distribution more equal'.[1] One question that comes to mind is whether inequality will deepen further with increases in *per capita* income in African countries ? Will the factors that have helped to reduce inequality in the advanced countries be effective in present-day Africa to produce the same result ?

Additional interest may spring from an investigation of the possible relationship between changes in income distribution and economic development through the impact of the former on the rate of saving. David Carney [2] investigating this in respect of Ghana and Nigeria was unable to go very far because of lack of adequate data. A similar exercise was carried out by O'Carrol [3] in respect of Cuba and Puerto Rico but the data referred to 1943 and 1946 respectively. No clearcut answer is possible since this depends on the assumptions we make about the relative propensities to save of the different income classes, of the size composition of these groups in the national total and on the extent of other mitigating factors, e.g., public investment, in the face of possible decline in private savings. O'Carrol found

[1] Irving Kravis, 'International Differences in the Distribution of Income', *Review of Economics and Statistics*, xlii, no. 4, 1960, p. 414. See also T. Morgan, 'Income Distribution in Developed and Underdeveloped Countries', *Economic Journal*, *63*, December 1953 ; United Nations Statistical Commission, *Statistics of the Distribution of Personal Income*, N.Y., 1957.

[2] David Carney, 'Income Distribution, Income Taxation and Economic Development', *The Indian Journal of Economics*, xli.

[3] F. M. O'Carrol, *Income Distribution in Relation to Economic Development* (Diploma Thesis, Institute of Social Studies, The Hague, 1959). See also K. J. E. Constas, *Personal Income Distribution in Australia* (Institute of Social Studies, The Hague, 1963).

that available evidence does not contradict the proposition that income distribution plays an insignificant role.

The main difficulties are first, that data on savings patterns are not available for most African countries. Surveys are few, and where they exist, they do not go far enough. Secondly, the lack of detailed demographic data makes it impossible to correlate changes in income distribution with changes in income per head. Obviously, therefore, there is an urgent need for data on population and on savings for a wide range of *per capita* income levels in African countries.

IV. CONCLUSION

From the foregoing discussion, we can only conclude that we are yet far from being able to undertake a thorough analysis of income distribution in African countries. The difficulties can, however, be overcome without putting undue strain on the limited statistical resources of the countries concerned. It is evident that the paucity of data stems from the concept of statistical priorities in the African countries : they are more concerned with measuring the increase in the national income than with measuring its distribution.[1] Consequently, the tabulation of existing data stops short just where it should begin to be interesting for an analysis of income distribution. For example, the tabulation of existing information on the tail of the personal income distribution obtainable from tax records in Nigeria need not impose a very heavy burden on the authorities. Yet, without this, it is impossible to use the tax data meaningfully to establish whether the process of growth has been accompanied by the immiseration of the poor. Social and fiscal policy, to be enlightened, must be based on some information on the progress of the incomes of the population.[2]

[1] This is not surprising. If incomes are rising fast enough for those in the lower income groups to move quickly into the higher income groups, distribution may no longer be a serious or urgent problem. See K. Galbraith's *The Affluent Society*.

[2] Dr. Okigbo was unable to be present at the Conference. In consequence his paper was not separately discussed in a seminar of the Conference, but it was available as background information to all participants.

PART IV

THEORIES OF DISTRIBUTION

Chapter 16

THE LAWS OF INCOME DISTRIBUTION
IN THE SHORT RUN AND IN THE
LONG RUN: AN AGGREGATIVE MODEL

BY

Dr. W. KRELLE
Bonn University

I. INTRODUCTION

MODERN distribution theories follow in the main three basic ideas.
The distribution of income is supposed to depend

(a) upon the *degree of monopoly*, i.e. political and sociological
factors determining the bargaining power of labour versus
capital (Oppenheimer [15], Preiser [16], [17], Kalecki [9], [10],
perhaps also Jean Marchal and Lecaillon [13]);

(b) upon the technological *laws of production*; this leads to the
neo-classical marginal productivity type of distribution theories
(v. Thünen [21], Jevons [7], Walras [22], J. B. Clark [4],
Wicksell [23], Douglas [5], Solow [19], and many others);

(c) upon the *consumption* and *saving habits* of the income receivers,
i.e. upon the general circulative process with particular
emphasis on the spending side (Boulding [3], Kaldor [8],
Bombach [1], [2], Erich Schneider [18], Föhl [6], Niehans [14],
Stobbe [20], and others). These authors follow more or less
the lines of the Keynesian system.

It should be evident that in each type of theory only one side of
reality is elaborated. To get a full picture of the reality, a theory
that would comprise all three ideas has to be developed. This — as
already undertaken in my book *Verteilungstheorie* [11], yet in a way
which made the theory incomprehensible for most of the readers —
will be the topic of this paper.

In addition the relation between the short-run and the long-run
laws of distribution will be discussed. There are some fundamental
differences indeed. This side of the problem has been rather
neglected in the literature.

413

The Distribution of National Income

The basic idea of this paper is to formulate a reasonable and realistic consumption and investment function describing the spending pattern of households and entrepreneurs. In real terms and in the long run the increase of demand cannot exceed or fall short of the increase in the capacity of production. Hence we may infer a difference equation for the real national income as a function of income distribution. It will be shown that there exists a stable growth path, the equilibrium rate of growth depending on the distribution of income. This income distribution will be shown to depend on the change of the wage rate, the degree of monopoly, technological relations, and under certain circumstances in the consumption and investment behaviour. Some other interesting relations will emerge also.

II. THE REAL SYSTEM: DEVELOPMENT OF CONSUMPTION, INVESTMENT, AND THE CAPACITY OF PRODUCTION

(a) The Consumption Function

For our purpose, the following consumption function seems to be the most suitable: [1]

$$C_t = c_L L_t + c_Q Q_t + c^{(1)} \cdot \frac{C_{t-1}}{p_{t-1}} p_t. \tag{1}$$

$c^{(1)}$ is estimated to lie between ·1 and ·2. Dividing by p_t and substituting for C_{t-1} the expression (1) for $t-1$, considering

$$Y_t = L_t + Q_t, \tag{2}$$

[1] The notation is

C_t = value of consumption expenditure in period t

$c_t = \dfrac{C_t}{p_t}$ real consumption of period t

p_t = price level in period t

L_t = wage bill in period t

Q_t = profits in period t

c_L = marginal propensity of wage-earners to consume

c_Q = marginal propensity of profit-earners to consume

c^1 = coefficient explaining the influence of the level of real past consumption on current consumption

$c_{L-Q} = c_L - c_Q$

Y_t = national income of period t in monetary terms

$y_t = \dfrac{Y_t}{p}$ real national income.

414

and putting $c^{(1)2}=0$ (1) becomes [1]

$$c_t = c_0 y_t + c_1 y_{t-1} \qquad (3)$$

where

$$c_0 = c_{L-Q} \cdot \frac{L_t}{Y_t} + c_Q$$

$$c_1 = c^{(1)} \left[c_{L-Q} \cdot \frac{L_{t-1}}{Y_{t-1}} + c_Q \right].$$

This is a first-order linear difference equation, its coefficients depending on the share of wages L_t/Y during the current as well as the previous period and on the marginal propensities to consume. For short-run purposes an exogenous and stochastic term $\bar{c}_t$ may be added on the right-hand side of (3) with a long-run average of zero :

$$c_t = c_0 y_t + c_1 y_{t-1} + \bar{c}_t$$

the long-run average of c_t being $\bar{\bar{c}}_t = 0$.

(b) *The Investment Function*

Economic theory has developed the following type of investment function : [2]

$$i_t = k \cdot \Delta y_t^* \left(1 + \epsilon_I \cdot \frac{Q_{t-1}}{Y_{t-1}} \right). \qquad (4)$$

Here the capital coefficient k is supposed to be constant. This seems to be a drawback ; there is no law of the Medes and Persians compelling the capital coefficient to remain as it is. But some theoretical reflection reveals that it must be at least asymptotically stable when the savings ratio remains constant ; on the other hand, a long time has elapsed since the beginning of industrialization in western countries, during which the proportion of saving remained reasonably stable and the capital coefficient in the long run in fact stayed constant so that this supposition seems to do not too

[1] Cf. the definitions in the footnote on previous page.
[2] Notations (not yet explained in former notes) :
I_t = net investment of period t in monetary terms
$i_t = \dfrac{I_t}{p_t}$ real investment
K_t = total capital in period t (in monetary terms)
$K = \dfrac{K_t}{Y_t}$ the average capital coefficient (supposed to be constant) : i.e. marginal equals average capital coefficient
Δy_i = extension of the capacity of production wanted by the entrepreneurs in period t, i.e. new demand for which the entrepreneurs would like to procure the capacity
ϵ_I = sensitivity coefficient of investment to changes in profits.

much harm. As to the planning of new production capacity by the entrepreneurs we assume a sort of longer time extrapolation of past demand :[1]

$$\Delta y_t^* = v_0 y_t + v_1 y_{t-1} + v_2 y_{t-2}. \tag{5}$$

The simple acceleration principle $\Delta y_t^* = y_t - y_{t-1}$ would be foolish from the point of view of the entrepreneurs, as they would have to adapt their productive capacity to all short-run stochastic movements of demand. A three-period regression scheme seems to be the minimum requirement for extrapolation. To determine the numerical values of v_0, v_1, v_2, we assume the entrepreneur to follow a policy of increasing the productive capacity in period t according to the change of demand in period $t-1$ corrected by a proportion v of the change of demand in period t against the change in period $t-1$:

$$\Delta y_t^* = \Delta y_{t-1} + v\,(\Delta y_t - \Delta y_{t-1}),\ 0 \leq v \leq 1, \tag{6}$$

where $$\Delta y_t = y_t - y_{t-1}.$$

It will be : $$v_0 = v,\ v_1 = 1 - 2v,\ v_2 = v - 1. \tag{7}$$

In our numerical example we assume to be $v = \frac{1}{2}$ so that

$$v_0 = \tfrac{1}{2},\ v_1 = 0\ ;\ \ v_2 = -\tfrac{1}{2}.$$

Using (2), (6), and (7) and introducing

$$\eta = 1 + \epsilon_I \tag{8}$$

our investment function (4) will be turned into :

$$i_t = i_0 y_t + i_1 y_{t-1} + i_2 y_{t-2},$$

where $$i_0 = kv_0\left(\eta - \epsilon_I \frac{L_{t-1}}{Y_{t-1}}\right)$$

$$i_1 = kv_1\left(\eta - \epsilon_I \frac{L_{t-1}}{Y_{t-1}}\right)$$

$$i_2 = kv_2\left(\eta - \epsilon_I \frac{L_{t-1}}{Y_{t-1}}\right).$$

(4) is a linear difference equation of the second order. The coefficients depend on the share of wages L/Y during the previous period.

---

[1] v_0, v_1, v_2 = weighing coefficients for extrapolation of future demand
v = correction proportion for longer-term adaptation of capacity.

For short-term purposes a stochastic term $\bar{\imath}_t$ with a long-run mean of zero may be added to the right-hand side of (9). But to follow the usual notations, it seems preferable to call $\bar{\imath}_t$ the exogenous investment and define it in such a way that it cannot be negative. This means the short-run induced investment becomes only a fraction α of total long-run average investment (9), the other part being made up by the exogenous or autonomous investment. The latter becomes now a non-negative stochastic variable with a long-run rising mean. Thus we arrive at a *short-run investment function* [1] of

$$i_t = \alpha(i_0 y_t + i_1 y_{t-1} + i_2 y_{t-2}) + \bar{\imath}_t, \quad \bar{\imath}_t \geq 0, \tag{9a}$$

the long-run average of $\bar{\imath}_t$ being

$$\bar{\imath}_t = (i - \alpha)(i_0 y_t + i_1 y_{t-1} + i_2 y_{t-2})$$

(c) *The Capacity of Production*

The capacity of production of period t is equal to the one of period $t-1$ plus the new capacity created in period t. The latter is calculated by dividing real investment i_t by the capital coefficient. For a long-run consideration we may identify capacity and production of period $t-1$. Hence [2]

$$y_t^* = y_{t-1} + \frac{1}{k} i_t. \tag{10}$$

(d) *Total Demand and Capacity in the Long Run*

Because of

$$Y_t = C_t + I_t \tag{11}$$

we have to add up c_t in (3) and i_t in (9) in order to get the total long-run demand y_t in real terms:

$$y_t = b_1^* \cdot y_{t-1} + b_2^* y_{t-2}, \tag{12}$$

where

$$b_1^* = \frac{c_1 + i_1}{1 - c_0 - i_0}$$

$$b_2^* = \frac{i_2}{1 - c_0 - i_0}.$$

---

[1] α = proportion of total long-run investment which forms the short-run induced investment.
[2] y_t^* = capacity of production of period t.

This second-order linear difference equation would yield an equilibrium rate of growth of demand which would be unstable for a reasonable range of the parameters — a fact that led Hicks to his theory of the trade cycle. But it would be wrong to consider only the development of demand in real terms (as in (12)) without taking into account the development of the capacity of production which procures the real commodities for the real demand. In a theory of growth we have to identify real demand with real capacity of production (of course, not *monetary* demand! Price changes may be quite arbitrary).

In the long run it is physically impossible that real demand grows faster than the real capacity of production; on the other hand it cannot grow at a smaller rate without changing the investment function. Thus, for any existing investment function, we must write

$$y_t = c_t + i_t = y_t^* \tag{13}$$

Considering the equation for y_t^* in (10), (13) becomes

$$y_t - y_{t-1} = 1 i_t \tag{13a}$$

showing that now a new condition is imposed to the path of economic development.

Substituting (3) and (9) into (13) and equalizing it to (10), we come to the formula:

$$y_t = b_1 y_{t-1} + b_2 y_{t-2} \equiv F(L_t / Y_t)$$

where

$$b_1 = \frac{1 - c_1 - i_1\left(1 - \dfrac{1}{k}\right)}{c_0 + i_0\left(1 - \dfrac{1}{k}\right)}$$

$$b_2 = \frac{i_2\left(\dfrac{1}{k} - 1\right)}{c_0 + i_0\left(1 - \dfrac{1}{k}\right)}.$$

(14) represents a *stable* equilibrium growth for reasonable sets of parameters.[1],[2]

---

[1] Regarding stability, the extrapolation of demand for the future investment, i.e. the parameters v_0, v_1, v_2 are of crucial importance; see section V.

[2] In order to make (12) and (14) compatible — as is necessary — the parameter v in (6) has to be considered as a variable. The paper does not cover this consequence.

III. THE LONG-RUN REAL SYSTEM : THE INFLUENCE OF INCOME DISTRIBUTION ON THE EQUILIBRIUM RATE OF GROWTH AND THE LONG-RUN LEVEL OF PRODUCTION IN A GIVEN PERIOD

The general solution of the long-run function (14) is [1]

$$y_t = y_0 \left\{ g_1 w_{y1}^t + g_2 w_{y2}^t \right\} \tag{15}$$

where g_1 and g_2 depend on the initial conditions. The coefficients of growth are

$$w_{y1} = \frac{b_1}{2} + \sqrt{\left(\frac{b_1}{2}\right)^2 + b_2} \tag{16}$$

$$w_{y2} = \frac{b_1}{2} - \sqrt{\left(\frac{b_1}{2}\right)^2 + b_2}$$

Estimations of the range of the numerical values of the parameters reveal that in general

$$\left(\frac{b_1}{2}\right)^2 + b_2 > 0,$$

i.e. there are no imaginary roots and, consequently, no periodic solutions ; the first coefficient of growth w_{y1} is just above unity, while the second coefficient w_{y2} is negative but greater than

$$-1 : -1 < w_{y2} < 0.$$

Of course these solutions depend on the share of wages

$$\frac{L_t}{Y_t} \text{ and } \frac{L_{t-1}}{Y_{t-1}}$$

because they determine the parameters b_1 and b_2.[2]

[1] $w_{yi} = 1 + \beta_i$, $i = 1, 2,$ =the coefficients of growth of the national product y
  β_i =rate of growth i of the national product.
[2] Supposing the following values of the parameters :
$c_L = \cdot 8$; $c_Q = \cdot 366$; $c^{(1)} = \cdot 2$; $k = 3 \cdot 07$; $v_0 = \cdot 5$; $v_1 = 0$; $v_2 = -\cdot 5$; $\epsilon_I = 1$; $\eta = 2$
one gets the solutions

for $\dfrac{L_t}{Y_t} = \dfrac{L_{t-1}}{Y_{t-1}}$	$\cdot 6$	$\cdot 7$	$\cdot 8$	$\cdot 9$
w_{y1}	1·074	1·059	1·046	1·031
w_{y2}	$-\cdot 650$	$-\cdot 629$	$-\cdot 608$	$-\cdot 583$

The parameters are chosen so that the following initial conditions are fulfilled :
$y_0 = 100$; $y_{-1} = 95$; $y_{-2} = 90$; $p_0 = 1$; $c_0 = 80$; $i_0 = 20$; $\dfrac{L_0}{Y_0} = \dfrac{L_{-1}}{Y_{-1}} = \cdot 7$

The second coefficient w_{y2} being negative but greater than -1, the influence of this root disappears with time elapsing so that the equilibrium rate of growth becomes a rather simple function of the wage share :

$$\beta_y = w_{y1} - 1 = \frac{b_1}{2} + \sqrt{\left(\frac{b}{2}\right)^2 + b_2} - 1 \equiv \phi\left(\frac{L}{Y}\right).$$

In the sequence we put $w_{y1} = w_y$.

Using the parameter values of footnote 2, p. 419, this function is pictured in Fig. 1. It demonstrates that a better income distribution will lower the rate of growth. A better income distribution will lead to a relatively higher consumption and, therefore, lower investment, so that the result is easily understandable.[1]

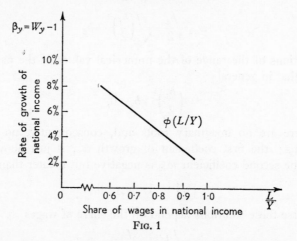

Fig. 1

Each point on the curve $\phi\ (L/Y)$ in Fig. 1 represents a stable equilibrium point; the distribution of income decides which one will be realized. The curve $\phi\ (L/Y)$ is determined by the consumption, saving, and investment behaviour of the wage- and profit-earners. Consequently, this aspect of determining the distribution of income is examined.[2]

Instead of looking at the rate of growth one may be interested in the equilibrium value of the real national product in period t, i.e. in solving (14) for the given parameters and the previous values of

---

[1] By varying the different parameters their influence on the ϕ-curve may be ascertained, e.g. a higher marginal propensity to consume c_L lowers the ϕ-curve: the same income distribution is now connected with a smaller rate of growth.

[2] Assuming the capital coefficient to be constant, part of the influence of technology is already taken into account.

the national product y_{t-1} and y_{t-2}. Since some of the parameters are functions of the income distribution L_t/Y_t, y_t may be considered as a function of L_t/Y_t, i.e. $y_t = F(L_t/Y_t)$. Figure 2 shows this function for different values of the propensity to consume c_L of the wage-earners for the same set of other parameters as indicated in foot-note 2, p. 419. The result is that *in the long run* the level of production

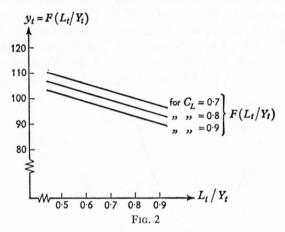

FIG. 2

declines if the labour rises and that the same is true if the propensity to consume c_L rises with income distribution remaining constant. This rather surprising result is due to the fact that in the long-run relationships high consumption means low investment and that the effect of investment on production is more important than the effect of consumption (given the investment and consumption functions). We can see how these relations change in the short run.

IV. THE SHORT-RUN REAL SYSTEM: THE INFLUENCE OF INCOME DISTRIBUTION ON LEVEL OF PRODUCTION IN THE SHORT RUN

Adding up (3a) and (9a) one gets the total demand in the short run

$$y_t = b_1^{**} y_{t-1} + b_2^{**} y_{t-2} + b_0^{**} \equiv f(L_t/Y_t) \tag{12a}$$

where

$$b_1^{**} = \frac{c_1 + i_1^*}{1 - c_0 - i_0^*}$$

$$b_2^{**} = \frac{i_2^*}{1 - c_0 - i_0^*}$$

$$b = {}_0^{**} \frac{\bar{c}_t + \bar{\imath}_t}{1 - c_0 - i_0^*}$$

$$i_j^* = \alpha i_j, \; j = 0, 1, 2$$

the difference to the long-run function (12) being that there is a considerable amount b_0^{**} of exogenously and stochastically determined production. Because some of the parameters depend on the labour share L_t/Y_t, y_t may be considered as a function of L_t/Y_t, i.e. $y_t = f(L_t/Y_t)$. Figure 3 shows this function for different propensities to consume c_L of wage-earners, using the other numerical values of footnote 2, p. 419 and putting $\alpha = \frac{1}{10}$ and $\bar{c}_t + \bar{\imath}_t = 18$. Now

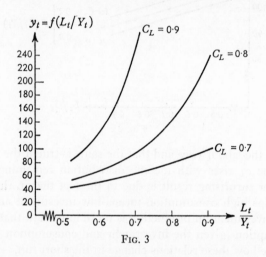

FIG. 3

the well-known short-run Keynesian relations emerge : the higher the labour share and the higher the propensity to consume of the wage-earners, the higher total production and employment. The same is true for higher investment coefficients v_0, v_1, v_2 and higher exogenous demand $\bar{c}_t$ and $\bar{\imath}_t$. The reason for the difference in the long-run and the short-run behaviour of the functions is due to the fact that in the short run the greatest part of investment is already decided upon in the past and in the process of being realized so that investment cannot be reduced if the rate of profit declines. This is only accomplished after a while, and then the long-run relations come into play.

V. STABILITY CONDITIONS FOR THE LONG-RUN
REAL SYSTEM

The solution of the long-run equation (14), which was given in equations (15) and (16) of section III, has to be dynamically stable in order that it makes sense to use this solution for the analysis of the long-run behaviour of an economic system. By 'dynamically stable' I mean in the context of the analysis of a growing economy :

1. that there is a trend in the development of the national product and no continuing cycles on the same level, i.e. that the expression under the square root in (16) is not negative :

$$\left(\frac{b_1}{2}\right)^2 + b_2 \geq 0. \tag{17a}$$

2. that this trend is a positive one ; that means that at least one root of (16) should be greater than 1. The condition is :

$$\text{if} \quad b_1 \leq 2, \quad \text{then} \quad b_1 + b_2 > 1. \tag{17b}$$

If $b_1 > 2$, no further condition except (17a) is imposed.

3. that eventually the system settles down to this positive trend. That means : no root in (16) should be smaller than -1. The condition is :

$$b_1 - b_2 > -1. \tag{17c}$$

This condition may seem a bit restrictive. One may be content with a slower approximation to the trend. This would lead to requiring the positive root to be greater than the absolute value of the negative root (if there is any) ; the condition is simply

$$b_1 > 0. \tag{17d}$$

But we shall use (17c) here. In either case, if there are negative roots at all, side conditions may turn out to be necessary.

Figures 4 and 5 show the value of b_1^* and b_2^* in (12) and the values of b_1 and b_2 in (14) as a function of the investment behaviour described by the parameter v in (6) and the ranges of dynamic stability as defined above. The numerical values of footnote 2, p. 419 are used with $L_t/Y_t = \cdot 7$. There is a point of discontinuity for $v = \cdot 0825$ in the case of function (12) (see Fig. 4), where the denominator of b_1^* and b_2^* becomes zero. There is no such point in Fig. 5 for function (14). Moreover, the range of dynamic stability is greater.

These are the mathematical reasons (besides the economic ones) which led to the conclusion to use (14) instead of (12).

One other comment may be added. Figures 4 and 5 confirm what was said at the end of the previous section. If investment is

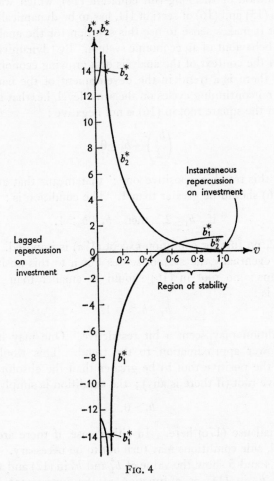

Fig. 4

totally or to a high degree determined by the past, i.e. if $v=0$ or nearly so, then the systems become unstable. But if changes in the period influence the investment of the same period to a major degree (i.e. v approaches 1) the opposite is true. This may be due to the special form of the investment and consumption function chosen. More research is necessary till this can be established beyond doubt.

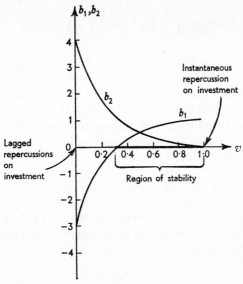

Fig. 5

VI. DETERMINATION OF THE WAGE SHARE : GENERAL RELATIONS

In sections III and IV real production in the short and in the long run and the long-run equilibrium rate of growth were shown to depend on income distribution. In this section the latter will be determined.

The wage bill is the mathematical product of the wage rate l, the labour coefficient a, and the real national product y : [1]

$$L_t = l_t \cdot a_t \cdot y_t. \tag{18}$$

The labour coefficient a_t depends on the wage-price relation (thus allowing for price substitution) and on the technical progress in the form of an improvement of labour productivity. It can be shown that the following function fits well into the general production theory : [2, 3]

[1] l_t = wage rate, = pay per hour of work
   a_t = labour coefficient, = hours of work per unit of real product.
[2] If the entrepreneurs wish to minimize their cost of production and if the production function has a constant elasticity of substitution, the input coefficients are necessarily of the form (19). Cf. [12]. Therefore (19) is equivalent to assuming a production function of constant elasticity of substitution.
[3] a_0 = constant = the labour coefficient at time 0, if the wage rate equals the price of production in the previous period
   $w_a = l + \beta_a$ the coefficient of the rise of labour productivity
   β_a = rate of growth of labour productivity
   γ = elasticity of price substitution of the labour coefficient.

The Distribution of National Income

$$a_t = a_0 \cdot \left(\frac{1}{w_a}\right)^t \cdot \left(\frac{l_{t-1}}{p_{t-1}}\right)^\gamma, \quad -1 < \gamma < 0. \tag{19}$$

A time lag of one period is assumed between wage-price changes and their repercussions on the labour coefficient. The wage rate will depend on the difference between the demand for labour by the entrepreneurs A and the supply of labour by the population $\alpha . N$, which in turn is influenced by the relative strength of the labour unions and the employers' associations called μ. The latter is an exogenous factor. So we have : [1]

$$l_t = l_{t-1} \left[1 + \zeta(A_{t-1} - \alpha N_{t-1}) + \mu_t\right]. \tag{20}$$

Here also a time lag of one period is assumed between an excess demand or supply of labour and its influence on the wage rate. Of course, by definition

$$A_t = a_t \cdot y_t. \tag{21}$$

The rate of growth of the population N is taken as exogenous :

$$N_t = N_0 \cdot w_N^t. \tag{22}$$

Prices and wages are connected by the profit calculations of the entrepreneurs. If they want to maximize their profits they equalize marginal revenue.[2]

$$E'_t = p_t \left(1 - \frac{1}{\epsilon_D}\right); \quad \epsilon_D > 1 \tag{23}$$

(marginal revenue in the form of the Amoroso–Robinson relation) to marginal cost

$$K'_t = \left(a_t l_t + \frac{1}{\lambda} k p_t\right) \cdot z_t \tag{24}$$

---

[1] A_t = number of working hours demanded by the entrepreneurs in period t
N_t = total population in heads
$w_N = 1 + \beta_N$ = coefficient of growth of the population
β_N = rate of growth of the population
α = number of working hours supplied per unit of population, so that αN_t = supply of working hours by the population in period t
ζ = a coefficient describing the influence of an excess demand or supply of labour on the wage rate ; $\zeta > 0$
μ_t = exogenous influence on the wage rate (influence of political and sociological force, etc.)
[2] ϵ_D = elasticity of demand ; $1/\epsilon_D$ may be taken as a measure for the degree of monopoly in the economy ; $\epsilon_D = \infty$ in the case of complete competition.

where
$$z_t = 1 + 2\kappa^* \frac{y_t - y_t^*}{y_t^*}.\ [1]$$

The marginal costs consist of the labour cost per unit of product $a_t l_t$ and the cost of the capital equipment $l/\lambda\ kp_t$. kp_t represents the total value of capital necessary to produce one unit of output, l/λ represents the depreciation quota. Factor z_t in (24) allows for the cost rising influence of over-utilization of capacity: $z_t = 1$, if production y_t is smaller or equal to capacity y_t^*, and $z_t > 1$, if the economy runs into bottlenecks of production. When (23) and (24) are equalized, then [2]

$$p_t = \frac{a_t z_t}{1 - \dfrac{1}{\epsilon_D} - \dfrac{1}{\lambda} kz_t} l_t. \tag{25}$$

Evidently, prices move proportionally to the wage rate (i.e. $z_t = 1$), if there is no over-utilization of capacity, and they rise more than wages if the economy runs into bottlenecks ($z_t > 1$). (25) may be improved by introducing a time lag between the change of the wage rate and the price level, i.e. by substituting l_t by $v_1 l_t + v_2 l_{t-1}$

$$p_t = \frac{a_t z_t}{1 - \dfrac{1}{\epsilon_D} - \dfrac{1}{\lambda} kz_t} (v_1 l_t + v_2 l_{t-1}).\ [3] \tag{26}$$

Taking into consideration (18) and (26), we arrive at the following

[1] The total cost function is assumed as
$$K_t = \left(A_t l_t + \frac{1}{\lambda} K_t^* p_t \right) \left[1 + \kappa^* \frac{y_t^*}{y_t} \left(\frac{y_t - y_t^*}{y_t^*} \right)^2 \right]$$
$K_t^* = k \cdot y_t =$ real capital in period t
$\lambda =$ average life-time of capital goods, so that $1/\lambda$ may be taken as the rate of depreciation
$y_t^* =$ average capacity of production, defined as that production where the marginal costs begin to rise
$\kappa^* =$ coefficient describing the rise of marginal costs ;
$\kappa^* = \begin{cases} 0, \text{ if } y_t \le y_t^* \\ > 0, \text{ if } y_t > y_t^* \end{cases}$
The cost function above supposes that each capitalist owns all of the nominal capital of his firm so that he gets the interest on the capital in form of profits. The opposite assumption would be that he pays interest for total capital. The term $K_t^* p_t \cdot \zeta_t$ had to be inserted into the first brackets and accordingly a term $kp_t \zeta_t$ in the brackets on the right-hand side of (24). The corresponding changes in the following equations are self evident. But all conclusions would remain the same.
[2] This relation may also be arrived at by starting from the Barone curve of average costs of firms. Then all profits are considered as differential profits in the same way as Ricardo considered the rent of land as a consequence of different qualities of the land.
[3] $v_1, v_2 =$ coefficients describing the time shape of the influence of changes of the wage rate on the price level ;
$$v_1, v_2 > 0,\ v_1 + v_2 = 1$$

expression for the determination of wage share :

$$\frac{L_t}{Y_t}=\frac{l_t a_t * y_t}{y_t p_t}=\frac{l_t a_t}{p_t}=\left[\frac{1}{z_t}\left(1-\frac{1}{\epsilon_D}\right)-\frac{1}{l}k\right]\frac{1}{v_1+v_2\dfrac{1_{t-1}}{1_t}}1_{t-1}\equiv\psi(l_t/l_{t-1}) \quad (27)$$

Herewith, the analysis of this section is completed. The share of wages in national income is shown to be a function of the degree of monopoly in the economy measured by $1/\epsilon_D$, the rate of depreciation $1/\lambda$, the capital coefficient k, the rate of change of the wage rate $1_t/1_{t-1}$, and the rise of marginal cost z_t in the case that the normal capacity $*y_t$ has been passed.

A short concluding remark may be in order to show how the determination of prices and of the wage share fits into the real system of section 2. Because of the relation $\dfrac{L_t}{Y_t}=a_t\cdot\dfrac{l_t}{p_t}$ (cf. (27)) determining the income distribution means determining the wage-price relation. By $\epsilon_D=$ construction an isolastic demand function is supposed to exist for each firm, i.e. a demand function of the form

$$p_t=\bar{e}\cdot y_t-\frac{l}{\epsilon_D},\quad\epsilon_D=-\frac{dy}{dp}\cdot\frac{p}{y}>l,$$ $\bar{e}$ being a constant describing the

position of the demand curve. This position depends on the monetary side of the system, i.e. of the purchasing power of consumers and investors. Given now the production y_t which is determined by the real system *as a function of income distribution* (or in other words : as a function of the wage-price ratio), prices are such that the entrepreneurs *given the cost function* are willing to offer just this amount y_t that is demanded by consumers and investors. This fixes $\bar{e}$ and therefore p_t.

VII. SHORT-RUN INFLUENCE OF THE WAGE RATE ON THE DISTRIBUTION OF INCOME AND EMPLOYMENT

Now we have all the tools together to analyse the laws of distribution in the short run. Space permits only to consider the influence of the wage rate. All other parameters may be treated in a similar way. The problem connected with a short-run influence of the wage rate is : given all values of the previous periods, what will be the influence of a change of wages on the distribution of income, on production

---

$v_1=$ ratio of a change of the wage level influencing the price level in the *same* period

$v_2=$ ratio of a change of the wage level influencing the price level in the *next* period.

(and therefore employment) and on the price level *in the next period* ? The influence of a change of wages on the distribution of income

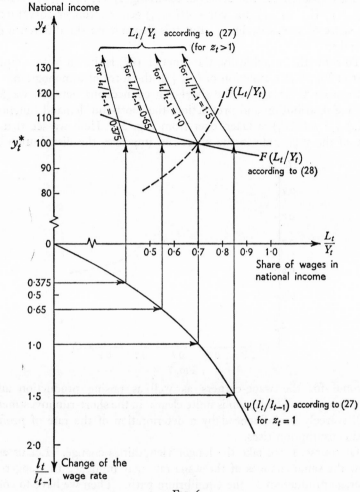

FIG. 6

may be seen from (27). Obviously, a wage rise will increase the share of wages in the short run ; this increase will be smaller if the economy is in a boom and its capacity is over-utilized ($z_t > 1$). The lower part of Fig. 6 shows the function (27) for $z_t = l$.[1] The increase

---

[1] The values of the parameters are

$$\epsilon_D = 5 \; ; \quad \lambda = 30 \cdot 7 \; ; \quad k = 3 \cdot 07 \; ; \quad \nu_1 = \nu_2 = \cdot 5 \; ; \quad \kappa^* = \begin{cases} 0 \text{ for } y_t \leqq y_t^* \; ; \\ \cdot 5 \text{ for } y_t^* > y_t \end{cases} \quad y_t^* = 100.$$

of the wage rate l_t/l_{t-1} is measured downward on the ordinate. The ψ-curve relates the change of wages to the distribution of income L_t/Y_t, measured on the abscissa, assuming $z_t=1$, i.e. $y_t \leqq y_t^*=100$. If $y_t>y_t^*$ (i.e. $z_t>1$), the curve $\psi(l_t/l_{t-1})$ gets a stronger curvature: the share of wages declines. But this depends on the difference of y_t and y_t^*.

To show that graphically, the function (27) is drawn in the upper part of Fig. 6 as a function of l_t/l_{t-1} in the form of a monogram.

In order to recognize the short-run connections between wages, income distribution and production, the short-run demand function (12a) $y_t=f(L_t/Y_t)$ is taken over from Fig. 3.[1] Here we see that a rise of the wage rate in the short run improves the distribution of

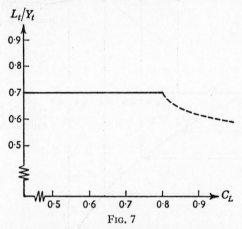

Fig. 7

income for the wage-earners as well as raising production and employment. The reason is quite clear : in the short-run investment will scarcely be influenced by a deterioration of the rate of profit, and consumption rises.

Of course, if we take the longer view things change. Let us ask how the same changes of the wage rate may influence the long-run average production on the equilibrium path. Then we have to consider (14) $y_t=F(L_t/Y_t)$. This function is also transferred from Fig. 2 to Fig. 6.[1] Now we see that a rise of the wage rate decreases production and employment in the long run. This testifies the equilibrating influence of wage changes in the long run : higher wages lead to unemployment, lower wages stimulate employment. Therefore the wage function (20) leads to full employment in the long run.

[1] Assuming $c_L=\cdot 8$.

This result is independent of the use of the more stable long-run function (14) where production is equal to capacity compared with the more unstable function (12).

The influence of other parameters on the short-run income distribution may be analysed along similar lines. Consider for example the propensity to consume c_L of the wage-earners. If it changes, the short-run demand fluctuation $f(L_t/Y_t)$ changes also as indicated in Fig. 3. By carrying over Fig. 3 into the upper part of Fig. 6, i.e. by solving (27) and (12a), one gets a relation as in Fig. 7.

VIII. LONG-RUN RELATIONS BETWEEN GROWTH OF POPU-LATION, INCOME, EMPLOYMENT, TECHNICAL PRO-GRESS, AND DISTRIBUTION OF INCOME

Because of the stability of the real system, the economy moves in the long run along the equilibrium path given by (17) and depicted in Fig. 1. Consequently, we only need to analyse the relations on this long-run equilibrium path of growth. On this path the degree of utilization of capacity y_t/y_t^* will be asymptotically constant (cf. (13) and hence also z_t (cf. (24)); therefore, we consider

$$z_t = z = \text{constant in the long run.} \tag{30}$$

The coefficient of the increase of the wage rate [1]

$$w_l = \frac{l_t}{l_{t-1}} \tag{31}$$

may be taken as exogenous because of the factor μ_t which is included in the wage function (20), thus reflecting the influence of bargaining power in determining the wage rate. It follows from (20):

$$w_l = 1 + \delta(A_{t-1} - \alpha N_{t-1}) + \mu_t \tag{32}$$

and from (26)

$$p_t = h_0 \cdot a_t \cdot l_t \tag{33}$$

where

$$h_0 = \frac{z\left(v_1 + \dfrac{v_2}{w_l}\right)}{1 - \dfrac{1}{\epsilon_D} - \dfrac{1}{\lambda}kz} \cdot [2]$$

---

[1] $w_l = 1 + \beta_l = $ coefficient of increase of the nominal wage rate
$\beta_l = $ rate of increase of the nominal wage rate.

[2] $h_0 = $ a coefficient reproducing the influence of the degree of monopoly $1/\epsilon_D$, the capital coefficient k, and of a steady increase of the wage rate w_1 on the price level in the long run.

The Distribution of National Income

Substituting (19) into (33) we come to :

$$p_t = h_0 \cdot a_0 \cdot \left(\frac{1}{w_a}\right)^t \cdot \left(\frac{l_{t-1}}{p_{t-1}}\right)^\gamma \cdot l_t. \tag{34}$$

Now we put

$$\frac{l_t}{p_t} = \frac{l_0}{p_0} w_l/p^{t.1} \tag{35}$$

Substituting (35) into (34) we may write after some modifications

$$(w_l/p)^{(1-\gamma)}{}_t = \left(\frac{p_0}{l_0}\right)^{1+\gamma} \cdot \frac{1}{h_0 \cdot a_0} \cdot w_l/p\gamma \cdot w^t{}_a. \tag{36}$$

Because this relation must hold for any time we conclude

$$w_l/p = w_a \frac{1}{1+\gamma}, \quad -1 < \gamma < 0 \tag{37}$$

and

$$\left(\frac{p_0}{1}\right)^{1+\gamma} \frac{1}{h_0 a_0} \cdot w_L/p\gamma = 1. \tag{38}$$

These then are the conditions governing the wage-price relation ; they will be observed by the *entrepreneurs when following their profit interests*.[2] According to (37), the wage-price relation in the long run is a function of the growth of the productivity of labour w_a, the latter being the variable which reflects the technical progress in the model. We shall come back to (38) later.

However, there is still another condition to be fulfilled in the long run : the maintenance of *full employment*. From the short-run analysis (cf. Fig. 2) we know that higher wages decrease employment and lower wages increase it in the short run. Supposing a wage function of the type described under (20), there will be full employment in the long run. Full employment means

$$A_t = \alpha N_t. \tag{39}$$

Substituting (19), (21), (22), (35) and remembering $y_t = y_0 \cdot w_y^t$ (39) will be turned into :

$$\left(\frac{l_0}{p_0}\right)^\gamma \cdot \left(\frac{1}{w_l/p}\right)^\gamma \cdot w_l/p^{yt} = \frac{\alpha N_0}{a_0 y_0} \cdot \left(\frac{w_a w_N}{wy}\right)^t. \tag{40}$$

---

[1] $w_l/p = w_l/w_p =$ the coefficient of growth of the wage-price relation
$w/p = 1 + \beta_l/p$ $\beta_l/p =$ the rate of growth of wages over prices.
[2] In the interpretation give n above. In the interpretation of the Barone curve (37) and (38) state the conditions that all firms necessary to produce y_t are able to stay in business.

Since this should be valid for all t, the conditions for *long-run full employment* are

$$w_{l/p} = \left(\frac{w_a w_N}{w_y}\right)^{\frac{l}{\gamma}}, \quad -1 < \gamma < 0 \tag{41}$$

and

$$\left(\frac{l_0}{p_0}\right)^\gamma \cdot \left(\frac{1}{w_{l/p}}\right)^\gamma \cdot \frac{a_0 y_0}{\alpha N_0} = 1. \tag{42}$$

(41) presents the further conditions for the coefficient of growth of the wage-price-relation : the condition to maintain full employment.

(37) as well as (41) must be valid in the long run. Equalizing these equations, it will be

$$w_y = w_N \cdot w_a \frac{1}{1+\gamma}. \tag{43}$$

This will say : the long-run equilibrium coefficient of growth of the national product is the mathematical product of the coefficients of growth of population and of labour productivity (i.e. of the technical progress), the latter taken to the $1/1+\gamma$th power.

From these basic relations many others are easily derived, all of them allowing a wide range of interpretation.

Because l_t is a function of time in the long run (cf. (35)), a_t in (19) $\bar{p}_t$ becomes

$$a_t = \hat{a}_0 \cdot \left(\frac{1}{w_{\hat{a}}}\right)^t \text{[1]} \tag{44}$$

where

$$w_{\hat{a}} = w_a \cdot \left(\frac{1}{w_{l/p}}\right)^\gamma \tag{44a}$$

$$\hat{a}_0 = a_0 \left(\frac{l_0}{p_0} \cdot \frac{1}{w_{l/p}}\right)^\gamma.$$

(44) is a 'technical progress function', where all effects of price substitution are included. From (41) follows :

$$w_a \cdot \left(\frac{1}{w_{l/p}}\right)^\gamma = \frac{w_y}{w_N}. \tag{45}$$

Comparing (44a) and (45) :

$$w_y = w_{\hat{a}} \cdot w_N. \tag{46}$$

[1] $w_{\hat{a}} = 1 + \beta_{\hat{a}} =$ coefficient of gross change of the labour coefficient.

The coefficient of growth of the national product is obtained by multiplying the coefficients of gross technical progress and of the growth of population. Comparing (43) and (46) the relation

$$w_{\hat{a}} = w_a \frac{1}{1+\gamma} \tag{47}$$

is obtained. It appears that in our case we may use a technical progress function as well as a production function with price substitution.

Substituting (47) into (37) will yield

$$w_l/_p = w_{\hat{a}}, \tag{48}$$

and substituting (48) into (46) :

$$w_l/_p = \frac{w_y}{w_N}. \tag{49}$$

All these relations are conditions for long-run full employment and simultaneously for profit maximization of the entrepreneurs. (48) has a very simple and well-known meaning. By putting $w_l/_p = \dfrac{w^l}{w_p}$ it follows that prices can only be stable in the long run if wages rise by the same rate as the gross productivity of labour. This is sometimes disputed, but it follows inevitably in the long run.

It is easily seen that under the conditions of long-run full employment and profit maximization the *share of wages in national income remains constant in the long run*, if a set of variables to be determined at once stay constant.

Considering (35) and (44) we come to

$$\frac{L_t}{Y_t} = \frac{l_t a_t y_t}{p_t y_t} = \frac{l_0}{p_0} \cdot \hat{a}_0 \cdot (w_l/_p)^t \cdot \left(\frac{1}{w_{\hat{a}}}\right)^t \tag{50}$$

which is constant because of (48) so that the index t may be cancelled. Hence it follows :

$$\frac{L}{Y} = \frac{l_0}{p_0} \hat{a}_0. \tag{50a}$$

Substituting $\hat{a}_0$ from (44a) and using (38) we get

$$\left(\frac{l_0}{p_0}\right)^{1+\gamma} = \frac{1}{h_0 \cdot a_0} \cdot w_l/_p^{\gamma}.$$

Now (50a) turns into the extremely simple expression

$$\frac{L}{Y} = \frac{1}{h_0}$$

considering the definition of h_0 in (33):

$$\frac{L}{Y} = \frac{1 - \frac{1}{\epsilon_D} - \frac{1}{\lambda} kz}{z\left(v_1 + \frac{v_2}{w_l}\right)} = \phi(w_l). \tag{51}$$

This, of course, is the function (27) but with the important difference, that z_t is substituted by the constant z.

This is the result we want to use in the long-run theory of distribution. If this distribution is realized the economy follows the stable long-run equilibrium path of growth, all workers are employed in the long run and the entrepreneurs maximize their profits.

IX. LONG-RUN INFLUENCES ON DISTRIBUTION AND THEIR RELATION TO THE RATE OF GROWTH

Looking at (51) it will be apparent that the distribution of income is insensitive to many, but not all, parameters of economic behaviour. It is especially the degree of monopoly $1/\epsilon_D$ which governs the distribution in the long run — or in another interpretation already mentioned in some notes, the shape of the Barone curve, i.e. the inequalities of efficiency among the firms. Technology exerts its influence through the capital coefficient k, the average life-time of a capital good λ, and the rise of marginal costs as measured by z.

The absolute level of wages is without influence on distribution, only a steady rise of wages, i.e. a positive w_1 may improve the income distribution for the workers even in the long run, if v_2 is positive, i.e. if there is a certain time lag between the rise of wages and the rise of prices. But since according to (48) prices and wages are tied to the technical progress in the long run such a policy leads to a deterioration of the value of money if the rise of wages exceeds that of labour productivity. Besides it has a negative effect on the rate of growth of the national income.

The influence of an aggressive wage policy on the rate of growth may be seen by substituting (51) into (14) and determining the rate of growth β_y according to (17). We do it graphically in Fig. 4.

The Distribution of National Income

The upper part of Fig. 8 reproduces Fig. 1. In the lower part the function $\phi\,(w_1)$ of (51) is drawn (using the numerical values of the parameters in footnote 2, p. 419, with $z = 1$). As already said, an

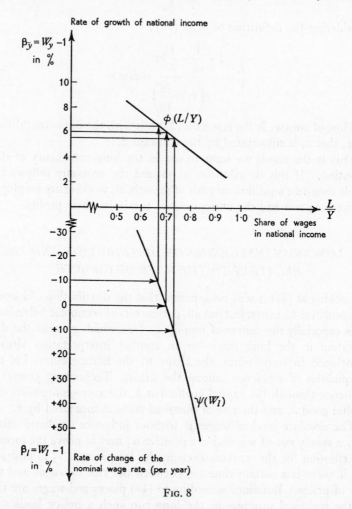

Fig. 8

aggressive wage policy may improve the distribution of income even in the long run, if there is a time lag between wage rise and price reaction ($\nu_2 > 0$) as assumed in Fig. 8 (there is $\nu_2 = \frac{1}{2}$). But this inevitably reduces the rate of growth, so that such a policy is to the disadvantage of the future generation.

With $\nu_2 = 0$ (which may be supposed if the unions pursue such a

436

policy for a while) the ϕ-curve is a vertical straight line : there is no influence of wage policy on distribution at all in the long run. Therefore, the rate of growth cannot be influenced by nominal wage changes. A lower degree of monopoly shifts the ϕ-curve to the right : it improves the wage share but lowers the rate of growth.

In such a way the influence of all other parameters contained in the model on production, prices, rate of growth, and distribution in the short and in the long run may be analysed.

VIII. CONCLUSION

Only a few results may be repeated here. There are different laws governing the short-run and the long-run relations of income distribution and employment. In the short run each rise of the wage rate improves the distribution of income for the wage-earners and raises production and employment. In the long run a single wage rise has no influence on distribution whatsoever. Only a *steady* increase of the wage rate *may* have a positive effect on distribution and a negative effect on the rate of growth of the national product. But this is only true if the process of adaptation of prices to the new structure of costs takes more time than one period. Besides, the long-run distribution is insensitive to most parameters of economic behaviour with the exception of the degree of monopoly (or in another interpretation, the shape of the Barone curve), the capital coefficient, the average life time of capital goods (or the depreciation rate), and the rise of marginal costs.

BIBLIOGRAPHY

[1] Bombach, *Die verschiedenen Ansätze der Verteilungstheorie*, E. Schnei der, *Einkommensverteilung und technischer Fortschritt*, Berlin, 1959.
[2] Bombach, 'Preisstabilität, wirtschaftliches Wachstum und Einkommensverteilung', *Schweiz. Zeitschr. f. Volksw. u. Stat.*, 95 (1959), pp. 1–10.
[3] Boulding, *A Reconstruction of Economics*, New York and London, 1950.
[4] J. B. Clark, *The Distribution of Wealth*, New York, 1899.
[5] Douglas, *The Theory of Wages*, New York, 1934.
[6] Föhl, 'Möglichkeiten einer künftigen Fiskalpolitik', *Weltwirtschaftl. Archiv*, 79 (1957), pp. 1–59.

The Distribution of National Income

[7] Jevons, *The Theory of Political Economy*, London and New York, 1871.

[8] Kaldor, 'Alternative Theories of Distribution', *The Review of Economic Studies*, 23 (1955/56), pp. 83–100.

[9] Kalecki, 'The Distribution of National Income', *Essays in the Theory of Economic Fluctuations*, London, 1939.

[10] Kalecki, *Theory of Economic Dynamics*, London, 1954.

[11] Krelle, *Verteilungstheorie*, Tübingen, 1962.

[12] Krelle, 'Ersetzung der Produktionsfunktion durch preis- und kapazitätsabhängige Produktionskoeffizienten', *Jahrbüche für Nationalökonomie und Statistik*, 1964.

[13] J. Marchal et Lecaillon, *La Répartition du revenu national*, Paris, 1958.

[14] Niehans, *Die Wirkung von Lohnerhöhungen, technischen Fortschritten, Stetern und Spargewohnheiten auf Preise, Produktion und Einkommensverteilung*, in E. Schneider, *Einkommensverteilung und technischer Fortschritt*, Berlin, 1959.

[15] F. Oppenheimer, *Der Arbeitslohn*, Jena, 1926.

[16] Preiser, Artikel 'Distribution' in the *Handwörterbuch der Sozialwissenschaften*.

[17] Preiser, *Bildung und Verteilung des Volkseinkommens*, Göttingen, 1957.

[18] E. Schneider, *Einkommen und Einkommensverteilung in der makroökonomischen Theorie*, in *L' industrie*, Milano, 1957, pp. 3–15.

[19] Solow, 'Technical Change and the Aggregate Production Function', *Review of Economics and Statistics*, 39 (1957), pp. 312–320 and *passim*.

[20] Stobbe, 'Kurz- und langfristige Bestimmungsgründe der Einkommensverteilung', *Schweizerische Zeitschr. f. Volksw. u. Stat.*, 96 (1960), pp. 131–155.

[21] v. Thünen, *Der isolierte Staat*, Heidelberg, 1826.

[22] Walras, *Éléments d'économie pure*, Lausanne, 1874.

[23] Wicksell, *Vorlesungen über Nationalökonomie auf der Grundlage des Marginalprinzips*, Jena, 1913–22.

THE DISCUSSION OF PROFESSOR KRELLE'S PAPER

Professor Bronfenbrenner said that Professor Krelle's paper was ambitious, eclectic, and difficult to introduce. It included in one single package elements from marginal productivity, the Kaleckian and the Kaldorian theories and even elements of the sociological approach. Professor Bronfenbrenner could not think of any such attempt, apart from Weintraub's model, to bring together the productivity, monopoly, and saving investment approach.

Another difficult feature was that the model included both short-term and long-term elements, the last one bringing full capacity and full employment into consideration. In contradiction to what was usually implied in sociological theories, Professor Krelle had made the growth

438

rate a function of income distribution rather than the reverse. Professor Bronfenbrenner would agree with him in the short run, though he was of the opinion that the reverse assumption might have been more realistic in the longer run. Professor Krelle's model included, in a single theory, both causes of the functional distribution and its effects. In general, distribution theorists attempted only the first.

On the other hand, this model postulated many functions, in fairly precise mathematical form, and it had not yet been tested for the existence or stability of its parameters. It postulated a great number of what Professor Bronfenbrenner in his own paper had called 'magic constants'; one did not really know how magic or how constant was, for instance, the capital-output ratio.

The first of the four major elements in the model was a Keynesian or saving investment approach. In Professor Krelle's consumption function the values of the coefficients depended on the labour share L/Y and on the size of the differences between marginal propensities to consume of the different social groups. Professor Krelle's investment function was more difficult. Δy^* was the increase in desired capacity; this depended on the income in the present and the two past periods. Since income = consumption + investment, investment was a function of income in the past two periods, the coefficients depending on the profit share, Q/Y. Thus for a capital coefficient K given as a technologically determined constant, the investment function could be written:

$$i = i[k, \Delta y^*, (Q/Y)_{-1}].$$

By combining this with the equation for the desired extension of productive capacity

$$\Delta y^* = v_0 y_t + v y_{-1} + v_2 y_{-2};$$

one obtained

$$i = i_0 y_t + i_1 y_{-1} + i_2 y_{-2}.$$

In the second expression of the investment function the coefficients (i_0, i_1, i_2) increased with the profit share, Q/Y.

Professor Bronfenbrenner stressed that there were no consumption or direct interest-rate terms, as in Lange's post-Keynesian model of 1938 on the optimum consumption propensity. He was of the opinion that had this been included in Professor Krelle's model some of his results might have been different and the outcome of it would have looked less 'classical'.

Professor Krelle's capacity function was definitional

$$y^* = y_{-1} + i/k.$$

His equilibrium function was rather a long-run one, in the sense that he equated income y to the output of 'desired capacity' y^* rather than equating investment i to income minus consumption s. Professor Krelle derived income as depending on income in the two preceding periods, but with coefficients dependent on distribution, b_1 and b_2 in equation (14) in the paper.

439

This worked out to be mathematically stable for 'reasonable' values of the underlying coefficients. That was to say, deviations turned out to be self-correcting. This was a moving equilibrium, not a stationary state. Income y was a declining function of the labour share L/Y, at least for the values which Professor Krelle considered realistic for the other coefficients. Professor Krelle stated that this resulted in a kind of dilemma whereby 'a better distribution lowered the growth rate'. Professor Bronfenbrenner did not like this terminology; he would rather have said 'a higher labour share lowers the growth rate' and let the reader decide for himself whether this was better or worse.

Professor Bronfenbrenner also did not think that this dilemma would have developed had Δy^* been related to c instead of y in the equation:

$$\Delta y^* = v_0 y + v_1 y_{-1} + v_2 y_{-2},$$

and if an interest rate term had been included. He thought that this had biased the results on the classical side. Instead Professor Krelle might, like Lange, have found an optimum propensity to consume in relation with growth and, correspondingly, an optimum share.

The second major element in Professor Krelle's paper was aggregated micro-economics. Professor Krelle had stated that total wage income L was the product of the nation income y, the wage rate l and a term α which was the labour coefficient. α was not a constant; it was related fairly precisely to the rise of average labour productivity:

$$\alpha = \alpha[\beta, \gamma(l/p) - 1].$$

The elasticity of substitution between labour and capital γ was thus taken into account. Variations between wage rate and price level were lagged one period, and in this way dynamics again entered into the model. Furthermore, the wage rate term was a function of three variables: the wage rate in the preceding period, the excess demand for labour in the preceding period and a coefficient μ which had a sociological aspect. It was an arbitrary constant making allowance for the 'relative bargaining strength' of unions of employees, although Professor Bronfenbrenner wondered how this could be measured.

Professor Bronfenbrenner pointed out that the model conformed to the marginal theory of cost and revenue in a strict sense. It represented adjustment to (exogenously determined) wage rates on its cost side. It actually worked from the assumption that employers related marginal revenue to marginal costs at given wage rates. Professor Bronfenbrenner proceeded by commenting on equations (23) and (24) in the model. He pointed out that by equating them Professor Krelle ignored possible 'all-or-none' bargaining by trade unions, or other conditions interfering with profit maximization. This made prices move proportionately with wages unless capacity was over-utilized, in which case they rose more. To admit the possibility of rising real wages Professor Krelle introduced a time lag (in equation (26) in the model); if the v terms were positive, prices adjusted to wages only with a lag and a rise in money wages raised real wages as well.

Finally the labour share became

$$\frac{L}{y} = \frac{l\alpha y}{py} = \frac{l\alpha}{p} = \psi[a,\ z,\ \gamma,\ \epsilon,\ \kappa,\ \lambda,\ \mu,\ \nu_1,\ \nu_2,\ (l/p_{-1})],$$

which included some coefficients not included in this brief summary. Professor Bronfenbrenner would agree with Professor Krelle in calling equation (27) in the paper insensitive to 'ordinary' economic relationships if the terms on the right were constants, but not in so far as they themselves depended on other economic variables.

The third major element in Professor Krelle's model was what he called a short-run analysis of the influence of the wage rate on income distribution and employment: if wages rose from one period to the next exogenously what would be the result? A rise in the wage rate increased the labour share but less so if there was over-heating of the economy, that is if z was bigger than unity. At the same time a rise in the wage rate lowered both production and employment. This was a classical view, with which Professor Bronfenbrenner was glad to agree. But he thought that whether Professor Krelle obtained this result depended on the constancy of the capital-output ratio k and on the assumption that investment was independent of consumption. Both of these features Professor Bronfenbrenner found questionable.

The fourth and final element of the Krelle model provided the influence of the wage rate on income distribution and employment in the long run, with exogenous population growth. Professor Bronfenbrenner wanted to stress again that the long-run evolution in this context meant a movement along a stable equilibrium growth path, and was distinct from any movement towards a hypothetical stationary state.

The rate of increase in wages was taken as autonomous at first. The rate of price increase was in the model a function of the rate of wage increase, w, the rate of labour productivity increase, α, and the elasticity of substitution between labour and capital, γ. (Later development required movements of the wage rate so that full employment was maintained). If employers maximized profits, this yielded a constant labour share. The price level either rose, or remained constant, equal to or smaller than the labour coefficient.

The mechanism by which this long-run equilibrium was reached and maintained was by no means clear to Professor Bronfenbrenner's mind. It seemed to him more like a pious hope than a necessary outcome of the system, and the hope could be wrecked, for example, by collective bargaining, holding real wages above their full employment level. This reminded Professor Bronfenbrenner of what the London *Economist* said a few years ago about an 'uneasy triangle': one could not have steady full employment, stable prices, and strong unions together — you could have no more than two of the three at the same time.

Professor Krelle had prepared a mathematical appendix which Professor Bronfenbrenner wished had been included in the distributed paper as it showed Professor Krelle to have prima facie evidence of a general over-determinacy at some stages, but he had not investigated the problem from this viewpoint. Under what conditions was there a stable and unique solution with 'reasonable' values ?

If Professor Bronfenbrenner might venture to give a general criticism of Professor Krelle's system, this would be that he tried to include four alternative distribution theories (i.e. productivity, monopoly, Kaldorian, sociological) whereas Professor Bronfenbrenner himself was not sure whether one needed more than one. The first of these four theories Professor Bronfenbrenner thought to give reasonably good predictions in developed countries. The monopoly theory was theoretically plausible, but it had not yet been shown to produce better predictions than those which one could obtain without it. The Kaldorian theory was a theory of effects of distribution rather than of causes, except over very long periods. With regard to the sociological theory, Professor Bronfenbrenner did not know what it could be said to predict, though it might explain past developments. Were Professor Krelle's functions the right ones ? Were they stable over time ? Were his constants really constants ? Professor Bronfenbrenner thought that it would be highly desirable to have statistical verification. And even if the model were verified, one would still be left with the problem of its applicability to problems of policy. Before the development of 'computerology', Professor Bronfenbrenner would have considered Professor Krelle's model too complex and cumbersome to be useful. As things stood he was much less sure.

Professor Reder referring to Professor Krelle's statement (p. 434 in the paper) that 'prices can only be stable in the long run if wages rise by the same rate as the gross productivity of labour', remarked that it was sometimes disputed whether what one statistically measured as wage rate and gross productivity of labour were related in the way Professor Krelle stated. Professor Reder was aware that what was then disputed was the behaviour of aggregates and as such was a different issue but this raised another sort of problem: that of the casual identification of variables in the model with variables which might be used more generally with a different meaning.

Professor Reder also remarked that in the real world the length of the working week should also be brought as a variable into the relationship between rising wages and rising labour productivity. But much more worrying to Professor Reder was the assumption of a constant degree of monopoly. Professor Krelle talked about an average degree of monopoly as alone determining distribution in the long run : this seemed to Professor Reder an enormous mouthful to swallow. He would be inclined to interpret it as packing up most of the factors affecting relations of prices to costs and therefore much of what determined distribution. But did

442

all these remain unchanged ? In concluding that 'the long run distribution is insensitive to all parameters of economic behaviour with the exception of the degree of monopoly, the capital coefficient, the average life time of capital goods (or the depreciation rate) and the rise of marginal costs', had Professor Krelle done more than attempt to classify the influences at work ? How useful this was empirically would depend on how stable the relations between these variables happened to be.

Unlike Professor Bronfenbrenner Professor Reder did not feel inclined to oppose marginal theory to the Kaldorian theory. It might be that all these factors were needed for constructing a complete model. For instance changes in propensities to spend might in a loose sense cause changes in the parameters of the production functions so that both needed to be determined simultaneously. On the other hand production functions might remain fairly stable. The real issue was not which of the two theories was true, but which of the two allowed the better chance of interpreting the real world.

Professor Lecaillon thought that Professor Krelle's paper had attempted with strict logic a synthesis of different theories of distribution : the degree of monopoly, marginal productivity, the post-Keynesian theory. He nevertheless wondered whether this did not involve some methodological difficulty. The marginal productivity theory was part of the theory of production and it explained distribution on the basis of the combination of factors according to their availability in a given sector of the economy.

Income distribution could thus be explained within sectors where there was no difficulty of imputing incomes to factors. But this analysis could not apply to income determination in sectors where there was no such possibility, for instance, the pre-capitalist sector or the public sector. The distribution theory based on factor costs and optimum allocation of resources was therefore limited in scope. Professor Krelle's model was essentially designed for analysing distribution in industrial sectors and excluded the public sector. This was partial analysis as opposed to general theory in the sense the Keynesian or the sociological approaches could claim to be when considering effective demand in the generating of overall income.

There was a gap to be bridged between the micro- and the macroeconomic approaches to income distribution. This could be done in two alternative ways. One way was to construct a purely partial model based on the device of the representative firm, but this was only relevant to primary distribution and was an unsatisfactory limitation ignoring the part played by the public sector's operations in distribution. At any rate this could apply only to the purest market economy. As a second alternative Professor Lecaillon suggested that one could assume that national income was generated within the industrial sectors and that incomes distributed outside them were purely transfer incomes and one should introduce in the model (as it then would probably be necessary) a

443

correcting coefficient making allowance for the redistributive effects of the government's operations.

Dr. Pasinetti said that whereas a rate of growth was determined in the first part of Professor Krelle's paper by a neat combination of two factors—consumers' demand and investment — as the building up of new production capacity, later many other elements were introduced into the model. It seemed, however, that in the long run the rate of growth of the product was exogenously determined by a given rate of productivity and population growth. Now, leaving out all other factors, was he right in thinking that the introduction of this exogenous rate of growth into the model determined which of the many alternatively possible rates of growth of the product relating to the first part of the model was the valid one ?

Professor Krelle replied that the natural rate of growth was determined in equation (46) of the model by the rate of increase in productivity and the labour force only in the long run. But there were shorter run movements around this and they were determined in the first part of the paper as he would not omit short-run movements.

Dr. Pasinetti still thought that, leaving aside the short-run factors and also the sociological factors, the degree of monopoly and other disturbing factors could still prevent the long-run rate of growth from materializing.

Professor Krelle pointed out that in his model the distribution of income was independent of the long-run rate of growth. It was determined by inventiveness, technical progress, and in short productivity increase and the growth of the labour force. Only in the short-run could distribution be affected, depending on whether or not production ran into bottlenecks in factor supply.

Dr. Pasinetti confessed that he was still puzzled. He thought that this left undetermined which of the many short-run rates of growth 'à la Domar' compatible with the natural (i.e long-run) rate of growth would prevail in the short run. *Professor Solow* referred Dr. Pasinetti to equation (51) of the model which described the income distribution compatible with the long-run rate of growth.

Dr. Pasinetti replied that there was in equation (51) no parameter which brought out the distribution of income. *Professor Krelle* referred to Fig. 4 in the paper which showed primary distribution and rate of growth, as a short-run function of change in nominal wage rate. This fitted in with equation (51) in the following manner : if z (i.e. the factor allowing for the cost-raising influence of over-utilization of capacity) remained constant, it brought out one of the curves set in Fig. 4 and the rate of growth of national income was thus fixed to what was given in equation (46). Professor Krelle regretted not to have stated this explicitly in his paper as it was in this way that short-run analysis came through to long run.

Professor Solow commented on this, saying that he was not sure that Professor Krelle had quite understood what had disturbed Dr. Pasinetti, i.e. that equation (51) did not contain the determinants of the natural rate of growth, or the natural rate of growth itself. They had to be deduced from the equation.

Dr. Jungenfelt said that he had tried to combine in a model the Kaldorian approach with the ordinary labour market approach under the assumption of perfect competition. The model turned out to be overdetermined if one assumed investment to be exogenous. But by treating investment in the long run as endogenous and postulating labour force, the model was perfectly determined.

If one wanted to treat investment as exogenously determined and still have full employment one had to go into disequilibrium analysis. This closely resembled the inflation model used by Bent Hansen in 1952: the higher the constant saving programme, the lower the labour share.

Professor Krelle said he thought it really important at this stage of the discussion to explain his idea of the short run. This was also connected with other points made by Professor Bronfenbrenner.

A short-run problem was usually thought of in the following terms; everything in the past being determined, what would be the effect of a change for the next year? But what he meant by short-run analysis was that the economy was not on an equilibrium path. To him a short-run change was a change in equilibrium value of the trend of growth. The short-run question then was: what would be the change of parameters over the next year?

By taking this real short-run disequilibrium approach things went quite the other way round. Next year's production was a function of income distribution and if, for example, the propensity to consume of the wage-earners changed it had a negative effect on short-run equilibrium.

If one did not want everything in the short-run to be determined by the past one had to introduce a chance variable. Now the most important stochastic term in the short-run should be investment because it did not depend on the value of the variables in the same year. If everything was determined by the past, investment could be more or less constant, but this induced investment was in real life only a small part of investments in the short run.

By making investment exogenous the whole outlook for the short period was changed as one got short-run functions which were whole economic values. In the long run, however, investment could not be exogenous.

An increase in the wage rate would bring out in the short run a 'better' distribution of income meaning by that a bigger labour share resulting in rising employment and production. In the short run the Keynesian views were right in this sense but in the longer run one obtained the opposite, classical, result: with a constant capital-output ratio the rentability of capital declined, then investment declined.

Professor Reder wished to add one more comment to the preceding discussion. He would suggest that the way out of Dr. Pasinetti's dilemma was to make the growth rate enter into equation (5) of the model via a change in the degree of monopoly power. This would be quite realistic as the planning of production capacity was not merely a kind of policy decision by employers. An increase in the labour share implied a higher degree of monopoly so that this should not be considered as a parameter.

Professor Krelle said that he was grateful to Professor Reder for his suggestion. He would think it over. Meanwhile he would abstain from commenting on this point.

Professor Föhl, referring to Professor Krelle's statement that the rate of growth was independent of income distribution in the very long run said that he had not a clear idea of what Professor Krelle meant by the very long run in this connection. Professor Krelle started out from a condition of full employment which to Professor Föhl was a long-run consideration. Had Professor Krelle not taken the degree of monopoly as exogenous he would never have come to the conclusion that the growth rate was independent of distribution. The rate of growth depended on investment and this depended on the degree of monopoly.

Professor Rasmussen said that he had difficulty in seeing the inter-relations between the determinants of long-run growth and distribution in the long run. It did not seem to him that Professor Krelle's assertion that in the long run the income distribution was independent of the growth rate held within his model. There might be several links, one of them being the influence of the growth rate on the optimal life time of capital and, in turn, on the distribution.

Professor Solow wished to ask Professor Krelle a question relating to the very beginning of the model. Starting out from consumption and investment in the short run Professor Krelle had arrived at equation (10) which was like the Domar relation between output, investment, and capacity. Professor Krelle added that in the long run output and capacity were the same. Then Professor Krelle arrived at equation (12) for an equilibrium rate of growth and concluded that this would be unstable. As real demand and real capacity should be the same in the long run, Professor Krelle came to equation (14) which led to a stable equilibrium rate of growth.

Both equations (12) and (14) appeared to be true in the framework of the model but it seemed to Professor Solow that this part of the model was overdetermined: the system of equations in section II of the paper exceeded by 1 the number of unknowns. Professor Krelle arrived at equations (12) and (14) by ignoring one of his too many equations but equations (12) and (14) were alternative, depending on which equation was ignored.

Professor Krelle answered that the core of his system consisted of equation (14). This was not alternative to equation (12) because it assumed that production could exceed the capacity of consumption. Professor Solow would be wrong in doing nothing more than counting the number of equations because many equations followed on a set of others and equations (3) and (9) were not independent of (12) and (14).

Professor Solow replied that equations (3) and (9) were certainly two equations independent of each other. Equation (10) was also independent. Equation (11) was an income identity, also independent, and equation (13) posited that $y = y^*$. Thus he thought that he had found five equations relating to the four variables c, y, i, y^*. By including (13) one deduced both (12) and (14).

Professor Krelle said that he had been very careful to avoid over-determinacy. He had started from the equation for $z_t = 1$. Then z_t was determined from equation (24). Then he put equation (10) for determining y_t^* and i_t was determined by equation (9). There were thus three additional variables and three additional independent equations. The extension of the system followed with eight more unknowns, P_t, a_t, C_t, C_{ti}, I, Y, L, Q_t, and eight more independent equations. Professor Krelle thought that he ought to have made it clear that he had put some of the relations not in the mathematical order but in the order significant for the purpose of economic analysis.

Professor Robinson thought that in his treatment of the short run Professor Krelle was by implication assuming the non-existence of the state. Between periods 1 and 2 the budget did nothing to modify the consumption function. One was left supposing that public finances were still run in a Gladstonian way by balancing the budget and doing nothing which could affect the emerging trend.

Professor Krelle said that before this he had constructed and published a model taking the state's operations into account but it was very cumbersome and nobody read it. Before devising a model one must decide on the scale. This was a model at a certain distance from reality. He had decided to limit it to the private capitalistic sector and allow nothing to interfere with it. He could have gone nearer to the complexity of facts but the verifying of a model of this sort was likely to be too great a task even with the help of the most efficient computers.

Professor Lecaillon had also regretted that his model had not included the public sector. Professor Krelle would answer that he had no objection to Professor Lecaillon's suggestion of bringing income redistribution into a model of this sort but again this would make the model much more cumbersome whereas his intention had been to make it operational.

Professor Krelle thanked Professor Bronfenbrenner for introducing his paper so clearly and so completely. He wished to stress that the dichotomy between growth and income distribution in his model related to the long run only, not to the short run. Professor Bronfenbrenner had asked him how the power of trade unions could be measured. Professor Krelle answered that if the wage rate grew faster than the full employment of the labour force made necessary, this would prove the power of the trade unions, although this could be just an 'ex post' measure of this power. Professor Krelle would agree that trade union power should be considered

447

as a variable (he would take the opportunity to remind the audience that all variables in his paper were indexed t), but then the principle of profit maximization would have to go.

Professor Krelle wished to make it clear that he had not assumed z to be equal to one in the long run; he only assumed the degree of capacity utilization to be constant in the long run. Nor did he regard μ as a constant, but as an exogenous variable, as the impact of political and sociological factors on the wage rate could change through time.

He admitted Professor Reder's criticism that he had not made any assumption about the length of the working week. A change in it could obviously affect the amount of work supplied by the labour force. He had also been criticized for supposing the degree of monopoly power to be constant. Although he had not meant it to be always constant, being an exogenous variable he assumed it to be constant here for simplicity's sake.

Professor Krelle could not agree with what Professor Reder had said about his concluding sentence. Was not packing up many different influences within one conceptual framework what theory ought to be ? Far from being afraid of putting too many things into a nutshell he had tried to construct a conceptual system in which all the influences were treated as variables having some precise meaning and an intuitive appeal as well.

Finally, he was fairly sure that his model was consistent because he had solved it numerically for feasible values. What he had had in mind had been to put together what was known about consumption and investment behaviours and technological change, and see how income distribution, employment and the rate of growth were affected.

Chapter 17

DISTRIBUTION IN THE
LONG AND SHORT RUN

BY

ROBERT M. SOLOW
Massachusetts Institute of Technology

I. ALTERNATIVE THEORIES OF DISTRIBUTION
IN THE LONG RUN

THE object of long-run theories of distribution, which is almost the only kind we have, is to explain the slow trend behaviour of the shares of wages and property income ('profits' for short) in the national product. It used to be thought that the long-run trend was adequately described by Bowley's Law of constant relative shares. More recent statistical work has suggested that, in the United States at least, the share of wages has been increasing slowly at the expense of profits.[1] Whatever one believes about these complicated facts, they are what the theory is supposed to explain.

There appear to be two main competing macro-economic theories of distribution in the long run.[2] One of them is the 'marginal productivity' theory (appropriately modified by considerations of the average degree of monopoly) and the other, for want of any more accurate name, may be called the 'savings-investment' theory. I think this characterization is misleading, and, so far as the factors behind the catch-phrases are concerned, there are not two theories but only one. The essential distinction has to be made on other grounds.

To begin with, the marginal productivity theory is fundamentally a micro-economic theory and its presentation in macro-economic terms is an act of empirical desperation. Secondly, there is no such thing as a marginal productivity theory all by itself. Suppose the

---

[1] For a summary of the broad facts and one way of accounting for them, see Kendrick and Sato, 'Factor Prices, Productivity, and Growth', *American Economic Review*, December 1963.

[2] These and other theories are well summarized in W. Krelle, *Verteilungstheorie*, Tübingen, 1962.

economy contains n goods and m factors of production. Then there is a subset of the equations of general competitive equilibrium which states that the value of the marginal product of each factor in the production of each good is equal to its price. This subset of equations is usually said to constitute the marginal productivity theory of distribution. But even if the supply of each factor is taken as given and m balance equations are added requiring each factor to be fully employed, there are only $nm+m$ equations. These equations involve as unknowns the nm allocations of factors to industries, the m factor prices, and the $n-1$ relative prices of goods, or $nm+m+n-1$ unknowns in all. Unless there is only one commodity, there are fewer equations than unknowns and these equations cannot in general determine anything at all. They have to be supplemented by demand equations for commodities, and that will bring in much the same considerations that appear in the savings-investment theory.

Nor can the savings-investment theory itself stand on purely macro-economic foundations. Savings, investment, and relative shares are, of course, macro-economic totals. But in any capitalist economy, income is actually distributed in firms and industries. The share of wages in the national income can always be exhibited as a weighted average of the wage shares in the income originating in the several industries, with weights equal to the proportion of national income originating in each industry. One can believe that there are macro-economic laws governing the macro-economic totals, but such a theory owes it to itself as well as to others to show how the laws governing the distribution of income within firms or industries are made *consistent* with the macro-economic laws. So micro-economics cannot be escaped.

There is a red herring to be avoided here. I am going to reason in this paper in terms of old-fashioned models in which capital goods are freely transferable from industry to industry, smoothly substitutable for labour, and not subject to technical progress or obsolescence. A realistic theory must naturally get rid of these assumptions. But recent research has shown that this can be done without essentially altering the long-run structure of the theory.[1] The intensive margin of substitution can be replaced by a moving extensive margin, with plant going into or out of operation as prices,

---

[1] See R. Solow, 'Substitution and Fixed Coefficients in the Theory of Capital', *Review of Economic Studies*, June 1962, and 'Heterogeneous Capital and Smooth Production Functions', *Econometrica*, October 1963 ; N. Kaldor and J. Mirrlees, 'A New Model of Economic Growth', *Review of Economic Studies*, June 1962 ; G. Pyatt, 'A Measure of Capital', *Review of Economic Studies*, October 1963.

wages, and its own technical characteristics permit it to earn or not to earn quasi-rents. Corners create indeterminacies, but small corners create only small indeterminacies.

If the true differences among alternative theories do not lie here, where are they ? One possible real source of difference is in assumptions about causality. Pre-Keynesian (pre-*General Theory*, that is) theories work on the assumption that real wages settle at a level which will ensure full employment of labour, and similarly for other factors of production, so that output is limited by the availability of resources. Post-Keynesian theories operate on the assumption that this does not or cannot happen, so that output is limited by effective demand. But even what is usually called the neo-classical theory of distribution can work on the Keynesian assumptions — though it may prove necessary to abandon the assumption of perfect competition, which would be a gain in any case. Moreover, so long as we keep to long-run steady-growth comparisons, with fluctuations in effective demand small relative to trend changes, the key variables mutually entail one another and theoretical predictions turn out to be much the same regardless of which set of assumptions one chooses about the determination of output. So while this is a very important distinction for other purposes, it is probably not the important one for discriminating between theories of long-run distribution.

I suspect that the really vital difference between the two theories lies in the kind of micro-economic behaviour that is explicitly or implicitly postulated. Marginal productivity theory rests on the assumption of profit maximization, with due modification for uncertainty and imperfections of competition. The savings-investment theory, at least in Mr. Kaldor's hands, seems to rest on the assumption that uncertainty and oligopoly require some other behaviour principle than profit maximization.

It is not hard to show how, in a simplified model operating under full employment and competition, the marginal productivity theory is incomplete by itself, but becomes complete when it absorbs something about saving and investment. For this purpose I take the two-sector model lately explored by James Meade and others. Let one industry produce consumer goods and the other investment goods, each under conditions of constant returns to scale and diminishing marginal rates of substitution between labour and a single kind of investment good. Then the marginal productivity equations tell us that

$$w = p_C M_{CL} = p_I M_{IL} \qquad r = p_C M_{CI} = p_I M_{II}$$

where w is the money wage, r the money rental on a unit of investment goods, p_C and p_I the prices of consumer and investment goods,
and M_{AB} is the marginal physical product of factor B in the production of good A. From these equations it follows that the share of
wages in the income generated in the C-sector is the elasticity of
C-output with respect to labour input, and analogously for profits
and the I-sector. These micro-economic relative shares are independent of other economic facts only if the separate production
functions for the two goods are of Cobb–Douglas type, which is not
required. If we let L stand for total employment, C for the annual
output of consumer goods, and I for the output of (for simplicity,
non-depreciating) investment goods, then the share of wages in
aggregate income is

$$\frac{wL}{p_C C + p_I I}.$$

It is obvious that this aggregate share is a weighted average of the
two sector shares, with weights

$$\frac{p_C C}{p_C C + p_I I} \quad \text{and} \quad \frac{p I^I}{p_C C + p_I I}.$$

The aggregate wage share must be between the two sector shares,
but it need not be constant even if they are, because the weights
will change as data change.

It is easily verified that these equations are indeterminate, as I
showed earlier. But suppose we know the savings function (or,
what is the same thing, the demand function for consumer goods),
and suppose that the government or Providence ensures that the
demand for new investment goods is just enough to offset the full-
employment demand for consumer goods. Suppose in fact that
expenditure on consumer goods is equal to a fraction $l - s_W$ of the
money wage bill plus a fraction $l - s_r$ of aggregate profits. Then we
can add the equation

$$p_C C = (l - s_W) wL + (l - s^-_r)(p_C C + p_I I - wL)$$

and the model becomes complete. One may call this the 'supply-
and-demand' theory, or The Good Old Theory, for short.

Let R be the share of profits in aggregate income, and e_C and e_I
be the elasticities of output with respect to inputs of capital goods in
the two sectors. Then, from what has already been said, we know that

$$R = \frac{p_C C}{p_C C + p_I I} e_C + \frac{p_I I}{p_C C + p_I I^e}.$$

Then, by substitution from the consumption function, we obtain

$$R = \frac{eC + s_W(eI - eC)}{1 - (s_r - s_w)(e_I - e_C)}.$$

By putting $s_w = 0$, we get the formula appropriate to what I may call the Joan Robinson version of the model:

$$R = \frac{e_C}{1 - sr(e_I - e_C)}.$$

By putting $s_w = s_r = s$, we get the formula appropriate to what may be called the Harrod version of the model:

$$R = e_C + s(e_I - e_C).$$

Needless to say, by juggling the consumption function and the income identity $Y = p_C C + p_I I = wL + P$ alone, one gets the Kaldor formulation

$$R = P/Y = \frac{1}{s_r - s_w} \frac{pI^I}{Y} - \frac{s_w}{s_r - s_w}.$$

This appears to make R independent of the elasticities e_C and e_I. But not really, because with full employment and given savings propensities, relative prices and therefore $p_I I / Y$ will depend on the elasticities.[1] If there is only one commodity, in effect, so that $e_C = e_I$, then R is independent of the savings function and equal to the common elasticity. This represents a real difference in 'prediction' between the two theories; if I am right, it must be explained by different assumptions about micro-economic behaviour.[2]

II. DISTRIBUTIVE SHARES IN THE SHORT RUN

There are fairly well-defined short-run changes in relative shares superimposed on whatever smooth trend-movement may

[1] From the formula for R as a weighted average of e_C and e_I, it follows that $\frac{pI^I}{Y} = \frac{R - e_C}{e_I - e_C}$. If this is substituted into the Kaldor formula and the result solved for R, one gets the general formula of the text giving R in terms of elasticities and savings coefficients. The two formulae are thus equivalent. The special character of the one-commodity case arises because then the investment quota is independent of relative prices. [This footnote, which was not available to participants in the discussion at Palermo, has been added by the author to meet a comment by Professor Rasmussen in the course of that discussion.—Ed.]

[2] If the isoquants have corners, e_C and/or e_I may be undefined at those points. There will always be right-hand and left-hand limits, however, and these can be used to set upper and lower bounds to distributive shares. If both goods are produced under strictly fixed coefficients, then the limits for the elasticities are one and zero and the formulas become useless.

exist.[1] As output falls away from near-capacity at the peak of a business cycle, the initial reduction in income is concentrated quite heavily on profits ; the share and total of profits may fall drastically. At the low point of the cycle, perhaps even a bit before, profits generally begin to recover their lost ground. There seems to be a fairly strong rate-of-change effect, so that at any given level of output profits are higher on the upswing than on the downswing. So much is obvious from the statistics.

Kuh has found for the United States (confirmed by Neild's findings for Britain) that, in the course of these fluctuations in output and employment, the ratio p/w of prices to money wages is much more stable (apart from trend) than the ratio Q/L of real output per manhour. Since the product of these two ratios is the reciprocal of the wage share, this amounts to saying that short-run changes in distributions are primarily a reflection of short-run changes in productivity. Differential movements of prices and wages are much less significant. (There are some differences between the two countries ; Kuh finds rather more sensitivity of p/w to demand conditions in the United States than Neild does in the United Kingdom. But the statement given above will do as a summary description.) Thus the fall in the share of profits during a downswing results mainly from a fall, or a slower-than-usual rise, in productivity, and much less from any crumbling of prices relative to money wages.

A good theory of distribution in the short run has to account for this pattern of behaviour. One could hope for more. One could hope, that is, for a short-run distribution theory which is *consistent* with some satisfactory long-run theory. By consistency I mean something fairly obvious. A long-run distribution theory is supposed to account for trend-movements in distribution. It should in principle say what relative shares would be if the economy were for a long time undisturbed by fluctuations in effective demand. A short-run theory is supposed to explain the characteristic changes in relative shares in the course of disturbances caused by fluctuations in effective demand. It would be desirable for a short-run theory to show how, as disturbances die away, the distribution of income tends more or less slowly to merge into that predicted by some

---

[1] The best references are : for the U.S.A., E. Kuh, 'Profits, Profit Markups and Productivity', Study Paper No. 15, Joint Economic Committee, Washington, 1960, and also an unpublished paper on 'Income Distribution over the Business Cycle', 1963 ; for the U.K., R. Neild, *Pricing and Employment in the Trade Cycle*, Cambridge, 1963.

companion long-run theory. In that case the theories are consistent.

It is possible to extend the Good Old Theory by fitting it with a consistent short-run theory. One way of doing so has been sketched by my colleague Paul Samuelson in an unpublished note.[1] He assumes, quite plausibly, that the output producible from given current inputs of capital and labour depends on how much time has been available to adjust to changes in the variable input labour. The long-run production function is thus the envelope of a sequence of short- and shorter-run production functions. Unexpected changes in output are met in the first instance by movements along the short-run production function, but as time passes and the proper adjustments are made the long-run production function becomes accessible. The relation between short- and long-run production functions is much like the standard relation between short- and long-run cost curves. It is natural to suppose that the elasticity of substitution between labour and capital goods is quite small along the short-run production functions, but becomes effectively larger as more time can be taken for adjustment. There is no need to assume that the long-run elasticity of substitution is exactly unity ; it may be larger or smaller than that, so long as it is larger than the short-run elasticity of substitution, and the latter is less than unity.

Now as output recedes from some established high level, the Samuelson model permits labour input to fall, while the input of capital goods may be treated as fixed. Initially the movement is along a very short-run production function, whose elasticity of substitution may be very much less than one. Conventional marginal-productivity reasoning leads to the conclusion that the relative share of profits will fall, perhaps drastically, since the capital/labour ratio is rising. But as the process of adjustment to changed output catches up with events, perhaps even by extrapolation, the effective elasticity of substitution rises towards its long-run value. The profit share will therefore recover some of its lost ground. If a new, lower, plateau of output should become established, then ultimately the long-run production function will become the effective one. Whether the share of profits in the new plateau is greater or less than in the original plateau depends on whether the long-run elasticity of substitution is less or greater than unity, and on what eventually happens to the stock of capital. But in the course of the short-run movement, the model will reproduce the kind of qualitative behaviour of distributive shares required by the facts.

[1] P. A. Samuelson, *An Integrated Macro-Micro Theory*, 1963.

Much the same kind of behaviour can be generated by a model which permits no intensive margin of substitution between capital and labour at all, but produces changes in output by a moving extensive margin, with the oldest or most labour-using or least profitable plant moving into or out of production as demand conditions require.

There is, however, a difficulty with all such models. If the short-run production, whatever its elasticity of substitution, is assumed to be of the normal shape, with constant returns to scale and diminishing returns as proportions vary, then as the capital/labour ratio rises in the short run, output per manhour should rise with it. But, as Kuh and Neild have documented, this is contrary to fact. Productivity falls in recessions, or rises more slowly than the trend of technical progress. A satisfactory short-run theory of distribution must be able to account for this.

Various more or less *ad hoc* explanations can be found for the cyclical behaviour of labour productivity. The intensity of the individual worker's effort may be variable for short episodes of increased or decreased output, though not for longer maintained changes. Or there may be falling unit costs in the short run. Mr. Kaldor prefers this second interpretation of the facts. The assumption of falling average costs is inconvenient for any theory based on profit-maximizing behaviour, though of course not in the slightest inconsistent with it so long as one does not insist on perfect competition. A Samuelson model with monopoly can accommodate a marginal product of labour higher than its average product. In the next section of this paper, I wish to propose a model of short-run behaviour which can account for the Kuh–Neild facts without invoking static falling unit costs. This model has the advantage of being consistent with the sort of long-run theory sketched in the first section of the paper. It amounts to a formalization of the widely, if casually, discussed notion of 'labour hoarding', and thus supplements the Samuelson model.

I propose this model not simply to escape from increasing returns, but because it captures aspects of industrial behaviour which seem to be real and important. Indeed, I have no particular objection to a bit of falling unit costs at below-capacity outputs. The labour-hoarding and increasing-returns models are complementary in the sense that both may be true and necessary parts of a full explanation of the facts.[1]

---

[1] After this paper was written, there appeared the excellent paper by T. Wilson and O. Eckstein, 'Short-Run Productivity Behavior in U.S. Manufacturing',

III. A SHORT-RUN MODEL OF LABOUR-HOARDING

My object in this section is to produce a simple and strong model capable of describing many of the buffer-stock characteristics of labour as a factor of production. I have not hesitated to make radical simplifying assumptions.

Consider a typical oligopolistic firm producing a perishable product, so that it holds no finished inventories. For the usual reasons, the firm has adopted a price policy — to be discussed later — and committed itself to adhere to the policy in the face of fluctuating demand. The firm produces its output with inputs of capital and labour according to a Cobb–Douglas production function. Since I shall be talking exclusively about the Keynesian short-run, I shall assume that the input of capital is fixed for the time being. By appropriate choice of units, therefore, we can say that

$$Q = L^j$$

where Q is the current rate of output (and sales), L represents current labour requirements, and the elasticity j is a positive number between zero and one.

Given its price policy, the firm knows that its sales will fluctuate cyclically. I have chosen the simplest possible time-shape for the course of sales. There is a regular cycle lasting for T months. At the current instant, $t = 0$, sales are at their peak, and current labour requirements (*not* current sales) are equal to $k + mT$. Current labour requirements are about to fall instantaneously to the level k, after which they will rise linearly according to the equation $L = k + mt$. At time T sales and labour requirements will have risen back to their current levels, whereupon L will fall instantaneously to k again, and the whole cycle will repeat itself. Fig. 1 on p. 466 shows what the time-graphs of L and Q will look like.

The only costs to be considered are labour costs. Since I want to introduce the notion of labour hoarding I must distinguish between

Review of Economics and Statistics, February 1964, 41–54. They show how one can account for observed productivity behaviour within a model derived from the Marshall-Viner apparatus of long-, short-, and shorter-run U-shaped cost curves. Their short-run total labour-cost curves are linear, for statistical purposes, and this implies always-falling unit labour costs. Wilson and Eckstein point out that the low labour costs at high outputs may be at the expense of incurring high costs of other kinds, and may in any case not be achievable except for short bursts of production. These two factors involve considerations exactly like those introduced in this paper. The two approaches seem definitely complementary.

current employment, E, and current labour requirements for production, already labelled L. I shall assume that the money wage is constant in the course of the cycle (there is no technical progress, though it would be merely difficult to allow some). The first component of current costs is just the wage bill wE, since all employed workers must be paid the going wage. I now wish to introduce two other categories of current costs which have become commonplace in the literature of Operations Research.[1]

The first category consists of costs associated with changing the level of employment. They occur because layoffs often require severance payments, because newly-hired workers must be trained at the company's expense, and in general because changing the level of employment is associated with some disorganization of the production process. There is no reason why hiring and firing costs should be symmetrical, but for the sake of simplicity I shall assume that they are and that they are proportional to the square of the rate of change of employment. Thus we have a component of current costs equal to $v\dot{E}^2$, where $\dot{E}=dE/dt$ is the instantaneous rate of change of employment.

Finally, I shall assume that employment at any moment can be greater or less than current production labour requirements. If greater, the excess employment can be set to work repairing equipment or doing general housekeeping of a kind that is not reflected in the measured output of the firm. These services are presumably less valuable to the firm than ordinary production labour, so there is a cost associated with excess employment; this cost is greater the greater the volume of excess employment. If employment (thought of as measured in manhours) is less than labour requirements, the difference is made up in overtime work and this incurs an additional cost; instead of simply charging overtime as $1\frac{1}{2}$ times the standard wage, I shall assume that overtime costs increase as the amount of overtime increases. The simplest way to introduce undertime and overtime costs is to add a component to current costs equal to

$$a(L-E)^2+b(L-E).$$

The disadvantage of this quadratic form is that eventually enough excess employment makes a negative contribution to production; perhaps this is plausible, but in any case it will make no difference

---

[1] See for instance, Holt, Modigliani, Muth, and Simon, *Planning Production, Inventories and Work Force*, London, 1960, esp. pp. 15–25, 47–63, 92–109; and Arrow, Karlin, and Scarf (eds.), *Studies in the Mathematical Theory of Inventory and Production*, Stanford, 1958, esp. chap. 6 by Arrow and Karlin.

if fluctuations in sales are not too extreme. If we assume that the first undertime minute can be employed at tasks only infinitesimally less profitable than production itself, and that the first overtime minute costs no more than the going wage, then we can specify that $b = w$. I shall make this specification, though it can very easily be lifted. The three elements of current cost are illustrated in Fig. 2.

The firm faces a known time series of sales and therefore of labour requirements. It regulates its employment policy in such a way as to minimize the costs incurred in the course of a complete cycle of sales. It would not be hard to minimize a discounted sum of costs over a complete cycle, but so long as the discount rate is small the solution would be only slightly affected and so I have not pursued refinement. The problem of employment policy for the firm is thus to minimize

$$C = \int_0^T [wE(t) + v\dot{E}(t)^2 + a(L(t) - E(t))^2 + b(L(t) - E(t))]dt$$

where $L(t) = k + mt$ and $b = w$. I will discuss the problem of deciding on initial and terminal employment, $E(0)$ and $E(T)$, in due course.

This is the simplest kind of problem in the calculus of variations. The cost-minimizing employment policy must satisfy the differential equation [1]

$$\ddot{E} = h^2E - h^2L + \frac{w - b}{2v} = h^2E - h^2(k + mt),$$

where $h = \sqrt{\dfrac{a}{v}}$. The solution of this equation is

$$E(t) = A_1 e^{-ht} + A_2 e^{ht} + k + mt \quad 0 \leq t \leq T$$

where the constants of integration A_1 and A_2 are determined in terms of initial and terminal employment by

$$A_1 = \frac{(E_0 - L_0)e^{hT} - (E_T - L_T)}{e^{hT} - e^{-hT}}$$

$$A_2 = \frac{(E_T - L_T) - (E_0 - L_0)e^{-hT}}{e^{hT} - e^{-hT}}.$$

To specify optimal employment policy completely, we must provide a rule for fixing E_0 and E_T. (Of course $L_0 = k$ and $L_T = k + mT$.)

[1] If discounted cost had been minimized instead, the differential equation would have the term $-r\dot{E}$ added to the right-hand side, where r is the rate of discount. For small r this would make little difference.

There is no dodging the fact that the best initial and terminal levels of employment will depend on what has preceded and what will follow the current cycle in sales. On the assumption that exactly similar cycles have been going on for a long time and will continue for a long time around a stationary trend, it seems natural to look for a repetitive employment pattern. (One could incorporate a smooth trend at the expense of a lot of arithmetic and an explicit treatment of investment, which I have preferred to avoid.) This leads to the following calculation : put $E_0 = E_T$, so that the firm ends each cycle with the same level of employment. Then calculate C, the minimum sum of costs over a typical cycle, treating the common value of initial and terminal employment as a parameter. Then choose the value of $E_0 = E_T$ that minimizes C. When this is done, it turns out that the firm should begin and end each cycle with a level of employment halfway between the peak labour-requirement and the trough labour-requirement. Thus

$$E_0 = E_T = k + \frac{mT}{2}.$$

The reason for this peculiarly symmetrical result is that the cost-function I have chosen is itself excessively symmetrical : increases and decreases in employment are equally costly and there is a corresponding symmetry in the extra gains from undertime and costs of overtime work. If, for example, I had assumed that hiring costs exceeded layoff costs, or overtime costs exceeded the gain from undertime, then it would have been optimal for fluctuations in employment to take place about a higher level with less overtime at the peak and more hoarding of labour at the trough.

In any case, with this choice of initial-terminal employment, we have

$$A_1 = \frac{\frac{mT}{2}(e^{hT} + 1)}{e^{hT} - e^{-hT}}$$

$$A_2 = \frac{-\frac{mT}{2}(1 + e^{-hT})}{e^{hT} - e^{-hT}} = -e^{-hT} A_1$$

$$E(t) = A_1(e^{-hT} - e^{h(t-T)}) + k + mt.$$

A rough comparative sketch of $L(t)$ and optimal $E(t)$ is shown in Fig. 3 on p. 466. When employment exceeds labour requirements early in the recession, there is labour hoarding. After the midpoint of the cycle, there is overtime work. Of course the precise characterization shown in Fig. 3 is not to be taken seriously. It depends on the particular assumption I have made about the nature of costs and the object of employment policy. What is important is that this kind of model has shown itself to be capable of explaining the observed pattern of labour productivity during short-term fluctuations in output and sales.

The precise course of apparent productivity during the business cycle will depend on how labour input is measured. If the statistical measure of labour input is employment, then output per man employed will be simply Q/E. If labour is measured in manhours, so that overtime work is taken into account (but not undertime) then measured labour input will be E when E exceeds L and L when L exceeds E, and productivity will be measured accordingly by either Q/E or Q/L. In either case, when output falls sharply at the peak, measured labour input will fall much more slowly, and productivity will fall in accordance with the facts. If output were to fall sharply, but not discontinuously as in the formal model, then productivity would continue to fall for a while. Sometime in the course of the upswing, presumably near the bottom, productivity begins to rise. The statistical course of events later in the upswing depends on the nature of the measure of labour input. If overtime work is fully reflected in labour input, productivity should begin to fall before the peak. But if labour input is measured in a way which corresponds fairly closely with the E-series, then productivity may increase sharply just before the peak because output is continuing to rise whereas employment may taper off and begin to fall even before output has reached a peak (to avoid the costs associated with rapid changes in employment). I must repeat that one should not take seriously the exact productivity pattern produced by the model, because the cost relations themselves are deliberately oversimplified and because the cyclical pattern of sales has been grotesquely sharpened to yield strong and easy results.[1] What is important is the demonstration that a pattern of productivity behaviour recognizably like that observed for manufacturing industry in the United States and United Kingdom can be produced as the result of entirely rational cost-minimization without invoking sharply-falling unit costs.

---

[1] Figures 1–2, 1–3, and 1–4 in Holt, *et al.* show how a quite realistic model, which includes production for inventory, can give a good representation of observed behaviour.

On the assumption that the ratio p/w is constant, or moves within narrow bounds, during short-term fluctuations in output, the distribution of income between wages and profits will simply mirror the movements of productivity. The profit share will fall early in the cycle when productivity falls and recover later on as productivity rises. Since this kind of model is capable of accounting for observed short-term movements in productivity, it provides also a short-run theory of distribution.

IV. A MODIFIED MARGINAL PRODUCTIVITY THEORY

Up to this point the sales of the typical firm have been taken as given. Correspondingly, nothing has been said about the price policy of the firm except that, for oligopoly reasons, it is committed to keeping the ratio p/w constant in the short run. Even taking that commitment for granted, there remains a question as to how the particular value of p/w is set by the firm. The answer to this question will also determine the level around which distributive shares fluctuate ; the model so far has thrown light only on the shape of the time pattern. There are as many answers to this final question as there are market structures which may be postulated with some degree of plausibility. I shall consider only a single simple case. In that case, it will turn out that the short-run theory sketched above is *consistent* in the long run with a slightly modified version of the marginal productivity theory.

The price policy I have in mind is this. Suppose the money wage rate constant. The firm must set a price on its product, to be held constant throughout the cycle in sales. The *shape* of the cycle in sales is independent of the firm's price decision ; it depends only on aggregate effective demand. But the *level* around which sales fluctuate does depend on the price. In particular, I assume that the peak (or average) level of sales depends on the price set, according to an ordinary downward-sloping demand curve for the firm, and that the cycle in sales is simply proportionate. Thus, for example, if one price should lead to peak sales of 100 and trough sales of 90, then a lower price which leads to peak sales of 110 will lead to trough sales of 99, with the same drop of 10 per cent.

Knowing this, and knowing its demand curve, the firm can calculate for any given price what its total sales will be over a full cycle. It can therefore calculate its total sales revenue (undiscounted for

462

simplicity). We have already had occasion to calculate total costs for that employment pattern which meets demands and minimizes costs. The difference between revenues and costs is the total of profits earned in the course of a complete cycle. The firm sets the price which maximizes this total of profits.

This leads to an elementary but laborious calculation whose details are omitted. The outcome, however, is interesting and important. We can represent the firm's demand curve as showing the peak output Q_T associated with each price. Let the elasticity of this demand curve (taken positively) be η. Since $Q_T = L_T^j$, we can read off the peak labour requirement L_T corresponding to any Q_T and therefore to any price. The marginal productivity of labour when the peak output is being produced is

$$jL_T^{j-1};$$

I shall call it MPL_T. Finally, let λ be the ratio of trough labour requirements to peak labour requirements,

$$\lambda = \frac{L_0}{L_T}.$$

In this notation, the profit-maximizing condition can be written in the form:

$$p\left(1 - \frac{1}{\eta}\right)\left[\frac{2(1-\lambda^{1+j})MPL_T}{(1-\lambda)(1+\lambda)(1+j)}\right] = w + \frac{2v}{1+\lambda}\frac{L_T}{T}\left(h - \frac{2(1-\lambda)^2}{T}\right).$$

The term in square brackets on the left-hand side of this equation can be given a straightforward interpretation. It is, in fact, a weighted average of the marginal productivity of labour at all phases of the business cycle, where the weights are the labour requirements at each phase of the cycle. We can call it $\overline{MPL}$; it is formally defined by

$$\overline{MPL} = \frac{\int_0^T jL(t)^{j-1} \cdot L(t)dt}{\int_0^T L(t)dt}.$$

The profit-maximization condition now becomes

$$\overline{MPL} \cdot p \cdot \left(1 - \frac{1}{\eta}\right) = w + \alpha$$

where α is an 'adjustment factor'. In words we can say that under the special assumptions made, profit-maximizing over the business cycle requires that the 'marginal revenue product of labour averaged over the whole cycle' be equal to the money wage plus an adjustment factor. The precise character of the adjustment factor depends on the particular cost function I have chosen and on the peculiarly simple cyclical pattern that is assumed to occur. The most I can do, therefore, is to speculate about its order of magnitude.

In the book by Holt, Modigliani, Muth and Simon cited earlier, a model very similar to this is applied to a paint factory. Values for the various constants are given which are at least close approximations to those characterizing a particular industrial enterprise. Labour is measured in man-months and costs in dollars per man-month. Employment is about 100. The approximate values of the parameter corresponding to those appearing in this paper are: $w=340$, $a=6\cdot4$, $b=290$ (so it is almost true that $w=b$), $v=64$. Therefore h is about $0\cdot3$. The adjustment factor α is thus approximately

$$\frac{2 \cdot 64 \cdot 100}{(1+\lambda)T}\left(0\cdot3 - \frac{2(1-\lambda)^2}{T}\right).$$

If we take a 10 per cent drop in labour requirements ($\lambda=0\cdot9$) as typical for modern industrial fluctuation and 3 years as the period of a full cycle ($T=36$ months) then α is about 55 or about 15 per cent of the monthly wage. Thus the required modification to the usual marginal productivity doctrine is not insubstantial. One would conjecture, however, that a cycle somewhat smoother than the rather jagged saw-tooth I have taken for convenience would reduce the significance of the adjustment factor.

The fact that the adjustment factor is proportional to v — the parameter corresponding to the costs of changing the level of employment — suggests that in a movement from one stationary state to another the adjustment factor might lose its significance entirely. This turns out to be the case. If at time zero sales fall suddenly to a new plateau level which is expected to be maintained thereafter, the optimal adjustment calls for employment to fall gradually towards the new lower labour requirement. If the stock of capital remain unchanged, productivity will fall sharply at first and then rise gradually toward the new (higher) level corresponding to the lower sales and labour requirements. If, as would be more natural, the stock of capital is reduced in the process, then the obvious amendments have to be made. As stationary conditions are re-established, the adjustment factor in the wage equation will disappear and eventually the wage will equal the marginal revenue product of labour, with due allowance for the degree of monopoly.

Evidently the correction factor α is likely to be positive. This implies that when output fluctuates, the money wage will be less than the average marginal revenue product of labour. The reason for this is that the cost to the firm of a unit of labour is more than the wage ; when employment fluctuates, there are hiring and firing costs, and these reduce the value to the firm of hiring a marginal worker. Moreover, when overtime rates are being earned, the straight-time wage, w, understates the earnings of labour.

V. A BRIEF COMMENT ON UNCERTAINTY

This analysis has been conducted on the assumption that the future course of sales is known to the firm. But the limitation to conditions of certainty is not intrinsic. Owing to the quadratic character of the cost function one can invoke a theorem of Theil and Simon [1] which states, roughly, the following : if under conditions of uncertainty the objective of the firm is to minimize expected cost, then an optimal policy is one which replaces uncertain quantities with their expected values and proceeds deterministically. In other words, when the criterion is quadratic, expected values are 'certainty equivalents'. This is an advantage of the quadratic formulation not shared by even simpler cost functions.

VI. CONCLUSIONS

(1) The essential differences among alternative theories of distribution are likely to be found in their assumptions about microeconomic behaviour, not in any of the fashionable slogans.

(2) In any theory of distribution, full weight has to be given to uncertainty and imperfection of competition.

(3) Short-run or out-of-equilibrium behaviour is likely to be the key element in the formulation and empirical testing of distribution theories.

[1] H. Simon, 'Dynamic Programming under Uncertainty with a Quadratic Criterion Function', *Econometrica*, vol. 24 (1956), pp. 74–81 ; H. Theil, 'A Note on Certainty Equivalence in Dynamic Planning', *Econometrica*, vol. 25 (1957), pp. 346–349.

The Distribution of National Income

(4) It is possible to construct a theory along profit-maximizing lines which can account for the observed short-run distributional facts and reverts to the Good Old Theory under conditions of long-run equilibrium.

(5) When output is fluctuating, the wage is likely to fall short of the marginal revenue product of labour.

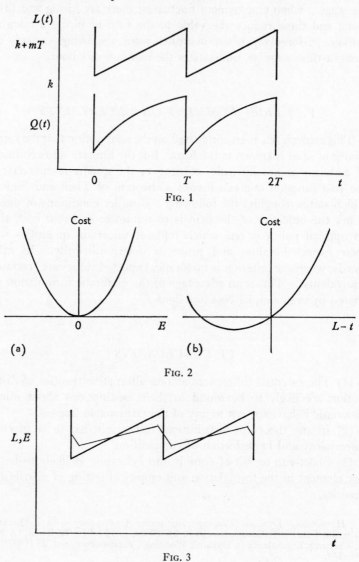

FIG. 1

FIG. 2

(a)

(b)

FIG. 3

DISCUSSION OF PROFESSOR SOLOW'S PAPER

Professor Phelps Brown said that it seemed to him that the interest and value of meetings such as these lay in the convergence on a common problem of the thoughts of economists who normally worked at a distance from one another. How was one to reconcile and combine several different theories of distribution each of which claimed allegiance because it rested on some observed propensity of behaviour or inescapable requirement of equilibrium ? It was with an essay on divided loyalty that Professor Solow opened. The discussion of the relations between the marginal productivity theory, appropriately modified by considerations of the average degree of monopoly on one side and the saving-investment theory on the other, had stimulated but also puzzled Professor Phelps Brown ; for it seemed to establish two propositions, (a) that each type of theory was incomplete without the other, (b) that the two types were basically incompatible.

The first proposition raised no difficulty. To show that the marginal productivity theory could not stand alone but had to be supplemented by an account of demand, Professor Solow had only to remind his readers that the equations expressing the basic postulate of the theory formed only one subset of equations within the whole pricing system. To show that the saving-investment theory could not stand alone, Professor Solow first argued that the division of the aggregate product did not occur in the aggregate : the shares found by the statistician arose only by the summation of shares formed firm by firm and any theory of the aggregate had to begin with the components. But second, and pressing his scalpel deeper into the savings-investment theory, Professor Solow showed that the very formulation that made it appear wholly independent of marginal adjustments in the firm, had in fact to take relative prices as given. For the Kaldorian ratio of the output of investment goods to the aggregate product was not given solely by entrepreneurs' decisions to increase capacity in a certain proportion, but also depended on the relative prices of investment goods in comparison with those of consumption goods. To complete a Kaldorian system, therefore, one needed to show how relative prices were determined and this related again to decisions taken in the firm.

Professor Solow then showed how the two kinds of theory could in fact be used to complete one another in a singularly compact two-sector model whose neatness Professor Phelps Brown thought largely due to an adroit use of the elasticities of output with respect to factor input as surrogates of the marginal adjustment in the firm. In this model the aggregate share of profits depended on both (from the marginal productivity theory) the elasticities of output with respect to the inputs of capital goods in the making of consumer and of capital goods, and (from the savings-investment theory) the propensity to save out of wages and profits, and on these alone.

Both theories could be brought into play without over-determination because Professor Solow had set out to work not with undifferentiated units of national product but with a two-sector economy in which the output of capital and consumption goods was distinguished, and Professor Phelps Brown hoped that the author would agree with him that one could think of a change in the aggregate share of profits as being brought about by a shift in the relative activity of the two sectors — a shift which would at the same time make an appropriate change in the relative output of capital and consumption goods.

Professor Solow's model did not display the process by which equilibrium would be reached or indeed give any assurance that equilibrium would be reached at all. A raised investment programme, for instance, would require a rise of the relative activity of the sector producing capital goods and how could one be assured that the elasticities of output would be such as to generate thereby just that rise in relative profits that was also required ? Nevertheless Professor Solow's model had the merit of simplicity, and Professor Phelps Brown thought it most illuminating in stating with all the emphasis of brevity that two conditions of equilibrium could be imposed together : namely that aggregate savings should equal aggregate investment ; and that in each sector factor compensation per unit should equal the marginal value product of the factor.

But Professor Phelps Brown regretted not to have been able to form a clear idea about what seemed to be Professor Solow's second conclusion, namely that the marginal productivity and the savings-investment theories were basically incompatible. Professor Phelps Brown thought that he would not misinterpret Professor Solow's thought by saying that if, instead of a two-sector, a one-product economy was envisaged, then, in Professor Solow's model, the share of profits ceased to depend on the propensities to save and became equal simply to the elasticity of output with respect to capital input, which was now one and the same throughout the economy. So in the Solovian model everything depended on marginal adjustments in the firm whereas in the Kaldorian nothing did, since in a one-product economy the relative price of capital goods became unity and the share of profits could be explained with a given investment programme solely by the propensities to save out of wages and profits.

But did this say more than that, if one left out some parts of the economy, one could leave out some conditions of equilibrium ? Treating the whole economy as a single firm with a single product, one could choose either with Solow to neglect the equilibrium between different kinds of product or, with Kaldor, to neglect the competitive equilibrium of the firm. But, on any view of the economy, did believing that firms made marginal adjustment force economists to deny that ex ante savings had to be made equal to investment ; or did believing the second require them to deny the first ? And if it did, how had it been possible for Professor Solow to combine the two beliefs in his own model whose great usefulness had been to show that the two could go hand in hand ?

Professor Phelps Brown wished to make a general observation in connection with this part of Professor Solow's paper. The actual division of the national product in Western economies in recent years had been marked, one might say universally, by steadiness or a mild upward trend in the share of pay. Now how much light did the savings-investment theory throw on the actual dynamic process of adjustment as distinct from the determination of an equilibrium condition ? Dr. Jeck's paper submitted to the meeting had shown that in Germany, from 1933 to 1939, the share of profits had changed so as to adjust savings to a change in investment. But where in the Western economies since 1945 could one see this process at work ? If the investment programme was stepped up in the present social and economic climate of these economies, which excluded any decrease of the share of pay, one possibility was inflation. But another, evidently, was that the government would provide compulsory savings through a budget surplus. Thus the division of the national product between pay and profits could surely vary over a wide range without any necessary upsetting of the balance of savings and investment. Instead of regarding the savings-investment theory as providing a complete understanding of the division of the national income, should we regard it as doing more today than setting public finance its task ?

In the remaining part of his paper, which was devoted to distribution in the short run, Professor Solow's basic assumption had been that the process of profit maximization (for a given output) continued through the short-run fluctuations subject only to the limitation that in general the shorter the run, the lower the elasticities of substitution. The adjustments of the short run, therefore, took place within a different production function from that which became effective as adjustment extended over a longer span ; but the production function that governed the long run trend might be regarded as the envelope of the short-run function. With this Professor Phelps Brown found himself in full sympathy. It was in the short run that managers had to take the relevant decisions so as to minimize costs through marginal adjustments, if they ever took these decisions at all. The fluctuations in sales that tended to be regarded as the major impact to which they had to react were in practice only one part of the changes, in design, technique, and the prices and availabilities of supplies, as well as in the markets which they sold in, through which they made their way from day to day. The decisions they took in that setting were aggregated to shape the trend. If there was a rationale of the trend this could be only because these day to day decisions had a rational tendency.

Professor Solow had singled out two facts of recent observation for special consideration. One was that the ratio of the unit price of the product to the rate of pay varied less in the short run than the output per manhour so that it was the changes in this output that governed short-run variations in the division of the product between pay and profits. The second fact was that these changes in output per manhour were, in a sense, perverse : when the labour force was reduced capital per man went up, yet output per man fell. This Professor Solow accounted for mainly by the effect on the firm's employment policy of the cost both of laying labour off and of taking it on again. These costs warranted some retention of labour in excess of requirements when these temporarily fell and some making do with less than requirements when these temporarily rose. But each of these expedients, in avoiding one cost, set up another — overtime rates, for example, when the number employed was kept below the number required. Employment policy had to strike a balance.

Professor Phelps Brown wished to comment on only two aspects of Professor Solow's shrewd and clear analysis of how this balance could be struck. The first was about 'labour hoarding', i.e. the retention of labour in excess of current requirements when output fell. Whereas Professor Solow had treated the cost of laying off and taking on again as the pre-dominant if not the sole reason for this, Professor Phelps Brown would put the stress on the physical impossibility of adjusting employment in strict proportion to requirements. He felt inclined to regard indivisi-bilities of indirect labour as the major cause of 'labour hoarding', the more so as technical development tended to raise the proportion of indirect to direct labour. It might be also that employers could simply not afford to lay labour off in a recession because there would be a strike if they tried to do so and they could not take labour on in a boom because there was just none available. This was an extreme case but more generally Pro-fessor Phelps Brown felt inclined to regard the technical compactness of indirect labour as the major cause of labour hoarding.

The fall in output per manhour appeared to Professor Solow to require explanation, especially because it occurred in the presence of a higher ratio of capital per man. But Professor Phelps Brown desired to point out that although there was a reduction in the labour force against a capital stock which, for the time being, was unchanged, the amount of capital co-operating with each worker was not necessarily raised : if 20 men had been driving trucks and now there was work only for 16, it was just that 4 trucks would stand idle. This consideration, it was true, did not explain why output per man fell ; but save in so far as the trucks kept in use were better than the others, it did remove any expectation that output per man would rise.

Professor Jean Marchal wished to comment on Professor Solow's implication that in a one-commodity economy (where the elasticities of output with respect to input of capital goods were the same for the two sectors producing capital goods and consumption goods) the profit share would be independent of the savings function and equal to the common elasticity. Professor Solow had added that this represented a real difference in 'prediction' between the marginal productivity and the Kaldorian theories which he thought to be based on differences in assumption about microeconomic behaviour. Did this mean that in a real, several-commodities economy there was no longer any difference between the two theories with respect to the determination of profit share ; or would it not rather be that the differences would be on other grounds ? Professor Marchal also wished that Professor Solow would specify the difference in assumption about microeconomic behaviour between the two theories.

In his model introducing 'labour hoarding' Professor Solow assumed that 'the firm faced a known time series of sales and therefore of labour requirements (p. 459) and that the sales would have a regular cyclical behaviour'. In so far as the cyclical pattern of activity was not easily predictable, this gave rise to a problem of uncertainty which Professor Solow had solved by giving a quadratic form to the cost function so that firms could still minimize their costs with expected values equivalent to certainty (p. 465). But supposing the actual cost functions not to be of a quadratic character, would the entrepreneurs still be able to plan their sales in a rational fashion and, if not, would Professor Solow's model still hold ?

As a more general observation Professor Jean Marchal thought that Professor Solow's model could be but a part of a theory of distribution. Being based on the technique of the representative firm, his model could only explain the division of income between labour and capital in certain branches of the economy ; the peculiarities of cost functions and demand functions in agriculture, for instance, were such as to exclude this sector from the scope of the model. Furthermore, short of assuming a complete fluidity of factor supply within the whole economy, it did not explain all differences in income shares between branches or sectors ; it did not explain for instance why the rate of profit was lower in agriculture than in other activities.

Professor Marchal also questioned Professor Solow's assumption that money wage rates remained constant all through the business cycle. This might be more or less true in the United States but it did not hold for France nor, for that matter, for Europe. Then Professor Marchal would ask Professor Solow what would become of his model when money wages went up.

It seemed to *Professor Rasmussen* that if Professor Solow's generalized macro-economic model could not be reconciled with the Kaldorian model in a one-commodity economy, this was for the simple reason that in the latter investment — or the share of investment — was exogenous. This being so, there was no reason why the rate of investment corresponding to full employment should involve the fulfilment of the marginal conditions of neo-classical theory for the individual firm. In a more than one commodity economy, however, changes in the relative prices could ensure Kaldorian as well as neo-classical equilibrium.

Professor Solow answered Professor Phelps Brown, Professor Marchal and Professor Rasmussen on a point which had been raised by the three of them referring to page 453 in his paper. Professor Solow said that whereas he had argued that both marginal productivity theory and savings-investment theory were incomplete within the framework of a more-than-one-commodity economy, he had suggested that a genuine inconsistency did arise in a completely aggregated economy with no more than one commodity. In that case the marginal productivity theory alone was complete : then one had to reason simply on many identical firms and if profits were maximized this determined only one income distribution.

Professor Solow pointed out that it was not true that the standard Kaldorian formula could not be derived from his earlier equations although it was in a very complicated way. Professor Phelps Brown had asked him what happened to the savings-equal-investment condition of equilibrium in his own model for a one-commodity economy in so far as it was incompatible with the Kaldorian model ; to this he would answer that the full employment condition on which the Kaldorian model rested became difficult to preserve. In a completely aggregated economy there were no longer relative prices and therefore no possibility was left of achieving full employment through price flexibility. In a one-commodity economy only one investment share was compatible with full employment — either the state saw to it or it did not, but full employment could no longer be a basic assumption. The Kaldorian economists wished to have simultaneously full employment and their own theory of distribution, but in general this was not compatible with the representative firm maximizing profits.

Dr. Pasinetti said that, looking at the long run and provided one did not think in terms of Cobb-Douglas production function, the gross rate of profits and the profit share would depend on savings and technological progress.

Professor Solow agreed with Dr. Pasinetti that in a one-commodity economy, if the technology was not of the Cobb-Douglas type, then the elasticity of output, which would not be constant for technological reasons, would depend on how much capital had been accumulated. In a steady state there would have to be enough accumulated so that income would be distributed by shares according to marginal productivity theory in such a way that the formation of savings would be equal to what was implied by the Kaldorian theory. But this was only one possible outcome on which Professor Solow would not rely because technological conditions could be such that income shares could vary only within very narrow bounds. If the equilibrium conditions required a labour share beyond the technological bounds, full employment of labour was what would have to yield.

Professor Reder admitted that there was no incompatibility between the Kaldorian and the marginal productivity theories of distribution in a more-than-one-commodity economy as long as the number of commodities and of distributive shares were equal. This clearly held in the special case of a two-commodity economy with two income shares. Now considering three categories of income recipients with distinct marginal propensities to save, one just needed to add another commodity and apparently there would be no problem as long as the numbers of commodities and shares were kept equal by dividing up income by shares and product by commodity.

The splitting up of a community into groups could however be made in different ways so that the same person might appear in more than one group. For instance in the United States the marginal propensity to save was different between Negroes and whites so that the differentiation of propensity to save was not simply between wage-earners and profit-earners. This might lead to overdetermination of the system.

What was to be the criterion for deciding which theory consistent with equilibrium should be chosen ? If the criterion retained were simplicity of theoretical relationship between the variables and predictability of what happened to income shares over time, the marginal productivity theory might be preferred to the Kaldorian on these grounds. On the other hand if the production functions were stable the Kaldorian theory would be preferable. Professor Reder would thus think that the choice between the two theories would just be a matter of convenience and to his mind the real problem of choice arose only on a question of overdeterminacy when one could classify social groups in several ways.

Professor Solow replied that whatever the social composition of the population, for any given set of prices there was a well-defined market demand. *Professor Reder* said that if two different ways of classifying people showed different predictions, one could not decide which one was right — obviously both were.

Professor Bronfenbrenner pointed out to Professor Solow that Professor Reder's worries over overdeterminacy did not relate to the number of commodities and of groups of income recipients but on how the microeconomics of the Walrasian price system got itself into adjustment with the Kaldorian system.

Professor Solow said that what he had done was to show how in a two-commodity world the savings-investment issue became incorporated in Walrasian economics. He could not imagine that a different principle would be involved by a more-than-two-commodities set-up — the reasoning indeed would be easier with *n* commodities.

Professor Föhl agreed with Professor Solow that there could not be any overdeterminacy in a situation of equilibrium although one could for a time have an excess of investment and of profits until final equilibrium was reached. But Professor Föhl wished to point out to Professor Solow that in a one-commodity world it should be stipulated whether this commodity was produced by a single firm — so that final equilibrium could be reached with monopoly profit — or whether it was produced by many firms under perfect competition — so that a no-profit equilibrium would obtain in the long run.

Professor Solow agreed with this observation.

Dr. Pasinetti, referring to the first part of Professor Solow's paper, and commenting on the differences between the two theories considered by Professor Solow, said that another difference seemed to him relevant, namely that the two theories implied different assumptions about elasticity of substitution.

Dr. Pasinetti observed that the concept of profit maximization implied by the model in the second part of the paper was not of the type normally used in marginal productivity theory nor was the demand function the usual one.

Professor Solow agreed with Dr. Pasinetti's first observation ; this was a question that Professor Solow would leave open and he was prepared to accept any reasonable values for the elasticities of substitution. About Dr. Pasinetti's second point, it was true that the process of maximizing profit in the model was not the usual one. In imagining it, Professor Solow had meant to meet the criticism made against the usual concept as implying an instantaneous process of short-run profit maximization. Accumulation of profits over the course of the business cycle should be considered as a more realistic description. He had tried to go nearer to the factual evidence and, in assuming that the standard manufacturing firm would set a price and hold it through the entire cycle, he had tried to fit into his model what Neild and others had described as the best way of summarizing the statistics.

Professor Solow said that his assumption about labour hoarding by entrepreneurs had been devised to meet the observed short-run behaviour of the productivity per worker. Professor Phelps Brown had questioned his assumptions and suggested that in Britain employees were not laid off in recession for fear of strike and not hired in boom because there were none available on the market. Professor Solow thought that this might be true in extreme cases but that in general this was not sufficient to prevent hiring and firing. After all, the observed unemployment rate fluctuated in Britain. He would not deny that special characteristics could play a part in labour hoarding but the same short-run productivity behaviour was observed if one took output per production worker only, so that he felt justified in arguing that functional phenomena must also be part of the explanation. The British economy had been nearer full employment over the last fifteen years than the U.S.A.; this might explain why statistical analysis showed this behaviour of productivity was more marked in Britain.

Professor Alchian said that one ought not to take data on productivity from the statisticians at their face value because they might be biased by accounting practices for cost allocation in industries where there was a peak-load problem (for instance bus drivers on long routes had a high productivity in the middle section of the line only), and some data should be reinterpreted.

Professor Solow had assumed (p. 458) that labour was a variable input in the short period, but Professor Alchian was not convinced that it was labour and not capital which was regarded as the variable input in the short run.

Professor Solow said that whereas in the tradition of economics the short run was defined as the period in which capital was fixed while labour was a variable input, he on the contrary regarded his paper as a first step towards thinking that labour was not freely variable in the short run.

In reply to Professor Jean Marchal's objection to applying the theory in his model to economies like the French which had not a regular cyclical behaviour he would say that if in these economies the output was always rising the rate would however vary through time and the same theory could apply as well to deviations from a rising trend, the slowing down of growth playing then the same role as the recession in other economies.

Concerning the treatment of uncertainty Professor Solow was fully aware that by paying attention to expected values one got only a first approximation. Obviously one needed a better theory of behaviour under uncertainty. He would also agree with Professor Jean Marchal that his theory of distribution in the end part of the paper was far from complete ; it applied to corporate manufacturing and mining but surely not to agriculture.

About his assumption of money wages keeping constant over the cycle, the same theory would hold good if wages rose smoothly, provided that they would not be too sensitive to fluctuations in demand for labour, and this was a generally accepted reading of the facts. It was also true that he had abstracted from institutional changes, but he had in mind only a short-run theory. When institutional changes occurred they obviously mattered but it was difficult to evaluate precisely how much influence institutions like collective bargaining had on income distribution. Trade unions did not operate in a social and economic vacuum and it was hardly feasible to isolate their impact.

Chapter 18

NEO-CLASSICAL MACRO-DISTRIBUTION THEORY[1]

BY

M. BRONFENBRENNER

I. INTRODUCTION

MACRO-DISTRIBUTION is about the relative shares of various classes in functional income distribution, as distinguished from micro- or 'pseudo-' distribution, which is about the prices of productive inputs or 'factors of production'. Neo-classical macro-distribution has, however, been based on two major notions derived and adapted from micro-distribution; these are the production function and the elasticity of substitution. It also accepts and applies some form of the marginal productivity theory of demand for inputs.

Rival theories of macro-distribution discard one or more of these elements as rubbish, or at least, include other elements as substantially more significant. For example, if we suppose all productive inputs ultimately reducible to simple abstract labour or labour-power, as in the systems of David Ricardo and Karl Marx (or in the mid-twentieth century, the systems of Wassily Leontief and Piero Sraffa), it makes little sense to discuss the marginal productivities of multiple independent inputs, based on substitution among them.

In this paper I assume, in one leading neo-classical tradition following my own preceptor Frank Knight, that 'land, labour, and capital make land, labour and capital'. To put it differently, I assume that civilized labour, if not all labour, is in large part a product of investment in 'human capital' in the same sense that capital instruments are in large part products of the application of direct labour. In this view, all productive inputs are logically on a par with each other, the distribution between 'original' and derived

---

[1] My principal debts in preparing this paper are to M. I. Kamien and Michael Nicholson (both of Carnegie) and to unpublished notes by Y. T. Kuark (University of Denver). The National Bureau volume *The Behavior of Income Shares* (*Studies in Income and Wealth*, vol. 27); Princeton: Princeton University Press, 1964) unfortunately appeared too late for more than patchwork utilization here.

inputs is largely meaningless, and each input has its substitutes at the margin, at least in the long run.

After the present introduction (Part I), Part II takes up the simplest and most common production function used in classical macro-distribution — namely, the Cobb–Douglas in its original form of 1927–28 — and also the elasticity of substitution between inputs. Part III will take up economic objections to the Cobb–Douglas function, and Part IV statistical (econometric) objections to it. Part V considers later modifications of production functions (by Douglas, his co-workers, and others) in the light of these objections, without summarizing explicitly 'where we stand'.[1] Part VI, which might easily have come sooner, is devoted to a few principal alternative versions of macro-distribution.

With Professor A. A. Walters's econometric survey of cost and production functions at hand [2] I need make no encyclopaedic pretensions. Rather, since I must pick and choose with some care (in the last four sections) and an eye to space limitations, I apologize in advance to writers whose work would have been treated more painstakingly under other circumstances.

II. THE COBB–DOUGLAS FUNCTION AND ELASTICITY OF SUBSTITUTION OF INPUTS

(1) The Cobb–Douglas function arose in the later 1920's from observations by Professor (later Senator) Paul H. Douglas on index numbers of labour, capital, and output for the U.S.A. and for the State of Massachusetts. Briefly, these indices (when related to common bases) rose in logarithmic straight-line patterns, indicating constant long-term growth rates. Capital rose most rapidly and labour most slowly ; the product line followed labour more closely than it did capital, whether the latter was defined to include or exclude working capital.[3] Searching for a mathematical formula to indicate these relations, and which also would combine constant

---

[1] For three such statements, see Tibor Scitovsky, 'A Survey of Some Theories of Income Distribution', *Behavior of Income Shares, op. cit.* pp. 15–31 ; William Fellner, 'Significance and Limitations of Contemporary Distribution Theory', *Am. Econ. Rev.* (May 1953) ; and Mary Jean Bowman, 'Theories of Income Distribution : Where Do We Stand?' *Journ. Pol. Econ.* (December 1948). These essays combine macro- and micro-economic propositions and conclusions.

[2] A. A. Walters, 'Production and Cost Functions : An Econometric Survey', *Econometrica* (January–April 1963).

[3] Douglas, *Theory of Wages* (New York : Macmillan, 1934), charts 10, 15 (pp. 135, 161).

returns to scale with diminishing returns to individual inputs, Douglas consulted Professor Charles W. Cobb, an Amherst College mathematician and amateur economist.[1] The result was a formula which has become standard: $P = bL^kC^{l-k}$ or in logarithmic form $\log(P/C) = \log b + k \log(L/C)$.

Here (P, L, C) represent 'homogenized' product, labour, and capital respectively, while (b, k) are statistical constants, presumably positive, fitted by least squares.[2] The k term is, as we shall see, the estimated macro-economic labour share. The simplest interpretation of the b term is as a statistical catch-all for the effect of omitted variables such as land, management, and (sometimes) working capital, as well as for incomplete homogeneity of the basic variables (P, L, C).

This function fits Douglas's data with high multiple correlation coefficients (above 0·95). It also generally over-estimated output, as it should have done, in periods of depression characterized by what we now call 'disguised unemployment' of labour and particularly capital. The reverse was generally true, as it should have been, during boom periods when labour and capital worked overtime, or when inflation caused systematic undervaluation of fixed capital.[3] Using index numbers, Douglas's constant term b (x_0, in footnote 2) was close to unity.

(2) We may possibly surmise that the Cobb–Douglas function's use for macro-distribution theory was something of an after-thought. At any rate, the principal applications to relative shares in *The Theory of Wages* come late and somewhat incidentally in their respective chapters.[4] Douglas did, however, compare observed labour shares, which we call s, with theoretical shares computed on

---

[1] This characterization may be unfair to Cobb, who authored or co-authored nine scholarly papers on economics, listed in the American Economic Association, *Index to Economic Periodicals* (Homewood, Ill.: Irwin, 1961), vols. ii–iii, over the period 1938–45.

[2] Douglas, *op. cit.* p. 132. Rewriting in the more usual notation $x = f(a, b)$:

$$x = x_0 a^\alpha b^{1-\alpha}.$$

We then have, for $(a = \lambda a, b = \lambda b)$, where λ is an arbitrary constant:

$$f(\lambda a, \lambda b) = \lambda x_0 a^\alpha b^{1-a} = \lambda x$$

showing constant returns to scale. To show diminishing returns to an input (say a), we take the second derivatives:

$$\frac{\delta^2 x}{\delta a^2} = x_0^\alpha (\alpha - 1)a^{\alpha - 2}b^{1-\alpha}.$$

This expression is negative for a fractional α, showing diminishing returns to input a when its product share is fractional.

[3] *Ibid.* charts 10-A, 17 (pp. 136, 164).

[4] *Ibid.* pp. 198–200, 221–224.

marginal-productivity lines — in our notation, $\left(a\dfrac{\partial x}{\partial a}/x\right)$ — and expressed satisfaction at the closeness of the results. He seemed more interested at the moment in the measurement of demand elasticities for labour, η. These are estimated as $\left(\dfrac{-a\partial p_a}{p_a \partial a}\right)$, or if a represents labour, or if the wage rate p_a equals the marginal product of labour, as $\left(\dfrac{a\partial x/\partial a}{\partial^2 x/\partial a^2}\right)$. When the Cobb–Douglas function applies, the relative share and the demand elasticity appear as :

$$s = \frac{a\partial x/\partial a}{x} = \frac{ax_0 a^{\alpha-1}b^\beta}{x_0 a^\alpha b^\beta} = \alpha$$

$$\eta = -\frac{a\partial x/\partial a}{\partial^2 x/\partial a^2} = \frac{-ax_0 a^{\alpha-1}b^\beta}{\alpha(\alpha-1)x_0 a^{\alpha-2}b^\beta} = \frac{1}{1-\alpha}.$$

With the measured labour share s and its statistical estimate α in the neighbourhood of ·60–·75,[1] the estimated elasticity of demand for labour η is in the range 2·5–4·0. Indeed, the elasticity must be greater than unity unless the share ratio is negative, an impossibility. There is then some feature of the Douglas method which holds the demand elasticity for productive inputs above unity. This makes payrolls, in particular, rise when wages fall, and *vice versa*, over-turning the 'purchasing power' case for wage increases. (The demand elasticity itself is not amenable directly to checking against actual data.)

(3) The Cobb–Douglas function made its formal bow to the American Economic Association in December 1927, and appeared in print early the following year.[2] It also appeared in Douglas's *Theory of Wages* (1934, reprinted 1957), and his presidential address to the American Economic Association (December 1947, just twenty years after the function's debut).[3]

In the generation since 1927 the Cobb–Douglas function has found applications around the world. It has been applied to firms, in-dustries, regional and national economies. It has been used with multiple inputs as well as with the original two. It has been applied

---

[1] It is *not true* that a is selected arbitrarily to equal the actual labour share s, although the writer has encountered this misconception persistently.

[2] Cobb and Douglas, 'A Theory of Production', *Am. Econ. Rev.* (March 1928), anticipated by Knut Wicksell (in Swedish).

[3] Douglas, 'Are There Laws of Production?' *Ibid.* (March 1948). (Reprinted as an additional foreword to the 1957 re-issue of *The Theory of Wages*.)

to production and growth as well as distribution problems.[1] It may prove useful in estimating such magnitudes as 'disguised unemployment'.[2] Applications, however, are being made increasingly to modified forms of the function, the modifications being responses to controversies discussed below. The most exhaustive testing of results to date may be found in the Walters survey already cited,[3] but controversy regarding the function's meaning and usefulness has never died out.

(4) By comparison, the elasticity of substitution has led a quiet life. It was devised independently by Professor J. R. Hicks and Mrs. Joan Robinson in connection with the abstract proposition, under what circumstances 'an increase in the supply of any factor [a] will increase its relative share, (i.e.) its proportion of the National Dividend'.[4] This turned out to depend, with absolutely price-

---

[1] If a competitive firm wishes to maximize profits π (with output price equal to unity) from a production process governed by the function

$$x = x_0 a^\alpha b^{1-\alpha}$$

and input prices (p_a, p_b), its demand functions for inputs are obtained by differentiating a profit function

$$\pi = x_0 a^\alpha b^{1-\alpha} - (a p_a + b p_b)$$

with respect to a and b respectively, and dividing one of the two derivatives by the other. The results are

$$a = \left[\frac{\alpha p_b}{(1-\alpha) p_a} \right]^{1-\alpha} \left(\frac{x}{x_0} \right) \text{ and } b = \left[\frac{(1-\alpha) p_a}{\alpha p_b} \right]^{\alpha} \left(\frac{x}{x_0} \right)$$

Its total cost function $(C = a p_a + b p_b)$ is :

$$C = \frac{p_a}{\alpha} \left[\frac{\alpha p_b}{(1-\alpha) p_a} \right]^{1-\alpha} \left(\frac{x}{x_0} \right) = \frac{p_b}{1-\alpha} \left[\frac{(1-\alpha) p_a}{\alpha p_b} \right]^{\alpha} \frac{x}{x_0}$$

Its supply or marginal cost is a constant. Differentiate C (above) with respect to x. (With output price equal to unity, the reciprocal of the derivative can be substituted.) The result is independent of a, b and x :

$$1 = x_0 \left(\frac{\alpha}{p_a} \right)^{\alpha} \left(\frac{1=a}{p_b} \right)^{1-\alpha}$$

These results require the output x to be given outside the system. Within the system, since the supply function is horizontal, x is indeterminate for the competitive firm.

[2] Computed labour requirements from the Cobb–Douglas function may be called a_0

$$a_0 = \left(\frac{x}{x_0} \right)^{1/\alpha} b^{\frac{\alpha}{1-\alpha}} \text{ or } \log a_0 = \frac{\log x - \log x_0}{\alpha} + \frac{\log b}{1-\alpha}.$$

If actual a exceeds a_0, the difference $(a - a_0)$ or the ratio (a/a_0) may be used as estimates of disguised unemployment.

[3] Walters, *op. cit.*, Tables I–V (pp. 26, 31–33, 36). Even these tables are incomplete. For example, material in Miyōhei Shinohara, *Growth and Cycles in the Japanese Economy* (Tokyo: Kinokuniya, 1962), ch. 13, might have been included.

[4] J. R. Hicks, *Theory of Wages* (London: Macmillan, 1932), p. 117. See also Mrs. Joan Robinson, *Economics of Imperfect Competition* (London: Macmillan, 1933), pp. vii, 256, 330 n. For a precursor, Stuart Wood, see Douglas, 'Are There Laws of Production?' *op. cit.* p. 2.

inelastic factor supplies, on whether the supply of *a* rises autonomously (relative to that of other factors *b*), more than its unit compensation n_a falls as a result, relative this time to p_b. (Both prices may in fact rise absolutely.) Or at the opposite extreme, with infinitely price-elastic factor supplies, the answer to Hicks's question depends upon whether p_a rises autonomously (relative to p_b) by a higher proportion than *a* falls as a result (relative to *b*). (Both quantities may in fact rise absolutely.) For intermediate cases, with factor price-elasticities positive but finite, the crucial condition must be defined in less convenient terms than relative quantities and market prices. In the standard elasticities of the elementary textbooks, which apply strictly for extreme supply-elasticity values only, the share of *a* will rise with its relative quantity if :

$$\frac{\text{percentage rise in } (a/b)}{\text{percentage fall in } (p_a/p_b)} = \frac{\text{percentage rise in } (a/b)}{\text{percentage rise in } (p_b/p_a)}$$

which Hicks calls σ, is greater than unity. The share of *a* will remove the same if σ is unitary, and fall if σ is a proper fraction. Quite generally, the elasticity of demand for either *a* or *b* taken singly will exceed in absolute value the elasticity of substitution between these two inputs.

The resultant σ is, of course, precisely the elasticity of substitution. For algebraic production functions without gaps or corners (which rules out input-output and activity-analysis cases), σ may be written in calculus notation, assuming p_a and p_b equal to their respective marginal productivities :

$$= \frac{d\left(\frac{a}{b}\right)}{a/b} \div \frac{\frac{\partial x}{\partial \partial b}\frac{\partial x}{\partial a}}{\frac{\partial x}{\partial b}\frac{\partial x}{\partial a}} = \frac{\frac{\partial x}{\partial a}\frac{\partial x}{\partial b}}{\frac{\partial^2 x}{\partial a \partial b}}.$$

The last derivation, found most conveniently in Professor R. G. D. Allen's *Mathematical Analysis for Economists*,[1] is important, first for its symmetricality, showing that the elasticity of substitution between *a* and *b* is the same in both directions, and second for assuming, like the Cobb–Douglas function, a productive function $x=(a, b)$ homogeneous in the first degree. Incidentally, it is easy to show that, in the Cobb–Douglas case

$$x=x_0 a^\alpha b^{1-\alpha}, \ \sigma=1.$$

[1] Allen, *op. cit.* (London : Macmillan, 1938), sec 13.7 (pp. 340–343). For more than two inputs, compare also *ibid.*, sec. 19.5 (pp. 503 f.).

Or, in other words, relative shares of labour and capital are independent of relative quantities.

In the aggregative domain, as several writers have pointed out,[1] the *economic* elasticity of substitution is a compound of the elasticities of *technological* substitution (between inputs along individual isoquants within individual industries) and of *demand* substitution (between the products of industries with different input-intensities). In micro-economic problems technological substitution is of primary importance, but it is erroneous to assume the same thing for macro-economic problems, and doubly erroneous to connect relative aggregate shares directly with elasticities of technological substitution.

(5) The elasticity of substitution has been, until recently, used more widely in theoretical analysis than in empirical work. Thus Hicks, in deriving the elasticity of demand for an input *a*, which he calls λ, obtains the result :

$$\lambda = \frac{(\eta+e)+ke(\eta-\sigma)}{(\eta+e)+k(\eta-\sigma)}$$

while Allen, deriving the cross-elasticity of demand for any input *a* with respect to a price change in any other input *b* has :[2]

$$\eta_{ap_b} = k_a(\sigma_{ab}-\eta).$$

One early empirical estimate of the labour-capital elasticity of substitution was, however, made by Professor Irving Kravis over a 58-year range of American data.[3] Kravis's arc-elasticity estimate of 0·64 added to his doubts of the constancy of relative shares. The value significantly below unity implies in this case that labour, which increased less than capital over the period of Kravis's study, should have increased its relative share — as 'standard' data suggest that it did.

[1] A. C. Pigou, 'The Elasticity of Substitution', *Ec. J.* (June 1934) ; Fritz Machlup, 'The Common Sense of the Elasticity of Substitution', *Rev. Econ. Stud.* (June 1935) ; Irving Morrissett, 'Recent Uses of the Elasticity of Substitution', *Econometrica* (January 1953). (The last-named article, a survey, includes an extended bibliography.)

[2] Hicks, *op. cit.* p. 244. Allen, *op. cit.* p. 509. In these equations η is the elasticity of demand for output, *e* the elasticity of supply of input *b*, and *k* the relative importance or loading of an input in total cost, thus $k_a = \frac{ap_a}{x}$.

[3] Kravis, 'Relative Income Shares in Fact and Theory', *Am. Econ. Rev.* (December 1959), p. 940.

III. ECONOMIC OBJECTIONS TO THE COBB–DOUGLAS FUNCTION

(1) The Cobb–Douglas 'verification' of marginal-productivity theory, or what we should today call their evidence for neo-classical macro-distribution theory, has seemed since 1928 'too good to be true'.[1] Objections have accordingly crowded thick and fast, which I am sorting out in arbitrary fashion between the economic and the statistical. (This section is limited to the former group.)

One immediate objection was anchored on the facts of technological change. Several of Douglas's critics of 1927–28 vintage[2] saw no economic rationale in forcing into one function (with no temporal term) the technology of 1890 (Massachusetts) or 1900 (U.S.A.) and the near-contemporary technology of the early 1920's. What some of them saw in the Cobb–Douglas function was only inter-relationship between the slopes of their trend lines.

(2) Somewhat later, after further developments in the theory of the firm, came the objection that a linear homogeneous production function, like the Cobb–Douglas one, is inconsistent with atomistic competition. This is because, for such a firm, one scale of plant is as good as any other. There is no optimum, and the scale is indeterminate.[3]

(3) What, after all, do we mean by a quantity like 'measured capital' in the sense of the C figures in the Cobb–Douglas function ? The issue involves the fundamentals of capital theory, along with the minutiae of its measurement. What is meant, asks for example

---

[1] Or, as Professor Edmund S. Phelps puts it in 'Substitution, Fixed Properties, Growth, and Distribution', *Int. Econ. Rev.* (September 1963), p. 284, 'The Cobb–Douglas production function . . . was adopted out of convenience rather than any evidence of its validity'. On the other hand, Phelps admits, 'there is no convincing evidence against it'.

[2] Particularly Professors John Maurice Clark and Morris Copeland. Compare Clark, 'Inductive Evidence of Marginal Productivity', *Am. Econ. Rev.* (1928), and Douglas, *Theory of Wages, op. cit.* pp. 214–216.

[3] Similar difficulties hold for any other homogeneous production function. If the degree of such a function is greater than unity we have increasing return to scale, and the larger firm can always undersell the smaller one. If the degree of a homogeneous production function is a (non-negative) proper fraction we have decreasing returns to scale, and the optimum firm is the smallest conceivable.

The first writer to suggest the advisability of independent estimates for the coefficients of log P and log C in the Cobb–Douglas function, without binding the sum of these coefficients at unity, seems to have been Dr. David Darand, 'Some Thoughts on Marginal Productivity, with Special Reference to Professor Douglas' Analysis', *Journ. Pol. Econ.* (December 1937).

Mrs. Robinson,[1] by 'a quantity of "capital" in the abstract ?' And she goes on : 'What is meant by saying that a quantity of "capital" remains the same when it changes its form is a mystery that has never been explained to this day.' With regard to distribution, to estimate the value of a physical capital stock by a capitalization process involves circularity when the capitalization factor is itself the (unknown) return per dollar's worth of capital. And when we proceed from the opposite direction, to estimate capital value as the cost of 'prudent investment', the investment cost too turns out to embody returns to investment in capital-goods production, also computed at the same (supposedly unknown) rate of return. In feigned exasperation, Mrs. Robinson concludes : [2]

> Just as the problem of giving an operational meaning to utility used to be avoided by putting it into a diagram, so the problem of giving a meaning to the quantity of 'capital' is evaded by putting it into algebra. K is capital, ΔK is investment. Then what is K ? Why, capital of course. It must mean something, so let us get on . . . and not bother about these officious prigs who ask us to say what it means.

(4) Measured capital figures and (in some countries) measured labour figures as well, include varying volumes of inputs available but not in use. For the best result in fitting production functions, we should limit ourselves to capital actually in use, depreciated as 'accurately' as possible. In taking depreciation data, Professor Robert M. Solow [3] has reduced measured capital by assuming equal proportions of capital and labour unemployed, while Dr. Burton Massell interpolated in a trend of full-employment capital-output ratios,[4] obtaining less variance than Solow in the ratio of capital in use to capital available.

(5) And what finally, are we to say of results 'forced' by the forms of the Cobb–Douglas function, meaning the elastic demand for labour, and the constant labour share, and the latter's cause, the unitary elasticity of substitution ? To quote Professor Nicholas

---

[1] Mrs. Robinson, *Economic Philosophy* (London : Watts, 1962), p. 60. For a standard 'orthodox' treatment of the definition of income while 'keeping capital intact', compare Hicks, *Value and Capital* (Oxford : Oxford University Press, 1939), ch. 14.

[2] Mrs. Robinson, *Economic Philosophy*, *op. cit.* p. 68.

[3] Solow, 'Technological Change and the Aggregate Production Function', *Rev. Econ. and Stat.* (August 1958).

[4] Massell, 'Capital Formation and Economic Change in the United States Manufacturing', *ibid.* (May 1960). Compare also Walters, *op. cit.* pp. 22 f. on parallel problems of 'homogenizing' labour and output data.

Kaldor,[1] whom we meet again in Part VI as the author of a rival macro-distribution theory : 'Existing theories are unable to account for such constancies as the constant relative functional share of labour except in terms of particular hypothesis (unsupported by any independent evidence) such as the unity-elasticity of substitution between Capital and Labour.' A quite different rebuttal was made by Solow, whose main stress is on the variability of the distributive shares within and between industrial groups.[2] Solow applies the statistical formula for the standard error of the arithmetic mean to show that the variability of the labour share is no less than one would expect from its substantial variability between industry groups and the number of such groups within the entire economy. Using the elasticity of substitution, the present writer has attempted to show that relative shares are somewhat insensitive even to large variations in σ, particularly to values in excess of unity.[3]

IV. STATISTICAL OBJECTIONS TO THE COBB–DOUGLAS FUNCTION

(1) There is little point, in a paper of this sort, to remind one's readers further of the imperfections of available data. Labour and output vary in composition, especially over time. Over and above the capital measurement problems touched on in Part II, there are others involving netness (deduction for depreciation and obsolescence) and others in adjusting investments of different ages and efficiencies to a common price level. These are real problems for the statistician ; questionable solutions may account for a sizeable proportion of the ridiculous results obtained occasionally from production functions in macro-distribution problems.[4] Our discussion here, however, will concern itself only with problems of *collineatity* and *identification*, which are of more general interest.

A standard econometric textbook defines multi-collinearity as 'the general problem which arises when the explanatory variables are so largely correlated with one another that it becomes very difficult, if

---

[1] Kaldor, 'A Model of Economic Growth' (*Econ J.*, December 1957), p. 592.
[2] Solow, 'Skeptical Note on the Constancy of Relative Shares', *Am. Econ. Rev.* (September 1958). Also Kravis, *op. cit. passim.*
[3] M. Bronfenbrenner, 'A Note on Relative Shares and the Elasticity of Substitution', *Journ. Pol. Econ.* (June 1960).
[4] Consider, for example, the results for Japanese rice-growing reproduced in Walters, *op. cit.* Table IV, or for U.S. agriculture and British cotton-spinning (*ibid.* Table II).

not impossible, to disentangle their separate inferences and obtain a reasonably precise estimate of their relative effect.[1]

Geometrically speaking, it results from fitting a line through a point, or a plane through a line or 'pencil' in space. Error terms aside, there are an infinite number of solutions each as bad as the other. This phenomenon was analyzed closely by Professor Ragnar Frisch in 1934.[2] It was applied to the Cobb–Douglas functions by Dr. Horst Mendershausen four years later,[3] since the dependent variables of Douglas's original data (his capital and labour index numbers) are highly correlated with each other.

(2) The identification problem is best explored by a standard illustration, drawn from the elementary 'law of supply and demand'. Suppose that both the quantity of, say, wheat demanded per year and the amount of wheat supplied per year depended exclusively upon the price of wheat in that year, but that both demand and supply functions were subject to random shifts. Suppose also that we had series of (price, quantity) data for a number of years. Without further information about, for example, shifts in the functions, we could not tell whether the plotted points represented a supply function, a demand function, or a hybrid of both. This problem was brought into the forefront of econometrics by Professor Trygve Haavelmo in 1944.[4] Its initial application to the Cobb–Douglas function came in the next year, by Professor Jacob Marschak and his co-workers.[5]

In addition to the production functions such as

$$x = x_0 a^\alpha b^{1-\alpha}$$

as Marschak and Andrews pointed out, another relationship connects the variables (x, a, b). This is the cost function. Under long-run competitive equilibrium, with p_x set equal to unity, we have the equation

$$x = ap_a + bp_b.$$

The problem of identifying the productive functions, i.e. of dis-

[1] John Johnston, *Econometric Methods* (New York : McGraw-Hill, 1963), p. 201.
[2] Frisch, *Statistical Confluence Analysis by Means of Complete Regression Systems* (Oslo : University Economics Institute, 1934).
[3] Mendershausen, 'On the Significance of Professor Douglas' Production Function', *Econometrica* (April 1938).
[4] Haavelmo, 'The Probability Approach in Econometrics', *Econometrica* (Supplement, July 1944).
[5] Marschak and William H. Andrews, 'Random Simultaneous Equations and the Theory of Production', *ibid.* (July–October 1944). For later developments, see the discussion among J. Kmenta, M. E. Joseph, and Irving Hoch, *ibid.* (July 1963).

tinguishing it from the cost function, is identical with the supply-demand problem we dealt with above. Figure 1 makes this point for two variables, a and x (with b constant). Marschak felt, on balance, that Douglas and his co-workers had fitted hybrid functions and confused them with true production functions. In a later critique, Professor E. H. Phelps Brown concluded that the functions fitted to Australian data were cost and not production functions at all.[1]

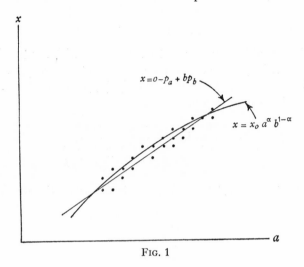

FIG. 1

V. MODIFICATIONS OF PRODUCTION FUNCTIONS TO MEET OBJECTIONS

(1) During the later 1930's, Douglas and his staff found it relatively easy to meet objections to having bound the sum of his coefficients at unity, and to refute suggestions that his results reflected fortuitous coincidences between true series. He unbound the sum of his coefficients, fitting the form :

$$x = x_0 a^{\alpha} b^{\beta} \quad \text{or} \quad \log x = \log x_0 + \alpha \log a + \beta \log b$$

and testing the closeness of his $(\alpha + \beta)$ to unity.[2] He also began the fitting of cross-section as well as time-series data (in cross-section

---

[1] E. H. Phelps Brown, 'The Meaning of the Fitted Cobb–Douglas Production Function', *Quart. Journ. Econ.* (November 1957).
[2] Walters (*op. cit.* p. 5 f.) uses this form as the most representative type of Cobb–Douglas function. It remains homogeneous, but its degree is now $(\alpha + \beta)$, since replacement of (a, b) by $(\lambda a, \lambda b)$ on the right, will yield $(\lambda^{\alpha+\beta} x)$ on the left.

analysis each point represents a different firm, industry, or location at the same point in time), with results no worse than he had achieved earlier with time series.

The freeing of $(\alpha+\beta)$ did not change the assumed elasticity of substitution, which remained equal to unity.[1] The anticipated sum of income payments, assuming marginal productivity analysis to hold, became :

$$a\frac{\partial x}{\partial a}+b\frac{\partial x}{\partial b}=(\alpha+\beta)x$$

rather than x itself as under Euler's Theorem with a linear homogeneous function, so that the computed relative shares of inputs a and b were no longer unambiguously (α,β), respectively. The usual practice was to compute

$$\frac{\alpha}{\alpha+\beta}, \frac{\beta}{\alpha+\beta}, \text{ i.e. } \frac{a\partial x/\partial a}{a\frac{\partial x}{\partial a}+b\frac{\partial x}{\partial b}}, \frac{b\partial x/\partial a}{a\frac{\partial x}{\partial a}+b\frac{\partial x}{\partial b}}$$

which added to unity. However, the simple proportionate shares

$$\frac{a\frac{\partial x}{\partial a}}{x}, \frac{b\frac{\partial x}{\partial b}}{x}$$

remained (α,β) as before. The resulting paradox remains unsolved, but one may consider a solution in terms of 'profits' and 'losses', which are not considered factor payments at all, making up the difference between $(\alpha+\beta)$ and unity.

(2) How is the aggregative Cobb–Douglas function, with its macro-distribution theory implications, related to the micro-functions for individual firms, from which it is supposedly derivable ? We have suggested (*vide supra*, Part III, paragraph 2) the economic difficulties of homogeneous production functions. How are they to be avoided ?

The conventional econometrics of the 'aggregation problem', as treated for example by Walters,[2] assumes micro- and macro-functions to be of the same mathematical form, and relates the coefficients of

---

[1] By the formula

$$=\frac{\dfrac{\partial x}{\partial a}\dfrac{\partial x}{\partial b}}{x\dfrac{\partial^2 x}{\partial a\partial b}}$$

[2] Walters, *op. cit.* pp. 7–11.

the macro-function to sums or averages of the micro-functions.[1]   In the present case, however, the micro-function may be of a quite different mathematical form from the macro-function, in which case this conventional theory is irrelevant.

This writer has felt for many years that the Cobb–Douglas or aggregative production function was most usefully to be regarded as an *envelope* of micro-functions.[2]   Each of the latter has the standard non-homogeneous shape of the intermediate textbooks, rising first by increasing and then by decreasing increments as in Fig. 2, with a clear inflection point.   The macro-function is tangent to these micro-functions at their equilibrium points, where the two have the same slope, but even at the points of tangency the micro-function has the larger curvature and the larger elasticity.

If (see Fig. 2) we measure on the horizontal axis *a*, and on the vertical axis the net marginal product of all inputs other than *b*, the macro-function and envelope may be of Cobb–Douglas form even if the marginal product of *a* alone is constant between firms.   (Three micro-functions are also shown, indicated by different amounts of *b*, presumably a more fixed input.)

(3) Unless a completely stationary state is postulated or unless we are comparing different economies, I cannot share the contemporary Cambridge concern with the indefinability of capital.   All we need to argue is that, in solving for the current interest rate r_t in terms of

---

[1] A Cobb–Douglas example is V. N. Murti and V. K. Sastry, 'Production Functions for Indian Industry', *Econometrica* (April 1957).   These writers average results for *branches* of Indian industry to obtain estimates for the total.

[2] Bronfenbrenner, 'Production Functions: Cobb–Douglas, Interfirm, Infrafirm', *Econometrica* (January 1944).   Here, on the diagram corresponding to Fig. 1, *x* was on the vertical axis, and the 'envelope' was a straight line to indicate uniform marginal productivity $\partial x/\partial a$ as between firms.   Professor Marvin Frankel, 'The Production Function: Allocation and Growth', *Am. Econ. Rev.* (December 1962) proposes an alternative distribution between *ex ante* and *realized* production functions in the individual enterprise.   The *ex ante* micro-function may be written, in our notation

$$x_i = x_0 \, H_i \, a_{i\,a}^{\alpha} \, b_i^{1-\alpha}$$

where H is the capital-labour ratio (b/a), and the subscript i refers to the ith firm. Frankel's aggregate or macro-function is, however,

$$x = x_0 \, H^{\partial} \, a^{\alpha} \, b^{1-\alpha} \text{ or } x = x_0 \, a^{\alpha - \partial} \, b^{1+\partial - \alpha}$$

As *b* and *a* approach each other, this reduces to what Frankel calls a realized Harrodian growth function :

$$x = x_0 b.$$

Yet another alternative approach involves the assumption that for each firm, input-output ratios (a/x, b/x) are completely fixed by reason of managerial limitations.   For efficient firms, these will be low ; for inefficient firms, they will be high.   But if the ratios are distributed in a Pareto distribution, Professor Hendrik Houthakker has shown that the resulting macro-function will approach the Cobb–Douglas type.   Houthakker, 'The Pareto Distribution and the Cobb–Douglas Production Function in Activity Analysis', *Rev. Econ. Stud.* (1955–56).

current capital values C_t, the latter must be related (say, by capitalization) either to the known prior interest rate r_{t-1} or more realistically to some set of weighted averages of past rates (r_{t-1}, r_{t-2}, . . . r_{t-n}) which determine our forward looking anticipation of what the current and subsequent rates (r_t, r_{t+1}, . . . r_{t+n}) ought to be.

Actually this circularity issue is a species of an ancient genus, a familiar member of which is the seasoned dispute about including money in the utility or preference functions which determine money prices. Ah, yes, but at what value of money? Doesn't that depend

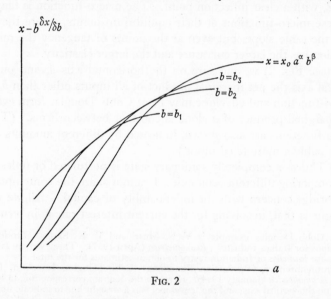

FIG. 2

on its purchasing power, i.e. on the (unknown) money prices? And so we once proceeded but (one may hope) need do so no longer.[1]

(4) Were the 'good' Cobb–Douglas results the rarities, and the freakish ones the common run, we might be justified in imagining, with Mendershausen, a multi-collinear universe, yielding encouraging results occasionally by pure chance. But the facts now seem clearly otherwise, however they appeared in 1938 when Mendershausen's essay appeared. The method gives too many 'right' answers to be accounted for by chance. Something more must be operating.

Quite generally, indeed, according to Professor Lawrence Klein, the multi-collinear bogey has been laid for sufficiently high multiple

[1] Much of the credit for clearing this matter up goes to Don Patinkin, *Money, Interest and Prices* (Evanston, Ill. : Row, Peterson, 1956), ch. 5, esp. pp. 71 f.

correlation coefficients. In a production function case, which Klein uses as an example,[1] if the multiple correlation is 0·95 or above with the output x the dependent variable and labour and capital cast as the dependent variables (a, b) there is no real multi-collinearity problem even though the sample correlation between labour and capital be as high as 0·90.

(5) A similar argument could perhaps be used against sceptical doubts on the scene of improper identification, but what is done instead to an increasing degree has been to introduce into the production functions one or more terms whose purpose is to allow, at least formally, for technical change — and often, at the same time, to unbind the elasticity of substitution as well. These changes make the function read for example

$$x = f(a, b, t)$$

where t is a new variable, a surrogate for technological change. These leave the production function identifiable, since it now contains a t term not found in the cost identity :

$$x = ap_a + bp_b.$$

(6) The earliest function usable for this purpose is by Solow : [2]

$$x = A^t a^\alpha b^\beta \quad \text{or} \quad \log x = t \log A + \alpha \log a + \alpha \log b.$$

This can be fitted as it stands, although Solow prefers a modification :

$$\frac{x}{a} = A^t \left(\frac{b}{a}\right)^\beta \quad \text{or} \quad \log\left(\frac{x}{a}\right) = t \log A + \beta \log (b/a).$$

A still more extreme device has been not to compute β at all but substitute s_k, the *observed* relative share of *capital*. If we denote (dx/dt), etc. by x, denote product per manhour (our x/a) by q, and capital per manhour (our b/a) by k, Solow derives a formula for rates of change over time :

$$\frac{\dot{q}}{q} = \frac{\dot{A}}{A} + s_k \frac{\dot{k}}{k}$$

and estimates (for the U.S.A.) that approximately seven-eighths of observed improvement in output per manhour arises from technological change (A) rather than increased capital.

[1] Klein, *Introduction to Econometrics* (Englewood Cliffs : Prentice-Hall, 1962), p. 101.
[2] Solow, 'Technical Change . . .', *op. cit.* (1958).

This equation retains the unitary elasticity of substitution. It also treats all technical change as 'neutral', since the marginal productivity ratio of labour and capital is independent of t. It is of course subject to criticism for using an entity so colourless as 'time' for its surrogate of technical progress.[1]

(7) A more exciting improvement, with Solow again playing a leading role, has been the homohypellagic, c.e.s., or SMAC production function, in which the elasticity of substitution, while still constant, need no longer be bound at unity, and which can therefore suggest directions of change in relative shares.[2] Its formula is:

$$x = \gamma[\sigma b^{-\rho} + (1-\sigma)a^{-\rho}] - \frac{1}{\rho} \text{ where } \rho = \frac{1-\sigma.}{\sigma}.$$

Although x represents product (or more accurately, value-added) a and b are no longer quantities of labour and capital but coefficients of the side-relation

$$\log y = \log a + b \log w$$

in which y is value-added *per capita* and w is a wage rate. It is further assumed that competitive conditions hold, including a linear homogeneous production function f, so that:

$$w = f\left(\frac{b}{a}\right) - \frac{b}{a}f'\left(\frac{b}{a}\right).$$

The use of this side relation, assuming a condition which in macrodistribution requires testing, naturally lessens the usefulness of this particular function for our purposes here, even though generalized elasticities of substitution can be derived with its aid.

A generalization of the c.e.s. formula to n inputs was subsequently achieved by V. Mukerji,[3] whose work exposed a remaining lack of generality. When there are n inputs, the c.e.s. formula implies that

[1] Studies using other surrogates include Robert J. Wolfson, 'Econometric Investigation of Regional Differences in American Agricultural Wages', *Econometrica* (April 1958); O. Niitamo, 'Development of Productivity in Finnish Industry, 1925–1952', *Productivity Measurement Review* (1958); and Frankel, *op. cit.* (The Niitamo study uses the coefficient h, representing the middle-school graduating class as a percentage of the labour force, to indicate technological advance. The Frankel study suggests the use of the capital-labour ratio H.) Compare Klein, *op. cit.* pp. 108–110.

[2] Kenneth J. Arrow, Hollis B. Chenery, Bagicha Minhas, and Robert M. Solow, 'Capital-Labor Substitution and Economic Efficiency', *Rev. Econ. and Stat.* (August 1961).

[3] V. Mukerji, 'A Generalized SMAC Function with Constant Ratios of Elasticity of Substitution', *Rev. Econ. Stud.* (October 1963).

all pairwise elasticities of substitution are equal, a condition which Mukerji succeeded in relaxing.

Further economic generalization has been made by Murray Brown and John S. de Cani.[1] Their suggested equation is, assuming a production function $x = f(a, b)$,

$$x = \gamma_1 \left(\frac{a^\alpha b^\alpha}{a^\alpha + \gamma_2 b^\alpha} \right)^{v/\alpha}.$$

The parameter α is related to the elasticity of substitution σ by the relation :

$$\alpha = (1 - \sigma)/\sigma \quad \text{or} \quad \sigma = 1/(\alpha + 1)$$

and the parameter γ_2 is derived, under the crucial assumption that input prices are proportionate to their marginal products, from the side relation

$$p / p_a = \frac{\partial x / \partial b}{\partial x / \partial a} = \frac{1}{\gamma_2} \left(\frac{a}{b} \right)^{1/\sigma}.$$

The remaining parameters γ_1 and v do not enter directly into the determination of the input ratio (a/b). In a time series including technological change, Brown and de Cani call them measures of neutral technological change, while γ_2 is an 'input intensity' parameter.

(8) Initial estimates of the elasticity of substitution on the basis of these formulae run considerably below unity. In a competitive world with a rising capital-labour ratio or, in Marxian terms, 'organic composition of capital', these results imply a rising labour share in the national product, such as has occurred in a number of countries.

The SMAC group, for example, estimated the elasticity of substitution in 24 industries (with results below unity in 23) by fitting the following function across countries for each of the 24 :

$$\log x/a = \log k + \sigma \log p_a$$

where x is value-added rather than total output.[2] Professor Victor Fuchs, however, added a dummy variable separating developed from

---

[1] Brown and de Cani, 'Technological Change and the Distribution of Income', *Int. Econ. Rev.* (September 1963), pp. 292–294, 305–309. For the relationship between the SMAC and Brown–de Cani formulae, I am indebted to Kamien, 'Comment on Alternative Deviations of the Two Input Production Functions with Constant Elasticities of Substitution', *Zeitschrift für Nationalökonomie* (1964), pp. 124-126.

[2] Arrow, Chenery, Minhas, and Solow, *op. cit.* p. 225.

underdeveloped countries,[1] after which the elasticities of substitution in fact clustered about unity (median 1·04, slightly above unity) suggesting constant relative shares of the Cobb–Douglas variety.

Other Solow studies (between U.S. regions for 10 manufacturing industries, 1956) yield a wide but generally higher range of estimates for the elasticity of substitution. The range is from ·06 to 1·96; 10 values exceed unity; 11 lie in the smaller range 0·60–1·50; the unweighted arithmetic mean is 1·02 and the median 1·01.[2] Criticizing these results, Robert Eisner suggests an upward bias due to transitory output variations, while John Kendrick produces lower results for the same industries over the interval 1953–57 by the naïve arc-elasticity formula (Sec. II, paragraph 4), whose applicability is itself questionable.

It has become quite common, as we have seen, to employ various devices for limiting the 'capital' term in production functions to capital instruments in actual use, evaluated at current prices. In another study aimed at ascertaining an empirical elasticity of substitution, Professor Mordecai Kurz and Alan Manne have used engineering rather than economic data for the American metal-machining industry and derived a value of 0·99 for the elasticity of substitution.[3]

(9) It is clearly no longer justifiable to refer, as Kaldor did in 1957, to the unitary elasticity of substitution as a 'particular hypothesis unsupported by independent evidence'.[4] On the other hand, results to date can hardly be said to have settled the question. Many estimates (including the SMAC originals) are far from unitary, and the use of marginalist 'side relations' to fit generalized production functions lessens the usefulness of these estimates testing marginalist distribution theory. Improvements are still in order on this last point.

An interesting combination of *changes* in the elasticity of substitution (always less than unity) with other factors in explaining distributional *changes* is found in the Brown–de Cani article already cited. Their variable S is the ratio of the labour to the capital share, and

---

[1] Fuchs, 'Capital-Labor Substitution : A Note', *Rev. Econ. and Stat.* Table 2 (p. 438). Fuchs' classification puts Puerto Rico in the 'developed' and Japan in the 'under-developed' group.

[2] Solow, 'Capital, Labor, and Income in Manufacturing', *Behavior of Income Shares, op. cit.* Table 2, p. 113. The Eisner and Kendrick criticisms are at pp. 131–135 and 141, respectively.

[3] Kurz and Manne, 'Engineering Estimates of Capital-Labor Substitution in Metal Machinery', *Am. Econ. Rev.* (September 1963), p. 676.

[4] Kaldor, *vide supra*, p. 485, note 1.

they are explaining changes in its logarithm over three technological 'epochs' in the U.S.A. : 1890–1918, 1919–37, 1938–58.

SOURCES OF LONG RUN CHANGES IN LOG S

Interval	Change in Elasticity of Substitution	Change in Labour Intensiveness of Technology	Change in Relative Input Prices	Total	Actual Change in Log S
Epoch 1 (1890–1918) to Epoch 2 (1919–37)	+0·399	−0·413	+0·055	+0·041	+0·113
Epoch 2 (1919–37) to Epoch 3 (1938–58)	−0·106	+0·202	+0·044	+0·140	+0·098

Source : Brown and de Cani, *op. cit.* Table 5, p. 303.

VI. ALTERNATIVE VERSIONS OF MACRO-DISTRIBUTION

(1) Admitting as one must the survival of gaps and ambiguities in neo-classical macro-distribution theory and its statistical supports, why does this writer persist in anticipating at least as much progress here as along the more modernistic lines fashionable in Britain, as well as much of Europe and Asia ? And more particularly, why the present overlong protest against discarding the Good Old Theory out of hand, and in favour of including it prominently in any future synthesis of macro-economic distribution models ?

Three obvious and related appeals of the Good Old Theory have been (1) its consistency with micro-distribution, (2) its acceptance (over the long period, at least) of the principle of substitution at the margin of inputs for each other, both directly and as a by-product of output substitution, and (3) its reasonably adequate record of empirical testing and application.

(2) On the importance of consistency between micro- and macro-economics, Professor Fritz Machlup has pleaded my methodological case better than I could plead it myself : [1]

Needless to say, it is not a duty for every macrotheorist to search for the hidden micro-relations that lie at the foot of the

[1] Machlup, 'Micro- and Macro-Economics : Contested Boundaries and Claims of Superiority', in *Essays on Economic Semantics* (Englewood Cliffs, N.J. : Prentice-Hall, 1963), pp. 109, 140.

macro-relations. . . . To specialize in the construction of macro-models without worry about the underlying micro-theories is neither unsound nor dishonourable. But to deny that all macro-theory requires a micro-theoretical underpinning, or to deride the efforts of those who do investigate it, would be unreasonable and obtuse.

While it is, of course, possible to concentrate on macro-theory, taking the macro-relations as given without being concerned about their composition, the macro-theorist wanting to understand his subject more profoundly will proceed to study the micro-theoretical underpinning of his macro-models.

In the short run, in societies with constant relative prices, or in societies insulated from market forces, input substitution may have no place and elasticities of substitution may be near zero. These cases aside, however, it is an obvious advantage to use a theory which, unlike most 'structural' ones, does *not* assume them to be zero, especially when statistical tests suggest that they are positive.[1] With regard to empirical testing, the record of neo-classical theory, while far from spotless, is better than any non-tautological rivals which have yet come to this writer's attention.[2]

(3) A further, and more controversial, reason for concentrating on neo-classical macro-distribution is what frankness compels me to call the unpromising character of those alternatives I have thus far encountered. I have mentioned the paucity of their empirical testing. The remainder of this essay will be devoted to some further objections, illustrated by the simplest forms of the alternative theories and accordingly perhaps unfair to some or all of their varieties.[3]

[1] In the particular case of labour-capital substitution, it is commonly supposed 'that substitution of labor for capital must mean the scrapping of machines and shifting of their functions to hand labor. Better care or maintenance work for equipment, postponing the need for replacement, constitutes a clear case of substitution of labor for capital. Increased utilization of plant capacity with increased employment and output also raises the ratio of labor to capital. So do alterations in the numbers of machines to be tended by one man, or in the size of the crew tending one machine.' The quotation is from Machlup, 'Marginal Analysis and Empirical Research', in *ibid.* p. 162, note 14.

[2] With respect to one alternative (Kaldor), however, see Melvin W. Reder 'Alternative Theories of Labor's Share', in Moses Abramovitz (ed.), *The Allocation of Economic Resources* (Stanford, Cal. : Stanford University Press, 1959) pp. 185-192.

[3] More comprehensive and sympathetic treatments may be found in Paul Davidson, *Theories of Aggregate Income Distribution* (New Brunswick, N.J., Rutgers University Press, 1959), chs. 5–9 ; Karl W. Rothschild, 'Some Recent Contributions to a Macro-Economic Theory of Income Distribution', *Scottish Journ. Pol. Econ.* (October 1961) ; Wilhelm Krelle, *Verteilungstheorie* (Tübingen : J. C. B. Mohr–Paul Siebeck, 1962), chs. 6, 8, 9 (esp. secs. 6–8) ; and A. K. Sen, 'Neo-Classical and Neo-Keynesian Theories of Distribution', *Econ. Record* (March 1963).

These rival theories seem divisible into five varieties, although some writers (notably Professors Sidney Weintraub [1] in America and Wilhelm Krelle in Germany) have sought to combine several of these.[2] The principal varieties appear to be : (1) theories of monopolistic exploitation, (2) theories of accounting identity, (3) theories of aggregate demand, evolving in many cases from Lord Keynes's *General Theory of Employment, Interest and Money*, (4) structural theories involving fixed proportions, 'stylized facts', 'magic constants', etc., and (5) power, bargaining, and 'sociological' theories, implying indeterminacy under market conditions.

(4) The prototype of monopolistic exploitation theories remains Dr. Michal Kalecki's famous article of 1938–39, whose argument has been simplified and clarified by Dr. Kurt W. Rothschild.[3] It yields a zero non-labour share in competitive cases, and an excessively small non-labour share in oligopolistic or monopolistically-competitive cases where monopoly power is low.

(5) Theories like Professor Kenneth Boulding's,[4] built up from accounting identities *ex post*, require interpretation *ex ante*, in the sense that they may more naturally be taken to represent *effects* than causes of distribution when viewed in this way. In Boulding's theory, to cite a well-known example, six key factors are : (a) household consumption of non-durables, (b) household accumulation

[1] This reference is to Weintraub, *An Approach to the Theory of Income Distribution* (Philadelphia : Clinton, 1958). Later publications have been less eclectic. See also Davidson, *op. cit.* ch. 8.

[2] Sen (*op. cit.*), omitting sociological theories, divides the analytical ones into neo-classical and neo-Keynesian categories, depending on the equation dropped in an over-determinate system of his own devizing. In Sen's notation, X is total output, of which $\bar{X}$ is used to reproduce itself ; L is the (given) amount of labour, and w its wage rate ; π is the total amount of profits, and I the amount of investment. Two saving propensities (s_w, s_p) are given for workers and capitalists respectively. There is also an autonomously-determined amount of investment I*. There are four unknowns (S, W, π, I). To solve, there are five equations (below). Equation (1) is a production function, assumed linear homogeneous ; (2) is a demand function for labour, along marginal-productivity lines ; (3) exhausts total product between labour and profits ; (4) equates saving and investment *ex ante* ; and (5) equates actual with autonomous investment. Neo-classical writers, says Sen, avoid over-determinacy by dropping equation (5) ; neo-Keynesian ones (but not Keynes himself) solve it by dropping the marginal productivity equation (2). The equations are :

$$(1)\ X = X(L, \bar{X})\ ; \quad (2)\ w = (\partial X)/(\partial L)\ ; \quad (3)\ X = \pi + wL\ ;$$
$$(4)\ I = s_p \pi + s_w L\ ; \quad (5)\ I = I^*.$$

[3] The most readily available version is Kalecki, 'The Distribution of the National Income', in American Economic Association, *Readings in the Theory of Income Distribution* (Philadelphia : Blakiston, 1949), Selection II. See also Rothschild, *The Theory of Wages* (New York : Macmillan, 1954), ch. 14.

[4] Boulding, *A Reconstruction of Economics* (New York : Wiley, 1950), ch. 14, and 'The Fruits of Progress and the Dynamics of Distribution', *Am. Econ. Rev.* (May 1953).

of durables, (c) household accumulation of money, (d) household debts to business, (e) business debts to households, and (f) business distributions of dividends and interest. *Ex post*, clearly, the identity involves no causation in either direction — or alternatively, equal causation in both directions. *Ex ante*, however, which is most intuitively reasonable, to view the volume of household consumption (say) as an *effect* or as a *cause* of the income distribution?

Consider also one form of the Kaldor formulation, in which the capital share equals the product of the growth rate of the economy and the aggregate capital-income ratio (a 'stylized fact'), divided by the

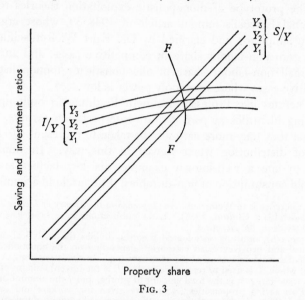

Fig. 3

capitalists' propensity to save.[1] *Ex post*, this is unexceptionable, accepting the approximation that workers' propensities to save are near zero. *Ex ante*, however, a more intuitively satisfactory interpretation might make the growth rate the dependent variable, that is to say, a result and not a cause of the income distribution.

(6) A representative Keynesian macro-distribution theory, also based on Kaldor's writings, is shown in Fig. 3.[2] The basic notion is that for any level of income Y_1, the saving ratio is a rising function of the property share while the investment ratio remains more or less

[1] N. Kaldor, 'Alternative Theories of Distribution', *Rev. Ec. Stud.* (1955–56).
[2] This figure is adapted from Krelle, *op. cit.*, Fig. 10, p. 77. The shape of the I/Y function, however, is based on the argument of Oscar Lange, 'The Rate of Interest and the Optimum Propensity to Consume', *Economica* (February 1938).

constant. Both S/Y and I/Y functions tend to move upward as income rises. The equilibrium property share may be constant (*FF* vertical) or follow a path or locus as in the figure. Two difficulties are that Keynesian theory has not yet been interpreted to tell us a great deal about the shape of the share function *FF*, and that it seems to assume in the background, with Keynes himself, marginalist notions of the determination of wage rates and profitabilities of investment.

The generalization has been suggested that all anti-classical macro-economic distribution theory (particularly the Keynesian variant) concentrates on developing the simple identity :

$$\frac{\pi}{Y} = \frac{\pi}{K}\frac{K}{Y}$$

which makes the profit share the product of the rate of return on capital and the aggregate capital-output ratio. 'If any two of these ratios can be shown to be constant, the remaining one is, by necessity, constant. . . . The chief problem, of course, is the determination of which ratios are fundamental, and which derived. Further, it is indeed possible that one or more of the above ratios may be more appropriately explained by the combined effect of factor substitution and technological change, as in the micro-economic theories.' [1]

(7) The trouble with 'magic constants' is that, in the long run and with variable prices, they may no longer be constant ; by the same token, an over 'stylized' fact is no longer a fact at all.[2] For instance, the Weintraub k, which is the ratio of business gross product to business wage payments, seems fairly clearly to be falling (albeit slowly), in Weintraub's own results for the U.S.A., now extended to the period 1899–1960, so that the wage share is rising.[3] A similar

---

[1] Charles L. Schultze and Louis Weiner, 'Introduction', *Behavior of Income Shares, op. cit.* p. 5. The formula in the text is used most openly by Krelle, *op. cit.* ch. 18, in his 'simple' distribution theory.

[2] Contrary viewpoints, however, are not lacking. See Klein's 'great ratios of economics' (*op. cit.* p. 183). More emphatically, Weintraub says in his 'Real Versus Price Theories of Distribution', reprinted in *Some Aspects of Wage Theory and Policy* (Philadelphia : Chilton, 1963), p. 243, n. 13 (running quotation) :

> 'It is distressing to find so much discomfort over evidence of certain important constancies in economics, not least the labor share. Why do we fear them? Why do we refuse to acknowledge them as empirical facts, even as we proceed to understand and explain them? I have even encountered the twisted argument that recognition of a functional relationship imparts more insight than an empirical near-constant. Is this anything short of arguing that a horizontal locus in a diagram is a weaker force than a curved locus whose shape we fix only vaguely, whose location is in doubt, and whose stability is in question? Does work with such fuzzy "functions" advance over science in the same way as empirical recognition and analytical utilization of (near) constants?'

[3] 'The Constancy in the Wage Share', Table 29, p. 87.

variability seems likewise observable in the marginal capital-output ratios, where alleged constancy has been an important argument for the constancy of the total ratios, as cited by Kaldor.[1]

The role of price changes in unhinging three magic constants in particular has been brought out by Edward Denison, referring to the trio we have called (π/Y), (π/K), and (K/Y). The first two are ordinarily presented in current prices, the last in constant prices. To preserve consistency, a fourth ratio is needed, namely, the price of capital goods divided by the price level of total national product. For the U.S.A. at least, Denison has found no set of definitions which, applied uniformly, show all three ratios stable in the long run.[2]

(8) We come finally to the sociological and institutional alternatives, which make distribution, following John Stuart Mill, 'a matter of human institution solely', or more precisely, within broad limits. The majority of these theories seem, to one accustomed to neat, tidy, and 'structured' economic theory, still inchoate and formless. Exactly what are these sociologists and institutionalists arguing, over and beyond the inapplicability of economic orthodoxy outside the realm of profit-seeking private industry ? Exactly what propositions, testable even qualitatively, can be distilled from a theory sufficiently general to apply to public employment, subsistence agriculture, and planned economy as well as Western-style private enterprise ? How, and to what extent, are sociological conclusions articulated with those achieved by economic theory of the ordinary sort which they do not usually propose to discard ?

And so I have recoiled, more puzzled than critical, awaiting for example the conclusion of the Marchal-Lecaillon treatise on distribution,[3] which is written from this point of view and may answer these sceptical questions.

One sociological rival to orthodoxy, more structured than marginalism itself, has however arisen from the Left-Keynesian, neo-Marxian wing of the Cambridge School, itself the very *fons et origo*

---

[1] N. Kaldor, 'A Model of Economic Growth', *op. cit.* For a (Japanese) example of planning which went awry in assuming constant coefficients, see Shigeto Tsuru, 'Empirical Testing of the Macro-Economic Planning in Japan', in *Essays on Japanese Economy* (Tokyo : Kinokuniya, 1958), pp. 109–115.

[2] Denison, in *Behavior of Income Shares*, *op. cit.* pp. 35–39. In another comment immediately following Denison's, Franco Modigliani strives to rehabilitate the magic constancies. He assumes a desired lifetime (K/Y) ratio toward which individuals progress normally from below. Progress may be faster or slower, or even negative, according as the rate of interest (π/K) exceeds or falls short of its permanent or long-term value. So long as both (K/Y) and (π/K) are constant in the long term, (π/Y) is naturally constant also. (*Ibid.* pp. 45–49.)

[3] Jean Marchal and Jacques Lecaillon, *La Répartition du revenu national* (Paris : Librairie de Médicis).

of economic tradition. This is Piero Sraffa's Ricardian *Commodities by Commodities*.[1] As in the Ricardian and (I conjecture) the Leontief input-output systems, with constant returns to scale, one 'original factor of production', average 'abstract' labour, and technologically fixed coefficients of production,[2] the wage rate can vary from 'subsistence' to the average product, and the labour share can move accordingly (given the labour force). To this reactionary writer, these assumptions appear, as said above, simply contrary to fact — skilled labour results from 'investment in human capital' in the same way as capital goods result from human labour, input-output coefficients are generally variable with relative input prices, constant returns to scale hold only in the small, etc. What remains to be seen is how important quantitatively these sceptical doubts may be. Planned economies with flexible plans certainly can (but need not) vary revenue distribution between wide limits. In a private or mixed economy dominated by profit-maximizing business, I suspect the range of variation to be very low, with attempts to extend it producing inflation, depression and/or chaos. But, of course, I may be wrong, which humble note is a good one to end this not-so-humble survey.

THE DISCUSSION
OF PROFESSOR BRONFENBRENNER'S PAPER

Dr. Pasinetti said that Professor Bronfenbrenner, in his review of alternative theories of distribution, had not disguised his strong preference for the marginal productivity theory, which he had presented in a neo-classical version, relying on macro-economic production functions of the Cobb–Douglas type.

Dr. Pasinetti said, by way of introduction, that the revival of interest in the theory of distribution had been stimulated by the appearance of the theories of growth characterized by the Harrod–Domar equation :

$$S = Ki,$$

relating the rate of savings S, the capital-output ratio K and the rate of

---

[1] Sraffa, *Production of Commodities by Means of Commodities — Prelude to a Critique of Economic Theory* (Cambridge Univ. Press, 1960). See also the three-part review article by P. R. Brahmanand 'Economics : The Sraffa Revolution', *Ind. Ec. Journ.* (January, April, and October–December 1963), esp. pp. 281–286.

[2] Professor Kamien reminds me of the theorem (by Professor Paul Samuelson) proving that fixity of production coefficients results from the other conditions posited, and need not be assumed additionally. This theorem applies to the Leontief system ; I conjecture that it applies likewise to the Sraffa one.

capital accumulation i. This equation could be looked at in two ways. One could state that if savings were, let us say, 12 per cent of national income and the capital-output ratio were 4, the economy could afford a 3 per cent rate of capital accumulation a year. Alternatively one could say that if the rate of population growth were, let us say, 1 per cent per annum and the rate of technical progress were such as to allow for a 2 per cent increase in productivity per annum so that the long-run 'natural' growth rate were 3 per cent, then, with a technologically given value of $K = 4$, the economy would have to save 12 per cent of national income to achieve the 'natural' rate of growth.

Either interpretation was possible. One could not, however, adopt both of them at the same time. There was one equation involving three magnitudes. Not all three of them could be taken as 'given', as Harrod had done. The post-Keynesian theory of distribution came out of the attempt to solve this difficulty, and the procedure consisted in taking K and i as given and in concentrating the attention on the left-hand side of the equation. Here, the propensities to save of the different groups of income recipients could indeed be taken as given; yet, the saving ratio S could be considered as a variable, defined as the average of the saving propensities, weighted according to the groups' shares in national income. Income distribution, in this way, immediately came in as a system of weights. In the usual two-group analysis, the weights represented the profit share and the wage share which were necessary to make up the saving ratio required for the system to work.

This 'natural' distribution would or would not be reached according to whether profit margins were flexible to changes in demand, as Kaldor assumed, or were not, as Kalecki assumed. But both Kaldor and Kalecki adopted the common assumption that K and i were not responsive to changes in income distribution.

Marginal productivity theorists, on the other hand, started from different preoccupations. The theory of marginal productivity was originally developed with reference to micro-economics. However, it proved later to be surprisingly flexible in extensions to macro-economic problems, by means of the 'production function'. This was an analytical tool which reduced output as a function of many physical inputs to output as a function of only two: capital and labour. At this point, marginal productivity theorists assumed S as a psychological constant and i as given in the long run by technological progress and population growth. The capital-output ratio K thus became the determined variable; production techniques would be chosen as compatible with factor prices so that K became a function of the relative price of capital and labour.

The consequence of all this was to take the process of determination of factor shares back again into the technological sphere of the economic system. In particular, there was one function that accomplished this task entirely: that was the Cobb–Douglas production function. Dr. Pasinetti said that Professor Bronfenbrenner's paper gave an excellent account of the characteristics of the Cobb–Douglas production function. This was a linear and homogeneous function. When used as a production function the marginal productivities of labour and of capital were equal to the wage rate and to the price of capital, and the elasticity of substitution between labour and capital was always equal to one, so that the shares of wages and profits in national income would be always the same, no matter what happened. If, for instance, the investment programme was stepped up, the capital-output ratio would react to the change in factor prices and the value of K would change in such a way that full employment would be reached with a different technology but with the same shares of wages and profits as before.

Dr. Pasinetti would not go into the details of Professor Bronfenbrenner's arguments to meet theoretical and statistical criticisms against the Cobb–Douglas functions in Sections III, IV, and V of his paper. Professor Bronfenbrenner's conclusion was that all the objections against the production functions were answerable and that the Cobb–Douglas function made a consistent micro- and macro-economic theory.

The last part of Professor Bronfenbrenner's paper was devoted to a strong criticism of all the other theories of distribution. Dr. Pasinetti confessed that he had not been convinced by Professor Bronfenbrenner's arguments. Could not the criticism against magic constants in other theories be turned against the Cobb–Douglas function ? If in the neo-Keynesian distribution theory K was a magic constant, was not α in the Cobb–Douglas production function another magic constant ? Could not the criticism against the neo-Keynesian theory for considering 'abstract labour' be turned against the marginal productivity theory for considering 'abstract capital' ? Indeed Dr. Pasinetti saw little difference between stating, on the one hand, that the wage share was constant because K was constant and stating, on the other hand, that the wage share was constant because α was constant.

Dr. Pasinetti thought that the Cobb–Douglas production function was also unsatisfactory in putting the whole task of adjustment on the sensitivity of the capital-output ratio to changes in the rate of interest whereas all empirical research in entrepreneurial behaviour had revealed the rate of interest to be of little significance in decision making. It was true that, according to some enquiries, changes in the rate of interest could influence the volume of investment but this was not the same as influencing the choice of production techniques.

Dr. Pasinetti said that he was disturbed that marginal productivity theory should consider the capital-output ratio so dependent on the rate of interest as to make all other processes of adjustment irrelevant. He wondered whether this was not a situation similar to the one that existed before Keynes when the rate of interest was considered as the only determinant of total savings.

The Distribution of National Income

Professor James said that he had been surprised to read in Professor Bronfenbrenner's paper (p. 500) that those in favour of the sociological theory of distribution were following Mill in making distribution solely a matter of human institutions. He had been rather shocked by Professor Bronfenbrenner's lumping together authors belonging to this school of thought with institutionalists and historicists. Nor was Jean Marchal the historicist Professor Bronfenbrenner accused him of being. Far from it, as Jean Marchal believed in economic laws. Nor could he be called an institutionalist as he was most respectful of the categories of traditional analysis. Nor could his sociological theory be called French as many French economists held other views. To the extent there was such a thing as a distinct French approach to distribution theory, this could not be described as ignoring economic laws but as trying to integrate institutional considerations into general economic theory.

As distinct from the traditional line of thought the French economists sought a synthesis between economic mechanisms and institutions instead of simply conciliating them. Thus Professor James could not agree with Professor Solow's remark in a previous discussion that it was not so much a matter of which theory of distribution one thought right as of choosing the one which was adequate to the purpose of the study in hand. Professor Solow's answer to Professor Jean Marchal in the discussion of his own paper had also revealed the real point of disagreement when he had said that he had thought himself justified in abstracting from institutions because his model had been devised for the short run. Professor James thought that even in the short run institutions had to be taken into account: the impact of trade unions, for instance, was relevant to the short run as well as to the long run. In wage bargaining, decisions did not relate to marginal productivity alone and the behaviour of institutions was not to be confused with the behaviour of individuals.

Professor Bronfenbrenner said that he had been provoked to state his objections to other approaches more strongly than he intended by no less strongly worded criticism of the marginal productivity analysis. In reacting to a trend of thought which questioned its significance he had tried to re-establish that it had a major part to play.

He agreed that Dr. Pasinetti's analysis fitted in with the way he felt about the direction of causation except in one particular : he considered the rate of growth as primarily a result of income distribution. He would also go a step further, and make the level of employment another resultant.

The level of employment was a resultant not only of distribution analysis but also of some sociological factors. The marginal productivity of labour might be ignored in wage-bargaining discussions as Professor James had suggested — Professor Bronfenbrenner would agree that the words 'marginal productivity' were never mentioned in these discussions — but the decisions reached on wage rates might affect the level of employment in that industry and, if generalized through the whole economy, might affect the level of employment.

Dr. Pasinetti had introduced the Cobb–Douglas function as answering a challenge set by the Harrod–Domar models. Professor Bronfenbrenner thought it worth while pointing out that it antedated these models. What made the Cobb–Douglas function fit so well into marginal productivity analysis was not the form of the function or the 'magic' of its constants but its proven reliability in interpreting observed facts. Although it made no allowance for a degree of monopoly or for the all-or-none type of collective bargaining, this had not prevented its application to market economies. On the other hand Professor Bronfenbrenner would be surprised if it worked equally well for subsistence and planned economies.

Professor Bronfenbrenner thought that most of Dr. Pasinetti's criticisms of the functions were directed against its original 1928 version. Since then it had been improved considerably and would doubtless continue to be improved.

Dr. Pasinetti had questioned the influence of the rate of interest on the choice of production techniques. But this was not simply a question of substitutability of labour and capital. In a country like Japan, with plenty of labour available, techniques were as modern as in the U.S.A. where labour was scarce: it was not a matter of Japan using less modern techniques, but of Japan using more workers per modern machine, with 'half the labour force serving tea to the other half'. Thus techniques tended to be the same in both countries, but capital-output ratio would none the less be higher in Japan.

Professor Bronfenbrenner said that he was grateful to Professor James for having pointed out the reasons why it was wrong to confuse a sociological theory of distribution with historicism or institutionalism. One of the best results of attending an international Conference was that one was able to form a clearer idea of what one's foreign colleagues were thinking, and he felt that he now knew better what the sociological approach aimed at.

Professor Solow told Professor James that he had never intended to say that one could freely choose between independent theories for studying different problems. In principle this was not possible. On the other hand one could not unify approaches, at least in their present state. It was clear that the collective actions of social groups affected price determination but the reverse was no less true: market mechanisms and marginal productivity had a bearing on the action of groups. As the gap between the two conceptions could not yet be bridged, all one could do at the present moment was to correct conclusions drawn from one theory with conclusions drawn from the other.

Professor Jean Marchal observed that the pressure of well-organized groups such as trade unions might well exceed the narrow margin imposed by marginal productivity on collective bargaining as implicit in Professor

Solow's reasoning. If trade unions were in a strong position they might thus obtain wage increases in excess of marginal productivity requirements in a few big firms and this might push up wage rates in the rest of the economy, leading to reactions in price formation and distribution of income between wages and profits. In the U.S.A. as in many other countries the fear of this had been enough to lead governmental authorities to interfere.

Professor Preiser said that after he had read the theoretical papers, especially Professor Solow's and Professor Föhl's, he felt justified in maintaining that there were no alternative theories of distribution. All were incomplete and their elements had to be combined. Certainly one could derive an equation for the share of profits on Keynesian lines like the Kaldorian equation. But this was looking only at the demand side. There was also a supply side. Or, better, one should take into account what happened in the process of production, which was, at the same time, the process of income formation. In this way, one came back, in fact, to micro-economics, which again seemed to mean productivity theory.

This theory was in his opinion not altogether satisfactory. First, it implied the law of decreasing returns which, as a general statement, was not always true. Secondly, it operated under the assumption of given amounts of factors instead of making use of supply functions of factors. Reasoning on the elasticity of output with respect to factor inputs might be realistic in production theory but not for a distribution theory as it implicitly conferred a purely passive role to factors.

Professor Preiser did not wish to go further into these points as there existed another way of approaching the micro-economics of distribution, making use of a sort of full-cost principle as Kalecki had done. Although at the cost of abandoning the profit-maximization principles (which might still remain relevant for short-period changes), such a theory fitted in well with the observed facts in a world of oligopolies and monopolistic competition.

In this way, one came nearer to the process of income distribution, generating in the process of production, considered as a struggle between groups, not only for money wages on the labour market but also of price setting by entrepreneurs. Workers aimed at a definite real wage ; they had no money illusion. Entrepreneurs aimed at a definite profit or rate of profit (in this respect they seemed to have a money illusion). What was meant by 'definite' was that both wanted to have at least what they always had, which was a historical link with the past. Needless to say they also wanted to have their share in productivity increase. Following this line of thought was recognizing that distribution was not simply the effect or, so to speak, the by-product of the whole process of producing, consuming, and investing. A certain distribution was planned by the actors. This was also the view of his French colleagues.

This planned distribution could be called the structural degree of monopoly. Obviously, then, actual distribution remained a function of all the variables of the system, but if it differed from the planned one, there would be no equilibrium because, for instance, of too much investment. Any deviation of actual from planned distribution would provoke reactions from the actors. In the usual models there was only one subject making decisions : the profit-maximizing entrepreneur ; but in real life there were two conflicting ones, acting and reacting upon each other.

To hold a production theory (which in effect was an input theory) and a price theory was not enough for a proper distribution theory. If one wanted one, one could not dispense with the concept of a structural degree of monopoly which *inter alia* led back to the primary distribution of property. Models were based on psychological and technical data ; they ought also to include sociological or institutional data. This by no means implied mixing history and theory. It could be shown that the insertion of such a structural degree of monopoly into the macro-economic model led to a consistent system, which was not, as was often maintained, over-determined. Of course if entrepreneurs planned prices they could not independently plan investment. If they attempted to do both the whole economic process would head for disequilibrium but this was no objection to the theory.

Professor Solow supposed one could say that the price theory in his paper in part tried to reconcile the full-cost principle with marginalist ideas by putting profit maximization in the long-run context. Entrepreneurs set prices by marking up their prime costs by how much ? The conditions of demand in the long run provided the answer, without daily adjustments to changes in the demand. A theory of market structure would thus help to determine intervals of mark-ups.

Professor Falise thought that there was some logical difficulty in using an aggregated production in so far as this was obtained by averaging sectoral production functions. Supposing that the increases in capital or labour inputs were not distributed between sectors according to their weights in the overall production function and that, for instance, the whole increase was in a sector where the production function was very different from the overall one, it would no longer be right to calculate marginal productivities of capital and labour by using the overall production function. If most of the increase in labour inputs went to the sector of services, as was the case in the Belgian economy, one had to keep in mind the fact that the production function in this sector was a peculiar one.

Professor Falise, contrary to Professor Bronfenbrenner, did not think that the question of whether sociological or marginal productivity theory was better for prediction could be answered *a priori*. It all depended on which of the technological and sociological basic conditions would prove the more stable. Group behaviours might be stable whereas production functions might change rapidly and unexpectedly. For instance within the last few years, contrary to expectations, the textile industry in Northern

France had changed from a labour- to a highly capital-using industry in response to scarcity of labour and trade-union pressure.

Professor Bronfenbrenner said that he entirely agreed with Professor Falise's objection about the difficulty in using aggregate production functions indiscriminately. Cobb–Douglas functions might or might not fit the observed data but one of the attractions of the production function approach was that, unlike some others, it could be proved wrong. As a matter of fact it had been generally proved successful in fitting the data in a variety of situations. For instance, productivity analysis applied to agriculture before and after price control. Before the break there would be one function and after the break there might be, in the second period, an entirely different function. This might be part of the reconciliation between the sociological and the market approaches but one would have to wait and see.

Professor Föhl said that to determine the share of wages as α and the share of profits as $1 - \alpha$ as in the Cobb–Douglas function was just another way of equating the labour share in the social product to marginal productivity of labour and the capital share to the marginal productivity of capital. This was typical long-run reasoning. It would apply to the employer of the last unit of labour. The determination of profits, however, was something quite different from the determination of wages by marginal productivity of labour. Entrepreneurs minimized costs but they did not equate share of profits. Profits, i.e. revenue above cost, were differential and the profit share could not be determined just by reciprocity with α. It seemed to Professor Föhl that the discussions had shown a consensus of opinion about the need to conceive models which would bring supply and demand functions into the picture. This implied that the profit share had to be determined independently of the wage share whereas it seemed to him that by using the Cobb–Douglas function one made everything depend on the given value of α.

Professor Reder was surprised that in discussing the theoretical papers there had been no reference to the alternative 'bargaining theory' of wages. There had been considerable empirical work in the U.S.A. on the effects of changes in the circumstances of bargainers on wage rates. The problem had been also approached through the theory of games, and while it was not yet clear whether simulating behaviour in laboratory experiments would throw any light on real bargaining, this was at least a first step towards an experimental approach.

The difficulty was that non-marginal theories could not be easily confronted with marginal theories because they did not work under the same assumptions: whereas the Cobb–Douglas theory applied to variations in the product, they could say nothing as yet about what would happen if one side in the bargaining had increased resources. Some initial results were, however, worth considering, as they suggested that effects of bargaining depended on how often bargainers met and confronted resolutions.

Professor Ducros wished to comment on the dynamics of the Cobb–Douglas function. One could go from the static to a dynamic formulation of the function by bringing in a new variable, t, as a surrogate for technological change as Professor Bronfenbrenner had posited $[x=f(a,\ b,\ t)]$. This obviously left open the issue as to whether increase in productivity through time should be related to labour or to capital: it was simply ascribed to labour and capital working jointly.

This, however, could only be a first step after which Professor Bronfenbrenner used Professor Solow's function: $x=A^ta^\alpha b^{1-\alpha}$. Professor Bronfenbrenner had reminded his readers that the outcome of Professor Solow's calculations based on the observed relative share of capital had been that, in the U.S.A., approximately seven-eighths of observed improvement in output per manhour was to be related to technological change rather than increased capital (p. 491).

Professor Ducros observed that this sort of calculation led to attributing the increase in production to the increase in the amount of labour and capital and in capital productivity alone. This seemed to imply that no increase in productivity ever originated in a rising level of labour's skill or know-how. In many cases an increase in productivity as a result of better production techniques would simply mean labour being combined with more efficient capital goods. But in other cases the reason for an increase in productivity might be, not that workers were using more efficient equipment but that there were more highly skilled workers available. Just as one took into account the changes in capital stock brought about by new more-efficient equipment substituted for the old, one ought to take into account the effect of productivity of a parallel change in manpower, i.e. an increasing proportion of people with better training or education. An increase in productivity could result from either changes in the proportion of modern equipment in the stock of capital goods or of changes in the proportion of people with higher skill in the labour force. Therefore one should not attribute all the increase in productivity per manhour to capital.

Professor Bronfenbrenner replied to the last four speakers. Professor Preiser had advocated eclecticism. Professor Bronfenbrenner thought it rather dangerous, as one might get inconsistent results through over-determinacy. It was true that marginal productivity theory was first a theory of demand for inputs. Nevertheless, on the supply side, it assumed a given quantity of factors only in the short run. Professor Bronfenbrenner was not clear on the significance of Professor Preiser's notion of planned distribution. The level of employment and the rate of growth might be affected by the implied group behaviour. Professor Preiser's planned distribution was different from distribution in a planned economy. At any rate, the degree of variability of distribution in a market economy ruled by the principle of maximizing was much less than in a planned economy. One could have a wider margin of variation in a mixed economy but Professor Bronfenbrenner was afraid this meant trying to fulfil three conflicting objectives at the same time : if one was committed to allowing large increases in wages, forcing firms to keep all the labour force in employment, and restraining increases in the money supply, this would lead to chaos in any but a centrally planned economy, and perhaps even there.

Professor Bronfenbrenner was not sure that Professor Föhl had not misinterpreted the Cobb–Douglas function : the relative shares were determined separately, by two independent computations ; β was equal to $1 - \alpha$ but this was just the result of the value of the elasticities being equal to one. The real issue was how close $\alpha + \beta$ were to unity. In short-run computations, this left an unexplained residual, but the Cobb–Douglas function was rather a long-period determination. (Professor Bronfenbrenner would agree with Professor Föhl on this.)

Professor Reder's observations related to applied economics whereas Professor Bronfenbrenner had meant his study to be pure theory and he would rather abstain from commenting on these points. Professor Ducros's point called for a mathematical answer. If one introduced in the Cobb–Douglas function an A term allowing for the effects of changes in technology so that : $P = A(t)L^{\alpha}K^{\beta}$, the marginal productivity of labour would vary according to changes in the quantity of capital K, the quantity of labour L, and the value of A. The quantities K, L, and A all being functions of time, marginal productivity itself should be a function of time, $\left(\dfrac{dP}{dL}\right) = f(t, A, L, K)$.

Chapter 19

ON THE INTERRELATIONS BETWEEN GROWTH AND THE DISTRIBUTION OF INCOME

BY

P. NØRREGAARD RASMUSSEN

Institute of Economics, University of Copenhagen

I. INTRODUCTION

ONE of the rewarding viewpoints in the recent theory of distribution has been its dynamic character in the form of attempts to unify the theory of distribution and the theory of growth. As dynamics opens up so many possibilities depending on the configuration of the structure of the models, it is not surprising that no unified (and unanimously accepted) pattern has as yet been reached. In what follows only bits and pieces of some of the relevant arguments will be presented. The following pages, in other words, do not in any sense claim comprehensiveness.[1]

Income is divided into wages (including salaries) and profits only. In other words, only two factors of production are considered: labour and capital. Payments of interest (and rent) are not considered to constitute factor incomes but are considered transfer incomes.[2]

Two alternative questions can be asked depending on the basis of comparison. An economy characterized by a given growth rate may be compared to the same economy deprived of growth, i.e. a stationary economy. Alternatively the distribution of income under a given rate of growth may be compared to the distribution under conditions of another rate of growth.

A positive growth rate as compared to stationary conditions by necessity involves certain shifts in the distribution of income. The

---

[1] I am indebted to Mr. Erling Olsen and Mr. Hector Estrup — both research associates in the Institute of Economics, University of Copenhagen — for valuable comments on a first draft of this paper. Likewise, discussions with Professor Jørgen H. Gelting have been rewarding.

[2] This is in accordance with theoretical reasoning and has in fact been adopted in the Danish national accounts, cf. *Nationalregnskabsstatistik 1947–1960*, Statistiske undersøgelser nr. 7, København, 1962, p. 10.

first argument to be considered is that of reinvestments. If reinvestments do not increase *pari passu* to the increase in the volume of capital, a gain for profits will appear under growth. The fact that it takes some time before new capital has to be scrapped means only a shift in income over time if a business cycle is considered. Under growth, however, this gain for profits becomes permanent. The shift in the distribution will be greater the longer is the lifetime of capital, because the decline in the average age of capital will be greater. *Ceteris paribus*, the shift also will be greater the faster capital is increasing, i.e. the higher the growth rate. The growth may, however, lead to a decrease in the lifetime of capital goods. This may weaken, neutralize, or reverse the reinvestment effect.

Other forces, however, may be at work and may strengthen or weaken the reinvestment effect. One such force is the effect following the inter-industry shifts. Two basically different types of inter-industry shifts can be considered. One type is intimately related to the theory of growth: the relative shift from the sectors producing consumer goods to the sectors producing capital goods. Another type is the well-known shift from sectors producing primary goods to those producing secondary or tertiary goods. Whether one or another of these shifts are considered it must be important to separate these consequences from those following the reinvestment effect. This will be attempted below, taking the starting point in a Wicksell–Solow model.

Obviously, the changes in the distribution of income depend exclusively on the type of growth theory relied upon. While the reinvestment effect as well as the effect of inter-industry shifts usually are based on the same type of growth theory involving production functions, a different mechanism is at work if prices are allowed to change. Two types of changes in prices may be considered. One is a change in the general level of prices. Under this heading, the transfer of wealth and real income from creditor to debtor has been dealt with at length in the literature. As interest is not considered a factor income and as only shifts between different types of factor income are considered, this problem is of no importance in the present context. However, another effect of changes in the general level of prices of goods may be an increase in profits due to a 'widow's-cruse' argument. It can be shown that if the increase in prices originates in an increase in investments, only the consumption behaviour of the capitalists — i.e. those receiving profits — is important.

Another type of price changes which has so far been rather neglected is a change in the system of relative prices. If the terms of trade are changed in favour of consumer goods versus capital goods, this may involve a shift in real income towards profits. This is the simple consequence of the fact that profits as compared with wages buy relatively less of consumer goods.

Finally, problems relating to technical progress will be mentioned, though here only in the form of a few notes to a Schumpeterian viewpoint. The notes presented in relation to Schumpeter's terminology are only interesting as a reminder : in present growth theory Schumpeter seems more or less forgotten.

II. THE ROLE OF REINVESTMENT

If — to take an extreme case — a unit of capital remains intact throughout its lifetime, it is easily seen that a positive growth as compared to stationary conditions means that the average age of capital will be lower. But this means that the drain on gross profits due to reinvestment will be relatively smaller. Consequently a shift towards net profits (as compared to wages) takes place.[1]

In a Wicksellian model, treated by Solow [2] this reinvestment effect is at work though mixed up with the effects of inter-industry shifts. One may take this Wicksell–Solow model and try to separate these two effects.

Retaining Solow's notations, Q_C is the rate of output of consumption goods while L_C and R_C are the inputs of labour and capital (machinery) in this sector. Q_R, L_R, and R_R are the corresponding symbols relating to the capital-producing sector. Q_R is measured in terms of consumer goods. Following Wicksell [3] and using proper

---

[1] Quite apart from the impact on the distribution, the same mechanism may be used for arguing against a predominant view : That the treatment of depreciations in the tax legislation only influences the distribution of income over time. Disregarding the effects of progressive taxation, a liberal policy towards depreciations is often claimed to mean a short-term gain for profits (net of taxes), but when the capital has been fully depreciated while it still generates income the punishment is inevitable. This, of course, may be correct under stationary conditions. Assuming growth, however, the gain becomes more than a temporary loan free of interest. It becomes a permanent gain. Cf. on this P. Nørregaard Rasmussen, 'En note om afskrivninger, skattepligtig indkomst og vækst', *Nationaløkonomisk Tidsskrift*, 1962.

[2] Cf. Robert M. Solow, 'Notes Towards a Wicksellian Model of Distributive Shares', published in F. A. Lutz and D. C. Hague (ed.), *The Theory of Capital*, London, 1961. For all details the reader must be referred to Solow's article.

[3] *Lectures on Political Economy*, London, 1934, Appendix 2.

units, two production functions of the Cobb–Douglas type are postulated :

$$Q_C = L_C^\gamma R_C^{1-\gamma} \tag{1}$$

and

$$Q_R = L_R^\alpha R_R^{1-\alpha} N_R^{-\beta} \tag{2}$$

The peculiar form of (2) is explained by reference to the two dimensions inherent in Wicksell's capital : increasing the input of L_R and/or R_R involves either an increase in the number of capital units produced (axes in Wicksell's presentation) or it involves a lengthening of the life period of each unit of capital. (A third possibility, of course, is a combination of these two extremes.) Thus N_R denotes the durability of capital (as measured in years) while β is a parameter expressing the technical difficulty of extending the lifetime of capital. It is assumed — and that is important in the present context — that machines keep their productive capacities fully throughout their lifetime. After N_R years their value is zero.

Solow's article is available in print and a complete survey of the reasonings is not necessary.[1] Under stationary conditions, the net national income is Q_c, i.e. the rate of output of consumer goods.

---

[1] Assuming competition and the related full adjustments it is shown (as already Wicksell did) that in equilibrium :

$$e^{\rho N_R} = 1 + \frac{\rho N_R}{\beta},$$

where ρ is the rate of interest. This relation shows that the optimal life period of a machine is determined by the rate of interest only, as soon as the technical conditions are given (β), cf. the following figure. In other words, the product of ρ and N_R depends on β only.

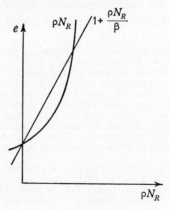

Denoting the value of real capital by V_R, Solow shows the share of profit to be

$$D_s=\frac{\rho V_R}{Q_C}=(1-\gamma)\frac{\rho N_R+e^{-\rho N_R}-1}{\rho N_R-(1-\alpha)(1-e^{-\rho N_R})}. \qquad (3)$$

Under growth, net investment will be positive. In a golden age where everything increases at a constant rate, g, the share of profits in total net income becomes

$$D_g=\frac{\rho V_R}{Q_C+\text{net investment}}$$

$$=\frac{\rho(1-\gamma)\left[\dfrac{1-e^{-gN_R}}{g}-\dfrac{1-e^{-\rho N_R}}{\rho}\right]}{(\rho-g)\left[\dfrac{1-e^{-gN_R}}{g}-\dfrac{1-e^{-\rho N_R}}{\rho}\right]+\alpha(\rho-g)\dfrac{1-e^{-\rho N_R}}{\rho}}. \qquad (4)$$

Needless to say, this expression is most difficult to give any simple interpretation. In this connection the interesting thing is whether $D_g>D_s$.

Two different factors affecting the share of profits, D_g, are at work in this model. These two factors may co-operate or they may work against one another. Firstly, growth as compared to stationary conditions involves as already mentioned that on average capital will be younger. Under the assumption stated as to the way in which capital is worn out it follows that reinvestment becomes less of a burden. This is easily seen when considering an economy in the take-off, i.e. being in the transition from stationary conditions to a golden age, where the extra capital coming into production needs not for the first N_R years be renewed at all. But this advantage is maintained even beyond the first N_R years — exactly because of the growth.

Secondly, growth involves a shift in the distribution of output towards the capital-producing sector. Now, it may happen that this latter sector is characterized by generating a higher share of profits than the sector producing consumer goods. In the Wicksell–Solow model this is so if $\gamma>\alpha$. In this case there will be two reasons for an increase in the overall share of profits. But, clearly, the two factors may work against one another in so far as the capital producing sector may yield a lower share for profits, i.e. $\gamma<\alpha$.

One way of analyzing this would be to isolate the two factors from one another simply by comparing the share of profits as shown above

S

The Distribution of National Income

to the share which would be the result of assuming profit to receive the same share in the two sectors, i.e. assuming $\gamma = \alpha$.

Under stationary conditions, of course, the share of profits will be higher if $\gamma > \alpha$ than if $\gamma = \alpha$. This is bound to be so and it is easily seen from (3). In a golden age things are more complicated. Denoting the overall share of profits as shown in (4) by D'_g in the case where $\gamma = \alpha$, it is easily found that

$$D_g - D'_g \frac{1}{BB'}(1-\gamma)(\rho-g)(1-e^{-\rho N_R})(\gamma-\alpha)K \tag{5}$$

where B is the denominator in (4), B' is the same expression for $\alpha = \gamma$, while

$$K = \frac{1-e^{-gN_R}}{g} - \frac{1-e^{-\rho N_R}}{g}.$$

Now, it can be proved that $D_g - D'_g$ is positive conditional on $\gamma > \alpha$ only. This is so because K and $\rho - g$ appear to have the same sign, i.e. $\rho \gtrless g$ involves $K \gtrless 0$.

(5) may be considered to measure the extra positive or negative gain in the profits share due to $\gamma \neq \alpha$. Another part of the gain for profit is due to the assumption about depreciations. Apparently this part may be measured by $D'_g - D_s$, where D'_s is the share of profits under stationary conditions [1] assuming $\gamma = \alpha$. It can be shown that a sufficient condition for $D'_g > D'_s$ is $\rho > g$.

Another way of demonstrating that the shift considered in the Wicksell–Solow model is composed of two parts is to use an alternative assumption as to the way in which capital disappears in the process of production. An alternative to the above-mentioned assumption according to which capital is supposed to maintain its productive capacity throughout its lifetime has in fact also been proposed by Solow. In his appendix (as well as in the discussion at the meeting) Solow shows the result of assuming 'radioactive' depreciation, i.e. a constant fraction of capital is assumed to disappear each year. In this case the share of profits under stationary conditions is shown to be [2]

$$\frac{1-\gamma}{1+\dfrac{\alpha\beta}{1-\beta}}$$

[1] This additive approach is simply based on the formal decomposition :
$$D_g = D'_s + (D'_g - D'_s) + (D_g - D'_g).$$
Thus $D'_g - D'_s$ remains to be considered.
[2] Cf. Lutz and Hague, *op. cit.* p. 383.

as compared to the share under growth

$$\frac{1-\gamma}{1+\dfrac{\alpha\beta}{1-\beta}+(\alpha-\gamma)\dfrac{g}{\rho}}.$$

Clearly, now the only positive gain for profits due to growth originates from an assumption about $\gamma > \alpha$.

A number of alternative rules for depreciations — in the sense of reinvestment needed to make up for the decline in the productive capacity of capital — might be considered. It seems quite clear that the two cases analysed above are extremes. These two cases imply that the productive capacity of a unit of capital through time behaves as indicated by A and B in the following figure. Alternative possibilities exemplified by C and D can be visualized.

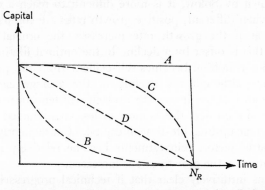

It is important to note that the case denoted by B (radioactive decay) indicates a lower limit because of the *form* of B. B will be linear on a semi-logarithmic scale. Any *form* which is convex in this scale will, *ceteris paribus*, imply a positive gain for profits due to growth. Any *form* which is concave on the semi-logarithmic scale must, *ceteris paribus*, imply that the reinvestment effect works against profits. This latter case may be difficult to visualize as of any importance. An illustration of such concave forms would be a rule stating that during the first year of use a unit of capital reduces its productive capacity by 50 per cent, during the next year by 40 per cent (of what remains), during the third year by 32 per cent, etc. (Tax legislation may sometimes assume such cases. One might also visualize such forms if due account is given to obsolescence in a world of innovations.) It would carry too far in the present context to go into details on the alternative cases.

It is also important to note that these conclusions on the reinvestment effect do not seem to depend on the form of the production function relied upon. In fact, they seem to hold even if the whole idea of a production function is discarded. However, it should also be noted that the effect depends on depreciations being a function of time rather than on the utilization of capital.

A preliminary conclusion consequently is that, depending on the assumption used for depreciations, growth may shift income distribution towards profits. This has been shown in relation to production functions of the Cobb–Douglas type but it seems as if the basic mechanism does not depend on this restrictive assumption. It also seems to hold under less restrictive assumptions about depreciations as long as depreciations do not increase proportionate to the volume of capital.

As shown by Solow, it is more difficult to reach a definite conclusion when different, positive growth rates are compared. Solow shows that if the growth rate increases, the crucial question is whether this is offset by a decline in the optimal lifetime of capital N_R.[1] This condition becomes self-evident from the present interpretation: although the decline in the average age of capital following an increase in growth in itself will tend to make reinvestment less of a burden, this is more or less counteracted by a decline in the average optimal life-time of capital. Consequently, depending on the latter factor, reinvestments become relatively more or less important when the growth rate is increased.

It seems intuitively clear that if technical progress is taken into account, the tendency for the average optimal lifetime of capital to be lower will be stronger the higher the growth rate. The consequence of this is that the reinvestment effect is weaker the more rapid is the technical progress.

III. INTER-SECTOR SHIFTS

As already stated this reinvestment effect may or may not be counteracted by the change in the composition of total output. It seems difficult to present any *a priori* reasonings for the capital producing sector to generate a higher or lower share to profit. As far as I know systematic empirical studies are not available.

---

[1] Cf. Solow, *op. cit.* p. 256. Whether a shift towards profits will take place depends on whether gN_R rises or falls when g increases.

In a broader field of consideration, using alternative break-downs of industry, a number of arguments under this heading may be presented. Taking into account that growth clearly is tantamount to a shift in output as between industries, i.e. from agriculture to manufacturing industries, etc., and, further, taking into account that the institutional framework for production is very different in different industries, the result will clearly be that growth will change the (observed) figures for the share of profits. One important reason for this is simply that in the statistics usually no attempt is made to impute a wage to the self-employed. For instance, in Danish agriculture the share of (gross) profits was 78 per cent in 1961 against 40 per cent in manufacturing industry. Consequently the *statistics* of profits share will change when the share of agriculture falls relatively to that of manufacturing industry, cf. Table 1 showing the number of self-employed as percentage of total occupied population.

The inter-industry shifts are bound to be more violent, the faster the rate of growth. In a rather mechanical way one may try to isolate these effects from the overall relation between wages and profits. Such attempts prove the importance (as measured by the statistics) of inter-sector movements, cf. Table 2, though it must be borne in mind that these calculations run into the same difficulties as any atomistic index number calculation. The figures in Table 2 attempt to show percentage points change in the share of wages in three post-war years as compared to that part of the change which is due to inter-sectoral movements. The latter figures are calculated by estimating 'what would have been the total share of labour income in the different years on the assumption that the share within each sector was constant at the 1950 level and that only the relative size of sectors changed' (*Economic Survey of Europe, 1956*, pp. viii–24). On the whole, it appears from the table that a notable part of the observed changes may be explained in this way.

It should be borne in mind that the observed distribution within a given industry may differ from the average for two reasons. Firstly, the rate of profits may be above or below average. (This may not indicate any disequilibrium because the statistics are bound to work on average figures while the question about equilibrium or disequilibrium must refer to marginal considerations.) Secondly, production may be more or less capital intensive. (Thirdly, what has been referred to as the 'institutional framework for production' may be such that a higher or lower part of manpower is counted as

The Distribution of National Income

TABLE 1

SELF-EMPLOYED PERSONS AS A PROPORTION
OF TOTAL OCCUPIED POPULATION IN DIFFERENT INDUSTRIES
(Percentages)

	Agri-culture	Manu-facturing	Con-struction	Trans-portation	Trade
Austria (1951)	67	14	7	6	36
Belgium (1947)	84	15	26	10	63
Denmark (1950)	49	15	21	13	40
France (1954)	60	13	18	5	44
Ireland (1951)	82	12	9	9	30
Norway (1953)	83	14	18	11	23
Switzerland (1950)	75	14	15	5	30
Sweden (1950)	70	10	13	10	23
United Kingdom (1951)	33	6	12	5	25

Source : *Economic Survey of Europe, 1956*, pp. viii–19.
Note.—For details on methods (and modifications), reference must be made to the source.

TABLE 2

CHANGES IN THE PERCENTAGE SHARE
OF WAGES AND SALARIES IN NET DOMESTIC PRODUCT
AS COMPARED TO 1950

A : Total change in percentage points.
B : Change due to inter-sector movements.

		1948	1952	1955
Denmark	A	+2·5	+1·0	+2·7 *
	B	+0·6	+0·4	+1·1 *
Finland	A	−0·4	+0·5	−0·5
	B	−3·0	—	+0·7
France	A	..	+2·7	+4·8 *
	B	..	+0·9	+0·6 *
Western Germany	A	..	−0·8	+1·0
	B	—	+0·7
Ireland	A	..	−0·5	+0·2
	B	..	−1·2	−0·7
Norway	A	−0·7	+0·9	+1·0
	B	+0·1	+0·3	+0·5
United Kingdom	A	+0·7	+3·2	+2·5
	B	+0·2	+0·5	+0·2

* 1954.

Note.—The figures have been taken from the *Economic Survey of Europe in 1956*, Geneva, 1957, pages viii–25. In the case of Denmark and the United Kingdom, the figures relate to gross domestic product. For details on sources and methods, cf. the source.

entrepreneurs because of the difficulty of imputing a wage or salary to, say, agriculturalists.)

It may be added that the reason why relatively little in terms of economic *theory* can be said under this heading, is because we have only fragments of a theory about the inter-relations between growth and inter-industry shift of production and factors of production. Following the tradition of William Petty and Colin Clark we have gone a long way to describe these shifts. But much remains in terms of theory. One difficulty confronts such theory. It can be argued that these shifts can be explained in terms of incentives and would from a *ceteris paribus* viewpoint carry the economy towards an equilibrium. However, because of changes — which are too regular to be called structural — *ceteris* are not *paribus* and an equilibrium has not been attained. In fact, it may be argued that an equilibrium between industries is just as far away as it was a few decades after the industrial revolution. This point was very clearly put by Colin Clark [1] 25 years ago :

'From Sir William Petty's day to the present time the transfer of working population from primary production to secondary and tertiary has been continuing, and perhaps will continue for as many centuries more. This is clear evidence that world economic equilibrium has not yet been obtained, and indeed that the world is still a very long way from obtaining it. In other words, certain agricultural countries and regions must be regarded as being "over-populated". This word is not used in the sense that they are in any way unable to support their present populations, but simply in the economic sense of the term, namely that their inhabitants could earn even considerably higher average real incomes per head in other industries or territories, and, if actuated by economic motives, will in the course of time do so.'

Since then the statistics have done nothing but verify Colin Clark's statement. The data, however, are still poor Data on changes in the distribution of the labour force are only available in a few countries — not to mention data on real capital.

On the whole it is difficult to argue on any firm basis that the shift in output (and demand) as between industries will necessarily involve any definite shift in the distribution between profits and wages. [2]

---

[1] *Conditions of Economic Progress*, London, 1940, p. 341.
[2] On the other hand, a definite shift in the distribution may be disguised because of inter-sectoral changes. This is — at least — exemplified by Solow, 'A Skeptical Note on the Constancy of Relative Shares', *American Economic Review*, September 1958.

IV. THE ROLE OF PRICES

Most growth models available are in terms of constant prices. There are very good reasons for this though everybody would admit that a process of growth is likely to involve important changes in prices. Such changes in turn may influence the growth process itself and have a bearing on the distribution of real income. Taking into account the importance attached to prices, it is rather surprising that the theory of growth has done so little to clarify the subject.

Two types of changes in prices can be considered. One is a change in the system of relative prices on finished goods, another is a change in the general level of prices. As to changes in relative prices, it may be justified in the present context to present only a loose idea, which most clearly can be stated by assuming an economy like the one known from underdeveloped countries in the process of developing.

On the whole it seems as if industrial revolutions do not originate in agriculture as such. It seems rather as if the crucial changes originate in the urban activities. This also seems to hold true in the underdeveloped, though developing, countries today. If so, it may be possible to generalize and argue in an extremely simplified form that the question of growth very often is reduced to the question whether it might be possible to speed up the rate of investment in urban activities, to increase the influx of manpower from rural to urban areas and — simultaneously — to increase agricultural output in order to cope with the increased demand for foods.

If in very general terms this (extremely vague) description can be accepted it seems quite clear not only that a rise in the general level of prices very often — if not always — goes hand in hand with a vigorous development policy but also that changes in the system of relative prices will be just as certain. In general terms it might be argued that because development is tantamount to a relative increase in demand for capital goods, these will increase in terms of consumers goods.

This, however, is a *ceteris paribus* statement to be modified by differences in the supply elasticities. For a closed economy it may be difficult to argue that the technology in producing capital goods would indicate the supply elasticities of capital goods to be systematically different from those of consumers goods. (A marginal change in the demand for the two categories of goods will change the terms of trade in favour of capital goods if the sum of the numerical values of demand and supply elasticities for capital goods is less than the equivalent sum for consumers goods.)

Institutional — though not less important — arrangements, however, may allow definite conclusions. In many countries, including those of Eastern Europe, the prices on capital goods are maintained at a low level throughout the growth process. In several under-developed countries the supply elasticity of capital goods is relatively great because of a liberal import policy particularly for these categories.

If the process of development for one reason or another increases the price of consumer goods versus capital goods, the distribution of *real* income may change in favour of profits. This is simply so because profits buy relatively more of capital goods and relatively less of consumer goods than do wages. Clearly, it is assumed that real income is measured in terms of the volume of goods acquired.

The importance of the influence of changes in the terms of trade between the two categories of goods considered may be difficult to indicate. What is needed is a comparison for individual countries of price indices for consumer goods as compared to investment goods, this relation in turn being compared to the rate of growth. Furthermore, such comparison in itself could not allow any definite conclusion as other factors may be at work.

An example illustrating the mechanism at work seems to be provided by Iran during the second part of the fifties.[1] During that period, a vivid expansion took place. The growth process was initiated by a very sharp increase in the revenue from oil production (after the Mossadeq period). This, in turn, was followed by an equally sharp increase in direct governmental spending as well as an increase in credit expansion partly through governmental and partly through private banks. One result was a significant increase in investments and a rate of growth of domestic product of the order of 6 per cent per year. At the same time, however, there was a significant change in the relative prices. Investment goods have a relatively high import content. As import prices were stable (and virtually no import control was enforced) the expansion took place without much increase in the prices on capital goods. On the other hand, because the import content is relatively low for consumer

---

[1] It would be appropriate to note my debt to Mr. Bahman Abadian (from the Iranian Plan Organization) and Mr. P. Bjørn Olsen (from the Danish Ministry of Finance) for lengthy discussions on the development of the Iranian economy during this period.

goods, the stable prices on imports could not prevent price increases on consumer goods, cf. Table 3 indicating a substantial change in the relative prices.

TABLE 3

PRICE CHANGES IN IRAN

(Index, 1955 = 100)

		Wholesale Prices		
	Retail Prices	Cereals	Metals	Construction Material
1956	109	115	99	112
1957	118	116	97	112
1958	117	116	90	121
1959	126	125	91	118
1960	139	179	96	118

Note.—The figures (including the base) refer to September of the years indicated. The table has been drawn from the *Outline of the Third Plan*, Division of Economic Affairs, Plan Organization, Iran, 1961 (1340).

In such countries where agriculture constitutes a very high proportion of output it seems, however, to be impossible to work on the basis of a consideration relevant to highly industrialized countries. At least it seems necessary to distinguish between the urban sector on the one hand and the rural on the other.

In the rural sector, the real income may not change at all when the terms of trade between capital goods and consumer goods are changed in favour of the latter. The money incomes, which to a large extent can only be estimated by an imputation, tend to increase in proportion to the increase in the cost of living. If rural capitalists exist, their real income may increase because they may also buy investment goods. It appears that most of the 'burden' will fall on the urban wage- and salary-earners, though they may — due to the growth — enjoy an increase in their real income in spite of a fall in their share.[1]

As already indicated such change in the system of relative prices

[1] In some of the socialized countries, a similar process seems to be at work. In Poland, the farmers have had a significant increase in real income while the urban workers have not as yet to the same degree enjoyed the benefits of the high rate of growth. In order to induce an increase in agricultural production necessary to feed the rapidly increasing urban population the terms of trade have been shifted in favour of agricultural products while at the same time the high growth rate has not allowed the same increases in real wages for the urban population. For political reasons such policy can only be pursued up to a point where a slowing down of the rate of growth becomes necessary.

in itself must involve a shift in favour of real profits. It can be argued that because of the higher propensity to save out of profit this shift is one of the ways in which the expansion of investment can be financed. Clearly, such development does not necessarily mean that the absolute level of real wages is declining. Even so it seems as if the process considered is closely akin to the old concept of 'forced saving'.[1]

It should not be overlooked that it is somewhat paradoxical to argue that a given growth rate (as compared either to stationary conditions or to a lower rate of growth) will shift the terms of trade in favour of investment goods. It seems necessary to rely on arguments like foreign trade (Iran) or a political decision on prices (Poland).[2] Generally one would as already stated be inclined to argue that growth must involve an increase in the prices of the expanding sector, i.e. investment goods.

An alternative approach to the question about prices is to consider changes in the general level of prices. This, generally, is the viewpoint in the discussions on 'growth and inflation'. It is also this type of price change which plays a main role in the well-known theory about 'widow's cruse' argued by Keynes, Schneider, Jørgen Pedersen, Kaldor, Föhl, and others.[3]

The essence of the theory can (in Kaldor's formulation) be presented as follows :

Let total income (Y) be divided into profits (P) and wages (W), i.e.

$$Y = W + P.$$

Let, further, total savings be divided into savings out of wages and savings out of profits, i.e.

$$S = S_w + S_p.$$

Assuming equilibrium, i.e. investment (I) equal to saving and assuming that the average (and marginal) propensity to save out of wages

[1] Quite apart from the fact that the word 'forced' may lead astray, it may well be that some of the objections against this concept lose ground in the light of growth considerations (as compared to those of the business cycle). For instance, when business cycle theory at length has discussed on the one hand what happens (during the up-swing) when investment increases relatively to consumption and on the other hand what happens when the newly created capital starts to produce consumers goods, a growth theory may more or less disregard the latter problem as 'the old proportions' will never be restored.

[2] Dr. Luigi Pasinetti has in private discussions at the Conference drawn my attention to the fact that these two cases might be interpreted as illustrating cases of biased technical progress.

[3] Cf., for instance, Nicholas Kaldor, 'Alternative Theories of Distribution', *Review of Economic Studies*, vol. xxiii (2), no. 61, 1955–56.

is s_w, while it is s_c in respect of profits, it follows that

$$I = S = s_w W + s_c P = s_w Y + (s_c - s_w) P.$$

Hence

$$\frac{P}{Y} = \frac{1}{s_c - s_w} \frac{I}{Y} - \frac{s_w}{s_c - s_w} \qquad (6)$$

The 'widow's-cruse' argument assumes inelastic output and a constant wage-bill. In other words, capital is limitational. Considering I (or I/Y) as an exogenous variable, a decline in savings out of wages will necessarily increase prices and hence the share of profits (the total wage bill being constant). Likewise, if the capitalists try to increase their consumption, profit (and its share) will increase because of the increase in prices.[1]

Now, take the case where the capitalists increase their consumption. The volume of consumer goods is unchanged (because the volume of output as well as investment is given) and, hence, prices must increase. This increase in prices, however, does not only mean that profits will increase but also that real wages will decline. The decline will depend on the extent to which wages buy consumer goods. Likewise, in so far as capitalists consume, they suffer from the increase in prices but this obviously is more than counteracted by the increase in profits. To put it otherwise, capitalists have a double advantage. The money value of profit is increased and as profit buys relatively little of consumer goods (as compared to wages), the share of profits will increase not only in current prices but even more so in terms of constant prices.

This result is the simple consequence of considering a change in the propensity to consume. In this case the consumer goods sector — having zero-elasticity of output — is bound to absorb the increase in demand by an increase in prices. As wages spend more on consumption they must carry more of the burden.

Considering (6) it may be slightly puzzling that a change in the demand for investment goods does not lead to exactly analogous results. This, however, is because a change in I/Y in equation (6) involves an assumption about changing the distribution of *real* output. As real income is given (at the full employment level) it is no wonder that also in this case, the consumer goods must take a price increase and that the share of profits will increase. It follows that the argument assumes implicitly that factors of production may readily be transferred from one sector to another — or, more pre-

[1] It is easily verified that $d(P/Y)/ds_w$ and $d(P/Y)/ds_c$ are negative.

cisely, a one-commodity economy. (Again it might be argued that the increase in investment is partly financed by 'forced saving'.)

It will be seen that if investment (or I/Y) is considered exogenous, an increase in the prices of consumer goods followed by a decline in workers' savings (out of current money income) must be exactly offset by the increase in savings out of profits. This, in general, is only possible for one, uniquely determined, distribution of total income between profits and wages. This is exactly the Kaldorian theory of distribution. It will also be seen that the same mechanism holds if it is assumed that capitalists maintain their consumption at a constant (real) level more or less independent of changes in prices and profits.

From (6) it follows that [1]

$$\frac{\Delta P}{\Delta Y}=\frac{1}{s_c-s_w}\frac{\Delta I}{\Delta Y}-\frac{s_w}{s_c-s_w}, \tag{7}$$

where ΔI denotes an increase in investments while ΔY and ΔP are the ensuing increase in income and profits. If, in accordance with the 'widow's-cruse' argument it is assumed that $\Delta P = \Delta Y$, it follows that $\Delta P/\Delta Y$ equals unity and consequently

$$\Delta Y = \frac{1}{s_c}\Delta I. \tag{8}$$

In other words, the increase in money income depends only on the propensity to save out of profits. This expresses the simple fact that the increase in investments will start a multiplier mechanism which runs until profits and in turn savings out of profits have increased sufficiently to finance the increase in investments. As the wage-bill is assumed unchanged no increase in savings can be assumed to come out of wages.[2]

[1] It should be stressed that the argument assumes that the workers are unable to obtain increases in their money wages.

[2] In the present context I am disregarding, though certainly not forgetting, the important extension of the arguments given by Luigi L. Pasinetti, 'Rate of Profit and Income Distribution in Relation to the Rate of Growth', *Review of Economic Studies*, vol. xxix (4), no. 81, October 1962. Pasinetti proves that if workers are assumed to get a return on their savings, the share of total profits (including that of workers) depends on the capitalists' propensity to save only, cf. (6) above. Clearly when s_c appears to be the only important parameter here, cf. (8), this is for completely different reasons. The mechanism (and the problem) considered here is far from that of Pasinetti. In passing it may be noted that the elegance of Pasinetti's arguments is due to the assumption about wage (and salary) earners receiving a rate of return on their accumulated wealth equal to the rate of profits. The whole model becomes heavy and clumsy if it is assumed (which may be more realistic) that the rate of return on workers' savings is lower than the rate of profit.

It should, however, be remembered that total output is constant. Consequently two things are assumed to happen at the same time: real resources are shifted towards the investment sector and prices are increased. However, the argument depends on the assumption that not only is labour income in money terms a constant but it is assumed that saving out of wages likewise is a constant in spite of the increase in prices. The consumption behaviour assumed is in accordance with a consumption function of the form

$$C_w = aW$$

or

$$\frac{C_w}{p_c} = a\frac{W}{p_c}$$

or

$$\frac{C_w}{p_c} = \frac{b}{p_c} + \frac{aW}{p_c},$$

where p_c is a price index for consumer goods. b/p_c can be interpreted as a minimum standard of living. (In a process of growth, it may simply be last year's income — equal to the last peak income.) The consumption function, however, is likely to be irreversible. In other words, a 'rachet effect' may be at work, the consequence of which is a tendency to maintain the standard of living in spite of increasing prices. This is tantamount to a fall in the propensity to save out of wages when prices increase. The consequence of this viewpoint is that in terms of the Kaldorian model one would have to analyse an increase in investment simultaneous to an increase in the propensity to consume out of wages. However, as an isolated increase in investments tends to increase the share of profits and as a decline in the propensity to save out of wages will have a similar effect, the conclusion holds *a fortiori*.

On the other hand, it may also happen that the increase in (money and real) profits tends to increase the propensity to save out of profits. This will have an opposite (i.e. dampening) effect. Of course, this cannot be sufficient to produce a net result in favour of wages. Even if wages and profits share fifty-fifty, the isolated effect of the increase in investments remains. Thus the wage-bill has to be lower than total profits if there should be any chance for an isolated increase in the propensity to save out of profits to be sufficient to give a total, net result in favour of wages. As this increase in the propensity to save out of profits assumes a redistribution towards profits it need not be further demonstrated that the net, total result must be in favour of profits.

It remains to be added that at least in the formulation of the 'widow's cruse' used above, the relationship between the distribution of income and the theory of growth has not been taken into account. For instance, considering the consequences of an increase in investments one would have to include the consequences of the increase in productive capacity following the increase in the volume of capital. The result would not only be a (short-run) change in the distribution but also a (potentially) higher level of output. The additional output, however, could perhaps be distributed according to a Kaldorian mechanism. It becomes much more difficult if capital is not considered a limitational factor and thus the wage-bill is assumed to increase as a response to an increase in the demand for labour. In this latter case an inflationary process may be inevitable. The consequences for the distribution cannot be analysed within the framework of the theory used above.[1]

V. CHANGES IN THE RELATION BETWEEN INPUT AND OUTPUT

This heading opens up the whole sphere of problems relating to the interrelationship between income shares and technical progress. The literature on this subject is very great,[2] though no unanimous viewpoint seems clear. This section is limited to a footnote on Schumpeterian theory.

The 'widow's cruse' in the form presented above is founded on the multiplier mechanism only. An extension of the model to include a production function has been attempted by Solow.[3] Such approach, however, is far from that of Kaldor, who relies on a 'technical progress function' to take care of the sphere of production. As will be known,[4] this function shows the relationship between the

[1] Cf. Bent Hansen, *A Study in the Theory of Inflation*, London, 1951.

[2] Cf. Wilhelm Krelle, *Verteilungstheorie*, Tübingen, 1962. The fact that this is the first reference to this treatise and the fact that also no reference has been given to Alfred Stobbe, *Untersuchungen zur makroökonomischen Theorie der Einkommensverteilung*, Tübingen, 1962, nor to the contributions of Niehaus, Bombach, and Ott in 'Einkommensverteilung und technischer Fortschritt', published in *Schriften des Vereins für Socialpolitik*, Neue Folge, Band 17, Berlin, 1959, goes to prove that this article cannot claim any comprehensiveness at all.

[3] *Op. cit.* Section V.

[4] Cf. 'A Model of Growth', *Economic Journal*, December 1957 (reprinted as chapter 13 in Nicholas Kaldor, *Essays on Economic Stability and Growth*, London, 1960). Kaldor has supplied more refined models than the one referred to. One model has been published in the volume edited by Lutz and Hague (*op. cit.*), another one (in co-authorship with James A. Mirrlees) was published in the *Review of Economic Studies*, vol. xxix (3), June 1962. However, the basic reasoning as presented seems to be the same.

rate of growth of capital (per man) and the rate of growth of output (per man). One of the arguments behind this relation is that investment (presumably gross investment) is always made in new techniques. In fact, it is through investment that the technical progress is ploughed into the production apparatus. Consequently, the higher investment the higher the rate at which innovations are made. The reasoning can be phrased the other way around : an increase in technical progress presupposes an increase in the volume of investment. This, however, has been shown to involve a shift towards profits.

This result seems to be in perfect accordance with a Schumpeterian theory.[1] If Schumpeter's terminology is maintained it does not make much sense to ask for the relation between growth and profit share. Under stationary conditions, the 'circular flow of economic life' repeats itself. On Schumpeter's definition, no 'profit' appears : 'As value is a symptom of our poverty, so profit is a symptom of imperfection'.[2]

Comparing growth to stationary conditions the answer seems a pure tautology as 'profit' only exists under growth. If a golden age only includes parallel increase in capital, income, and population, Schumpeter seems to argue that there is no 'growth' : 'Nor will the mere growth of the economy, as shown by the growth of population and wealth, be designated here as a process of development. For it calls forth no *qualitatively* new phenomena . . .' (p. 63, my italics).

It becomes more difficult in a golden age to allow for technical progress, because it is the entrepreneurs who introduce technical progress and they receive a return which is Schumpeterian 'profits'. One difficulty, however, is that we may visualize a growth process in equilibrium, where the rate of technical progress is constant. From the whole concept of 'profit' in Schumpeter's building, it is difficult in this case to conceive the income of the entrepreneur as profit. The difficulty is that Schumpeterian 'profit' cannot easily be associated with equilibrium. (Growth is inevitably associated with business cycles — and *vice versa*.) Clearly, during the process of *increasing* from one growth rate to another (higher), the share of profits will increase. But again, it becomes difficult to compare two equilibrium growth rates in Schumpeter's theory. It all depends on the imputation. On the micro-level, there may well be true Schumpeterian 'profit'. One may argue that this is the way in which a

---

[1] See *The Theory of Economic Development*, Cambridge (Mass.), 1934.
[2] Schumpeter, *op. cit.* p. 31.

given growth rate is maintained. Hence, a higher rate of growth would involve a higher Schumpeterian 'profit'.

If profit is taken to mean residual income it might be argued that the profit received by successful entrepreneurs may cancel out against a loss in 'ordinary', competitive business. However, using Schumpeter's notations, a positive 'profit' received by *entrepreneurs* cannot be counterbalanced by a negative income received by *managers*. In other words, there is — according to Schumpeter — a fundamental difference between a manager and an entrepreneur. Consequently, it would be logical that technical progress — this being taken in a very wide sense, as also Schumpeter does — must by necessity involve a shift towards 'profit'. This depends on whether the entrepreneur is successful. However, by definition he is bound to be successful if we have a growth which includes technical progress.

It seems quite easy to conclude that the share of 'profits' (in the Schumpeterian sense) will be higher if growth (in the sense of an increase in income *per capita*) is compared to stationary conditions and also that the share of 'profits' will increase if a stage of a higher growth rate is compared to a stage of a lower growth rate.

It seems more doubtful whether profit in the ordinary sense (equal to residual income) is bound to increase its share in a Schumpeterian world. During the transition from a zero-growth rate to a positive growth or from one growth rate to a higher one there is no doubt. But comparing different equilibrium processes (including a zero-growth rate), it is much harder within Schumpeter's model to find an answer.

———

DISCUSSION OF PROFESSOR RASMUSSEN'S PAPER

Dr. Jeck said he had pleasure in introducing Professor Rasmussen's very interesting paper. Nobody could hope to solve all the problems of interrelations between growth and distribution in a few pages and Professor Rasmussen had been wise in restricting himself to four major issues.

The first section of the paper dealt with the part played by capital depreciation. Professor Rasmussen started out from what one could call a Wicksell–Solow model but with intent to dissociate the effects of depreciation from those of inter-sector shifts which were closely associated with them.

The issue at stake was whether the share of profit ought to be higher in a growing economy than in a stationary one. The answer was not obvious because there were two factors influencing the distribution of income and they might easily work against one another. On the one hand, in a growing economy capital on average would tend to be younger than under stationary conditions and this made for a higher share of profits. On the other hand, growth involved a shift in the distribution of output towards the capital-producing sector.

Instead of summarizing Professor Rasmussen's treatment of this problem, Dr. Jeck thought it more useful to draw attention to one of the author's conclusions, namely that the effects of the alternative ways of depreciating capital did not depend on a given form of the production functions (the Cobb–Douglas functions in Professor Solow's model) and perhaps were independent of even the idea of a production function. Professor Rasmussen had concluded that the normal effect of depreciation was to increase the share of profits in a growing economy, but that this might be offset by a decline in the average optimal life-time of capital.

As a second problem Professor Rasmussen had dealt with the influence of inter-sector shifts on income distribution. As a growing economy was characterized by change in the composition of total output, if there were differences in the labour share within the various sectors, these shifts might influence the distribution of national income leading either to a higher or a lower wage share. The effect of depreciation could thus be either reinforced or counteracted.

In ascertaining this, obstacles were encountered arising not only from the insufficiency of available statistical data on sectoral income shares but also from the difficulty of correctly interpreting the figures. For instance, if a decreasing share of agriculture and an increasing share of manufacturing industry in the total product seemed to bring forth a higher wage share, this was because in the former sector the share of labour was much smaller. But this might merely be the result of the statisticians' convention of considering the self-employed as profit earners as these were proportionately more important in the agricultural sector than in industry. Dr. Jeck would thus think that what might on statistical grounds look like a genuine shift in the distribution by income shares would to a large extent on theoretical grounds appear only as a change in the classification of incomes by name.

Stating that the inter-industry shifts were bound to be more marked the faster the rate of growth, Professor Rasmussen had made in Table 2 a cautious attempt at isolating and calculating the effects of intersectoral movements on distribution. Dr. Jeck thought, incidentally, that there must be a mistake in the figures for Finland. The results presented by Professor Rasmussen tended to show that these kinds of structural changes could not be neglected in income distribution models. Dr. Jeck thought, nevertheless, that operating and theorizing with structural changes could be risky because the weight of intersectoral movements was highly influenced by the number of sectors which were retained. Whereas if in taking one single sector one naturally could not find any structural effect, in taking one million sectors — supposing figures were available — one would, no less forcibly, come to the not less inevitable conclusion that intercostal shifts were of the highest importance.

The third issue considered by Professor Rasmussen was the effects of price changes on distribution. Although Professor Rasmussen had studied the effects of changes both in relative prices and in the average level of prices, Dr. Jeck would limit his comments to the latter.

Starting out from the Kaldorian model, Professor Rasmussen introduced further realistic assumptions that capitalists maintained their real consumption at a constant level irrespective of changes in prices and profits. Assuming this and still supposing, as in the Kaldorian model, that the increase in profits was the same as the increase in national income, Professor Rasmussen came to the conclusion that the increase in national income depended only on the propensity to save out of profits.

Professor Rasmussen also assumed that wage-earners tried to keep their real consumption at a constant level despite rising prices and that the rise in prices would lead to a lower rate of saving out of wages, hence a second effect in addition to the effect of increasing investment for lowering the labour share. Dr. Jeck wished to point out that, as Professor Rasmussen had admitted, the scope of these conclusions was limited to short-run analysis and this was a rather severe limitation in so far as the relations between price level and distribution referred to a growing economy.

In the last pages of his paper Professor Rasmussen had studied the effects of technical progress on distribution. Although he mentioned in this context Kaldor's 'technical progress function', Professor Rasmussen's argument went the other way round: whereas Kaldor had stated that investment led to innovations, Professor Rasmussen stated that advancing technology presupposed an increase in the volume of investment.

As he had already come to the conclusion that an increase of investment led to a higher profit share, Professor Rasmussen arrived at a Schumpeterian theory. In this line of thought no profit appeared under stationary equilibrium conditions and profits existed only under growth. Professor Rasmussen had had, however, some difficulty in combining his findings with the restricted Schumpeterian concept of profit. The desire to conciliate Schumpeter's theory of profit, which excluded equilibrium conditions, with his own conclusions based on growth equilibrium led Professor Rasmussen *in fine* to some rather sophisticated theoretical developments.

Dr. Jeck thought that such a varied paper would stimulate discussion. He had one question to ask. Professor Rasmussen had stated that the decline in the average age of capital which was caused by growth would lead to a tendency towards a higher profit share because depreciation became 'less of a burden' under such a situation. Unfortunately Professor

Rasmussen's developments on this had been so condensed that Dr. Jeck had not fully understood the mechanism which was operating behind the scene. What, for instance, did 'less of a burden' mean ? As became an economist writing in English, Professor Rasmussen was far from wordy, but other economists had some trouble in interpreting his statements and Dr. Jeck for one would like to benefit from Professor Rasmussen's further comments on this point.

Professor Rasmussen pointed out that the statement to which Dr. Jeck had just referred would be more easily understood if the word 'reinvestment' was substituted for 'depreciation'.

Professor Lecaillon said that he had been convinced by Professor Rasmussen's arguments explaining why growth should tend to increase the share of profits. However in the discussions of the papers on income distribution as observed in several countries the share of wages had proved to be stable or even increasing.

This led Professor Lecaillon to ask Professor Rasmussen what factors, in his view, had caused the observed evolution of income shares to differ from that in his model. Had not Professor Rasmussen been thinking in terms of a model applying to a newly growing economy whereas his conclusions would not apply to mature economies ? If it were so, would there not have been a tendency in industrial economies for the rise of the labour share to slow down the rate of growth ?

Professor Solow wished to comment on Professor Lecaillon's question. It would be easy, he thought, to reconcile the statement that a high rate of growth meant a higher profit share with what one could find in observed data because these data related to growth economies as opposed to stationary ones. Had they been stationary the share of profits would have been lower than observed. Professor Rasmussen's model was consistent with a rising or stable wage share.

Concerning Professor Lecaillon's last observation Professor Solow said that it was presumably true that the rate of saving from wages was lower than from other forms of income ; thus a higher share of wages would lead to a lower rate of savings and, in so far as saving influenced the rate of growth, that too would be lower. But state intervention had then to be brought in : not only was the state budget a medium of income redistribution but also of the formation of public saving, and this allowed economies where the labour share was increasing to invest enough for sustaining the rate of growth.

Professor Phelps Brown questioned Professor Rasmussen's treatment of reinvestment. He could easily see how the carrying out, in the present period, of large programmes of new investment would lower the average age of capital, but postponing expenditure on replacement should produce fluctuations in the proportion of reinvestment to gross investment in future years. If, for instance, to meet the needs of new shipping lines new ships were built with a twenty-year life-time, for the next nineteen years they would count for nil in gross investment programmes whereas in the twentieth year their replacement would add substantially to investment demand.

What would be the effect of this on the share of profits in national income ? Professor Phelps Brown wished to point out that firms did not distribute their gross profits without allowing for amortization needs. Profits reported would be after allowance for depreciation and these allowances would provide savings in the meantime.

Thus whereas Professor Phelps Brown clearly understood the bearing of Professor Rasmussen's analysis on physical depreciation in relation to the proportion of net investment in the total of gross investment expenditure, the link between this and profits reported by firms according to accountancy practices eluded him.

Professor Ohkawa said that he had been much interested by Professor Rasmussen's treatment of inter-sector shifts. He had noted in Table 2 that, for certain countries like Finland and Ireland, the B figure, i.e. the isolated effect of intersectoral movement on the percentage wage share, was bigger than figure A, i.e. the total change in the wage share.

This he thought possible. But he thought it might be useful to compute another figure, which he would call C, by taking income share as constant in each sector, C being then the product of the constant (base year) income share and the changed sectoral income shares. The product of these two terms would yield figures comparable to those in series B as $(B + C)$ would ordinarily approximate to A, after smoothing the short-run fluctuations.

Such a statistical procedure had been used for measuring the 'shift effect' of productivity change. Since labour's share was derived from wage-earnings and labour productivity, these two approaches could be combined.

Professor Ohkawa suggested that another kind of structural change could profitably be studied, namely the effects of the shift of the labour force from small-scale establishments to larger ones, that is roughly speaking the effect of the shift from the traditional to the modern sector, because, taking Japan as an instance, the labour share was bigger in the former than in the latter.

A procedure of income imputation would then be desirable. Short of this it would be misleading to use figures such as the data in Table 2 for measuring the intersectoral shifts. In Professor Rasmussen's paper the figure of 78 per cent quoted for the profit share in Danish agriculture in 1961 appeared abnormally high in comparison with the corresponding 40 per cent figure for the industrial sector, and this should be redressed by imputing to the self-employed of the agricultural sector an income for their labour according to what was the current wage rate in Danish agriculture.

As a last and minor point Professor Ohkawa disagreed with Professor

Rasmussen's statement that the data on the distribution of the labour force by sector were available only for a few countries as he thought that as compared with the period when Colin Clark's book was published far more data were now available.

Professor Jean Marchal observed that Professor Rasmussen to a certain extent took into account changes in the institutional framework in so far as they reflected intersectoral movements and changes in the relative prices of capital goods and consumer goods. But should he not have taken into consideration other institutional changes in his analysis of the effects of a changing general price level on distribution ? In discussing the 'widow's-cruse' argument Professor Marchal wondered how far to assume a constant wage-bill remained realistic. Once a certain stage of growth was attained institutional factors, such as the trade unions' bargaining power, intervened. Professor Rasmussen had not ignored this, but he had restricted himself to stating that a process of inflation would then evolve. This seemed to Professor Marchal to put an end to the analysis at the stage when it became most interesting and relevant to the present conditions in economies like the French.

Professor Rasmussen's conclusion about the effects of depreciation had been that a high rate of growth led to a higher share of profits as long as depreciation did not increase parallel to the volume of capital. But it seemed to Professor Marchal that the passing from a low to a high rate of growth might shorten the optimal life-time for capital and this should work against the tendency towards a bigger share of profits. On the other hand, growth was normally accompanied by technical progress and this was conducive to a higher profit share. Professor Marchal thought that the net effect would depend on the respective intensities of these two antagonistic forces.

Professor Falise asked Professor Rasmussen whether in studying the effects of intersectoral shifts on distribution it would not be advisable to consider the differences in income elasticities of final demand according to the industries' products. Quoting as an example the low income elasticity of consumers' expenditure on food and clothing, Professor Falise suggested that these differences might help to explain changes in the intersectoral distribution of profits in periods of rapid growth of incomes. Then this could also contribute to explaining an overall change in the distribution of national income between the profit and the wage shares as wages might resist better than profits a downwards pressure in the sectors where the income elasticity of demand was insufficient. Thus the wage rate in these sectors would tend to remain nearer the overall average than the rate of profit and this would tend to bring down the overall share of profits.

Professor Krelle, commenting on Professor Rasmussen's argument (p. 521 in the paper) said that when the propensity to consume of either the wage-earners or the profit-earners increased, the volume of real consumption should remain constant and the labour share go down as a result of the rise in the price level. Professor Krelle pointed out that there was no need to assume consumption to be stable in order to get this, provided that production was not supposed to be inelastic. If consumption and production were allowed to be completely elastic the same consequences would follow.

Professor Bronfenbrenner said that he was afraid that in the third part of the paper there had been some confusion between the effects of inflation and of changes in relative prices, because the results shown there did not fit in with the fact that the relative prices of capital goods tended to be rising. Professor Bronfenbrenner was not sure about the interpretation of the 'widow's-cruse' argument. The factors under consideration could lead to increases in output, so that the share of labour might remain the same.

Professor Bronfenbrenner observed that the Schumpeterian concept of profit excluded rent and interest from factors' income ; they were then considered as transfer incomes out of profits and this did not tally with the usual, much grosser, definition of profits in international statistics. Before using shares in the Schumpeterian sense had Professor Rasmussen corrected this ? In Table 2 the figures in series *B* might have been affected by the labour force shifting from industries where interests and rents might have been more important to sectors where they were less so.

Professor Rasmussen in answering the discussants, pointed out to Dr. Jeck that although it might seem rather odd, the total change in the percentage share of wages could be smaller than the change due to intersectoral movements in figures in Table 2, e.g. for Finland, because the share within each sector could change in the opposite direction. Professor Rasmussen agreed with Dr. Jeck that the quantitative effects of the inter-sector shifts of course depended on the number of sectors considered.

Professor Rasmussen wished to show Professor Lecaillon that there was no inconsistency between the reinvestment effect and data showing an increase in the share of wages. The reinvestment effect worked only to a clear conclusion if one compared a stationary economy with an economy in process of growth. Furthermore other factors — which Professor Rasmussen had mentioned in his paper — might be at work. Thus there did not on these grounds seem to be any reason for distinguishing between an economy in the take-off period and a more mature economy. The possible tendency to have a slowing down of the growth rate when the share of wages increased, mentioned by Professor Lecaillon in this context, could not be studied within the framework of the models and arguments of the paper.

To Professor Phelps Brown, Professor Rasmussen pointed out that the reinvestment effect on the distribution would disappear if the marginal case of 'radioactive decay' was considered. It would also disappear if reinvestment was made a function of the utilization of capital rather than of time. On the contrary, case A in the paper was another extreme when it worked with the maximum effect.

Professor Ohkawa had wanted the calculations in Table 2 to be supplemented by a direct calculation showing the changes in the share of wages due to a change in the share within each sector. Professor Rasmussen agreed that this might be a useful check on the figures although the calculation would of course have all the inherent weaknesses of the usual index numbers. It might also, as suggested by Professor Ohkawa, be useful to supplement it by data on productivity, however difficult that might be. As to the advisability of using imputations in order to reduce the (only partly apparent) shift in the distribution following inter-sector shifts, Professor Rasmussen would just refer to the well-known difficulties of such a procedure.

Professor Rasmussen thought that it would be interesting, as suggested by Professor Ohkawa, to study the change in the distribution following a shift in the labour force from smaller to larger establishments. It might, however, be difficult to get the necessary data. Finally Professor Rasmussen argued that, at least according to his experience, the data on the labour force seemed to be rather poor. They might be particularly poor for Denmark, but also for many other countries the material seemed weak, for instance, for the service sector.

He agreed with Professor Jean Marchal that it was tempting to go a step further in the analysis of the effect of price changes on the distribution, taking into account the effects of wage increases. That kind of analysis, however, would have gone very far beyond the framework of the present paper.

He agreed with Professor Falise that one might extend the analysis to take into account the distribution effects of a shift in the distribution of demand following a growth in income.

In answering Professor Krelle, Professor Rasmussen admitted that he had only considered marginal cases when discussing the 'widow's-cruse' argument. More realistic cases might be considered. For instance it seemed rather extreme to assume that capitalists would maintain their real consumption in spite of an increase in prices, but he did not think that modifying such points would substantially change the conclusions. In order to see the mechanism at work these marginal cases were useful.

Professor Rasmussen agreed that the 'widow's-cruse' argument should be modified along the lines suggested by Professor Bronfenbrenner. The assumption about inelastic output was very abstract and ought at a later stage to be changed. As to the exclusion of interest and rent from profits in actual data, this Professor Rasmussen thought to be only of minor importance in this context. His figures were consistent and based on ordinary definitions.

Chapter 20

THE SCALE OF RETURNS:
A MISSING LINK IN THE THEORY
OF DISTRIBUTION

BY

CARL FÖHL
Freie Universität, Berlin

I. INTRODUCTORY

IN his paper on 'Alternative Theories of Distribution', published in
1955, Kaldor mentions a letter by Ricardo to Malthus. In this
letter Ricardo expresses his conviction that the theory of distribution holds the key to an understanding of the whole mechanism of
the economic system. It seems indeed that Ricardo thought it
might be possible to develop from a theory of distribution something
which we would call today a simple macro-economic model. My
personal opinion is that Ricardo, if he thought so, was perfectly
right. However, in spite of the numerous attempts made since, we
have not yet succeeded in solving, in a satisfactory way, the problem
which Ricardo may have had in mind.

Ricardo's own attempt to split the social product into the components rent, wages, and profits succeeded only because he, basing
himself on the Malthusian population thesis, assumed that the wage
rate was given as the minimum subsistence rate necessary for the
reproduction of labour. With this hypothesis, which later on proved
unrealistic, and with his splendid explanation of the differential rent
on land of different qualities which became the starting-off point of
marginal theory, he was able to explain profits as a residue. Profits
thus defined, being at the same time an incentive for and a source of
the accumulation of capital, gave at least a faint idea of the factors
determining the growth of the capital stock and employment capacity
to which, according to Ricardo, the supply of labour would adapt
itself in the course of economic development.

If we drop the hypothesis of an infinitely elastic supply curve of
labour, on which the assumption of minimum-subsistence-wages

was based, and if we assume instead that the supply of labour be nearly inelastic, and that therefore wages can rise above the minimum-subsistence-rate, it is far more difficult to deduct the shares of capital and labour in the national product. An attempt under rather restrictive conditions has been made by the marginalists. However, what their theory has been able to say refers to that optimal factor combination which is supposed to emerge 'in the long run' and not to the transitory period, in which we are mainly interested. In the transitory phase entrepreneurs even in competition make profits and their decisions on investment depend on expectations of profits and on the interest rate, while at the same time profits and possibly expectations of profits again may depend on the amount of investment.

The pre-classic approach of Hume, Turgot, and Thornton in the eighteenth century had well prepared the ground for an investigation of the share of profits in an economy where competition has not yet taken full effect. The division of capital yield into profit and interest, the first conception of a functional relation between investment and the rate of interest and the observation that the interest rate is determined by demand and supply in the capital market were indeed promising suggestions. That they did not lead to a solution of our problem — even after Irving Fisher and Knut Wicksell started thinking along the same lines — may be due to the lack of an equilibrium theory of employment.

When finally a macro-economic theory of employment was presented in the 1930's it created the impression that the share of profits now could be derived simply from total net investment and the propensity to consume. This however — as I shall try to show — proved to have been a vain hope. In the end it had to be acknowledged that an outside determination of the share of profits in national income is still indispensable.

The authors of the theories of the monopoly degree have offered such an outside determination and thus — though only formally — solved the problem. All they offer is the suggestion that the entrepreneurs obtain a share on behalf of their bargaining position. This of course does not explain much. What will their reaction be if they get more or less than they claim ? How big will profits have to be to make the entrepreneurs' demand for labour just equal to the supply ?

Even a complete price theory could not sufficiently answer these questions as it would only explain how the single entrepreneur will react to a change of his own expected profit. What we need in addition is an explanation of the distribution of individual profits to the different enterprises, a scale of returns from which we can deduct a functional relation between total profits and the entrepreneurs' total demand for labour.

As the scale of the returns depends on the productivity and thus on the age of the equipment used in the different enterprises it is of course not possible to calculate its slope and shape theoretically. But it can be measured empirically and theory can help us to explain its shape and how it will probably change according to changes of other factors.

A macro-economic model which will explain distribution must necessarily comprise at least two groups of income receivers. The purpose of this paper is to show that we need a distribution function, a functional relation between the components of income and total income to make any such model consistent. Such a distribution function can be derived from the scale of returns.

II. THE MARGINALIST THEORY OF DISTRIBUTION

The great achievement of marginal theory consists in the demonstration that there exists only one optimal combination of factors, if the utility function of each consumer and the production function of the commodities and the quantity of each factor are given. This combination of factors guarantees that each consumer is granted the maximum utility he can obtain under the prevailing distribution of wealth. The marginalists' statement that the optimal combination of factors automatically materializes if everybody tends to improve his economic situation has considerably contributed to the scientific foundation of the system of liberal market economy.

The marginalists have restricted their enquiry into macro-economic distribution to this 'long-run' optimal factor combination. In their micro-analysis they have clearly shown that competing entrepreneurs can make a profit and that their profit is maximized if they combine their invested capital with such a quantity of labour that marginal costs equal prices. Marginalist micro-economics did by no means deny that prices can be above average costs. Turning to macro-economic distribution, however, the marginalists have supposed that competition — wherever it exists — has already come to full effect extending productive capacities in all branches so much that prices are lowered to average costs. In this 'long-run' situation therefore profits can no longer exist — with the exception of monopoly profits. All categories of total income then are factor remunerations. The height of each remuneration results from the factor's marginal productivity function and its relative scarcity.

Rent in marginal theory is something quite different from the Ricardian differential rent, which resulted from the different qualities of land. It is a function of the quantity of labour employed on a given area of land of homogeneous quality. Its size is the difference between the average yield, obtained when the optimal amount of labour is employed, and the marginal yield of the last employed hour of labour, which labour gets as a return, both multiplied by the quantity of labour employed per acre.

Rent corresponds to the scarcity profits which competing entrepreneurs receive as long as competition has not fully taken effect on the extension of capacities. The difference is that rent does not disappear in the 'long run', since only a limited amount of land is available which cannot be increased by competition. Lands of different qualities are considered as separate factors. Ricardo's differential rent appears as the difference between the rents of these different factors. In addition to these differences between their rents, however, all qualities of land can earn a scarcity-rent if the total land available is so scarce that agricultural products obtain a price above marginal cost of the production on land of the lowest quality.

The share of *wages* is established entirely differently from Ricardo's reasoning, as the marginalists assume available labour to be given as a scarce quantity. If the quantities of the other factors of land and capital are given as well, the wage rate can be derived from labour's marginal productivity function.

Interest is considered by marginalists as the return for capital, and — as they concentrate their reasoning on the optimal factor combination materializing 'in the long run' and assume capital even then to remain scarce just as the other factors — it is considered as that return for capital which persists under 'long-run' conditions. Marginal theory by no means neglects that capital as a whole is not homogeneous and that therefore each kind of means of production has to be treated as a separate factor. In the 'long run', however, once the optimal factor-combination has materialized, the relative quantities of each of these separate factors will have been chosen in such a way that all of them have the same marginal productivity.

542

Profits in the sense of a surplus over interest, with the exception of monopoly gains, are eliminated altogether from the marginalists' explanation of macro-economic distribution by the assumption that competition has completely taken effect.

Monopoly profits can result from the scarcity of the goods supplied to the market or from differences in cost. The monopolist maximizes his scarcity profit by choosing such a capital-labour combination that marginal costs equal *marginal returns*, not prices. He thus is definitely in a better position than the landlord who, in spite of the limited land, behaves as a competitor employing on his acres so much labour that marginal costs equal price. What both have in common is that the quantity of products supplied to the market cannot be increased by the impact of competition so that both rent and the monopolist's scarcity profit persist in the long run.

The monopoly, however, can as well consist in the possession of secret or protected highly economical means of production, by which commodities are produced which sell in a competitive market. In this case the monopolists obtain a cost-difference benefit, which corresponds to the difference of the rents on land of different quality.

Some critical remarks may be permitted. The basic assumption of scarce factor quantities seems justified as far as the factors land, labour, and even the means of production, which are monopolists' property, are concerned. However, with regard to other means of production, which can be produced by any competitior in any quantity he thinks wise, and consequently with regard to the quantity of the entire group of 'capital factors', the justification of this assumption seems utterly questionable.

What is going to stop the process of capital accumulation once the capital stock has reached a size which marginal theory would suppose to remain constant in the 'long run' ? We cannot argue that investment stops because it is no longer attractive with the 'long-run' interest rate, for this interest rate itself results, according to the marginal productivity function of capital, from the amount of capital supposed to be given as a scarce quantity. The assumption that in the 'long run' capital will remain constant at a size which yields a positive marginal return can only be sustained if we are able to find for it a justification which is independent of the capital-marginal productivity-function.

The marginalists have not given any such justification for their assumption. Their argument thus is not conclusive — not even for the long-run optimal-factor combination. What remains are their statements regarding wages and rent or monopoly income, resulting from scarcity which cannot be eliminated by competition. The return for the factor capital however — the yield of capital and its components profit and interest — needs another careful investigation for the 'long-run' and especially for the 'short-run' transitory conditions.

III. AUTONOMOUS SAVING AND THE MARGINALISTS' ANALYSIS OF LONG-RUN DISTRIBUTION

Adam Smith, Ricardo, and the marginalists have treated interest and profits as synonymous for the total yield of capital whereas in modern economic theories they are clearly two different things. This is the more surprising as Turgot as early as in 1770 has presented a theory which comprises all the important elements of capital formation.

Turgot was familiar with the idea that entrepreneurs share the yield of capital with the capitalists who supply the funds and that the share that goes to the latter (the interest) is determined like all other prices by the play of supply and demand.[1] Turgot held, as Hume did before him, that the funds supplied were equivalent to the savings. Moreover, his conception that the rate of interest was negatively correlated with the rate of saving proves that he had a notion of a functional relation between the demand for funds and the interest rate.[2] This idea was elaborated a little later by the banker Henry Thornton to a rather complete analysis of the loan fund market in which the author states 'that the loan rate tends to equal expected marginal profits of investment'.[3]

It is indeed one of the most curious facts about the history of economic science that these fundamental ideas had to remain hidden in the basement until eventually — about a century and a half later — Irving Fisher and Knut Wicksell prospected the same ground. We have to give Schumpeter credit for having given due recognition to the admirable work of the pre-classics.[4]

It is worth while making it quite clear to ourselves that according

[1] A. R. I. de Turgot, Réflexions LXXV, LXXVI, quoted from the original edition of the *Ephémérides 1769–70*, by J. A. Schumpeter, *History of Economic Analysis*, London, 1934.

[2] *Ibid.* LXXXIX.

[3] Henry Thornton, 'Inquiry into the Nature and Effects of the Paper Credit of Great Britain', 1802, quoted from Schumpeter, *op. cit.*

[4] J. A. Schumpeter, *op. cit.*

to this theory the rate of economic development is exclusively governed by the consumers' decisions on saving and not by the entrepreneurs' initiative to invest. What depends on the entrepreneurs' expectations of returns is the interest rate and not the amount of net investment. New technical inventions contribute to the growth of the social product only to the extent that their higher productivity allows an increased production at a given amount of investment.

This consequence is the less satisfactory since autonomous saving decisions have nothing to do at all with the question of optimal capital equipment of the economy. Autonomous saving decisions are the result of the consumers weighing the utility of present consumption against that of future consumption. Saving means the formation of a reserve for satisfying a demand expected in the future. It would be strange if such a consideration alone would be responsible for the rate of progress.

The assumption of autonomous saving might, however, have provided the marginalists with a plausible foundation for their thesis that capital remains constant in the long run. If people save because they want to accumulate a reserve for future consumption, then saving must stop as soon as the population's desire to hold wealth is fully satisfied.

And if annual autonomous saving limits annual net investments the growth of the capital stock must come to an end when no more savings are forthcoming. The value of the total capital stock, integrating all positive and negative annual net investments, must then be equal to the savings fund which satisfies all consumers' desire to hold wealth. Like this fund, the capital stock must remain unchanged. Whether or not capital stock, once it has reached this size, will still have a positive marginal productivity is indeed a question which nobody can answer.

Let us assume for the moment that the capital stock, grown to perpetual size, still has a positive marginal productivity. The interest rate then would be equal to this marginal productivity. This rate would reflect on the cost of the consumer goods, and, as in the long run prices are equal to average cost, it would influence prices and the distribution of the consumers' expenses unfavourably for those goods which are manufactured by methods of high capital intensity, the more the intensity, the higher the rate. For the entrepreneur choosing the most economic equipment, a process of less capital intensity would become more economical. Both arguments

545

lead to the conclusion that the optimal combination of capital and labour in the economy and hence the optimal size of the capital stock are a function of the interest rate. The higher the rate is, the smaller is the optimal capital stock. If its size is given as the equivalent of the consumers' desire to hold fortune, the interest rate will hold itself at a level at which the so given size of the capital stock is the optimal size and combination.

Can the interest rate remain constant at this level? To curtail investment to the level of autonomous savings, the interest rate will have to be at a height which depends on the entrepreneurs' expectations of the rate of capital return over cost. What are the expectations of capital yield, which determine the demand for investment funds, going to be when the capital equipment of the economy has reached its optimal size at the prevailing rate of interest?

If we assume that, when this happens, autonomous saving has not yet come to an end, then the supply of savings will continue to be offered in the capital market when the economy is fully equipped with all means of production which are economical at the given rate of interest. No surplus of the yield of capital over and above the interest on capital can then be expected for further investment. The demand for investment funds will have dropped to zero. The continuing offering of savings would bring the interest rate down and thus create new expectations of capital yield.

If, however, autonomous saving stops before the economy is fully equipped with the most economical equipment for a given rate of interest, and if the demand for investment funds at this time still has a positive value, then the interest rate must rise to a level which reduces the demand to zero. Net investment then stops. The value of the capital stock remains constant. The replacement of economic equipment by other equipment which is optimal for the resulting rate will nevertheless continue in the margin of reinvestment. The whole economy thus will eventually become equipped with means of production, the utilization of which will grant a yield equivalent to the interest rate. In this case there is nothing to prevent the interest rate from remaining constant at a positive value.

The marginalists' assumption that, in the long-run analysis of distribution, capital can be assumed to be constant and to have a positive marginal productivity, thus implies the condition that autonomous saving ceases before the interest rate has decreased to zero. The observation that some people, in spite of the considerable fortunes they hold, still don't have enough, certainly does not support the probability of this expectation. We should, however, not forget that the concept of the long-run state of things supposes constant exogenous data: stagnation of the population and a given book of blue prints. Growth of population and technical inventions enhance the expectations of capital yield. The demand for funds for net investment, and thus, with a given rate of savings, the level of interest, will rise, while on the other hand the desire to hold wealth will grow with the population and the rising standard of living.

The exogenous data determining the 'long-run' distribution will have changed again before we ever reach such equilibrium. This should not lead to the conclusion that a careful analysis of long-run distribution is not worth while. Today's reality should be understood as a point on the curve of adaptation to the equilibrium — although the equilibrium may be a moving one. A mathematical description of the dynamic process of adaptation in a simplified model would not be possible without a clear definition of the equilibrium towards which reality moves.

It is evident that profits and interest will play a leading role in this dynamic process. The incentive to invest results from the interaction of profits and interest while profit-incomes and income from interest are the main sources of savings financing the build-up of real capital. On the other hand, the shares of capital- and labour-income in today's social product are the main object of the political discussion on distribution. Thus for good reasons economic thought has concentrated on the question : what determines the share of income from capital-ownership in the short-run transitory state of things ?

The problem might have found an earlier solution if the ideas of Hume, Turgot, and Thornton had not been forgotten for such an incredibly long time. New hope arose when economists in the 1930's returned to macro-economic considerations. Although at first they concentrated on nothing but a short-run theory of employment they soon gave a new start to the macro-economic theory of growth and to the theory of distribution. The discussion is still open.

IV. THE CONTRIBUTION OF MACRO-ECONOMIC THEORY

It could hardly be expected that the theory of employment as represented in Keynes's *General Theory* would supply us with a solution to the problem of functional distribution. The model underlying his theory comprises besides the enterprises just one group of households, within which the receivers of all kinds of income are combined. The Keynesian model is, like the model of Jean Baptiste Say, a two-sector model. The whole difference between the two models is that Keynes has split the incomes of the group of all households into expenses for consumption and savings according to a consumption-function which was already known to Malthus.

Nevertheless right here, in its explanation of the factors on which saving depends, the theory of employment has hit on a new thesis which is essential for the analysis of functional distribution. To the classical assumption of autonomous saving it opposes the undeniable fact that in the whole economy real savings and real net investment are identical. As net investment is nothing else but that part of the social product which is not consumed during the period in which it is produced, and thus represents an increment to wealth, this newly created wealth must necessarily become somebody's property as the difference of his income and his consumption expenditure, i.e. as his saving. Contrary to the assumption of autonomous saving, this conclusion would leave open the possibility that it is not the consumers' decisions on savings but rather the entrepreneurs' decisions on investment that decide on the formation of capital and thus on the rate of progress. The theory of employment itself barred this possibility by the deduction of a functional relation between net investment and the rate of employment.

This functional relation says that investment determines the rate of employment at which the economy can be in equilibrium, which means that entrepreneurs do not want to employ more or less labour than corresponds to this rate of employment. As consumption is a function of the social product and on the other hand investment is that part of the social product which is not consumed it is evident that the sum of both must be equal to the social product which results at a given rate of employment, if demand shall equal supply. Taken as an equilibrium, this condition means that the entrepreneurs have to adapt their investment to the margin between the social product which can be produced at a certain rate of employment and that part of it which is consumed. If they don't do so the consequence will be a non-planned alteration of stocks, i.e. an unintended positive or negative investment which will induce a demand for labour deviating from present employment.

The algebraic expression for this equilibrium condition is

$$\mathcal{J} = Y - C(Y)$$

where $\mathcal{J}$ means investment, Y the social product which can be produced at a chosen rate of employment, and $C(Y)$ consumption given as a function of Y. Klein and Samuelson have illustrated this relation in their well-known graph, plotting consumption $C(Y)$ over the social product Y as abscissa.

The Keynesian theory of employment assumes $C(Y)$ as one of the system's exogenous data just as the classics did with autonomous saving. Indeed autonomous saving is nothing else but the non-consumed part of the social product shown in the graph by the vertical distances between Y, represented by a 45° line, and $C(Y)$. However, not the $C(Y)$-function but only the propensities to consume may be considered as given. In a two-sector model, where all receivers of income are comprised in one single group, this does not make any difference. If, however, we disaggregate into several groups and if we consider different groups to have different propensities to consume, total consumption is no longer an unbiased function of the social product but becomes a function of the distribution of incomes to the different groups. The condition of equilibrium then reads

$$\mathcal{J} = Y - C\left(Y, \frac{P}{Y}\right).$$

In the graph we then have to represent consumption no longer by a single curve but by a group of curves.

Whatever the prevailing distribution may be — in other words whichever curve out of this group may represent the actual distribution — the Keynesian condition of equilibrium can always be satisfied if only investment is adapted to the margin between Y and $C(Y)$. This holds even for a distribution where profits P are zero and investment equals the savings S_F out of the factor incomes.

It certainly does not prove that the entrepreneurs' demand for labour should be quite independent of the size of their total profits. Total expenditure is by no means allocated to the individual enterprises proportionally to their costs of production. Different positions in the market and the different productivity of equipment will result in a wide variation of entrepreneurial profits. This leads up to the conclusion that total profits must have a certain value if all entrepreneurs together shall demand a certain quantity of manhours.

What we need and what so far is missing is a functional relation between profits and the demand for labour.

Keynes passed by this problem already in his *Treatise on Money* where he defined his Q-profits in such a way that they designate only the deviations from that size of profits which makes the demand for labour just equal to the quantity of labour employed. How big, however, profits had to be to maintain this equilibrium of employment he never said. In his *General Theory* which deals with the national income as an aggregate and no longer with its components factor income and profits, the question how profits and demand for labour are related has completely submerged.

The problem would be solved if a way was found to define the share of profits in total income P independently of the Keynesian equilibrium formula. This Y has been attempted by the theorists of the monopoly degree, especially by Kalecki and Preiser. They suppose that the entrepreneurs are willing to claim and able to obtain an arbitrary surplus over prime cost, either as a percentual mark up (Kalecki) [1] or as an absolute amount charged per manhour (Preiser).[2] They thus obtain a ratio P/Y which is what they call the 'monopoly degree'. By inserting this value for P/Y into the formula

$$\mathcal{J} = Y - C\left(Y, \frac{P}{Y}\right)$$ it is easy to obtain equilibrium values for

$Y, \mathcal{J}, C, P$ and for the entrepreneurs' demand for labour.

The drawback is that we can by no means be sure that entrepreneurs do not change their mark up in case of a changing demand for their products. If they increase prices when demand exceeds production and if prices give way when demand falls below production, then equilibrium is undetermined again. Not even a complete theory of entrepreneurial price and production behaviour could sufficiently solve the problem.

A different way towards an independent definition of P/Y has been suggested by Kaldor and Mirrlees [3] in their article 'A New Model of Economic Growth'. They argue that investment $\mathcal{J}$ is given as the product of the number n of men becoming available to man new equipment and the cost i of equipment per man. Once $\mathcal{J}$ is given in this way P and P/Y can be calculated for given propensities to consume. However, n depends on the entrepreneurs' decisions to put

[1] M. Kalecki, *Theory of Economic Dynamics*, London, 1954.
[2] E. Preiser, 'Wachstum und Einkommensverteilung', Heidelberg, 1961.
[3] Kaldor–Mirrlees, 'A New Model of Economic Growth', *Rev. Econ. Stat.*, vol. 29, 1961/62, pp. 174–192.

older equipment out of production. These decisions again depend on the profitability of the old equipment as compared to that of new equipment. Once new equipment is ready to produce it requires not only labour to man it but it attracts away a part of the expenditure stream from old equipment. The consequence is that the entrepreneurs are forced to shut down old equipment because decreasing returns make the operation of old equipment uneconomical. The number of men set free to man new equipment thus depends on the entrepreneurs' own decisions to invest in new equipment.

Thus even in Kaldor's model the question of what determines J and hence P remains open. We cannot determine an equilibrium value of J without knowing P/Y, and we cannot determine P/Y either, because P, with the propensities to consume given, depends on J. J itself puts out of work the number of men (n) which Kaldor uses to determine J at full employment.

On the other hand we can find in Kaldor's article some very interesting remarks regarding the profits earned on machinery of different age. 'Machines', he says, 'earn quasi-rents which are all the smaller the older they are so that for the oldest surviving machine the quasi-rents are zero'.[1] Kaldor evidently had a clear notion of a scale of profits depending on the different age of equipment, ending at zero with the oldest machine in use. This is the line of thinking I propose to follow. I shall try to show that this concept holds the clue to an independent determination of P/Y. My argument will confirm Kaldor's conclusion that in economic development 'everything depends on past history, on how the collection of equipment goods, which comprises (the capital stock) K_t has been built up'.[2]

V. THE SCALE OF RETURNS

The question which factors decide the demand for labour brings us back to marginal theory. From the supposed tendency to maximize profits the marginalists have deduced that entrepreneurs with given means of production employ so many manhours that the marginal cost of the product of the last employed hour of labour equals the marginal return which is obtainable by this product's sale in the market. If equal products manufactured in an enterprise are

---

[1] Kaldor–Mirrlees, 'A New Model of Economic Growth', *op. cit.*, p. 188.
[2] *Ibid.* p. 188.

sold at the same price, this gives a clear connection between the total returns of this enterprise and its demand for labour.

Enterprises operating in a competitive market, if their offer has no remarkable influence on the market price, will employ so much labour that their marginal cost per unit of the goods produced equals the unit's price. In the period of transition, when competition has not yet had its full effect upon capacities, the price is above the minimum of the average cost, and all competitors will obtain scarcity profits. Those who operate more economical equipment than their competitors will in addition obtain a cost-difference profit.

Monopolistic enterprises, whose obtainable price depends on the size of their offer, will, if they want to maximize profits, keep their capacity short. Their capital costs remain low, and they will employ only so many manhours that marginal costs equal marginal returns and not price. Their monopoly gain is a scarcity profit. In oligopolies the participants operating with more economic equipment moreover obtain a cost-difference profit. The tendency to maximize profits leads even in the case of monopoly to a clear connection between total returns and demand for labour. If the tendency to maximize profits is replaced by any other chosen aim of profit policy, a different demand for labour will result, which, however, will again be a function of total returns.

If we divide the total returns of an enterprise by the amount of manhours worked, we obtain the returns per manhour. This figure has the dimension 'monetary units per hour' and is equal to the quotient of the price of the product and the productivity of labour. The returns per manhour worked depend on the height and shape of the price-demand function of the goods produced and thus on the preferences of the consumers for the different goods offered in the market. As they will be different in size, we can arrange the enterprises according to the height of their returns per manhour. In this order we plot — as has been done in Fig. 1 (p. 571) — the returns per manhour of all enterprises over an abscissa which shows the manhours L worked in the whole economy. To each enterprise a margin is given corresponding to the manhours it employs. In this way a curve falling continuously to the right is obtained.

Over the same abscissa L we can show as well the enterprise's costs per hour worked. These are the costs of goods and services purchased, depreciation of capital, interest, and wages. We can, however, exclude from the returns and from total cost the cost of goods and services purchased and of depreciation, so that we obtain the curve ϵ, the scale of returns of the net value added per manhour and that of the corresponding net costs κ. This offers the advantage that the area below the ϵ-curve represents the total of returns of all enterprises, which is equal to the national income Y, as a function of the quantity L of the labour employed, while on the other hand only the factor incomes, wages and interest, are left as components of cost.

The vertical distances between the ϵ- and the κ-curves represent the profits per manhour of the different enterprises.[1]

The cost curve, like the profit curve, will have a tendency to fall towards the right side as the enterprise making high profits will be prepared to pay somewhat higher wages and also will have, as they probably use equipment of higher capital intensity, higher interest charges per manhour than their less profitably-operating competitors. However, the falling trend of the κ-curve will be less steep than that of the ϵ-curve, so that both curves intersect at a certain value of the abscissa.

As only those entrepreneurs whose returns exceed cost will continue to exercise a demand for labour, the abscissa of the intersection of the ϵ- and κ-curves shows the size of the total demand for labour D_L of all enterprises. We thus have found a relation between the total demand for labour and the national income Y, which is represented by the area below the ϵ-curve, limited on the left side by the ordinate and on the right side by the vertical line through the point of intersection.

The demand for labour D_L can be equal to, smaller than, or larger than the supply of labour S_L. We can mark S_L on the abscissa, then if the ϵ-curve has such a position that D_L is just equal to S_L, we have an employment equilibrium at full employment. In case the ϵ-curve is situated at a lower level, so that the point of intersection is to the left of S_L and $D_L < S_L$, our diagram shows a situation of under-employment. This is a case of disequilibrium of employment if — contrary to Keynes — we assume for the general case that the unemployed are prepared to work for lower wages and thus cause a decreasing demand for money and a lower rate of interest. In case the ϵ-curve is situated above the equilibrium position, so that

---

[1] As we have arranged the enterprises according to the height of their net value added per manhour, it cannot be expected that the cost curve κ has a continuous shape. We propose for the present argument to assume that the κ-curve be replaced by a continuous curve averaging the oscillations. If we plot profits separately, rearranging the enterprises according to the height of their profits per manhour, we obtain a continuous shape of the profit curve.

the point of intersection is to the right of S_L and thus $D_L > S_L$, which represents a boom situation of excessive entrepreneurial activity. Here unsatisfied demand for labour bids up wages. With the propensity to consume given, expenses for consumption and as a consequence commodity prices and the demand for money will rise and consequently cause a higher rate of interest. This is a disequilibrium situation as well. We see that unemployment and inflation as caused by over-activity are just two possible consequences of the same phenomenon, a discrepancy between D_L and S_L.

Just as the area below the ϵ-curve represents the national income Y, the area below the κ-curve represents the factor income Y_F. If we plot as a third curve the wages per manhour worked — which is nothing else but the enterprise's average wage rate — we can split Y_F into its components : income from labour Y_L and income from interest Y_r. The triangular area between the ϵ- and the κ-curves shows the total profit P. P and Y_r together are property income which we may call Y_p. The scale of returns thus pictures the functional distribution which we have been looking for, the division of national income into its components : wages, interest, and profit as functions of the demand for labour D_L.

For any chosen rate of employment represented on the abscissa of our diagram as the number of manhours actually worked, the areas show the resulting distribution of any assumed national income. That size of national income at which the ϵ- and the κ-curves intersect at the values of the abscissa corresponding to the chosen rate of employment is the equilibrium income — in the Keynesian sense — belonging to this rate. The relation of the areas in this case shows the equilibrium distribution for the chosen rate of employment.

Contrary to marginalist theory, which only tried to explain functional distribution in the 'long run', our diagram is able to show the distribution in the 'short-run' transitory period for equilibrium of employment in the Keynesian sense as well as for all possible situations of disequilibrium.

The results of our considerations differ from Kaldor's conclusions, i.e. that 'the total profit is determined quite independently of the structure of these "quasi-rents" . . . by the factors determining the share of investment in output and the proportion of profit saved.'[1] Kaldor's so determined profit may not ensure that the entrepreneur employing the last manhour supplied obtains returns just covering

[1] Kaldor–Mirrlees, p. 188.

his cost. As the profit then earned 'on the oldest machine' would not be zero, the economy would not be in equilibrium at the given rate of employment. To reach and sustain equilibrium at this rate the entrepreneurs will have to increase or decrease investment until a size of profits is obtained which allows the last entrepreneur to just cover his costs. If they do so then — contrary to what Kaldor states — it is indeed 'the age-and-productivity structure of machinery which will determine what the aggregate share of quasi-rents will be'.[1]

Functional distribution, at Keynesian employment equilibrium — as a function of the amount of labour employed — is illustrated in Fig. 2. In this graph we have plotted as ordinates over the abscissa L, measuring the manhours worked, the areas resulting from Fig. 1 if the ϵ- and the κ-curves intersect at the corresponding value of the abscissa.[2]

The ordinates of Fig. 2 again are monetary values. They have the dimension 'monetary units per year'. We have assumed the wage rate to be the same for all rates of employment. Moving to higher rates of employment in Fig. 1 thus means moving along the same cost-curve κ but shifting upwards the scale of returns ϵ so that the two intersect at the considered value of the abscissa. This gives in Fig. 2 a factor income rising at a diminishing rate but a progressively rising curve of equilibrium total income Y.

The ordinates of the three curves $\bar{Y}$, Y_f, and Y_L indicate the distribution of income which guarantees that the entrepreneur's demand for labour D_L just equals the amount of labour employed at this rate of employment. All points outside the $\bar{Y}$-curve represent situations of disequilibrium and cause dynamic changes. The vertical distances between the $\bar{Y}$- and Y_F-curves indicate the equilibrium profit P. Every $\bar{P}$ causes the entrepreneurs to demand not more and not less labour than indicated by the corresponding abscissa value. If we mark on the abscissa L the supply of labour S_L, then the vertical line through S_L indicates the national income $\bar{Y}$ and the profit $\bar{P}$, which at a given nominal wage rate are compatible with equilibrium at full employment.

From the components of income as represented by the ordinates in Fig. 2 we can, by applying the consumption functions, derive the outlays for consumption. However, it does not make sense to attribute a propensity to consume to functional incomes as only individual

---

[1] Kaldor–Mirrlees, p. 188.
[2] Remember that if we do so, the discontinuity of the κ-curve in Fig. 1 disappears.

income receivers, or the households in which they live, have a propensity to consume. To be able to apply a consumption function in a reasonable way, we have first to step from functional distribution to personal distribution. We allocate functional incomes to certain interesting groups of households, e.g. the households of dependent working people and the households of the self-employed. This can be done by means of coefficients which we can compute from statistics on the actual distribution of wealth to the different groups.

Curve C in Fig. 2 shows the expenditures on consumption we would obtain in this way. The vertical distance between the C-curve and the $\bar{Y}$-curve indicates for each value of L how big the outlays on investment $\mathcal{J}$ must be to make total expenditure $Y = C + \mathcal{J}$ just equal to the equilibrium national income $\bar{Y}$. The equilibrium value of investment $\bar{\mathcal{J}}$, which is a function of L, is related to the equilibrium value of the profit $\bar{P}$ in a way which depends on the propensities to consume of the different groups of households. If C_p indicates the consumption of the proprietor group and S_w the savings of the wage- and salary-earners, then $\bar{\mathcal{J}}$ must be

$$\bar{\mathcal{J}} = \bar{P} - Cp + S_w.$$

Thus completed, Fig. 2 shows a remarkable similarity with the diagram by Klein and Samuelson. This becomes even more evident if we draw our diagram not in monetary value, as done in Fig. 2, but in real values. Then $\bar{Y}$ as a function of L, equal productivity of labour assumed all over, becomes a straight line. It makes no sense to speak of an equilibrium value of the national income Y in real units. Here instead the factor income $\bar{Y}_F$ and the profit $\bar{P}$ are equilibrium values and the same goes for the consumption expenditures $\bar{C}$. This brings out very clearly the difference between our diagram and the graph of Klein and Samuelson. In the latter, $C(Y)$ has been assumed as being given by nothing else but the propensity to consume. In our diagram $\bar{C}(Y)$ is that height of consumption expenditures which results, with the propensities to consume of the different groups of households given, from that distribution of Y on P and Y_F which must prevail, if, at a chosen rate of employment, employment shall be in equilibrium.

The Keynesian condition $\mathcal{J} = Y - C(Y)$, according to which investment has to fill the gap between the national income related to a chosen rate of employment and the consumption resulting as a function of this income, can be satisfied with all possible wage quotas

Y_L/Y or profit quotas P/Y. These different quotas P/Y result at given propensities to consume of the different groups of households but with a varying distribution of income to these groups. For each of the possible quotas P/Y we can draw the corresponding consumption line $C(Y)$ in the Klein-Samuelson graph. But not all these possible profit quotas satisfy the Keynesian condition that the entrepreneurs' demand for labour shall equal the amount of labour employed at the chosen rate of employment. Among the whole group of possible P/Y ratios there is just one which satisfies this condition, the equilibrium ratio $\bar{P}/\bar{Y}$, which results from the scale of returns. Thus in addition to the Keynesian formula $\mathcal{J} = Y - C(Y)$ we have found a separate second condition, which Keynes did not mention and which was hidden implicitly behind his assumption that C is a function of Y. This second condition is

$$P = \bar{P}.$$

Keynes justified calling a situation of underemployment one of equilibrium through the assumption that trade unions prevent wages from falling as a consequence of unemployment. There are good reasons to suppose this for the present Western economic systems and Keynes was certainly right to start out from this assumption, as he wanted to explain why an economy can remain in a situation of underemployment. In a basic theoretical model, however, which is to serve to explain how the whole mechanism works without political intervention, we should renounce this assumption and only regard it as one possible intervention, which blocks part of the sequence of 'natural' reactions. If we do so, then the Keynesian equilibrium at underemployment is only a partial equilibrium of employment, whereas total equilibrium of employment requires a third condition to be satisfied, the condition that the demand for labour D_L be equal to the supply of labour S_L.

The three conditions of total equilibrium of employment thus are

(1) $\quad \mathcal{J} = Y - C(Y)$
(2) $\quad P = \bar{P}$
(3) $\quad D_L = S_L$.

These can all be combined in one formula, if we write

$$\mathcal{J} = \bar{\mathcal{J}}(S_L) = \bar{Y}(S_L) - C(\bar{Y}).$$

If this condition is satisfied then the wage rate and the interest rate, employment, the price level and distribution remain constant

The Distribution of National Income

in the short run. The equilibrium of employment thus defined is
the short-run internal equilibrium of the economy.

VI. THE MACRO-ECONOMIC MODEL

By splitting households into two different categories we have
replaced the two-sector model, underlying the theories of Say and
Keynes by a three-sector model. It seems that Keynes, speaking
in his *Treatise on Money* of the Q-profits of the entrepreneurs and of
the savings S of the non-entrepreneurs, and submitting his famous
formula $Q = \mathcal{J} - S$, was on his way to develop a three-sector model.
In the *General Theory* he abandoned this attempt. It is for good
reason that no such attempt has succeeded since.

The system of equations by which we can describe a simplified
three-sector model, as shown in Fig. 3, contains 9 variables and
5 identity-equations which are given by the branching-off and joining
points of the income flow. To make the model consistent we therefore need four behaviour equations, out of which two are given as
the consumption functions of the two groups of households. The
third one is the investment function, which can be dispensed with if
we regard investment, as Keynes did, as an independent variable,
i.e. as one of the exogenous data. The fourth behaviour equation,
however, has been missing so far in all models. A look at the scheme
of the three-sector model shows clearly where it is missing. What is
missing is an equation which indicates how the national income Y
branches off into its components P and Y_F. The missing equation is
the distribution function $Y_F(Y)$. The scale of returns has supplied
us with the function which was missing, to make a three-sector model
consistent.

The information flow in Fig. 4 helps us to check whether our model
is consistent or not. The only exogenous variable in this model is
$\mathcal{J}$ which together with C adds up to Y. C is composed of $Cp = Cp(Yp)$
and $Cw = Cw(Yw)$. All this is easy to draw but to split up Y into
its components Yo and Yw would clearly have been impossible without a distribution function $Yw(Y)$ shown in the upper right part of
the information flow scheme.

This simplified model can be brought a lot closer to reality by
including the labour market and the money market as we have done
in Fig. 5. The basic scheme corresponds to that of the simplified
model in Fig. 4. In Fig. 5 the splitting of Y into Y_P and Y_F, how-

558

ever, is achieved by a distribution function which contains explicitly the demand for labour D_L, the national income Y and the capital stock K, which determines the slope of the scale of returns. We obtain the factor income Y_F by multiplying D_L with the wage rate w. The profit P is obtained by subtracting Y_F from Y.

As to the determination of the wage rate, we assumed that a positive (negative) deviation of the demand for labour D_L from the supply S_L causes a continuous rise (decline) of the wage rate. We can express this by

$$\frac{D_L - S_L}{S_L} = T_L : \frac{d\omega}{dt}; \quad \omega = \frac{w}{\bar{w}}$$

where the coefficient T_L has the dimension of time.

Correspondingly we have assumed for the money market that a positive (negative) deviation of the demand for money D_M from the supply of money S_M causes a rise (decline) of the rate of interest r so that

$$\frac{D_M - S_M}{S_M} = T_M \cdot \frac{d\rho}{dt}; \quad \rho = \frac{r}{\bar{r}}$$

where again the coefficient T_M has the dimension of time. The demand for money is supposed to be given as a function of C, $\mathcal{J}$ and the liquidity preference LP, which is considered an exogenous factor.

The rate of interest r interacts with the entrepreneurs' investment-function $\mathcal{J}(r)$ in determining investment $\mathcal{J}$. The investment-function $\mathcal{J}(r)$ results from the entrepreneurs' expectations of capital yield and has been determined by the two exogenous factors supply of labour S_L and technical progress T.P., furthermore by the size and structure of the existing capital stock K which itself results from previous investments $\mathcal{J}$. This step may be justified because increasing supply of labour requires an extension of productive equipment whereas technical progress encourages investment for rationalization.

The core of our information flow scheme is the rather complex function $D_L(Y, K, U)$. This function describes the position and slope of the scale of returns, as shown in Fig. 1 and depends on the national stock K and a fifth exogenous factor U, the consumer's preferences for the goods offered in the market. If we consider the latter two factors constant, the scale of returns shows the functional relation between D_L and Y. It may be that future empirical research will make it possible to analyse the influence the two other factors have on the scale of returns and on D_L.

In Fig. 5 we have shown the four exogenous factors: supply of labour, technical progress, supply of money and liquidity preference, as vertical lines entering the information flow from above. These exogenous data define the equilibrium of the model, i.e. the equilibrium values: $\bar{Y}, \bar{P}, \bar{\jmath}, \bar{D}_L, \bar{w}$ and $\bar{r}$ of the endogenous variables of the system. A situation of disequilibrium prevails if any of the mentioned variables deviate from their equilibrium value as defined by the exogenous data. The reason for such a deviation can be a change of any of the exogenous data or a disturbing interference with one of the endogenous variables, e.g. an arbitrary change of the interest rate or some autonomous investment independent from the rate of interest. In each case, such changes cause a process of adaptation or re-adaptation towards an equilibrium defined by the changed or unchanged exogenous data.

The adaptation process will certainly not be smooth in all cases. Time lags in the reaction of the wage rate and of the interest rate, of consumer expenditure on changes in income, of investment on changes of the interest rate, and the demand for labour on changes in returns, may cause oscillations around the new equilibrium position. If the exogenous data do not change abruptly but steadily and continuously, as is the normal case in reality, endogenous variables will follow the change of the exogenous data either with or without oscillations.

Once the model has been made consistent by the introduction of the distribution function, it is only a question of mathematical technique to track the time path of adaptation and to calculate the conditions of stability. This would not be possible without the $Y_F(Y)$ or $D_L(Y)$ function we derived from the scale of returns. Ricardo thus was perfectly right in saying that a satisfactory theory of distribution holds the key to an understanding of the mechanism of the economic system.

VII. SOME EMPIRICAL EVIDENCE FOR THE SCALE OF RETURNS

We have shown that by marginalist reasoning the relation between the returns per manhour worked and the entrepreneurs' demand for labour can be traced back to the consumer's utility functions, to the entrepreneurial price and profit policies and to the structure of the economy's capital stock, which itself is the result of previous investments and depreciation. Thus the reasoning for the assumed $\epsilon(L)$-function is well founded, and we can, to a certain extent, even make some assumptions concerning its shape. But we certainly cannot calculate its shape exactly, since we have no quantitative knowledge of all the data mentioned from which it is derived.

This must not be considered a special disadvantage of our function, as the same is true for all similar functions on which we base our theoretical deduction, e.g. the $C(Y)$-function, the $J(r)$-function and also the price-demand-function of all kinds of commodities. Generally we are satisfied if such hypothetically assumed functional relations do not qualitatively contradict our experience. However, if possible, we should of course try to test them empirically.

The attempt to verify the $\epsilon(L)$-function meets with some difficulties. Certainly the required data on returns, cost, and hours of labour employed are known in every enterprise. But they are not published, they do not show in any statistics, and the managers are not enthusiastic about communicating them to outsiders.

First information on the approximate position of the scale of returns can be based on data from national income accounting, if the incomes from labour and from capital are shown separately.

If national income is split only into incomes of wage-earners and of entrepreneurs, the income from property of the former group must be added to capital income, and an adequate remuneration for the entrepreneurial working hours must be attributed to labour-income. The income from interest can be estimated by multiplying the private capital invested with an average rate of interest for long-term loans. If the total manhours worked per year are known, the components of income, i.e. wages, interest, and profit, can be shown as rectangles over the manhours employed in the economy. The expected triangular area, representing profits, must be equal to the rectangular profit area we just obtained. We now have to tilt the upper horizontal line of the profit-rectangle. If we can be sure that the period to which the statistical data refer was no boom-period and if the cost line was horizontal, then the right end of the tilted line of returns should cut through the upper right corner of the cost rectangle.

A first proof that indeed the ϵ-curve has such a slope is supplied by Fig. 6, which is based mainly on data taken from the *Statistisches Jahrbuch der BRD* (1963). In this graph net returns per man (net value plus interest on borrowed capital) and net costs per man (personal costs plus total interest) are plotted over the number of persons employed for six different sectors of the German economy.[1]

Further evidence has been supplied by the Deutsches Institut für Wirtschaftsforschung (DIW) in its 1963 analysis of the net production value of 40 different sectors of the German manufacturing industry. Grouping the results of this analysis in four subsectors enabled us to tilt the horizontal return and cost lines of the largest block in Fig. 6. The result is shown in Fig. 7, which displays the slope of ϵ even more clearly than Fig. 6.[2]

As was to be expected, the cost lines in Figs. 6 and 7 do not show a continuously falling trend but rather wide variations. In Fig. 8 we have therefore rearranged the 9 sectors according to the height of their profits per man. The resulting profit-scale offers quite a surprise. The profit area — far from resembling a rectangle — has not only the expected triangular shape but it shows a rather sharp peak of profits concentrated in a few sectors and a long tail of low profits for the rest. This means that the economy's demand for labour is much more sensitive to a variation in the relation of total cost to total expenditure than would have been the case if the profit line was widely horizontal with a steep decline at its end.

However, before drawing any conclusions, we should, just as has been done for manufacturing industry, tilt the horizontal lines of all other columns. Unfortunately the corresponding statistical data are not yet available. We shall try to get a more reliable picture of the ϵ-curve by questioning a representative sample of enterprises. The analysis of commercial balance sheets may not be very illustrative. It would be welcome if the fiscal authorities, who year by year receive the tax statement sheets of each enterprise, would be prepared to co-operate in analysing this material for the whole economy. It would certainly be possible to ensure that the data are treated confidentially and that only anonymous results are published.

[1] The net returns have been calculated from the figures of the net domestic product of the sectors given in the *Statistisches Jahrbuch*, deducting depreciation and indirect taxes from the net production values. Depreciation has been estimated as 3·3 per cent of the replacement value of fixed capital (Brutto-Anlagekapital) as currently calculated by the Deutsches Institut für Wirtschaftsforschung (DIW). Personal costs have been estimated by correcting data taken from DIW's income analysis for 1955 with the help of the wage indices of the *Statistisches Jahrbuch* (1963). Total interest has been calculated as 5 per cent on the DIW replacement value of fixed capital, assuming that the balance sheet value of the fixed capital amounts to about half of the DIW figure and that total capital required is about twice the book value of fixed capital.

[2] The returns per man have been calculated from the value added to materials as given in the DIW analysis in prices of 1950, using the price-indices of the *Statistisches Jahrbuch* (1963). Indirect taxes have been derived from the latter source. Personal costs, depreciation, and total interest have been estimated the same way as for Fig. 6.

If we succeed in measuring with some precision the curves of returns and cost for a number of different economies and for some subsequent years, this would enable us to compare changes of the position and the shape of the ϵ-curves according to the known changes of the exogenous data and of the structure of our model. We would learn to interpret the observed curves and to draw from their changes more reliable conclusions as to the behaviour of entrepreneurs regarding their demand for labour and their decisions on investment than we have been able so far with our traditional tools.

VIII. INCOME COMPONENTS AND INCOME QUOTAS

Given the scale of returns and wages per manhour, we can express the functional distribution in a number of algebraic formulas. This may help us to survey the income components wages, interest, and profits and their share in the social product, the quotas.

If $\epsilon\phi$ designates the average value of $\epsilon(L)$, and if $w\phi$ is the average and w_m the marginal nominal wage rate, then with $\alpha = \dfrac{w\phi}{wm}$ we obtain

for the

national income $\qquad Y = \epsilon\phi \,.\, L$ and the

labour income $\qquad Y_L = \alpha \,.\, w_m \,.\, L$

The income from interest is $Y_r = rK$, where $K = w_\phi$. R is the replacement cost of the total working capital of the enterprises and R the amount of manhours necessary to produce its replacement. If we put $i = R$ for the capital intensity (dimension : unit of time) we obtain for the

income from interest $Yr = r \,.\, i \,.\, \alpha \,.\, w_m \,.\, L.$

From $P = Y - Y_L - Yr$ then is derived the

income from profits $P = [\epsilon\phi - (1 + ri)\, \alpha w_m]\, L.$

The shares of the income components in total product thus are

$$\text{wage share } \frac{Y_L}{Y} = \alpha \frac{w_m}{\epsilon\phi}$$

$$\text{interest share } \frac{Y_r}{Y} = ri\, \alpha \frac{w_m}{\epsilon\phi}$$

The Distribution of National Income

$$\text{profit share } \frac{P}{Y}=1-(1-ri)\,\alpha\frac{w_m}{\epsilon\phi}.$$

If we set λ for the wage share, so that

$$\lambda=\alpha\frac{w_m}{\epsilon\phi}$$

we obtain for the shares of the income components :

$$\text{wage share} \quad =\lambda$$

$$\text{interest share} =ri\,.\,\lambda$$

$$\text{profit share} \quad =1-(1+ri)\,.\,\lambda.$$

The quota of the income from property ownership is then of course $1-\lambda$.

If we want to explain the marginal wage rate w_m by the marginal returns per hour of labour ϵ_m we have to start from the formula

$$w_m+r_m=\epsilon m,$$

which means that the sum of the marginal wage rate w_m and the marginal interest cost per hour of labour r'_m is equal to the marginal return per hour of labour ϵ_m, as the profit of the marginal producer is zero. The marginal interest costs per hour of labour are

$$r'_m=r\left(\frac{K}{L}\right)_m=r\,.\,\alpha\,.\,w_m\,.\,i_m$$

where i_m designates the marginal capital intensity. We thus obtain

$$w_m=\frac{\epsilon m}{1+\alpha\,.\,r\,.\,i_m}$$

and

$$\lambda=\frac{\alpha}{1+\alpha\,.\,r\,.\,i_m}\,.\,\frac{\epsilon m}{\epsilon\phi}$$

As λ may be in the order of 1·1, which already corresponds to a difference of 20 per cent between maximal and marginal wages and as the marginal capital intensity may be between 1·5 and 3, we find that the quotient

$$\frac{\alpha}{1+\alpha\,.\,r\,.\,i_m}$$

will not differ much from unity. We thus come to the conclusion that the wage share primarily depends on the ratio $\epsilon m/\epsilon\phi$, of marginal and average returns per manhour, i.e. from the slope of the ϵ-curve.

The other way round, we can guess what the ϵ-curve will look like if the wage quota λ is given. If, e.g., λ is given as 0·666 the average returns per manhour $\epsilon\phi$ will be about 1·5 times the marginal returns and the maximal return about twice the marginal returns.

With the wage share given at 0·666 we can, using our formulas, calculate the other shares. With an interest rate of 5 per cent and values for the capital intensity between 1·5 and 3 we find that the profit quota will vary between 0·29 and 0·24 and the interest quota between 0·05 and 0·1. This means that the income from interest may amount to between 5 and 10 per cent of the national income. The profit share and the interest share together of course give for the share of income from ownership $1 - 0 = 0·333$.

Assuming propensities to save or to consume we can calculate from the income shares the ratios C/Y and S/Y, the latter being identical with I/Y. If, e.g., the average propensity to save is 0·1 for the group receiving income from labour and 0·5 for the group receiving capital income, we obtain a total savings quota $S/Y = 0·233$ and correspondingly a total consumption quota $C/Y = 0·766$. In accordance with this we obtain from the formula

$$\mathcal{J} = Y_p - C_p + Sw$$

the investment quota which, under the assumption made, is necessary to maintain equilibrium at full employment. Its value of 0·233 means that investment must amount to 23·3 per cent of the national income.

IX. THE SCALE OF RETURNS AND THE GROWTH RATE

With the capital coefficient given, the growth rate depends on the investment quota. If the slope of the ϵ-curve, and hence the profit share, would remain unchanged, then according to the formula

$$\mathcal{J} = P - C_p + Sw$$

investment would depend exclusively on the consumption expenditures of the receivers of capital incomes and on the savings of wage and salary earners. The growth rate would then be determined by the decisions of the consumers, just as the theory of autonomous saving supposed.

However, the slope of ϵ will not remain unchanged in the course of economic development. The position and slope of the scale of returns will depend on how fast the endogenous variables have been able to adjust to changes of the exogenous data.

Scarcity profits and cost-differential profits will be the higher the slower the economy's means of production get adjusted to the optimal factor combination which becomes possible through changes in the supply of labour and of technical know-how, the exogenous data of our model.

New commodities are manufactured and marketed in relatively small quantities. They can be sold at high prices so that the enterprises manufacturing them obtain high returns per manhour. The production of goods already known with more rational equipment reduces the manhours per unit of goods produced and — selling prices unchanged — results as well in higher returns per manhour. The scale of returns will change according to the height of the returns per manhour which the enterprises manufacturing new commodities and using more productive methods have so far been able to obtain.

Normally we shall find the pioneers — as Schumpeter used to call the innovators — among the entrepreneurs who already previously made good profits. They have the facilities to finance their own research work, to develop new products and to buy better equipment before their less-earning competitors can afford it. If their returns, which are already relatively high, grow, then the slope of the ϵ-curve will become steeper.

If, however, there are neither new commodities nor new economic methods invented, and if the new ways opened previously by the pioneers are more and more adopted by all the other enterprises, then their returns per manhour will rise in relation to the returns of the so far pioneering competitors and the ϵ-curve will flatten out.

In a period of stagnation of inventive activity, the ϵ-curve will get closer and closer to the κ-curve, which in itself will flatten, until both curves approach a horizontal position. Profits will have decreased to zero. The classics thus were quite right in saying that 'in the long run' profits have the tendency to disappear. This, however, will only happen once technical progress has completely stopped and the economy has fallen into stagnation.

Every invention will first create expectations of capital yield and raise the $\mathcal{J}(r)$-function. There is yet no influence on the ϵ-curve. But as soon as the first pioneers have applied the invention, the ϵ-curve becomes steeper, so that a higher rate of investment is required to keep the supply of labour fully employed. With the money supply inelastic, the interest rate, falling as a consequence of unemployment and a falling wage rate, enhances investment with the effect that the required investment rate is realized. If the supply of money is elastic, the central bank, if its aim is to safeguard full employment, has to foster the same effect through a corresponding manipulation of the bank rate. In this way technical inventions, through a steepening of the scale of returns, themselves bring about higher investment and thus a quicker realization of the possibilities they offer.

The growth of the population has a similar effect. With an increased supply of labour S/Y, the equilibrium values of the national income $\overline{Y}$, the profit share $\overline{P}/Y$ and in consequence the investment quota $\overline{\mathcal{J}}/Y$, rise more than proportionally, as can be seen from the ordinates of Fig. 2. A more than proportional rise would already result if the ϵ-curve would shift upwards, parallel, so that it intersects the cost curve at the new value of S_L. Both P and $\mathcal{J}$ will grow even faster in relation to S_L if the ordinates of the ϵ-curve increase proportionally as a consequence of unchanged consumer preferences.

An increased supply of labour thus also increases the investment quota which is necessary to obtain and maintain full employment and therefore induces a faster growth of the economy's productive equipment. The expansion will automatically fade out as soon as the productive equipment approaches the size which corresponds to the new supply of labour.

We thus gain a result, quite contrary to the classical thesis of autonomous savings — probably the most important conclusion we can draw from the theory of functional distribution we have presented — that it is not the consumers alone who, by making provisions for future needs, decide on the pace of economic progress, a concept which, as we have mentioned above, has always been unsatisfactory. What makes and what keeps economic growth going, what accelerates and what throttles down the creation of productive capital, is first of all the change in the exogenous data, the invention of new commodities and of more economic means of production and the growth of the population.

X. CONCLUSIONS FOR DISTRIBUTION POLICIES

What interests us for distribution policies is not the functional but the personal distribution. We have shown, while discussing the macro-economic model in section IV, that once functional distribution is known, we can transform it into a personal distribution on relevant socio-economic groups of households, if the structural co-efficients of the distribution of wealth are known.

The distribution of wealth and of its annual increment cause complaints of the injustice of personal distribution in our Western market economies. Certainly also the market's valuation of services according to their scarcity does not always correspond to popular ideas of justice. But astronomical salaries are exceptions and, moreover, they show that relatively high remuneration is necessary to attract labour to under-supplied branches and thus in course of time incomes are automatically normalized. Unanimously condemned by the working classes as injustice, however, is the concentration of wealth in the hands of a relatively small group of the population, and the fact that the members of this group draw unearned incomes, which allow them to live on a standard far above average and even to increase their fortune year by year without any special effort.

What does this one-sided distribution of wealth result from ? To explain this it is not necessary to suppose the distribution to be unequal from the outset. It is sufficient that there exist entrepreneurs who employ labour to produce consumption goods *and* investment goods, and that the workmen spend nearly their whole income on consumption goods. The consequence will be that entrepreneurs get beside their own consumption all the newly created capital with the exception of that part of it which corresponds to savings from labour income.

Naturally there is only little saving out of small individual labour incomes, whereas a high percentage is saved out of the big incomes from capital. As the increment to capital is divided between the socio-economic groups according to their share in total savings, it follows that the biggest part of it always goes to those who already possess. In the Federal Republic of Germany the group of wage-earners, which comprises about 87 per cent of the income receivers, got during the years 1950 to 1960 not more than one-quarter of the increment to private wealth. The excessive concentration of capital formation among the top-income receivers is not shown in any statistic.

In Western Germany politicians and economists begin to realize that this problem of concentration cannot be tackled by conventional means. A number of plans and propositions to foster the formation of wealth out of labour incomes have been discussed and criticized. Attention has been given to the fact that any successful redistribution might lead to increased expenditure on consumer goods. According to the Keynesian formula $\mathcal{J} = Y - C(Y)$ investment then would be reduced, and as the critics have pointed out, then redistribution, if no change in working people's propensity to consume occurs, will slow down the growth rate. It has generally been taken for granted that if investment was adjusted to the thus reduced margin between the social product and consumption no harm would be done to the employment-equilibrium. A few examples may show that a careful consideration of the relative position of the ϵ-curve and the κ-curve can lead to different conclusions with regard to full employment equilibrium.

First of all, every author of redistribution plans should keep in mind that if full employment is to be sustained, we have to generate a gross profit which is given as a structural datum — whether from the point of view of distribution policies we like it or not. Second, in a closed economy a general increase in nominal wages does not disturb equilibrium, but does not have the intended influence on distribution either. It shifts upwards both the ϵ- and the κ-curve. With an elastic supply of money it drives prices to a higher level.

The erroneous idea that higher nominal wages mean a higher rate of consumption is the ground on which the plan of 'investive wages' has grown, which has lately been discussed in Germany. This plan proposes that additional nominal wages should — instead of being paid out to the wage-earners — be transferred to an investment fund. The wage-earners would according to the plan receive certificates of the fund, which they could not sell within a period of six years. It is significant that critics of this plan were quite satisfied with the idea that this way 'forced saving' would prevent a rise in consumption, so that the growth rate would not decline. No attention was paid to the consequence that costs would rise while returns would remain unchanged, which would be detrimental to employment. If full employment then were re-established by increased investment, the price level of consumer goods would rise and wage-earners themselves would pay for their 'forced savings' by a lowering of their standard of living.

We can draw another important conclusion from the scale of returns. Contrary to increases in nominal wages all proposals which are based on an effective reduction of entrepreneurs' net profits may lead to a successful redistribution. Profit taxation or profit sharing will not affect employment, as it leaves the marginal producer unaffected and does not change the gross profit. But even gross profits can be reduced without causing unemployment, if we manage to influence entrepreneurial price and investment policies, which might be achieved, for example, by a progressive taxation based on the ratio of profits to total sales.

It is well known that all these redistributive schemes, if they are successful, increase consumption and decrease growth as long as they are not combined with effective provisions to increase savings either out of labour income or out of taxes by exactly as much as the equilibrium investment quota needs to remain unchanged. Keeping this in mind certainly will prevent us from making some of the worst mistakes.

But once we start to co-ordinate our ways and means for a simultaneous control of employment, price level, growth, distribution, and the foreign trade balance, we need quantitative data. One of the most valuable pieces of information we shall have is the gross profits which we have to generate in order to sustain full employment. Once we have some nearly exact data on this, we can plan taxation of the different income groups, expenditure on consumption and savings to secure the margin for investment and the means to encourage investment to such an extent that it fills the gap and that a chosen growth rate results.

The scale of returns per manhour has proved to be useful in quite a number of investigations of a qualitative nature. Let us hope that once we have succeeded in putting it on reliable numerical ground by more empirical research, it will be helpful in solving the many problems we have still ahead of us.

Föhl — Scale of Returns and Distribution

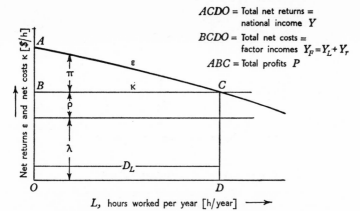

$ACDO$ = Total net returns =
national income Y

$BCDO$ = Total net costs =
factor incomes $Y_F = Y_L + Y_r$

ABC = Total profits P

The scale of returns per man hour [p.m.h.]

ε = Net returns p.m.h. = NVA p.m.h. + non-material outside services p.m.h.

κ = Net costs p.m.h. = personal costs p.m.h. (λ) + interest on own and borrowed
capital p.m.h. (ρ)

$\pi = \varepsilon - \kappa$ = Profit per man hour

FIG. 1

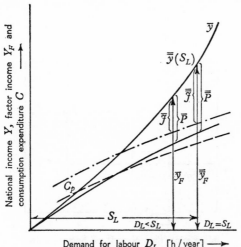

The $\overline{P}/\overline{y}$ = function for equilibrium of employment

S_L = Supply of labour
P = Profits
$\mathcal{J}$ = Net investment
$\overline{Y}, \overline{P}, \overline{\mathcal{J}}$ = Equilibrium values for $D_L < S_L$
$\overline{\overline{Y}}, \overline{\overline{P}}, \overline{\overline{\mathcal{J}}}$ =   ,,   ,,   ,, $D_L = S_L$

FIG. 2

571

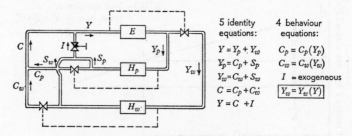

5 identity equations:

$$Y = Y_p + Y_w$$
$$Y_p = C_p + S_p$$
$$Y_w = C_w + S_w$$
$$C = C_p + C_w$$
$$Y = C + I$$

4 behaviour equations:

$$C_p = C_p(Y_p)$$
$$C_w = C_w(Y_w)$$
$$I = \text{exogeneous}$$
$$\boxed{Y_w = Y_w(Y)}$$

Circular flow scheme of a Three-Sector-Model

E = Enterprises H_p = Households of property owners
H_w = Households of wage-earners
Behaviour functions represented as control valves

FIG. 3

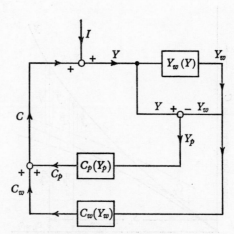

Information flow of a Three-Sector-Model
with exogeneous investment

FIG. 4

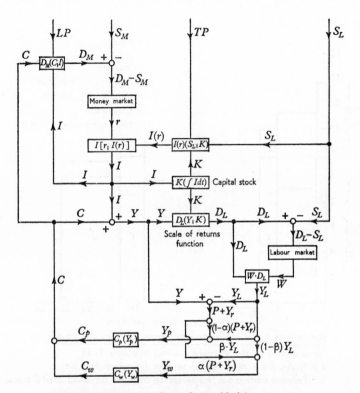

Information flow of a Three-Sector-Model
with liquidity preference LP, money supply S_M, technical
progress TP and labour supply S_L as exogeneous variables

Fig. 5

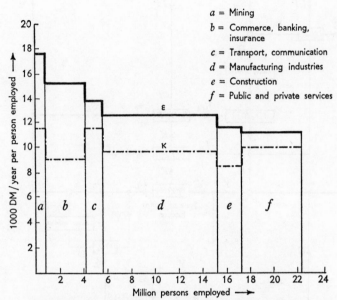

a = Mining
b = Commerce, banking, insurance
c = Transport, communication
d = Manufacturing industries
e = Construction
f = Public and private services

Net returns ε and net costs κ per person employed (p.p.e.)
for 6 sectors of the Western German economy 1961
ε = NVA p.p.e. + non-material services from outside p.p.e.
κ = Personal costs p.p.e. + interest on own and borrowed capital p.p.e.

FIG. 6

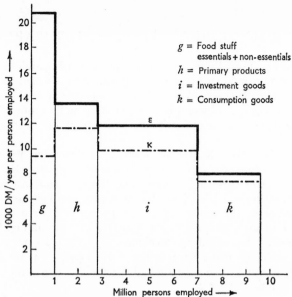

Net returns ε and net costs κ p.p.e. (like fig 6)
for 4 subsectors of the West German manufacturing industry 1961
ε and κ see fig 6

FIG. 7

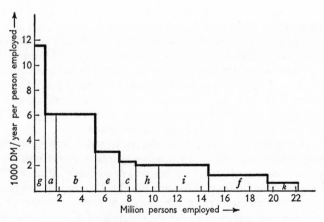

The scale of profits per person employed
for 9 sectors of the West German economy 1961
for the different sectors see fig. 6 and 7

FIG. 8

DISCUSSION OF PROFESSOR FÖHL'S PAPER

Professor Reder said that Professor Föhl's paper required a careful reading as it offered so many new ideas and concepts. As it covered such a broad area Professor Reder could but salute the scholarship displayed in the first three sections and, to save time, concentrate upon Professor Föhl's own contribution to the theory of distribution which began with section IV of the paper.

Professor Föhl's analysis started by positing a relationship between returns (net value added) per manhour and manhours employed. He also posited a relationship between net costs per manhour and manhours employed. Both these variables diminished as employment increased, but net value added decreased more so that it cut the net cost per manhour relation from above and determined an equilibrium (as shown in Fig. 1 on p. 571) where net value added per manhour minus net costs per manhour, i.e. net profit per manhour, was zero. Total profit was the area between the returns and the cost curves and the profit share was the ratio of total profit to total factor cost.

The relations portrayed in Fig. 1 were not as simple as they looked. They seemed to Professor Reder to be first cousins to Marshall's 'Particular Expenses' curves. Professor Reder would propose to interpret them as follows : supposing the system to be put into equilibrium at any quantity of manhours, L_0, then at that value of L_0 there would be, for each firm, an equilibrium value (per manhour) of net value added and net cost. These equilibrium values might be arrayed *à la* Föhl from highest to lowest, generating his two curves for L_0. But at some other value, L_1, all relative prices might well be different. The net value added and net cost for each firm would also be different, and so would the rank order of firms in the net profit (per manhour) hierarchy. Hence in moving from L_0 to L_1 the firms would have to be re-arrayed and the curves reconstructed. Only if the equilibrium value of L was determined from another relationship — as in the Föhl model — might we determine the shapes and positions of the curves as in Fig. 1 and compute the relative shares.

As Professor Reder understood it, the model was strictly short-run. If so, entrepreneurs maximized by making marginal prime cost equal to marginal revenue, neglecting overheads. Accordingly, Professor Reder would suggest that Professor Föhl amend Fig. 1 to exclude interest from his cost relationship and replace the concept of profits with that of quasi-rents. This would not greatly alter the conclusions of his analysis though the expenditure plans of firms operating at short-run losses might differ from those making short-run profits.

Professor Föhl contended (rightly) that in order for the level of income to be determined by a conventional Keynesian model it was necessary to know the distribution of income since the level of consumption would vary with relative shares, the level of income being constant.

The relative shares depended upon the relationship portrayed in Fig. 1. These relationships in turn depended upon the technological history of the economy ; upon its history of capital accumulation ; upon the extent to which collective bargaining forced the more profitable firms to share their differential profits with their workers, etc. . . . Professor Föhl rightly stressed the importance of these sources of differential profitability as determinants of the profit share and he was correct in disputing Kaldor's contention that 'the total profit is determined quite independently of the structure of these "quasi rents" . . . by the factors determining the share of investment in output and the proportion of profit saved'. In general, short-run variations in the ratio of investment to output and in the relationship in Fig. 1 interacted, and to determine an equilibrium position it was necessary that both sets of variables be taken into account.

However, Professor Föhl's statement (p. 554) that 'contrary to marginalist theory, which only tried to explain functional distribution in the long run, [his] diagram was able to show the distribution in the short-run transitory period for equilibrium of employment in the Keynesian sense as well as for all possible situations of disequilibrium' was surely wrong. That which explained all conceivable states of affairs explained none ; if the theory was to have empirical content it had to be incompatible with some observations.

Professor Reder suspected that the above quotation was not intended literally because in sections VI and VII Professor Föhl offered empirical evidence for his theory. In section VII he presented data concerning the shape of his net return curve of Fig. 1 from various sections of the German economy for 1963 and these showed that the curve was negatively inclined as posited in his theory. Professor Reder did not feel as surprised at this result as apparently Professor Föhl had been (p. 562 in the paper). But he was puzzled by Professor Föhl's statement that the high degree of concentration of profits in certain branches of industry made 'the economy's demand for labour much more sensitive to a variation of total cost to total expenditure than would have been the case if the profit line [had been] widely horizontal with a steep decline at its end '. The analysis underlying this statement required considerable elaboration.

The main empirical implication of the paper was that the variation in the dispersion of profits (or rather quasi-rents) among firms was a more important determinant of the profit share than alternative variables such as the ratio of investment to output *à la* Kaldor. The test of such an hypothesis — not yet made — would be to compare (i) the correlation over time and/or in a cross-section between profit dispersion (among firms) and profit share for the economy and (ii) a parallel correlation between profit share and the investment-output ratio. It was possible that the latter could better predict variations in the profit share than profit dispersion, by raising the average profit per manhour for each firm proportionately but holding interfirm

577

dispersion constant. But the reverse was also possible, and both factors might contribute to an explanation of the behaviour of the profit share. Only time and hard work could tell.

Professor Bronfenbrenner thought that Professor Föhl was only half right in supposing that marginal analysis was entirely short-run analysis. Marginal analysis was also long-run. On the other hand profit maximizing and marginal analysis applied in the short run too. But there was then a residual and this corresponded to the profits which Professor Föhl had in mind.

In the long run, Professor Föhl had said, there was a certain level of employment and he proposed the income distribution which gave that level of employment. This was what he meant by the scale of output having been neglected. This interpretation seemed to Professor Bronfenbrenner to be rather Kaldorian. Professor Föhl brought in whole series of profits as a vector, thus modifying the Kaldorian scheme. What was there in the long run which resulted in full employment, or the provision of an optimum degree of unemployment ?

Professor Jean Marchal said that he rather fancied the central idea, the necessity of introducing a distribution function, in Professor Föhl's model. But the function which Professor Föhl proposed seemed to him too crude as it related only to primary distribution, in other words only to two kinds of income, profits, and other factor incomes. Small entrepreneurs' and self-employed peoples' incomes could not fit into this distinction. Besides, Professor Marchal would not put interest and labour incomes into the same category; interest on loan capital was charged on profits and distribution was a two-time process : first, profits, gross of interest versus labour incomes; in a second stage interest was paid by profit-earners according to conditions on the capital market.

Professor Föhl had nevertheless been obliged to consider personal distribution later when he turned from primary distribution to consumption and investment. Professor Marchal would agree on the necessity of substituting personal for functional distribution but in so doing had not Professor Föhl overlooked two difficulties ? He had not tried to define homogeneous categories of income recipients in personal distribution. He made use of constant coefficients and had said that in order to step from functional to personal distribution 'one could allocate functional incomes to certain interesting groups of households, e.g. the households of dependent working people and the households of the self-employed. This could be done by means of coefficients which (one could) compute from statistics of the actual distribution of wealth to the different groups' (p. 556). Professor Marchal would object to using constants for this purpose because this distribution was influenced by the level of national income and by exogenous factors.

Professor Marchal turned to Professor Föhl's three conditions of total equilibrium of employment (listed p. 557). He had no objection to the first Keynesian one. About the third, $D_L = S_L$, i.e. equating supply and demand for labour, he thought that full employment was not a point of equilibrium if there were strong trade unions since full employment would mean cost inflation.

In order to take into account the scale of returns, Professor Föhl had proposed as his second condition an equilibrium ratio of profits to national income $\overline{P}$, at which there was full employment. Professor Marchal had found this very interesting. He wondered, however, whether the same reasoning could apply to wages. There was also a scale of wages according to skill, occupations, etc. Would there not be thus an equilibrium condition of a mininum wage share ? If so, what then would be the relationship between these two conditions ?

Professor Preiser said that, if he understood him rightly, Professor Föhl could not agree with the Kaldorian approach nor with the productivity approach because in neither theory had he been able to find the missing link in the usual models, namely a behaviour equation about the distribution of profits and factor incomes. Professor Preiser would agree with him.

Now, in order fully to understand Professor Föhl one had to remember that he defined profits in a narrow sense, excluding interest. Thus, if we had perfect competition, profits became zero and it seemed that we could not then get an equation about distribution at all. But there were always differential profits which could be shown by comparing the returns of the individual firms and plotting a curve which, as Professor Reder has rightly said, was like the Marshallian particular expense curve. Professor Föhl had referred to this scale of returns. Although Professor Preiser thought this correct, he would rather follow another line, as he had already pointed out in the course of the discussion of Professor Bronfenbrenner's paper.

Professor Delivanis referred to Professor Föhl's statement that the incentive to invest resulted from the interaction of profits and interest (p. 547 in the paper). It seemed to him, nevertheless, that under permanent inflationary conditions many investments were made not with a view to anticipated profits but to making capital gains or to avoiding the consequences of inflation on the real value of cash holdings.

Professor Solow thought that Professor Föhl's Fig. 1 was an attractive way of studying income distribution. Professor Föhl, however, had availed himself of the theorists' licence of making things smooth. He had first drawn the uppermost curve of net returns, firms being arrayed according to their ranking in value added per manhour, then the curve κ on which presumably each point represented the same firm as on the curve above. But there was nothing to guarantee that it would be smooth. The curve might rise to cross the curve ϵ.

Another difficulty was that changes might occur in the economy so as to make the ϵ- and κ-curves shift in unpredictable ways. For instance, the κ-curve would shift peculiarly if wage rates rose and interest rates fell. One ought not to abandon this way of looking at distribution, but it was a radically simplified view and it had to be remembered that the passage from

U

micro- to macro-economics here did not evade difficulties in an economy with many firms and many industries.

Professor Föhl wished first to explain why he thought that the scale per manhour might be called a missing link. The beginning of the search for this element went back nearly thirty years, to the time when Keynes in his *General Theory*, confining himself to a two-sector model, defined the conditions of the equilibrium of employment, a conception which later on found its convincing expression in Klein and Samuelson's famous graph. Professor Föhl said that his ambition, even before the *General Theory* had been published and ever since, had been to deduce these conditions of equilibrium for a three-sector model consisting of a least two groups of households besides the group of the firms, i.e. a model which could at the same time indicate something about the distribution of the national income to these groups.

In order to make such a simple model consistent, one needed not only the consumption functions of the two groups of households and an investment function of some kind, but also an independently given distribution function so as to know how the total income earned in the firms was split in its two branches, the incomes of the groups of households, i.e. the entrepreneurs, and the working class. Many attempts had been made to find this missing distribution function. The authors of the theory of monopoly degree, especially Professor Preiser and Professor Kalecki, based it on the scarcity profits of monopolists which, however, were just one element and did not seem to Professor Föhl to explain much. For a long while he had tried to bring in the cost-difference profits by referring to the Barone function mentioned in Professor Krelle's paper. This, however, only held for one single commodity. It became evident that the consumers' preferences for the different goods offered by the firms played a leading role in determining the firms' profits and that consumers' preferences, monopoly positions and Barone cost-differences had to be combined in order to arrive at a sufficiently realistic distribution function.

This was what Professor Föhl had aimed at by plotting the returns per manhour of the different firms and the cost per manhour over the manhours employed. In this graph, surprisingly, areas below and between the curves pictured macro-economic distribution, and at the same time this led to a function of entrepreneurs' behaviour, namely a functional relation between national income and the entrepreneurs' demand for labour. This was exactly what he had been looking for to make his three-sector model consistent and therefore he believed the scale of returns to be the missing link.

The value of the abscissa of the point of intersection of the returns and the cost curves indicated the entrepreneurs' total demand for labour. For a given cost curve the volumes of employment would be determined by the shape of the curve of returns. This meant that a structurally given volume of gross profits had to be formed in order to reach a certain level of employment. The distribution between profits in factor income had thus to be structurally given if equilibrium was to be sustained at any chosen level of employment.

Whereas the Keynesian equilibrium of employment meant only that entrepreneurs had no incentive to employ more or less labour than they had done up till then, i.e. a situation which could persist at any level of employment, Professor Föhl's internal equilibrium indicated a situation where the entrepreneurs' demand for labour was equal to the supply of labour so that, even for a model without trade unions, no reaction on the level of wages resulted. This might answer Professor Jean Marchal's question regarding the three equilibrium conditions on page 557 of his paper.

The equilibrium value of maximal income thus depended on the shape, slope, and position of the returns curve for each level of employment. Starting from a situation of full employment, a shift upwards meant that even the entrepreneur employing the last available manhour would make a profit ; the entrepreneurs' total demand for labour would exceed the supply of labour, wages would rise and, for a given propensity to consume on the part of the wage-earners, consumption expenditure and prices would rise, thus leading to inflation. A downward shift conversely meant a situation of underemployment. Therefore Professor Föhl hoped that Professor Reder would admit that his graph was able to depict any possible situation of disequilibrium. Professor Föhl wished to stress that the scale of returns was a demand curve, namely a demand curve for labour. When plotting the curve of returns each firm had been given a place on the abscissa measuring exactly the amount of manhours this firm wanted to employ with a given capital according to marginal productivity theory. This might answer another of Professor Reder's doubts. If this was convincing to him he must agree that the inclination of the scale of returns at its right-hand end must have no small bearing on the reaction of employment to a shift of the return and cost curves. If, for instance, the cost curve remained in the same position while the curve of returns made a parallel downwards, employment would fall very little if the curve of returns was steep at its end. On the contrary employment would be significantly reduced if the curve of return was as flat as it seemed in the German economy.

Of course both curves might change in shape and position as Professor Solow had pointed out. Professor Föhl was quite aware of this contingency. He was still unable to predict how they would change, but empirical research could be done on the reactions of the scale of returns to innovations, changes in the tax system, etc. Once this was done one would be able to predict with some accuracy the effect of, say, a new invention or a planned alteration of the tax system on distribution, employment, and growth.

Professor Föhl did not agree with Professor Reder's remark that his model was strictly short-run. This was only true on the assumption of a given shape and position of the curves. One could, however, use it for developing a growth theory by making empirically tested or at least plausible assumptions on the influence of investment on the shapes of the curves. In studying the influence of changing inclination of the scale of returns on the growth rate he had tried to give a rough outline for further research.

It might appear that the suggestion to introduce into the model the changes in the scale of returns caused by investment, by an increasing saturation of the consumers' demand for specific commodities and by the shifting over of the consumers' demand to new commodities, would make the long-run analysis overcomplicated. Professor Föhl thought, however, that what was complicated was not his way of representing the interdependence but rather, as Kaldor had said, the fact that in our changing economy 'everything depended on past history, on how the collection of equipment goods had been built up'. What mainly depended on the past history of the economy was the distribution function, the ratio P/Y, which was an indispensable element of any three-sector model. This was what he had wanted to make evident by the scale of returns.

It had been suggested by both Professor Reder and Professor Bronfenbrenner that somehow marginal theory should be brought in again. Professor Föhl said that he would welcome any attempt to find a workable solution. Once it had been made clear on what factors the distribution function depended, one might be able to compress the result into some suitable function of the Cobb–Douglas type. But such a formula would by no means be simple. One could of course, as Professor Bronfenbrenner had said during the discussion of his own paper, consider an assumed percentage of profit over interest by choosing the exponents n and m of L and K so that $n+m>1$. But was this not the theory of the monopoly degree? What one really wanted was exponents in the Cobb–Douglas function which were themselves endogenous variables of the system linked to the other factors by just those functional relations which he had tried to represent by the scale of returns.

Chapter 21

THE SIZE DISTRIBUTION OF EARNINGS [1]

BY

M. W. REDER
Stanford University

INTRODUCTORY

THE purpose of this paper is to develop a theory of the size distribution of earnings or income from work, as distinguished from property income. The theory that is to be sketched is abstract and limited in reference to positions of long-run equilibrium ; i.e. it purports to show how earnings would be distributed as various assumptions are made about long-run forces. By long-run forces, we mean those forces that determine relative factor rewards in a neo-classical stationary state or on a balanced growth path.

Our analysis is quite far removed from recorded data on the size distribution of (annual) incomes. It is concerned with a model that relates the parameters of hypothetical distributions of expected lifetime earnings to (1) related parameters of distributions of personal characteristics that are presumed to act as causal determinants of the distribution of earnings and (2) the characteristics of the reward (payoff) mechanism implied by the demand functions for factor services. Specifically, in Section I we attempt to show how the nature of the preference for superior *vis-à-vis* inferior workers affects the distribution of expected lifetime earnings under conditions of long-run equilibrium and certainty, and to deduce some empirical implications of the analysis. In Section II, we attempt to show how still under conditions of long-run equilibrium and certainty, the distribution of inherited ability influences the distribution of earnings and how differences in training among individuals interact with differences in inherited ability to affect the distribution of earnings. Training and

[1] This paper is part of the research done on a Ford Faculty Fellowship in 1961–62. The final product has been greatly improved by the suggestions of a number of the participants at the Conference. The written comments of Professors E. H. Phelps Brown and B. F. Haley were especially helpful as were the oral remarks of Professor Armen Alchian. Of course, the author remains solely responsible for remaining errors and infelicities of expression.

inherited ability act upon the earnings distribution from the supply side ; but the effect of their action depends upon the intensity of the demand for superior performance. Therefore we must also consider the interaction of the forces emanating from the two sides of the market. In Section III we abandon the assumption of certainty — though not that of long-run equilibrium — and investigate the implications of risk and risk-hedging for the distribution of lifetime earnings.

Before commencing the argument, let us define terms and specify assumptions :

(1) We abstract explicitly from the (important) forces that bear upon the earnings distribution during the course of movement from one stationary state or growth path to another. The earnings concept appropriate to this (long-run equilibrium) frame of reference may be defined in either of two ways : (a) as annual earnings that are the same for every year of an individual's working lifetime or (b) as capitalized lifetime earnings. This implies, *inter alia*, that we ignore that part of earning differences that results from individuals being in different phases of their lifetime earning cycles.[1]

(2) Unless otherwise specified, pure competition in all markets is assumed.

(3) For simplicity we assume that any distribution of earnings can be completely described by two parameters, which we shall call the 'mean' and the 'dispersion'. 'Inequality' increases with dispersion.

(4) All individuals maximize their earnings, and earnings are identical with 'net advantages' ; i.e. they include all non-pecuniary satisfactions.

(5) Except where the contrary is specifically stated, it will be assumed that all individuals can borrow capital for training purposes on identical terms.

I. THE DISPERSION OF LIFETIME EARNINGS UNDER CONDITIONS OF CERTAINTY: DEMAND CONSIDERATIONS

To facilitate discussion, consider an economy in which everyone follows the same occupation or, alternatively, assume that we are

---

[1] This aspect of the matter is well discussed by Jacob Mincer, 'Investment in Human Capital and Personal Income Distribution', *Journal of Political Economy*, August 1958, pp. 281–302.

analysing the distribution of earnings within a specific occupation. In order to fix ideas let us treat a foot-race as a paradigm, with the prizes awarded to the various runners being analogous to economic rewards. The dispersion of these rewards will depend crucially upon the basis for distributing them ; if prizes depend only upon the order (rank) in which the runners finish, the distribution may be quite different than if they are a function solely of the differences in runners' speed, or of some combination of differences in both speed and rank.

Let us suppose that the prizes offered are employment contracts to deliver messages. The economy under consideration is one in which messages must be delivered on foot and great store is placed on being able to have one's messages delivered more swiftly than those of other people. Individuals wishing the services of particular runners for (say) a given day, bid for them in a competitive market. Since we assume that the speeds of the various runners are determined once for all by the outcome of the race, and that there are no problems arising from chance variations in performance or from variations in effort, the daily wage (or capitalized life earnings) of a runner will, given the state of demand for runners' services, depend entirely upon the outcome of the race.

In general, equilibrium implies that each employer of runners (labour) be satisfied with the speed (quality) of those he hires, given the prices associated with the various qualities. This means that the demand prices for different qualities — indivisibilities aside — must be proportional to the marginal utilities of different speeds to each employer. Thus the difference between the reward of the fastest runner and that of the next, between those of the second and third place runners, etc., reflects the marginal utility of greater speed to employers. Given tastes and the level and distribution of wealth, the amount of each prize — the wage of each runner — is determined.

If (1) preference functions are identical among employers of runners, and (2) the distribution of wealth (among these employers) is given and (3) better service quality (greater speed) is a superior good, then the fastest runner will be employed by the wealthiest individual, etc.[1] Also, if each employer hires no more than one runner and the *per capita* wealth of the employers is given, then *the dispersion of runners' wages will increase as the dispersion of the wealth distribution increases.* Further, given the dispersion of wealth among employers and the assumption that greater speed is a superior good,

---

[1] Assume for simplicity that each would-be employer hires no more than one runner at a time.

the dispersion of wages will increase with their (the employers') per capita wealth.

The forces operative in this very abstract model throw some light upon those at work in determining the relative incomes of performers in highly competitive activities such as professional athletics, concert and theatrical performing, real estate selling, practise of law, etc. All of these activities are characterized by (a) the existence of great differences in the demand price for association with a higher ranked performer (or team) than with a lower ranked and (b) strong consensus in the ranking of the various performers.

(a) *Variations in Demand Price*

Differences in demand for performers' services are usually expressed through differences in demand for tickets to their performances.[1] This in turn is reflected in the compensation of the performers. (Where a game has little public interest, e.g. soccer in the United States, the pecuniary rewards of proficiency are slight.) Differential demand prices for the services of lawyers, real estate salesmen, etc., usually reflect desire to share in their (differential) earnings.[2]

(b) *The Role of Consensus*

The above types of activity are characterized by a strong degree of consensus in ranking performers. There is *the* baseball team that won the World Series, there is *the* heavyweight (boxing) champion, etc. But what about teaching performance ? No one knows who is the world's best teacher, and (perhaps) no one cares. But knowing and caring are not independent ; e.g. local school boards, in setting teachers' salaries, are frequently insensitive to the importance of attracting better teachers. One reason for this is that there is no widely accepted way of demonstrating that 'superior' teachers, as these can be identified, have any pronounced tendency to produce superior students (judged by any given criterion). Coupled with this is disagreement as to what criteria should be used for judging students ; e.g. 'well-roundedness' versus academic performance, etc.

[1] I.e. what is rewarded is 'Box Office Appeal' rather than proficiency *per se.* There is a strong relation between the two, but the cases where they diverge cause much comment and bitterness.

[2] The sharing often takes place through commission arrangements of various kinds : lawyers often accept compensation in damage suits as a percentage of the awards ; salesmen get a percentage of the proceeds of their sales, etc.

Ambiguity of ends interacts with uncertainty of means to produce relative indifference toward alleged differences in quality. Hence the dispersion of teachers' earnings is far less than that of trial lawyers.

Though disagreement on ranking is quite different from indifference toward it, the effect on relative incomes is similar. Consider : suppose some patrons strongly preferred one painter while others (equally wealthy) preferred another. The demand prices for their paintings would be the same as though all patrons liked both painters equally well, provided that each person bought the same number of paintings in both cases.

(c) *Economies of Scale and Quantitative Differences in Productivity*

The paradigm of the foot-race tends to focus attention upon the qualitative differences among occupational practitioners — their relative ranking — rather than the quantitative aspects of the matter. Obviously, this is not always appropriate. If the best violinist can play in only one place at one time, then only the person bidding the most for his services (and his guests) will hear him. Clearly there will be a market for inferior violinists. But if, through recordings, the best can be heard in many places simultaneously, his productive capacity will be enormously increased and he will become a devastating competitor for inferior artists.

Obviously, the economies of scale created by sound and visual reproduction have changed drastically the earnings distribution for entertainers. A small number of highly successful performers now earn stupendous incomes while most others are condemned to a semi-professional existence in which their meagre earnings as performers are combined with other gainful employment.[1] This situation is very different from that (say) among surgeons, where only a few persons can be cared for by any one man.

(d) *The Pay-off Mechanism: Quality versus Quantity*

In the paradigm of the foot-race, relative rewards may depend upon the rank of the runners, their relative speeds, or both. But apart from

---

[1] Cases where reproduction makes for such huge economies of scale as to make it possible for everyone to enjoy 'the best' may be termed satiation cases. In such cases, all or most persons can indulge their taste for superior quality to the point where its marginal utility is at or close to zero. This ignores the great premium some persons put on 'live' performance, but this abstraction does not really affect our argument.

the requirement that faster runners receive more than slower, our argument does not require that we go behind the employers' demand functions. The relative premium placed 'by the market' on the services of the fastest runner *vis-à-vis* the next swiftest will reflect both the marginal utility, if any, of having messages delivered faster than anyone else (e.g. for reasons of prestige), and that of faster communication.

If running speed alone determined the speed of message delivery, and the marginal utility of increased communication speed were the same for all persons and independent of the rate of speed, then the relation between the dispersion of running speeds and the dispersion of earnings would be simple : the latter would be the same as the former up to a multiplicative constant. But these conditions will not always be satisfied. One type of situation where they would be satisfied is where the marginal physical productivities of various individuals can be measured directly (i.e. without making use of information concerning their earnings), and their dispersion (presumably) equals the dispersion of individual earnings up to a multiplicative constant (which would represent the marginal revenue from selling the product).[1]

However, more often one encounters situations where the marginal physical productivities of individuals cannot be ascertained (directly) and the best that can be done is to measure various physical or mental attributes of individuals that are presumably related to their productivities.[2] One may try to relate differences in these attributes to differences in earnings, but notoriously the relationship is complicated. The main reasons for this complexity are (1) the marginal contribution of any given attribute in a particular occupation (e.g. intelligence as measured on an I.Q. scale) may diminish sharply beyond a certain level and (2) the marginal utility of superior performance may diminish — after a certain level is reached. Where either of these statements applies, the dispersion of rewards may differ greatly from that of any single personal attribute (or average of attributes) that is presumably associated with inter-personal differences in marginal productivity.

To put the same idea differently : the distribution of earnings is related to the distribution of any set of personal capacities only after the latter are subjected to one or more transformations reflecting the

[1] The relation of earnings differences to quantitative differences in personal productivities is discussed by A. D. Roy, 'The Distribution of Earnings and of Individual Output', *Economic Journal*, September 1950, pp. 489–505.

[2] E.g. measures of physical strength, intelligence, etc.

marginal productivity of the capacity in terms of the service for which the reward is paid. This observation is hardly startling, but it dispels the 'paradox' (noted by many writers [1]) that while measurements of skill and ability are distributed normally, the distribution of earnings to which they give rise is skewed.

(e) *The Scale of Operations and Marginal Productivity*

Now let us approach the real world more closely and consider why demand prices for the services of some occupations are so much more variable with respect to differences in 'quality' than in others. In this subsection of the paper, we shall be concerned primarily with the (derived) demand of employers rather than the direct demand of consumers. But this introduces no difference of principle.

Some outstanding cases of widely unequal earnings, within given occupations, arise when individuals operate virtually alone, and not as part of a team. Salesmen of real estate, life insurance, securities, automobiles, etc., are instances.[2] In these occupations it is customary for individuals to be paid, partly or entirely, on the basis of commissions from sales made. This is not accidental; the marginal product of a salesman (in these lines) to a firm is easily measured, and a successful salesman can readily go elsewhere (including into business for himself) if he is offered less. But before probing more deeply into the case of commission salesmen, let us examine another occupation where rewards are very unequal.

Because of their great dispersion, it might be supposed that the earnings of corporate executives are determined by roughly the same forces as those of salesmen-entrepreneurs. However, the available evidence suggests that the compensation of corporate executives reflects, to a considerable degree, factors other than disguised profit sharing.[3] The most important piece of this evidence is that the relationship between executive compensation and profits, sales constant,

---

[1] S. Lebergott, 'The Shape of the Income Distribution', *American Economic Review*, June 1959, pp. 328–347, contains a lucid discussion of this problem along with a full bibliography.

[2] Of course many salesmen (e.g. in department stores) are akin to clerks and work on a straight salary with little or no commission on their sales. Sales jobs of this sort occur where dollar sales per hour are small and the return to superior skill is negligible.

[3] See, for example, D. R. Roberts, *Executive Compensation*, Free Press, Glencoe, Ill., 1959, chap. iii; A. Patton, *Men, Money and Motivation*, New York, 1961; and J. W. McGuire, J. S. Y. Chiu, and A. O. Elbing, 'Executive Incomes, Sales and Profits', *American Economic Review*, September 1962, pp. 752–761.

is much weaker than that between executive compensation and sales, profits constant.[1]

Superficially, this might seem inconsistent with the explanation of the dispersion of individual salesmen's earnings ; i.e. salesmen's rewards are strongly associated with the profits of the enterprise. However, a reconciliation is possible : the marginal product of an executive to a firm is not indicated by the *amount* of profit that the firm earns, but by the *difference* in its profit that results from his guidance. Clearly, precise measurement of this difference is impossible. However, corporate directors act as though they had an estimate of it when they choose a top executive (or team) and establish his level of compensation. Whom they can obtain for the job varies, to some extent, with the compensation they are willing to offer, and in the selection process they balance cost against return in the usual manner. The greater the size of the difference in profit that it is believed would result from obtaining a better executive, the greater the increase in salary that a rational firm will pay in order to obtain him. Now if we suppose that executive skill and capital [2] are co-operant factors in producing profits (i.e. a given degree of skill can generate more profit the greater the value of the resources over which it is exercised), it follows that the marginal product of an executive would have a strong positive association with the value of the resources under his control ; i.e. with his 'scale of operations'. The current profits of the firm need not, in the first approximation, have anything to do with his compensation ; a good executive is worth as much to a company in holding its losses to $10 million when, with ordinary management they might have been $15 million, as in augmenting its profits by $5 million.

However, there is a (relatively weak) relation between current profits and executive compensation stemming from the desire of employers of executives to create a pecuniary incentive to maximum effort.[3] Another link between profits and compensation is the liquid asset position of the firm ; unprofitable firms are more likely than others to be pinched for working capital and inclined to hold down

---

[1] That is, in correlating measures of executive compensation with both the profits and the sales of the firms that employ them, one finds a much stronger association (in a given year) between compensation and sales, profits constant, than between compensation and profits, sales constant.

[2] 'Capital' is used here as a synonym for the value of resources under the control of the chief executive of the firm. So defined, capital is highly correlated with sales. Nevertheless, interfirm differences in turnover could becloud this relationship and, in principle, should be allowed for.

[3] See, for example, L. R. Burgess, *Top Executive Pay Package*, Free Press, Glencoe, Ill., 1963, pp. 40–48.

salaries; this tendency becomes stronger the longer the period during which a firm has been making losses.[1] Finally, where the labour services of its executives are a major part of a firm's assets (e.g. a firm created to sell the professional services of one or several doctors, lawyers, actors, salesmen, etc.) its income depends mainly on the successful performance of its 'executives'. In such cases wages and profits become intertwined and considerations both of solvency and risk sharing require that 'executive' compensation be closely geared to current profits with the 'scale of operations' effect becoming negligible.[2]

In short, if executive compensation were studied over the whole range of firm sizes, and not confined to large corporations as it has been, I surmise that the regression of compensation on profits [3] would be very large for small firms, but would shrink as sales rose. However, the partial regression of compensation on sales, profits constant, would rise with sales.[4]

So far we have discussed the scale of operations effect only in relation to executive compensation. However, this effect is pertinent to explanations of relative earnings at all levels of an organizational hierarchy, and a number of writers have used it.[5] Unfortunately these discussions have stressed the relation of an employee's relative compensation (within an organization) to the *number* of his

[1] This relationship is probably curvilinear, being (possibly) quite strong for firms with big losses, but negligible among firms showing a profit.

[2] An employer's scale of operations may be indicated as follows : imagine that a firm's operations may be divided into a number of processes such that every job can affect the outcome of at least one. Also suppose that a firm decides how much the performance of each job in the firm can affect the net revenue yielded by each of its processes. Then the scale of operations effect of a particular job increases, *cet. par.*, with the number of processes affected, and with the amount (in net revenue terms) by which it affects each one.

[3] For very small businesses whose outputs are services and whose only source of labour is their owners, the correlation between sales and 'profits' might be so high as to make partial correlations involving their separate variation meaningless.

[4] An alternative explanation of the inter-relation of firm size, profits, and executive compensation might be the following : executive compensation is related to 'permanent' profits (rather than current profits) which in turn is highly correlated with firm size. ('Permanent' profits, analogous to Friedman's permanent income, would be measured by a weighted moving average of lagged profits.) Under competitive conditions, in the long run there is a very strong correlation between firm size and *amount* of profit (not rate of return) so that it may be difficult, in practice, to test this hypothesis against the 'scale of operations' hypothesis. The two hypotheses are not incompatible and both may contribute to explaining interfirm variations in executive compensation.

[5] One outstanding example is R. H. Tuck, *An Essay on the Economic Theory of Rank*, Basil Blackwell, Oxford, 1954; Thomas Mayer, 'The Distribution of Ability and Earnings', *Review of Economics and Statistics*, May 1960, pp. 189–195, contains a very good general discussion of this subject. Also see H. A. Simon, 'The Compensation of Executives', *Sociometry*, March 1957, pp. 32–35.

subordinates rather than to the *value* of the resources that he and they utilize. Surely, a superior supervisor of five diamond cutters is 'worth' more than a superior supervisor of five pick-and-shovel coal miners. But, if the five miners are working with the whole panoply of modern tools and equipment, the value of their gross output and of the tools they employ may make 'superiority' in their supervisor quite as important as in the supervisor of the diamond cutters.

The essence of the matter can be seen most clearly if we treat each human agent of production as though he were an independent contractor (entrepreneur) hired to perform a particular task.[1] The employer behaves as though he thought the particular task could be done more or less well, and that to secure a man who would do the task better, more must be paid. How much more the employer will pay for a superior employee depends upon how important it is to him that the task be done better ; the extra cost of getting a presumptively superior performer tends to be equalized at the margin to the expected value of having him.

The value of the director of a productive process to an employer depends upon the expected dispersion of performance levels considered possible. If the process is purely mechanical with little opportunity for discretion, then all that is wanted is willingness and ability to follow directions ; greater capacity than this is of no utility. The greater the opportunity for unusual human capacity of any kind — but usually qualities of intelligence — to add to the level of performance, the greater (*cet. par.*) the desire to secure (and reward) superiority.[2] This aspect of a job we may term its 'sensitivity' ; the sensitivity of a job varies with the expected dispersion of performance levels, given a lower cut-off point at a minimum level of acceptability. In general greater sensitivity and larger scale of operations go together, but there are exceptions.

As Mayer points out, the scale of operations effect is very similar to what writers on job evaluation refer to as 'responsibility'.[3] In

[1] This parallels the distinction made by H. A. Simon ('A Formal Theory of the Employment Relationship', *Econometrica*, July 1951, pp. 293–305) between an employment contract and a sales contract.

[2] I am indebted to my colleague, Professor Paul David, for discussion on this point.

[3] T. Mayer, *op. cit.*, especially footnotes 15–18. S. Lebergott, 'The Shape of the Income Distribution', *op. cit.* pp. 340–343, develops a special application of the scale of operations effect to explain the overall skewness of the income distribution. He argues that the credit rationing methods of lending agencies act to expand the resources (scale) of those adjudged more credit-worthy relative to those adjudged less.

terms of price theory, the scale of operations effect amounts to the following : the greater the intensity with which a particular job is used in a given productive process — i.e. the greater its average net value product — the greater is the gain to the employer from using better quality labour. In other words, the demand price for the labour used in a particular job will rise, *cet. par.*, with the value of the complementary resources employed. This, of course, implies nothing about the quantitative relations between factor inputs and product outputs that are the essence of the 'laws of return'. However, it does account for the inverse association that has been found between sales per dollar of wages and hourly earnings of 'unskilled' labour ; [1] it also accounts for the association of size of firm with level of executive compensation noted above.

Since this result may be new to the reader, let me describe its theoretical underpinning in somewhat more detail. It is hypothesized that for each job in a firm, there is a range of net value products ; net value product equals profit minus compensation of job holder. Where the firm lands in this net value product range depends upon how well the job is performed. To maximize profit, the firm balances the gain from superior performance against the cost of obtaining it (i.e. against the extra compensation necessary to obtain a superior performer).

The range of net value products for any given job will depend partly upon the complementary inputs with which the employer finds it profitable to equip the incumbent. In particular, we assume that the range will be greater, *cet. par.*, the greater the value of the complementary resources used ; this is the scale of operations effect. The greater this range, the greater the premium employers will pay for superior performance.

The scale of operations affects the dispersion of earnings via its effect on the dispersion of the value of complementary resources used by different workers in the 'same' occupation; the greater the dispersion of the value of the complementary resources used, *cet. par.*, the greater the dispersion of the earnings within the occupation. As between occupations, the higher the average value of the complementary resources used by workers in a given occupation, *cet. par.*, the higher the average compensation within it. [2]

But value of complementary resources is not the only determinant

---

[1] See S. H. Slichter, 'Notes on the Structure of Wages', *Review of Economics and Statistics*, February 1950, pp. 80–91.

[2] I am indebted here, as elsewhere in this section, for the comments of A. A. Alchian.

of the range of net value products attainable from a given job ; there is also the 'sensitivity' of the job. Formally, we might define the sensitivity of a job as an indicator of the range of attainable net value products, holding value of complementary resources constant ; however, this does not help much. It is perhaps more useful to define a routine or insensitive (low sensitive) job as one where there is but a negligible marginal product to a higher degree of any aptitude beyond that commonly possessed by persons filling such jobs.

Bank-teller is a good example of a job with low sensitivity, though utilizing a large volume of complementary resources. Despite numerous jokes about the dangers of absconding, banks do not normally seek or pay high salaries to unusually honest men in order to induce them to become tellers. Character references, a bond, and minimum standards of aptitude and education suffice. Toward the other extreme, the job of (independent) salesman is highly sensitive. Differences in complementary resources used among salesmen are small and (probably) not closely related to differences in earnings which mainly reflect differing degrees of 'salesmanship'.

In concluding this subsection, let us note one further implication of the scale of operations effect ; i.e. the partial correlation of compensation per worker with firm size is greater the higher the organizational rank of the employee. Consider, the effect of a company's chief operating official applies to the whole of its output. But the scale of operations of the next tier of officials is not uniquely determined by the size of the firm. The largest firm might consist of the same number of (say) divisions as the next largest, but with each division larger ; however, it might consist of more divisions, with each one no larger than its counterpart in the smaller firm. In the former case, the scale of operations effect would lead the larger firm to pay higher wages to its second rank personnel ; in the latter case it would not.

At the very highest rank, the difference between resources managed per 'top executive' in very large firms (say the 200 largest corporations) and those managed per 'top executive' throughout the rest of the economy far exceeds the differences in capital per gainful worker in these two sectors. This would suggest that the scale of operations effect would be far stronger among top-ranking employees than among employees as a whole. This, in turn, would suggest that variations in compensation among firms of different sizes are much greater at high organizational ranks than at low ones. All this would seem to be consistent with the real world — at least at first glance.

However, much data collection is needed before this statement can be regarded as anything more than a conjecture.[1]

II. THE ROLE OF SUPPLY

In the previous section we argued as though the distribution of skill and ability among a work force was completely independent of the reward for using it. Clearly this is not the case. Demand conditions, especially the willingness of employers to substitute (directly or indirectly) inferior for superior labour services in response to variations in relative rates of reward, determine the premia for superior qualities of labour service, given their supplies. But, in the long run, supplies are not data.

If each individual's capacity (and desire) for rendering labour service were immutably determined by his genetic characteristics, then supply could not respond to relative rewards. But, in general, if a given degree of a particular capacity is highly rewarded, investment in training can often increase its supply — or that of good substitutes — thereby reducing its relative reward. In general, the earnings of a given degree, y, of any capacity, A (call it A_y), cannot exceed those of B_z (or A_z) by more than the marginal cost of transforming (training) persons with B_z to A_y.

To appreciate the role of training in limiting the dispersion of earnings, suppose a given set of employer demands initially confronts a group of individuals with identical training but varying native talents.[2] (The lower the elasticity of substitution on the demand side among different kinds and qualities of service and the greater the dispersion of degrees of each kind of native talent, *cet. par.*, the greater will be the dispersion of earnings.[3]) In the distribution of earnings

---

[1] There are, so far as I am aware, no studies comparing resource quantities controlled by persons of comparable organizational rank in different size firms. However, the data on concentration of capital and employment, at least in the American economy, suggest the allegation in the text. Similarly, what is said about interfirm variation in compensation levels, at different ranks, is consistent with 'general knowledge' of wage and salary structures.

[2] Native talent is obviously not an easy concept to define, and its proper definition varies with the problem. For this purpose, we may suppose it to be the capacity of individuals at any age at which further training or education ceases to be universal. Obviously, this definition ignores all-important differences in training within the family whose effects are interrelated with those of genetic factors.

[3] If employers generally accepted inferior services as substitutes for superior ones because of arbitrarily small differences in price, the dispersion of earnings would be zero (in long-run equilibrium), no matter how great the dispersion of talent. Conversely, if all individuals had the same native talent and training, the dispersion of earnings would be zero, no matter how anxious employers were to obtain superior quality.

that results, some differences (e.g. $A_y - B_z$), will exceed the marginal cost of transforming (through training) the lower earner into the higher. In order to reach equilibrium all such training opportunities must be exploited which will lower the earnings of the initial A_y's relative to those of the initial B_z's, thereby making the dispersion of earnings less than if training were technically impossible. The greater the price of the resources used in training and the greater the physical quantities needed to accomplish given results, the fewer will be the 'scarce native talents' subjected to competition from trained substitutes and the fewer the individuals whom it will pay to train in order that they might compete with initial high earners. Hence, the greater the general level of training costs, *cet. par.*, the greater the dispersion of earnings.

In practice, differences in earnings reflect differences both in the amount of capital invested in training and in native talent. Only if (1) native talent were the same for all individuals; (2) they all had the same tastes; and (3) could obtain capital for training on the same terms would their earnings be the same in long-run equilibrium.

It is probable that relatively high costs of securing capital for training are associated with relative deficiencies in native talent,[1] and also that perceptions of relative deficiencies in learning capacity tend to discourage investment in training the less talented.[2] In either case, it is likely that there will be a positive association of training, natural talent, and earnings.

(a) *Differential Access to Training*

Differential capacity of individuals (or their families) to finance or otherwise obtain access to training has been, historically, an integral part of the association of superiority in training, talent, and earnings. Consequently, it is reasonable to suppose that a reduction in the difference in the marginal costs of borrowing for training purposes (as between any pair of individuals) will alter their relative earnings. That is, a reduction in the dispersion of borrowing costs would tend to increase the relative amounts of training undertaken by the less

---

[1] This may be due to a correlation of genetically associated incapacity with low wealth of parents. Because of their poor credit standing, relatively poor parents can borrow for training their off-spring only at relatively high rates of interest, if at all, and hence are deterred from doing so. But irrespective of genetic factors, capacity to benefit from training is strongly associated with home environment, so that children of low-income families — who can't 'afford to invest in training' — appear, from an early age, to be relatively deficient in intellectual capacity.

[2] See G. S. Becker, 'Investment in Human Capital: A Theoretical Analysis', *Journal of Political Economy*, October 1962, Supplement, pp. 9–49.

talented who are also the relatively low earners, which would tend to raise the earnings of low earners relative to high earners. However, if, initially, native talent had a negative correlation with access to training, the effect of making access to training more equal might be to increase the inequality of earnings.

A further analytical consideration, and one with considerable practical importance, complicates the relation between unequal access to training and unequal distribution of earnings. The relative returns to native talent and training will surely vary as investment in training becomes greater and more widespread.[1] Jobs which have paid well in the past because of great training required, but demand relatively little native talent will decline in relative earning power *vis-a-vis* those requiring greater degrees of native talent, as appropriately trained persons become more abundant. If it should happen that those individuals who initially got more training, because of superior access, should also happen to have more native talent, the effect of equalizing access to training might be to widen the dispersion of earnings and not the reverse.

That is, as the relative advantage (of the initial high earners) from greater training diminishes, the earning advantage from greater native ability may increase sufficiently (because of its increased scarcity relative to investment in training) to overbalance the equalizing force of the training factor.[2]

The practical importance of this point stems from the world-wide trend toward equalizing opportunities for education and training, at least within individual countries. On grounds both of ethics and efficiency, I approve of this trend. However, it is by no means clear that its consequences will be egalitarian ; i.e. that it will make the distribution of earnings more equal. As indicated in the previous paragraph, it is possible — though by no means certain — that reducing differences in access to opportunities for training (combined with an increase in the general level of training) will *increase* the

---

[1] It is important to note that this argument requires both an increase in total investment in training and making access to it more nearly equal. Most people intend both when they demand equal opportunity in education. It is unlikely that merely transferring opportunity for training without increasing the total 'amount' available, would have the possible effects alleged in the text.

[2] Though it is not likely, it is possible that as training became more abundant and more nearly equal, the relative value of training and native talent would so shift that the dispersion of earnings increased, even though the initial correlation between native talent and access to training had been negative. In such cases, individuals initially at the top of the earnings ladder would tend to sink to the bottom, and *vice versa.*

dispersion of earnings. A 'meritocracy' may be more just than an aristocracy of birth, but it is not clear that it will be more egalitarian.[1]

(b) *Native Talent*

In the discussion thus far we have treated native talent as though it had but one dimension. This obscures certain problems as well as being patently false. Accordingly, let us consider a two-dimensional (two-capacity) concept; let native talent be a vector of two components which might (in the paradigm of the foot-race) be called speed and endurance.

The difference between the one- and two-capacity cases arises from the possibility of various correlations between the capacities. If the correlation between them is very strong and positive, the two-capacity case degenerates to the one-capacity. But if the correlation is strongly negative and the two capacities are of roughly equal economic importance, this case will exhibit less dispersion of earnings than the one-capacity. For example, suppose that the capacities are so scaled that earnings are a function of the sum of the 'scores' on each. Then, if the summed scores of all individuals were equal, earnings would be distributed equally. Although negative correlation between two capacities would be an equalizing factor, it is not hard to construct examples where moving from a one-capacity to a two-capacity case would increase the dispersion of earnings even though there were negative rank correlations of these two capacities among individuals.[2] Increasing the number of capacities beyond two does not suggest qualitatively different results.[3]

Another important aspect of the earnings distribution is revealed by examining the case where 'capacity' is identified with ability to

[1] This point is analogous to an argument in A. D. Roy's interesting paper, 'Some Thoughts on the Distribution of Earnings', *Oxford Economic Papers*, June 1951, pp. 135–146.

[2] For instance, consider the case where the rewards are paid in the form of $1 for each 'point' on each capacity; the capacities have a bivariate normal distribution, with negative correlation and different variances, and the pay-off is on the sum of points. Suppose that, initially, earnings depended only upon the capacity with the smaller variance. Then the effect of introducing the second capacity into the pay-off mechanism upon the dispersion of earnings will depend upon the relative sizes of the two variances and the strength of the (negative) correlation. If the variance of the second capacity is sufficiently larger than that of the first, earnings dispersion could increase even with perfect negative correlation.

[3] For another discussion of the role of different capacities in determining relative earnings see J. Tinbergen, 'On the Theory of Income Distribution', pp. 243–263 of *Selected Papers*, North Holland Publishing Co., Amsterdam, 1959. Also B. Mandelbrot, 'Paretian Distributions Income Maximization', *Quarterly Journal of Economics*, February 1962, pp. 57–85. The analogy between 'capacities' and the 'factors' of factor analysis is quite obvious.

work in a particular occupation. Assume, for simplicity, that an individual can practise only one occupation at a time, and that the dispersion of capacity for occupation A is greater than for occupation B, where capacity is measured in 'points'. Then an increase in demand for the services of A relative to B will increase the value of a point of A capacity relative to a point of B capacity thereby increasing the overall dispersion of earnings ; the reverse will apply where there is an increased relative demand for B services. Clearly the overall size distribution of earnings will be affected by the inter-occupational pattern of demand for labour. The greater the tendency for employers to demand those services the capacity for whose production (allowing for training) varies greatly among persons, the greater the dispersion of income, and *vice versa*.[1]

(c) *Firm Sizes*

Given demand conditions, the smaller the dispersion of any one capacity (after optimum investment in training) the smaller will be the dispersion of rewards ; i.e. the smaller will be the difference between the market prices of the services of the best and those of the next best person, etc. Also a smaller dispersion of capacities will tend to promote a smaller dispersion of 'value of resources controlled' ; i.e. a reduction in dispersion of managerial capacity, *cet. par.*, will make it possible for owners of resources used in small-scale activities to obtain *relatively* better managers [2] thereby inducing relative expansion of these smaller enterprises. This will tend to reduce the dispersion of earnings among managers, and the dispersion of the sizes of the resources — firms — they direct. Thus, dispersion of firm sizes is increased by employer (resource owner) rigidity concerning the quality of managerial capacity and also by dispersion of managerial capacity.

III. RISK AND DISPERSION OF EARNINGS

(a) *The Significance of Risk Hedging*

Assume a situation similar in all respects to the foot-race discussed in Section I, except that there is uncertainty as to the outcome. The

---

[1] I do not elaborate on this point, despite its importance. One reason is that it would take us too far afield ; a second is that it is well discussed, though very briefly, by A. D. Roy, 'Some Thoughts on the Distribution of Earnings', *op. cit.*
[2] 'Manager' may refer to any human agent of production, but in this section we mean director of a firm. For more general discussion see Section I (c) above.

schedule of prizes is arbitrary; it may be anything from winner-take-all to equal shares. Assume the mathematical expectation of the speeds of the various runners to be equal so that, prior to the race, one runner's chance for prize money is as good as another's.

To avoid risk of faring badly in the race, the runners might, in principle, voluntarily enter into an insurance scheme such that the recipients of large prizes agree to give some (or even all) of the excess value of their prizes over the (pre-race) expected value to those whose prizes fall below the expected value. Thus the observed distribution of prizes (wealth) after the race might, in an extreme case, have nothing whatever to do with either the relative speeds of the runners or the characteristics of the schedule of prizes, but only upon the willingness of the runners to engage in mutual insurance, and the cost of doing so.[1]

If there were no costs associated with such insurance transactions then, under our restricted assumptions, observed inequalities of wealth would be due solely to the tastes of individuals for risk-bearing as these interact through a system of markets for shares in prize money. The significant element of cost in buying shares in another runner's prize is the adverse incentive effect — the 'moral hazard'.[2] This hazard makes the cost of hedging 'contestant's risk' very costly (where it is even legally and socially permissible), and also makes it difficult to create institutions that accomplish such hedging.

The difficulties of arranging risk hedges are vastly increased when there is great uncertainty and disagreement about relative abilities. In the real world, the lifetime earning prospects[3] of different individuals, even in childhood, are known to differ substantially. Without even considering genetic factors, the differential advantages of a 'good' family life create quite obvious differences by (say) age 12 in

---

[1] One way in which the insurance scheme could work would be for each runner to sell shares in his prize to other runners. Abstracting from the 'moral hazard', a runner could assure himself of the expected value of his prize by buying equal shares in the prizes of all runners. If he wished to gamble, he could vary his investment accordingly. The argument of part (a) of this section is very similar to that of Milton Friedman, 'Choice, Chance and the Personal Distribution of Income', *Journal of Political Economy*, August 1953, pp. 277–291.

[2] I.e. if a runner sells shares in his prize and uses the proceeds to buy shares in the prizes of other runners, so that he is financially indifferent as to the outcome, there is reason for concern about the intensity of his effort. If he bets more heavily on other runners than himself, the moral hazard is even greater. For this reason, insurers often insist that some part of a risk be borne by the insured, and refuse to 'over-insure' against adverse events where the insured can affect the outcome.

[3] We shall define the 'earning prospect', at a given stage in an individual's or cohort's life cycle, as the mathematical expectation of earnings for the duration of life.

capacity to absorb training, and strongly correlated advantages in ability to finance its acquisition.[1] Because of this, progressive taxation and related devices inevitably confound risk hedging with wealth redistribution. Indeed, the latter aspect so dominates debate on income-tax structure as almost to obliterate the former.

(b) *Second Chances*

The economic significance of the opportunity to hedge risks depends very much on how important chance factors are in determining the distribution of lifetime earnings. In this connection a crucial circumstance is the number of 'chances' one gets in a lifetime. If all prizes in our foot-race were divided into (say) thirds, and one set were awarded after each of three races, the expected difference between the expected and actual lifetime earnings of each runner would be less than if the total prize money were awarded after one race.

It is obviously not a simple matter to decide how many races an individual runs in one lifetime, but let us try. To define second, third, and higher order chances suppose that on the date at which an individual enters the labour force, he adopts a course of action which appears (to him) to entail a given probability distribution of lifetime earnings ;[2] call this distribution the earnings prospect at t_0. At t_1 another earnings prospect emerges, influenced by the events transpiring between t_0 and t_1. The individual's optimal course of (planned) action as of t_1 will therefore depend upon what happened between t_0 and t_1. In the event that the optimal outcome at t_1 (as seen from t_0) emerges, the individual will continue on his initially chosen course. If some other outcome emerges he may alter his course by changing his employer, moving to another town, commencing a new course of training, etc. Whether an individual will alter his course depends upon whether there is an earnings prospect at t_1 from a new course of action that is preferable to the prospect from continuing the course adopted at t_0. If so, there is an *effective* second chance at t_1 ; otherwise there is not. (The meaning of a third chance at t_2 and so forth

---

[1] This, I think, is responsible for a very large part — most — of the observed inequality in the distribution of earnings. However, Friedman (*op. cit.* p. 290) seems to advance the reverse view.

[2] 'Course of action' is not easy to define completely, and the precise content given the term should vary with the person or group under discussion. However, a given course of action will usually imply association with a specific employer, occupation, and location of economic activity. A change in either of these at a given moment, t_1, that had not been planned at some previous moment, t_0, will usually indicate that there has occurred a change in the planned course of action.

can be conceptualized in a similar manner.)

In any free society, there is always the technical possibility of a second chance ; the important question, however, is whether such a chance is of sufficient value to affect the distribution of expected life-time earnings for a cohort entering the labour force at t_0. Because life is short, an individual starting 'at the bottom' with a new firm at t_1 will inevitably have a less attractive prospect than one starting at t_0 ; investment in training will simply have a shorter expected pay-off period. But the value of the second chance may be reduced by much more than is implied by the loss of time between t_0 and t_1. If firms generally believe that job changers are less likely to be desirable employees than others, second chances will be obtainable only on relatively unfavourable terms and hence worth less than if the reverse is the case.

Manifestly, it would be impossible in a brief paper to characterize different economies or even occupations in terms of the opportunities they afford for second chances. However, a few brief remarks are offered to exemplify the point being made.

In a caste society where occupation is determined by birth and migration forbidden, it is pretty much one race per lifetime. Effective freedom to move from place to place, of itself, helps to give 'failures' a second chance, but the presence of new and rapidly growing com-munities enhances the value of the chance. In new communities, most individuals start afresh on equal terms, without the differential advantage of reputation. In such places men can (or could in the nineteenth century) get a second, third, or fourth chance at a career ; i.e. they could get a New Deal. Thus in the last century, the fron-tiers of America and Australia and newly developing cities throughout the world made it possible for individuals to start successful new careers at advanced ages.

This aspect of the opportunity-creating role of the frontier is less widely appreciated than another aspect ; i.e. in frontier communities, the relative value of capital intensive training is less, and that of sheer animal vitality, ingenuity, and determination greater, than in more developed ones.[1] As the former virtues are more strongly correlated with the possession of inherited wealth than the latter, the distribu-tion of earning prospects (presumably) were less dispersed in frontier communities than at 'home' — or at least the rankings of individuals were negatively correlated in the two (frontier and home) distribu-

[1] On this point, see S. Lebergott, *Manpower in Economic Growth*, McGraw-Hill, New York, 1964, pp. 120–123.

tions of earning prospects.[1] While it is not my intention to minimize the significance of this aspect of 'discontiguous development', it is to the second chance aspect that I wish to direct attention.[2]

It would be rash and quite possibly wrong to contend that in the economy of the nineteenth century, second chances were relatively better than at present. However, the tendency for individual firms to offer (combined with the tendency of young men to seek) jobs with life-long career prospects, serves to worsen the earning prospect of second chances. That is, the greater the fraction of jobs in the community to which access is closed except through promotion from within a given organization, the less will be the earning prospect of any individual who starts afresh with a new organization some time after entering the labour force.[3]

Thus the value of a second chance is enhanced by the presence of new and growing firms. Such firms flourish most where the rate of economic growth is high, and where turnover in the population of business firms is large. But though economic turbulence fosters second chances, by the same token it generates economic insecurity at later stages in life. A second chance for a first race loser is a source of insecurity for a first race winner.

Second chances have no effect on the distribution of expected lifetime earnings at t_0, or would have none if individuals maximized their expected utilities. However, second chances do reduce the expected variance of lifetime earnings at t_0. Therefore, if individuals wish to hedge earning risks,[4] the greater the number of independent chances

[1] The mere fact that the rankings of individuals in the two distributions were negatively correlated made the presence of the second a force for equalizing overall income dispersion. That is, it was possible for those low ranked at home to go to the frontier where they were relatively more advantaged, while those who were high ranked could stay put.

[2] 'Discontiguous development' occurs where new economic opportunities arise in a manner that induces individuals to enter new economic environments where their personal histories are much less well known than in their previous environment. The creation of new cities, removed in space and limited in communication with old ones, is an obvious example of discontiguity. However, the creation of new firms, new industries, new universities, as distinguished from expansion of old ones, also exemplifies the process even when there are no significant locational changes.

[3] The implications of such employment policies for labour mobility and relative wage rates are lucidly expounded by Clark Kerr, 'The Balkanization of Labor Markets', in *Labor Mobility and Economic Opportunity*, John Wiley, New York, 1954, pp. 92–110.

[4] If individuals maximize expected utility, they will not pay to avoid fair gambles. Without becoming involved in the dispute as to whether individuals are, typically, maximizers of expected utility, I would like to point out that their observed behaviour, which is 'at the margin' and reflects the influence of substantial hedging through institutional arrangements, is no indicator of what their behaviour would be in the absence of such institutional hedging.

they have in a lifetime, the smaller the incentive to pay for such hedges.

Since many of the institutional devices that serve to hedge risks (see below, 'Promotion from Within') also reduce the value of second chances, it is impossible to judge whether such devices serve to reduce risk (expected variance of lifetime earnings) as of t_0 (the date at which a cohort enters the labour force). But they do serve to reduce risk as of t_1 and subsequent dates. Hence attempts to reduce risk (increase security) for those persons who have obtained given positions at t_1 may work to favour the fast starters — the 'hares' — at the expense of the tortoises. The result may be not so much to reduce risk as to concentrate it in the early phases of the life-cycle.

(c) *Promotion from Within*

The tendency to 'promote from within', and not to hire from outside except for jobs at the lowest rank, acts much like a mutual insurance scheme for the members of an organization. Let us exaggerate and treat hiring by a corporation as consisting of a guarantee of some minimum earning prospect plus a lottery ticket for one of a number of prizes (careers). (Assume for the moment that in exchange for hiring the employer obtains an enforceable lifetime commitment, and that the moral hazard is somehow avoided.)

Whether such a guarantee costs the employer anything depends upon the desire of job applicants to hedge their risks. If they are sufficiently anxious to hedge, the employer can arrange his prizes so that the more able workers (i.e. those who rise to high rank) are paid less than they would have earned in the absence of a guarantee, while the less able are paid more. That is, the guarantee could be simply a disguise for a (costless) mutual insurance arrangement. Of course, it could also happen that a cohort of recruits taken as a group, accept less (or obtain more) than the expected value of their earning prospects in order to obtain the guarantee.

However, it is not only desire of workers to avert risk that might lead to the institution of such guarantees. Firms, too, have hiring risks they might wish to hedge by promoting only from within. These hiring risks of incompetence, dishonesty, psychological instability, etc., increase sharply with the rank of the job; to hedge them, employers seek to learn as much as possible about the individuals they appoint, prior to appointment. Often this can be best accomplished by promoting someone from within the organization with whom there is complete familiarity. Moreover, persons within the organization can be (and are) given specific training for the precise jobs for which they are being groomed. Outsiders, even when well and favourably known, may suffer from this lack of training.[1] As a result, the demand price of a firm for a given number of bottom rank employees consists of the value of their marginal product in their first job, plus the value of the information about the individuals (relevant to assessing their probable performance in higher ranked jobs) plus the value of the opportunity to give them specific training. This increases the number of persons of given quality a firm would hire at a given starting wage, as compared with a situation in which there was no incentive to promote from within.

The net effect of the desire to hedge risks, on both sides of the labour market, is to increase the fraction of the labour force hired (for the bottom rung) by firms offering lifetime careers.[2] But the effect of risk hedging (of this kind) on the dispersion of earning prospects is not clear, *a priori*.

Case 1. Assume that all economic activities were completely independent of risk hedging arrangements, so that the dispersion of earning prospects with hedging could be derived from the dispersion without hedging by suitable lump sum transfers. Then the fact of hedging (via the offering of lifetime careers, etc.) would not affect the pre-hedging dispersion, and therefore the post-hedging dispersion would necessarily be smaller than the pre-hedging.[3] In this special case, the obligation to retain individuals (and pay them a wage determined by their rank in the organization without reference to the current market value of their services) after it has been decided not to promote them further, entails a loss which must be offset (for each firm) by the 'underpayment' of those whom it wishes to consider for further promotion. That is, those who make it to the top are paid less (over their entire careers) than they would have been if their careers had been perfectly foreseen at the time of hiring. As a result, in this case hedging reduces the pre-hedging dispersion of earning prospects.

[1] The distinction between training, which is specific to the firm, and general training is stressed by Becker, *op. cit.* pp. 9–30.
[2] Both by the transfer of jobs from non-career to career categories within firms, and by the relative expansion of firms specializing in the latter type of job. For concreteness, assume a lifetime career to mean the following : each person hired is paid a wage, at all times, determined solely by his rank in the organization. He can never be discharged or demoted ; the firm can merely decide whether to promote or not promote.
[3] If individuals voluntarily engaged in hedging at all.

Case 2. But hedging may well interact with the organization of economic activities. In particular, it may be that were it not possible to hedge the risks of selecting high-level managers for large organizations through a process of selective promotion, the risks entailed in assembling huge aggregations of capital would be too great for potential investors and such firms could not survive (if they were even born). As we have seen, dispersion of firm sizes leads to (increased) dispersion of earnings among employees, especially managers, of different firms. Therefore by facilitating an increase in the dispersion of firm sizes, hedging may increase the overall dispersion of earnings even though its effect is to reduce the earning dispersion within each firm.[1]

Of course, all this is very abstract and of limited application to concrete situations. Firms that engage in promoting from within do not offer guarantees of lifetime careers in the literal sense ; they offer vague presumptions of permanence conditioned upon a variety of factors of which the most important is the financial condition of the company. One reason for a firm to live up to its implicit promise of a lifetime career is the desire to preserve its reputation as a good employer. However, adverse earnings statements and/or a very unsuitable collection of employees may, at times, exert sufficient pressure to over-balance this desire. Because the nature of the commitment to new employees is not spelled out in detail, the day-to-day treatment of employees by a firm is subject to considerable variation of an unpredictable kind. Employee complaints of unfair treatment under permanent employment relationships lead trade unions to demand detailed specification of the terms of employment with explicit provisions governing lay-off, recall, promotion, etc., which transform rather vague unilateral company policies into imperatives of collective agreements.

If employers never hired workers except at the bottom rank, workers would never have the full protection of the market once they advanced above this level. That is, if they were dissatisfied, they could not leave without going back to the bottom rank with another firm. (Moreover, the older an individual, the shorter his remaining productive life and the less his value to a new firm as a candidate for

---

[1] There may also be interaction between risk hedging and labour supply. For example, individuals may desire the security of a lifetime career sufficiently to accept a guarantee of the same at expected lifetime earnings for less than their expected earnings without it. This would tend to enhance the relative profitability of firms large enough to offer such guarantees on attractive terms (and make the guarantee credible), thereby increasing their relative importance as employers of labour.

promotion.) But some firms do hire workers at ranks above the bottom, depending upon circumstances. Thus, at various places in a job hierarchy the existence of an external market constrains the policies of employers. The points where market forces impinge upon the wage and personnel policies of employers cannot be predicted in advance, but their occasional collisions create crises for 'job evaluation plans' which are aimed at maintaining internal equity irrespective of market conditions.[1]

There has been much debate as to the relative importance of the internal wage policies of firms (mediated in some cases by the policies of trade unions) and the external pressure of labour markets in determining the relative wages of employees at different ranks within a firm. It is not necessary for our purpose that we join this debate. However, it is worth noting that internal forces are more potent in the short run than in the long. This is because the attraction of alternative opportunities will always affect the supply of persons entering an organization at the bottom rung, but the resulting pressure may be resisted (or not even felt) at higher levels for a considerable period so that the relative wage scales, rates of promotion, etc., within a firm do not respond. During this more or less extended 'transitory period' wages at ranks above the starting level will be set as in a bilateral monopoly[2] except in so far as they are subjected to external market pressures as a result of shocks. These shocks result, on the demand side, from sharp and unanticipated changes in the value of the marginal physical product for labour of particular ranks within the firm and, on the supply side, from changes in the external demand for labour at particular ranks. If all firms followed promotion from within for all employees at all times, these shocks could not affect wage and personnel behaviour. Since this is not the case, shocks generated externally in quarters where promotion from within is never followed (or where it has broken down) may bring market pressure to bear upon internal wage structures in the short run. However, the chance of any internal wage structure being subjected to market shock increases with the period of time considered.

In short, the very imperfect attempts at mutual insurance represented by a policy of promotion from within enormously complicate

---

[1] The classic paper on this topic is Clark Kerr and Lloyd H. Fisher, 'Effect of Environment and Administration on Job Evaluation', *Harvard Business Review*, May 1950, pp. 77–96.

[2] It will be bilateral monopoly even without a trade union if the worker embodies some training specific to the firm, i.e., he is not worth as much to another firm as to his present employer, but his present employer would have to spend a considerable sum (in training costs) to obtain an equivalent replacement.

the relation between the value of the current marginal contribution of a productive agent and its reward, and alter the distribution of earnings in a variety of ways. Mutual insurance against unduly low incomes may be arranged through a variety of channels : through the firm, the extended family, the state, etc. But it would be far beyond the scope of this paper to explore these in detail.

IV. SUMMARY

This paper has surveyed the determinants of the size distribution of lifetime earnings as these would operate in situations of long-run equilibrium, either in a stationary state or on a balanced growth path. For simplicity the distributions discussed have been assumed to have only two parameters, measuring central tendency and dispersion, respectively. Hours worked are assumed to be the same for all persons.

The first two sections assume that all variables are known with certainty. *Section I* deals with demand factors, and *Section II* with supply. The principal conclusions of *Section I* are :

(1) If all employers of labour had identical tastes, the greater the dispersion in the demand prices for different qualities of labour service, the greater would be the dispersion in the rewards (earnings) of those who furnish them.

(2) The greater the degree of consensus as to what is superior quality of labour service, the greater the dispersion of earnings.

(3) Given tastes and the distribution of wealth, the greater the level of *per capita* wealth of employers, the greater the dispersion of earnings among those hired.

(4) The important determinants of the relative demand prices for different qualities of labour services are (1) the value of the complementary resources (scale of operations) used by the employees and (2) the sensitivity of the (outcome of) the production process to differences in quality of labour service. Wages increase with either the employee's scale of operations or the sensitivity of the production process, the other determinant constant. This result is used to explain observed inter-firm differences in executive salaries.

(5) Because of (4), the dispersion of earnings increases with the dispersion of scales of operation, and with the dispersion of degrees of sensitivity. This result is used as the basis for the

conjecture that interfirm differences in earnings associated with size of firm are greater for higher ranking employees than for lower.

In *Section II* it is argued that the ability to render superior quality of service is a result of two factors, training and native talent, which are complementary to one another.

(1) If tastes and native talents of workers are identical and access to training is available to all on equal terms, then earnings will be identical, no matter what the state of demand.

(2) Dispersion of earnings induced by demand factors is limited by the ability to improve worker quality through training. The greater the ease with which training can be substituted for natural talent in producing given worker quality (assuming equal access to training facilities), the less the dispersion of earnings resulting from a given state of demand.

(3) Differences in native talent would make it rational to invest more in training those individuals with greater native talent (thereby inducing a syndrome of native talent, training, and earnings) even if the marginal costs of training were equal to all. However, in practice, differences of native talent are positively correlated with superior (cheaper) access to training so that there is a further reason for the aforementioned syndrome.

(4) A lessened degree of inequality in access to training coupled with an increase in aggregate *per capita* investment in training would alter the distribution of earnings but not necessarily make it more equal. This is because it would alter the relative scarcities of native talent and training with the result that the former would become relatively more valuable. Consequently, *if* the correlation between native talent and initial advantage in access to training is sufficiently positive, the effect of making opportunity more equal *may* be to make the distribution of earnings more unequal. This, however, is a possibility ; it is by no means certain.

Section III discusses some of the problems that arise from the existence of risk and attempts to hedge against it. The principal conclusions are :

(1) If individuals mutually agree to share their earnings in excess of mathematical expectations with those receiving less than their mathematical expectations, the final earnings distribution

may differ greatly from what it would have been in the absence of such agreements. However, such agreements entail costs which limit the extent to which they are adopted.

(2) Overt risk hedging in the form of an agreement that the more fortunate will share with the less fortunate is rare. However, many institutions work to accomplish this result indirectly ; e.g. systems of progressive taxation and the practice of 'promoting from within'. Promoting from within affects the size distribution of firms (and that of the earnings of their managers) through both demand and supply. It is impossible to predict, *a priori*, the net effect of the practice on the dispersions of the relevant distributions.

(3) When chance factors affect the distribution of lifetime earnings, the greater number of (approximately) independent chances individuals have over the course of their lifetimes, the smaller the variance of lifetime earnings. Therefore, the greater the number of chances per lifetime, *cet. par.*, the less the incentive to hedge risks.

In this paper, an attempt has been made to cover a great deal of ground and to pull together many hitherto unconnected threads of analysis. As a result we have constructed a very small-scale map which indicates, let us hope, most of the broad outlines of the terrain. Inevitably, however, much of the detail remains to be filled in.

DISCUSSION OF PROFESSOR REDER'S PAPER

Professor Alchian said that during the past few days facts about the various distributions of income had been presented for contemplation. As a means of introducing the paper by Professor Reder he would like to note that the conference's prior attention to the distribution of income by size, classes, and by wages and salaries seemed to place unwarranted emphasis on equality or on the growth of labour's share as being, in and of themselves, good or desirable results. But even Marx had said ' to each according to his needs ', and he knew of no prescription of his that said needs would be declared equal for all people. But Marxist dogma aside, a change in the distribution of income, towards or away from equality, had to be evaluated in the light of what had produced that change — and even more fundamentally in terms of what factors had been determinants of the existing distribution. Without some understanding of these factors

— let alone the incentive effect — Professor Alchian for one was unable to attach any significance, either positive or normative, to the existing or changing distribution of income, or, more pertinently, the distribution of wealth.

Professor Alchian asserted that it would have been delightful to have been born into an economy in which labour's share was only one per cent while the capitalist owner of non-human goods got 99 per cent. This could mean that people did almost no work and lived off a highly automated economy. Or it might mean that (with appropriate elasticities of demand, supply, and substitution) most people were very poor with one person possibly owning the 'capital'. Obviously the situation depended on the distribution of ownership of various forms of wealth and not basically on the human/non-human division of income.

Hoping that these comments were sufficient to direct attention to underlying factors, Professor Alchian said how happy he was to initiate discussion on Professor Reder's fine introductory analysis of some of the basic determinants of the size distribution of the allocation of income within occupations.

Instead of summarizing the paper's contents, Professor Alchian preferred to indicate portions that left his interest unsatisfied. He would do this not because of manifest defects in Professor Reder's analysis, but simply because he had touched on so many ideas that the time and space constraints had surely prevented him from saying all he could have said on most of them.

First, Professor Reder's discussion of 'rank and absolute performance' implied a change in the distribution of allocated income from the skill or ability distribution. Professor Alchian's reading of Professor Reder's references (Lebergott and Stigler) had aroused rather than satisfied his interest and he would be grateful if Professor Reder could comment more fully on this point.

Second, Professor Alchian referred to the positive correlation between the amount of investment in people and native inherent talent. He was uneasy about this presumption. Was there a correlation between investment in people and native ability, or one between investment and capital goods used jointly with native ability? Or was he mistaken in supposing there was any difference? Leaving this aside, the important feature was the implication that if capital for training was available to all on equal terms the dispersion of income would be increased. This related to Professor Alchian's opening remarks. Did it imply that reduced inequality was really not so good after all?

Third, on the aspect of risk hedging, Professor Alchian would like to offer some suggestions. He thought that much could be learnt by studying the behaviour of professional athletes, especially in baseball, football, and golf. Their remuneration involved salaries as well as competition for rank prizes. What he thought interesting was that they also engaged in side bets or negotiations to modify the 'official' distribution of prizes. They also had recourse to lifetime contracts. This last feature was especially pertinent to Professor Reder's discussion about the cases in which there was great uncertainty about marginal productivities of different people. This led further to another powerful (if true) implication of economic theory : the higher the cost of discerning the marginal productivities, the smaller the dispersion of income within occupations. Again, the implication was disturbing in the face of evidence suggesting reduced inequality of overall income distribution, even though Professor Alchian was aware that within an occupation and among occupations dispersions did not need to be in the same direction.

Fourth, Professor Alchian ventured to suggest that the discussion of 'second chances' was the most tenuous. Professor Alchian was not clear as to what 'another chance' corresponded. The concept was still very ambiguous, as Professor Reder had been careful to emphasize, and here Professor Alchian was unable to discern any implications.

Fifth, in respect of Professor Reder's discussion of promotion within a firm as an economical means of acquiring information about productivities and as a risk-hedging device, Professor Alchian thought that these were different. Would not the former imply greater dispersion while the latter implied a narrower one ? He was perhaps confused. If so, he hoped that his mistake was the result of Professor Reder's exposition and not of his own 'native ability'!

Sixth and most interesting to Professor Alchian was Professor Reder's discussion of the correlation between the amount of wealth whose value would be affected by the decision of a person and the dispersion of income of those persons. Again Professor Alchian wished to stress the connection between this and judgments about the desirability of any observed reduction in inequality of income.

Lastly, after having been justifiably kind to the author, Professor Alchian would try to detect an error. He had the sneaking suspicion that in discussing correlation of executive wages and profits Professor Reder had departed from his stricture about using lifetime earnings (or equivalent value annuities) when he referred to the correlation with measured profits — which, Professor Alchian suspected, were measures of transient concepts and not wealth. His own conjecture was that the correlation should be with wealth and not transient profits, to make the analysis consistent throughout.

Professor Reder answered Professor Alchian's observations before the meeting proceeded further. Concerning the correlation of ability and training, Professor Reder saw in what he had written no reason for disagreement with Professor Alchian : correlation of ability with training contrasted with correlation of ability with capital used. Professor Reder would have supposed that the people who got most training were those with the greatest native ability. It was the generally accepted view that there was an advantage to be derived from an early good training and a better environment and that people with money were healthier, had a better personal infrastructure and were more likely to win scholarships. However, upon examination such views often turned out to be incorrect. Therefore he would consider Professor Alchian's comments carefully.

With regard to risk hedging, Professor Reder would not be so optimistic as Professor Alchian about studying the behaviour of atypical groups, but he felt that a great deal of hedging against the vicissitudes of an uncertain future was inherent in the institutions of any society.

Professor Reder did not understand Professor Alchian when he related his remarks in the paper about the cost of discerning marginal productivity to reduced income dispersion. It was not clear whether there was such a connection, and Professor Reder thought that he might expand on this later in a revised version of his paper.

Professor Reder was sorry that his remarks about second chances did not appeal to Professor Alchian. Taking the frontier society as an extreme case, the implication was that a boy who had, for instance, run into trouble with the law and then had difficulty in finding employment could go to the frontier where no questions were asked and start all over again. This was very close to a genuine second chance. The United States bankruptcy laws, in making it easier than in France for entrepreneurs to start afresh, provided second or even third or fourth chances. Distribution of income on a life-time basis would be made more equal in communities which would some-how allow for multiple chances. As an example, supposing an instructor had had an unfortunate experience in his first job in one of the older universities, it would make it difficult for him to increase his earnings there, but he could improve his position if he had a chance to move to another university where his full record would not follow him. Of course this was but a paradigm and Professor Reder agreed that a paradigm was an abstract idea, but he would not think this was any different from the usual ways of theoretical reasoning in economics. Any time that there was a prospect of recovering from a first failure there was a second chance and this concept of multiple chances could help to improve the still very crude theory of income.

On promotion within the firm as a risk-hedging device, Professor Alchian's concern made Professor Reder think that he had not been suf-ficiently explicit. Supply factor and demand factor were both involved in determining the terms on which individuals were tried out on long-term contracts. Risk hedging related to the supply side in the sense that in so far as young people preferred a more certain lifetime earning prospect to one with higher expected income but wider dispersion, a corporation could hire labour more cheaply by offering lifetime earnings. Conversely, if individuals were not prepared to sacrifice any expected income in order to hedge uncertain prospects, employing firms would be compelled to offer higher initial wages in order to have a second chance in deciding whether to retain their employees.

Finally Professor Reder commented on Professor Alchian's criticism concerning the correlation of the level of executive salaries with the level of current profits. Professor Alchian thought him wrong to use temporary income for the purpose of this analysis. Professor Reder thought, however, that the association between corporate earnings and executive salaries would also hold if permanent profits rather than current profits were used. The observed relationship between corporate salaries and the size of firms was quite strong and the principal officers of the very large profitable firms appeared regularly at the top of the list of salaries of the highest executives. Professor Alchian's reasoning was correct but Professor Reder thought that the empirical evidence would refute his statement.

Professor Falise asked Professor Reder whether he did not think that hedging by means of mutual insurance had the result of prolonging income distribution according to aptitudes rather than of altering it drastically. Professor Falise believed that people were led to hedge not so much on account of uncertainty about winning the race as of the risk of being prevented from competing because of accidents or disabilities which would deprive them of the deserved reward of their aptitudes. Thus people would insure against the risk of not starting the race rather than against the chance of poor ranking at the finishing post. Professor Falise thought that the wealthier people would be disposed to pay more in order to get the reward they expected from their abilities. Hedging must therefore make dispersion of incomes more conformant with distribution according to aptitudes rather than less so.

Professor Falise also wanted to draw to Professor Reder's attention the consequence of market imperfections as he was under the impression that they were neglected in the paper. Political favouritism in civil servants' careers, nepotism in private businesses, might make the actual distribution of personal incomes differ from distribution according to aptitudes.

Professor Reder answered Professor Falise, saying that on the first point Professor Falise's question made him fear some misunderstanding. He should have made it explicit that he had reasoned under the usual assumption that individuals try to maximize the sum total of expected utilities. But as long as one stuck to this assumption hedging would not affect expected lifetime incomes or level of wealth. Of course wealthy people were rich even before starting the race and they could and would pay more for insuring than the poorer who were initially handicapped.

On the second point, surely the notion of earning prospects over a lifetime at the start of the race could take such facts as favouritism and nepotism into consideration. The chances of gain did not necessarily depend on personal aptitudes alone but on a combination of different factors obtaining at the start of the race. It might be that winning the race was a matter of having the right family connections as well as good legs!

Professor Bronfenbrenner wondered which would be the correct way of interpreting the general view that increased information would increase the dispersion in income distribution as two different kinds of errors could result from imperfect knowledge : either the mistake in entrusting assets to an incompetent individual or in not entrusting them to an individual who would make an acceptable executive for lack of discerning his aptitudes. It seemed to Professor Bronfenbrenner that increased information was meant by Professor Reder as correcting the first kind of error. But if it meant correcting the second kind of error, would Professor Reder still be disposed to deduce that increased information about aptitudes tended to increase income dispersion ? Would not the reverse be the case ?

Having this in mind, Professor Bronfenbrenner felt that he should defend the man in the street's avowed preference for a higher labour share against the author and the discussants of the paper. One still lived in a society where there was a great deal of poverty and everywhere where people lived in poverty their abilities were inadequately developed. Professor Bronfenbrenner thought it very difficult to do anything about this in the short run without a measure of income redistribution from richer to poorer people. Professor Reder's paper had aristocratic undertones and even if he could accept all its aristocratic implications, he would argue that the bleeding heart liberal type still had a leg to stand on.

Professor Patinkin remarked thereupon that in his opinion Professor Reder and Professor Bronfenbrenner did not refer to the same notion of 'aptitude'. This might be a semantic misunderstanding : whereas Professor Bronfenbrenner thought of latent aptitudes, Professor Reder meant aptitude as the result of conditioning in childhood as his assumption of a high correlation between ability and education proved.

Professor Reder said that the answer to be given to the question at issue would depend on the age at which people were supposed to start the race — and some people had an enormous handicap by the age of five. Professor Bronfenbrenner had suggested that one should redistribute income so as to help children otherwise at a disadvantage. Professor Reder would not make these transfers by giving such people more cash income, but by distributing free certain services which could only be used to improve the children's lot. But Professor Reder thought one should be explicit about the implications of such actions. If one were in a hurry for more equality, one must be prepared to interrupt family life in an unpleasant way.

Professor Alchian said that Professor Bronfenbrenner's two types of error could exist but in their effect on income dispersion they would work in opposite directions.

Professor Phelps Brown said he was grateful to Professor Reder for his distinction between reward by place and reward by speed as this could help in removing an obstinate difficulty in applying marginal productivity analysis to everyday life.

Marginal productivity analysis imposed itself as a condition for minimizing costs by means of changing the combinations of factors until marginal productivities and prices of factors were equal. This would be achieved by entrepreneurs competing together even if the process were partially blind. But when one came to judgment of particular management, one then started to run into trouble as it was very hard for the ablest manager to relate quantities and productivitites. Managers could estimate the marginal productivity of the labour employed only for that part of the labour which could be directly related to a given product. A great part of labour input, however, was only indirectly used in producing output and it was hard to determine whether one used too much or too little of the indirect factor.

Now Professor Reder had proposed two alternative methods of measurement, cardinal and ordinal, and where the cardinal failed it was worth trying the ordinal. One was thus able to arrange marginal productivities of present labour intakes in a ranking order and try to insure that intakes were so ranged that the order corresponded to unit prices at which labour was available.

There was, however, a difficulty. Even if there were a perfect rank correlation with marginal productivities, wage bills would remain cardinal figures and one could not be assured that at the margin productivities and pays would be perfectly equal for each line of labour intake. Nevertheless, no matter how great were cardinal disparities between wages and productivities, the ordinal measurement would be an improvement in narrowing the blank area in managers' calculations.

Professor Reder said that he wished he had expressed his ideas in the way Professor Phelps Brown had done. He had nothing to add to Professor Phelps Brown's comments so long as the reasoning was restricted to one firm. If reasoning referred to more than one, the operation of markets tended to narrow the range of wage rates possible for any one firm for any one job.

To this Professor *Phelps Brown* remarked that the wider the market the more likely there were to be trade unions with strong views about conventional wage differentials.

Dr. Pasinetti said that Professor Phelps Brown's comments pointed out both the possibilities of marginal analysis applied to the relationship between productivity and reward and its limitations, which Professor Reder doubtless had in mind.

Professor Reder had been concerned in his paper with the explanation of differentials — and this was a most appropriate field for marginal analysis. He had not been concerned with the explanation of average levels of rewards per head. Dr. Pasinetti nevertheless thought that it would be easy from the paper itself to go on to the analysis of relations between differentials and average rewards, as one could superimpose on the theory explaining the former a distinct theory which would explain the latter.

Concerning differentials, Dr. Pasinetti thought that whereas Professor Reder's analysis could be applied to explaining differentials amongst people within a specific occupation, he was not sure whether this analysis was as appropriate for explaining differentials between wide categories of workers, e.g. coal-miners versus railwaymen. In this case one would have to bring in many other factors : institutional factors, relative strength of trade unions, comparative rates of growth in productivity, etc.

Finally this analysis would have to be completed according as it was to be applied to a stationary economy or to a dynamic one with long-run equilibrium growth. In a growing economy there were investments and therefore savings. This involved some assumption about people's saving behaviour. If people saved, then they would own property. Since profits were distributed in proportion to ownership of the capital stock, different people would receive different amounts of profits, according to their ownership of property and this would contribute to income inequality.

Professor Reder did not agree with Dr. Pasinetti in limiting the scope of his analysis to explaining differentials within specific occupations. There were no occupational categories *per se* in his analysis : whether a category was broad or narrow depended on the cost of acquiring information so as to discriminate ; the less this cost the more complete the differentiation should be between workers. He had abstracted from trade unionism and other institutional factors, and of course trade-union pressure might force the employers to award the same salary to all the workers within the same occupation. But it might be that even in the absence of trade unions employers would treat all, say, coal-miners as alike just because it would cost too much to differentiate between them.

Professor Reder said that in his paper he had been narrowly concerned with earnings. Thus he had not dealt with the question which had been the subject of Dr. Pasinetti's last comment, but if there was capital accumulation the community would grow wealthier and of course somebody must own the wealth. Clearly the distribution of wealth would then have to be considered. Although Professor Reder had meant to study the earnings distribution alone, he had to acknowledge the fact that the rate of investment in human capital was a function of the growth rate itself. It had not occurred to him that the higher the rate of growth the greater the amount of investment for differentiating human abilities because he had regarded the saving function as implied in marginal analysis of general equilibrium.

He was therefore grateful to Dr. Pasinetti for his observation.

Chapter 22

INFLATION AND DISTRIBUTION OF INCOME AND WEALTH

BY

ARMEN ALCHIAN
University of California

INTRODUCTORY

INQUIRIES into the income distributive effects of inflation have been performed in several ways. Easiest is a count of assertions and allegations in the fashion of a public opinion poll. Obviously our task is not to conduct such a survey of opinion, for then we could dispense with the science of economics. Instead we take it to be that of reviewing briefly what presently validated economic theory implies about the wealth and income distributive effects, only, of inflation and to what extent we have empirical evidence supporting those implications.

Wealth and income effects are the same thing. Wealth is a present value measure of income, and conversely. But for people whose wealth is essentially human talents, a market place for observing changes in their wealth is not readily available. As a surrogate variable, current rates of wage receipts are often used to detect wealth changes.

I. INFLATION AND CONCURRENT EVENTS

In investigating the effects we had best be certain that it is an inflation whose effects we are investigating, and not the effects of other events which also cause or are concurrent with an inflation. Therefore we should separate the side (non-inflationary) effects of such things as increases in the quantity of money, war damages, blockades, droughts, plagues, unemployment, or any events that can instigate a *policy* of inflation. For example, we should not jump to the conclusion that an increase in the quantity of money affects

618

employment and output only by raising the general level of prices. Nor should one blame inflation for the effects of a war that initiates an inflationary finance policy. Yet that is exactly what has been said for every war episode by many responsible writers on economic affairs. The fall in real income in the South during the Civil War, the rise in the real wages during the early plagues, the shifts in demands from peacetime-type jobs and goods to munitions-type goods with the resultant shift in relative prices and wages have also been blamed on the inflation rather than losses of wealth and resources and on the demand shifts. Our first conclusion must be that by utilizing this distinction we can separate confusion and myth from verifiable and verified analysis.

Let us see what validated economic theory has to say. We have been warned that this is a dangerous approach — apparently because there is presumed to be no body of valid, useful economic theory — a false judgment which one sometimes is tempted to accept when surveying the assertions about inflation. It is because that core of theory is not consistently applied that disparate and inconsistent analyses of inflation can result. Of course, each person is free to set up his own special assumptions and grind out the implications. After all, anything is conceivable and so anything must be possible.[1] But we are here bound by a more severe constraint — that of using valid economic theory and its verified implications. We must recognize and accept that constraint, for it is the economist's source of comparative advantage in analysing this question.

II. UNANTICIPATED AND ANTICIPATED INFLATION

By inflation we mean a rise in the general level of prices. We can agree also on certain episodes as having been inflations, even if this is not possible for all episodes.[2]

[1] For excellent illustrations, see the survey called a 'Survey of Inflation Theory' (M. Bronfenbrenner and F. Holzman, *The American Economic Review*, September 1963, pp. 593–661). A more accurate title would have been a 'Survey of Inflation Literature', for it is an excellent survey of opinions, assertions, and models, many inconsistent with each other as well as with what we had thought were well validated economic theorems. One can hardly conceal dismay at what that survey has so ably exposed. Mistake us not ; this is no criticism of the authors. Anyone should have been delighted to have discharged a duty so well.

[2] For example, has there been any inflation in the United States from 1952 through 1963 ? Despite a rise in the official price index, its margin of error or confidence interval, and its biases are sufficiently large that it would take a rise in the various respected indices of at least 3 per cent a year to provide persuasive evidence of inflation. But for present purposes, surely, we can all agree there are lots of episodes that we would all quickly agree to classify as inflations.

We hope it will be agreed there is no point to having different techniques of analyses of inflations according to the rate of inflation (e.g. creeping, chronic, galloping, hyper). In Fisherian and Keynesian fashion (provided we confine ourselves to the Keynes of the *Tract on Monetary Reform*) we classify inflations into unanticipated and anticipated.[1] Anticipated inflations are characterized by market phenomena implied by the postulate that prices are expected to rise. Unanticipated inflation, as you can guess, is characterized by market phenomena implied by the postulate that the contemporaneous level of prices is 'expected' to persist.

(1) *Net Monetary Status Effects*

The economic analysis of the effects of inflation is simple. Since inflation is a rise of prices in terms of money units it follows, by definition, that monetary assets (claims to fixed amounts of money) fall in relative value. In contrast, non-money (real) assets rise in value with the price level. The nominal yields of real assets rise along with the price level, whereas those of monetary assets do not. Examples of real assets are common stock, real estate, buildings, inventories. Monetary assets are exampled by money, bonds, and accounts receivable, to name a few.[2]

Since the price rise is unanticipated, the increased cost of holding money fails to affect the quantity of money people want to hold, in real terms (i.e. relative to nominal wealth and income). Because of the imperfect foresight, interest rates on *monetary* assets do not reflect the change in the price level so as to maintain pre-inflation economic relations between *net* monetary debtors and creditors

---

[1] I. Fisher, *The Purchasing Power of Money*, rev. ed., New York, 1926 ; J. M. Keynes, *A Tract on Monetary Reform*, London, 1923, p. 18.

[2] Let R and M be net real and net monetary assets, respectively, and E, the initial equity. Thus :

$$E = R + M.$$

If E' is the new equity when prices rise by proportion, P, then :

$$E' = PR + M.$$

Finally, let Q be the proportionate increase in the money value of the equity :

$$Q = E'/E.$$

Now, substituting and rearranging :

$$Q = \frac{PR + M}{E}$$

$$= P - (P-1)\frac{M}{E}.$$

Whether Q is larger than, equal to, or smaller than P (assumed larger than 1) depends on whether M is negative, zero, or positive.

(monetary assets minus monetary liabilities). As a result there are transfers of wealth from net monetary creditors to net monetary debtors. What is true of debtors and creditors linked by inter-personal monetary claims in the form of bonds is equally true of monetary debtor creditor relationships created by mortgages, notes, bills, leases, demand deposits, prepayments, and fiat money.

A rise in the price level — whatever its cause — reduces, by definition and in fact, the value of the non-interest bearing money, in units of which prices are expressed. Those whose debts form the money, if it be debt money, gain real wealth because of their reduced real liabilities.[1] If the inflation was induced by an increase in printed fiat government money, the government gains wealth and then exchanges one form of wealth for another when the money is spent — with the gain being at the expense of those who held money at the time the price level rose.[2]

(2) *Other Presumed Effects of Inflation*

No income effects other than those flowing from the wealth transfer among net monetary creditors–debtors are implied. There are implied no wage lags, no forced saving, no suffering by widows, orphans, and old people, no profits to business men and speculators, and no price distortions. Then so much the worse for the validity of economic theory — unless these phenomena are illusions, as we are convinced they are. The available evidence and data simply do not support the presumption of the presence of those alleged phenomena. The reconciliation of observation and analysis lies, we are convinced, in avoiding a prevalent, earlier mentioned, confusion between the effects of events initiating an inflation and the effects of the inflation itself. Let us look into these briefly.

There is nothing in economic analysis that says an inflation must first occur with a more rapid rise in consumer goods prices. Yet this preconception underlies many of the statements of the wage lag doctrine.[3] Another preconception is that wages are naturally sticky,

---

[1] We note that if the money were bank debt money, it does not follow that banks will gain wealth on *net*, because every bank is a net monetary *creditor* and loses more than it gains from the inflation. R. Kessel, 'Inflation-Caused Wealth Redistribution : A test of a Hypothesis', *American Economic Review*, March 1956, pp. 128–141.

[2] See Appendix.

[3] A. Alchian and R. Kessel, 'The Meaning and Validity of the Inflation-Induced Lag of Wages Behind Prices', *The American Economic Review*, March 1960, pp. 43–66.

rigid, and immobile relative to consumer-goods prices. Finally, another preconception is that during an inflation, with the increase in wealth to those who gain from the inflation, there must be a reduced income left to the rest of the community. If, for example, the government gains from an inflation by printing new money and taking some of the wealth and income from the community, the smaller remaining income must imply a reduction in real wages. Given the preconceptions, one hardly needs to look at evidence, for if he does he can certainly find support for his belief if he is a little careless in his evaluation of the evidence or use of statistical principles.

(a) *Wage Lags*. As every economist understands, real wages can be affected by real forces like changes in the relative supplies of labour and capital, changes in the quality of the labour force, changes in the pattern of consumer demand, and changes in the state of the arts. Only if one abstracts from the effects of known real forces can one determine the effects of inflation upon an observed time series of real wages. To illustrate, real wages and money prices since 1889 show a very high positive (not negative) correlation. Is this evidence against the wage lag? Certainly not. Real wages rose during this time according to informed observers, because of *per capita* increases in skill, capital, technology, etc. Those who believed in the wage lag would not have denied this. Their position would have been that real wages rose despite inflation and that if the effects of real forces upon real wages were accounted for properly, one would observe a fall in real wages attributable to inflation.[1]

No amount of examination of time series will convince some people of the absence of a wage lag. The theory they have adopted simply requires its presence, and if the data do not show it, so much the worse for the statistical data. But once the implications of economic theory are pointed out and once it is shown that a wage lag is not implied, even with a decrease in real income or wealth for the rest of the community during an inflationary expropriation of wealth by, say, the government, everything falls into place. What, as we now know, happens is that the wealth transfer is accomplished via a tax on

---

[1] Note momentarily a common and humorous error of statistical interpretation and evaluation of evidence. Given the presence of a myriad of 'random' forces on wages and prices, one would expect that during inflation, deflation, or price stability, there would be observed a negative relationship between changes in prices and real wages half the time, and a positive correlation half the time. It is no inaccuracy to say that some observers cite the negative relationships as evidence, while ignoring the positive relationships — exclaiming that the wage lag operates for about half of the cases, just as a gambler could claim that a roulette wheel is biased toward red half the time !

money — a transfer of wealth from net monetary creditors to net monetary debtors (and money is an important form of monetary credits). The lower income to the rest of the community is borne by those who have lost that claim to wealth. There is no implied real wage-rate decline. Instead there is a lower share of wealth and income to net monetary creditors. Wage-earners have the same income as formerly. A failure to recognize the process as a specific form of *wealth* transfer rather than a kind of *generalized income* transfer was, we believe, the responsible culprit in causing so much confusion of analysis.

A careful review of all the available evidence simply does not support the wage-lag contention, even if one goes back as far as 1350 ! On the other hand, the available evidence of a wealth transfer according to net monetary status is overwhelming.[1]

(b) *Forced Savings.* Associated with the wage-lag contention is the well-known, but still mysterious, forced savings doctrine — a doctrine as vulnerable as it is ambiguous. At least three versions exist.[2] One identifies it with the wage lag, often with the explicit additional addendum that wealth so saved is necessarily or usually devoted to investment. A second contention is that those who first spend new money get wealth by driving up prices and depriving those who held the prior existing money. Finally there is the argument that since the government gets wealth, or more income, by inflation, all the rest of the community *must* have less income and this smaller income therefore must result in a rise in consumer-goods prices relative to factor prices. Now the fact is that none of these

---

[1] A. Alchian and R. Kessel, 'Redistribution of Wealth through Inflation', *Science*, 4 September 1959, pp. 535–539; G. L. Bach and A. Ando, 'The Redistributional Effects of Inflation', *Review of Economics and Statistics*, February 1957, pp. 1–13, D. Felix, 'Profit Inflation and Industrial Growth: The Historic Record and Contemporary Analogies', *Quarterly Journal of Economics*, August 1956, pp. 441–463, B. Pesek, 'Distribution Effects of Inflation and Taxation', *American Economic Review*, March 1960, pp. 147–153.

[2] Jacob Viner, *Studies in the Theory of International Trade*, Harpers, New York, 1937, pp. 187–197, finds two versions. The first citation of the wage lag is to Henry Thornton, while a quote from T. Joplin contains a nearly correct version of the money tax, which Viner calls forced saving, despite the fact that he later implicitly denies it when saying Ricardo did not have a 'forced savings' thesis. Gottfried Haberler, *Prosperity and Depression*, United Nations, Lake Success, 1946, pp. 42, 43, 138, and 310, has all three versions. J. M. Keynes in *The General Theory of Employment, Interest and Money*, Macmillan, London, 1936, pp. 79–81, 123–124 contains a well-directed and potentially effective attack on the idea that savings in any of the three above versions are forced in any sense different from that which results from a change in circumstance like a loss of wealth, whatever the cause ; but he blunted his attack by his simultaneous acceptance of the wage-lag doctrine, which to many economists (e.g., Robertson, Haberler, Viner) is the forced savings doctrine.

will stand up to either theoretical analysis or to empirical evidence. As we have indicated, the wage-lag assertion is neither theoretically nor empirically sound. The second version implying a forced saving on those who do not get the new money, comes close, but is fundamentally wrong. The interpretation simply fails to distinguish between the fact of a wealth transfer and the way in which it is achieved. A change in consumer-goods prices relative to factor prices simply is not implied by a loss of wealth.[1]

(c) *Losses by Economic Classes.* Although our interest in the net monetary status of business firms was based on a desire to obtain economic ownership units of different net monetary status in order to test the wealth redistribution effect, there is interest also in relating net monetary status to other personal or occupational characteristics. In other words, who are the net monetary debtors and the creditors ? Their incidence in various occupations and wealth levels is still unknown. Some attempts have been made in this direction, but these have relied on aggregative data for a class as a whole. They tell us nothing about the proportions within the class. Furthermore, the data so far available by groups or classes involves much ambiguity in assigning assets and liabilities to monetary or non-monetary status. Even if data were available accurately and for individuals there is a disturbing element in the attempt to classify occupational or wealth *groups* on this basis.

In the first place, it invites attention to superficial characteristics, especially if not everyone in that class or category is of the same net monetary status. Second, it suggests policy action toward one class as if everyone were of the same net monetary status within that class. For example, comparisons of the progressivity of the inflation tax on monetary assets with the progressivity of the graduated income tax leads precisely to that policy.

And again, the impression that widows, orphans, and retired people suffer from inflation is also wrong, even if more of the widows, orphans, and retired people are net monetary creditors than debtors. We think it is clearer, and more relevant to say simply that net monetary debtors gain at the expense of net monetary creditors whatever their other attributes, and that if one wishes to take action to 'correct' that, attention should be directed to the net monetary status, not some other superficial classification criterion. However, this is a

---

[1] Despite the logical vacuity and empirical falsity of all versions of the forced savings doctrine, we predict a continued vigorous and long life. Its emotional appeal and obviousness is too strong to kill with reason and evidence.

matter of conjecture as to what the consequences and general interpretation of such studies will be, and of course does not mean that it is wrong to make such studies nor that they are useless. We merely wish to emphasize and warn of a source of potentially dangerous misinterpretation.

Disclaiming any implication that inflation-induced gains to those of a net monetary debtor status justify a special tax on net monetary debtors, we can nevertheless enquire whether business men as a class typically are net monetary debtors or creditors. In general, the evidence is that it varies in time and by countries. In the United States, the proportion of firms that are net monetary debtors has varied from a high of close to 90 per cent down to about 50 per cent, from 1915 to 1946.[1] Most recent data for 1956 indicates the proportion is about 60 per cent.[2] These data refer to firms whose stock is traded on the organized security exchanges. In England in the post-war period, the fraction has run higher, running at about three-fourths of all firms (although the type of business seems to be a determining factor).[3] In Japan for the post-war period the proportion runs close to 90 per cent.[4]

An amusing example of reliance on casual empiricism and abandonment of analysis is provided by Keynes's discussion of the 'gains' to businessmen from inflation. In his *Tract* he had the analysis straight.[5] There he had no wage lag, no inventory gains, just debtor status — but no supporting statistical data. Yet within ten years Keynes had abandoned the analysis and was asserting that businessmen gained from inventories and from wage lags. At some place between the *Tract* and the *Treatise* he had been induced to change his mind (we believe by Professor E. Hamilton's persuasive publications as evidenced by the extensive reference to his work in Keynes's *Treatise*).[6] It is hard to believe that Keynes could have thrown aside all his theoretical rigour and seized upon the wage-lag hypothesis — especially in view of the inadequacies of the data and the more consistent alternative interpretations of which Keynes showed appreciation in his *Tract*. But he did. In any event, in the *Treatise* he defended and interpreted the excess profits tax during World War I

---

[1] Alchian and Kessel, *Science, loc. cit.*
[2] Unpublished doctoral dissertation of V. Brousallian at UCLA.
[3] L. De Alessi, 'The Redistribution of Wealth by Inflation: An Empirical Test with United Kingdom Data', *Southern Economic Journal*, October 1963, pp. 113–127.
[4] Unpublished doctoral dissertation of J. Kuratani at UCLA.
[5] J. M. Keynes, *loc. cit.*
[6] J. M. Keynes, *A Treatise on Money*, II, Macmillan, London, 1930, pp. 148–181.

as a means of appropriating inflation-induced 'gains' of businessmen resulting from the wage lag. In a sense, his behaviour is more a tribute to his open-mindedness than to his confidence in economic theory.

(d) *Price Distortions.* Price distortions are commonly alleged to be results of inflation. Sticky, inflexible customary prices are the usual basis of the alleged distortion of prices. If we recognize that inflations often are the result of changes in factor supplies or are policy responses to desires to revise relative demands (e.g. armaments versus retail clerks) we should not be surprised to see changes in relative demands at times of inflation. Again, it is said that government employees have fixed wages. Even though this may be true it does not indicate that job reclassification or job shifting is not equally efficient as a wage-rate reviser. Sticky, inflexible, customary or rigid prices are easy to talk about but harder to substantiate. We suspect the illusion arises partly from a comparison of the price of a single good with an index of many prices. If all prices are equally flexible and responsive, each single price will appear to lag (or lead !) the smoother changing average of all other prices.

The only available evidence germane to the presumption of increased dispersion of prices during inflation is that presented by Wesley Mitchell.[1] And that evidence does not show any increase in relative price or wage dispersions in inflation as compared to non-inflations. We would have expected an increase at the onset and termination of an inflation — in response to changes in relative demands — not because of relative price stickiness. Suffice it to say that here is an unexplored, but we think, tractable and useful area of empirical research. And while performing that research it will be desirable to see if there are any relative price effects arising from relative demand shifts associated with changes in real value of money stocks.

III. LOSSES OF INTEREST RECEIVERS

Income data can be used to supplement wealth statistics. Here, too, the evidence about shares going to various factors shows no wage lag nor, for that matter, any substantial changes in factor incomes systematically related to inflation, except for *explicit contractual* interest receipts.[2] But notice that we have emphasized the *explicit*

[1] W. Mitchell, *The Making and Using of Index Numbers*, U.S. Department of Labor, Bulletin No. 656, 1938. [2] Bach and Ando, *op. cit.*

contractual interest. We emphasize that because the share going to interest is *measured* with a serious bias.

We are accustomed to measuring the interest rate as a form of payment for loans. It is, of course, a payment or reflection of differences in present prices of present consumption rights and future consumption rights — a payment for deferral of consumption. But not all such deferrals are in the form of contractual loans in monetary amounts. Consumption rights can be deferred in many ways ; one need not lend money in return for a monetary asset claim ; he can invest in long-lived assets to put the matter allegorically. These investors receive interest, not in the form of pre-assigned monetary amounts, but in real terms and also stand to receive profits or losses. Therefore it is not entirely correct to say that interest receivers lose from unanticipated inflation. It is only those interest receivers who take their interest claims in monetary forms rather than in non-monetary forms ; they lose because they have chosen to express their interest claims in monetary units and have underestimated the extent of future price rise.

We are forced to return to our initial implication of economic analysis for unanticipated inflations. It is the net monetary status that is the source of income and wealth redistributions — not even the interest receiver can, in strict accuracy, be claimed to be a loser from even unanticipated inflation. It is his tie to fixed monetary contracts for the interest that is the source of the redistribution. All other contentions have as yet failed to be supported by the available empirical evidence. We must exclude from this generalization the effects of price control and tax policies adopted by governments (e.g. the effect of a graduated income tax in the face of rising prices). We make this exclusion not because they could not be considered effects of inflation, but because they represent effects of discretionary actions and laws. Rather than associate them with the inflation *per se* we have chosen to separate them as policy variables. However, if you wish, you may put them wherever you wish and modify the conclusion in a consistent fashion, without, we think, changing one's understanding.

IV. ANTICIPATED INFLATION

A fully anticipated, in contrast to unanticipated, inflation implies interest rates that do accurately allow for the inflation that will occur. As a result net monetary assets bearing explicit interest do not impose a loss on the creditor. It is difficult to imagine an economy without some non-interest bearing monetary assets. But, only difficult, not impossible. Some major banks would find it profitable to issue purchasing power or interest-bearing securities or monies — unless prohibited by government edict. The switch to such money would of course mean the inflation would come to an end — since there would be no inflation in terms of this money. What is difficult to imagine is any government permitting that kind of competition in issue of money. Implicitly, we are assuming that anticipated inflations are results of government policy — an *ad hoc* presumption, but one which we think is justified by historical fact. Therefore we say that we cannot imagine interest-bearing or purchasing-power money really being issued by any non-government agency, and we cannot bring ourselves to imagine a government willing to cut off its power to claim a share of the community's wealth and income by inflation, and that is what a really effective purchasing-power money would do.

In the absence of perfect purchasing-power or interest-bearing money the inflation, anticipated or not, will continue to impose a loss of wealth on money holders. Also imposed is a general loss of efficiency and consequently of wealth on the community at large as a result of its resort to less efficient means of exchange and specialization in production. This revision in exchange procedures will of course imply a gain in wealth (and hence income) for people who provide services that facilitate economizing on money. But this is essentially identical to the analysis of the effects of a tax on any resource. In this case the resource is money. We conjecture that non-human capital is a better money substitute than human labour. If so, there is a shift in relative demand from labour to non-labour wealth as a money substitute, with a consequent fall in real wage rates.

Again we have come full circle. The decrease in real wages is now not a result of a wage lag but of a shift in relative demand for money substitutes — if it is correct that non-human goods are a better money substitute than labour. Unfortunately empirical evidence on these implications for anticipated inflations is sparse and we can only wish for more evidence, while waiting for others to obtain it.

APPENDIX

This appendix presents a simple numerical illustration of a wealth transfer via net monetary status in the context of a simultaneous revision of relative demands. We emphasize that this is an illustration of the process implied by economic analysis ; it is not evidence in support of that theory. Because it helps clarify the meaning of some of the implications contained in the text we have taken the liberty of including it as an appendix.

Let us suppose that the government — which we shall arbitrarily use as our source of inflation — decides to shift its relative demands. People for whose services or goods there has been a relative increase in demand will experience an increase in income and wealth. These demand-revision effects neither cause nor are caused by the net monetary status inflation-effects. The gross effect is a sum of both inflation and demand shift effects. This can be illustrated by the following numerical illustration. Suppose that the government wishes to obtain wealth by printing fiat money. Assume that it creates and spends new money for services, rather than for the purpose of existing capital goods (although this does not affect the wealth transfer process). Futhermore, let the money creation and resulting inflation be a one-shot operation. Let the individuals in a community be typified by five individuals whose wealth and income positions are summarized in Table 1.

TABLE 1

PRE-INFLATION WEALTH, DEBTS, AND INCOMES OF INDIVIDUALS

Persons	Wealth	Cash	Goods	Interpersonal Debts (−) or Credits (+)	Income
A	15·15	2·40	12·75	0	2·25
B	9·85	·85	9·00	0	1·00
C	16·10	·60	14·25	1·25	·75
D	4·65	·40	4·75	− ·50	·25
E	4·25	·75	4·25	− ·75	·75
	50·00	5·00	45·00	0	5·00
Govt.	10·00	1·00	9·00	0	1·00
Total :	60·00	6·00	54·00	0	6·00

All sorts of assumptions are possible about the ratio of income from capital assets and from labour. Assume, for simplicity, that the total income flow per period from labour and capital is equal to 10 per cent of the community's capital, and that all income is consumed. Capital goods can be used up if consumption is to be changed. For the redistributive process that assumption would make no difference. Only the numerical results would be modified. In equilibrium, assume the community jointly (but not severally) holds 10 per cent of the total wealth (including money) in the form of money. ($6 of money equals 10 per cent of the community's wealth of $54 + $6 = $60.) Let the government inflate the money supply by $1.20 of fiat money and spend $1.00 of it — all for the services of individual B.[1] When $1.00 per period increased money demand impinges on B, the price of his service is assumed to double (his income was formerly $1.00 per period). The government gets only half of B's services, since the private sector was offering $1.00 for all of B's services prior to the government's additional demand of $1.00 None of this increased demand goes to anyone except B in the first stage. The rise in service prices is reflected in captial goods prices.

Looking at each individual we see what this implies. A's balance sheet initially is:

A (before inflation and demand revision)

Cash	$ 2.40	Equity	$15.15
Goods	12.75		

$15.15

In the first period, his income stays at $2.25, while the price level of services rises to, say, $1.20. If he spends all his income, his consumption in real terms falls to $2.25(1.20 = $1.875), a decline of $.375 in original price units. In the next period he receives a larger income, $2.70 as B spends part of his increased earnings. A has the choice of spending $2.70 or saving part of it to restore some of his wealth. If he spends it all in order to maintain his consumption at its original level, his balance sheet position will be:

A (No Saving)

Cash	$2.40	Equity	$17.70
Goods	15.30		

$17.70

His equity, in original price level units, would be $17.70/1.20 = $14.75, a decline in wealth of $.40 (from $15.15). He experienced a decline in real income in the first period of $.375. The wealth loss, $.40 is his wealth redistribution loss due to the *inflation*, and the second is the loss of income consequent to the *demand revision* as relative demand is shifted towards B.

---

[1] By the time the government has spent $1.00, prices will be 1·20 of the former level. At this price level the government, given its propensity for liquidity will want to hold larger cash balances — because like everyone else, the demand for cash is in part a function of one's level of nominal wealth. If prices have risen by 20 per cent, we shall suppose the government wants to hold $1.20 in money. The upshot is that only $1.00 of the new money is spent.

In fact, no matter what the demand shift, the inflationary loss is unaffected. Only if the degree of demand shift is tied to the degree of inflation are the two effects related, but this tie is a policy correlation, completely independent of the fact of inflation.

Suppose that A decides to save the increment of money income in order to increase his stock of money. His balance sheet would now appear :

A (saving all his increased money income)

Cash	$2.85	Equity	$18.15
Goods	15.30		
	$18.15		

In real terms his equity is $18.15/1.20 = $15.125, a decline of $.25 from the original level. He has to save still more if he wants to restore his equity to its original real level. Although he can choose any level of saving and resultant equity, he will have suffered the same loss of $.40 in wealth because of the *inflation* and the reduced real income of $.375 consequent to the *demand revision*. How he choses to bear these two separate losses, that is, whether to maintain consumption by eating up his wealth, or to restore his wealth by saving, or to not save at all is entirely up to his discretion. He is forced into no particular way, but he is forced into making a choice among them — a choice forced on him by both the inflationary wealth redistribution and the revised demand effect on income and asset values.

In the same manner B's experience can be examined. Initially, his balance sheet is :

B (before inflation and before demand changes)

Cash	$.85	Equity	$9.85
Goods	9.00		
	$9.85		

During the first period he has received $2.00 of income and has spent $1.00. With the higher prices, his real income is $2.00/1.20 or $1.666, an increase of $.666 in original price units. He has lost wealth by being a net monetary creditor ; the real value of his money stock falls to $.85/1.20 = $.70833, a decline of $.1416 — exactly the same loss as if there were no demand shift. He can choose any combination of saving and consequent level of wealth that he wishes. If he saves all of his increase in real income, $.666, this will more than offset the inflationary loss of wealth of $.1416. He will have a net increase in wealth of $.525. If, instead, he saves, say, only $.20, his balance sheet will be :

B (*after restoring cash ratio*)

Cash	$ 1.05	Equity	$11.85
Goods	10.80		

$11.85

His equity (in original price level units) is now $11.85/1.20 = $9.875, an increase of .025. This increase is the result of his voluntary decision to save $.20. In summary, he loses $.1416 (original price level units) by being a net monetary creditor during the inflation, and he gains a transitory one-period increase of $.666 in income by the demand shift. He chose to save $.20 of that increase in income ($.1666 in original price level units), so his wealth increased by $.1666 − $.1416 = $.025. The rest of the increased real income, in original price level units, $.666 − $.1666 = $.50 is devoted to increasing his consumption. Similar analysis for C, D, and E yields the results given in the appropriate rows of Table 2. Columns (1) and (3), when summed, give Column (4).

This table shows that all of the income gain, $.666, accruing to B, is at the expense of the rest of the community (proportionate to their income) and not from inflation. Also the net wealth redistribution due to inflation is independent of the degree of demand revision. With the demand revision, income revision has occurred, as shown in the second column,

TABLE 2

SUMMARY OF EFFECTS OF INFLATION AND DEMAND
SHIFTS ON INCOME AND WEALTH

(All in original price level units)

	(1) Net Wealth Redistribution from Inflation	(2) Income Change Caused by Demand Revision : One period of Income	(3) Voluntary Savings Increments	(4) Net Changes in Wealth of Private Sector
A	− $.4000	− $.3750	$.3750	− .025
B	− .1416	.6666	.1666	.025
C	− .3083	− .1250	.1250	− .1833
D	.0166	− .0416	.0416	.0583
E	.0000	− .1250	.1250	.1250
	− $.833 (to Govt.)	0	$.8333	0

whereas the inflation wealth redistribution went from the money holders to the government, and from private net creditors to private net debtors. In this particular example, the amount of savings increments was simply assumed to be just sufficient to restore the private community's stock of real wealth. Under different assumptions about the desire to hold cash and to save, the numerical results would be different. The government could get the services without at the same time inducing the rest of the community to do any saving or dissaving. Or the community could insist on maintaining its consumption rate (and consume some wealth). In our example the community saved enough to restore its wealth to the pre-inflation level. But in any event, the inflation effect is one thing, and the shift in relative demand another, and the resultant saving decision still another thing.

———

DISCUSSION OF PROFESSOR ALCHIAN'S PAPER

Professor James appreciated Professor Alchian's scientific scruples ; his reluctance to make gratuitous statements had led him to the conclusion that inflation had no significant influence on income distribution and little even on wealth distribution. Such a conclusion, however, ran counter to conventional wisdom and, thought Professor James, to actual experience.

Professor Alchian placed his readers before a dilemma because, in his view, the theory of inflation implied 'no wage lags, no forced saving, no suffering by widows, orphans, and old people, no profits to businessmen and speculators, and no price distortions' (p. 621), so that either there was no value in economic theory or these phenomena were illusions. Professor Alchian concluded that they were so.

This implied that 'the available evidence and data simply (did) not support the presumption of the presence of those alleged phenomena' as Professor Alchian stated (p. 621). But did they not ? 'Widows' sufferings', old people reduced to misery as a result of monetary depreciation, had been common experience in France even though it could not be statistically demonstrated. Professor Alchian's systematic denial of money wages lagging behind rising prices for consumer's goods and of forced saving as implied by this was also surprising. It was true that wages were not always found to be lagging behind prices in actual observation, nor did they lag for ever. The lag appeared in the initial period of inflation, but wages tended later to overcome rising prices. At any rate the presence of an actual wage lag was too often observed in the course of inflation for logical reasoning to be sufficient proof to the contrary. Professor James did not possess statistical evidence on the spot to prove it, but the fact that wage-earners, far from having a money illusion, felt so urgent a need for a better adjustment of their wages to rising prices and made claims for a sliding scale in periods of inflation tended to prove that they did not think prices were sufficiently flexible.

Neither could Professor James agree with Professor Alchian's statement that inflation did not result in price distortions. He wished that a distinction had been made between open and suppressed inflation. In a situation of suppressed inflation surely there must be distortions since the prices of some commodities and services were strictly controlled — housing rents, for instance — whereas other prices were left free to rise or could not be prevented from doing so. In a situation of open inflation this disparity was perhaps not so marked. However, suppressed inflation was the kind of inflation usually observed today. It would seem, therefore, more realistic to take price distortions into account. Inflation did not work to the advantage of the great majority of people but differentially — to the benefit of certain sectors with increased production demand. Professor James would think that anyway even in an open inflation and supposing no discriminating price control, price distortions would tend to appear.

Professor Alchian reasoned on the grounds that what were commonly held to be the results of inflation could not be proved to be so using the available statistical evidence. (In an appendix to his paper he gave numerical illustrations of his own reasoning, warning readers that this was just an illustration of the implications of economic analysis, not evidence in support of his theory.)

Professor Alchian had had, however, to give an explanation for the observed data displaying a change in income distribution in concomitance with inflation which then had to be related to causes other than inflation. 'Sufferings by widows and orphans', for instance, were a consequence of war — but, asked Professor James, what was the mechanism if not inflation ? Price distortions were related by Professor Alchian to differences in the elasticity of demand for different commodities. Again, one had to find out the reason why the change in demand was sectorally differentiated— inflation was the most plausible explanation. Losses experienced by holders of interest-bearing assets were attributed by Professor Alchian to their having failed to hedge against price increase by contracting in monetary terms. Again, creditors would be harmed if they held claims in the form of debentures only in so far as prices rose.

Despite his references to historical evidence, what Professor Alchian had had in mind seemed to be only the U.S. type of inflation, i.e. latent inflation with creeping rises in prices, nothing like the European type of inflation. Had he considered open inflation his conclusions would probably have been entirely different. Even though there was no general agreement on the analysis of the U.S. type of inflation, one might venture to suggest that rising prices resulted from money wages increasing faster than productivity of labour — a situation which would be the reverse of a wage lag. This might explain why he and Professor Alchian disagreed.

Professor Rasmussen expressed full agreement with the criticisms offered by Professor James. He, however, did not think the main point to be that Professor Alchian had perhaps only considered creeping inflation while other types should also have been considered. His disagreement was more basic. Professor Alchian's paper consisted of a series of statements without any detailed analysis of the 'origin' and type of inflation considered and without any attempt to analyse the functioning of the economy during the process of inflation.

Professor Rasmussen did not want to go into details and repeat Professor James's statement. He wished, however, to express strong disagreement with Professor Alchian's statement in Section II (2) (c). It was argued that a study of the gains or losses of social groups might be misleading because no social group was homogeneous. However, it seemed to Professor Rasmussen that this could be taken into account in the analysis. In the more simple cases one might simply utilize not only the mean of the distribution but also measures of deviation, etc. Secondly, it was stated that such research work might lead to 'incorrect' policy action. Quite apart from the value judgment involved, such argument could and should never be an argument against valuable fact finding.

Professor Delivanis said that he was grateful to Professor Alchian for having put the stress on the principles that inflation would be to the detriment only of holders of net money claims ; that its effect ought not to be confused with those of concomitant events ; that gains and losses should not be related to social groups as such.

He would disagree, however, with Professor Alchian on two points. Wages could lag behind prices. Statistical evidence supplied by Professor Alchian, e.g. a positive correlation between the rise in prices and in real wages since 1889 was no proof of the absence of a wage lag because it ignored increases in productivity. He could not agree either with Professor Alchian's criticism of forced saving as being an empty concept. In each of the three versions given by Professor Alchian forced saving did operate as an actual transfer of income allowing those who benefited from it to spend more than they would have been able to do otherwise.

Professor Reder said that Professor Alchian had written his paper as an attempt to arouse critical examination of the way words were used. He had wanted to provoke debate and achieved his purpose with such success that Professor Reder thought it opportune to bring the discussion back to pure theory. Professor Alchian was not minimizing the sufferings of widows and orphans but inviting us to substitute one model for another. Thus he had reduced the phenomenon of a wage lag to a change in relative prices which might easily occur without any time lag. The implication was that inflation accompanied a relative change in food prices *vis-à-vis* other commodities having less weight in the cost of living index so that real wages must appear to decline even when in fact they had not. However, there might be a 'true' wage lag. How could we determine this ? One might consider a case such that there was a marked increase in the supply of money with all relative supply and demand functions unchanged. If it were found that money-wage rates increased less rapidly than other prices while simultaneously an unfilled vacancy index increased *vis-à-vis* indices of excess demand for other goods and services, this would indicate the existence of a wage lag.

Professor James pointed out to Professor Reder that he did not accept his definition of inflation. Professor Reder thought of inflation as a money injection : excess demand was a consequence of inflation. Professor James would consider excess demand as inflation *per se*. Non-monetary factors could equally well cause the rise in prices. All his reasons for disagreeing with Professor Alchian stemmed from conflicting views about the definition of inflation.

Professor Brochier did not think that one could argue, from the observation of a positive correlation between wages and prices since 1889, that such a phenomenon as a wage lag did not exist because this was long-period analysis. Wages lagged behind prices only for a limited period of time and the lag could only be measured within such a period as a short-run phenomenon. Over a longer period leaving time for the wages to adjust to the price rise one would obviously find no lag. Nevertheless wage-earners did incur an actual loss of real income.

Professor André Marchal said that Professor Alchian's approach to the subject from the point of view of income earners defined according to their legal status as creditors and debtors instead of social groups was stimulating and original. Professor Alchian had postulated that distribution could be affected by inflation only to the extent that the rise in prices would change the relationship between creditors and debtors. However, he thought that Professor Alchian had been very biased in his argument, brushing aside facts which contradicted his thesis.

Was the assumption that inflation could start by an increase in consumers' prices to be rejected as a preconceived idea ? It would depend on the origin of the inflationary process — in other words, whether this was demand inflation or cost inflation.

Neither was the assumption of wages being more sticky than prices a preconceived idea. It seemed to Professor Marchal to be founded not only on logic but also on the observation of facts. To refute it Professor Alchian would have had to produce statistical evidence bearing on short-run analysis. Not only was the argument about a positive correlation between real wages and money prices a long-run consideration but it implicitly referred to the classics' idea of long-run in which in a system of equilibrium there would be complete adjustments of the variables to an exogenously given change.

Professor Alchian's reasoning which led to a denial of price viscosity did not convince him. Professor Alchian had written that the illusion came from comparing 'the price of a single good with an index of many prices. If all prices (were) equally flexible and responsive, each single price (would) appear to lag — or lead! — the smoother changing average of all other prices' (p. 626). This criticism would hold against the comparison of the change in the price of one single commodity with the percentage variation of the average of all the prices retained for calculating a price index. However, the customary procedure was to use for the comparison the average of all indices, not the index of average prices. One would compare, e.g., the percentage variation in the price of one consumers' good with the percentage average of the actual variations of the prices of all the other goods contained in the cost of living index. This was the correct method of calculation. Professor Alchian's argument was not significant unless one used an average instead of an index — but an index made up of unequally flexible prices, and this was begging the question.

Professor Marchal still believed that inflation had a bearing on the distribution of income and wealth not only through the creditors versus debtors relationship but, more fundamentally, through changes in the structure of demand and the uneven flexibility of prices.

Professor Robinson hoped that he would be forgiven for broadening out the discussion. There had been ten papers on models of distribution. As a fly on a spider's web he admired the ability of spiders. What were the characteristics of a good model ? It had to disregard the unimportant and include enough important phenomena. Those who wrote papers on models produced them in anticipation of facts. Did the ten authors feel that their models were sufficient to explain the facts which had been produced in the first part of the Conference ?

If one went back to Feinstein's and Lecaillon's facts, their first important phenomenon was an increased share of labour in national income ; the second, the great decline in incomes from rent and land property, leading to a decline in the share going to owners of property.

Even supposing that model makers had a complete foreknowledge of economic trends, Professor Robinson would be sceptical about their ability to forecast the evolution of distribution in the long run because of institutional changes. He had heard hardly any comment on the way state intervention had operated to modify distribution. Another momentous change had been overlooked : whereas in early days corporations had tended to distribute all the profits they earned, they had since acquired an identity distinct from their shareholders ; the major part of earned profits was retained within the firm instead of rewarding the owners of shares, so that distributed profits no longer reflected the category of capital.

There were these unassimilated facts and there were the theories. The two groups were almost holding separate conferences. Professor Solow had said that there was an econometric model behind his spider's web. Professor Robinson would like more assurance that using an econometric model with no more variables it was possible to explain the very big changes over the past ten years.

Professor Solow said that he proposed to follow Professor Robinson's detour. Professor Robinson suspected that there was a spider behind every web and not much else. Professor Solow said that his own paper was not designed to explain long-run changes in distribution and no paper had been given on short-term changes, i.e. quarter to quarter changes. His paper was begun to explain a particular set of facts, working on productivity changes in the U.S. and Canada since the war, using productivity data. It was not fair to ask a model to do more than it set out to do.

Professor Alchian wished to thank Professor Reder for the way he had interpreted his paper. It was true that he had meant to be blunt and decisive. Professor Robinson had criticized the ten model makers for having neglected the part played by the state. Professor Alchian did not know whether he was included in the ten but he had, he thought, attempted to explain one of the ways a government redistributed wealth through inflation.

His point about the absence of a wage lag had been much commented on in the course of the discussion. However, no evidence of the phenomenon had been produced. No matter how provocative his position had seemed to be it was in no way original. It was stolen from Irving Fisher and Keynes, at any rate the earlier Keynes, in the *Tract on Monetary Reform*. (Later, Keynes had changed his mind, and in the *Treatise on Money* he had asserted time and again that there was a wage lag — yet presented example after example of cases where wages had risen faster.) If wages were to lag behind prices it implied that wages had to be stickier than other prices but there was nothing in economic theory to support this assumption.

In its positive aspects inflation was a tax on cash holdings. It could only weigh upon those who held wealth in cash. Some people had been shocked by the way he had treated 'the sufferings of widows and orphans' in theory. What, however, he had meant was that widows and orphans were hurt by inflation in so far as they were holders of fixed debentures in money terms and not as widows and orphans. If they were all net monetary creditors all would be affected, but it was not intrinsically so.

He had insisted on the distinction between unanticipated and anticipated inflation. This was crucial; if inflation was perfectly anticipated by creditors the rates of interest would be adjusted to monetary depreciation so that there would be no redistribution of wealth to their detriment.

PART V

INCOME POLICIES

Chapter 23

THE INFLUENCE OF GOVERNMENT ACTIVITY ON THE DISTRIBUTION OF NATIONAL INCOME [1]

BY

G. U. PAPI

University of Rome,
President of the International Economic Association

I. AGGREGATE INCOME AND PERSONAL INCOME, REAL AND MONEY INCOME

WE call income all those direct, or consumer, goods which accrue to an economic subject over time and which, by implication, can be consumed without impairing the source from which this flow of goods originates, except for such losses as can be covered by amortization and insurance. Unlike the static concept of wealth, the concept of income is dynamic, in so far as it deals with the time flow of goods to the economic subject. Given the money stock and the prices of consumer goods, the sum of all the products of quantity of each good or service times its price constitutes the aggregate money income of any country. A few words may be said right at the outset about how aggregate income, or the sum total of consumer goods, is distributed at all stages of production among those who contribute to its creation. Aggregate income is distributed in the first place among stages of production ; within any one stage, it is, secondly, distributed among the various production units taking part in the process of production ; and within any one production unit, it is, thirdly, distributed among the factors of production employed therein.

Take, for example, bread. The first link in the chain of production of this direct consumption good is, maybe, a firm which makes ploughs and carts ; the second link is a wheat farm, the third a flour mill and the last a baker who turns the flour into bread. Following this division of labour, we get an 'economic complex' associated with the consumer good bread. The producers of ploughs can make their

[1] Translation by Elizabeth Henderson.

product, and sell it at a price which becomes their income, for the sole reason that bread is demanded by consumers and commands a price. On the market, the price of ploughs is, therefore, a function of the price of the consumer good bread. Similarly, the wheat growers can sell their product for a price which becomes their income, only because the consumer good bread has a price which makes it possible for the intermediate good wheat also to have a price and so on and so forth. Money is a token of advance income pending the production of the direct good bread. Money facilitates the exchange of all the goods needed to produce a direct good. In extreme synthesis, we can make the following statements :

(a) The income of a community is the sum total of the direct goods, or services, produced in the course of more or less numerous stages of production.

(b) Any production unit which makes a producer good can, through its sale, get an advance on what we call the real income, that is, the sum total of direct goods, say bread, to the production of which the components of any one economic complex contribute by their activities.

(c) Money is the means by which the direct good — on which, so long as it is not yet produced, advances are drawn — is eventually distributed among the successive stages of production.

(d) Within each stage of production, the direct good is distributed among all units which contribute to its production.

(e) Within each unit, the direct good is distributed among the owners of factors of production.

For each owner of a factor of production, income is then the flow of direct goods or money which accrues to him over time without diminishing the source of its origin. Aggregate income and personal income are, thus, complementary concepts, whether they are expressed in real or in monetary terms.

II. THE CONCEPT OF TAX AS THE INCOME OF PUBLIC ENTERPRISE

Apart from entrepreneurs and firms at every stage of an economic complex we have to consider also, at the very beginning of any kind of productive process, the state which provides the indispensable public services without which there could be no production at all. It follows that the state, too, has a right to a share in the distribution of real income, that is, the sum of direct goods produced by each economic complex ; the state equally has a right to collect its share in advance, and it does so through taxation.

In the old days of taxation in kind, the government would levy the tithe from any one of the producers — say, the wheat growers — and simply take part of the produce at once, leaving the rest to be distributed among the production units at other stages of production and, within each unit, among factors of production.

With growing division of labour, taxation in kind became somewhat complicated and, in any event, money enables every final sales transaction to be decomposed into a series of intermediary transactions. The government now lays down a tax rate and collects accordingly part of the money income of the firm making the producer good furthest removed from the final good. Successively, the government then collects a tax of equal or different rate on the money income of the firm at the next stage of production. That second firm, however, to avoid excessive taxation, will deduct from its declared and taxable money income its own prior payments to the firm at the preceding stage of production, say, the ploughmakers. By taxing the money income of each firm forming part of an economic complex, the government will, since each firm deducts from its own taxable income the costs of producing that income, get exactly the same result that the old tithe system could have yielded, and at the same time make sure there is no tax evasion.

It can be said, therefore, that the process of refining income for purpose of taxation, that is, deducting all expenses incurred in producing the income, follows the same lines as the process of distribution : it takes place as between various stages of production, firms at every stage, and the various categories of factors of production within each firm. To make this process really effective, it is necessary, on the other hand, to do away with tax evasion which might impair tax revenue, and on the other hand to avoid double taxation — both conditions of an organic system of taxation.

III. THE PRODUCTION OF GOODS FOR PERSONAL AND PUBLIC CONSUMPTION

The productive activities of any society as a whole may be divided into two broad categories according to their results :

(a) Production of goods for individual consumption, such as food, clothes, houses, and others which directly satisfy a wide range of human needs. These consumption goods are produced with the help of producer goods, such as fuel and power, machinery, raw materials, transport vehicles, etc., and in the course of successive stages, the number of which depends on the state of technology.

(b) Production of public services, or, as some might prefer to say, goods for consumption by the community, even though the latter as such has no faculty of consumption. These include the administration of justice, national defence, the creation of roads and railways, public works. From the point of view of the individual, all these may, in turn, be considered as producer goods, in so far as they help to produce a more secure and ample supply of consumer goods. Like producer goods properly speaking, these too are linked to consumer goods by typical technical relations.

The first kind of production is carried on by individuals, alone or in groups, and it is financed by the proceeds of sales of consumer goods, for instance bread, regardless of the number of stages through which production has to pass. From this process we can derive fairly precise notions of national and personal income, real income and money income.

Real national income, or, as some might prefer to say, the real national dividend, is the sum of consumer goods produced or consumed in the time unit — generally a month, or a year — in a more or less regular flow and which can be consumed without impairing the source from which the flow of goods originates. Given the money stock and the prices of consumer goods, the sum of all the products of quantity times price constitutes the monetary national income of a country.

Side by side with the production of consumer goods by individuals, and financed by the sale of the products, there is also a public production of goods and services. The goods so produced are consumer goods from the point of view of the community as a whole and producer goods from the point of view of the creation of a country's real or monetary income. Production by the state, however, is financed by other means : by taxation, saving, capital consumption, and inflation. It does, like other production, distribute incomes to those who contribute to it.

So long as the production of public goods and services by the state is financed solely by taxes on the incomes of the inhabitants, real income, that is the sum of consumer goods produced and consumed in the time unit, still coincides with monetary income, that is the sum of the products of the prices times the quantities of these same consumer goods. It can certainly not be assumed *a priori* that the incomes which the state subsequently distributes through the production of public services are additional to the incomes distributed prior to the tax levies through individual and independent production, and therefore there is no reason for any divergence between aggregate and money income, as defined above.

A divergence between real income and money income does appear, however, as soon as the government begins to draw on sources other than the incomes of the inhabitants, or, in other words, as soon as ordinary finance gives way to extraordinary finance. By ordinary finance is meant here a process of financing which is indefinitely reproduceable, as seems to be true at first sight of income-tax collection from the country's inhabitants in order to pay for the activities of government. Extraordinary finance, on the other hand, is characterized by taxes which the taxpayer cannot pay out of current income, without drawing on capital. But if capital is to be drawn upon, this presupposes that someone must have some savings which he is willing to spend on acquiring some part of the wealth of the taxpayer who is unable to pay the tax.

It may, furthermore, happen that saving is not in ample supply, or that savers are unwilling to subscribe to public loans, or that it proves impossible to increase the tax burden. In that case a government which cannot finance its activities with the proceeds of the taxes it levies on the incomes of citizens, can raise additional funds by using up capital, or, as is sometimes said, by disinvestment.

The mere recourse to these two sources of government revenue, saving and capital consumption, can cause the sum of disposable resources to diverge widely from aggregate real income. We are in the presence of what might be called generic inflation, which greatly increases the possible scope of government activity.

Finally, the government can yet further increase the resources with which to finance its own activities by tapping a fourth source : specific inflation, or the creation of money without any corresponding increase in consumer goods. Such money creation offers to its originator ever increasing chances of gaining disposal over more and more of the goods he needs. As soon as the new money is distributed in the form of incomes which remain within the country, these new incomes swell the country's money income, which originally was defined as equal to its real income.

Recourse to this fourth source of government finance causes the gap between money income and real income, which appeared first under the impact of generic inflation, to widen enormously and also keeps increasing the scope of government activity, regardless of the economic results and of the destruction of goods which are bound to follow from this mistaken, though convenient, concept of monetary income.

To correct this concept and to examine all its real implications seems a necessary preliminary to the study of any economic, financial, or social phenomenon.

IV. THE THREE ECONOMIC ACTIVITIES OF GOVERN-
MENT. THE CONCEPT OF AN ORGANIC SYSTEM
OF TAXATION

The modern state carries its economic activities into ever-expanding and more varied fields. For more than a century the literature of many languages has analysed the causes and consequences of this expansion of government activity.

It is hard to see how one can progress very far with any theory of the distribution of national income without taking account, on the one hand, of the growing portion of income accruing to government, and on the other hand, of the influence which the activities of government and other public agencies exercise on the formation and growth of income at given rates. Before we can work on the theory of income distribution, we have to analyse the consequences of the multiple activities of government and public agencies : we need a theory of state activities. Without it, any theory of income distribution is bound to remain incomplete in relation to the realities of the life of society.

Government economic activities may conveniently be considered under three broad headings : the raising of revenue, more generally referred to as taxation, expenditure, and intervention. None of these can be considered separately without running the risk of serious gaps in the analysis, for the simple reason that, just like the activities of individuals, the activities of government have profound repercussions on real national income.

Since it is clearly impossible to discuss the whole range of government activities in this paper, we shall here merely point to the consequences and then to the economic limits of the three activities of taxation, expenditure, and intervention.

A system of taxation which is adapted to the country's situation and to its targets of economic growth, should fulfil the following conditions:

(a) there must be no tax evasion ;

(b) there must be no double taxation ;

(c) the tax burden must, on the whole, be proportional to taxable income ;

(d) the tax system must be flexible with respect to cyclical fluctuations ;

(e) recourse to extraordinary finance (extraordinary taxes, loans) must be adapted to the country's available liquid resources or to the banking system's ability to advance credit on future real income without incurring excessive risks.

These few conditions serve to define in practice the optimum taxation of both income and savings, and indeed to define the concept of an organic system of taxation, both ordinary and extraordinary. They also define the minimum cost of taxation for any given community and, by the same token, the economic limits of taxation. The more any government departs from these conditions under the pressure of day-to-day vicissitudes, the higher is the cost to the community and the greater the damage to the formation of the country's real income.

V. THE CONCEPT OF AN ORGANIC SYSTEM OF PUBLIC EXPENDITURE

Public funds may be spent on the production of general public services, such as the administration of justice, security, or public health, or on the production of special public services, that is to say services divisible into sales units, like transport and communication, or on investment, such as railways, ports, roads, electric power stations, or, finally, on subsidies and subventions.

Unless public expenditure generates new incomes for consumers and producers, it encourages consumption to the detriment of saving, impedes the formation of new saving, may give rise to inflationary pressure, and will hardly call forth private investment apt to increase national income. The so-called transfer payments, for example, which simply break up existing savings into a series of small income flows, destroy a great stock of disposable savings and are not suitable

647

for promoting the growth of either production or income.

It is a general belief that the effects of public expenditure tend to offset those of taxation in diminishing the incomes of taxpayers. The truth is that public expenditures have an expansionary effect on the country's economy only on condition that their use in general or special public services, investment, subsidies to firms or price supports to the benefit of particular groups of individuals eventually generates in every consumer and producer budget new incomes which, via the reduction of risks and costs, become additional to the country's existing incomes. Unless this happens, the harmful effects of public expenditure, far from offsetting those of taxation, are added to the latter. This is why care should be taken in the formulation and presentation of national and local government budgets to give preference to such public expenditures as are capable of generating new incomes for consumers and producers, and to cut down all other public expenditures.

The concept of an organic system of public expenditure applies to a set of expenditures so organized that most of them are always capable of generating new incomes for consumers and producers. As in the case of an organic system of taxation, the concept of an organic system of public expenditure also implies the economic limits to government expenditure.

We see that the techniques both of raising revenue and spending it have their influence on national income. Given the aim of encouraging a steady growth of real *per caput* income, the principle of organic taxation requires techniques of revenue which minimize both the total tax burden and, by appropriate tax distribution, the burden on individual incomes. In its turn, public expenditure must also aim at the growth of national income. The effects of the relevant techniques are coming to be understood much better ; the important point is that governments must stop allocating expenditures under the pressure of emergency situations — which, incidentally, most often means also seeking revenue from those taxpayers who offer the least resistance. The principle of organic expenditure requires techniques which maximize income-creating expenditure at the expense of unproductive expenditure.

VI. GOVERNMENT INTERVENTION

Alongside these two vast fields of government activity, there is a third, no less extensive one : that of government intervention. It, too, exercises great influence on national income and very often its effects are not confined to the country under consideration, but spread to all the countries having trade relations with it. It is of great interest, therefore, to try to establish the economic limits of such government intervention.

We define government intervention as public action designed to achieve an aim which the community has set itself. A first useful classification is to distinguish between intervention in the general interest — that is, in the interest of all or most of the members of a given community, and intervention in the interest of specific groups. The latter kind of intervention tends to multiply as the political identity and value of certain groups of interests becomes a factor to be reckoned with.

Let me give some examples.

In the field of production, general intervention may take the form of the creation of government monopolies, nationalization of certain branches of industry, the timing of public works; as special intervention we may note the enforcement of certain production plans — for instance, particular crops, government control of particular firms, the formation of industrial associations by government order or on public initiative.

We may ask : What are the reasons which lead government to intervene in this or that economic activity ? The answer is that government tends more and more to relieve the individual of the responsibility of organizing his own life according to his own discretion. This tendency accompanies the growth of public expenditure, but remains distinct from it. It is due, among other causes, to the successes of the labour movement. A lot of new forms of insurance for the workers have developed : labour exchanges, more and more numerous types of social insurance, new types of direct and indirect relief, general education and vocational training. With the growing political power of the working classes these forms of individual insurance have in many countries been assumed or at least encouraged by government.

But the rapid evolution and spreading of this new kind of claim caused the insurance principle to be extended beyond the sphere of the individual. Gradually it came to be realized that government action was also needed to assure the development of productive undertakings, which, being the sources of income, are rightly considered as eminently important for the community.

If, to take an example from the production sector, the government authorizes or refuses permission for the establishment of new firms or the enlargement of existing ones, it relieves the entrepreneur of the risk of a wrong investment choice. It is in effect the government and not the entrepreneur that makes the decision whether or not to set up or enlarge a firm, and it is thus up to the government to assess the expediency of intensifying or not intensifying this or that line of production.

Or if the government reaffirms the principle of private enterprise in the face of political strikes which endanger the country's economy, this amounts in effect to relieving private capital, private activities, and the faculty of saving — the mainsprings of any expansion of production — from the uncertainties to which compromise or the temporary toleration of political strikes give rise. Anti-monopoly legislation to safeguard even small-scale production, control of profit distribution, compulsory production programmes for firms in certain branches — all these are examples of government taking away from entrepreneurs the responsibility of organizing their own business according to their own judgement.

This growing interference of government in economic life therefore tends to relieve first individuals, and then firms, of certain risks. Economically speaking, the government extends the principle of risk insurance first to individuals and then to firms.

VII. THE COST OF INSURANCE

In practice, the insurance principle amounts to substituting certain present cost for uncertain future cost. This uncertain future cost is the cost which individuals or firms would have to incur if the insured event should take place. The former cost should be lower than the latter, and the difference between the two represents the benefit accruing to the individual or firm through insurance. It is this margin between the two costs which induces the individual or firm to incur the certain present cost of insurance, that is the insurance premium.

The notion of the cost of insurance becomes more complicated when we pass from private insurance companies and individuals to government insurance of individuals and firms against certain risks.

For instance, the government may wish to insure all the members of a community, including the well-to-do, against such risks as a shortage of goods and services due to excess demand ; in this case it will have recourse to rationing. Or the government may wish to protect specific groups — those in the lowest income brackets, for example — by exempting certain consumer goods from taxation. Or it may wish to protect firms in some branch of industry against a fall of domestic prices due to a large influx of foreign goods, and this can be done by customs duties, quotas and other obstacles to imports, or else by purchase or sales monopolies on the home or foreign market. All these latter measures aim at avoiding price falls, production stoppages, unemployment, idle capital resources, inventory losses. And even though such measures may be taken at the instance of certain interest groups of producers, they may still be regarded as general intervention in the sense that they benefit all members of the community.

Lastly, the government may decide on intervention not in the interests of individuals or firms, but to protect itself against certain risks. For instance, if the government fails to avert certain harmful developments, it runs the political risk of being upset by a coalition of the damaged interests.

The point to note is that all government intervention, whether in the general interest, or in the interest of specific groups, or in its own interest, is always based on the principle of incurring certain present cost rather than uncertain future cost. And the authorities responsible for the decision on intervention are always also themselves responsible for the assessment of the two costs, especially of the magnitude of the damage to be expected in the absence of intervention. The officials on whom the responsibility of this decision rests may of course exaggerate in one direction or the other. But if, to avoid contradictions, they acquire the habit of thinking of all intervention in terms of an insurance principle with respect to individuals, firms and government itself, they cannot escape weighing the certain and immediate economic consequences of government action against its ultimate beneficial results.

How are we to define the cost and benefits of government intervention ? As I have had occasion to explain at length elsewhere, the cost includes all the direct and indirect charges incurred by the government itself and by all those on whom the intervention has unfavourable effects. The benefits include not only the achievement of the purpose of the intervention, that is the avoidance of the harmful consequences — or in other words the uncertain future cost — of developments which might occur in the absence of intervention, but they include also the beneficial consequences of the intervention itself. Examples of such beneficial consequences are low consumer prices due to rationing, lower production costs due to appropriate allocation of factors of production, more remunerative sales prices as a result of customs duties, provided these latter do not act as disincentives to an expansion of output.

All these favourable consequences are additional to the minimum beneficial result of intervention, which is the elimination of a future possible cost. They reinforce the benefits in relation to the cost of intervention. Unlike ordinary public expenditure, government intervention is, therefore, economically justified even if it does not create new incomes ; it is justified by the difference between present certain cost and minimum beneficial result — or we might say, between the certain present cost of the insurance and the possible future cost which it eliminates.

The insurance principle can certainly also be assumed to apply to the economic activities of government in the fields of revenue and public expenditure. But it is convenient to discuss it and its implications under the heading of intervention — partly because research into this branch of government activity is generally less advanced, and partly because, given its multiple aspects, it provides the best support for the validity of the insurance principle as a standard of economic behaviour.

VIII. THE INSURANCE PRINCIPLE AND REGIONAL ECONOMIC INTEGRATION

Like all other government intervention, the introduction or abolition of customs duties, quantitative import restrictions, or export subsidies may be based upon the insurance principle, and justified economically by the difference between present certain cost and minimum beneficial result. In my view the same principle is applicable also to the wider field of economic integration between countries belonging to the same region, say Europe.

Integration implies for every participating government a whole series of interventions other than taxation, public loans, and public expenditure. These interventions have to do with the establishment of a common policy, with a better organization of the domestic market through such measures as rationing, stock-piling, or the abolition of price supports, and with the better organization of foreign trade through the gradual elimination of the various kinds of obstacles to trade. If the process of integration is to have durable results, it can neither neglect economic phenomena nor do without the economic and therefore the insurance principle.

The only difference between national intervention and regional integration lies in the source of insurance. On the national plane, it is the government which assumes the function of insurance on behalf of individuals and firms, and it is government intervention which protects all the members of the community, or certain defined groups, or the government itself, against certain risks. On the regional plane, this function of insurance is assumed by the concerted action of member governments.

Let us take an example. Certain trade barriers, such as customs duties, import restrictions or export subsidies, set up by governments for the protection of national interests, are to be suppressed. The question arises : When can these obstacles to trade be removed at least loss ? The answer is : when the concerted efforts of governments to build a common market enable each member country to expand its own exports enough to offset the cost of importing from other member countries goods which, in the absence of integration, might have been bought elsewhere or not at all.

In other words, economic integration begins to have chances of success as soon as concerted action by governments begins to be capable of replacing insurance by national governments in the form of obstacles placed in the way of foreign trade, and to offer each country a definite net advantage. As in all forms of national intervention, the economic justification of regional integration lies in the difference between cost and benefit. The certain present cost of concerted action by governments is the disappearance of national insurance measures in the form of obstacles to international trade ; the minimum beneficial result is elimination of the risk that trade between the member nations will diminish. So long as a clear difference between cost and benefit is not demonstrable, so long negotiations may continue, treaties may even be signed, but that integration which would confer a minimum of benefits on each country will not yet be achieved. It will be achieved only when regional insurance can replace the various forms of government insurance on the national plane.

IX. EXAMPLE OF GOVERNMENT INTERVENTION — GOVERNMENT CONTROL OF COMPANIES

The complexities of modern life keep driving individuals and groups to call for ever-expanding public activities. The counterforces tending to limit the economic sphere of government are definitely on the losing side. And as government activities grow, so grows the damage they can do if their cost exceeds any reasonable valuation of minimum beneficial results. It behoves experts and statesmen alike to concern themselves with the losses this may entail for the community.

The damage may for a time be offset or disguised by certain factors such as population growth, increasing productivity, credit expansion, or disinvestment. But if we leave those factors aside and postulate the condition *ceteris paribus*, then the red light shows as soon as real national income, as well as capital accumulation and new saving, decline. This is the point where government must heed the economic principle, and must confine its intervention within the limits of a positive ratio between cost and benefit.

To show what dangerous consequences for the country's economy may result from the government's failure to observe these limits, let us take the example of government participation in a company producing goods or services.

What have now become known as public firms, that is, companies in which the government has a financial, and usually a majority interest, have to be distinguished from private companies on the one hand, and from public enterprise properly speaking on the other. Government-controlled companies differ from private enterprise in so far as they may pursue purposes other than to earn a profit, and from a public agency producing special public services in so far as the latter, while non-profit-making, yet has economic behaviour forced upon itself by the very purpose of providing services at least cost to the public. In relation to private enterprise, both autonomous government agencies and government-controlled companies are public. It is often said nowadays that government finds the latter form preferable because it is more suitable for competitive, and even imperfectly competitive, markets. Market differences are used to explain the different principles of management : monopoly is associated with public agencies, competition with government-controlled companies.

But the alleged difference between these two forms of public enterprise really has no basis of precise fact. It is true that autonomous government agencies are monopolistic, but they are so not for the purpose of profit, but only for the purpose of producing as cheaply as possible certain divisible public services, and thereby maximizing their consumption. It bears repeating that this purpose imposes strict economic behaviour.

However, monopolistic elements are not absent from government-controlled companies either. They may, for instance, be given savings to transform into capital which other firms have to borrow ; or they may be granted, or indeed simply arrogate to themselves, other kinds of privileges, such as not to pay certain taxes. Given that both types of public enterprise are monopolistic, it can no longer be said that they operate in different market conditions. Even on the unrealistic assumption that a government-controlled company really does form part of a competitive market, it still remains true that precisely in a competitive market survival depends upon the strict observance of the economic principle. Whether, for some reason or another, the government chooses one or the other form of public enterprise, strict adherence to the economic principle is always of the essence. The economic principle must rule autonomous government agencies, even though they are typically monopolistic, because they have to provide a special public service at the lowest possible price ; and it must rule government-controlled companies, because they are in competition with private companies. No vague notions of market differences can justify the adoption of different principles of management in the two cases, namely, strictly economic ones for autonomous government agencies, and non-economic ones for government-controlled companies.

X. THE ECONOMIC PRINCIPLE AS AN ATTRIBUTE OF EACH SEPARATE FIRM

The economic principle is always the same in all cases ; it is the same for private companies, government-controlled companies, and autonomous government agencies. Furthermore, the economic principle is translated into facts through the judgements of individual entrepreneurs, that is, in each separate firm producing goods or services, with or without government participation. There simply is no substitute for the judgement of the entrepreneurs and managers responsible ; it is useless to look for the economic principle, for instance, in any comparison between the aggregate figures pertaining to all firms, such as aggregate investment and aggregate return on capital.

In practice it may well happen, of course, that firms producing goods at joint costs or at related costs are run by one and the same entrepreneur, whose unity of purpose enables him for a time to offset the losses of one firm by the other's profits. Such an entrepreneur may also impute to one of the firms a larger share of total costs than to the other, because, say, the former's products are in greater demand on the market. This sort of thing does, in fact, happen often enough. But it can happen only because the two firms are really only one, and under the management of one entrepreneur only, and because that single entrepreneur can decide, on technical grounds, how much of the joint or related costs he is to impute to both firms in the light of market conditions.

However, the technical decisions which an entrepreneur takes on the basis of the data and calculations pertaining to several firms under his own management are one thing ; it would be quite another thing to expect such decisions from, say, a Ministry of State Participations (as in Italy), or from a Joint Ministerial Committee, let alone from the Cabinet. Such bodies are generally worlds apart from the possibilities of arriving at technical judgements concerning the management of separate companies ; yet it would be up to them, for instance, to decide — and to decide without reference to any *a priori* limitations — that companies showing a loss should nevertheless stay in business. The consequences for the country's whole economy are, of course, known well enough : they are an increase in the public debt ; the need for more and more government funds. And this sort of thing can go on so long as the losses of some firms are offset by the profits of others, even though the latter are in no way connected with the former. To say the least, decisions of this kind are somewhat disconcerting.

All this goes to show that even in the case of government-controlled companies, the question as to whether management is economically rational can be answered only with reference to each separate firm, or in other words, to each separate government intervention. Aggregate figures, like aggregate investment and aggregate return on capital, are useful enough in presenting past results with reference to global phenomena ; but they are no substitute for economic analysis, that is, an enquiry into the behaviour of individual business men, nor for the assessment of the economic justification of government intervention, in the sense that every public investment generates, within a reasonable period, new incomes in addition to those that already exist. In Great Britain, for instance, public firms are allowed to run at a loss for up to five years only.

XI. GOVERNMENT-CONTROLLED FIRMS AND SOCIAL
COSTS

There is another illusion against which one must be on guard. Whether they run at a loss or at a profit, government-controlled companies as such can do nothing to avoid certain social costs — the costs, for instance, due to differential rates of development in different regions of one and the same country. This is a problem which requires long-term structural changes in the country's economy. It is somewhat naïve to pretend that any contribution can be made to the solution of this problem by production through government-controlled companies — especially if they run at a loss.

There is another type of social cost which it is often considered government-controlled companies can help to avoid, even if they run at a loss : the cost, that is, of inadequate utilization of factors of production. This is a problem with which I have repeatedly dealt in other writings, explaining how an improvement in the public health of depressed areas, the battle against illiteracy, widespread vocational training, and an informed structural policy designed to lead to a durable increase in agricultural incomes can eventually shift excess population from the land to other sectors of production, where these people can produce more and therefore get more pay. But this is surely not a task for government-controlled companies, especially not if they run at a loss. These are problems, I repeat, which can be solved only by structural changes which take a long time. Italy's own experience is ample proof that it is vain to look for the solution of problems of regional imbalance either in massive and unprofitable public investment or in production by government-controlled, and possibly equally unprofitable, companies.

Finally, it is sometimes argued that government-controlled companies can be used to keep prices down. But, surely, a company in the red can hardly be expected to have any sort of beneficial influence on the market. In some form or other the losses of government-controlled firms must be offset at the expense of all citizens, either through increased taxation or through an increase in the public debt. The question then arises what damages are the greater : those deriving from monopoly, or those which all citizens have to sustain to make good the continuing losses of government-controlled industry. The comparison does not always confirm the alleged price-reducing functions of government-controlled firms.

XII. THE NEED FOR CLARITY IN THE ACCOUNTS AND PLANS OF GOVERNMENT-CONTROLLED COMPANIES

Nowadays, the conviction is gaining ground that any expansion of the activities of government-controlled industry, or indeed, of government intervention generally, in a country deliberately bent on economic development, definitely requires prior proof that worse results are to be expected if the production of the good, or service, in question were left to private enterprise. In the absence of such proof, there is no valid reason at all why government should make further inroads into the field of private enterprise.

Like all other agencies in which the government has a direct or indirect stake, government-controlled companies should be under an obligation to make available full documentation and accounts, which make it possible to follow the effective business conduct of every firm and enable both Parliament and government :

(a) to assess the economic and financial aspects of the management of every single company ; and

(b) to scrutinize the expansion and investment plans of every firm with a view to enforcing the principle that all public intervention be in line with the balanced development of the country's economy as a whole.

XIII. THE NEED TO HARMONIZE THE POLICIES OF THE TREASURY AND OF THE CENTRAL BANK

In the past, the clearing banks' capacity to extend credit was limited by the ratio between their deposits with the Central Bank and outstanding cheques, and the observance of this ratio was reinforced by open market operations.

But this system was practicable only until 1914. By 1931, the whole concept had become highly questionable, and today, when Treasury Bills and bonds keep swelling the Treasury's short- and medium-term indebtedness, it breaks down completely. Clearing banks today have enormous holdings of Treasury Bills and bonds, and, whenever bank reserves are depleted by open market operations, the banks buy Treasury Bills and other government securities and borrow against them from the Central Bank. As a result, it is no longer the Central Bank, but the Treasury which controls the credit base, as indeed is confirmed by the circumstance that the supply of Treasury Bills and bonds to the market and bank liquidity tend to move in the same direction.

Since the issue of Treasury Bills and bonds is a prerogative of government, it follows that the Central Bank's monetary policy can be effective only if it is co-ordinated with the Treasury's policy concerning the public debt. It is in theory open to the Central Bank, of course, to refuse to give the clearing banks any advances against Treasury Bills or bonds, but this would run counter to established tradition in many countries.

Nor should the government plan public expenditure consistently and increasingly in excess of revenue, lest it deprive the Central Bank's monetary policy of its stabilizing functions. It cannot be said too often that any divergence between the Treasury's and the Central Bank's policies ends up in inflation. It is up to the government to make sure that there is no contradiction between the interventions of its own agencies.

XIV. THE CONCEPT OF AN ORGANIC SYSTEM OF GOVERNMENT INTERVENTION

Government intervention is bound to have harmful effects on the economy unless there is a clear excess of minimum beneficial results over certain present cost, and unless it is free of internal contradictions between the policies of the various authorities responsible. These harmful effects come to be added to those of other government activities in the field of revenue and public expenditure, in so far as they diverge from the economic principle. We are, therefore, led to the concept of an organic system of intervention, to take its place beside organic systems of taxation and public expenditure. This concept implies the analysis of all the economic consequences of each separate intervention, and a clear excess, in each separate case, of minimum beneficial result — that is, elimination of some determined risk — over certain present cost — that is, the losses inflicted on the community by each intervention.

In practice, then, an organic system of intervention means a set of different plans put into effect either through one single intervention with a favourable cost/benefit ratio, or, as happens more frequently, through several interventions each having a favourable cost/benefit ratio.

When it comes to combining several interventions, the government and other public authorities involved must, furthermore, make sure

659

that there is no internal contradiction between policies. To the extent possible, the marginal principle must be observed, the future correctly discounted, certain risks insured, and flexibility maintained in relation to market changes.

If public plans rest on these principles, they become compatible not only with each other, but also with the plans of private producers and consumers. The economic principle is always the same, whether the plans are those of government or of private individuals, and the economic principle requires that government plans should not upset private plans by making them more costly, in the sense that additional provision has to be made for insurance against the harmful effects of government intervention. In that case the cost/benefit ratio would be compromised by an increase in the present certain cost of any form of public intervention.

If, on the other hand, government plans are carefully prepared, an organic system of intervention maximizes the efficiency of government action, maximizes the compatibility between different government interventions, and, by maximizing also the compatibility between private and public plans, minimizes the losses inflicted upon private producers and consumers. These are the conditions of an organic system of government intervention ; they define the economic limits of intervention, just as the concept of an organic system of taxation defines the economic limits of taxation, and the concept of an organic system of public expenditure defines the economic limits of public expenditure.

It may be asked : what is the use of all these concepts ?

Well, the individual can act rationally without too much difficulty : it is a question of attaining a given end with the least amount of scarce resources. But government is always exposed to a variety of pressures and for this reason the concept of rational economic behaviour has remained rather vague. The concepts here developed serve to define the conditions of maximum economic efficiency through an analysis of the consequences of government action in the broad fields of taxation, public expenditure, and intervention.

Government may, of course, be led to diverge from these conditions by a host of circumstances and considerations of the most varied order. Nevertheless, the conditions we have outlined and which culminate in the creation of organic systems of taxation, expenditure, and intervention, always remain a standard of reference for enlightened government. This is especially important if the aim of government is the growth of real national income in the interests of all, and if organized society is considered as an organic whole whose equilibrium depends upon balance of all parts in the common direction of economic expansion, rather than as a random collection of groups of citizens, each ready to press its own interests and to claim that its alleged services entitle it to special privileges and advantages at the expense of other groups.

In the perspective of the state as an organic whole, the three organic systems of taxation, public expenditure, and government intervention define *ex post* also the ultimate concept of an organic system of purposes which a community may set itself — but this is the logical conclusion rather than the premise of government action in all its multiple forms.

Our analysis so far suggests that any government activity trespassing beyond its economic limits tends to destroy existing resources without any certainty that they can be reconstituted in the same measure for given uses, and that it tends also to impair the rate of formation of real income, saving and investment alike. The definition of the economic limits of the various forms of government activity shows up the fact that the portion of real national income accruing to government exceeds the revenue raised by government and other authorities either by taxing incomes or by borrowing savings; the government's portion of national income is increased by every form of waste consequent upon non-economic behaviour on the part of government and other public agencies. Whenever it goes beyond the economic limits of taxation, public expenditure, and intervention, the government behaves like a pressure group — and a pressure group, at that, whose power is incomparably greater than that of any private one, because government can ultimately take a much bigger portion of national income than would have been necessary and equitable under the economic principle.

No theory of the distribution of a country's real income can be complete without the most searching examination of the origin and size of the portion which the government takes for its own purposes or else more or less consciously destroys by uneconomic behaviour.

XV. CONTINUITY OF GOVERNMENT ACTION CONCEIVABLE ONLY IN A PROGRESSIVE SOCIETY

The continuity of government action in defiance of the economic principle, and therefore destructive of real income and prejudicial to the people's standard of living, is conceivable only in a society whose real income expands at a rate which at least offsets the damaging effects of public activities not confined within the three organic systems we have outlined.[1] It is hardly conceivable in a stationary society, and still less in a regressive one, unless people are prepared to accept a considerable lowering of their standard of living.

In all three cases — progressive, stationary, or regressive society — it is of course difficult to estimate how much national income might increase if the cost of public activities were lower. But it is quite certain that the greatest possible reduction of the cost of government activities by means of organic systems of taxation, expenditure, and intervention is an essential condition both of the continuity of government action and of the economic development of the country.

DISCUSSION OF RECTOR PAPI'S PAPER

Professor Fauvel said that Professor Papi's paper gave the Conference the opportunity, before turning to incomes policy, to consider state intervention and income distribution. Professor Papi had treated his subject in its more general aspects, taking the three principal activities of government to be levying taxes, spending, and state interventions proper.

With regard to the first of these, Professor Papi thought that the tax burden ought to be proportional to incomes defined as value added. This was one of the conditions for minimizing the cost to the community of financing state activities and for defining optimum taxation.

The object of the theory of government spending was to determine overall public expenditure in such a way as to maximize expenditure which had an income-creating effect and reduce to a minimum unproductive expenditure. Reasoning under the assumption that private savings were always employed according to an optimum allocation, Professor Papi would thus reject public expenditure which led to increasing consumption to the detriment of savings, in particular public transfers. It seemed, however, to Professor Fauvel that Professor Papi considered only the direct effects of transfers on the national expenditure, excluding income redistribution by transfers which might induce investment.

The paper was nevertheless centred on the last of the three principles of government activity, the notion of state intervention as such. Professor

---

[1] This means that in the last resort the progress of the economy depends on individuals. Government, in its turn, can enhance the efficiency of private activities, and it can do so the better the more it bases its own actions on the economic principle and tries to establish the three organic systems as a standard of its far-flung activities.

Papi defined this as an attempt by the state to protect individuals and firms against risks according to the principle of insurance, i.e. substituting certain present known cost for uncertain future cost.

Professor Fauvel thought that in many instances public policy, in guaranteeing individuals and firms a given level of either prices, incomes, or investments, had resulted in perpetuating economic disequilibrium. He could not help thinking that the social cost of the insurance had in this way been more than the social benefit. However, Professor Papi had envisaged a rational insurance policy. But if the individual when confronted with the scarcity of resources could act in a fairly rational way, governments were always subject to various organized pressures, as Professor Papi had pointed out (p. 660). What the rational conduct for the state was could not easily be defined.

Surely the main point of discussion was whether all government interventions could be reduced to insuring private people against risks, especially when contemporary societies seemed to be moving towards collective consumption. One might try to include this by saying that state intervention aimed at insuring any consumer against, for instance, poor education or housing. But was not social solidarity a better justification for such public expenditure ? Therefore, he felt, the theory ought to have been founded on collective choice. One would then have been confronted with the problem of determining the share of public and private consumption. Without being unduly austere, many economists thought that in a world invaded by gadgets, private consumption was artifically boosted and that the free choice of the individual made for much wastage of resources. Professor Fauvel wondered whether in this environment the extent of public activities could still be determined by reasoning under the assumption of the *homo oeconomicus* type of rational behaviour. The trend towards more collective consumption brought to light the conflict between the state's and the individual's scales of values.

Professor Tress said that he had approached with some excitement a paper written by the successor of the Italian masters of public finance who had taught English economists that public expenditure bore an integral relationship to public taxation about which principles could be stated and applied.

Professor Tress had no quarrel with Professor Papi's definition of income provided that, in the phrase 'those direct, or consumer, goods which accrue to an economic subject', the word 'accrue' be replaced by 'could accrue' in order to accommodate the saving of consumer's purchasing power and its use to purchase investment goods. He would, however, question Professor Papi's approach to income as it appeared in his treatment of taxation, i.e. through the output of consumer goods by firms rather than through the national accounting concepts of national output, national income, and national expenditure. Professor Tress thought this to be the Italian tradition at its most exasperating for it then represented the typical form of tax as the turnover tax — in its most satisfactory form, the 'value-added tax'.

But a universal tax on value added to consumption goods resulted in a proportional tax on income (or strictly, income spent and not saved). It was not surprising that Professor Papi represented later this pattern of taxation as the most desirable tax structure. This was the Italian tradition and it set aside the use of public finance to redistribute income.

It would seem to Professor Tress that when Professor Papi commented on public expenditure he departed from the Italian tradition by speaking of the principle of public expenditure as 'a set of expenditures so organized that most of them (would be) always capable of generating new incomes for consumers and producers' (p. 648). The Italian tradition was to invoke the activity of the state where the market failed, i.e. in the provision of 'corporate wants' which might be public goods of their own nature (e.g. defence) or private goods which have a public-interest element (e.g. private-public health).

Professor Tress was concerned at Professor Papi's application of his criterion of income-creation effects, particularly in the case of government-controlled companies. He would take as an example housing policy. If one asserted that housing was simply an object of private consumption, then the provision of housing could be left to private enterprise supplying at market rents; but if one inserted a public interest in how people were housed, then provision and subsidization became legitimate. In order to determine the amount which ought to be spent out of public funds on providing or subsidizing housing, one had, however, to apply cost/benefit analysis. Professor Tress could not see that the setting up of, say, a housing corporation, which was purely a device of administrative convenience, would affect the application of the cost/benefit criterion, e.g. why the corporation, because it took the form of a government company, should be required to operate as a commercial enterprise.

Professor André Marchal remarked that Professor Papi had treated tax as the income of the state considered as an enterprise. This was a stimulating way of approaching taxation; it was true to say that the state, in providing for corporate wants, the provision of which was a prerequisite to the conduct of productive activities, was entitled to a share of real income through taxation.

If the idea was pushed to its extreme consequences it would, however, become a dangerous notion. Ought we to reduce the state to just an enterprise ? Surely the state had functions of its own as only it could and did further the corporate interests of the nation and make public interest prevail. Conversely, an enterprise as such was under no obligation to perform its functions ; when it operated at a loss it could either change its activity towards more profitable outlets or just disappear.

Another and even more convincing difference was that the enterprise's or the household's spending was a function of their income, i.e. of what they earned as a return for their activity ; they could, by running into debt, finance expenditure over their current income, but only in so far as they

anticipated increasing income receipts in the future. The state was under
an obligation to spend and had to levy taxes. Taxation was a function of
public expenditure whereas private spending was a function of private
income. This difference was illustrated in public finance by the universal
rule of Parliament voting the budget's expenditure prior to taxes, the
state being entitled to levy taxes only after its expenditure had been
fixed.

Professor James congratulated Professor Papi on having gone beyond the
study of techniques of state intervention to try to base them on a general
principle which would at the same time justify all the interventions and
limit their scope. This common ground was found to be an insurance
principle.

Professor James had been very interested by the concept of common costs.
Professor Papi had rightly emphasized it as a way of justifying state intervention. Had not, however, the concept other implications ? In a free
market economy Professor Papi's concept of common costs would mean
that the profits of some firms would not necessarily correspond to their own
outlay. Would not this justify controls and integrated planning ?

Professor Papi's ultimate preoccupation was with the wisdom of state
intervention. In order to prevent the state from yielding to demagogic
group pressures he proposed to set up agencies which would abide by the
principles of rational economic behaviour. Professor James wondered,
however, whether the criterion of common costs would not in its application
lead to intervention far beyond the principle of free enterprise which Professor Papi defended. How would these agencies be made sufficiently independent from the state and how could one be sure that they would act
according to an economic rationale ?

Professor Papi wished to make clear that the function of the agencies
which he proposed to establish would be to co-ordinate state activities ;
they would be part of the state and not autonomous bodies with specific
functions. By an 'organic system of government interventions' he did not
mean the creation of a new institutional framework of public administration
but the enforcement of a set of principles and criteria.

Professor Reder wished to comment on the insurance principle. If
insurance was desirable, why would it not be provided by private institutions ? Apart from obvious differences (e.g. in private insurance, payments
had to be guaranteed by the companies' reserves), Professor Reder did not
think there was a really basic difference between private and public insurance so long as prices were parameters. This implied that there was no
governmental intervention in fixing them.

As long as public insurance was on a small scale it could be very like
private insurance. But the basic difference appeared when the scope of
public insurance was enlarged so as to insure, say, the consumer against a
rise in food prices and guarantee his food consumption from falling below
a certain level. To make good the guarantee the state might have to tax

The Distribution of National Income

or even to raise a levy in kind on the producers. The producers' output, however, might not be enough to meet the guarantee. Then the way out of the problem was food rationing. This showed how ambiguous the notion of a guaranteed fixed share was. State intervention occurred when a government had to behave as a monopolist in achieving pay-off.

Professor Reder observed that the Paretian notion of optimum was not far beneath the surface of Professor Papi's paper. What was the amount of public intervention which would lead to the optimum ? The answer would depend on the alternative methods which would be available in a given situation for achieving certain results. In Adam Smith's time the alternative was between able entrepreneurs and incompetent government. But there were nowadays other situations which might call for more state intervention in order to reach the conditions of optimum. One could take as an example the Israelian economy in which there was a scarcity of able entrepreneurs whereas the standard of competence of the staff in public administration was high. Economists, however, were much too prone to reason under the assumption that the marginal cost of state intervention was nil. One should always guard against too abstract reasoning on the issue of optimum state intervention.

Professor Brochier said that economists should approach state intervention from a cost/benefit analysis. The principle of balancing marginal cost and marginal benefit in appraising public intervention ought, however, to be applied in terms of social costs and benefits. A given situation would call for more or less public intervention according to whether social costs and benefits diverged greatly or little from private costs and benefits. For instance, the reasoning in terms of social costs and benefits might lead to locating a post office in a remote mountain village whereas a village of the same size in an area where road communications were easier would not get one.

Nevertheless Professor Brochier did not believe that all state interventions were subject to the cost/benefit criterion: those measures which were taken in order to redistribute national income and, generally speaking, measures which meant reallocating a given amount of resources through state intervention, could not be appreciated according to a strict, narrow criterion of efficiency. In decision-making efficiency could not be the sole criterion, but even for measures intended to redistribute income between groups, it was advisable to estimate the anticipated cost of state intervention.

Professor Gannagé observed that to appraise public investment in development projects the cost/benefit analysis had to be in social terms. This calculation was subject to great statistical difficulties. Social benefit and private profitability were concepts of a different order. The former could not be reduced to the latter. Whereas the state in providing public utilities just completed the functioning of private market economy, its intervention could have specific objectives, i.e. the redistribution of national income. Income redistribution was a form of social solidarity, but the state redistributive function, Professor Gannagé thought, could not be reduced to an insurance principle.

Professor Papi thanked Professor Fauvel for introducing his paper. Professor Fauvel and several of the speakers had commented on the relationship between public and private activities. In any economy, capitalist or socialist, there were corporate wants for which the state provided through public utilities when the goods and services produced could not be divided up and sold.

The efficiency of state intervention could be tested by whether it led to reduced cost or risk for private producers or consumers. Public spending did not always have this result. A good part of it was unproductive. The effect of public expenditure on the rate of growth of national income provided a good criterion.

By an organic system of intervention he did not mean particular public bodies but a certain line of economic policy. One should aim at co-ordinating the action of the existing bodies, for instance National economy, Budget, Treasury, which in Italy were separate ministries. Their activities ought to be co-ordinated through the principle of efficiency, whereas in fact their interventions led all too often to reducing national income.

Professor Papi said that Professor Tress's objection to the way he had defined income was the expression of a long-standing quarrel between theoreticians and statisticians or national accounting specialists in Italy. De Viti di Marco had already stressed the distinction between the pure economic notion and the statistical notion of income. It was expedient for social accounting purposes to include instrumental goods within income, but for logical purposes income should only refer to consumption goods because otherwise income thus measured would overlap from one year to the next.

Professor Tress had criticized the value-added tax for being proportional. Professor Papi, however, thought that the state revenue ought mainly to be out of proportional, not progressive, taxation because progressive taxes fell on savings and would thus be detrimental to economic growth. If heavy, progressive taxation might result in reducing taxable income in the future.

Professor Tress had been surprised that in his analysis of public expenditure he had substituted an income generating criterion for the usual cost/ benefit criterion. Far from ignoring cost considerations, he, however, had insisted on the principle that public spending should result in diminishing costs and risks for the individual. Nevertheless the costs and benefits of state interventions were not on the same footing and could not be strictly compared ; whereas costs could be valued as immediate consequences of the interventions, benefits were more indirect and more uncertain and would only appear in the longer run.

In regard to the example of housing policy on which Professor Tress had reasoned, Professor Papi said he would admit Professor Tress's alternative:

direct spending by the state out of budgetary appropriation might eventually be preferred to the setting up of a public corporation, but if the state's policy was not consistent with efficiency, this again would be detrimental to national income and growth.

Professor André Marchal had expressed doubts about the comparison between state revenue and private incomes. Professor Papi did not deny that the state had certain specific duties to perform. The rationale of the comparison was that, in the same way as private people had to accept to limit their expenditure to their income, the state ought to limit its spending to the amount of resources it could levy by taxation or borrowing without diminishing real national income thereby.

Professor Papi wished to thank Professor James for having underlined the interest of the common cost notion. He did not think that its application would result in lessening economic freedom. The concept was rather devised so as to keep the scope of state intervention within its proper limits.

Professor Reder had been right in analysing the differences between private and public insurance. Evaluating cost and benefit was more uncertain in the case of public insurance. The logic of the insurance principle, however, was relevant to both. Professor Reder had stressed the ambiguity of the pay-off of the guarantee in public insurance, but Professor Papi thought that a case by case examination would remove this ambiguity. For example, in the case of the European Common Market, farmers had been much more effectively insured against falling prices compared with the previous system of each nation protecting its own farmers. European farmers were not just promised a price guarantee : they were guaranteed access to a wider market which was the condition for better and less unstable farm prices.

Professor Brochier and Professor Gannagé had commented on the shortcomings of the marginal cost/benefit analysis in its application to public finance and both had emphasized social costs and benefits. But who could measure them ? Scales of preferences were individual and collectivity as a corporate subject of economic calculation was a void notion. Professor Papi had no intention of denying the fact of social solidarity, but the appreciation of its results ought to be subject to the criterion of rational economic behaviour.

Chapter 24

'INCOME POLICY' AND THE FRENCH PLANNING SYSTEM

H. BROCHIER
Université de Grenoble

I. INTRODUCTORY

DURING the past few months 'income policy' has emerged from the stage of expert discussion to make its appearance on the political scene. Indeed it is now among the topics dwelt on by the Head of the State in his public addresses in which he has come to allude not only to a 'fair sharing out of the national income', a figure of speech time-honoured and limited in scope, but also to an 'income policy comprising a set of coherent measures embodied in our national plan'.[1]

This prominence given to a form of public action, comparatively unnoticed hitherto, is based upon various grounds and sources of expectancy. In the first place, it would seem to be the logical adoption of a complement to the French planning system. This method, on which the preparation of the plan is based, actually assumes that an ultimate demand, reflecting both the supposed preference of the consumer and the political choices of the state, can be projected five years ahead. This ultimate demand is the starting point for the calculation of the rate of increase and of the investments entailed. It used to be assumed that, in this process, the sharing out of income was constant or, at all events, that such variations as occurred had little effect on demand. This hypothesis erred on the side of over-simplification. To quote M. Massé : 'the experience of the first two years of the IVth Plan goes to show that *planning in terms of volume*, as practised by us hitherto, is liable to be impaired by the absence of what might be called *planning in terms of value*'.

It is feasible to suppose that this logical gap did not escape economists on the Planning Commission. If no effort was made to fill it in,

[1] Television address on 18 April 1964.

669

this was mainly due no doubt to serious problems of method ; planning 'in terms of value' is *a priori* a further step towards economic intervention — an intervention which, there is reason to fear, might easily be more coercive, involving as it does a type of data less amenable to 'pilot' action. A method thus had to be found thanks to which the income policy would have an appreciable impact while providing, like the plan itself, a 'framework and source of guidance'. It is still too soon to say whether such a method has been discovered, but the importance assumed by preoccupations of this kind at the Conference on Income and in the drafting of the final report is unmistakable.[1]

In the second place, a certain 'income policy' might easily respond to the quest for an economy in which strife would make way for colloquy, the outlook would be well in keeping with that of a 'concerted'[2] economy, and social groups would mould the sharing out of the national income and also no doubt its rate of progression by common consent on the basis of multilateral discussion. What is more, such an 'income policy' might easily take pattern by the struggle against social inequality or, at all events, certain forms of it, and might accept as its own that yearning for equality which seems to have lost its appeal in modern societies since the last century, but which might well be nurtured afresh by the conspicuous discrepancies and inequalities attendant on economic expansion during the past two decades.

However, the sudden favour enjoyed by the income policy is ultimately due to the imperative needs of equilibrium without. France has experienced several times since the end of the war a high rate of increase in prices and has had to resort to devaluation — a state of affairs made possible by a certain isolation which has now come to an end. To go back on the option in favour of the liberalization of trade, as M. Massé has written, 'would seem an impossibility today'. Be it added that devaluation would give rise to awkward problems inside the EEC and would seem incompatible with our international commitments.

Thus the stabilizing of prices or the limiting of their rate of increase at least seems a dictate of the growing interpenetration of Western economy ; it is bound up with the end of a protectionist phase in the economic policies of France.

Now, as compared with what seems a necessity in the field of

[1] Report on income policy drawn up following the Conference on Income (October 1963–January 1964), Doc. Française, 1964, No. 47.
[2] To quote the now famous expression of M. Bloch-Lainé.

international competition, means of action look poor and inadequate. The inadequacies of conventional policies based on the conjuncture are perfectly familiar : in order to stem an inflationist trend, drastic monetary measures are needed, so much so that it often happens that expansion is throttled without there being any certainty that inflation can be curtailed. Measures of budgetary inflation are highly unwelcome in view of the succession of public tasks to which the authorities grant a certain priority : nuclear armament and public investments made necessary by growing population and the need to modernize the country. Finally, the various 'stabilization plans', resorted to by various governments, are too sporadic in character to constitute a policy.

The income policy thus seems to be a stand-by in many ways. To those — and they are many — who deem that the cause of inflation resides in the increase of wages at a rate faster than that of the National Revenue, it will convey the impression of delving into the deep-lying causes of the ill. In any case, it will seem less belated than would any other policy.

Moreover, it might well be the only rational policy whereby the rate of growth would not be impaired and expansion without inflation might ultimately be obtained. It thus responds to the logic of a society that requires a constant rate of economic power, but will not hear of fluctuation in the rhythm of activity.[1]

Thus income policy owes its topical interest not only to the logical requirements of planning and therewith to the moral obligation to reduce inequality : it is also and solely perhaps a technical means of regularizing income, made necessary by the opening up of the country to outside markets and to the inadequacy of the traditional methods of policies based on the conjuncture.

It now remains for us to specify what its methods will be and to what institutional context it belongs.

II. INSTITUTIONS AND METHODS OF INCOME POLICY IN FRANCE

The government approach during and after the Conference on Income was one of the utmost caution. The responsible authorities

[1] Cf. P. Massé, Report on the Conference on Income, *op. cit.*, 'only conscious action at the income-formation stage will make for rapid and balanced expansion . . . in an economy open to the outer world where competitiveness has become the law that rules us '.

The Distribution of National Income

are obviously desirous of defining a method acceptable to all groups involved and especially to the trade unions. It is clear that, without a minimum of good will on the part of the unions, income policy is bound to remain a dead letter. Thus the institutions on which the French Government will fasten no doubt and to which the finishing touches are now being put are peculiarly redolent of this desire for prudence.

According to the proposals made by the General Commissioner for Planning after the Conference on Income, the implementation of an income policy would involve three distinct phases :

(1) A phase of *exploration and enquiry* in which the 'social partners'[1] and the public authorities (the INSEE in particular) would jointly look for and establish the statistical data on which the later phases would be based. This phase, preliminary though it would be, could not but be highly significant since the various incomes are not well known and such knowledge as exists is incomplete. This was why various organizations spoke of a 'statistical prerequisite' to any income policy.

(2) *A defining and guide-line* phase. This phase will be left for the present to government responsibility ; however, another formula might have been worked out for defining a 'contractual' policy in which representative organizations, acting in common, would have been responsible for the views and judgements at the basis of the income policy. The government will therefore be responsible for defining the guide-lines through which the income policy is to be guided, but only after the 'social partners' have been consulted through the medium of the Economic and Social Council or other suitable bodies.

Practically speaking, these guide lines should be included in the planning process ; they would go to make the essential element of pilot programming in terms of value which will be perfected by the General Planning Commission and brought forward every five years at the same time as planning in terms of volume. They would affect the 'main body of income' (wages, health insurance, social-welfare benefits, agricultural earnings, and profits) together with the ways and means of balancing savings and investments, and public receipts and expenditure. As soon as statistical data permits it is planned to break down into various sectors and allot them to sectors, indices of

[1] The appellation used in the terminology of the Conference for the various groups interested in the sharing out of the national income who will be taken into consideration when the policy to be followed is worked out.

672

added value and prices being established for branches of activity whose number remains to be determined.

Provision will be made, however, for differences of scope in the guide-lines thus defined which will vary with the types of income : wherever free discussion is the rule, they would be purely indicative (wages, profits) ; for incomes dependent on government authority, they might imply some sort of official commitment. This would be the case with the SMIG (minimum guaranteed wage), health-insurance benefits, agricultural prices and transfers.

Guide-lines will be specified and overhauled if need be every year ; the government would then define a recommended rate of progression for every class of income (including wages and civil-service salaries). The variable factor on which these guide-lines depend will give rise to accurate delimitation and to an exact statistical definition (a distinction being made for instance between the recommended progression of the wage per hour, the average annual wage and the mass of wages . . . etc.). The drawing up of these recommendations raises the problem of adopting criteria. It would seem, in the light of work at the Conference, that the standard adopted will usually be the average rate of productivity increase throughout the economy as a whole. It is agreed, however, that the growth of re-muneration might be higher in backward sectors and that, more generally speaking, rates of increase recommended should be adapted to the requirements of the conjuncture and reconcilable with the maintenance of those disparities on which manpower mobility relies.

It has often been felt that social transfers of wealth are a type of income that give rise to peculiar problems and are susceptible of specific treatment. It is conceivable indeed that transfers of wealth could be granted priority in allotting productivity gains and thus be enabled to grow faster than the national revenue: this idea has been advanced by the (Socialist and Christian) trade unions FO and CFTC in whose view the income policy might be confined, at an initial stage, to social transfers of wealth and to the SMIG — which would make it possible to carry out an initial experiment in a restricted field. It would not seem that this suggestion has the slightest chance of being adopted by the government.

Finally, agricultural income gives rise to specific problems which it is not easy to deal with in brief.[1] Suffice to say that it will be

---

[1] Cf. in this connection the reports submitted to the 8th seminar of the French Economic Science Association at Royaumont in May 1963, especially that of M. Milhau on 'Farmers' Earnings and the Parity Problem'.

necessary to look for a delicate balance between conflicting pre-occupations and more especially:

—to make good the 'lag' in agricultural earnings as compared with other sources of income without impairing the balance of prices ;
—to remunerate equitably the services rendered by farmers while facilitating at the same time reconversion and transfers of activity ;
—to decide what place should be given to action through the price medium, in ascertaining the methods of such a policy, and what role should be reserved for economic and social transfers and transfers of wealth.

(3) Finally, the income policy in France will entail a third phase devoted to appraisal and checking *a posteriori*, visibly inspired by British and Dutch procedures. A body whose nature is still in the discussion stage but will presumably be a small college of experts, the CEAR (College for the Study and Appraisal of Income) would be called upon to decide how far policies followed by the various social partners were in conformity with government directives. Its evaluations would be public but not legally binding, which is logical enough since the limits imposed on the growth of remuneration are purely indicative in character. It is feasible to assume even so that this moral sanction would not be devoid of efficacy and that publicity given to what would be construed as breach of contract on the part of a group may serve to curb a good deal of impatience.

Many questions remain outstanding with respect to these institutions : it is of the utmost import, for instance, to know how and by whom the CEAR will be advised and at what level (firm or professional branch) its opinions will be made known. These problems are under study at the time of writing, and an initial college of three experts is busy drawing up the standards and methods to be used for appraising *a posteriori* how government recommendations are being applied. It is expected that these institutions could be set up early in 1965 and that they could thus be run in to some extent by the time the Vth Plan comes into effect in 1966.

III. ECONOMIC PROBLEMS ATTENDANT ON THE INCOME POLICY

Problems arising from the implementation of the income policy are new, important, and numerous. Moreover, many of them depend on institutional forms still to be defined in this country. It would thus be impossible to list them summarily. For the sake of convenience we shall in this outline regroup these problems in two categories : the first affects the practical efficacy of the measures contemplated, the second the economic problems due to the standards that have to be adopted in defining official recommendations. We shall wind up with a word on the part that the income policy seems called upon to play in the planning system and political economy of France.

(1) *The Efficacy of an Income Policy*

If an income policy is to be defined as a series of recommendations made by the government with regard to the limits that ought to be respected by the growth of remuneration and enjoying a single moral sanction in the form of a check *a posteriori* by a group of wise men, it may well be wondered in the first place whether there would be authority enough to dictate or influence the reactions of the 'social partners' (i.e. in point of fact to limit trade-union claims or rising prices).

The doubts that may be entertained are not due to the fact that the checks imposed are devoid of legal value : publicity given to the views of the CEAR might well bring moral pressure to bear on the various groups engaged in the process of sharing out the national income with appreciable results. However, it is feasible to doubt whether the efficacy of this procedure would be the same if the conformity approved by CEAR referred no longer to the reciprocal obligations of a contractual policy but to official recommendations liable to be challenged from the outset and towards which representative organizations would not feel really committed.

The whole issue consists in ascertaining which would carry the most weight in times of crisis — recommendations and appreciations on the one hand, or economic incentives on the other. It is during such periods that the income policy should prove its efficacy, but it is then precisely that trade-union organizations and employers will feel it most tempting to share the gains made available by the combined rise of wages and prices. The example of the Netherlands is not encouraging in this respect for it shows that, despite the 'wisdom' of the unions and a comprehensive arsenal of institutions whose authority is administrative as well as moral, the wage 'slide' proved unavoidable. Were this 'slide' to become the rule in times of tension on the labour market, it would deprive the income policy of any significance by enabling it to be efficacious only when it would be of no avail.

In point of fact, many passages in the Massé report go to show that the General Commissioner for Planning feels that the efficacy of the procedures perfected by him resides not in the coercive value of such and such a device but in the 'common discipline freely consented to' by all concerned. It is thus reasonable to suppose that the authority of government recommendations will largely depend on the way in which they are drawn up (the consultation phase will be significant in this respect), and on whether they seem to be inspired by equity or aim solely at freezing wages. . . . In this respect, initial experience will be capital and the caution, which was ever present when the institutions were drawn up, must watch over the initial guide-lines.

In the second place, the efficacy of the institutions provided for relies on structural factors the impact of which is still hard to gauge. The first of these factors lies in the number of trade unions. This plurality has become a standing feature of the social situation in France ever since the great cleavages took place ; it has its advantages but it also has drawbacks and may well lead to overbidding or, at all events, place bodies most willing to accept the wage limitations recommended in an awkward predicament. More generally, it may be wondered whether the structures of representative organizations (both of employers and wage-earners) are adapted to this process of multilateral negotiation at summit level and whether industrial federations will enjoy the authority required to impose respect for decisions taken on the national scale on their recalcitrant members. In all probability the structures of representative organizations in France will have to be reviewed before an income policy can be really efficient : changes will have to be made in the delimitation of competence between the various bodies and the role of confederation should be reinforced. None of these changes can be brought about rapidly and all will give rise to keen opposition.

Lastly it should be noted that the main obstacle that holds up the implementation of an income policy lies in the differences in nature between various types of income and in the ensuing difficulty of making them obedient to any single procedure of guide-line and limitation.

Not only indeed are various incomes hard to pin down, statistically speaking, with the same degree of accuracy [1] and to grasp in the same

---

[1] This problem was forcibly emphasized by J. Lecaillon in his book, *Croissance et politique des revenus* (Income Growth and Policy), Ed. Cujas, Paris, 1964.

manner — civil-service salaries are better known and, in any case, under better control than wages in private industry which, in turn, are easier to ascertain and keep in hand than profits — but it is hard to see how equality of treatment could be achieved. We thus run the risk of seeing recommendations applied where they are easily applicable and of finding them a dead letter elsewhere.

Hence the controlling and limitation of profits — two indispensable corollaries, from the wage-earner's point of view, of limitations on wage claims — would entail the setting up not only of a still non-existent statistical control system, but also of a co-ordinated series of measures relying on credit, fiscality, and even on price-control in certain cases and which would seem to brim over the bounds of the proposed policy deliberately framed on the most liberal lines. However, one cannot but note in other respects that 'equality of treatment' between social categories is a prerequisite to the voluntary participation of the trade union in the task of defining and applying an income policy.

(2) *Income Policy and Economic Equilibrium*

This first group of difficulties affects the technique and efficacy of an income policy; the second refers to economic problems more fundamental in character. They may be listed rapidly as follows :

No standard for the distribution of income is to be found either in political ideologies or in economic theory. It is thus hard to specify to what extent existing inequality should be reduced and how far it should be maintained. Certain forms of inequality seem to have a quite definite link with the incentive to work, with risk and with the growth of the overall product ; others are visibly bound up with speculation or chance and, as such, have little in common with the growth of the national product. But the difference between productive and unproductive inequality is solely one of vocabulary for the present and, while it is feasible to hope in Keynesian terminology that the game can be played with lower stakes, complete uncertainty prevails as to the rigour of the connection between the extent of inequality and the rate of growth.

Other delicate problems arise with respect to discrepancies desirable at sector level. Socially speaking, there exists a powerful trend towards equality of gain between various branches of activity in spite of persisting and considerable inequalities in the rate of productivity increase inside each branch. Moreover, the fruits of productivity development are known to be distributed inside the economy less, as might be expected, thanks to the fall in relative prices than to the contagion of rising wages. However, this sectoral equalization is not without its limits, at any rate those brought about by labour-mobility needs. In this respect, government recommendations ought to be cautious and empirical lest desirable equalization impede the man-power movements required.[1]

Another series of uncertainties as to the economic impact of the income policy affects problems attendant on incentives to technical progress. There seems little doubt for instance that, in various industries during different periods of economic history, significant headway was solely due to the influence of growing labour costs. Thus it may be wondered whether there is no danger involved in trying to limit the increase in wages to the rise in average productivity in the economic system. As A. Gorz writes in connection with the experience and views of the Italian trade unions : 'the most powerful incentive to technical progress would disappear with the standing tension between wages and productivity — a tension kept alive only by the unions' freedom to make demands'.[2]

Finally the most important problem arising from a coherent income policy and tending to reduce inequality, is without doubt the problem of savings and ultimately of financing investment. If inequalities are really reduced and if, more simply, the increase in remuneration is reduced to 3 per cent per annum in accordance with the wish of the Prime Minister, M. Pompidou,[3] the savings total would dwindle in every likelihood. Moreover, the importance of self-financing in French investments is a well-known phenomenon : it is thus to be feared that any limitation of profits would have a drastic impact on the level of investments during the year that followed.

This maintenance of a minimum rate of investment — and conse-quently of the overall rate of increase — thus seems to be a new variable factor to be added to the ones that would enter into the framing of government recommendations on income. There would seem to be an element of contradiction in French financing policy ; thus, on the one hand we are intent on proceeding with the policy of 'debudgetizing' investments which is already under way ; on the

[1] It should be noted even so that the government has many other means of facilitating professional reconversion (housing, vocational training, reconversion financing policies, etc.).

[2] André Gorz, *Stratégie ouvrière et néocapitalisme*, Éd. du Seuil, Paris, 1964, p. 20.

[3] In an interview granted to the journal *Entreprise* on 20 June 1964.

other, we contemplate measures that would reduce the volume of spontaneous saving, while denying our willingness to accept the reduction in the rate of increase. There are potential contradictions here of a serious character, for costly fiscal measures to provide an incentive to saving may well be the inevitable palliative ; it might even be necessary to resort to compulsory savings as suggested by M. Chalandon in a recent article! But what a singular paradox it would be that a policy, in order to maintain the free negotiation of income, should be induced to forbid its being spent!

IV. CONCLUSION

If the existence of such difficulties is recognized, it may be wondered what chance the income policy would stand of being used successfully as a technique of political economy. However, it must not be forgotten that the policy actually pursued will probably be unambitious and that the fight against inequality is unlikely to have a high target priority ; far more probably its place on the list will be a long way behind limitations in the growth of remuneration. In this more restricted connotation, the income policy may stand a chance of success provided that those concerned are amenable and structural factors, giving rise to inflation in certain countries, do not get the best of the good effects of restraint in the matter of claims. It looks in any case as though many governments and experts, after using various anti-inflation devices with a varying degree of success, are now pinning their hopes to techniques for the planned limitation of income.[1]

In any case, to keep to our national framework, it is to be hoped that, in addition to its principal anti-inflation aims, an income policy confined to limiting the growth of remuneration and to modest adjustments of inequality, might have various additional advantages. First and foremost, the process of planning the minimum wage and transfers of wealth granted to certain social categories (elderly persons or people in retirement, etc.) might prevent the burden of possible price increases from being borne by those who are unlucky or bereft of bargaining power, as has been the case hitherto. It might also curtail the arbitrary proceedings of the state, towards its own employees who have often borne the brunt of 'stabilization' and wage-freezing measures.

---

[1] For example, the experts commission planned in Germany. We may note also the comments in the last annual survey of the CEE.

Finally the income policy may have yet another role to play in France with regard to the national planning system. At a time when the French plan finds its efficacy threatened both by the growing impingement of international competition and by measures brought about by the conjuncture and fashioned solely by short-term development regardless of the aims of the Plan, income policy and planning in terms of value, which would be its expression, would no doubt be conducive to a better equilibrium between middle-term objectives and the requirements of conjunctural policy and prevent the former from being sacrificed systematically to the latter. This, it is easy to see, would be a modest ambition. In our opinion it is impossible to follow M. Edgar Faure when he construes it as being a new 'social contract'. Nor does it seem feasible to interpret it as 'socialism reduced to common property'. Yet it is an aim that seems to correspond to the necessities of the times we live in and to add a fresh element to the working out of a rational economic policy.

Chapter 25

INCOMES POLICY IN THE
UNITED KINGDOM

BY

R. C. TRESS
University of Bristol, U.K.

I. REAL AND MONEY INCOMES

In this paper I propose to consider the attempts by the British government to formulate and apply an 'Incomes Policy' in the sense in which that phrase is currently used. First, however, I must relate 'Incomes Policy' in this especial sense to the more traditional uses of it and kindred phrases relating to the distribution of the national income.

The meaning which might have been attached to the term 'Incomes Policy' at any time prior to the last quarter-century is that which features most strongly in the programme of this Conference, namely, in relation to the distribution of income. When we speak of 'the distribution of income' we are usually referring to the distribution of real income in one or other of two ways : either to the distribution of the national product between the factors of production contributing to it, or to the distribution of the command over that national product between persons having claims to it. The first of these two ways may stop short as a purely economic interest in 'imputation', but it is more likely to be extended to a concern with the 'distributive shares' in the national product accruing to types of factors of production — profits, rents, and wages — and with the social classes broadly regarded as being dependent upon those types of income. The second of these two ways, of course, constitutes a social interest from the outset. When pursuing it we are concerned with the distribution of purchasing power between social classes, income-groups and age-groups not only as it is initially effected through the markets for the factors of production, nor yet with the qualifications to the amounts of personal receipts which may be imposed upon that pattern by the policies of enterprises in retaining

681

or distributing profits ; we pursue the further effects, some deliberate and some accidental, which result from the operations of public finance, through the taxation of property and income, through the taxation of goods and services, and through the redistribution of incomes brought about, in cash, by pensions and other state payments and, in kind, by the provision of free and subsidized state services.

The current use of the term 'Incomes Policy' in the United Kingdom relates only incidentally to any of these matters. It refers, not as do these to the amount of real income in an economy and the way that real income is shared out among its members, but to the relationship between changes in that real income and changes in the aggregate of money incomes taking place in the same economy at the same time. This problem is epitomized in the Royal Warrant of the National Incomes Commission established in 1962. The Warrant requires the Commission, in considering the matters referred to it,

. . . to have regard to the circumstances of the case concerned and to the National interest, including in particular :
(a) The desirability of keeping the rate of increase of the aggregate of monetary incomes within the long-term rate of increase of national production ; . . .[1]

Clearly, this undertaking is a pursuit distinct from that of trying to formulate a policy for the dividing up of the real national product. Yet it is important to recognize the connections between the two, as an appreciation of some of the difficulties in formulating an incomes policy in the current sense — and of some of the obstacles to its application — stems from them.

The first connection which we have to record is that the British economy is a money economy. Seemingly trite, the significance of this statement is that it is not only the new type of incomes policy which seeks to influence the flow of money incomes ; any policy directed to affecting the distribution among persons of real income has to operate by manipulation of the claims of those persons to real income, i.e. by manipulation of the flow of money incomes. Secondly, despite all the interventions and ameliorations undertaken by the state through public finance and in other ways, it remains the fact in the British economy that the initial receipts accruing to the factors of production continue to be the most important single determinant of the distribution among persons of claims to real income. From these

[1] National Incomes Commission, *Report on the Scottish Plumbers' and the Scottish Builders' Agreements of 1962*, Cmnd 1994, HMSO, 1963, pp. ii–iii.

two observations two conclusions of great political significance follow. First, the owners of factors of production cannot surrender their powers to affect the money receipts accruing to those factors of production without at least seeming to surrender their rights to influence their real incomes by the means most directly under their control. Secondly, an external authority cannot intrude upon the flow of money incomes arising out of production without at least seeming to intervene in the distribution of real incomes among persons.

The resistance of the trade unions to intervention in the process of wage-bargaining by the government on behalf of an incomes policy stems from these conclusions. It is a principle of the British trade-union movement that every worker has an inalienable right, as a person, to make his own terms with his employer, and to withhold his labour if there is no agreement. It may be true that it is now the trade union and not the individual worker which conducts the bargaining, but it does so on his behalf. It may be true that the state has introduced laws and institutions into the bargaining process, but it has done so to give a fairer balance to the bargaining, not to usurp it. The pattern of trade-union reaction to government intervention was set as long ago as the early war year of 1941 when Mr. Churchill's Cabinet had decided on a policy of subsidization with a view to stabilizing the official cost-of-living index and thereupon sought a parallel restraint in wage demands. Mr. Bevin, the most powerful trade unionist of his time, was Minister of Labour and the official historians' account of his arguments on that occasion is worth recalling :

> . . . the Minister of Labour argued that any attempt to reach an agreement to stabilise wage rates would be unwise ; for good industrial relations depended upon the unions' authority in the day-to-day adjustment of wages and conditions. Freedom of opportunity to make claims and to have them discussed, said Mr. Bevin, was essential to industrial peace ; it would, moreover, be a dangerous thing if the Government made the independence of statutory wage-fixing and arbritration bodies suspect by offering them ' guidance.'[1]

Since 1941 there has been a continuous insistence by government spokesmen on the dangerous futility of money incomes rising in aggregate faster than the national output. Moreover, there have been various attempts by governments to secure the voluntary co-operation of the two sides of industry in translating this precept into the practical

[1] W. K. Hancock and M. Gowing, *British War Economy*, HMSO, 1949, p. 338.

terms of their wages and profits policies. The most notable instance was the policy of 'wage restraint' introduced by the Labour Government in 1947–48 ; [1] an accompanying 'dividend restraint' served the purposes of industry seeking finance for post-war reinvestment. So far, however, logic of this kind has been unable to absorb or accommodate either the traditional urges of trade-union behaviour or the stresses of the labour market ; and, wages and salaries representing two-thirds of all factor incomes, there has seemed to be no obligation on the recipients of profits and investment income to conform to the requirements of an incomes policy while wage- and salary-earners have declined to come to order.

II. THE PRESENT STAGE IN INCOMES POLICY

The present stage in the development of an incomes policy in the United Kingdom dates from July 1961. In that month there appeared the *Fourth Report* of the Council on Prices, Productivity, and Incomes. It was also the month of a sterling exchange crisis.

The Council on Prices, Productivity, and Incomes was set up by the government in August 1957, as an independent body of 'three wise men' whose duty it should be to 'keep under review' changes in the three variables contained in its title. It was the obvious hope of the government that negotiators and arbitrators of wage claims might read these independent reviews before arriving at their decisions, but they were placed under no obligation to do so and even the hope was unexpressed. Moreover, the thinking which was needed to make these reviews relevant to the incomes issue was not immediately forthcoming. The first economist on the Council was the late Sir Dennis Robertson and the Council's initial analysis held firmly to the doctrine that the main cause of the rise in prices and incomes in the post-war period had been excessive demand. The Council's *First Report*, published in February 1958, argued for the damping down of demand ; the *Second Report*, in August 1958, allowed no more than that there might now be cautious expansion.

The turn came with the succession of Professor Phelps Brown to the Council in February 1959. The Council's *Third Report*, in July of that year, saw the beginning of an analysis of the cost inflation

---

[1] See *Statement on the Economic Considerations affecting Relations between Employers and Workers*, Cmd 7018, HMSO, 1947, and *Statement on Personal Incomes, Costs and Prices*, Cmd 7321, HMSO, 1948.

problem, and it also dared to outline, albeit without comment, possible modes of government intervention. The Council reviewed both 'proposals which would limit the employer's ability to raise rates of pay' and 'proposals for influencing the agreements and decisions by which rates of pay and profit are arrived at in individual industries'.[1] (The reaction of the Trades Union Congress, when it met in October, was to reject any form of wage freeze and to declare its support for a policy of wage increases and a shorter working week.) Two years later, in July 1961, the Council's *Fourth Report* [2] struck the contemporary note. The *Report* ascribed to 'the persistent tendency of our production to rise more slowly than our pay and profits', the harm of the depreciation of savings, the difficulty of raising funds for public economic and social development and, above all, recurrent trouble with the balance of payments which led governments to impose restraints on demand with consequent loss of production. But contraction of demand was not enough to prevent too rapid a rise of money incomes (unless it cut too deeply into employment to be acceptable). Customary wage differentials at local level and chain reactions between industries at national level ('the annual round') made the pay rise more than it would be under the pull of demand alone ; and an integral part of all these processes was that profits rose as much as pay.

These thoughts appeared at a moment when their pertinence could not have been more obvious : in a sterling exchange crisis. But, by the self-same token, the choice of that moment by the government for the launching of an incomes policy could not have been less auspicious. Reaction to the crisis took the familiar form of a squeeze of demand through expenditure curbs, budgetary pressures and credit restrictions. To these measures Mr. Selwyn Lloyd, as Chancellor of the Exchequer, now added a 'pay pause', imposed, as he put it, 'in order that an Incomes policy could be worked out empirically'.[3]

From the short-term view, the move was a heroic one and, in the next nine months, though it took no new powers, the government actively intervened in wages settlements whenever existing powers permitted it to do so. Mainly, however, this was in the public sector, affecting school teachers, employees in naval dockyards, and post-office engineers ; in the private sector, the government's authority

---

[1] Council on Prices, Productivity and Incomes, *Third Report*, HMSO, July 1959, ch. vi.   [2] *Ibid., Fourth Report*, HMSO, July 1961, ch. iii.
[3] *H.C. Debates*, 25 July 1961.

did not extend beyond the industries supervised by wages councils, where awards required their approval. Without the co-operation of private employers and trade unions, the 'pause' could not be maintained and, with the rate of national production at a standstill, such co-operation was far from forthcoming. By February 1962, the government had conceded that the 'pay pause' could not be held beyond, say, the end of March. The object thereafter should be to keep the rate of increase of incomes within the long-term rate of growth of national production and, on the trend of recent years, that rate could not be taken to be more than 2 to $2\frac{1}{2}$ per cent a year. This range of figures, therefore, should be the 'guiding light' for 1962, to be observed by both negotiators and arbitrators.

The White Paper setting out these conclusions [1] also recorded, not surprisingly, that the government had failed to secure the collaboration of the Trades Union Congress in working out this 'next phase'. No one will ever know if the introduction of an interventionist policy in more prosperous circumstances than those of 1962 would have evoked a more accommodating response. What was abundantly clear was that, without faster economic growth than 2 to $2\frac{1}{2}$ per cent, there was no prospect of trade-union co-operation in the future. Equally, however, the commitment to an interventionist policy having been made, it was impossible for a government to relent from intervention pending union agreement.

Subsequent developments are indicative of the dilemma. Even before the publication of the new statement on incomes policy in February 1962, the Chancellor of the Exchequer had secured agreement to the setting up of a National Economic Development Council composed of Ministers, employers, trade-union representatives, and independent members, with a full-time staff, 'to increase the rate of sound growth'.[2] The Council's explorations of the possibility of a steady 4 per cent per annum, pursued simultaneously through global analysis and by consultations industry by industry, has been instructive and, up to a point, encouraging. That point is incomes policy, the inescapable condition for 'sound' growth. The Council's first Statement [3] on the subject, made more than twelve months after it had been set up, had less of substance in it than had earlier, cautiously drafted statements made by the government alone. Subsequent

[1] *Incomes Policy : the Next Step*, Cmnd 1626, HMSO, February 1962.
[2] National Economic Development Council, *Growth of the United Kingdom Economy to 1966*. HMSO, February 1963, p. viii.
[3] National Economic Development Council, *Conditions Favourable to Faster Growth*, HMSO, April 1963, paras. 212–215.

labours in the Council, it is reported, have been directed to two ends : the one, some kind of understanding on prices and profits to go along with any commitment on wages and salaries ; the other, some kind of combined statement on the need for short-term restraint as, in early 1964, production advances and government spending grows. The prospect of a General Election and forecasts of a victory for the Labour Party have added their own tensions.

Side by side with the government's unsuccessful efforts to secure tripartite agreement on an incomes policy, therefore, has gone its insistence that, in default of agreement, government intervention in income determination must go on, at least to the extent of retrospective investigation. It was for this purpose that the National Incomes Commission, of five independent members, was set up in November 1962. The terms of reference of the Commission [1] hopefully provide for the possibility of a pay claim being referred to it by the contending parties themselves, but it must be confessed that the only questions of pay at present likely to be remitted to the Commission in advance of settlement are those, separately provided for under another clause, where the cost or part of it falls directly on the Exchequer, for example, the salaries of university teachers. The principal operating clause, given the hostility of the trade unions to the Commission, is that which allows of the government referring particular settlements to the Commission for examination after the event ; awards at arbitration are specifically excluded from this clause. Cases of this kind thus far referred to the Commission are :

(1) (a) the Scottish plumbers' agreement of May 1962 ;
    (b) the Scottish builders' agreement of November 1962 ;
(2) (a) the heating, ventilating, and domestic engineering agreement of February 1963 ;
    (b) the electrical contracting agreement of March 1963 ;
    (c) the exhibition contracting agreement of March 1963 ;
(3) (a) the engineering agreement of November 1963, and other recent agreements in the engineering industries ;
    (b) the shipbuilding agreement of December 1963.

III. WORKING OUT AN INCOMES POLICY

The procedure of the National Incomes Commission is to examine a particular case referred to it and to pass retrospective judgement

[1] See (1) above and also *National Incomes Commission*. Cmnd 1844, HMSO, November 1962.

687

having regard both to the circumstances of the case and to the national interest. The particular features of the national interest specifically referred to in the Commission's warrant do not stop at 'the desirability of keeping the rate of increase of the aggregate of money incomes within the long-term rate of increase in national production'. There are other elements :

the desirability of paying a fair reward for the work concerned ;
the manpower needs of the service, industry or employment concerned . . . and the importance of securing the most efficient deployment and use of national resources ;
the policies and practices in the service, industry or employment concerned in such matters . . . as pricing, profit margins, dividends, efficient use of manpower and equipment, and organisation ; and
the repercussions which a particular settlement . . . might have in other employments.

In reaching conclusions in particular cases, the Commission has certainly given some mind to all of these considerations. But it will be appropriate for the present purpose to concentrate on the first consideration and the Commission's interpretation of it as the main component of an incomes policy.

The terms under which the Commission operates provide it with two features distinguishing it from past attempts at formulating an incomes policy. On the one hand it cannot halt at generalities. Any criteria of good behaviour with respect to incomes which the Commission wishes to see maintained it must itself apply to an agreement in specific terms and set in a concrete situation. On the other hand, except in so far as what it may say carries implications for other cases, the Commission is not obliged to elaborate its criteria further than is necessary to cope with the particular case in hand. Provided that consistency is maintained, there can be a gradual unfolding of the Commission's interpretation of incomes policy as case follows case.

Besides providing the Commission with some opportunity for learning on the job, this time-factor also has bearing on the way in which the Commission may deal with the tactical situation in which it finds itself. The Commission has been brought into action at a particular date in the history of incomes policy and in a particular institutional complex accustomed to operating in a particular way. The Commission's first duty is to try to affect the immediate situation. In so far as it succeeds, it thereupon becomes a factor in the institutional complex, with the possible result that the complex may behave differently in the future from the way it has behaved in the past. Let me illustrate. The Commission has been established at a time when annual increases in money incomes regularly exceed the rate of growth in real national output by a wide margin. Since this proposition holds whatever may be the precise definitions attached to these two variables, the Commission is not obliged to single out a particular pair of definitions in order to make its arguments effective : the need for restraint obtains whatever the choice. Again, it appears at the present time that, in the sphere of wages and salaries, the main initiative derives from the formal processes of collective bargaining between employers' associations and trade unions. At this point in time, therefore, the Commission may usefully address itself to infusing some reality into the terms on which formal bargains are reached. That the successful introduction of the principles of an incomes policy into formal negotiations might lead to their being displaced in importance for the course of incomes by local agreements and private bargains is a problem that can come later.

We may trace this progressive unfolding of doctrine through the chapters on 'Incomes Policy' in the successive reports of the National Incomes Commission and, from the premises there outlined, speculate on its further stages. The record begins with the initial, almost puritanical, statement of the fundamental rule of incomes policy applied to wages and salaries, closely followed by a parallel statement applicable to profits. At both these stages, while the possibility of exceptions to the rule are hinted at, such hints are almost invariably accompanied by an insistence on the simple arithmetic that must embrace them, namely that more for one means less for others. Discussion of the circumstances in which exceptions are admissible comes later.

In its first report the National Incomes Commission laid down that it was to the long-term rate of growth of national production per head of the working population that increases in money incomes should be related, that this rate should be taken as that which 'would be achieved if the pressure of demand remained constant for some time' (the phrase of the National Economic Development Council) and that (despite the advice of the government spokesman in favour of the past rate of 2 to $2\frac{1}{2}$ per cent) a rate of 3 to $3\frac{1}{2}$ per cent was the practical minimum for an incomes policy to have a chance of being acceptable. This figure for the permissible rate of increase in money incomes was no compromise invention, however. A figure of 3 to $3\frac{1}{2}$ per cent was

the rate of increase in real productivity per head of which the
NEDC had shown the British economy to be capable over the period
1961–66. It was therefore a hard figure, as the second report
emphasized :

> the range of 3 to $3\frac{1}{2}$ per cent has been substituted for that of 2 to
> $2\frac{1}{2}$ per cent but it is still the case, if inflation is to be avoided and
> the value of money incomes maintained and possibly enhanced,
> that any increases in incomes beyond the new range must be
> matched by other increases which are proportionately smaller or
> by no increases at all.[1]

But the Commission did not stop at arithmetical tautology. As
against the forces of demand and supply on the one hand and
sectional claims to the fruits of increased productivity on the other,
it enunciated a single 'fundamental rule' : 'all wage settlements
must reflect the overall national average increase in productivity'.[2]
The Commission made clear in its first report that, in its view, the
mere experience of difficulties in recruitment and retention of labour
did not justify exceptional increases in earnings ; the manpower
needs of an industry had themselves to be 'exceptional' to justify
exceptional treatment.[3] When, in its second report, the Commission
tackled the 'lack of understanding' of the proper basis for the 'distribution of the fruits of greater productivity', it repeated in less
accommodating form the argument which the Council on Prices,
Productivity, and Incomes had used as long ago as 1959 : 'the notion
that it is the right of every industry to appropriate for itself the whole
of the fruits of its own greater productivity is mistaken and should be
abandoned'.[4]
The basis for both these propositions and hence for the fundamental rule is a statement about our institutions, namely, that :

> If any group by a private bargain at national, local, or works
> level seeks and is granted more than its proper share, this excess
> can be achieved only at the expense of others and sooner or later
> even the temporary advantage will be in large measure cancelled
> as these others seek to bring their own position to the same level.[5]

---

[1] National Incomes Commission, *Report on the Agreements of February–March
1963 in Electrical Contracting, in Heating, Ventilating and Domestic Engineering and
in Exhibition Contracting.* Cmnd 2098, HMSO, July 1963, para. 15.
[2] *Ibid.* para. 17.
[3] See Cmnd 1994, paras. 141, 169, 179, and 196.
[4] Cmnd 2098, para. 22. See also para. 18 and cf. Council on Prices, Productivity, and Incomes, *Third Report*, para. 76.
[5] Cmnd 1994, para. 29.

In other words, in the cases of wages and salaries, the institutional facts of collective bargaining on a national scale, together with the disposition in bargaining behaviour to appeal to comparabilities, mean that historically established relativities in wage rates are not easily altered. This being so, there is no point in trying to alter the relative offer prices for labour in different industries or occupations as a means to altering the distribution of labour : relative wage rates have ceased to perform their allocative function. Instead of deploring this circumstance, however, and seeking to change it, e.g. by breaking up national wage bargaining, the Commission would seem to be aiming at making a virtue out of necessity. If it is useless to try to change relative wage rates, then do not try to do so : keep all wage rates moving along together, all at the same rate. The prescription for an incomes policy is immensely simplified.

One can swallow this doctrine more easily, however, if one can see other means than altering relative wages for affecting the distribution of labour. Here, I think, the work of Mr. Brian Reddaway is of value, namely, his 'suggestion' that :

 . . . It is probably not worthwhile to undertake a difficult campaign to induce wage-negotiators to change their practices, when redistribution seems to be obtainable without such a campaign, largely via the (socially more acceptable) route of varying job opportunities.
 . . . Very substantial changes in the distribution of labour have been secured (with relatively small changes in relative wages) with the existing system of wage-fixing. . . .[1]

Of course, as Mr. Reddaway observes, 'if one wants to secure a redistribution of the labour force, then obviously it is all to the good if the force of "wage attraction" is on the whole pulling in the right direction'. Moreover, the Commission allowed from the outset the possibility of *exceptional* changes being allowable. But 'their justification . . . must be sought, found and be seen to be found in some circumstances of a truly exceptional nature'.[2]

The opportunity for a closer examination of these exceptional circumstances — and incidentally of taking practical incomes policy beyond that of the 'guiding light' — was furnished by the remission to the Commission of a review of the remuneration of the academic staff of universities and colleges of advanced technology, classed as one of the employments of which the cost is met in part by the

---

[1] W. B. Reddaway, 'Wage Flexibility and the Distribution of Labour', *Lloyds Bank Review*, October 1959. [2] Cmnd 1994, para. 19.

Exchequer. In their report on this reference the Commission, while resisting categorizing the exceptional circumstances which might justify a departure from the normal standard of increases in incomes, pointed to two such situations which might arise. Each represented a case for a long-term adjustment and action on each was conditional on its being generally recognized and accepted as a desirable long-term alteration and not made, therefore, the lever for a self-defeating sequence of increases in incomes elsewhere. One was where, given this general standstill, an outstanding and unusual shift in the relative rate of remuneration of some specific occupation could be shown to be and be seen to be desirable on economic grounds, to restore its competitive strength. The other was where there could be shown to be and be seen to be an exceptional case on social grounds for raising the remuneration of one of the lowest paid groups whose position was the consequence of past social and historical factors which have ceased to apply to modern conditions.[1]

In a developing society there comes a time when in one respect or more the existing pattern of differentials is outmoded. For instance, in the case of the first kind of exception a deeply rooted and persistent decline of manpower amounting to a long-term phenomenon in a given occupation may be so inimical to the national interest that it requires to be corrected by monetary means : or, before this situation has occurred, these means may be required to be employed to restore the competitive strength of the occupation when it has been weakened and thus to prevent a critical situation arising in the occupation. In the case of the second exception a change in social outlook may make an alteration in relativities desirable as a matter of long-term policy. When and if such situations occur and when and if they can be plainly seen and accepted for what they in fact are, an incomes policy by its very nature can and will make provision for them.

IV. PROFITS AND PRICES

Thus far I have spoken mainly of wages and salaries. These are indeed the classes of incomes with which an incomes policy must begin since together they add up to the major fraction of all factor incomes and because their terms are in large part negotiated and therefore most openly susceptible to the influence of an incomes policy. Of the remaining categories of factor incomes — profits,

[1] National Incomes Commission, *Remuneration of Academic Staff in Universities and Colleges of Advanced Technology.* Cmnd 2317, HMSO, March 1964, ch. 2.

interest and rents — profits are both quantitatively and qualitatively the most important. An incomes policy affecting wages and salaries will never become politically acceptable if it is not also made to apply to profits.

In its Second Report, the National Incomes Commission made its first sally into the field of profits as a source of income to be brought under the discipline of an incomes policy.[1] The Commission's approach to the subject, as there exhibited, displays two features. First, the Commission is at some pains to insist that the same principles of incomes policy must be applied to profits as are to be applied to wages and salaries. Secondly, however, the policy applied to profits must take cognisance of the institutional features of profit determination which are different from the institutional features of wage and salary determination to suit which the Commission's statements on wages and salary policy were devised.

The publication of the Commission's Second Report brought a number of comments from industry insisting that these institutional differences made any common policy for both classes of income impossible and it must be recorded that the Commission's terms of reference had lent some encouragement to that view. The Commission having been given general instructions on how it should proceed and what considerations it should have in mind when dealing with 'pay or other conditions of service or employment', there followed in a separate clause in its Warrant the requirement that it should report from time to time on any action which might need to be taken in order that 'any undue growth in the aggregate of profits which may follow from restraint in earned incomes shall also be restrained, by fiscal or other appropriate means'. While acknowledging in its second Report that 'some ways of using profits may yield greater benefits than others', the Commission insisted that it was first and foremost as factor income that profits must be considered and brought within the ambit of an incomes policy:

Increases in incomes arising from the annual gross domestic product must be related to the rate of growth in that product; profits as they accrue are one such set of incomes.

The fundamental principle of an incomes policy has thus to be applied to all profits arising from the production of goods and services, irrespective of whether they are subsequently retained in a business or distributed to its shareholders and bondholders, and irrespective of the uses to which they may subsequently be put.

[1] Cmnd 2098, paras. 23–26 ; see also ch. 6.

The peculiar institutional features attaching to profits were remarked by the Commission through its initial definition — 'profits
are the contingent reward for the capital invested in a business, for the
risks that have been accepted in earning the profits and for the skill
and enterprise with which the affairs of the business have been conducted' — and through points of elaboration on this definition : that
'profits are a contingent receipt, not a contractual one' ; that 'profits
arise from a collection of causes for which a unit of reference is
difficult to find' ; and that 'profits vary between one firm and another
to a notably greater extent than do the other categories of earnings
originating in the individual enterprises which make up the total of
an industry'. In view of these three points and the Commission's
discussion of them, it may seem a little surprising that the Commission was charged in some quarters with having demanded that the
aggregate profits of individual enterprises should be stabilized within
a 3–3½ per cent rate of annual growth. In fact, the Commission contrasted the position of profits with other incomes in that 'even after
a relatively stable rate of economic growth has been established, a
fairly long-term view of profit rates will be necessary' ; it contrasted
the comparative ease with which a measurable base could be established for calculating the unit of reference for wages and salaries
relative to the problems in finding an appropriate unit by which to
calculate profit-earning, observing difficulties in each of the two most
obvious bases, namely, capital employed and value of turnover.

If there was any omission on this score it is probably to be explained by the fact that the Commission, rather than impose its own
arbitrary solution on these definitional questions, sought an alternative route by which to advance the purposes of an incomes policy.
That route is through the measure, not of profits themselves, but of
prices. If incomes policy is concerned with keeping the aggregate of
factor incomes within the long-term rate of increase of national production and if this principle is applied to wages and salaries, the proof
of its having been applied to the remaining factor incomes (of which
profits are the main component) is that the prices of the goods and
services produced will, on average, have been held stable. Hence the
Commission's conclusion in the matter :

> In relation to the distribution of the fruits of greater produc-
> tivity . . . what has been said in respect of wage settlements has
> its no less firm counterpart in respect of profits. It is no less
> incumbent on employers than it is on workers not to appropriate
> an unfair share of the fruits of increased productivity. . . . It

should not be necessary to wait for the promised fiscal measures to impose restraint on profits ; the signs should be visible from the outset in the trend of prices. It is the duty of employers and workers alike to extract no more than their proper rewards as indicated by the overall rate of increase in *national* productivity. If, in their own industry there is then a balance of enhanced productivity outstanding, the prices of the products of that industry should be reduced and the benefit thereby dispersed to the community at large.

It may not be without significance that the National Economic Development Council in its efforts to coax support for an incomes policy out of its trade unionist members is promoting a prices policy among its business members as a workable *quid pro quo*.

But is it workable ? As I observed earlier, the basis for the propositions relating to a wages policy as here advanced is that changes in relative wage rates, except in rare and recognized circumstances, are short-lived in their effect and are therefore expendable as a means to effecting changes in the allocation of labour. The use of profits in the allocation of capital and enterprise cannot be dismissed so easily. As the Commission in its second Report itself remarked, 'the opportunity to earn increased profits is a prime source of the incentive by which greater national productivity may be secured'.

I suggest that there are three components making up the notion of profits as an incentive to enterprise and innovation. First, there is the abnormally high rate of profit per unit of output obtainable temporarily as the result of the initial seizure of a production opportunity. Secondly, there is the rate of profit per unit of output which comes to be established as normal within a particular line of production ; the actual rate of profit per unit of output may fluctuate about the norm, but the norm itself is only disturbed intermittently in consequence of change or innovation either in the industry concerned or in its competitors. And thirdly, there is the volume of sales in any period which, in the determination of *aggregate* net receipts, is the multiplier of the rate of profit, whether in the first or second of the above two definitions.

Of course, the first situation is important in a dynamic economy and there must be adequate accommodation to give it scope. Consideration of profits in this situation, as the Commission has suggested, is not unlike that which is to be accorded, in the area of wage incomes, to *well-devised* schemes of payment by results : 'they may achieve not only an increase in productivity greater than could reasonably be expected to be obtained in their absence, but theoretically at least an approximate equation between the rates of effort and of reward'. It may be contended, however, that it is the second situation which provides the main source of profit earning and that therein the origin of the rate of profit per unit of output (though not of sales and therefore of aggregate profit) is much more the product of convention. In support of this hypothesis one may cite the interpretation of business behaviour attributed by Mr. Robert Neild to Mr. Wyn Godley :

> . . . that business men have in their minds an idea about what the long-term trend of output is and fix their prices on the basis of the costs implied by this trend, and keep them there when output in fact fluctuates about the trend ; so profit margins rise when output rises faster and fall when output rises less fast, or declines.[1]

In this regard, the conclusion of Mr. Neild's own empirical investigations lends support :

> The pricing results seem to be consistent with the view that manufacturers' prices are set by reference to costs when operating at some normal level of capacity and that they are not sensitive to moderate fluctuations in demand. As noted earlier, if prices are set on this basis, the long-run productivity trend will tend to be accommodated in the wage-price relationship, since new costings will generally be made when the new techniques and the new productive equipment which give rise to the productivity trend are introduced.[2]

Thus it would appear that the attempt to stabilize rates of money wages and salaries by reference to the long-term rate of increase in national productivity and to represent a corresponding stabilization of profit rates as being achieved through the determination of prices may be a valid interpretation of the requirements of an incomes policy and one not inconsistent with the habits and practices of the institutions involved.

V. ERRORS AND OMISSIONS

None of the above is intended to suggest, of course, more than that some ideas for the interpretation of an incomes policy appear to have an immediate usefulness. Even if their present suitability were to be

---

[1] R. R. Neild, *Pricing and Employment in the Trade Cycle*, C.U.P., 1963, p. 4.
[2] *Ibid.* p. 51.

established, however, three large problems would remain. First, the Commission may be able to establish certain criteria by which it may itself judge the legitimacy of a movement of incomes after the event : within such judgements there is scope for the exercise of impartial discretion in the admission of special circumstances. But to lay down criteria by which trade unions and business organizations may mark their own behaviour in advance — without allowing all to be admitted as exceptional cases — is many times more difficult. Secondly, in so far as all incomes policy achieves success in respect of formal arrangements, e.g. in collective wage bargaining, economic forces may break through in more private and less regular — and therefore less controllable — fashion, e.g. in such phenomena as 'wage drift'. Thirdly, the imposition of an incomes policy, though having an economic purpose, is a political undertaking. Hence, like all other political undertakings, there can be no final conclusion to it. All is contingent. If an incomes policy is to be progressively unrolled, the phenomena with which it deals are also set in history and the subjects of change.

Chapter 26

THE EFFECTS OF POLICIES OF PRICE
SUPPORT ON AGRICULTURAL INCOMES

BY

LUC FAUVEL AND ULLRICH KLAMM

Faculté de Droit et des Sciences Économiques, University of Paris

INTRODUCTORY

THE absolute or relative declines in agricultural incomes which became particularly evident after the 1929 crisis, gave rise in a number of countries to a series of measures 'to organize the markets'. These measures have taken various forms : price support, exemption from taxes, harvest and livestock insurance, credit facilities, bonuses for reductions in areas under cultivation, subsidies intended to increase incomes directly or to reduce the prices of products necessary for agriculture, and others of the same kind. The support of agricultural prices was the most important element amongst these.

An indication of its importance is furnished by the cost of the various measures to the state : in the United States, 53 per cent of the money allocated for the subsidy of agriculture is absorbed by price support (including certain export subsidies) whilst the figure for the United Kingdom is 45 per cent.[1]

This system was introduced in France between the wars. One of the most notable institutions created was the Wheat Office in 1936. General outline schemes for the 'organization' of markets were circulated in 1953. These were applied in various ways to the major products (meat, dairy products, vegetable oil products, wine, and so on). Since then, this form of support has constantly been modified (particularly in 1955, 1957, and 1958). It underwent additional modification in the Law of Agricultural Orientation of 5 August 1960. The aim of this law was to establish parity between the incomes of farmers and those derived from other productive activities entailing a comparable degree of skill ; in addition, under Section V it pro-

[1] FAO, *Report by Working Group of Experts on Measures for the Support of Agriculture* (December 1956), Rome, 1960.

vided for complete organization both of production and of markets. In France, as elsewhere, the aim of price support has been to raise agricultural income. Now the relation between the rise of a price and the rise in the net income obtained from selling the goods concerned is not certain : it depends on the conditions of production and demand.

A measure of the effects of price support would, however, be doubly useful :

(1) at the national level, it would enable authorities to tell to what extent their policies had achieved their objectives ;
(2) at the international level, it would facilitate comparison of the degree of protection of agriculture in different countries.

This proposition is to be found already in Haberler's report to GATT and it was taken up again by FAO.[1] FAO also pointed out that budgetary expenditure is only a rather rough index : in fact, the costs that fall on the state only constitute part of the increase in agricultural income ; the rest is borne by the national consumers and, possibly, by foreign consumers and users of the product.

Three methods of approach will be considered here :

(i) an approach through national accounting ;
(ii) an approach through price theory ;
(iii) an empirical approach through analysis of particular cases.

I. APPROACH THROUGH NATIONAL ACCOUNTING

Hitherto French national accounting has not attempted the calculation of agricultural income by branches. It could do no more than supply the necessary statistical data. In the industrial sector, there is a detailed breakdown by branches of industry ; by contrast, agriculture continues to be treated as a single branch. This fact is obviously not due to any supposed greater homogeneity of agricultural production, but to a somewhat misleading simplification because of the multiple agricultural activities carried on by most agricultural enterprises, because of self-subsistence, and because of the difficulty of evaluating joint expenditures on different products of the enterprise.

[1] FAO, Experts' report of April 1959, Rome, 1960.

II. APPROACH THROUGH PRICE THEORY

(i) It is worthwhile to define and explain the concept of 'agricultural income by branches' or by product. In the general theory of prices, which is primarily concerned with industrial production, the notion of income per product is simple : in the case of perfect competition, this revenue is represented by the area bounded on the one side by the curve of marginal costs and on the other by the line of price ; in the case of a monopoly, this area is bounded by the curve of marginal costs and that of the marginal revenue up to the point of intersection.

These diagrammatic representations cannot be applied here because of a special property of agricultural supply : the curve of marginal costs, or its intersection with the curve of marginal revenue does not have any influence in fixing the quantity supplied. Marginal costs have little or no relevance because :

(1) it is practically impossible to determine the variable costs and fixed costs effectively *ex-ante*, or in many respects *ex-post*, or to evaluate the common charges amongst the different products, as a result of multiple products and self-subsistence activities ;

(2) the variable costs (which form the basis of marginal costs) are of little importance compared with the fixed costs ; in the case of a fall in the selling price, a reduction in production does not cause the total cost of production to drop appreciably.

On the other hand the quantity supplied is generally determined by the uncertainties of the harvest, and thus in the short term by exogenous factors such as the weather.

This implies great inelasticity of agricultural supply in the short term. Let us consider Diagram 1 : the supply curve is represented by a straight line parallel to the ordinate for which the point of intersection with the abscissa is given by the volume of the harvest. However, it should be emphasized that this straight line only becomes a supply curve after the point (*S*) where the price obtained is sufficient to cover the costs of harvesting and of bringing to market a unit of the product. If this is not the case, the farmer will abandon any sale.

On the other hand, the demand curve *DD* for agricultural products is theoretically no different from that for industrial products and its intersection with the straight line of supply defined above (A) gives the price which will be established on the market if the state does not intervene (p_0). The total return is given by the rectangle $p_0 A x_0 O$.

Now it is clearly no longer possible to calculate from our diagram the *revenue* obtained by producing and selling the harvest since our supply line is no longer related to the production costs and the difference between returns and costs can no longer be determined. This problem is not serious in the short term but becomes so in the long term because it is this net revenue which in the end constitutes the objective of agricultural activity.

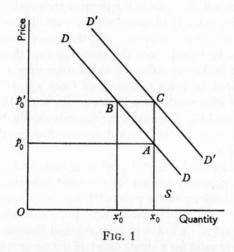

FIG. 1

In the long term it is the variations in this difference between receipts and costs per unit of product which lead to changes in the quantities supplied.

However, this difficulty can be avoided within the framework of our reasoning : all that is involved, in fact, is the determination of the increase in receipts which can be attributed to measures of intervention. This increase will serve either to raise a positive revenue or to diminish a negative revenue ; it will therefore have a direct effect on the magnitude of the difference between receipts and costs and can be considered as the increase in the net revenue.

Let us now assume that the price p_0 which would be established on the market is considered insufficient, and that the authorities wish to increase the income of farmers. In this case the state must intervene in the market to absorb a certain volume of the product either by stocking it, or transforming it, or by exporting it, any of which amounts to subtracting this volume from private demand during the current period. Thus this demand will be added to that represented by DD (to give $D'D'$). The state will have spent the sum given by the area of the rectangle BCx_0x_0'. The increase in the agricultural revenue is given by the rectangle $p_0'p_0AC$.

But a practical difficulty arises : the demand curves are not known for individual agricultural products ; what is more, some of these curves are subject to continual changes which destroy a large part of their practical significance. However, in the case of products with a high rate of (non-seasonal) consumption, one point on the demand curve can be identified : that is the point corresponding to the price and the quantity actually obtained on the market after intervention (B). As the form of the curve beyond this point is not known, the point A cannot be found ; nor therefore can the 'theoretical' price p_0 which must be known in order to determine the revenue which can be attributed to price maintenance (area $p_0'p_0AC$). In actual fact we are not interested in the whole of the curve but only in the price p_0 which would be obtained if the quantity supplied to the market had been increased by the amount represented by the difference between x_0' and x_0.

It seems that a knowledge of the price elasticity of demand could be utilized. It is generally known for the most important food stuffs. Knowing this elasticity of the point (B), we can answer the question asked and find the desired 'theoretical' price corresponding to the point A. However, it must be remembered that an elasticity by definition is only valid for a single point on the curve. If an elasticity is applied over a whole arc, it is implicitly assumed that the curve is iso-elastic over the part under consideration. Thus when the part of the crop absorbed by the authorities is too large, the method becomes inexact.

(ii) Thus far the proposed model has been very simple. We have limited ourselves to a single market and to one well-defined period : that which precedes the availability of the next harvest for commercial disposal.

To isolate the marketing of a product in this way both in time and in respect of the complex interplay that results from the general interdependence of markets, is obviously, however, a great simplification of reality. The problem arises of extending the analysis over time and space. What is more, this problem arises both for supply and for demand. We shall now examine the issues involved.

(a) *Demand*

(1) Since the time of Alfred Marshall it has been recognized that the value of any elasticity varies considerably according to the period to which one refers. This is true of the demand for agricultural products which are bought not by the final consumer but by intermediary speculators. Consequently a price change gives rise to a chain of reactions in the quantities bought, the direction and strength of these reactions being determined by the values of the elasticities in the short, medium, and long terms. But a short-term reaction in turn gives rise to a new chain of reactions and so on. To take into account this interplay between reactions, a large number of models of the distribution of lags have been developed, notably by Working, Ladd, and Tedford and by Nerlove.[1] The value of these elasticities clearly changes depending on the product under consideration, but we tend to assume that frequently the demand for agricultural products is fairly elastic in the short term (because of stocking by intermediaries), that it diminishes thereafter and increases again in the long term (because of adjustment of the demand of final consumers due to substitution within the total of family expenditure).

(2) Thus far we have limited ourselves to the effects which the absorption of a given quantity of a certain product will have on the price of *that* product ; the elasticity assumed has been direct. Now, in view of the effects of substitution and complementarity, this absorption will have repercussions on the price of *other goods*. Similarly measures intended to maintain the prices of these other goods will have repercussions on the demand, and therefore the price, for the first product.

Thus an analysis which is limited to a single product will clearly be insufficient : as is indicated by the interplay of cross-elasticities, the prices and the quantities demanded for all different agricultural goods are in a situation of interdependence. This has to be taken into account in determining the agricultural revenue for any branch which can be attributed to a policy of price maintenance. The failure of this policy in one branch may be due to concurrent measures in adjoining branches, and the implications of these indirect effects need to be analysed before taking action to absorb part of the crop in a given market.

[1] E. J. Working, 1944, *Demand for Meat*, University of Chicago ; Nerlove, Marc, 'Distributed Lags and Estimation of Long-Run Supply and Demand Elasticities : Theoretical Considerations' (*Journal of Farm Economics*, vol. 40, no. 2).

The importance of these indirect effects can be appreciated by measuring the cross-elasticities which are generally represented in a double-entry table such as that developed for the United States by Brandow [1] (we shall not, however, go into the details of the model proposed by this author).

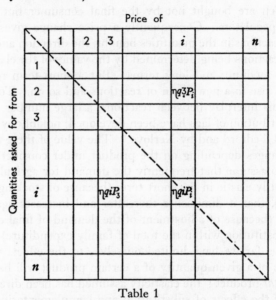

Table 1

Let us consider Table 1 : for each elasticity under consideration, the nature of the goods for which the dependence is to be investigated is written at the head of the column for which the price is being considered and at the head of the line for which the quantity is being considered. Thus the direct elasticities are found on the diagonal since the same product appears both at the head of the column and the head of the line. An individual column gives all the elasticities relating to the price of one product and the quantity demanded for each of the others.

To determine the indirect effects arising from price maintenance for a particular product (i), the elasticities in column (i) are used to calculate the relative variations in the quantities demanded for the other goods. Using the information obtained and taking into account the direct elasticities given by the diagonal, the variations in the corresponding prices can be found. But these changes in price will

[1] G. E. Brandow, *Interrelations among Demands for Farm Products and Implications for Control of Market Supply*, Univ. Penns., 1961.

in turn give rise to a change in the quantity of the product (i) demanded with the result that a new chain of causality is set up which is liable to be perpetuated until the initial effect ceases to be operative and a new equilibrium is attained.

What will be the significance of the process defined by the chain of causality described above ? It all depends on the nature of the different goods and whether they are complementary or substitutes for one another. The values calculated by Brandow for the United States demonstrate that in general the cross-elasticities are positive, i.e. that different foodstuffs are in a situation of substitution.[1]

(b) *Supply*

Thus far we have ignored the elasticity of supply or, more precisely, we have assumed that it was zero. This seems valid when we limit ourselves to the annual case : in fact, as in the case of the demand, the annual elasticity of supply is lower than the elasticity from day to day, on the one hand, and than the long-term elasticities, on the other hand. However, it should be pointed out that, unlike the elasticities of demand which have been the subject of large numbers of investigations and are relatively well known, the elasticities of agricultural supply are, in general, very little known.[2] This is due, particularly in the case of long-term elasticities, to the difficulty of isolating the influence of price changes on the quantity supplied. Whereas the factors which shift the demand curve — such as the national income, its distribution, the prices of other goods and the like — can all be taken into consideration, in the case of supply the corresponding factors are represented by elements which are often exogenous to purely economic explanation, such, for example, as weather conditions.

This is why hitherto one has confined oneself to limited investigations of individual or regional cases or to constructing supply curves obtained by linear programming.[3] In this respect it would be necessary to calculate these direct elasticities for different periods in order

[1] The only exception is beverages, for which a third of the cross-elasticities are negative. However, in view of the low values of these elasticities, none of which is greater than 0·0023, this exception is not significant.

[2] With the exception, however, of the elasticity of pork supply where the 'pork cycle' has led to complete and relevant estimations such as that of Howard J. Stover. In the case of France the great work of M. Dubos for cereals should also be mentioned.

[3] Krenz, Baumann, and Heady, 'Normative Supply Functions by Linear Programming Procedures', *Agricultural Economic Research*, USDA, January 1962. Cited by Shepherd.

to complete the models involving the interaction of the elasticities of demand with a corresponding model for the elasticities of supply. Actual results (notably for pork) lead us to assume that these elasticities of supply can be high for the short term (the case where stocking by the exploiter is possible), then diminish for the medium term, and rise again for the long term.

The rise in the long term is clearly due to the phenomenon of substitution of production, the importance of which is generally recognized although we know little about its real implications. For certain goods (for example, vineyards), this elasticity will, for technical reasons, probably be small. For other products (such as beet), technical conditions allow easy substitution of another crop such as cereals or fodder plants.

In view of the enormous practical problems which arise when calculating a simple direct elasticity of supply, there is all the more reason why the cross-elasticities of supply, which express these possibilities of substitution, are far from being known. They are, however, extremely important : it was on them that the classical mechanism of the market rested to a large extent. That this mechanism should, in fact, be judged intolerable for agriculture does not basically alter anything. The surpluses in production of certain goods benefiting from price support which result after a number of years, in France notably in the case of corn, are a proof in reverse of the importance of the interdependence of agricultural supplies. In practice, the prices have not dropped sufficiently for operators to be obliged to think of substitution.

(iii) *Conclusion to the Approach by way of Price Theory*

Having demonstrated a simple mechanism for determining the revenue per unit of product attributable to price support, we have then introduced complications. These complications have arisen both on the side of supply and on the side of demand ; they have been linked with two problems of elasticity. This has led us to consider the elasticities according to periods and, as far as possible, to analyse their interaction. Finally we have shown that the interdependence of agricultural markets, as expressed by the cross-elasticities, involves the phenomenon of substitution both in supply and in demand.

A complete model intended to calculate the influence of price maintenance on the revenue of farmers must therefore take into account this double extension over time and space — that is to say, over adjoining agricultural markets. In concrete terms, it would be a question of establishing the link between Brandow's studies and the different models of the distribution of lags, both for supply and for demand.

Brandow has, nevertheless, reached some interesting conclusions on a basis of his model. He has provided an estimate of the effects of programmes of 'supply-diversion' in 1955–57.

'Government programs in the 1950's diverted supplies from the market by accumulating stocks and subsidizing disposal of supplies outside the commercial channels. Estimates of prices and incomes expected in the absence of these programs are instructive about the sensitivity of farm income to prices and to the total value of products to be cleared from the market. If all crops available from current production had cleared the market during 1955–57, livestock production would have been a little larger than it was. Crop prices would have averaged perhaps 20 per cent lower, livestock prices 11 per cent lower, and all farm prices 15 per cent lower. Since production expenses would have declined only slightly, the realized net income of farm operators would have fallen about 35 per cent. Retail food prices would have decreased about 4·67 per cent and the urban cost of living as measured by the Consumer Price Index would have dropped perhaps 1·5 per cent — one tenth of the decline in farm prices' (*ibid.* pp. 8–9).

Brandow then adds some remarks to the same effect as those made above : 'The demand model yields no information on supply response for crop production, however. Thus this study cannot show whether high crop production would persist in face of the low prices and incomes it created, nor how long free market adjustment of output might require (p. 94)'.

III. THE EMPIRICAL APPROACH BY ANALYSIS OF INDIVIDUAL CASES

The obstacles which the two previous approaches have encountered lead us to consider the possibilities of analysis by case studies limited to the principal products.

In the case of France, moreover, the policy of price support did not result in a set of uniform measures. Thus there is no price support at all for fruit and vegetables (including potatoes) whereas the production of beet alcohol and wines 'for everyday consumption' (often wines of mediocre quality) benefited, from before 1914, from various forms of preferential treatment, some of them substantial. Yet the revenue from beet and vineyards is considerably less important for agriculture than that from 'fruit and vegetables'. An analysis by product (or group of products) is therefore entirely justified.

The special support of certain prices has for a long time been connected with complex collective pressures. In the last few years (during a period of full employment, comparative monetary stability and political stability), some of the income to peasants has been gained by various actions against the authorities. On several occasions the government has been forced to go beyond the policy of price support which had been decided. The result has been an increase in agricultural income varying according to crops, regions and methods of cultivation, and equally variable repercussions on the trends of the structures of production.

We shall limit ourselves to some remarks relating to two groups of essential products : (i) dairy products and beef ; (ii) cereals.

(i) *Dairy Products and Beef*

(a) Although milk producers are also livestock raisers (60 per cent of beef comes from discarded cows), the pressures exerted on the authorities have been much stronger in the case of price support for dairy products. The farmers wish the price of milk to be considered as a sort of 'wage', that is an income guaranteed by the state and received throughout the year by the farmer's family, whilst the sale of beef retains its speculative nature as a result of the length of the production process (several years) and the risks of fluctuations in market prices. In 1961–62, each litre of milk sold in France cost the taxpayers 5 centimes in a guaranteed price of about 35 centimes. This support covered the losses in exporting butter surpluses. Now dairy products supply 20 per cent of the gross return from agriculture. It should not, however, be concluded from this that the budgetary support is the source of 3 per cent of agricultural revenue. It is the processed products which are exported at a loss, not only butter but condensed milk, powdered milk, certain cheeses and other products. Collection costs, and the margins for processing and commercial disposal, are particularly high in France. Price support is divided between the farm and the subsequent stages of the process of disposing of the product.

Moreover it is difficult to determine what the market price would be without price support on a basis of clearance of the surpluses (point *A* on graph 1): in other words, it is difficult to calculate the over-payment demanded from French consumers as compared with what the price would be in conditions of competition. All that is known is that the guaranteed price of French milk is the lowest in the EEC — a little below the Dutch price.

Thus the impression remains that the acceleration of technical progress in dairy production is the principal cause of the flood of the 'white river' in France; the surpluses result from ill-considered support of the price of production.

(b) Since 1957 the authorities have tried unsuccessfully to deflect farmers from the production of milk to that of beef. Beef is also exported at a loss, but differences from the 'world' market price (meat from Argentine) in the long run should be smaller for meat. It was estimated in 1961–63 that the relative price of beef would have to be raised by 30 to 50 per cent to have a serious chance of limiting the milk surplus. Now, we are dealing with the main family expenditure for foodstuffs. At present 6 to 9 per cent of the family income is spent on cattle meat (beef and veal). The primary effect on the cost of living of such a rise at the farm would be 2 to 3 per cent. There is a risk of a cumulative process being triggered off by successive rises in the 'minimum guaranteed wage'. It is almost unthinkable that a government should deliberately engage on such a foolhardy path to discover whether this would happen or not. France has already experienced 'beef steak' inflation.

There is thus a problem of substituting meat for milk in French agricultural production. Meat production is only developing in regions where industrial expansion is significantly raising the level of rural incomes, since milk production involves labour costs which are considerably higher than those for meat. In most regions the dominant tendency remains in the converse direction: substitution of milk for meat, that is contrary to the trend desired on structural grounds.

To summarize, the repercussions of price support have been as follows. From 1957 onwards the government clearly adopted a policy of orientating agricultural production through prices. It was a question between 1958 and 1961 (the period of the third plan) of making French agriculture become more and more an exporter of beef rather than of wheat. This result should have been obtained by creating a disparity between the target prices for these two products: a relative drop in the guaranteed price for wheat and a relative increase in the price for meat.

This policy failed for very varied reasons :

(1) Since 1959 the wheat producers, who are numerous and well organized, have secured a relative increase in the guaranteed price for wheat ;
(2) The raisers of livestock were more pressing in demanding rises in the price of milk than a rise in the price of meat ;
(3) Industrial expansion has given rise to a large exodus from rural areas but has not been sufficient for substitution of meat for milk to become general ;
(4) Farm management investigations (in most regions) have shown that milk production is considerably more advantageous in the present agricultural structure (there are reserves of family labour in the small enterprises).

Thus the policy of orientation of production through prices has been held in check by the collective action of established interests. The producers have secured increases in their incomes in accordance with their immediate interests. By industrial agitation they have slowed down the structural development that their representatives had designed in agreement with the administration for the period 1958–66 ; this aspect of the concerted planning of the French economy has failed.

(ii) *Cereals*

Wheat producers have enjoyed a guaranteed price for their crop since 1936. This advantage was later extended to other cereals. The price is about 30 to 50 per cent higher than the world price. Now France has been an exporter for the last ten years. Wheat production tends to exceed 100 million quintals for a human consumption which has stabilized at about 55 million quintals. The surplus of secondary cereals is much smaller. Since 1953 this system has resulted in part of the cereal crop being exported at a loss. The authorities have tried to limit these losses by levying a tax to re-absorb the surpluses, which is deducted from the guaranteed price to producers ; the guaranteed price is restricted to a certain 'quantum' (about 70 million quintals). Thus the state only bears about two-thirds of the export losses. The quantities delivered over and beyond the quantum are paid for at the world price (price for re-absorption of the surplus). But this system does not restrain the rise in production resulting from technical progress. The quantum paid at the guaranteed price approximately corresponds to the output of a bad harvest and the surpluses due to good harvests constitute a windfall beyond this quantum : they are only paid at the world price, but King's law does not hold for the crop as a whole. There is no complete collapse of prices : the price remains stable within the limits of the quantum.

This system has now been in use for more than a quarter of a century. At the beginning, at the time of the great depression, it had primarily a social aim : to guarantee the small producer against a collapse of the market prices or seasonal speculation by grain merchants. Since about 1953, with the return of prosperity, the system seems to have favoured sclerosis of the agricultural structures. More than 500,000 'small suppliers', marginal or infra-marginal producers, continue to devote part of their activities to the cultivation of wheat (or secondary cereals) because it is one of the forms of cultivation (particularly south of the Loire) with the best guaranteed income. Rural migration, the regrouping of farms and their conversions to the cultivation of other crops have also been held up because of the slight advantage of continuing to cultivate wheat.

Moreover, it is known from studies made by the 'centres of administration' that the 55 million quintals of wheat required for human consumption could be produced by the large farming enterprises alone. Thus the farms of 150 to 300 hectares in the region of Paris, in spite of high wages, could continue to produce without loss at a price comparable to that guaranteed to American farmers. The social objective of price support, as defined in 1936, has lost its significance : by neutralizing the incentives to migration and structural development, the policy followed has rebounded against its beneficiaries. '*Les marginaux protègent l'armée.*' The beneficiaries are the efficient producers who obtain prices only a little lower than those of the 'small suppliers'.

There are cases, however, where the over-payment for wheat helps the development of more efficient farms. Thus in Seine-et-Marne, near Paris, farmers operating with less than 100 hectares frequently succeed year by year in buying land which is available close to their own, so as to increase the area under cultivation. In doing this they run into debt, but the guarantee of the price of cereals practically removes any risk of failure. There is no extension of the area under cultivation in the case of farm enterprises with over 200 hectares ; they are largely rentable ; but concentration is proceeding between 50 and 150 hectares. In this case price support results in a greater efficiency in the use of farm equipment.

IV. CONCLUSION

There is no contradiction between the various approaches discussed. The approach through the theory of prices and the interplay of cross-elasticities is encouraging and invites quantitative global investigation. The approach through socio-economic case-studies of the principal sectors of production gives another insight, perhaps more blurred, but which may usefully shade in the previous representation. The complementary nature of the two methods has, moreover, for long been recognized.

THE JOINT DISCUSSION OF
PROFESSOR BROCHIER'S, PROFESSOR TRESS'S,
AND PROFESSOR FAUVEL'S PAPERS

Professor D. J. Delivanis, introducing Professor Brochier's paper, recalled that since the end of World War II conditions of full or over-employment in Western European countries had led to an increase in the wage share and to a higher overall propensity to consume. The pressure on demand had been strengthened by a further pressure on costs as wage rises had tended to overtake the increase in productivity.

There were three traditional methods of coping with the ensuing inflationary disequilibrium. The securing of a budget surplus was not often practicable in view of continuously increasing public expenditure. Monetary policy could be effective in reducing profits and investments in so far as liquidity was controlled by the central bank. It had been so before 1914 but it had proved less successful in curbing inflation during the inter-war period ; repercussions were felt abroad when deflationary policy was applied in countries with key currencies. One could resort to devaluation but this only succeeded when the international market was a buyers' market, as was proved by the sterling devaluation of 1931, whereas in 1949, under different international conditions, devaluation had been far less successful. There were strong arguments against further devaluations in the future.

This explained the need for a new approach to the problem in the guise of an incomes policy aiming at planning the unavoidable increases in money incomes in order to prevent deadlocks and disequilibrium. Professor Brochier had given rather limited aims to an incomes policy for the French economy. He was of the opinion that it should try to slow down increases in monetary incomes saying that in conditions of full employment it would prove impossible to stop them altogether. Professor Brochier was not averse to monetary wages increasing at a somewhat higher rate than productivity because he believed that this was necessary in order to put pressure on entrepreneurs who otherwise would not be induced to cut labour costs by substituting capital for manpower in production processes.

In Professor Brochier's view an incomes policy was also a way of avoiding a tendency towards intersectoral income equalization as this would otherwise hamper the shift of manpower from depressed areas and sectors like agriculture. Finally it could, up to a certain point, reduce social injustice. These were limited objects which, Professor Delivanis thought, could be achieved within the present framework of the French economy.

Professor Lecaillon said that Professor Tress's paper gave both the reasons for an incomes policy in the U.K. and the difficulties encountered in enforcing it. In Professor Tress's opinion incomes policy was not a distribution policy. Its bearing was not on how national income in real terms was shared but on the relationship between variations in real income and in money income. It seemed thus that the main object in establishing an incomes policy in Britain had been to keep the rate of increase in overall monetary income below the ceiling of the long-run rate of increase in production. It had therefore been thought of as a means of curbing inflation. This was giving incomes policy a more restricted aim than in its French version where it was devised as a way of supplementing the planning of production with some measure of planning of income and also as a means of achieving a more equitable income distribution.

If the incomes policy was conceived as an alternative way of dealing with inflation it had to be related to the failure of more traditional, mainly monetary, policies in curbing a new form of inflation, i.e. cost inflation as distinct from demand inflation. However, as rightly emphasized by Professor Tress, it was not possible to influence monetary incomes without changing, in some degree, the distribution of real income. One then had to be prepared to face trade unions' hostile reactions to government intervention. An institutional issue was therefore involved.

Without entering into Professor Tress's developments about the historical circumstances under which incomes policy was conceived in Britain, Professor Lecaillon wished to observe that from 1961 onwards the official view had related the shortage of savings and the recurring balance of payment crises to cost inflation ; thus, as in France, the need for redressing the balance of payment's equilibrium had been one of the main reasons for designing an incomes policy. As in France, the government had been more successful in checking the rise of wages and salaries in the public sector than in the rest of the economy, thus creating income disparities between both. But an incomes policy, to be generally acceptable, would have to achieve the same measure of efficacy in dealing with all kinds of incomes.

The third and fourth parts of Professor Tress's paper related to the ways of enforcing an incomes policy. One point of special interest to Professor

Lecaillon was the fundamental rule laid down by the National Income Commission in its first report, namely that 'all wage settlements must reflect the overall national increase in productivity', the Commission making it clear that, in Professor Tress's words, 'the mere experience of difficulties in recruitment and retention of labour did not justify exceptional increases in earnings' (p. 690 of the paper). It seemed therefore that the Commission was resigned to let wages increase at roughly the same rate and therefore to allow for no changes in relative wage rates as a general rule.

This seemed to Professor Lecaillon to imply that changes in relative wage rates would no longer have a significant influence on the distribution of labour between industries. Would this mean that relative wage rates were no longer instrumental in allocating labour resources ? Would not such a rigid incomes policy hamper the sectoral shifts of manpower ? This indirectly raised the issue of whether an incomes policy was compatible with a market economy. An incomes policy had also to consider profits. However, special difficulties had been encountered in measuring them. The Incomes Commission had had to resort to a price criterion because, had the policy been successful in keeping wage increase within the ceiling of the overall growth rate, the test of its success in keeping the increase of profits and other factor incomes within the same limit would have been whether prices had remained stable in the same period. If not, what sort of measures was the Government to apply to prevent prices from rising ? Would these measures, especially direct price control, not alter a free enterprise economy ? Professor Lecaillon hoped that Professor Tress would answer these questions.

In his conclusion, Professor Tress had been careful to say that the imposition of an incomes policy was a political undertaking and therefore subject to many contingencies. Professor Lecaillon was not altogether sure whether it would prove successful. Was success possible without triggering off a process which would change some of the basic features of the economic system ? More state intervention might be required especially on investment as well as more centralization in trade unions' organization. Trade unions might have to participate in policy decisions in which case advancing wage claims would cease to be their main objective.

A general discussion on Professor Brochier's and Professor Tress's papers then followed.

Professor Gendarme emphasized the difficulties which occurred in France in computing wages and in comparing labour earnings because of bonuses, fringe benefits, and the like. Upgrading was frequently practised so that the classification of workers in similar jobs depended on the industries or even the firms in which they were employed and they were correspondingly paid at different wage rates for the same skill.

Professor Gendarme observed that in a period of growth the distribution of savings between individual and corporate savings changed. When personal incomes rose individual savings increased steadily, whereas the returns on capital did not increase at the same rate. Self-financing of investment by ploughing back profits became more difficult ; entrepreneurs were not likely to resign themselves to a diminishing share of profits in national income and they would welcome any opportunity to push profits rates up. This made the enforcement of an incomes policy more difficult.

It would be wrong to overlook incomes earned in the distributive trades. *Ceteris paribus* the higher the profit margin the lower the real wages. One would have to control the marking up of prices by middlemen and this was no easy task.

Dr. Feinstein, referring to Section IV in Professor Tress's paper, wondered whether it was sufficient to think in terms of national income categories as relevant to non-wage incomes. He would think that incomes accruing from capital gains were important in maintaining a balance between wage and non-wage incomes.

Referring to the figure of 3 to $3\frac{1}{2}$ per cent for the rate of increase in real productivity per head retained by the Incomes Commission in its second Report, Professor Tress had written that 'the N.E.D.C. had shown the British economy to be capable (of it) over the period 1961-1966' (p. 690 in his paper). Dr. Feinstein wished that the N.E.D.C. could have shown the economy to be capable of a 3 to $3\frac{1}{2}$ per cent increase in productivity *per annum*. At most one could say that this was the figure which they suggested might be possible. It was not just a matter of words. An incomes policy was difficult to achieve under any circumstances but particularly difficult when the rate of growth of productivity was very low as had been the case in the U.K. in the post-war period. A successful incomes policy had therefore to be integrated with a policy to increase the rate of growth of the economy.

Dr. Bruzek said that Professor Tress's assertion (p. 690 of the paper) that all wage settlements must reflect the overall national average increase in productivity seemed to him not quite correct as the growth of wages and salaries had to be related only to the increase in productivity of labour in consumer goods and services.

In devising an incomes policy the principles which applied to profits could not be the same as those applying to labour incomes. Dr. Bruzek did not think it sufficient to justify the difference of treatment by saying that profits were 'the contingent reward' for risk in investing capital as had been written in the Incomes Commission's Report quoted by Professor Tress (p. 694). This did not explain how profit was generated and by whom. What was Professor Tress's opinion on this ?

Professor Reder agreed with Professor Tress's careful conclusions about the chance of success in implementing an incomes policy. He would, however, rather put the stress on the possibilities of failure. Was not this a task for which market economies were ill-equipped ? Could it be imposed upon unions without undermining in the long run the rank-and-file loyalty to union bosses and entailing wild strikes?

Professor Reder would agree with the principle held by both the Council on Prices, Productivity and Income and the Incomes Commission that 'the notion that it (was) the right of every industry to appropriate for itself the whole of the fruits of its own greater productivity (was) mistaken and should be abandoned' (quotation p. 690 of the paper). But then why not let the industry, where the rate of productivity increase was faster, experience falling prices, wages remaining stable ? An incomes policy was no feasible alternative to letting the prices go down because it meant asking workers in progressive industries to give up rises when profits were high without their being guaranteed corresponding increases later : if they held back their claims in times when their bargaining position was exceptionally good, how could they be assured that they would get more later, when profits might be lower ? One of the worst difficulties which had to be encountered in enforcing an incomes policy was that it might be impossible to spread the differential gains of productivity over a longer period than the year when they appeared. Thus they had to be reflected either in higher profits or in lower prices in the industries where they had been generated.

Professor Reder wondered whether an incomes policy could be an appropriate policy against inflation. The root of the trouble was to be found in the conditions of full employment and the best cure for the disease would be to relax to some degree these conditions.

Professor Bronfenbrenner believed that as an incomes policy seemed to encounter so much difficulty one would do better without one. It seemed the conventional notion that one could at the same time guarantee full employment at any cost, aim at price stability, and yield to the leading producer pressure groups. As consumers were not organized, the condition that usually yielded was price stability. If something had to yield, Professor Bronfenbrenner would instead choose the guarantee of full employment : if people raised their prices, the penalty would then be unemployment for somebody, not always the ones who lead raised prices in the first place.

There was however an alternative way of dealing with this three-pronged problem, by substituting control of the supply of money for an incomes policy.

Professor Solow said he would like to dissociate himself from Professor Reder and Professor Bronfenbrenner. It was perfectly obvious that there were serious difficulties in formulating and enforcing an incomes policy in the U.K. and France and the recent developments of the incomes policy in the Netherlands were far from encouraging. No doubt success would require a certain degree of centralized bargaining, which would make it still more difficult to enforce in the U.S. where trade unions in many industries were not centralized. Even so, he believed that the alternative of disciplining prices by unemployment, as suggested by Professor Reder and Professor Bronfenbrenner, would prove a remedy far worse than the disease. How much unemployment would have to be imposed to avoid, say, a 1 per cent rise per year in the price level? If the cost were, say, 1 per cent of the GNP this would amount to a lot over a period of time.

Professor Gannagé said that the drafting of the Fifth Plan had been the occasion for a move in France from planning in volume to planning in value as had been emphasized by Professor Brochier. Professor Gannagé observed, however, that in setting the objectives for the Fifth Plan, the French planners had allowed for a wider margin of variation between forecast and achieved targets. This was going back to indicative planning at a moment when the enforcement of an incomes policy in Britain pointed to an evolution towards a greater measure of planning. It seemed to Professor Gannagé that although French planning had resulted in closer bargaining between groups it had not seemed to amount to much more than adjusting overall quantities which was disappointing.

Dr. Bruzek observed that planning in value as distinct from planning in volume implied that the planners were able to determine final demand. On which principles was this done in France ?

Planning in France as in other Western countries was only in the form of recommendations to firms. It could only succeed under the assumption that firms had enough inducement to achieve the proposed objectives. Dr. Bruzek feared that incentives to fulfil the plan would not be sufficient. In socialist countries when it could to some extent be compared with planning within the firm in Western countries, the pattern of planning was vertical. The reaching of targets was an obligation. Professor Brochier had written (p. 677) that no standard of income distribution could be found in either ideologies or economic theory. Dr. Bruzek could not agree with this statement because he believed that in a Marxist economy there were principles based on quality, quantity and importance of work done which provided for such a standard.

Professor Brochier thanked Professor Delivanis for introducing his paper. He thought, however, that Professor Delivanis had misunderstood him when he said that he (Professor Brochier) was in favour of money wages increasing at a higher rate than productivity. Professor Brochier had written that there was some danger in limiting the rise in wages to the average increase in productivity, meaning, however, by that statement that there was some danger in proportioning the rise in all wage rates to the average increase in productivity. It seemed to be the principle favoured by the British incomes policy. It had the disadvantage of making the rate structure rigid. The French were in favour of more flexibility. In some branches wages should increase more than average productivity, but in others less than average.

Professor Delivanis had interpreted Professor Brochier as pleading for maintaining the inter-sectoral gap in income level to the detriment of farmers through incomes policy so as to encourage the shift of manpower away from farming. On the contrary Professor Brochier believed that one of the objectives of incomes policy should be to reduce the gap in income levels. It was true that he was in favour of helping farmers to move to other sectors but only in so far as this shift from agriculture was the condition for reducing the income disparity through a diminishing number of farmers.

With regard to the practical difficulties which stood in the way of the incomes policy, Professor Brochier agreed with Professor Gendarme that the wage drift made it difficult to compare wage rates. Recent developments in the Netherlands had shown that any attempt to contain the rise in wages led to a speeding-up of the drift. In fixing, however, a feasible order of magnitude of the wage rises, the incomes policy could not and should not go into details. In the post-war years in France the policy had been to set a detailed wage-rate structure, but in a period of steady growth this was out of the question. One ought to leave the task of fixing the rates in detail and such matters as the payment of bonuses to the collective wage settlements. Although this was not usually the practice, both labour and employers unions were apparently not far from agreeing that wage settlements ought to be more detailed. This, however, had a bearing on the organization of the unions.

Dr. Bruzek's first question led Professor Brochier to refer to modifications introduced in French planning procedures in the drafting of the Fifth Plan in order to forecast final demand. In its first stage planners tried from the centre and in general terms to fix a feasible rate of growth projected for the duration of the Plan ; then, in the new procedure, the draft was sent for examination to varied peripheral bodies ; finally, it returned to the planning commissions whose task it was to adjust the detailed objectives to the overall rate of growth which had been set in the first stage.

Dr. Bruzek's second question and also Professor Gannagé's comments related to indicative planning. Dr. Bruzek had seemed to be rather dubious about the prospect of achieving the targets set by the planning authority if their fulfilment was not compulsory for the production units. French planning, however, was not purely indicative. One should say rather that the degree to which it was compulsory varied according to the sectors. First of all the state controlled roughly half of the whole expenditure on investment through public ownership. At the other end of the scale there were branches of industry for which planned objectives were not much more than pious wishes ; in these the fulfilment of the targets remained subject to the condition that the planned objectives met the interest of the private ownership.

In commenting on his statement that no standard of income distribution could be found in either theory or ideology, Dr. Bruzek had said that the Marxist theory provided such standards. Professor Brochier would, however, remark that their application had left room for much variation in the scale of wage rates in the U.S.S.R. where at one stage a policy of considerable income inequality had been carried through. Professor Brochier maintained that the question of how much inequality was most conducive to the growth of national income in a given situation was determined on empirical, not theoretical, grounds.

Professor Brochier was not far from sharing Professor Reder's pessimism about the implications of the incomes policy on the functioning of trade unions. If their leaders agreed to behave in such a way that they appeared to the rank and file as merely a medium for conveying the injunctions of the wage policy makers, they might well be in for a downfall. This, however, only showed that the incomes policy ought to be in the nature of a deal, with reciprocal commitments on both sides, and this was exactly the sort of policy he had been advocating.

Nevertheless, there remained a major reason for the union's reluctance to accept the new policy to be found in the way the overall increase of the wage bill was apportioned: supposing wage increases to be voluntarily limited in the most advanced industries, how would labour as a group be assured that what it gave up in these would be compensated by higher increases in others? Despite all these objections Professor Brochier still thought it worth while trying to enforce the new policy and he could only agree with the way Professor Solow had already answered Professor Reder's objections.

Professor Tress said that he would first answer Professor Reder's and Professor Bronfenbrenner's comments as they had presented the case against having an incomes policy at all. They were in favour of giving up the attempt and trying instead a policy of relaxing full-employment conditions. Professor Bronfenbrenner proposed also the control of the supply of money as a better alternative to the incomes policy. The Chicago policy had been tried in Britain. It had not worked. The stop-go policy had resulted in a loss of real income and it had slowed down the pace of growth and created balance of payments difficulties through a cyclical movement of stocking and de-stocking. The failure of all the conventional policy measures gave some ground for trying the new policy.

It had come to be considered as orthodox economics that each industry could not appropriate all its increase in productivity and that the overall increase in productivity should be allocated on a national rather than sectoral basis. Professor Reder had objected that in branches which did best employees would be reluctant to withhold their claims for a rise when profits were high for fear of not being able to get more later when profits went down. But this argument ignored the annual round of collective bargaining in Britain which gave labour an assurance that a momentary withholding of a claim was not giving it up altogether.

Dr. Feinstein had been very doubtful about the feasibility of the 3 to 3·5 per cent rate of increase in productivity assumed by the Incomes Commission. Professor Tress said that he was well aware that the Treasury assumed a 2 to 2·5 per cent rate. But this would not be politically acceptable. If incomes policy was to have the assent of the unions it was conditional on the provision of a sufficiently high overall rate of increase in wages and therefore a sufficiently high overall rate of productivity increase. A 3 to 3·5 per cent figure was not over-ambitious in so far as the enforcement of an incomes policy would make it possible to obtain a higher rate of increase in productivity. The terms of the comparison ought to be between the actual 2·5 per cent rate without an incomes policy and the projected 3·5 per cent rate with the enforcement of the incomes policy and trade unions co-operating in the drive for a higher increase in productivity.

Dr. Bruzek was in favour of allocating productivity increases on a national basis but only as a means of relating the increase in incomes to increase in output of consumers' goods alone. Professor Tress could not agree with him ; it should be related to the growth in national output, both in consumption and capital goods. An increase in personal incomes would tend to result in an increase in savings.

Professor Lecaillon, whom Professor Tress wished to thank for introducing his paper, had expressed strong doubts about the compatibility of the incomes policy and the market economy. Like Professor Reder, he was particularly worried by its implications on the functioning of the labour market and its effects on trade unionism. But, as had already been pointed out by Professor Solow, in comparison with the United States a large amount of collective bargaining existed already in Britain at the national level and took place every year on the almost institutional basis of the annual round.

Such considerations led, however, to an examination of another issue of the wage policy : would not the national regulation of wages induce a speeding-up of the phenomenon known as the wage drift as a reaction of the market forces to the enforcement of the policy ? Professor Tress said that his paper had been written before the National Income Commission had made an attempt to define the wage drift in the case of the shipbuilding and engineering industries. Professor Tress wished to quote from the evidence of K. G. J. C. Knowles and D. Robinson at the hearings of the commission : 'The trouble is that increases in all these components are economically ambivalent unless one is clear about their causes. If an increase in above-standard payments is in fact, in present circumstances, the best practicable means of ensuring an appreciably better distribution of labour, or serves to obviate some intolerable anomaly which would otherwise lead to breakdown, it would appear to be justified ; if it does not, or is bigger than is needed to serve its purpose, or sets up severe pressures elsewhere, it would not. If a rise in piecework earnings is caused by an increase in productivity, it should not perhaps be considered as contributing to drift at all ; but if this condition is not fulfilled, it should — as should any emulative reaction from workers whose productivity has not increased. If overtime working is necessary from the standpoint of production and is paid for at no more than the agreed rate of premium, it should presumably not be included in a reckoning of drift; but if it is merely a backstairs way of raising earnings, it should.'

Professor Tress cast strong doubts on the usefulness of systems of payments-by-results. There was the question of the pull exerted by piecework earnings on the earnings of time workers. He was dubious about the validity of the reasons for resorting to increased overtime working. But one should try, in a systematic way, to detect which components in a wage rise were in the nature of a drift and in this way it was possible to get the phenomenon under control.

Professor Tress then turned to questions relating to the profits policy, or, more generally speaking, to the policy with respect to incomes other than wages. Professor Gendarme had emphasized the specific character of incomes earned in the distributive trade. Professor Fauvel's paper had dealt with farmers' incomes in connection with price policy. A policy for non-wage income had to be a policy for factor incomes through prices as well as for what was distributed. Dr. Feinstein had, however, remarked that there could be in non-wage income a component other than a factor income, i.e. a capital gain. One way of controlling non-wage income would be through fiscal policy but it was only a way of regulating the distribution of profits ; a profits policy to be complete would also include a price policy. Professor Lecaillon had raised the question of what would happen if prices rose nevertheless. The answer was that in order to succeed, an incomes policy, far from making it unnecessary, implied a greater measure of fiscal policy.

Several times in the course of the debate comments had been made on the chances of failure of the policy. Professor Tress said that he had already underlined in the concluding sentences of his paper the importance of political contingencies as a condition of success. A fair measure of opportunism was required to make the policy work. What was sought above all was trade union assent to lowering the rate of the annual wage round. Only if this was achieved would an incomes policy meet with success.

Professor Gannagé introduced Professor Fauvel's paper on price policy for farm products and its repercussions on farmers' incomes saying that it was also related to incomes policy in the wider sense of a policy bearing on the growth of sectoral incomes. Professor Fauvel had chosen to approach his subject through price theory rather than from the point of view of national accounting because in his opinion French social accounts were oversimplified in considering agriculture as a simple industry and did not make it possible to break down costs of production in the multi-product farm between different kinds of output.

Professor Fauvel had based his study on three peculiarities of price determination for farm products : whereas the usual theory gave much significance to the point of intersection of the marginal cost curve with the marginal revenue curve, marginal cost did not play any part in fixing the volume of supply ; supply was exogenously determined and thus was highly inelastic in the short run ; consequently it was not possible to determine producers' incomes from the usual supply and demand graph : supply not being related to the cost of production, the difference between revenue and cost could not be reckoned in this fashion. It was, however, possible to determine the increase in farmers' revenue brought about by government intervention if one knew the price elasticity of demand for farm products.

Professor Fauvel's paper showed how this notion could be improved and its application widened by distinguishing short-, medium- and long-run elasticities as suggested by E. J. Working and other authors. The problem being further complicated by substitutability relations between products, this was a case for using cross-elasticities and Professor Fauvel had quoted G. E. Brandow's calculations showing that they were usually positive for farm products in the United States.

Professor Fauvel had completed his general theoretical study by a more empirical case study of milk, meat and corn products. This was still a market approach to farmers' incomes. Professor Gannagé could not feel entirely satisfied with a micro-economic approach ; only a macro-economic approach would determine the overall farmers' income and its share in national income. To do this one would probably need longer and more detailed statistical series than were available within the present framework of national accounting in France.

Professor Bronfenbrenner, commenting on Professor Fauvel's paper, said that a policy for supporting farm prices could be described in the following way. State intervention in setting a price p' above the equilibrium price p at the point of intersection of the supply and demand curves (see Fig. 1 below) would result in the substitution of a demand function described by the line D', drawn at the price p' at which the public authority bought the crop, for the demand curve D. Professor Bronfenbrenner assumed the supply function to be described then by the line S' drawn as a parallel to the price ordinate at a distance depending on the amount AC of excess supply at the price p' which the public authority would permit to be marketed.

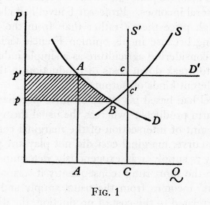

FIG. 1

What would be the costs of this policy ? First, there would be a cost for the consumer measured by the loss of consumer's surplus. This was the studied area in Fig. 1. The cost of this policy for the taxpayers had also to be considered ; even if one assumed the government could get rid of the accumulated stocks by exporting, they could only be sold out at a price below p'.

There might, however, be a less expensive way of dealing with the problem. Professor Bronfenbrenner would suggest that it might resolve itself. The reason for the price policy was that the position of the curve A in Fig. 2 (see below), the average cost function, counting farm labour, land and other

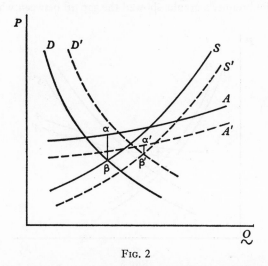

FIG. 2

inputs at market value, was such that farmers did not meet their cost at the market price to the extent of $\alpha\beta$. Would this gap, $\alpha\beta$, tend to widen or to disappear as time elapsed? Professor Bronfenbrenner thought that it might disappear for three reasons : an increasing population would result in a shift of the demand curve to D' ; technological progress might lead to a shift of the average cost curve to A' ; there might be a fall of the supply function to S'. These three changes would tend to work towards a new market price at which there might still be a gap, $\alpha'\beta'$, but it might be proportionately much less than before. The real issue was whether the gap would tend to grow larger or to resolve itself through time. Only if it was proved to remain constant or to increase should supportive policy be considered.

Professor Fauvel thanked Professor Gannagé for introducing his paper. He did not think it necessary to restate his reasons for thinking a macroeconomic approach to his problem in terms of national income to be unsatisfactory. He had had no intention of writing a thorough study on the determination of the farmers' share in national income. The policies designed for ensuring farmers income parity with other producers, however, operated most often through governmental price fixing. His object had thus been to study the conditions, forms and results of farm price policy, leaving aside their repercussions on incomes policy.

Professor Bronfenbrenner had suggested a graphic analysis of the results of governmental price-fixing for farm products which raised the problem of an alternative policy — or rather made it possible to develop out of anticipated changes in equilibrium conditions in an alternative situation of no state intervention. Then what ought to be forecast ? Professor Bronfenbrenner's graphs showed the gap $\alpha\beta$ between what farmers'

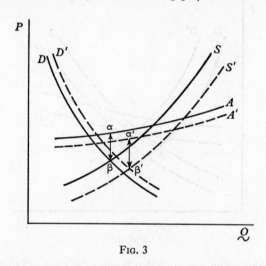

FIG. 3

earnings should be and what they actually were. However, as Professor Bronfenbrenner had admitted, the desirability or not of government intervention on price determination depended on whether or not the gap would tend to disappear of its own accord and this was contingent on changes in demand, average cost and productivity. In point of fact, taking account of the behaviour of the demand for farm products, the average cost and production in farming, Professor Fauvel thought it far from certain that the gap $\alpha\beta$ would lessen within a few years. Under these conditions, to reject the farmers' claim for price support would not help to bring about the sort of adjustments which would make the problem self-solving — it would indeed aggravate the imbalance.

If one reasoned under the assumption (more or less in accordance with the data over the last ten years) that the demand for farm products would increase at a rate of 1·0 per cent p.a., i.e. in the case of France at roughly the same rate as the increase in population, whereas productivity was assumed to rise at a 5·0-7·0 per cent rate p.a. and supply at a 4·0 per cent rate, the D', A' and S' curves on Professor Bronfenbrenner's graph no. 2 (see p. 723) should be redrawn as in graph no. 3 (see above), showing that the gap would not be reduced, but enlarged in comparison with its initial value. To postpone the decision to enforce a price policy would then be sheer procrastination.

INDEX

Page numbers in the index in black type under the Names of Participants in the Conference indicate their Papers or Discussions of their Papers. Page numbers in italic type indicate Contributions by Participants to the Discussions

Index

Lenin, V. I., 200–1, 202, 203, 210, 211, 223, 371
Leontief, W., 476, 501
Lergott, S., 353
Leroux, H., and Allier, J. P., 402
Levy, M. J., 355
Liebenberg, M., and Fitzwilliams, J. M., 28 ; Goldsmith, S. F., Jaszi, G., and Kaitz, H., 28
Life-time earnings, 36
Lim, T. B., 353
Lininger, C. A., Kosobud, R. F., and Katona, G., 28
Lipinski, E., *290–1*
Long-term trends in factor shares, xxv–xxx
Long-term trends of distribution, in Belgium, 149–70, 170–6 ; in France, 42–55, 67 ; in Japan, 178–88 ; in U.S.A., 31–2, 37–8 ; in West Germany, 78–105
Lorenz curve, 5 n., 328, 372
Lutz, F. A., and Hague, D. C. (eds.), 513 n., 516 n., 529 n.
Lydall, H. F., 354 ; and Lansing, J. B., 403 n.

McGuire, J. W., Chiu, J. S. Y., and Elbing, A. O., 589 n.
Machlup, F., 482 n., 495, 496 n.
Malthus, T. R., 53, 539, 548
Mandelbrot, B., 598 n.
Manne, A., and Kurz, M., 494
Mao Tse-tung, 370–1
Marchal, A., *195, 314–16, 636–7, 664–5*
Marchal, J., *32–4, 35,* 56 n., 72 n., 158 n., *170–3, 190–1, 242–3,* 302, *322, 359,* 362, 374–5, 378–9, 382, 384, *470–1, 505–6, 536, 578–9* ; and Ducros, B., xiii–xxx ; and Lecaillon, J., 45 n., 302, 413, 438, 500
Marginal productivity analysis, xiv
Marginal productivity theories of distribution, 169–70
Marginal productivity theory, Solow's modified, 462–5, 467–75
Marschak, J., 487 ; and Andrews, W. H., 486
Marshall, Alfred., 367, 457 n., 576, 579, 703
Marxist theories of distribution, xxiii, 38–9, 146, 199–293, 297–303, 370–2, 388–9, 395–9
Massé, P., 669–71 *pass.,* 676

Massell, B., 484
Matthews, R. C. O., 115 n.
Mayer, T., 591 n., 592 n.
Meade, J. E., 451
Mendershausen, H., 486, 490
Micro-distribution, neo-classical, 476–501
Milhau, J., 673 n.
Mill, J. S., 367, 500, 504
Miller, H. P., 11, 28, 29
Mincer, J., 37, 584 n.
Minhas, B., Arrow, K. J., Chenery, H. B., and Solow, R. M., 492 n., 493 n.
Mirabella, G., *29–32*
Mirrlees, J. A., 529 n. ; and Kaldor, N., 450 n., 550–1, 554 n., 555 n.
Mitchell, W., 626
Modigliani, F., 500 n., Muth, J. F., Simon, H. A., and Holt, C. C., 458 n., 461 n., 464
Monopoly, effect of, on distribution, 413–38, 497–501
Morgan, E. V., 139
Morgan, J. N., 15 n., 18, 29, 328 n., 353
Morgan, T., 329 n., 353, 386, 408 n.
Morice, J., and Delefortrie, N., 45
Morrissett, I., 482 n.
Mukerji, V., 492–3
Müller, J. H., 91 n. ; and Hoffman, W. G., 78 n., 81 n., 83 n., 86 n., 94 n.
Murti, V. N., and Sastry, V. K., 489 n.
Muth, J. F., Simon, H. A., Holt, C. C., and Modigliani, F., 458 n., 461 n., 464
Myrdal, G., 353, 385–6

National accounts, difficulties of using, to measure distribution, 32–4
National income, calculation of, in the U.S.S.R., 204–7
Negreponti-Delivanis, M., *174, 194, 240, 265–7, 274, 275, 290,* **297-325,** *322–5,* 353, *357*
Neild, R., 454, 456, 474, 696
Neo-classical theories of distribution, 32–4, 297–303, 362–70, 388–91, 393, 395–9, 438–48, 451–3, 476–501, 501–503, 539–47
Neo-classical theory, opportunity for testing, in West Germany, 108, 110
Neo-marginalist theories of distribution, xiv–xix, xviii, xxiii
Nerlove, M., 703

731